Pelican Books

Philosophy As It Is

Ted Honderich has been Reader in Philosophy at University College London since 1972, before which he was Lecturer in Philosophy there and at the University of Sussex, and has been a Visiting Professor at Yale and the City University of New York. He is the author of *Punishment, The Supposed Justifications* (1969) and *Three Essays on Political Violence* (1976) the editor of *Essays on Freedom of Action* (1973) and *Social Ends and Political Means* (1976), and the general editor of several series of books, including the International Library of Philosophy and Scientific Method.

Myles Burnyeat was Lecturer in Philosophy at University College London from 1965 to 1978, when he moved to Cambridge to be Lecturer in Classics. At Cambridge he is also Fellow and Lecturer in Philosophy at Robinson College. He has held visiting appointments at Princeton, Harvard and the University of Pittsburgh. He was awarded a Radcliffe Fellowship for 1974–5, and has contributed articles to philosophical and to classical journals.

Ted Honderich and Myles Burnyeat are also joint editors of *Philosophy Through Its Past*, the companion volume to *Philosophy As It Is*.

PHILOSOPHY AS IT IS

**Edited by Ted Honderich
and Myles Burnyeat**

Penguin Books

Penguin Books Ltd, Harmondsworth,
Middlesex, England
Penguin Books, 625 Madison Avenue,
New York, New York 10022, U.S.A.
Penguin Books Australia Ltd, Ringwood,
Victoria, Australia
Penguin Books Canada Limited, 2801 John Street,
Markham, Ontario, Canada L3R 1B4
Penguin Books (N.Z.) Ltd, 182–190 Wairau Road,
Auckland 10, New Zealand

Published in Pelican Books 1979

Copyright © Ted Honderich and Myles Burnyeat, 1979
All rights reserved

Printed in the United States of America by
Offset Paperback Mfrs., Inc., Dallas, Pennsylvania
Set in Monotype Bembo

The Acknowledgements on pages xi–xii constitute an extension of
this copyright notice.

For Helen Marshall

Contents

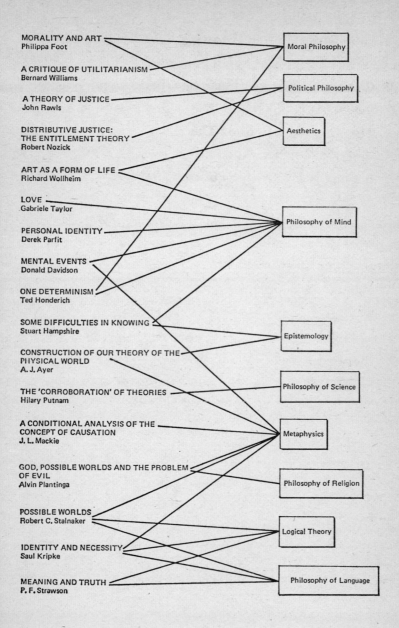

MORALITY AND ART
Philippa Foot

A CRITIQUE OF UTILITARIANISM
Bernard Williams

A THEORY OF JUSTICE
John Rawls

DISTRIBUTIVE JUSTICE:
THE ENTITLEMENT THEORY
Robert Nozick

ART AS A FORM OF LIFE
Richard Wollheim

LOVE
Gabriele Taylor

PERSONAL IDENTITY
Derek Parfit

MENTAL EVENTS
Donald Davidson

ONE DETERMINISM
Ted Honderich

SOME DIFFICULTIES IN KNOWING
Stuart Hampshire

CONSTRUCTION OF OUR THEORY OF THE
PHYSICAL WORLD
A. J. Ayer

THE 'CORROBORATION' OF THEORIES
Hilary Putnam

A CONDITIONAL ANALYSIS OF THE
CONCEPT OF CAUSATION
J. L. Mackie

GOD, POSSIBLE WORLDS AND THE PROBLEM
OF EVIL
Alvin Plantinga

POSSIBLE WORLDS
Robert C. Stalnaker

IDENTITY AND NECESSITY
Saul Kripke

MEANING AND TRUTH
P. F. Strawson

Moral Philosophy

Political Philosophy

Aesthetics

Philosophy of Mind

Epistemology

Philosophy of Science

Metaphysics

Philosophy of Religion

Logical Theory

Philosophy of Language

Acknowledgements

'Morality and Art' by Philippa Foot, Henrietta Hertz Lecture, *Proceedings of the British Academy*, LVI (1970). With permission of the author and of the British Academy. Retrospective notes and minor revisions by the author.

'A Critique of Utilitarianism' by Bernard Williams, reprinted from 'A Critique of Utilitarianism' by Bernard Williams in *Utilitarianism: For and Against* by J. J. C. Smart and Bernard Williams copyright © Cambridge University Press. With the permission of the author and publisher.

'A Theory of Justice' by John Rawls. Reprinted by permission of the publisher from *A Theory of Justice* by John Rawls, Cambridge, Mass.: The Belknap Press of Harvard University Press, copyright © 1971 by the President and Fellows of the Harvard College. Also by permission of Oxford University Press.

'Distributive Justice: The Entitlement Theory' by Robert Nozick. From Chapter 7, 'Distributive Justice', in *Anarchy, State and Utopia* by Robert Nozick © 1974 by Basic Books, Inc., Publishers, New York. English edition by Basil Blackwell, Publisher, Oxford. Reprinted by permission of the author and the publishers. Slight revisions by the author for this reprinting.

'Art as a Form of Life' by Richard Wollheim. From *Art and Its Objects: An Introduction to Aesthetics* (New York: Harper & Row, 1968) copyright © 1968, 1971 by Richard Wollheim. Reprinted by permission. Text arranged and modified for this volume by the author.

'Love' by Gabriele Taylor. Reprinted from *Proceedings of the Aristotelian Society* LXXVI (1975/76), pp. 147–64 © 1975/76 The Aristotelian Society with the permission of the author and by courtesy of the Editor of the Aristotelian Society.

'Personal Identity' by Derek Parfit. Reprinted by permission of the author and publisher from *The Philosophical Review* LXXX (1971), pp. 3–27.

'Mental Events' by Donald Davidson. Reprinted from *Experience and Theory* edited by L. Foster and J. W. Swanson copyright © 1970 by the University of Massachusetts Press. English edition by Gerald Duckworth & Co. Reprinted by permission of the author and publishers. Slight revisions by the author.

'One Determinism' by Ted Honderich. From *Essays on Freedom of Action* © Routledge & Kegan Paul Ltd, 1973. Reprinted by permission of author and publisher. Revised for this printing.

'Some Difficulties in Knowing' by Stuart Hampshire. Reprinted from *Philosophy, Science and Method* edited by Sidney Morgenbesser, Patrick Suppes and Morton White (New York: St Martin's Press, Inc.: London and Basingstoke: Macmillan, 1969), pp. 26–47. With permission of the author and publishers. Minor revisions by the author.

'Construction of our Theory of the Physical World' by A. J. Ayer. Reprinted from *The Central Questions of Philosophy*, copyright © A. J. Ayer, 1973. Published by Weidenfeld and Nicolson. Reprinted by permission of the author and publisher. Slight revisions by the author for this reprinting.

'The "Corroboration" of Theories' by Hilary Putnam. Reprinted with permission of the author and publisher from *The Philosophy of Karl Popper*, edited by Paul Arthur Schilpp (La Salle, Illinois: Open Court, 1974), pp. 221–40. Additional note by the author for this reprinting.

'A Conditional Analysis of the Concept of Causation' by J. L. Mackie. From *The Cement of the Universe* by John Mackie, copyright © Oxford University Press, 1974. Reprinted by permission of the author and publisher. Slight revisions by the author for this reprinting.

'God, Possible Worlds and the Problem of Evil' by Alvin Plantinga. From *God, Freedom and Evil* (New York: Harper & Row, 1974; London: George Allen & Unwin, 1975), pp. 29–55. Copyright © 1974 by Alvin Plantinga. Reprinted by permission.

'Possible Worlds' by Robert C. Stalnaker. Reprinted by permission of the author and of the editor of *Noûs*, X (1976): pp. 65–75.

'Identity and Necessity' by Saul Kripke. Reprinted by permission of the author and New York University Press from *Identity and Individuation*, edited by Milton K. Munitz, copyright © 1971 by New York University.

'Meaning and Truth' by P. F. Strawson © Oxford University Press. Reprinted by permission of the author and the publisher.

Introduction

The best introduction to philosophy is philosophy itself. This is not an original thought, but it is not common for it to be taken as literally and as seriously as we have taken it in bringing together this volume of essays and introductions.

Good philosophy is *rigorous*, and has been since Socrates and before. The quality of rigorousness is not preserved in dilution. Reflection on philosophy (by which we mean attempts to introduce it or describe it or survey it or explain its nature), as distinct from attempts to do it, may be more or less instructive. Some books *on* philosophy, as contrasted with books *of* philosophy, are excellent. At its best, however, this sort of thing still lacks an essential quality of its subject matter. There is not much less difference between reading philosophy and reading about philosophy than there is between reading original history and reading about the writing of history or reading a second-hand survey of the results of historical research.

Good philosophy is also in several ways *imaginative*, and this again is a quality which is best appreciated in original work. It does not come across well in paraphrase or in generalities about the philosophical endeavour.

It is no accident that rigour and imagination should be two prime characteristics of good philosophy. They are qualities called for by the nature of the questions with which philosophy deals. The questions of philosophy are fundamental ones about our understanding of ourselves and the world, questions of a kind for which we lack settled and defined methods of answer. They are often highly general questions, but they are not on that account distant from the real world. Many of them are questions about the very same reality which is the subject-matter of the sciences; philosophy traditionally has as one of its functions the attempt to reach a synoptic understanding of the results of other fields of inquiry. Many of the questions are also within the practical world, indeed the world of personal, social and political struggle. Many of them, finally, are questions which enter into the very stuff of the wider culture of our society; they contribute vitally to the shared fund of ideas on which action and reflection of diverse kinds can draw.

Our first concern, then, as editors of this volume, has been to provide examples of good and therefore rigorous and imaginative philosophy *as it actually is*. The papers, lectures and sections from books which are reprinted here exemplify the kinds of philosophical inquiry which are taken seriously by those who teach and learn philosophy in the English-speaking countries of the world. A good number of the examples have proved to be seminal contributions of the kind which carry their subject forward and become the focus of ongoing discussion.

Our second concern has been to represent the whole range of philosophy. One has something less than philosophy as it is if one or more of the major parts of the subject, perhaps logical theory or the philosophy of science, is left out as being too specialized or too challenging for the general reader. What is missing is not just a portion of the subject, but the essential interconnectedness of the problems of philosophy and of the subject areas into which they are conventionally distributed. This interconnectedness is an important part of what one learns from an education in philosophy. Equally, creative work in philosophy is often hard to classify by the conventional lines of division because it trespasses, fruitfully, into more than one branch of the subject.

We have therefore included logical theory, philosophy of language, epistemology, metaphysics, philosophy of science, philosophy of mind, aesthetics, moral philosophy, political philosophy and the philosophy of religion. But the diagrammatic map following the table of contents displays the fact that many of the contributions resist easy classification under these headings. We have regretfully omitted outlying subjects such as philosophy of history and philosophy of law. We have also omitted philosophy of education, which has not since John Dewey been in touch with the mainstream of philosophy.

An omission of a different order is the history of philosophy. It is noteworthy that a good number of the contributors to this volume have done distinguished work in the history of philosophy. Philosophy has a peculiarly close relation with its own traditions. The problems and arguments of the great thinkers of the past are a permanently present element in the contemporary debate. At any time a significant portion of the best work in philosophy is historical, enriching the current practice of philosophy with ideas arrived at by thinking through and reassessing the work of one of the great philosophers in the near or distant past. If, then, we have omitted to represent the history of philosophy, this is because it is too large a dimension of philosophy to represent adequately here. It needs a companion volume to itself.

Our third concern has been to find a representative selection of *recent* work, as philosophy understands 'recent'. The contributions were all written within approximately the last ten years, during which time philosophy has been developing rapidly on every front. There is more adventurous thinking and imaginative construction in this collection than would have been apparent ten years ago; at the same time, the concern for careful argument is, if anything, more pronounced than ever. The problems discussed are a fair balance of the traditional and the new, but all of them come from among the central concerns of the several branches of philosophy listed above. Taking the problems more or less by the order of that list, starting with logical theory, the contributions have to do with meaning and truth, necessity and identity, perception and the physical world, knowing, possible worlds, causation, freedom and determinism, the acceptance of scientific theories, the nature of mental events, personal identity, love, art and the idea of a form of life, the objectivity of moral judgements, Utilitarianism and moral integrity, justice in society, God and the problem of evil.

It may be that at this point a member or two of the class of 'general reader' will consider that our book offers too bracing a challenge. We very much hope not, and with reason. It is not, of course, that the book offers *no* challenge. It seems sometimes to be supposed that the reading of philosophy can be, or ought to be, as straightforward as the reading of a novel. It cannot. The way of philosophy is not the way of literature, or the rest of literature. Philosophical arguments are not for *drifting through*, and never have been. (Descartes once suggested that the reader should ponder the first of his *Meditations* for weeks, even months, before continuing further.) For the reasons already given, however, this should not be taken to justify giving the reader potted philosophy or philosophy-made-simple, or for weighting the selection towards more tractable issues which are peripheral to the mainstream of philosophy. The right response, we believe, is to offer material which is deserving of the sustained, careful attention that philosophy requires, and then try to provide help and guidance for the reader with little or no experience of these matters. So this has been our fourth concern: to provide help and guidance to lead the reader into a series of challenging but rewarding discussions.

In accepting the challenge, to ourselves as editors, of this fourth aim, we have tried to select, so far as was compatible with our other aims, work which is within the reach of those who have not previously studied the subject. We looked for clear, reasonably untechnical writing, and for the most part we have found it. Where the going gets tough, technical or obscure, we have said so. Better to share in the experience of difficulty, which for *anyone*, professional and amateur alike, is a normal part of doing the subject, and to appreciate where technical knowledge comes in, than to be fobbed off with easier, less representative material. Better too to be aware of what also exists – a fair measure of controversy and sharp disagreement.

We have furnished each piece with an introduction, often quite a long introduction. The aim of these introductions is pedagogical. In most cases they are summaries or abstracts of what follows, highlighting the main themes and arguments. If, as a result, the reader finds himself taken through two different presentations of the same argument, our hope is simply that this will aid his understanding of the author's original.

The introductions include a certain amount of explanation of philosophical notions and terms of art. Those who want more of this may find it useful to have to hand a reference work such as the *Dictionary of Philosophy* by A. R. Lacey (London: Routledge & Kegan Paul, 1976). Where symbolic formulae occur in the text, we have supplied an ordinary-language version in the introduction or by additional footnotes.

It is perhaps worth mentioning that behind these introductions lies the experience of one of the editors (M.F.B.) in taking a University of London Extra-Mural class through a large part of the material here assembled. Very few members of the class had any extensive acquaintance with philosophy, but with this type of introduction, and careful preparatory study of each piece by the class, it proved possible to achieve a level of discussion which would have done high credit to a university seminar. Our thanks to the members of that class for showing that good rigorous philosophy can become accessible to a wider public in a more than superficial way.

These, then, have been our four intentions – to represent philosophy as it is; to represent the whole range of its concerns; to represent recent developments in the subject; to bring the reader by way of the introductions and by choosing clear, reasonably non-technical selections to a decent understanding of arguments. The philosophy of which we speak is philosophy as it is carried forward by professional philosophers in the universities of the English-speaking countries of the world, and some others. (It is sometimes labelled 'analytic philosophy' in contrast with the various traditions of Continental philosophy.) We have aimed to present the best aspects of that philosophy. Indeed, to a large extent the book is the distinguished work of distinguished contemporary philosophers. It comes about as close as a single book can, we feel, to recording the achievement of ongoing philosophy in the English language at this time.

Our thanks are due to Christine Jones for cheerful typing and retyping, and to Colin McGinn for good advice.

Philippa Foot

Morality and Art

Philippa Foot's paper 'Morality and Art' is written to communicate a sense of unease about morality. It escapes from the orthodoxy, one might almost say the piety, which makes a good deal of modern moral philosophy less than challenging. We are invited to consider the proposition that in certain ways the character of our moral thinking is shaped by fiction and pretence, reaching even to the forms of language we use. The plan is to compare the way we think about moral questions with the way we treat roughly parallel questions about works of art, where, Mrs Foot suggests, our thinking is more open and candid. The comparison provides touchstones by which we may become aware how often in morality we represent things as other than they are.

In working out her comparison, Mrs Foot sets before us three fictions which, she argues, occur in morality but not in the field of art. It should, however, be understood at the outset that two of them occur, in Mrs Foot's view, only within a limited part of morality. What part that is, and how it is delimited, we will consider after first identifying the three fictions which are to be the focus of discussion.

Briefly, then, there is the fiction of objectivity, the fiction of a superior, non-relative point of view, and the fiction of inescapability. The idea of objectivity in morals is the idea that moral judgements can be backed by principles which are true or false independently of the attitude of persons who hold or reject them; the principles are something more than the expression of our attitudes and feelings. The idea of a superior, non-relative point of view is, again, the idea that judgements issuing from such principles are true as they stand, not just true within the context set by some individual or some community holding these principles and not others; on the contrary, moral principles define a point of view with claims to superior, absolute validity. Finally, such principles are binding on all of us without exception, no matter what we happen, contingently, to want in life – that is the idea of inescapability.

Now in the long history of moral philosophy these ideas have always been at the centre of controversy. Philosophers since ancient times have debated whether moral judgements are objective or subjective, absolute or relative, categorical or hypothetical (that is, dependent for their force on a man's contingent desires). The originality of Mrs Foot's contribution lies in a double suggestion. First, and regardless of where we stand on these issues in our reflective moments, all of us in practice use language which presupposes that moral judgements are objective, absolute and categorical. But secondly, Mrs Foot suggests, it is not in fact the case that these three presuppositions invariably hold good; in *some* instances the first two are fictitious, and the third is *always* that.

Here we must draw attention to the argument on p. 13f, further amplified in the Retrospective Note which follows the paper, for the conclusion that *certain* criteria of good and evil are objectively fixed as part of the very concept of morality. The argument is this: If there were no conceptual limitation on what could count as good or evil, a man might select, however arbitrarily or eccentrically, *any* form of behaviour, such as clapping his hands, and insist that he regarded this as a morally admirable or morally evil thing to do – and we would have to accept that his claim made sense, that his moral system, while it might be different from ours, was still conceptually intelligible to us as the morality he had chosen to follow.

Some anti-objectivist philosophers have indeed written as if this was correct. R. M. Hare, to mention the most distinguished recent exponent of such a view (see bibliography), holds that what counts as a moral principle depends on certain formal requirements to do with a man's preparedness to make his principle a universal one, applying to everybody (himself included) without exception; there are no restrictions as to the *content* of a moral system. Against this, Mrs Foot maintains, and has argued in detail elsewhere (see bibliography), that the hand-clapping example does not make sense as a moral principle. If, as in the example, clapping one's hands is not thought of in terms which relate it to human good or harm, a man who claimed that it mattered morally to him whether he clapped his hands would be confused or in error about what morality is. Of course, we could imagine a background of belief by which the action has some religious significance, was conceived as aggressive or treacherous, or brought some fancied benefit or harm –

but the point is that the formalist position makes no such requirement of connecting beliefs on what may count as a moral principle.

Reflection on such examples as the above shows, then, that the content of a moral system is not entirely open for anyone to choose, but has necessarily to do with human good and harm. It is necessary, not optional, that a moral system concern itself with such things as the effect of an action on the lives of innocent persons. Not that every morality will count that a decisive consideration in every case, but if it *is* a consideration that has to be taken seriously, then there are going to be cases in which it is the only or the most important consideration for the moral assessment of an action. That is, in some cases it will be decisive. In the case, for example, of the judgement that Hitler's murdering of innocent Jews was morally indefensible, there is, Mrs Foot argues, no option but to count the judgement objectively true. It is demonstrable on the basis of considerations fixed by the concept of morality itself.

The question now is: How far will these considerations take us? No general answer is given, but Mrs Foot cites examples on p. 14 to illustrate her contention that 'the concept of morality while it fixes a great deal also leaves quite a lot open'. It is one thing to say there is a moral objection to the taking of human life, another to say how this is to apply to the difficult problems of abortion and euthanasia or to determine what, in detail, is to count as murder. Further principles will be involved in these decisions, principles which are not derivable from the concept of morality alone. Mrs Foot calls them 'elective principles', suggesting that there is a genuine choice within an individual's or a community's moral system in regard to what these further principles are to be.

We have now sketched the general position from which Mrs Foot starts her inquiry into the three fictions. She is concerned about the fact that, when we get down to the details of difficult cases, where one person says, for example, that abortion is permissible and another says that it is wrong, these judgements are to all appearances delivered in the same objective terms and with the same assertive claim to objective truth as judgements which can be fully supported by definitional criteria of moral good and evil. We have reached a point where those criteria are not enough to guide us, where we must rely on elective principles, yet we speak and think as if the case was the same as before. Even those who in a reflective moment would say they are conveying their own moral viewpoint rather than claiming that the issue is objectively decidable, still use the objective form of expression 'It is right', 'It is wrong'.

Here we have the first point of comparison between morality and art. For Mrs Foot thinks that in aesthetic matters we find it easier to accept subjectivity where it genuinely exists. And she has a suggestion to make as to why this should be so.

Relativism is her next topic (p. 17). It arises naturally at this point since what Mrs Foot has been calling elective principles are often held in common by the members of a group or community. Where that is so, a moral judgement may be true in relation to the standards of one group and false in relation to those of another. It will be an objective matter that the judgement has these truth values in relation to each set of standards, but there will be no answer to the question, 'Is the judgement true or false, really?', where the question is asked without reference to the principles of any group, as if from a superior point of view with claims to absolute validity. We accept, to cite Mrs Foot's engaging comparison, that 'Rancid yak's butter gives a good flavour to tea' is true as said by a Tibetan, false as said by us. Why should we not accept a parallel relativistic account of moral judgements which depend on shared elective principles? (The reader should note the careful way in which Mrs Foot's relativism is formulated: in particular, it should not be thought that where a relativistic account is correct, it follows that a speaker cannot make a mistake about what is true or false by the relevant standards. Relativism is not the doctrine that 'my thinking it so, makes it so'.)

Thus far Mrs Foot has been arguing that we should not fear to accept *some* moral judgements as subjective and *some* moral truth as relative – some, not all, since, as explained earlier, her belief is that the core of morality is objective and non-relative. Her third comparison between morality and art is not in this way limited to a part of morality. Take a ruthlessly cruel or dishonest man, who does not care about the suffering his behaviour brings to others, and let us grant that it is objectively wrong and reprehensible of him not to care. We insist, and feel we must be able to insist, that he *should* care. He should care even if we can show him no connection between his doing so and something he already wants in life, or will want in the future. This is the idea that the moral 'should' necessarily give a reason for acting to any man, a reason that no-one can escape no matter how amoral his desires may be. Otherwise put, it is the idea that moral judgements are categorical, not dependent for their binding force on what a man contingently wants in life.

It is Mrs Foot's contention that this idea is fictitious in all cases. Faced with a man who is indifferent to the ends of morality, we cannot in fact produce the inescapable reason which our use of 'should' insists upon. Since Plato, philosophers have sought to show that wickedness is foolish or irrational, but the uncomfortable truth is that to show a man that something in his conduct or attitudes is a piece of foolishness, which he has reason to change, requires showing him that it tends to frustrate his purposes or desires; and in the case of the ruthlessly amoral man that just cannot be done. Once again, the comparison with art provides the illumination of a parallel situation where we find it easier to accept things as they are.

It is not difficult to understand why the fictions, if Mrs Foot is right in saying that is what they are, should be so important to us in morality. The reason is fear of what other people and, perhaps most of all, we ourselves, might do. But would we? Would we break out into violence and self-seeking if we abandoned the pretence that moral restraints on these things are somehow laid down for us in every detail? Why should not those who care about peace and co-operation, justice and fair dealing, continue to care about them as strongly as before? If we follow Mrs Foot's argument, we are led into fundamental questions about the social and psychological function of morality. It is these questions she is raising when, at the end of the paper, she says that she would like to open a debate which might lead us to consider changes in the way we talk about what is morally good or bad.

M.F.B.

Philippa Foot

Morality and Art

Henrietta Hertz Lecture, *Proceedings of the British Academy*, LVI (1970). With permission of the author and of the British Academy. Retrospective note and minor revisions by the author.

The title of this lecture will, I am afraid, have suggested many fascinating topics about which nothing is to be said. I am not going to argue, with G. E. Moore, that aesthetic experience is an intrinsic good which ought to be pursued for its own sake. Nor shall I join in the debate as to whether moral considerations are relevant when we judge works of art. I shall talk about moral and aesthetic judgements, but in order not so much to relate as to contrast them, and that from a special point of view. What I want to do is to follow a hunch, originally a mere suspicion, hard even to formulate, that there is some element of fiction and strain in what we say about right and wrong, while our appraisal of aesthetic objects is relatively free from pretence. How far others share this uneasiness about morality I do not know but I am certainly not the only one to have such thoughts or to find this contrast. One often hears those not conditioned to suppress all thought of the mere possibility of an attack on morality say that they are sceptical about moral judgements, and it may be a successful tactical move, always supposing that one wants to ride them off the sceptical position, to ask whether they are also sceptical about the merits of works of art. My present intention is to pursue the matter rather than to close down the debate. I shall argue that the original, half-formed, thought about morality, and the contrast between moral and aesthetic judgement, has something behind it. If I am right we do maintain certain fictions about morality, and they are even reflected in the forms of language that we use, while there is no comparable lack of candour in what we say and think about works of art.

I must begin by raising, yet once more, the old question as to whether moral judgements are subjective or objective. That they are, simply, subjective seems to me certainly false. For to impute subjectivity implies a comparison with the words in which a man expresses or reports his feelings, sensations, aims, allegiances, and so on. Here questions of truth or falsity either do not arise at all or else arise only in a special way. Where we have the verbal form of an exclamation, as when someone says 'alas!' or 'ow!' or 'how nice!' we cannot tell him that what he said was false, though we can suggest that he is pretending or being insincere. Where he uses a declarative sentence, as in saying 'I am dismayed' or 'that hurts' or 'I like that', we may say 'that is not true', but only if we think he is lying or at least insincere. Whichever form of words he chooses there is no room for the kind of mistake that he can make when his eyes have deceived him, or when he has drawn the wrong conclusion from some piece of evidence or other, which might of course, in a special case, be evidence about himself.

That all moral judgements are subjective in this sense is ruled out, rather trivially, by the fact that some, at least, are not asserted directly but rather derived; this at once breaks the analogy with subjective utterances by introducing a possibility of error not due to insincerity. Nothing follows, however, about the premises from which such conclusions are drawn, and we are not yet committed to any view about what their status may be. Now about this there has been a great deal of controversy, some philosophers arguing that a man can choose for himself, so long as he meets formal requirements of generality and consistency, what his ultimate moral principles are to be; while others insist that certain criteria of good and evil belong to the concept of morality itself. The first, or formalist, position seems to me indefensible, implying as it does that we might recognize as a moral system some entirely pointless set of prohibitions or taboos, on activities such as clapping one's hands, not even thought as harmful, aggressive, treacherous, or cowardly by the community in which the prohibitions exist. A moral system seems necessarily to be one aimed at removing particular dangers and securing certain benefits, and it would follow that some things do and some do not count as objections to a line of conduct from a moral point of view. There may be

strict proof of some moral propositions, such as that Hitler's treatment of the Jews was morally indefensible. Many philosophers have
rejected this possibility on the general theoretical grounds of a logical
gap between 'is' and 'ought'. I shall not here renew the arguments
against this supposed refutation. It seems to me that there is no
difficulty in principle in making such a derivation, and that there are,
as I said, starting-points fixed by the concept of morality. We might
call them 'definitional criteria' of moral good and evil, so long as
it is clear that they belong to the concept of morality – to *the* definition
and not to some definition which a man can choose for himself.
What we say about such definitional criteria will be objectively true
or false.

So far we have been describing elements of objectivity in a moral
system, but there is still some room for subjectivity for all that has yet
been said. For even if the arguments against fixed starting-points in
ethics are invalid, and even if there actually are definitional criteria of
moral good and evil, allowing some moral propositions to be proved
from the facts, it does not follow that we can settle all moral questions
in this way. There could be both fixed starting-points and an element
of 'play' in the system, allowing different and irreconcilable points of
view about certain things. I think that this is probably the actual
position, and that the concept of morality while it fixes a great deal
also leaves quite a lot open. It seems, for instance, that while one can
determine from the concept of morality that there is an objection to
murder one cannot determine completely what will count as murder.
Thinking about the problem of abortion I come to the conclusion that
there is a genuine choice as to whether or not to count as a human
being, with the rights of a human being, what would become a
human being but is not yet capable of independent life.[1] Again there
seems to be a more general choice of starting-point involved in the
decision as to how far we are going to protect an individual against
the claims of the community, where the interests of the majority
clash with his. It is extremely difficult to find a clear and obvious
principle when we start looking into the problems, e.g., of medical
ethics. We ourselves have a strong objection to the idea of *using* one
person for the benefit of others, and it probably guides our intuitions
in many cases. It does not seem clear, however, that one could rule

out of court the principles of a strict utilitarian who would, at least if he were consistent, allow things that we will not allow in the interests of cancer research. And so it may be that *at some points* we really do find the kind of ultimate breakdown in moral argument that has been suggested as a quite general possibility by those who refuse to admit definitional criteria of right and wrong.

It seems, therefore, that philosophers on both sides of this line of controversy must ask themselves about the status of what we might call 'elective principles' used in forming moral judgements. My contention is that if we really reach such starting-points in a man's morality we have something that can only be stated subjectively. By this I mean that the words will operate subjectively however much we insist on an objective form. Let us see what the arguments against subjectivity are worth at this point.

It is often said that no moral utterance could simply state a fact about one's own attitudes, the objection being that when one person says 'X is permissible' and another 'wrong' or 'not permissible' both statements cannot be true. But that, in a discussion of subjectivity, is just the point at issue. If the declaration of an elective principle really has the characteristic given to it in the hypothesis, if, that is, it really is a starting-point, why not say that the only truth of which it is capable is that (depending only on veracity and sincerity) which can belong to a subjective report such as 'that hurt' or 'I am hostile to that man'? No doubt it will be objected that this cannot be right, because we actually use 'true' and 'false' in a different way in connection with 'moral judgements', saying 'false' not to charge a man with lying or insincerity but to state an opposed point of view. That we do this is, of course, true, but the question is what the role of this piece of usage is once a statement of an elective principle has been reached. It is certainly not necessary in order to allow us to speak of the man who says '*p*' and the one who says 'not *p*' as disagreeing. 'Disagree' is (to use an expression of Miss Anscombe's applied by her in a different context) 'a light word'. If you find something pleasant and I do not, or you find some food delicious and I do not we can say 'how we disagree'. My suspicion is that the existing use of 'true' and 'false', and the choice of an objective form of expression ('it is right') does have a role but a rather disreputable role. When we say that something 'just is' right or wrong we want to give the *impression* of some kind of fact or authority standing behind our words, though by hypothesis both are here ruled out, maintaining the trappings of objectivity though the substance is not there. Perhaps there is not, in the language already, a subjective form of words which will say just what we want, but we do not have to keep the language as it is.[2]

This, then, is the first place where we see a statement of moral position dressed up to look like something other than it is. Do we find the same gap between appearance and reality at a similar point in our appraisal of works of art?

There is, of course, a great deal of difference between the activity of passing moral judgement and that of aesthetic appraisal and it is perhaps strange that philosophers have often tried to find a theory to cover them both. In the first place Nelson Goodman is surely right in insisting that the decision about what is good and bad does not play an all-important part in the critic's work: '... works of art are not race-horses, and picking a winner is not the primary goal'.[3] Secondly, the picture of an ultimate breakdown in argument does not have the same hold on us in aesthetics as it does in ethics. This is partly because a critic tries to display the characteristics of his subject but rarely to offer *proof* that it is good or bad. Moreover, description does not present the object of art as it presents the object of moral judgement, so that it is not obvious even what would be meant by saying, of a work of art, that two people might agree on all the facts and still disagree about the values. The idea of 'all the relevant facts' seems to have no application if we are thinking about works of art. Nor is it clear that there could be elective principles in aesthetics as in morals. This may sound surprising, for, of course, there have been many conflicting announcements about what makes a work of art 'good' or 'great'. One has only to think of Tolstoy's insistence that good or true art must produce a feeling, quite distinct from all other feelings, of 'joy and spiritual union' with the author and with others who appreciate the work. Such an announcement does not, however, have the status of our 'elective principles' in ethics. For there is a touchstone by which Tolstoy's judgement may be tested, and by which, incidentally, it may be shown to be insufficient. Someone may, if he chooses, restrict his own attention to works of art that satisfy certain criteria. What is great or good is determined, however, by what people find in certain objects that is deeply interesting and significant to them. If someone insists that what is thought of as a defect is really a merit he says something that relates necessarily, though of course in no simple way, to the reactions of others. He has the alternative ready to hand in an overtly subjective statement of his own appreciation or taste. In matters of moral judgement it is hard to accept subjectivity where it genuinely exists. It seems far easier in aesthetics, and this may be because it is not our own conduct that is in question. We are apt to be haunted by the thought of a law-giver when it is a question of what we are to do, and the thought that some-how and somewhere it is written down is very compelling indeed. It is not very tempting to refer aesthetic values to the will of God.

We find, I think, the same pattern if we raise the question of the relativity of judgements in morals and aesthetics. I will first try to show that we are over-resistant to theories of ethics that allow the relativity of some moral judgements. Relativism is often these days said to be absurd as a theory of moral judgement. As a theory of *all* moral judgement it is, of course, false if the thesis of definitional criteria is correct. (There would be nothing relative about the truth of the proposition that Hitler was a moral monster.) But if what we have also said about contingent, alternative, starting points for a moral system is true it should follow that there are moral judgements for which a relativistic account will be right.

Since there is a good deal of confusion about what is meant by a relativistic theory of ethics, we should discuss this before going on. Sometimes, for instance, relativism is contrasted with absolutism, so that a relativistic theory says that circumstances may always alter cases while its rival holds that certain kinds of action are always and everywhere good or bad. So, to deny relativism in this sense, which is not the one in which I am interested, one would need to say for example that if the description 'torture' or 'judicial condemnation of the innocent' applied to an action it was, *in any circumstances*, morally inadmissible. I mention this distinction only to set it aside. It belongs to our present topic only indirectly in providing other examples of what might be elective principles.

Perhaps it will be best to begin not with a definition of relativism but with some examples of judgements outside ethics for which a relativistic account would be correct. Many could be taken from the province of taste, as when, for example, clothes are said to be elegant or smart. Again we might consider the statement that someone is good-looking or fair of face. Other examples could come from gastronomy. The food at a certain restaurant is said to be good; or it is said that a particular process, say burying eggs for long periods, or letting yak's butter go rancid before floating it on the tea, gives the product a delicious flavour. Presumably no one will deny that the truth of such judgements is relative, not, of course, to the speaker's tastes, since one may *make a mistake* in thinking one's wife good-looking or the flavour of one's cooking good, but rather to the reactions of certain people at certain places and times. This is not to suggest that there is some simple connection between, say, the preferences of a majority and the judgement of taste; to give a proper account one would have to look at each case separately and ask, for instance, whether connoisseurs are recognized in the given area, and if so what kind of authority they are allowed. The relevant point for this discussion is that reactions do vary a great deal from time to time and place to place, and that while sentences predicating such things as handsomeness or good flavour have a truth value as uttered in a given context they cannot be used 'across cultures' as it were, since it is impossible to extract the utterance from both contexts and ask questions about the truth. It would quite obviously be ridiculous for us to say that our opinion about the Tibetans' tea is correct and theirs mistaken, nor would we necessarily dispute questions of female beauty even with a traveller from the eighteenth century, never mind with a representative of the ancient Maya peoples who practised cranial deformation and on purpose made their children cross-eyed. It is not that such judgements do not have a truth value, but they do not have one unless relativized in a particular way.

Another example, which may be more controversial, is to be found in the use of the sentence 'that's a good thing'. Moral philosophers have sometimes spoken of this proposition in a portentous way, as if it passed judgement on the state of the universe from some lofty point of view. And indeed it may do so, if the speaker has lofty interests, and knows or supposes that his hearer has them too. But

'It's a good thing that such and such' may be said by the robbers as well as the cops, and by those interested only in making money on the next race and getting safely home. It would be ridiculous to say that when the backers of rival horses, reacting to some news affecting their prospects, say 'a good thing', 'a bad thing', the truth of what they say is to be judged by the interests of racing, never mind the welfare of mankind; nor can a third speaker say 'which of them is right'. Yet this type of utterance is once more to be contrasted with subjective statements such as 'I am glad'. One may make a mistake in thinking it a good thing that such and such has happened, and two speakers who have the same desires and allegiances may challenge each other's opinion about whether it is.

So far all the examples of truths relative to a context of utterance have been from the class of evaluative judgements, but there are others from elsewhere. We might think here of the sentence 'N. M. is tall'. For suppose that our man, N. M., being about 5 ft. 9 in. goes to live first in Southern Italy and then in California; he will properly be called first tall and then not tall without any change in his height, while in mid-Atlantic 'N. M. is tall' may have no use at all.

It will be apparent that the relativity in which we are interested is a special case of that belonging to any sentence containing indexical expressions such as 'I' or 'here', or tensed verbs, since these too are true as uttered in one context but not in another. It is not easy to give an account of the distinctive mark of relativity as we want to consider it in ethics. Something must be said about this, however, since one would not call a theory of ethics relativistic in that it allowed for an element of relativization coming merely from the use of indexical expressions in making moral judgements. If we speak of relativism in ethics we mean something more than this. Roughly we might say that the relativity in which we are especially interested is truth relative to standards or tests. So we know that when 'he is tall' is said in California the height of Californians must be appealed to; when an Eskimo speaker talks to an Eskimo audience about good food what he says is to be tested by Eskimo tastes.

Since the context of utterance is necessary to determine the truth or falsity of these sentences for which relativization is necessary there is, of course, no question of contradiction between speakers saying '*p*' and 'not *p*' in relevantly different contexts. The meaning of '*p*' may nevertheless be the same, though it is a difficult problem as to when we will say that this is so. It seems unproblematic in the case of sentences containing indexical words (such as 'I am English') and also for the case of being tall, since we would be inclined to gloss 'N. M. is tall' as meaning, in all contexts, 'N. M. is well above average height' rather than in one context one thing and in another context another. What of the sentence 'the flavour is good' as uttered by people of different gastronomic backgrounds? One would say that the words do have the same meaning, especially if the relation of the judgement to preferences were exactly the same in the two communities. (It would be harder to know what to say if in one community but not the other there were connoisseurs of flavour with a position like that of our connoisseurs of wine.) Luckily this problem does not have to be solved just now, since it is only where '*p*' is thought to have a constant meaning that there will be any question of contradiction between '*p*' and 'not *p*'. What is important to us is that a difference of context of utterance will often remove apparent contradiction even here.

Let us now consider whether a relativistic account should be given of moral language. It was pointed out earlier that a completely relativistic account is out of the question for those of us who believe that there are some criteria of good and evil implied in the concept of morality. Moreover no moral judgement will depend for its truth solely on its utterance in a given context, since all are subject to the definitional criteria. Nevertheless, if it is the case that different speakers can validly relate their conclusions to different elective principles there is an element of relativity in morality. Perhaps a good model for comparison would be that of a discussion between two or more people about what it would be best to do where certain aims were implied in the question that had been raised, as e.g., what would be best for the college as discussed in a college meeting, but where some other aims and principles might nevertheless not be shared. In such a case we would talk together about what was best until some divergence of principle actually appeared, though after that the discussion might have to end. This seems to be how we often do talk about morality with those whose principles resemble our own.

I think it likely that even this modest amount of relativity will not easily be accepted where ethics is concerned. For if it is accepted we must admit that in certain cases 'it is wrong to do X' will be true as said by A who has one set of elective principles, and false as said by B who has another, the description and circumstances of X being taken as the same for A and B. And we do not like to admit this, particularly when thinking of ourselves as A or B, as if we felt that the word 'true' in the sentence 'As uttered by him p is true' somehow implied a weakening of our own allegiance to principles from which not p can be concluded. Yet we have to say that a Tibetan uttering a sentence meaning 'Rancid yak's butter gives a good flavour to tea' would be saying something true, and that we could find similar examples having to do with elegance or personal beauty. As said by some other person the sentence might be true though as said by us it would be false. No compromise of our own position is involved, and if we refused to apply the word 'true' here this could only support the *fiction* of a superior point of view. This is, of course, exactly the point about the moral divergencies we have been considering, i.e. the ones stemming from the adoption of different elective principles. So long as we still have something to bring forward to show why particular principles should not be adopted we have a genuine possibility of showing that ours is a superior point of view, and it is very important that nothing that can really be said should be squeezed out. But if someone merely *asserts* that something is right or wrong, as for instance he may say when discussing euthanasia 'to kill a human being is never permissible' he should admit the relativity of judgements based on this elective principle. If his allegiance to it really requires a fiction about its status there is something wrong, and it may be that some people who do not mean to base their morality on religion would change their moral views on such matters if they no longer covertly referred to an authority such as God. On the other hand some elective principles would surely survive. People do care, for example, that individuals should not in everything be sacrificed for the good of others, or that the unborn should be counted as in the human community. They are ready to fight for such things; why should they not continue to do so?

When thinking about art we do not, it seems to me, have the same worry about relativism as we do when thinking about morals. Or at least we do not have the same resistance to taking things as they come. If we actually have something to say in criticism of the art of some other time or some other culture, as that it is sentimental, we expect to be able to show that this is so, and to be backed up by the reaction of other generations as well as by our contemporaries. If there were genuinely nothing to say and nothing to show, as we suppose may be the case at certain points in morals, we would be most unlikely to insist that somehow, nevertheless, we must be right. In fact, as everyone knows, there is a most surprising, and rather moving, agreement between peoples whose civilizations are completely different, and who may even be culturally isolated from each other. It was not to be taken for granted for instance that we would recognize the expressiveness of figures made by Han craftsmen, or in pre-Columbian Mexico, or that this would have the importance for us that it does. Sometimes recognition or appreciation fails. But then we are increasingly likely to think of the matter like that, and not to condemn what we do not understand or like. Obviously this has something to do with the fact that we are, psychologically speaking, much freer from anxiety in relation to art than to morality, and also that our thoughts about artistic merit are not haunted by a historical connection with religion. Moral judgements regulate our conduct in just those areas which arouse the deepest feelings of guilt, so that we want to erect the strongest possible barriers against what we fear we might do; aesthetic judgements guide our conduct in relatively calm waters when they guide it at all. Thus we are not nearly so likely to speak and feel as if things have been laid down for us in spite of the overt belief that they have not.

These considerations are no doubt connected with the final contrast that I shall draw between the way we think about morality and the way we think about art. In the first case, I want to say, we maintain a fiction of inescapability, while in the second we do not. In a sense, of course, it is right to think of moral judgement as inescapable. A man does not cease to be cruel or dishonest because he does not mind if he is cruel or dishonest, and these characteristics may also wreck his life. But suppose that he does not care, and moreover argues (it just might be truly) that in his position wickedness is likely to bring him more benefit than virtue. He is a ruthless amoral man, and moreover in such a special situation that we are not able to insist that even from the point of view of his own good he has reason to abandon his cruelty and dishonesty. We ask him if he does not care, for example, about the suffering his action will bring to others, and he says, and we believe him, that he does not care. What can we say to such a man? What we do say is that he *should* care, and that he *should not* do the things he does; we must, however, look carefully at this use of 'should', and in particular ask whether it implies that he has *reason* to change his life. Normally 'should' does carry a necessary connection with reasons for acting, since we use the word, for example, in giving advice, and advice must relate to what the agent wants (for himself or others) or to what he will care about at some future time.[4] We also use 'should' in contexts such as that of a college meeting, where common aims and principles are presupposed, and so far the use of 'should' is parallel to that of 'a good thing'. It is different, however, in that 'should' is not here applicable to someone not sharing in the common enterprise. If, for instance, it is important for the college that a certain shopkeeper moves his business we cannot on these grounds say that he *should* move, although we do say that it would be a good thing if he did. If we are to say that he should move, then, unless we are urging some duty upon him, we must bring considerations related to his desires, as for instance the lack of custom where he is. I am not, it should be stressed, saying that these nonmoral uses of 'should', carrying a necessary connection with reasons for acting, must relate a course of action to something by which the agent will be *moved*. For it is often the case that one should do something, like getting up in the morning for the sake of something one does want (and it is true *now* that one wants it) as for instance to be a good philosopher, but which, at this moment leaves one cold. (Compare being fond of someone though just at the moment one feels one never wants to see him again.) Moreover the 'should' of advice can be properly backed up by some consideration about what the subject *will* want even if there is no sense in which he wants it now, and this too is enough to give reasons for acting. It is a clear case of irrationality if a man takes no account of the future penalty of his present action. When backed by moral considerations 'should' is used differently, and as we noticed earlier a man may be told that he should do something required by morality without any connection being traced between such action and his present or future desires. So though in some ways we may think of the 'should' of morality as comparable to any other, as if members of the community were meeting together with the particular aim of making good arrangements for a common life, the analogy breaks down where a man who explicitly puts himself outside the common enterprise is still told what on moral grounds he *should* do. That this is what we say is among the data, and it is obvious why we have this usage in the language. Firstly we do not expect people to stand outside the moral community as does our ruthless amoral man, and secondly we want to be able to influence those who do. What is not, however, clear is why they should do what we want. Someone who is a lover of justice, and who cares about the good of other people has the best of reasons for taking account of morality. Can we say the same of our uncaring man? If he does what we say he should do what will his motivation be? Will he not simply be afraid of our disapproval, or following a training which he is too timid or conventional to throw off?

I am sure it will be replied that the 'should' of morality necessarily gives reasons for acting to any man, but this is what I want to question. Why should we think that the connection with reasons exists necessarily even in the case of a 'should' that works like this? In one sense it is true that moral judgements necessarily give reasons for acting, but in that sense it is also true that, for example, codes of etiquette must do so. (We would not speak of a code of etiquette unless people in general guided their conduct by such rules.) Yet a man may ask whether he has any reason to obey some other code that he has been taught. Why should he not ask this also about the moral code, claiming to free himself from morality as many have freed themselves from codes of manners? It is no use our reiterating the word 'should' and 'shouldn't', since this piece of usage is not being questioned, only the connection with reasons for acting when 'should' is used like this. If we want to use the moral 'should' as we do in applying it even to a man indifferent to the ends of morality must we not accept the penalty that the connection between what a man should do and what he has reason to do breaks down? What we are inclined to do is to ignore all this, insisting on the word 'reason' without being able to show why we should use it in the case of morality though not, like this, in the case of etiquette. The rationale is lacking though the motive is clear. We are, naturally, concerned about the man who doesn't care what happens to other people, and we want to convict him of irrationality, thinking that he will mind about that. Outside moral philosophy we would not think of the cool and prudent, though wicked, man as specifically irrational in his conduct; outside philosophy we also know that there is nothing one can do with a ruthless amoral man except to prevent him from doing too much damage. To say that since his conduct is immoral we can tell him of some reason why he should change it, or that he necessarily has reason to alter his ways, seems yet another case of keeping up a pretence. We speak as if there were an authority in the background to guarantee that wickedness is necessarily foolishness, though the 'binding force' of morality is supposed to be independent of such an appeal. Would it not be more honest either to change the language or else to recognize that the 'should' of moral judgement is sometimes merely an instrument by which we (for our own very good reasons) try to impose a rule of conduct even on the uncaring man?

Once again, when we turn to aesthetics we find that the same problem does not arise, and this is connected with a fundamental difference in the judgement of art and of conduct. If we ask, as Plato might have done, what good is rendered by good conduct, and again by good art, and to whom it is rendered in each case, the answers will not be the same. The good of good action, while it may indeed accrue to the man who does the action, will very often go rather to another. A man who is just or honest or charitable produces a benefit for others rather than for himself, which is why we may not always be able to show that an unfeeling man, no lover of justice, has reason to be moral whatever the situation he is in. The good of good art, on the other hand, lies in such things as the pleasures of the imagination, and in general in the interest and enjoyment that a man gets from works of art. And since the one who chooses the book to read, the picture to look at, the music to hear, is usually the one to whom that good will come, there is no difficulty in seeing that he has reason to choose the good and reject what is bad. Where this connection breaks down, as it does in the atypical case of someone choosing a work of art but not able to appreciate it, we would not say that nevertheless he should choose what was good, unless in the hope that he might later come to appreciate it. We would recognize it as nonsense to say, 'The fact that a work of art is a good work of art is itself a reason for choosing it, and never mind whether you will get anything out of it or not.'

I have now drawn contrasts at three different points between moral judgement and the judgement of works of art, in each case with a conclusion unfavourable to moral judgement. I know that what has been said about the appreciation of works of art has been inadequate, and I hope that if you reject my remarks on aesthetics you will consider the discussion of moral judgement as standing on its own. My main interest in these topics is from the point of view of moral philosophy rather than aesthetics, and what I should most like to do is to open a debate which might lead us to consider changes in the way we talk about what is morally good or bad. Why, after all, should we take it for granted that the form of language already developed is the one we want?

Notes

1. It would be quite another matter to suggest that one could put the distinction between what is and is not a human being where one chose, and still have an interpretation of the principle that there is a moral objection to the *killing of human beings*.

2. Anyone who suggested that we could use the existing expression 'think it right' would be very far out indeed. For this implies just the contrast between truth and opinion that is being denied.

3. *Languages of Art* (Indianapolis and New York: Bobbs-Merrill, 1968), p. 262.

4. I am not here committing myself to a simplistic view of advising. As a corrective to this see B. J. Diggs, 'A Technical Ought', *Mind* LXIX (1960), pp. 301–17.

'Morality and Art': a Retrospective Note (1978)

Rereading this paper I realize that its main theses are not as clearly stated as I should wish. I therefore append a few remarks which may help the reader.

What I need to make clear is the general theory of moral judgement that I was more or less taking for granted, having argued for it in more detail elsewhere,[1] and the suggestions about fictitious elements in our thought about morality which are the special theme of this paper.

The background thought is that there are some objective criteria by which the moral character of actions and persons must, on pain of error, be judged. It is not conceptually possible that such considerations as the common good, the maintenance of liberty, and the lives of innocent persons, should be irrelevant to questions of morality. Whatever exactly the list, such are the kinds of things that must be taken into account when questions of morality, as opposed for instance to questions of law or manners or political or military strategy, are at issue. And since these considerations are sometimes decisive there are moral judgements – as that the Nazi treatment of the Jews was morally indefensible – which are objective, and whose truth is not relative to the standards of any particular community.

In this paper, however, I argued that there may be other moral judgements whose truth or falsity is not guaranteed by the criteria implied in the moral standpoint, but rather depend on principles which we may call 'elective'. (In the original version of the paper I called them 'contingent'.) Since elective principles may differ from individual to individual or community to community, the moral judgements based on them may be (a) subjective or (b) objective but only in relation to the standards of a particular community. It was about *these* moral judgements (be they few or many) that I was talking when I said that we may be maintaining the mere appearance of objectivity in insisting on forms of speech that suggest it. Perhaps we should make some judgements in these areas in an openly subjective way. But it is also possible, where there are elective principles shared by the members of a community, to have judgements objectively true or false, but only in relation to the standards of a particular community. If some moral judgements have this status then relativism is a true account of some moral judgements, as it is a true account, for example, of things said about good-tasting food or handsome people.

I was arguing, therefore, for the recognition of a modicum of subjectivism and relativism in moral judgement, though I was doing this against the background of the belief that there is a core of morality which is objective and whose truth is non-relative. I thought that in refusing to accept some moral judgements as subjective and some moral truth as relative we might be maintaining fictions about morality which we would not maintain about art.

In retrospect this part of the paper seems to me not to be satisfactory, just because the nature of the criteria built into the concept of morality is still so unclear, and because this leaves uncertainty about the amount of 'play' in the system. I am happier about the final section of the paper in which I argue that we are inclined to ascribe a wholly spurious *authority* to moral considerations. We like to think that morality is compelling, in a way that it is not; as if every rational man must let it guide his conduct, and this not because of some facts about human life but because moral considerations automatically give reasons for acting to everyone. I argued that not even the most central and objective judgements of morality do this: a man may simply not care whether his conduct is morally defensible or not, and it is an open question whether he nevertheless has reason to act morally.[2]

Notes

1. E.g. in 'Moral Beliefs', *Proceedings of the Aristotelian Society*, 1958–9.
2. This point of view was argued in a later paper, 'Morality as a System of Hypothetical Imperatives', *Philosophical Review*, 1972.

Biographical Note

Mrs Philippa Foot is Professor of Philosophy at the University of California at Los Angeles, and Senior Research Fellow of Somerville College, Oxford, where she was previously Fellow and Tutor. She is the author of a number of influential articles on moral philosophy, and editor of *Theories of Ethics* (1967). Her book *Virtues and Vices and Other Essays in Moral Philosophy* will be published shortly.

Further Reading

For Mrs Foot's defence of the claim that there is objective truth in morals, see her papers 'Moral Arguments', *Mind* LXVII (1958), pp. 502–13, and 'Moral Beliefs', *Proceedings of the Aristotelian Society* LIX (1958/9), pp. 83–104, reprinted in Philippa Foot (ed.), *Theories of Ethics* (Oxford Readings in Philosophy, Oxford University Press, 1967).

The 'formalist' position she is opposing in these papers and the present one is best represented by R. M. Hare, *Freedom and Reason* (Oxford: Clarendon Press, 1963).

Mrs Foot's critique of the idea that moral judgements are categorical is further developed in a more recent paper, 'Morality as a System of Hypothetical Imperatives', *Philosophical Review* LXXXI (1972), pp. 305–16.

Recent discussions of relativism and related matters include Bernard Williams, *Morality: An Introduction to Ethics* (Harmondsworth: Penguin, 1973); Bernard Williams, 'The Truth in Relativism', *Proceedings of the Aristotelian Society* LXXV (1974/5), pp. 215–28; and Gilbert Harman, 'Moral Relativism Defended', *Philosophical Review* LXXXIV (1975), pp. 3–22.

A recent argument for a thoroughgoing subjectivism about values, coupled with the idea that ordinary moral judgements include (erroneously) a claim to objectivity, is J. L. Mackie, *Ethics* (Harmondsworth: Penguin, 1977).

Bernard Williams

A Critique of Utilitarianism

Utilitarianism has been a considerable thing in moral philosophy, indeed too considerable a thing for those who have been appalled by the terribleness of certain consequences which it seems to have. The principle of utility had exponents before Jeremy Bentham recorded his satisfied conviction in about 1830 that 'the greatest happiness of the greatest number is the foundation of morals and legislation'. In one way or another the principle persists in a good deal of English, American and other moral and political philosophy. Certainly, despite the fact that it has never been without severe critics, its essential idea is a formidable one. Although it has become clear that this idea has to be brought into compromise with other ideas, it is very unlikely that it can entirely be left out of any tolerable morality.

Despite the reference to 'the greatest number' in Bentham's phrase above, the fundamental versions of the principle of utility are to the effect that the right choice in any situation is the one which can reasonably be expected to produce the greatest *total* of happiness, no matter who enjoys it and how many such people there are. In one fundamental version, the principle is that the right action, policy or whatever is the one which on the basis of the available evidence would produce more satisfaction or less dissatisfaction than any of the others, taking into account everyone affected in each case. This is how we are to guide ourselves in private morality, in politics, in fact in all of life. It is all very rational, in some sense of that unprotesting word. If we sign on as utilitarians, we can have a determinate answer, at least in theory, to every problem. That is the appeal of this philosophy. If we cannot just *add up*, as Bentham half supposed, we can do something like it. We can reckon the consequences of each alternative before us and judge which alternative comes out best overall. In the area of social decision-making, indeed, it seems that mathematical cost-benefit analysis has brought the utilitarian idea to a fine art. There are obvious comforts to be had, both philosophically and politically, from the hope that sufficient thought will deliver an unambiguous solution to every predicament.

But what if the calculated solution involves great hardship for someone who must be sacrificed for the sake of the overall sum of satisfaction? The recurring objection to utilitarianism is that its solutions may prescribe injustice, even victimization. The objection rests on the claim that there are situations where the action which would produce the most satisfaction or utility is also one which involves injustice. The utilitarian replies are to the effect that close and more acute examination of these situations reveals that either (a) utilitarianism does not, after all, prescribe the hardship, or (b) it does, and in fact it is morally acceptable – a terrible action is the right one, because it is the least terrible.

Once again this can seem the only rational and indeed responsible approach. But Professor Bernard Williams's first objection to the utilitarian outlook is directed precisely at its ability to find unambiguous answers in certain difficult situations. There are situations such that it is an objection to any morality if it makes some particular answer not only the right answer but so *obviously* the right answer as to leave no room for an adequate sense of dilemma.

Williams's objection, moreover, has to do with more than utilitarianism. Given the traditional objection to the principle of utility, that it issues in injustice, it has seemed to many philosophers that an addition must be made to it. There is the necessity of adding a principle of justice or equality, thereby producing a kind of compromise. What one must do in life, according to views of this kind, is to strike some sort of balance between the demand which we feel to increase satisfaction and, more important, to decrease distress, and, on the other hand, the demand of justice. In a sentence, what one must do in life is to act in such a way as to produce those consequences which best realize both utility and justice. Right actions are the ones which have these consequences.

Utilitarianism is evidently a morality of consequences – a consequentialism. We are to maximize consequences which consist in satisfaction. So too is this successor to utilitarianism a consequentialism. We are to act so as to produce, as we may say, consequences of satisfaction and equality. Williams's reflections comprise not only a critique of utilitarianism but also of this succeeding consequentialist morality.

Moralities of the consequentialist kind, to look at their general definition a bit more closely, have to do with two kinds of states of affairs:

those which *follow on* a person's doing something, and those which *consist in* his doing a thing. We have satisfaction from health, but also from exercise itself. We may have pleasure in seeing Peking, and, as the travel agents promise, also have pleasure in getting there. An action may thus be the right thing, from the utilitarian point of view, in large part because of the satisfaction or enrichment got by the person *in doing it*. It may be wondered, once this latter kind of intrinsic consequence of an action is noted, how any quite different kind of recommendation of an action can be distinguished. More precisely, what room is there for a *non-consequentialist* morality? Consequentialism may seem to have appropriated all the possible reasons for action that there can be.

In a section of 'A Critique of Utilitarianism' which comes before the three sections reprinted below, Williams discusses this matter acutely, and clarifies an essential perception. It is that for a consequentialist an action is right because the state of affairs of the person's doing it is better than any other state of affairs open to him, while on a non-consequentialist morality, it may be that a state of affairs is better than the alternatives because it consists in the right action being done. Very briefly, that is the contrast.

As already remarked, Williams's argument escapes from traditional disputes about utilitarianism and injustice, and strikes instead at all consequentialisms. He describes two dilemmas: that of George, the chemist who has to decide whether to take a job involving research in chemical and biological warfare, and that of Jim, who has to decide whether to take part in a political killing. These two examples are of real importance to the argument. They bring before us situations in which, contrary to utilitarian and related doctrine, it seems clear enough which choice will realize the best consequences overall but not at all clear that this choice is the right one for the agent to make. For George at least, it may even be the wrong solution to his predicament. The examples are also important in that they make the transition from abstract argument to concrete detail – a transition too rare in moral philosophy – and contribute vividly to clarifying what it would be like to live with a non-consequentialist morality. Two key concepts recur throughout the discussion, those of *negative responsibility* and of *integrity*.

It is a feature of both George's and Jim's dilemmas that if they do not undertake the morally repellent course of action offered to them, someone else will – someone who will make the evil worse. Their refusal, their inaction, will have a certain outcome; a worse state of affairs will come about than would result from the alternative choice. They know that this is part of their dilemma. From a consequentialist viewpoint, however, what matters is simply whether a better or a worse state of affairs results. From this viewpoint, they must see themselves as just as responsible for what comes about if they do *not* do something (negative responsibility) as they are for what comes about if they do it. A consequentialist cannot regard the two cases differently. In this sense he is committed to a strong doctrine of negative responsibility.

Yet it is also part of both George's and Jim's dilemma that the choice with the foreseeably better consequences is a choice which involves them in actively undertaking a morally repellent action. The thought 'I will have to do it' is bound to weigh heavily on their consciences. It is this thought, or more precisely, the contrast between *my* doing it and its being done (by someone or other), which brings in the difficult but important notion of integrity. A man cannot be expected to step aside, so to speak, from projects central to his life and to his sense of himself, allowing the mere circumstance of other people's intervention to affect the value at which his projects are to be assessed. The question is: what can the utilitarian say about integrity? Is it a value of which he can make sense at all? And if not, can he make a case for denying it a place in our moral thinking?

These questions Williams pursues with a rare combination of cogency and sensitivity. It only remains to say a word about 'the brain-electrode man' who puts in an appearance on p. 51. Williams's 'A Critique of Utilitarianism' is one half of *Utilitarianism: For and Against*. The other half is J. J. C. Smart's 'Outline of a System of Utilitarian Ethics', and from time to time Williams makes reference to Smart's careful and courageous defence of utilitarianism against various objections. One of the objections at issue is the familiar one that men have, and ought to have, higher ends than the maximizing of pleasure as such. It is claimed that utilitarianism would have nothing adverse to say about a man who gives over most of his life to electro-stimulation of the pleasure centres in his brain, effortlessly securing at the push of a button a continuous series of delectable pleasures. Were this science-fiction fantasy to come true, the objection runs, utilitarianism would have to approve of the man. Smart has things to say about the case. It is one part of Williams's argument, and indeed not just a response to the example of the brain-electrode man, that consequences which consist in happiness and the like are not enough.

T.H.

Bernard Williams

A Critique of Utilitarianism

Reprinted from 'A Critique of Utilitarianism' by Bernard Williams in
Utilitarianism: For and Against by J. J. C. Smart and Bernard Williams
copyright © Cambridge University Press. With the permission of the
author and publisher.

Negative Responsibility: and Two Examples

Consequentialism is basically indifferent to whether a state of affairs
consists in what I do, or is produced by what I do, where that notion
is itself wide enough to include, for instance, situations in which other
people do things which I have made them do, or allowed them to do,
or encouraged them to do, or given them a chance to do. All that
consequentialism is interested in is the idea of these doings being
consequences of what I do, and that is a relation broad enough to
include the relations just mentioned, and many others.

Just what the relation is, is a different question, and at least as obscure as the nature of its relative, cause and effect. It is not a question
I shall try to pursue; I will rely on cases where I suppose that any
consequentialist would be bound to regard the situations in question
as consequences of what the agent does. There are cases where the
supposed consequences stand in a rather remote relation to the action,
which are sometimes difficult to assess from a practical point of view,
but which raise no very interesting question for the present inquiry.
The more interesting points about consequentialism lie rather elsewhere. There are certain situations in which the causation of the situation, the relation it has to what I do, is in no way remote or problematic in itself, and entirely justifies the claim that the situation is a
consequence of what I do: for instance, it is quite clear, or reasonably
clear, that if I do a certain thing, this situation will come about, and if
I do not, it will not. So from a consequentialist point of view it goes
into the calculation of consequences along with any other state of
affairs accessible to me. Yet from some, at least, non-consequentialist

points of view, there is a vital difference between some such situations and others: namely, that in some a vital link in the production of the eventual outcome is provided by *someone else's* doing something. But for consequentialism, all causal connexions are on the same level, and it makes no difference, so far as that goes, whether the causation of a given state of affairs lies through another agent, or not.

Correspondingly, there is no relevant difference which consists *just* in one state of affairs being brought about by me, without intervention of other agents, and another being brought about through the intervention of other agents; although some genuinely causal differ-ences involving a difference of value may correspond to that (as when, for instance, the other agents derive pleasure or pain from the transaction), that kind of difference will already be included in the specification of the state of affairs to be produced. Granted that the states of affairs have been adequately described in causally and evalua-tively relevant terms, it makes no further comprehensible difference who produces them. It is because consequentialism attaches value ulti-mately to states of affairs, and its concern is with what states of affairs the world contains, that it essentially involves the notion of *negative responsibility*: that if I am ever responsible for anything, then I must be just as much responsible for things that I allow or fail to prevent, as I am for things that I myself, in the more everyday restricted sense, bring about. Those things also must enter my deliberations, as a responsible moral agent, on the same footing. What matters is what states of affairs the world contains, and so what matters with respect to a given action is what comes about if it is done, and what comes about if it is not done, and those are questions not intrinsically affected by the nature of the causal linkage, in particular by whether the out-come is partly produced by other agents.

The strong doctrine of negative responsibility flows directly from consequentialism's assignment of ultimate value to states of affairs. Looked at from another point of view, it can be seen also as a special application of something that is favoured in many moral outlooks not themselves consequentialist – something which, indeed, some thinkers have been disposed to regard as the essence of morality itself: a principle of impartiality. Such a principle will claim that there can be no relevant difference from a moral point of view which consists just in the fact, not further explicable in general terms, that benefits or harms accrue to one person rather than to another – 'it's me' can never in itself be a morally comprehensible reason.[1] This principle, familiar with regard to the reception of harms and benefits, we can see consequentialism as extending to their production: from the moral point of view, there is no comprehensible difference which consists just in my bringing about a certain outcome rather than someone else's producing it. That the doctrine of negative responsibility represents in this way the extreme of impartiality, and abstracts from the identity of the agent, leaving just a locus of causal intervention in the world – that fact is not merely a surface paradox. It helps to explain why consequentialism can seem to some to express a more serious attitude than non-consequentialist views, why part of its appeal is to a certain kind of high-mindedness. Indeed, that is part of what is wrong with it.

For a lot of the time so far we have been operating at an exceedingly abstract level. This has been necessary in order to get clearer in general terms about the differences between consequentialist and other outlooks, an aim which is important if we want to know what features of them lead to what results for our thought. Now, however, let us look more concretely at two examples, to see what utilitarianism might say about them, what we might say about utilitarianism and, most importantly of all, what would be implied by certain ways of thinking about the situations. The examples are inevitably schematized, and they are open to the objection that they beg as many questions as they illuminate. There are two ways in particular in which examples in moral philosophy tend to beg important questions. One is that, as presented, they arbitrarily cut off and restrict the range of alternative courses of action – this objection might particularly be made against the first of my two examples. The second is that they inevitably present one with the situation as a going concern, and cut off questions about how the agent got into it, and correspondingly about moral considerations which might flow from that: this objection might perhaps specially arise with regard to the second of my two situations. These difficulties, however, just have to be accepted, and if anyone finds these examples cripplingly defective in this sort of respect, then he must in his own thought rework them in richer and less question-begging form. If he feels that no presentation of any imagined situation can ever be other than misleading in morality, and that there can never be any substitute for the concrete experienced complexity of actual moral situations, then this discussion, with him, must certainly grind to a halt: but then one may legitimately wonder whether every discussion with him about conduct will not grind to a halt, including any discussion about the actual situations, since discussion about how one would think and feel about situations somewhat different from the actual (that is to say, situations to that extent imaginary) plays an important role in discussion of the actual.

(1) George, who has just taken his Ph.D. in chemistry, finds it extremely difficult to get a job. He is not very robust in health, which cuts down the number of jobs he might be able to do satisfactorily. His wife has to go out to work to keep them, which itself causes a great deal of strain, since they have small children and there are severe problems about looking after them. The results of all this, especially on the children, are damaging. An older chemist, who knows about this situation, says that he can get George a decently paid job in a certain laboratory, which pursues research into chemical and biological warfare. George says that he cannot accept this, since he is opposed to chemical and biological warfare. The older man replies that he is not too keen on it himself, come to that, but after all George's refusal is not going to make the job or the laboratory go away; what is more, he happens to know that if George refuses the job, it will certainly go to a contemporary of George's who is not inhibited by any such scruples and is likely if appointed to push along the research with greater zeal than George would. Indeed, it is not merely concern for George and his family, but (to speak frankly and in confidence) some alarm about this other man's excess of zeal, which has led the older man to offer to use his influence to get George the job . . . George's wife, to whom he is deeply attached, has views (the details of which need not concern us) from which it follows that at least there is nothing particularly wrong with research into CBW. What should he do?

(2) Jim finds himself in the central square of a small South American town. Tied up against the wall are a row of twenty Indians, most

terrified, a few defiant, in front of them several armed men in uniform. A heavy man in a sweat-stained khaki shirt turns out to be the captain in charge and, after a good deal of questioning of Jim which establishes that he got there by accident while on a botanical expedition, explains that the Indians are a random group of the inhabitants who, after recent acts of protest against the government, are just about to be killed to remind other possible protestors of the advantages of not protesting. However, since Jim is an honoured visitor from another land, the captain is happy to offer him a guest's privilege of killing one of the Indians himself. If Jim accepts, then as a special mark of the occasion, the other Indians will be let off. Of course, if Jim refuses, then there is no special occasion, and Pedro here will do what he was about to do when Jim arrived, and kill them all. Jim, with some desperate recollection of schoolboy fiction, wonders whether if he got hold of a gun, he could hold the captain, Pedro and the rest of the soldiers to threat, but it is quite clear from the set-up that nothing of that kind is going to work: any attempt at that sort of thing will mean that all the Indians will be killed, and himself. The men against the wall, and the other villagers, understand the situation, and are obviously begging him to accept. What should he do?

To these dilemmas, it seems to me that utilitarianism replies, in the first case, that George should accept the job, and in the second, that Jim should kill the Indian. Not only does utilitarianism give these answers but, if the situations are essentially as described and there are no further special factors, it regards them, it seems to me, as *obviously* the right answers. But many of us would certainly wonder whether, in (1), that could possibly be the right answer at all; and in the case of (2), even one who came to think that perhaps that was the answer, might well wonder whether it was obviously the answer. Nor is it just a question of the rightness or obviousness of these answers. It is also a question of what sort of considerations come into finding the answer. A feature of utilitarianism is that it cuts out a kind of consideration which for some others makes a difference to what they feel about such cases: a consideration involving the idea, as we might first and very simply put it, that each of us is specially responsible for what *he* does, rather than for what other people do. This is an idea closely connected with the value of integrity. It is often suspected that utilitarianism, at least in its direct forms, makes integrity as a value more or less unintelligible. I shall try to show that this suspicion is correct. Of course, even if that is correct, it would not necessarily follow that we should reject utilitarianism; perhaps, as utilitarians sometimes suggest, we should just forget about integrity, in favour of such things as a concern for the general good. However, if I am right, we cannot merely do that, since the reason why utilitarianism cannot understand integrity is that it cannot coherently describe the relations between a man's projects and his actions.

Two Kinds of Remoter Effect

A lot of what we have to say about this question will be about the relations between my projects and other people's projects. But before we get on to that, we should first ask whether we are assuming too hastily what the utilitarian answers to the dilemmas will be. In terms of more direct effects of the possible decisions, there does not indeed seem much doubt about the answer in either case; but it might be said that in terms of more remote or less evident effects counter-weights might be found to enter the utilitarian scales. Thus the effect on George of a decision to take the job might be invoked, or its effect on others who might know of his decision. The possibility of there being more beneficent labours in the future from which he might be barred or disqualified, might be mentioned; and so forth. Such effects – in particular, possible effects on the agent's character, and effects on the public at large – are often invoked by utilitarian writers dealing with problems about lying or promise-breaking, and some similar considerations might be invoked here.

There is one very general remark that is worth making about arguments of this sort. The certainty that attaches to these hypotheses about possible effects is usually pretty low; in some cases, indeed, the hypothesis invoked is so implausible that it would scarcely pass if it were not being used to deliver the respectable moral answer, as in the standard fantasy that one of the effects of one's telling a particular lie is to weaken the disposition of the world at large to tell the truth. The demands on the certainty or probability of these beliefs as beliefs about particular actions are much milder than they would be on beliefs favouring the unconventional course. It may be said that this is as it should be, since the presumption must be in favour of the conventional course: but that scarcely seems a *utilitarian* answer, unless utilitarianism has already taken off in the direction of not applying the consequences to the particular act at all.

Leaving aside that very general point, I want to consider now two types of effect that are often invoked by utilitarians, and which might be invoked in connexion with these imaginary cases. The attitude or tone involved in invoking these effects may sometimes seem peculiar; but that sort of peculiarity soon becomes familiar in utilitarian discussions, and indeed it can be something of an achievement to retain a sense of it.

First, there is the psychological effect on the agent. Our descriptions of these situations have not so far taken account of how George or Jim will be after they have taken the one course or the other; and it might be said that if they take the course which seemed at first the utilitarian one, the effects on them will be in fact bad enough and extensive enough to cancel out the initial utilitarian advantages of that course. Now there is one version of this effect in which, for a utilitarian, some confusion must be involved, namely that in which the agent feels bad, his subsequent conduct and relations are crippled and so on, *because he thinks that he has done the wrong thing* – for if the balance of outcomes was as it appeared to be *before* invoking this effect, then he has not (from the utilitarian point of view) done the wrong thing. So that version of the effect, for a rational and utilitarian agent, could not possibly make any difference to the assessment of right and wrong. However, perhaps he is not a thoroughly rational agent, and is disposed to have bad feelings, whichever he decided to do. Now such feelings, which are from a strictly utilitarian point of view irrational – nothing, a utilitarian can point out, is advanced by having them – cannot, consistently, have any great weight in a utilitarian calculation. I shall consider in a moment an argument to suggest that they should have no weight at all in it. But short of that, the utilitarian could reasonably say that such feelings should not be encouraged, even if we accept their existence, and that to give them a lot of weight is to encourage them. Or, at the very best, even if they are straightforwardly and without any discount to be put into the calculation, their weight must be small: they are after all (and at best) one man's feelings.

That consideration might seem to have particular force in Jim's case. In George's case, his feelings represent a larger proportion of what is to be weighed, and are more commensurate in character with other items in the calculation. In Jim's case, however, his feelings might seem to be of very little weight compared with other things that are at stake. There is a powerful and recognizable appeal that can be made on this point: as that a refusal by Jim to do what he has been invited to do would be a kind of self-indulgent squeamishness. That is an appeal which can be made by other than utilitarians – indeed, there are some uses of it which cannot be consistently made by utilitarians, as when it essentially involves the idea that there is something dishonourable about such self-indulgence. But in some versions it is a familiar, and it must be said a powerful, weapon of utilitarianism. One must be clear, though, about what it can and cannot accomplish. The most it can do, so far as I can see, is to invite one to consider how seriously, and for what reasons, one feels that what one is invited to do is (in these circumstances) wrong, and in particular, to consider that question from the utilitarian point of view. When the agent is not seeing the situation from a utilitarian point of view, the appeal cannot force him to do so; and if he does come round to seeing it from a utilitarian point of view, there is virtually nothing left for the appeal to do. If he does not see it from a utilitarian point of view, he will not see his resistance to the invitation, and the unpleasant feelings he associates with accepting it, *just* as disagreeable experiences of his; they figure rather as emotional expressions of a thought that to accept would be wrong. He may be asked, as by the appeal, to consider whether he is right, and indeed whether he is fully serious, in thinking that. But the assertion of the appeal, that he is being self-indulgently squeamish, will not itself answer that question, or even help to answer it, since it essentially tells him to regard his feelings just as unpleasant experiences of his, and he cannot, by doing that, answer the question they pose when they are precisely not so regarded, but are regarded as indications of what he thinks is right and wrong. If he does come round fully to the utilitarian point of view then of course he will regard these feelings just as unpleasant experiences of his. And once Jim – at least – has come to see them in that light, there is nothing left for the appeal to do, since *of course* his feelings, so regarded, are of virtually no weight at all in relation to the other things at stake. The 'squeamishness' appeal is not an argument which adds in a hitherto neglected consideration. Rather, it is an invitation to consider the situation, and one's own feelings, from a utilitarian point of view.

The reason why the squeamishness appeal can be very unsettling, and one can be unnerved by the suggestion of self-indulgence in going against utilitarian considerations, is not that we are utilitarians who are uncertain what utilitarian value to attach to our moral feelings, but that we are partially at least not utilitarians, and cannot regard our moral feelings merely as objects of utilitarian value. Because our moral relation to the world is partly given by such feelings, and by a sense of what we can or cannot 'live with', to come to regard those feelings from a purely utilitarian point of view, that is to say, as happenings outside one's moral self, is to lose a sense of one's moral identity; to lose, in the most literal way, one's integrity. At this point utilitarianism alienates one from one's moral feelings; we shall see a little later how, more basically, it alienates one from one's actions as well.

If, then, one is really going to regard one's feelings from a strictly utilitarian point of view, Jim should give very little weight at all to his; it seems almost indecent, in fact, once one has taken that point of view, to suppose that he should give any at all. In George's case one might feel that things were slightly different. It is interesting, though, that one reason why one might think that – namely that one person principally affected is his wife – is very dubiously available to a utilitarian. George's wife has some reason to be interested in George's integrity and his sense of it; the Indians, quite properly, have no interest in Jim's. But it is not at all clear how utilitarianism would describe that difference.

There is an argument, and a strong one, that a strict utilitarian should give not merely small extra weight, in calculations of right and wrong, to feelings of this kind, but that he should give absolutely no weight to them at all. This is based on the point, which we have already seen, that if a course of action is, before taking these sorts of feelings into account, utilitarianly preferable, then bad feelings about that kind of action will be from a utilitarian point of view irrational. Now it might be thought that even if that is so, it would not mean that in a utilitarian calculation such feelings should not be taken into account; it is after all a well-known boast of utilitarianism that it is a realistic outlook which seeks the best in the world as it is, and takes any form of happiness or unhappiness into account. While a utilitarian will no doubt seek to diminish the incidence of feelings which are utilitarianly irrational – or at least of disagreeable feelings which are so – he might be expected to take them into account while they exist. This is without doubt classical utilitarian doctrine, but there is good reason to think that utilitarianism cannot stick to it without embracing results which are startlingly unacceptable and perhaps self-defeating.

Suppose that there is in a certain society a racial minority. Considering merely the ordinary interests of the other citizens, as opposed to their sentiments, this minority does no particular harm; we may suppose that it does not confer any very great benefits either. Its presence is in those terms neutral or mildly beneficial. However, the other citizens have such prejudices that they find the sight of this group, even the knowledge of its presence, very disagreeable. Proposals are made for removing in some way this minority. If we assume various quite plausible things (as that programmes to change the majority sentiment are likely to be protracted and ineffective) then even if the removal would be unpleasant for the minority, a utilitarian calculation might well end up favouring this step, especially if the minority were a rather small minority and the majority were very severely prejudiced, that is to say, were made very severely uncomfortable by the presence of the minority.

A utilitarian might find that conclusion embarrassing; and not merely because of its nature, but because of the grounds on which it is reached. While a utilitarian might be expected to take into account certain other sorts of consequences of the prejudice, as that a majority prejudice is likely to be displayed in conduct disagreeable to the minority, and so forth, he might be made to wonder whether the unpleasant experiences of the prejudiced people should be allowed, *merely as such*, to count. If he does count them, merely as such, then he has once more separated himself from a body of ordinary moral thought which he might have hoped to accommodate; he may also have started on the path of defeating his own view of things. For one feature of these sentiments is that they are from the utilitarian point of view itself irrational, and a thoroughly utilitarian person would either not have them, or if he found that he did tend to have them, would himself seek to discount them. Since the sentiments in question are such that a rational utilitarian would discount them in himself, it is reasonable to suppose that he should discount them in his calculations about society; it does seem quite unreasonable for him to give just as much weight to feelings – considered just in themselves, one must recall, as experiences of those that have them – which are essentially based on views which are from a utilitarian point of view irrational, as to those which accord with utilitarian principles. Granted this idea, it seems reasonable for him to rejoin a body of moral thought in other respects congenial to him, and discount those sentiments, just considered in themselves, totally, on the principle that no pains or discomforts are to count in the utilitarian sum which their subjects have just because they hold views which are by utilitarian standards irrational. But if he accepts that, then in the cases we are at present considering no extra weight at all can be put in for bad feelings of George or Jim about their choices, if those choices are, leaving out those feelings, on the first round utilitarianly rational.

The psychological effect on the agent was the first of two general effects considered by utilitarians, which had to be discussed. The second is in general a more substantial item, but it need not take so long, since it is both clearer and has little application to the present cases. This is the *precedent effect*. As Burke rightly emphasized, this effect can be important: that one morally *can* do what someone has actually done, is a psychologically effective principle, if not a deontically valid one. For the effect to operate, obviously some conditions must hold on the publicity of the act and on such things as the status of the agent (such considerations weighed importantly with Sir Thomas More); what these may be will vary evidently with circumstances.

In order for the precedent effect to make a difference to a utilitarian calculation, it must be based upon a confusion. For suppose that there is an act which would be the best in the circumstances, except that doing it will encourage by precedent other people to do things which will not be the best things to do. Then the situation of those other people must be relevantly different from that of the original agent; if it were not, then in doing the same as what would be the best course for the original agent, they would necessarily do the best thing for themselves. But if the situations are in this way relevantly different, it must be a confused perception which takes the first situation, and the agent's course in it, as an adequate precedent for the second.

However, the fact that the precedent effect, if it really makes a difference, is in this sense based on a confusion, does not mean that it is not perfectly real, nor that it is to be discounted: social effects are by their nature confused in this sort of way. What it does emphasize is that calculations of the precedent effect have got to be realistic, involving considerations of how people are actually likely to be influenced. In the present examples, however, it is very implausible to think that the precedent effect could be invoked to make any difference to the calculation. Jim's case is extraordinary enough, and it is hard to imagine who the recipients of the effect might be supposed to be; while George is not in a sufficiently public situation or role for the question to arise in that form, and in any case one might suppose that the motivations of others on such an issue were quite likely to be fixed one way or another already.

No appeal, then, to these other effects is going to make a difference to what the utilitarian will decide about our examples. Let us now look more closely at the structure of those decisions.

Integrity

The situations have in common that if the agent does not do a certain disagreeable thing, someone else will, and in Jim's situation at least the result, the state of affairs after the other man has acted, if he does, will be worse than after Jim has acted, if Jim does. The same, on a smaller scale, is true of George's case. I have already suggested that it is inherent in consequentialism that it offers a strong doctrine of negative responsibility: if I know that if I do X, O_1 will eventuate, and if I refrain from doing X, O_2 will, and that O_2 is worse than O_1, then I am responsible for O_2 if I refrain voluntarily from doing X. 'You could have prevented it', as will be said, and truly, to Jim, if he refuses, by the relatives of the other Indians. (I shall leave the important question, which is to the side of the present issue, of the obligations, if any, that nest round the word 'know': how far does one, under utilitarianism, have to research into the possibilities of maximally beneficent action, including prevention?)

In the present cases, the situation of O_2 includes another agent bringing about results worse than O_1. So far as O_2 has been identified up to this point – merely as the worse outcome which will eventuate if I refrain from doing X – we might equally have said that what that other brings about is O_2; but that would be to underdescribe the situation. For what occurs if Jim refrains from action is not solely twenty Indians dead, but *Pedro's killing twenty Indians*, and that is not a result which Pedro brings about, though the death of the Indians is. We can say: what one does is not included in the outcome of what one does, while what another does can be included in the outcome of what one does. For that to be so, as the terms are now being used, only a very weak condition has to be satisfied: for Pedro's killing the Indians to be the outcome of Jim's refusal, it only has to be causally true that if Jim had not refused, Pedro would not have done it.

That may be enough for us to speak, in some sense, of Jim's responsibility for that outcome, if it occurs; but it is certainly not enough, it is worth noticing, for us to speak of Jim's *making* those things happen. For granted this way of their coming about, he could have made them happen only by making Pedro shoot, and there is no acceptable sense in which his refusal makes Pedro shoot. If the captain had said on Jim's refusal, 'you leave me with no alternative', he would have been lying, like most who use that phrase. While the deaths, and the killing, may be the outcome of Jim's refusal, it is misleading to think, in such a case, of Jim having an *effect* on the world through the medium (as it happens) of Pedro's acts; for this is to leave Pedro out of the picture in his essential role of one who has intentions and projects, projects for realizing which Jim's refusal would leave an opportunity. Instead of thinking in terms of supposed effects of Jim's projects on Pedro, it is more revealing to think in terms of the effects of Pedro's projects on Jim's decision. This is the direction from which I want to criticize the notion of negative responsibility.

There are of course other ways in which this notion can be criticized. Many have hoped to discredit it by insisting on the basic moral relevance of the distinction between action and inaction, between intervening and letting things take their course. The distinction is certainly of great moral significance, and indeed it is not easy to think of any moral outlook which could get along without making some use of it. But it is unclear, both in itself and in its moral applications, and the unclarities are of a kind which precisely cause it to give way when, in very difficult cases, weight has to be put on it. There is much to be said in this area, but I doubt whether the sort of dilemma we are considering is going to be resolved by a simple use of this distinction. Again, the issue of negative responsibility can be pressed on the question of how limits are to be placed on one's apparently boundless obligation, implied by utilitarianism, to improve the world. Some answers are needed to that, too – and answers which stop short of relapsing into the bad faith of supposing that one's responsibilities could be adequately characterized just by appeal to one's roles.[2] But, once again, while that is a real question, it cannot be brought to bear directly on the present kind of case, since it is hard to think of anyone supposing that in Jim's case it would be an adequate response for him to say that it was none of his business.

What projects does a utilitarian agent have? As a utilitarian, he has the general project of bringing about maximally desirable outcomes; how he is to do this at any given moment is a question of what causal levers, so to speak, are at that moment within reach. The desirable outcomes, however, do not just consist of agents carrying out *that* project; there must be other more basic or lower-order projects which he and other agents have, and the desirable outcomes are going to consist, in part, of the maximally harmonious realization of those projects ('in part', because one component of a utilitarianly desirable outcome may be the occurrence of agreeable experiences which are not the satisfaction of anybody's projects). Unless there were first-order projects, the general utilitarian project would have nothing to work on, and would be vacuous. What do the more basic or lower-order projects comprise? Many will be the obvious kinds of desires for things for oneself, one's family, one's friends, including basic necessities of life, and in more relaxed circumstances, objects of taste. Or there may be pursuits and interests of an intellectual, cultural or creative character. I introduce those as a separate class not because the objects of them lie in a separate class, and provide – as some utilitarians, in their churchy way, are fond of saying – 'higher' pleasures. I introduce them separately because the agent's identification with them may be of a different order. It does not have to be: cultural and aesthetic interests just belong, for many, along with any other taste; but some people's commitment to these kinds of interests just is at once more thoroughgoing and serious than their pursuit of various objects of taste, while it is more individual and permeated with character than the desire for the necessities of life.

Beyond these, someone may have projects connected with his support of some cause: Zionism, for instance, or the abolition of chemical and biological warfare. Or there may be projects which flow from some more general disposition towards human conduct and character, such as a hatred of injustice, or of cruelty, or of killing.

It may be said that this last sort of disposition and its associated project do not count as (logically) 'lower-order' relative to the higher-order project of maximizing desirable outcomes; rather, it may be said, it is itself a 'higher-order' project. The vital question is not, however, how it is to be classified, but whether it and similar projects are to count among the projects whose satisfaction is to be included in the maximizing sum, and, correspondingly, as contributing to the agent's happiness. If the utilitarian says 'no' to that, then he is almost certainly committed to a version of utilitarianism as absurdly superficial and shallow as Benthamite versions have often been accused of being. For this project will be discounted, presumably, on the ground that it involves, in the specification of its object, the mention of other people's happiness or interests: thus it is the kind of project which (unlike the pursuit of food for myself) presupposes a reference to other people's projects. But that criterion would eliminate any desire at all which was not blankly and in the most straightforward sense egoistic.[3] Thus we should be reduced to frankly egoistic first-order projects, and – for all essential purposes – the one second-order utilitarian project of maximally satisfying first-order projects. Utilitarianism has a tendency to slide in this direction, and to leave a vast hole in the range of human desires, between egoistic inclinations and necessities at one end, and impersonally benevolent happiness-management at the other. But the utilitarianism which has to leave this hole is the most primitive form, which offers a quite rudimentary account of desire. Modern versions of the theory are supposed to be neutral with regard to what sorts of things make people happy or what their projects are. Utilitarianism would do well then to acknowledge the evident fact that among the things that make people happy is not only making other people happy, but being taken up or involved in any of a vast range of projects, or – if we waive the evangelical and moralizing associations of the word – commitments. One can be committed to such things as a person, a cause, an institution, a career, one's own genius, or the pursuit of danger.

Now none of these is itself the *pursuit of happiness*: by an exceedingly ancient platitude, it is not at all clear that there could be anything which was just that, or at least anything that had the slightest chance of being successful. Happiness, rather, requires being involved in, or at least content with, something else.[4] It is not impossible for utilitarianism to accept that point: it does not have to be saddled with a naïve and absurd philosophy of mind about the relation between desire and happiness. What it does have to say is that if such commitments are worth while, then pursuing the projects that flow from them, and realizing some of those projects, will make the person for whom they are worth while, happy. It may be that to claim that is still wrong: it may well be that a commitment can make sense to a man (can make sense of his life) without his supposing that it will make him *happy*.[5] But that is not the present point; let us grant to utilitarianism that all worthwhile human projects must conduce, one way or another, to happiness. The point is that even if that is true, it does not follow, nor could it possibly be true, that those projects are themselves projects of pursuing happiness. One has to believe in, or at least want, or quite minimally, be content with, other things, for there to be anywhere that happiness can come from.

Utilitarianism, then, should be willing to agree that its general aim of maximizing happiness does not imply that what everyone is doing is just pursuing happiness. On the contrary, people have to be pursuing other things. What those other things may be, utilitarianism, sticking to its professed empirical stance, should be prepared just to find out. No doubt some possible projects it will want to discourage, on the grounds that their being pursued involves a negative balance of happiness to others: though even there, the unblinking accountant's eye of the strict utilitarian will have something to put in the positive column, the satisfactions of the destructive agent. Beyond that, there will be a vast variety of generally beneficent or at least harmless projects; and some no doubt, will take the form not just of tastes or fancies, but of what I have called 'commitments'. It may even be that the utilitarian researcher will find that many of those with commitments, who have really identified themselves with objects outside themselves, who are thoroughly involved with other persons, or institutions, or activities or causes, are actually happier than those whose projects and wants are not like that. If so, that is an important piece of utilitarian empirical lore.

When I say 'happier' here, I have in mind the sort of consideration which any utilitarian would be committed to accepting: as for instance that such people are less likely to have a break-down or commit suicide. Of course that is not all that is actually involved, but the point in this argument is to use to the maximum degree utilitarian notions, in order to locate a breaking point in utilitarian thought. In appealing to this strictly utilitarian notion, I am being more consistent with utilitarianism than Smart is. In his struggles with the problem of the brain-electrode man, Smart (p. 22) commends the idea that 'happy' is a partly evaluative term, in the sense that we call 'happiness' those kinds of satisfaction which, as things are, we approve of. But *by what standard* is this surplus element of approval supposed, from a utilitarian point of view, to be allocated? There is no source for it, on a strictly utilitarian view, except further degrees of satisfaction, but there are none of those available, or the problem would not arise. Nor does it help to appeal to the fact that we dislike in prospect things which we like when we get there, for from a utilitarian point of view it would seem that the original dislike was merely irrational or based on an error. Smart's argument at this point seems to be embarrassed by a well-known utilitarian uneasiness, which comes from a feeling that it is not respectable to ignore the 'deep', while not having anywhere left in human life to locate it.[6]

Let us now go back to the agent as utilitarian, and his higher-order project of maximizing desirable outcomes. At this level, he is committed only to that: what the outcome will actually consist of will depend entirely on the facts, on what persons with what projects and what potential satisfactions there are within calculable reach of the causal levers near which he finds himself. His own substantial projects and commitments come into it, but only as one lot among others – they potentially provide one set of satisfactions among those which he may be able to assist from where he happens to be. He is the agent of the satisfaction system who happens to be at a particular point at a particular time: in Jim's case, our man in South America. His own decisions as a utilitarian agent are a function of all the satisfactions which he can affect from where he is: and this means that the projects of others, to an indeterminately great extent, determine his decision.

This may be so either positively or negatively. It will be so positively if agents within the causal field of his decision have projects which are at any rate harmless, and so should be assisted. It will equally be so, but negatively, if there is an agent within the causal field whose projects are harmful, and have to be frustrated to maximize desirable outcomes. So it is with Jim and the soldier Pedro. On the utilitarian view, the undesirable projects of other people as much determine, in this negative way, one's decisions as the desirable ones do positively: if those people were not there, or had different projects, the causal nexus would be different, and it is the actual state of the causal nexus which determines the decision. The determination to an indefinite degree of my decisions by other people's projects is just another aspect of my unlimited responsibility to act for the best in a causal framework formed to a considerable extent by their projects.

The decision so determined is, for utilitarianism, the right decision. But what if it conflicts with some project of mine? This, the utilitarian will say, has already been dealt with: the satisfaction to you of fulfilling your project, and any satisfactions to others of your so doing, have already been through the calculating device and have been found inadequate. Now in the case of many sorts of projects, that is a perfectly reasonable sort of answer. But in the case of projects of the sort I have called 'commitments', those with which one is more deeply and extensively involved and identified, this cannot just by itself be an adequate answer and there may be no adequate answer at all. For, to take the extreme sort of case, how can a man, as a utilitarian agent, come to regard as one satisfaction among others, and a dispensable one, a project or attitude round which he has built his life, just because someone else's projects have so structured the causal scene that that is how the utilitarian sum comes out?

The point here is not, as utilitarians may hasten to say, that if the project or attitude is that central to his life, then to abandon it will be very disagreeable to him and great loss of utility will be involved. I have already argued in section 4 that it is not like that; on the contrary, once he is prepared to look at it like that, the argument in any serious case is over anyway. The point is that he is identified with his actions as flowing from projects and attitudes which in some cases he takes seriously at the deepest level, as what his life is about (or, in some cases, this section of his life – seriousness is not necessarily the same as persistence). It is absurd to demand of such a man, when the sums come in from the utility network which the projects of others have in part determined, that he should just step aside from his own project and decision and acknowledge the decision which utilitarian calculation requires. It is to alienate him in a real sense from his actions and the source of his action in his own convictions. It is to make him into a channel between the input of everyone's projects, including his own, and an output of optimific decision; but this is to neglect the extent to which *his* actions and *his* decisions have to be seen as the actions and decisions which flow from the projects and attitudes with which he is most closely identified. It is thus, in the most literal sense, an attack on his integrity.[7]

These sorts of considerations do not in themselves give solutions to practical dilemmas such as those provided by our examples; but I hope they help to provide other ways of thinking about them. In fact, it is not hard to see that in George's case, viewed from this perspective, the utilitarian solution would be wrong. Jim's case is different, and harder. But if (as I suppose) the utilitarian is probably right in this case, that is not to be found out just by asking the utilitarian's questions. Discussion of it – and I am not going to try to carry it further here – will have to take seriously the distinction between my killing someone, and its coming about because of what I do that someone else kills them: a distinction based, not so much on the distinction between action and inaction, as on the distinction between my projects and someone else's projects. At least it will have to start by taking that seriously, as utilitarianism does not; but then it will have to build out from there by asking why that distinction seems to have less, or a different, force in this case than it has in George's. One question here would be how far one's powerful objection to killing people just is, in fact, an application of a powerful objection to their being killed. Another dimension of that is the issue of how much it matters that the people at risk are actual, and there, as opposed to hypothetical, or future, or merely elsewhere.[8]

There are many other considerations that could come into such a question, but the immediate point of all this is to draw one particular contrast with utilitarianism: that to reach a grounded decision in such a case should not be regarded as a matter of just discounting one's reactions, impulses and deeply held projects in the face of the pattern of utilities, nor yet of merely adding them in – but in the first instance of trying to understand them.

Of course, time and circumstances are unlikely to make a grounded decision, in Jim's case at least, possible. It might not even be decent. Instead of thinking in a rational and systematic way either about utilities or about the value of human life, the relevance of the people at risk being present, and so forth, the presence of the people at risk may just have its effect. The significance of the immediate should not be underestimated. Philosophers, not only utilitarian ones, repeatedly urge one to view the world *sub specie aeternitatis*,[9] but for most human purposes that is not a good *species* to view it under. If we are not agents of the universal satisfaction system, we are not primarily janitors of any system of values, even our own: very often, we just act, as a possibly confused result of the situation in which we are engaged. That, I suspect, is often an exceedingly good thing.

Notes

1. There is a tendency in some writers to suggest that it is not a comprehensible reason at all. But this, I suspect, is due to the overwhelming importance those writers ascribe to the moral point of view.

2. For some remarks bearing on this, see my *Morality*, the section on 'Goodness and roles', and Cohen's article there cited.

3. On the subject of egoistic and non-egoistic desires, see 'Egoism and altruism', in my *Problems of the Self* (Cambridge University Press, London, 1973).

4. This does not imply that there is no such thing as the project of pursuing pleasure. Some writers who have correctly resisted the view that all desires are desires for pleasure, have given an account of pleasure so thoroughly adverbial as to leave it quite unclear how there could be a distinctively hedonist way of life at all. Some room has to be left for that, though there are important difficulties both in defining it and living it. Thus (particularly in the case of the very rich) it often has highly ritual aspects, apparently part of a strategy to counter boredom.

5. For some remarks on this possibility, see *Morality*, section on 'What is morality about?'

6. One of many resemblances in spirit between utilitarianism and high-minded evangelical Christianity.

7. Interestingly related to these notions is the Socratic idea that courage is a virtue particularly connected with keeping a clear sense of what one regards as most important. They also centrally raise questions about the value of pride. Humility, as something beyond the real demand of correct self-appraisal, was specially a Christian virtue because it involved subservience to God. In a secular context it can only represent subservience to other men and their projects.

8. For a more general discussion of this issue see Charles Fried, *An Anatomy of Values* (Harvard University Press, Cambridge, Mass., 1970), Part Three.

9. Cf. Smart, *Utilitarianism: For and Against*, p. 63.

Biographical Note

Bernard Williams is Provost of King's College Cambridge. He was Knightbridge Professor of Philosophy at Cambridge from 1967 to 1979; before that Professor of Philosophy at Bedford College, London, Lecturer at University College London, and Fellow of All Souls and of New College, Oxford. His books are *Morality* (1971), *Problems of the Self* (1973), *Utilitarianism: For and Against* (with J. J. C. Smart, 1973), from which the excerpt in the present book is taken, *Descartes: The Project of Pure Enquiry* (1978) and, as editor, with A. C. Montefiore, *British Analytical Philosophy* (1966). He is a Fellow of the British Academy.

Further Reading

Other relevant writings by Bernard Williams are *Morality: An Introduction to Ethics* (New York: Harper & Row, 1972, Harmondsworth: Pelican, 1973; Cambridge: Cambridge University Press, 1977) and *Problems of the Self* (Cambridge: Cambridge University Press, 1973). Readers may also consult *Utilitarianism: For and Against* (Cambridge: Cambridge University Press, 1973) for the parts of Williams's discussion not reprinted in the present volume and for the defence of utilitarianism by J. J. C. Smart; David Lyons, *Forms and Limits of Utilitarianism* (Oxford: Clarendon Press, 1965); J. L. Mackie, *Ethics: Inventing Right and Wrong* (Harmondsworth: Pelican, 1977); and Jonathan Glover, *Causing Death and Saving Lives* (Harmondsworth: Pelican, 1977).

A Theory of Justice

There is no question in political philosophy more fundamental and encompassing than the question of how the goods of the world and the goods of society ought to be distributed among us. What is the *just* sharing-out of material goods and of such goods as liberty, power, respect, standing and so on? It is near to being an overwhelming question, and it is no oddity that it has not had many full answers. One such answer is given by Professor John Rawls in his book, *A Theory of Justice*.

It is a work which derives from a great and straightforward conviction, and it is guided by a few ruling ideas. It is also a work of diligence and elaboration. If its ruling ideas are few, each of them is of many sides, aspects, details and consequences. Many of these latter things, it sometimes seems, are at first anticipated, later brought into full view and examined, still later looked at in another light, at other moments related to other things, and finally contemplated in retrospect. *A Theory of Justice* is a completed exploration, comprising 600 pages divided into 87 sections. The five sections reprinted here (3, 4, 11, 21 and 29) serve as an introduction. They do convey essentials of the principal argument and the conclusion of that argument.

In the history of political philosophy a good deal of attention has been given to a question smaller than the question of justice. It has to do with our obligation as citizens to comply with the demands of the law or the state. One ancient argument for the conclusion that we have a weighty obligation is essentially that our forebears or ourselves, explicitly or tacitly, entered into a contract or agreement. This answer has given rise to the tradition of thought about what is called a 'social contract'. Rawls is certainly in this tradition, but he is concerned with something more general than our obligation as citizens. The particular contract of which he writes is not merely an agreement to comply with a society or to be ruled by a government, but to accept a certain pair of principles of justice: to accept, that is, that this pair of principles, taken in a particular order of priority, should govern the distribution of all goods. This is not any actual agreement, not even a tacit one, made by ourselves or our forebears. It is a purely hypothetical or conceivable or imaginable agreement. Nevertheless, the whole importance of the agreement, and the argument concerning it, has to do with real people, ourselves in our actual societies.

To reduce the argument and conclusion to a few quick sentences, it is this. One can conceive a certain circumstance in which people are agreeing on the principles that will govern a society about to be set up, and of which they will be members. The circumstance, for particular reasons, would be a *fair* one for the making of such an agreement. Thus the principles that would be chosen in such a circumstance – though it has never obtained – are good principles and indeed the right principles for our own actual societies. In fact, the people in the given circumstance would choose the principle of liberty and the principle of difference (of which more in a moment), along with certain rules about the priority or ranking of these principles and their parts. Therefore these are the right principles for us in the actual world.

The circumstance is named the 'original position', and it is carefully defined – defined, in fact, by way of the people in it. (i) They are self-interested, and (ii) they are equal to one another in their freedom to advance principles and ideas for consideration in connection with their coming society. (iii) They are rational, which is mainly to say that they choose effective means to the ends which they all have, the possession of goods. They will not choose principles that turn out to defeat their own desires. (iv) They believe or know many things of a general nature about human psychology, society, politics and economics. They are far from ignorant of *general* facts. (v) Perhaps most important, they are absolutely ignorant of their own individual futures in the society to come. No one knows if he will be intelligent or otherwise, rich or poor, of this race or that, this colour or that, healthy or sick, of this class or position or that, industrious or otherwise, of this or that particular moral outlook. In short, there is a veil of ignorance over the future, such that no person in the original position knows what his own situation and indeed what he himself will be like.

It can obviously be argued that this circumstance, very different from life as it is, would be a fair one for making an agreement on principles. It can also be argued that the people in it would choose the principle of liberty, to the effect that each person in the coming society is to have the maximum amount of liberties consistent with each other person having the same. It can be argued, too, that the people in the original position would choose, as of second importance, the principle of difference, which has to do with differences or inequalities in socio-economic goods. This principle is to the effect that it is acceptable and also obligatory to have *only and all* those inequalities in a society which make the worst-off people better off than they would be without the inequalities in question. (There is a supposition here about the *general* effect of an incentive system.) Also, as part of the principle of difference, there is to be equal opportunity for anyone to get into any of the positions of favourable inequality.

The first section below from *A Theory of Justice* sets out its main ideas and also some others, one being that we acquire an *understanding* of the given conception of justice, an explanation of its nature, as well as see that it is the right conception, by seeing that it would be chosen in the original position. It is the sort of thing that would be supported in that circumstance.

The second section below has to do with the fact that one might have proceeded by imagining some choosing-situation different from the original position. One would very likely have concluded that in that situation different principles would be chosen. What is the merit of proceeding by way of the original position? The short answer, already given, is that it would be a *fair* situation. But there is more to be said, part of which complicates in a certain way the basic argument sketched above.

The third section is Rawls's first statement of his two principles and their ordering, and also the general conception from which they come. The final statement, from section 46 of *A Theory of Justice*, includes some modifications, and is given in the footnote on p. 76. The 'just savings principle' mentioned there is to the effect that a given generation must keep back certain resources for coming generations. The principle of efficiency is to the effect that we are to seek an 'efficient' distribution of things, one such that there is no possible redistribution which improves the situation of one or more individuals and does not disimprove anyone's situation. The principle which is said to call for maximizing the sum of advantages is the classical principle of utility. According to it, we are to choose the particular distribution of goods which produces the greatest total of satisfaction of desires, no matter how evenly or unevenly the total sum is shared out. The related average principle of utility is that we are to choose the distribution of goods such that the average satisfaction produced is higher than the average satisfaction for all other possible distributions.

The fourth section below pertains to the essential proposition that the people in the original position would in fact choose the two principles of justice as ordered. They would choose this particular conception of justice, A, rather than any of a number of alternatives. Conceptions mentioned under B keep the principle of liberty but substitute the average principle of utility, with or without modification, for the difference principle. Another possibility, related to the principles of utility, is the principle of perfection, which is that things ought to be distributed in such a way as to allow for the realization of human excellence in its various forms. Intuitionistic conceptions (D) are those that involve two or more principles, perhaps the classical principle of utility and some principle of equality, but do not specify an order of importance. The idea is that in some contexts equality is given more importance and in others the total of satisfaction. One decides on the basis of the merits of the particular case. Lastly, there are egoistic conceptions, which are included despite the fact that strictly speaking they do not consist in alternative *principles*.

The last section indicates something of the reasoning for the proposition that the people in the original position would in fact choose the given two principles. Rawls takes utilitarian conceptions of justice to be the main alternatives to his own. There is one fundamental reason for thinking that a utilitarian conception would not be preferred. It must be a possibility that if the future society secured the greatest sum of satisfactions, or even the highest average of satisfaction, this would involve a striking disadvantage to some class of individuals – and no person in the original position can be sure that he would not be in the given class. The thought that he might would surely deter him powerfully from choosing utilitarian principles. Given the whole of Rawls's argument, then, there is the conclusion that utilitarian principles are unjust. Another feature of this section, incidentally, is the use made of propositions about the psychology of a person who is committed to the principles of justice. This is one of a number of ways in which Rawls has sought to enlarge the scope of political philosophy.

A Theory of Justice is a distinguished renewal of the liberal–democratic tradition of political thought. It is a renewal which shows that that tradition, rather than being exhausted, has great potential.

T.H.

John Rawls

A Theory of Justice

The Main Idea of the Theory of Justice

My aim is to present a conception of justice which generalizes and carries to a higher level of abstraction the familiar theory of the social contract as found, say, in Locke, Rousseau, and Kant.[1] In order to do this we are not to think of the original contract as one to enter a particular society or to set up a particular form of government. Rather, the guiding idea is that the principles of justice for the basic structure of society are the object of the original agreement. They are the principles that free and rational persons concerned to further their own interests would accept in an initial position of equality as defining the fundamental terms of their association. These principles are to regulate all further agreements; they specify the kinds of social cooperation that can be entered into and the forms of government that can be established. This way of regarding the principles of justice I shall call justice as fairness.

Thus we are to imagine that those who engage in social cooperation choose together, in one joint act, the principles which are to assign basic rights and duties and to determine the division of social benefits. Men are to decide in advance how they are to regulate their claims against one another and what is to be the foundation charter of their society. Just as each person must decide by rational reflection what constitutes his good, that is, the system of ends which it is rational for him to pursue, so a group of persons must decide once and for all what is to count among them as just and unjust. The choice which rational men would make in this hypothetical situation of equal liberty, assuming for the present that this choice problem has a solution, determines the principles of justice.

In justice as fairness the original position of equality corresponds to the state of nature in the traditional theory of the social contract. This original position is not, of course, thought of as an actual historical state of affairs, much less as a primitive condition of culture. It is understood as a purely hypothetical situation characterized so as to lead to a certain conception of justice.[2] Among the essential features of this situation is that no one knows his place in society, his class position or social status, nor does any one know his fortune in the distribution of natural assets and abilities, his intelligence, strength, and the like. I shall even assume that the parties do not know their conceptions of the good or their special psychological propensities. The principles of justice are chosen behind a veil of ignorance. This ensures that no one is advantaged or disadvantaged in the choice of principles by the outcome of natural chance or the contingency of social circumstances. Since all are similarly situated and no one is able to design principles to favour his particular condition, the principles of justice are the result of a fair agreement or bargain. For given the circumstances of the original position, the symmetry of everyone's relations to each other, this initial situation is fair between individuals as moral persons, that is, as rational beings with their own ends and capable, I shall assume, of a sense of justice. The original position is, one might say, the appropriate initial *status quo*, and thus the fundamental agreements reached in it are fair. This explains the propriety of the name 'justice as fairness': it conveys the idea that the principles of justice are agreed to in an initial situation that is fair. The name does not mean that the concepts of justice and fairness are the same, any more than the phrase 'poetry as metaphor' means that the concepts of poetry and metaphor are the same.

Justice as fairness begins, as I have said, with one of the most general of all choices which persons might make together, namely, with the choice of the first principles of a conception of justice which is to regulate all subsequent criticism and reform of institutions. Then, having chosen a conception of justice, we can suppose that they are to choose a constitution and a legislature to enact laws, and so on, all in accordance with the principles of justice initially agreed upon. Our social situation is just if it is such that by this sequence of hypothetical agreements we would have contracted into the general system of rules which defines it. Moreover, assuming that the original position does determine a set of principles (that is, that a particular conception of justice would be chosen), it will then be true that whenever social institutions satisfy these principles those engaged in them can say to one another that they are cooperating on terms to which they would agree if they were free and equal persons whose relations with respect to one another were fair. They could all view their arrangements as meeting the stipulations which they would acknowledge in an initial situation that embodies widely accepted and reasonable constraints on the choice of principles. The general recognition of this fact would provide the basis for a public acceptance of the corresponding principles of justice. No society can, of course, be a scheme of cooperation which men enter voluntarily in a literal sense; each person finds himself placed at birth in some particular position in some particular society, and the nature of this position materially affects his life prospects. Yet a society satisfying the principles of justice as fairness comes as close as a society can to being a voluntary scheme, for it meets the principles which free and equal persons would assent to under circumstances that are fair. In this sense its members are autonomous and the obligations they recognize self-imposed.

One feature of justice as fairness is to think of the parties in the initial situation as rational and mutually disinterested. This does not mean that the parties are egoists, that is, individuals with only certain kinds of interests, say in wealth, prestige, and domination. But they are conceived as not taking an interest in one another's interests. They are to presume that even their spiritual aims may be opposed, in the way that the aims of those of different religions may be opposed. Moreover, the concept of rationality must be interpreted as far as possible in the narrow sense, standard in economic theory, of taking the most effective means to given ends. I modify this concept to some extent,[3] but one must try to avoid introducing into it any controversial ethical elements. The initial situation must be characterized by stipulations that are widely accepted.

In working out the conception of justice as fairness one main task clearly is to determine which principles of justice would be chosen in the original position. To do this we must describe this situation in some detail and formulate with care the problem of choice which it presents. It may be observed, however, that once the principles of justice are thought of as arising from an original agreement in a situation of equality, it is an open question whether the principle of utility would be acknowledged. Offhand it hardly seems likely that persons who view themselves as equals, entitled to press their claims upon one another, would agree to a principle which may require lesser life prospects for some simply for the sake of a greater sum of advantages enjoyed by others. Since each desires to protect his interests, his capacity to advance his conception of the good, no one has a reason to acquiesce in an enduring loss for himself in order to bring about a greater net balance of satisfaction. In the absence of strong and lasting benevolent impulses, a rational man would not accept a basic structure merely because it maximized the algebraic sum of advantages irrespective of its permanent effects on his own basic rights and interests. Thus it seems that the principle of utility is incompatible with the conception of social cooperation among equals for mutual advantage. It appears to be inconsistent with the idea of reciprocity implicit in the notion of a well-ordered society. Or, at any rate, so I shall argue.

I shall maintain instead that the persons in the initial situation would choose two rather different principles: the first requires equality in the assignment of basic rights and duties, while the second holds that social and economic inequalities, for example inequalities of wealth and authority, are just only if they result in compensating benefits for everyone, and in particular for the least advantaged members of society. These principles rule out justifying institutions on the grounds that the hardships of some are offset by a greater good in the aggregate. It may be expedient but it is not just that some should have less in order that others may prosper. But there is no injustice in the greater benefits earned by a few provided that the situation of persons not so fortunate is thereby improved. The intuitive idea is that since everyone's well-being depends upon a scheme of cooperation without which no one could have a satisfactory life, the division of advantages should be such as to draw forth the willing cooperation of everyone taking part in it, including those less well situated. Yet this can be expected only if reasonable terms are proposed. The two principles mentioned seem to be a fair agreement on the basis of which those better endowed, or more fortunate in their social position, neither of which we can be said to deserve, could expect the willing cooperation of others when some workable scheme is a necessary condition of the welfare of all.[4] Once we decide to look for a conception of justice that nullifies the accidents of natural endowment and the contingencies of social circumstance as counters in quest for political and economic advantage, we are led to these principles. They express the result of leaving aside those aspects of the social world that seem arbitrary from a moral point of view.

The problem of the choice of principles, however, is extremely difficult. I do not expect the answer I shall suggest to be convincing to everyone. It is, therefore, worth noting from the outset that justice as fairness, like other contract views, consists of two parts: (1) an interpretation of the initial situation and of the problem of choice posed there, and (2) a set of principles which, it is argued, would be agreed to. One may accept the first part of the theory (or some variant thereof), but not the other, and conversely. The concept of the initial contractual situation may seem reasonable although the particular principles proposed are rejected. To be sure, I want to maintain that the most appropriate conception of this situation does lead to principles of justice contrary to utilitarianism and perfectionism, and therefore that the contract doctrine provides an alternative to these views. Still, one may dispute this contention even though one grants that the contractarian method is a useful way of studying ethical theories and of setting forth their underlying assumptions.

Justice as fairness is an example of what I have called a contract theory. Now there may be an objection to the term 'contract' and related expressions, but I think it will serve reasonably well. Many words have misleading connotations which at first are likely to confuse. The terms 'utility' and 'utilitarianism' are surely no exception. They too have unfortunate suggestions which hostile critics have been willing to exploit; yet they are clear enough for those prepared to study utilitarian doctrine. The same should be true of the term 'contract' applied to moral theories. As I have mentioned, to understand it one has to keep in mind that it implies a certain level of abstraction. In particular, the content of the relevant agreement is not to enter a given society or to adopt a given form of government, but to accept certain moral principles. Moreover, the undertakings referred to are purely hypothetical: a contract view holds that certain principles would be accepted in a well-defined, initial situation.

The merit of the contract terminology is that it conveys the idea that principles of justice may be conceived as principles that would be chosen by rational persons, and that in this way conceptions of justice may be explained and justified. The theory of justice is a part, perhaps the most significant part, of the theory of rational choice. Furthermore, principles of justice deal with conflicting claims upon the advantages won by social cooperation; they apply to the relations among several persons or groups. The word 'contract' suggests this plurality as well as the condition that the appropriate division of advantages must be in accordance with principles acceptable to all parties. The condition of publicity for principles of justice is also connoted by the contract phraseology. Thus, if these principles are the outcome of an agreement, citizens have a knowledge of the principles that others follow. It is characteristic of contract theories to stress the public nature of political principles. Finally there is the long tradition of the contract doctrine. Expressing the tie with this line of thought helps to define ideas and accords with natural piety. There are then several advantages in the use of the term 'contract'. With due precautions taken, it should not be misleading.

A final remark. Justice as fairness is not a complete contract theory. For it is clear that the contractarian idea can be extended to the choice of more or less an entire ethical system, that is, to a system including principles for all the virtues and not only for justice. Now for the most part I shall consider only principles of justice and others closely related to them; I make no attempt to discuss the virtues in a systematic way. Obviously if justice as fairness succeeds reasonably well, a next step would be to study the more general view suggested by the name 'rightness as fairness'. But even this wider theory fails to embrace all moral relationships, since it would seem to include only our relations with other persons and to leave out of account how we are to conduct ourselves toward animals and the rest of nature. I do not contend that the contract notion offers a way to approach these questions which are certainly of the first importance; and I shall have to put them aside. We must recognize the limited scope of justice as fairness and of the general type of view that it exemplifies. How far its conclusions must be revised once these other matters are understood cannot be decided in advance.

The Original Position and Justification

I have said that the original position is the appropriate initial *status quo* which ensures that the fundamental agreements reached in it are fair. This fact yields the name 'justice as fairness'. It is clear, then, that I want to say that one conception of justice is more reasonable than another, or justifiable with respect to it, if rational persons in the initial situation would choose its principles over those of the other for the role of justice. Conceptions of justice are to be ranked by their acceptability to persons so circumstanced. Understood in this way the question of justification is settled by working out a problem of deliberation: we have to ascertain which principles it would be rational to adopt given the contractual situation. This connects the theory of justice with the theory of rational choice.

If this view of the problem of justification is to succeed, we must, of course, describe in some detail the nature of this choice problem. A problem of rational decision has a definite answer only if we know the beliefs and interests of the parties, their relations with respect to one another, the alternatives between which they are to choose, the procedure whereby they make up their minds, and so on. As the circumstances are presented in different ways, correspondingly different principles are accepted. The concept of the original position, as I shall refer to it, is that of the most philosophically favoured interpretation of this initial choice situation for the purposes of a theory of justice.

But how are we to decide what is the most favoured interpretation? I assume, for one thing, that there is a broad measure of agreement that principles of justice should be chosen under certain conditions.

To justify a particular description of the initial situation one shows that it incorporates these commonly shared presumptions. One argues from widely accepted but weak premises to more specific conclusions. Each of the presumptions should by itself be natural and plausible; some of them may seem innocuous or even trivial. The aim of the contract approach is to establish that taken together they impose significant bounds on acceptable principles of justice. The ideal outcome would be that these conditions determine a unique set of principles; but I shall be satisfied if they suffice to rank the main traditional conceptions of social justice.

One should not be misled, then, by the somewhat unusual conditions which characterize the original position. The idea here is simply to make vivid to ourselves the restrictions that it seems reasonable to impose on arguments for principles of justice, and therefore on these principles themselves. Thus it seems reasonable and generally acceptable that no one should be advantaged or disadvantaged by natural fortune or social circumstances in the choice of principles. It also seems widely agreed that it should be impossible to tailor principles to the circumstances of one's own case. We should ensure further that particular inclinations and aspirations, and persons' conceptions of their good do not affect the principles adopted. The aim is to rule out those principles that it would be rational to propose for acceptance, however little the chance of success, only if one knew certain things that are irrelevant from the standpoint of justice. For example, if a man knew that he was wealthy, he might find it rational to advance the principle that various taxes for welfare measures be counted unjust; if he knew that he was poor, he would most likely propose the contrary principle. To represent the desired restrictions one imagines a situation in which everyone is deprived of this sort of information. One excludes the knowledge of those contingencies which sets men at odds and allows them to be guided by their prejudices. In this manner the veil of ignorance is arrived at in a natural way. This concept should cause no difficulty if we keep in mind the constraints on arguments that it is meant to express. At any time we can enter the original position, so to speak, simply by following a certain procedure, namely, by arguing for principles of justice in accordance with these restrictions.

It seems reasonable to suppose that the parties in the original position are equal. That is, all have the same rights in the procedure for choosing principles; each can make proposals, submit reasons for their acceptance, and so on. Obviously the purpose of these conditions is to represent equality between human beings as moral persons, as creatures having a conception of their good and capable of a sense of justice. The basis of equality is taken to be similarity in these two respects. Systems of ends are not ranked in value; and each man is presumed to have the requisite ability to understand and to act upon whatever principles are adopted. Together with the veil of ignorance, these conditions define the principles of justice as those which rational persons concerned to advance their interests would consent to as equals when none are known to be advantaged or disadvantaged by social and natural contingencies.

There is, however, another side to justifying a particular description of the original position. This is to see if the principles which would be chosen match our considered convictions of justice or extend them in an acceptable way. We can note whether applying these principles would lead us to make the same judgements about the basic structure of society which we now make intuitively and in which we have the greatest confidence; or whether, in cases where our present judgements are in doubt and given with hesitation, these principles offer a resolution which we can affirm on reflection. There are questions which we feel sure must be answered in a certain way. For example, we feel confident that religious intolerance and racial discrimination are unjust. We think that we have examined these things with care and have reached what we believe is an impartial judgement not likely to be distorted by an excessive attention to our own interests. These convictions are provisional fixed points which we presume any conception of justice must fit. But we have much less assurance as to what is the correct distribution of wealth and authority. Here we may be looking for a way to remove our doubts. We can check an interpretation of the initial situation, then, by the capacity of its principles to accommodate our firmest convictions and to provide guidance where guidance is needed.

In searching for the most favoured description of this situation we work from both ends. We begin by describing it so that it represents generally shared and preferably weak conditions. We then see if these conditions are strong enough to yield a significant set of principles. If not, we look for further premises equally reasonable. But if so, and these principles match our considered convictions of justice, then so far well and good. But presumably there will be discrepancies. In this case we have a choice. We can either modify the account of the initial situation or we can revise our existing judgements, for even the judgements we take provisionally as fixed points are liable to revision. By going back and forth, sometimes altering the conditions of the contractual circumstances, at others withdrawing our judgements and conforming them to principle, I assume that eventually we shall find a description of the initial situation that both expresses reasonable conditions and yields principles which match our considered judgements duly pruned and adjusted. This state of affairs I refer to as reflective equilibrium.[5] It is an equilibrium because at last our principles and judgements coincide; and it is reflective since we know to what principles our judgements conform and the premises of their derivation. At the moment everything is in order. But this equilibrium is not necessarily stable. It is liable to be upset by further examination of the conditions which should be imposed on the contractual situation and by particular cases which may lead us to revise our judgements. Yet for the time being we have done what we can to render coherent and to justify our convictions of social justice. We have reached a conception of the original position.

I shall not, of course, actually work through this process. Still, we may think of the interpretation of the original position that I shall present as the result of such a hypothetical course of reflection. It represents the attempt to accommodate within one scheme both reasonable philosophical conditions on principles as well as our considered judgements of justice. In arriving at the favoured interpretation of the initial situation there is no point at which an appeal is made to self-evidence in the traditional sense either of general conceptions or particular convictions. I do not claim for the principles of justice proposed that they are necessary truths or derivable from such truths. A conception of justice cannot be deduced from self-evident premises or conditions on principles; instead, its justification is a matter of the mutual support of many considerations, of everything fitting together into one coherent view.

A final comment. We shall want to say that certain principles of justice are justified because they would be agreed to in an initial situation of equality. I have emphasized that this original position is purely hypothetical. It is natural to ask why, if this agreement is never actually entered into, we should take any interest in these principles, moral or otherwise. The answer is that the conditions embodied in the description of the original position are ones that we do in fact accept. Or if we do not, then perhaps we can be persuaded to do so by philosophical reflection. Each aspect of the contractual situation can be given supporting grounds. Thus what we shall do is to collect together into one conception a number of conditions on principles that we are ready upon due consideration to recognize as reasonable. These constraints express what we are prepared to regard as limits on fair terms of social cooperation. One way to look at the idea of the original position, therefore, is to see it as an expository device which sums up the meaning of these conditions and helps us to extract their consequences. On the other hand, this conception is also an intuitive notion that suggests its own elaboration, so that led on by it we are drawn to define more clearly the standpoint from which we can best interpret moral relationships. We need a conception that enables us to envision our objective from afar: the intuitive notion of the original position is to do this for us.[6]

Two Principles of Justice

I shall now state in a provisional form the two principles of justice that I believe would be chosen in the original position. In this section I wish to make only the most general comments, and therefore the first formulation of these principles is tentative.

The first statement of the two principles reads as follows.

First: each person is to have an equal right to the most extensive basic liberty compatible with a similar liberty for others.

Second: social and economic inequalities are to be arranged so that they are both (a) reasonably expected to be to everyone's advantage, and (b) attached to positions and offices open to all.

By way of general comment, these principles primarily apply, as I have said, to the basic structure of society. They are to govern the assignment of rights and duties and to regulate the distribution of social and economic advantages. As their formulation suggests, these principles presuppose that the social structure can be divided into two more or less distinct parts, the first principle applying to the one, the second to the other. They distinguish between those aspects of the social system that define and secure the equal liberties of citizenship and those that specify and establish social and economic inequalities. The basic liberties of citizens are, roughly speaking, political liberty (the right to vote and to be eligible for public office) together with freedom of speech and assembly; liberty of conscience and freedom of thought; freedom of the person along with the right to hold (personal) property; and freedom from arbitrary arrest and seizure as defined by the concept of the rule of law. These liberties are all required to be equal by the first principle, since citizens of a just society are to have the same basic rights.

The second principle applies, in the first approximation, to the distribution of income and wealth and to the design of organizations that make use of differences in authority and responsibility, or chains of command. While the distribution of wealth and income need not be equal, it must be to everyone's advantage, and at the same time, positions of authority and offices of command must be accessible to all. One applies the second principle by holding positions open, and then, subject to this constraint, arranges social and economic inequalities so that everyone benefits.

These principles are to be arranged in a serial order with the first principle prior to the second. This ordering means that a departure from the institutions of equal liberty required by the first principle cannot be justified by, or compensated for, by greater social and economic advantages. The distribution of wealth and income, and the hierarchies of authority, must be consistent with both the liberties of equal citizenship and equality of opportunity.

It is clear that these principles are rather specific in their content, and their acceptance rests on certain assumptions that must be explained and justified. A theory of justice depends upon a theory of society in various ways. For the present, it should be observed that the two principles (and this holds for all formulations) are a special case of a more general conception of justice that can be expressed as follows.

All social values – liberty and opportunity, income and wealth, and the bases of self-respect – are to be distributed equally unless an unequal distribution of any, or all, of these values is to everyone's advantage.

Injustice, then, is simply inequalities that are not to the benefit of all. Of course, this conception is extremely vague and requires interpretation.

As a first step, suppose that the basic structure of society distributes certain primary goods, that is, things that every rational man is presumed to want. These goods normally have a use whatever a person's rational plan of life. For simplicity, assume that the chief primary goods at the disposition of society are rights and liberties, powers and opportunities, income and wealth.[7] These are the social primary goods. Other primary goods such as health and vigour, intelligence and imagination, are natural goods; although their possession is influenced by the basic structure, they are not so directly under its control. Imagine, then, a hypothetical initial arrangement in which all the social primary goods are equally distributed: everyone has similar rights and duties, and income and wealth are evenly shared. This state of affairs provides a benchmark for judging improvements. If certain inequalities of wealth and organizational powers would make everyone better off than in this hypothetical starting situation, then they accord with the general conception.

Now it is possible, at least theoretically, that by giving up some of their fundamental liberties men are sufficiently compensated by the resulting social and economic gains.[8] The general conception of justice imposes no restrictions on what sort of inequalities are permissible; it only requires that everyone's position be improved. We need not suppose anything so drastic as consenting to a condition of slavery. Imagine instead that men forego certain political rights when the economic returns are significant and their capacity to influence the course of policy by the exercise of these rights would be marginal in any case. It is this kind of exchange which the two principles as stated rule out; being arranged in serial order they do not permit exchanges between basic liberties and economic and social gains. The serial ordering of principles expresses an underlying preference among primary social goods. When this preference is rational so likewise is the choice of these principles in this order.

In developing justice as fairness I shall here, for the most part, leave aside the general conception of justice and examine instead the special case of the two principles in serial order. The advantage of this procedure is that from the first the matter of priorities is recognized and an effort made to find principles to deal with it. One is led to attend throughout to the conditions under which the acknowledgement of the absolute weight of liberty with respect to social and economic advantages, as defined by the lexical order of the two principles, would be reasonable. Offhand, this ranking appears extreme and too special a case to be of much interest; but there is more justification for it than would appear at first sight. Or at any rate, so I maintain. Furthermore, the distinction between fundamental rights and liberties and economic and social benefits marks a difference among primary social goods that one should try to exploit. It suggests an important division in the social system. Of course, the distinctions drawn and the ordering proposed are bound to be at best only approximations. There are surely circumstances in which they fail. But it is essential to depict clearly the main lines of a reasonable conception of justice; and under many conditions anyway, the two principles in serial order may serve well enough. When necessary we can fall back on the more general conception.

The fact that the two principles apply to institutions has certain consequences. Several points illustrate this. First of all, the rights and liberties referred to by these principles are those which are defined by the public rules of the basic structure. Whether men are free is determined by the rights and duties established by the major institutions of society. Liberty is a certain pattern of social forms. The first principle simply requires that certain sorts of rules, those defining basic liberties, apply to everyone equally and that they allow the most extensive liberty compatible with a like liberty for all. The only reason for circumscribing the rights defining liberty and making men's freedom less extensive than it might otherwise be is that these equal rights as institutionally defined would interfere with one another.

Another thing to bear in mind is that when principles mention persons, or require that everyone gain from an inequality, the reference is to representative persons holding the various social positions, or offices, or whatever, established by the basic structure. Thus in applying the second principle I assume that it is possible to assign an expectation of well-being to representative individuals holding these positions. This expectation indicates their life prospects as viewed from their social station. In general, the expectations of representative persons depend upon the distribution of rights and duties throughout the basic structure. When this changes, expectations change. I assume, then, that expectations are connected: by raising the prospects of the representative in one position we presumably increase or decrease the prospects of representative men in other positions. Since it applies to institutional forms, the second principle (or rather the first part of it) refers to the expectations of representative individuals. Neither principle applies to distributions of particular goods to particular individuals who may be identified by their proper names. The situation where someone is considering how to allocate certain commodities to needy persons who are known to him is not within the scope of the principles. They are meant to regulate basic institutional arrangements. We must not assume that there is much similarity from the standpoint of justice between an administrative allotment of goods to specific persons and the appropriate design of society. Our common-sense intuitions for the former may be a poor guide to the latter.

Now the second principle insists that each person benefit from permissible inequalities in the basic structure. This means that it must be reasonable for each relevant representative man defined by this structure, when he views it as a going concern, to prefer his prospects with the inequality to his prospects without it. One is not allowed to justify differences in income or organizational powers on the ground that the disadvantages of those in one position are outweighed by the greater advantages of those in another. Much less can infringements of liberty be counterbalanced in this way. Applied to the basic structure, the principle of utility would have us maximize the sum of expectations of representative men (weighted by the number of persons they represent, on the classical view); and this would permit us to compensate for the losses of some by the gains of others. Instead, the two principles require that everyone benefit from economic and social inequalities. It is obvious, however, that there are indefinitely many ways in which all may be advantaged when the initial arrangement of equality is taken as a benchmark. How then are we to choose among these possibilities? The principles must be specified so that they yield a determinate conclusion.*

* At a later point in *A Theory of Justice*, after a careful introduction, Professor Rawls gives the following final statement of his two principles and of the priority rules, and of the general conception from which the principles and the rules derive:

'*First Principle*
Each person is to have an equal right to the most extensive total system of equal basic liberties compatible with a similar system of liberty for all.

Second Principle
Social and economic inequalities are to be arranged so that they are both:
(a) to the greatest benefit of the least advantaged, consistent with the just savings principle, and
(b) attached to offices and positions open to all under conditions of fair equality of opportunity. ·

First Priority Rule (The Priority of Liberty)
The principles of justice are to be ranked in lexical order and therefore liberty can be restricted only for the sake of liberty. There are two cases:
(a) a less extensive liberty must strengthen the total system of liberty shared by all;
(b) a less than equal liberty must be acceptable to those with the lesser liberty.

Second Priority Rule (The Priority of Justice over Efficiency and Welfare)
The second principle of justice is lexically prior to the principle of efficiency and to that of maximizing the sum of advantages; and fair opportunity is prior to the difference principle. There are two cases:
(a) an inequality of opportunity must enhance the opportunities of those with the lesser opportunity;
(b) an excessive rate of saving must on balance mitigate the burden of those bearing this hardship.

General Conception
All social primary goods – liberty and opportunity, income and wealth, and the bases of self-respect – are to be distributed equally unless an unequal distribution of any or all of these goods is to the advantage of the least favoured.'

The Presentation of Alternatives

Let us now turn to the description of the original position. I shall begin with the question of the alternatives open to the persons in this situation. Ideally of course one would like to say that they are to choose among all possible conceptions of justice. One obvious difficulty is how these conceptions are to be characterized so that those in the original position can be presented with them. Yet granting that these conceptions could be defined, there is no assurance that the parties could make out the best option; the principles that would be most preferred might be overlooked. Indeed, there may exist no best alternative: conceivably for each conception of justice there is another that is better. Even if there is a best alternative, it seems difficult to describe the parties' intellectual powers so that this optimum, or even the more plausible conceptions, are sure to occur to them. Some solutions to the choice problem may be clear enough on careful reflection: it is another matter to describe the parties so that their deliberations generate these alternatives. Thus although the two principles of justice may be superior to those conceptions known to us, perhaps some hitherto unformulated set of principles is still better.

In order to handle this problem I shall resort to the following device. I shall simply take as given a short list of traditional conceptions of justice, together with a few other possibilities suggested by the two principles of justice. I then assume that the parties are presented with this list and required to agree unanimously that one conception is the best among those enumerated. We may suppose that this decision is arrived at by making a series of comparisons in pairs. Thus the two principles would be shown to be preferable once all agree that they are to be chosen over each of the other alternatives.

Now admittedly this is an unsatisfactory way to proceed. It would be better if we could define necessary and sufficient conditions for a uniquely best conception of justice and then exhibit a conception that fulfilled these conditions. Eventually one may be able to do this. For the time being, however, I do not see how to avoid rough-and-ready methods. Moreover, using such procedures may point to a general solution of our problem. Thus it may turn out that, as we run through these comparisons, the reasoning of the parties singles out certain features of the basic structure as desirable, and that these features have natural maximum and minimum properties. Suppose, for example, that it is rational for the persons in the original position to prefer a society with the greatest equal liberty. And suppose further that while they prefer social and economic advantages to work for the common good they insist that they mitigate the ways in which men are advantaged or disadvantaged by natural and social contingencies. If these two features are the only relevant ones, and if the principle of equal liberty is the natural maximum of the first feature, and the difference principle (constrained by fair equality of opportunity) the natural maximum of the second, then, leaving aside the problem of priority, the two principles are the optimum solution. The fact that one cannot constructively characterize or enumerate all possible conceptions of justice, or describe the parties so that they are bound to think of them, is no obstacle to this conclusion.

It would not be profitable to pursue these speculations any further. For the present, no attempt is made to deal with the general problem of the best solution. I limit the argument throughout to the weaker contention that the two principles would be chosen from the conceptions of justice on the following list.

A. The Two Principles of Justice (in serial order)
1. The principle of greatest equal liberty
2. (a) The principle of (fair) equality of opportunity
   (b) The difference principle
B. Mixed Conceptions. Substitute one for A2 above
1. The principle of average utility; or
2. The principle of average utility, subject to a constraint, either:
   (a) That a certain social minimum be maintained, or
   (b) That the overall distribution not be too wide; or
3. The principle of average utility subject to either constraint in B2 plus that of equality of fair opportunity
C. Classical Teleological Conceptions
1. The classical principle of utility
2. The average principle of utility
3. The principle of perfection
D. Intuitionistic Conceptions
1. To balance total utility against the principle of equal distribution

2. To balance average utility against the principle of redress
3. To balance a list of prima facie principles (as appropriate)
E. Egoistic Conceptions (Strictly speaking, however, these are not alternatives.)
1. First-person dictatorship: Everyone is to serve my interests
2. Free-rider: Everyone is to act justly except for myself, if I choose not to
3. General: Everyone is permitted to advance his interests as he pleases

The merits of these traditional theories surely suffice to justify the effort to rank them. And in any case, the study of this ranking is a useful way of feeling one's way into the large question. Now each of these conceptions presumably has its assets and liabilities; there are reasons for and against any alternative one selects. The fact that a conception is open to criticism is not necessarily decisive against it, nor are certain desirable features always conclusive in its favour. The decision of the persons in the original position hinges, as we shall see, on a balance of various considerations. In this sense, there is an appeal to intuition at the basis of the theory of justice. Yet when everything is tallied up, it may be perfectly clear where the balance of reason lies. The relevant reasons may have been so factored and analysed by the description of the original position that one conception of justice is clearly preferable to the others. The argument for it is not strictly speaking a proof, not yet anyway; but, in Mill's phrase, it may present considerations capable of determining the intellect.[9]

The list of conceptions is largely self-explanatory. A few brief comments, however, may be useful. Each conception is expressed in a reasonably simple way, and each holds unconditionally, that is, whatever the circumstances or state of society. None of the principles is contingent upon certain social or other conditions. Now one reason for this is to keep things simple. It would be easy to formulate a family of conceptions each designed to apply only if special circumstances obtained, these various conditions being exhaustive and mutually exclusive. For example one conception might hold at one stage of culture, a different conception at another. Such a family could be counted as itself a conception of justice; it would consist of a set of ordered pairs, each pair being a conception of justice matched with the circumstances in which it applies. But if conceptions of this kind were added to the list, our problem would become very complicated if not unmanageable. Moreover, there is a reason for excluding alternatives of this kind, for it is natural to ask what underlying principle determines the ordered pairs. Here I assume that some recognizably ethical conception specifies the appropriate principles given each of the conditions. It is really this unconditional principle that defines the conception expressed by the set of ordered pairs. Thus to allow such families on the list is to include alternatives that conceal their proper basis. So for this reason as well I shall exclude them. It also turns out to be desirable to characterize the original position so that the parties are to choose principles that hold unconditionally whatever the circumstances. This fact is connected with the Kantian interpretation of justice as fairness.

Finally, an obvious point. An argument for the two principles, or indeed for any conception, is always relative to some list of alternatives. If we change the list, the argument will, in general, have to be different. A similar sort of remark applies to all features of the original position. There are indefinitely many variations of the initial situation and therefore no doubt indefinitely many theorems of moral geometry. Only a few of these are of any philosophical interest, since most variations are irrelevant from a moral point of view. We must try to steer clear of side issues while at the same time not losing sight of the special assumptions of the argument.

The Main Grounds for the
Two Principles of Justice

In this section my aim is to use the conditions of publicity and finality to give some of the main arguments for the two principles of justice. I shall rely upon the fact that for an agreement to be valid, the parties must be able to honour it under all relevant and foreseeable circumstances. There must be a rational assurance that one can carry through. The arguments I shall adduce fit under the heuristic schema suggested by the reasons for following the maximin rule. That is, they help to show that the principles are an adequate minimum conception of justice in a situation of great uncertainty. Any further advantages that might be won by the principle of utility, or whatever, are highly problematical, whereas the hardship if things turn out badly are intolerable. It is at this point that the concept of a contract has a definite role: it suggests the condition of publicity and sets limits upon what can be agreed to. Thus justice as fairness uses the concept of contract to a greater extent than the discussion so far might suggest.

The first confirming ground for the two principles can be explained in terms of what may be referred to as the strains of commitment. The parties have a capacity for justice in the sense that they can be assured that their undertaking is not in vain. Assuming that they have taken everything into account, including the general facts of moral psychology, they can rely on one another to adhere to the principles adopted. Thus they consider the strains of commitment. They cannot enter into agreements that may have consequences they cannot accept. They will avoid those that they can adhere to only with great difficulty. Since the original agreement is final and made in perpetuity, there is no second chance. In view of the serious nature of the possible consequences, the question of the burden of commitment is especially acute. A person is choosing once and for all the standards which are to govern his life prospects. Moreover, when we enter an agreement we must be able to honour it even should the worst possibilities prove to be the case. Otherwise we have not acted in good faith. Thus the parties must weigh with care whether they will be able to stick by their commitment in all circumstances. Of course, in answering this question they have only a general knowledge of human psychology to go on. But this information is enough to tell which conception of justice involves the greater stress.

In this respect the two principles of justice have a definite advantage. Not only do the parties protect their basic rights but they insure themselves against the worst eventualities. They run no chance of having to acquiesce in a loss of freedom over the course of their life for the sake of a greater good enjoyed by others, an undertaking that in actual circumstances they might not be able to keep. Indeed, we might wonder whether such an agreement can be made in good faith at all. Compacts of this sort exceed the capacity of human nature. How can the parties possibly know, or be sufficiently sure, that they can keep such an agreement? Certainly they cannot base their confidence on a general knowledge of moral psychology. To be sure, any principle chosen in the original position may require a large sacrifice for some. The beneficiaries of clearly unjust institutions (those founded on principles which have no claim to acceptance) may find it hard to reconcile themselves to the changes that will have to be made. But in this case they will know that they could not have maintained their position anyway. Yet should a person gamble with his liberties and substantive interests hoping that the application of the principle of utility might secure him a greater well-being, he may have difficulty abiding by his undertaking. He is bound to remind himself that he had the two principles of justice as an alternative. If the only possible candidates all involved similar risks, the problem of the strains of commitment would have to be waived. This is not the case, and in this light the two principles seem distinctly superior.

A second consideration invokes the condition of publicity as well as that of the constraints on agreements. I shall present the argument in terms of the question of psychological stability. A strong point in favour of a conception of justice is that it generates its own support. When the basic structure of society is publicly known to satisfy its principles for an extended period of time, those subject to these arrangements tend to develop a desire to act in accordance with these principles and to do their part in institutions which exemplify them. A conception of justice is stable when the public recognition of its realization by the social system tends to bring about the corresponding sense of justice. Now whether this happens depends, of course, on the laws of moral psychology and the availability of human motives. At the moment we may observe that the principle of utility seems to require a greater identification with the interests of others than the two principles of justice. Thus the latter will be a more stable conception to the extent that this identification is difficult to achieve. When the two principles are satisfied, each person's liberties are secured and there is a sense defined by the difference principle in which everyone is benefited by social cooperation. Therefore we can explain the acceptance of the social system and the principles it satisfies by the psychological law that persons tend to love, cherish, and support whatever affirms their own good. Since everyone's good is affirmed, all acquire inclinations to uphold the scheme.

When the principle of utility is satisfied, however, there is no such assurance that everyone benefits. Allegiance to the social system may demand that some should forgo advantages for the sake of the greater good of the whole. Thus the scheme will not be stable unless those who must make sacrifices strongly identify with interests broader than their own. But this is not easy to bring about. The sacrifices in question are not those asked in times of social emergency when all or some must pitch in for the common good. The principles of justice apply to the basic structure of the social system and to the determination of life prospects. What the principle of utility asks is precisely a sacrifice of these prospects. We are to accept the greater advantages of others as a sufficient reason for lower expectations over the whole course of our life. This is surely an extreme demand. In fact, when society is conceived as a system of cooperation designed to advance the good of its members, it seems quite incredible that some citizens should be expected, on the basis of political principles, to accept lower prospects of life for the sake of others. It is evident then why utilitarians should stress the role of sympathy in moral learning and the central place of benevolence among the moral virtues. Their conception of justice is threatened with instability unless sympathy and benevolence can be widely and intensely cultivated. Looking at the question from the standpoint of the original position, the parties recognize that it would be highly unwise if not irrational to choose principles which may have consequences so extreme that they could not accept them in practice. They would reject the principle of utility and adopt the more realistic idea of designing the social order on a principle of reciprocal advantage. We need not suppose, of course, that persons never make substantial sacrifices for one another, since moved by affection and ties of sentiment they often do. But such actions are not demanded as a matter of justice by the basic structure of society.

Furthermore, the public recognition of the two principles gives greater support to men's self-respect and this in turn increases the effectiveness of social cooperation. Both effects are reasons for choosing these principles. It is clearly rational for men to secure their self-respect. A sense of their own worth is necessary if they are to pursue their conception of the good with zest and to delight in its fulfilment.

Self-respect is not so much a part of any rational plan of life as the sense that one's plan is worth carrying out. Now our self-respect normally depends upon the respect of others. Unless we feel that our endeavours are honoured by them, it is difficult if not impossible for us to maintain the conviction that our ends are worth advancing. Hence for this reason the parties would accept the natural duty of mutual respect which asks them to treat one another civilly and to be willing to explain the grounds of their actions, especially when the claims of others are overruled. Moreover, one may assume that those who respect themselves are more likely to respect each other and conversely. Self-contempt leads to contempt of others and threatens their good as much as envy does. Self-respect is reciprocally self-supporting.

Thus a desirable feature of a conception of justice is that it should publicly express men's respect for one another. In this way they insure a sense of their own value. Now the two principles achieve this end. For when society follows these principles, everyone's good is included in a scheme of mutual benefit and this public affirmation in institutions of each man's endeavours supports men's self-esteem. The establishment of equal liberty and the operation of the difference principle are bound to have this effect. The two principles are equivalent, as I have remarked, to an undertaking to regard the distribution of natural abilities as a collective asset so that the more fortunate are to benefit only in ways that help those who have lost out. I do not say that the parties are moved by the ethical propriety of this idea. But there are reasons for them to accept this principle. For by arranging inequalities for reciprocal advantage and by abstaining from the exploitation of the contingencies of nature and social circumstance within a framework of equal liberty, persons express their respect for one another in the very constitution of their society. In this way they insure their self-esteem as it is rational for them to do.

Another way of putting this is to say that the principles of justice manifest, in the basic structure of society, men's desire to treat one another not as means only but as ends in themselves. I cannot examine Kant's view here.[10] Instead I shall freely interpret it in the light of the contract doctrine. The notion of treating men as ends in themselves and never as only a means obviously needs an explanation. There is even a question whether it is possible to realize. How can we always treat everyone as an end and never as a means only? Certainly we cannot say that it comes to treating everyone by the same general principles, since this interpretation makes the concept equivalent to formal justice. On the contract interpretation treating men as ends in themselves implies at the very least treating them in accordance with the principles to which they would consent in an original position of equality. For in this situation men have equal representation as moral persons who regard themselves as ends and the principles they accept will be rationally designed to protect the claims of their person. The contract view as such defines a sense in which men are to be treated as ends and not as means only.

But the question arises whether they are substantive principles which convey this idea. If the parties wish to express this notion visibly in the basic structure of their society in order to secure each man's rational interest in his self-respect, which principles should they choose? Now it seems that the two principles of justice achieve this aim: for all have an equal liberty and the difference principle explicates the distinction between treating men as a means only and treating them also as ends in themselves. To regard persons as ends in themselves in the basic design of society is to agree to forgo those gains which do not contribute to their representative expectations. By contrast, to regard persons as means is to be prepared to impose upon them lower prospects of life for the sake of the higher expectations of others. Thus we see that the difference principle, which at first appears rather extreme, has a reasonable interpretation. If we further suppose that social co-operation among those who respect each other and themselves as manifest in their institutions is likely to be more effective and harmonious, the general level of expectations, assuming we could estimate it, may be higher when the two principles of justice are satisfied than one might otherwise have thought. The advantage of the principle of utility in this respect is no longer so clear.

The principle of utility presumably requires some to forgo greater life prospects for the sake of others. To be sure, it is not necessary that those having to make such sacrifices rationalize this demand by having a lesser appreciation of their own worth. It does not follow from the utilitarian doctrine that it is because their aims are trivial or unimportant that some individuals' expectations are less. Yet this may often be the case, and there is a sense, as we have just noted, in which utilitarianism does not regard persons as ends in themselves. And in any event, the parties must consider the general facts of moral psychology. Surely it is natural to experience a loss of self-esteem, a weakening of our sense of the value of accomplishing our aims, when we must accept a lesser prospect of life for the sake of others. This is particularly likely to be so when social cooperation is arranged for the good of individuals. That is, those with greater advantages do not claim that they are necessary to preserve certain religious or cultural values which everyone has a duty to maintain. We are not here considering a doctrine of traditional order nor the principle of perfectionism, but rather the principle of utility. In this instance, then, men's self-esteem hinges on how they regard one another. If the parties accept the utility criterion, they will lack the support to their self-respect provided by the public commitment of others to arrange inequalities to everyone's advantage and to guarantee an equal liberty for all. In a public utilitarian society men will find it more difficult to be confident of their own worth.

The utilitarian may answer that in maximizing the average utility these matters are already taken into account. If, for example, the equal liberties are necessary for men's self-respect and the average utility is higher when they are affirmed, then of course they should be established. So far so good. But the point is that we must not lose sight of the publicity condition. This requires that in maximizing the average utility we do so subject to the constraint that the utilitarian principle is publicly accepted and followed as the fundamental charter of society. What we cannot do is to raise the average utility by encouraging men to adopt and apply non-utilitarian principles of justice. If, for whatever reasons, the public recognition of utilitarianism entails some loss of self-esteem, there is no way around this drawback. It is an unavoidable cost of the utilitarian scheme given our stipulations. Thus suppose that the average utility is actually greater should the two principles of justice be publicly affirmed and realized as the basis of the social structure. For the reasons mentioned, this may conceivably be the case. These principles would then represent the most attractive prospect, and on both lines of reasoning just examined, the two principles would be accepted. The utilitarian cannot reply that one is now really maximizing the average utility. In fact, the parties would have chosen the two principles of justice.

We should note, then, that utilitarianism, as I have defined it, is the view that the principle of utility is the correct principle for society's public conception of justice. And to show this one must argue that this criterion would be chosen in the original position. If we like, we can define a different variation of the initial situation in which the motivation assumption is that the parties want to adopt those principles that maximize average utility. The preceding remarks indicate that the two principles of justice may still be chosen. But if so, it is a mistake to call these principles – and the theory in which they appear – utilitarian. The motivation assumption by itself does not determine the character of the whole theory. In fact, the case for the principles of justice is strengthened if they would be chosen under different motivation assumptions. This indicates that the theory of justice is firmly grounded and not sensitive to slight changes in this condition. What we want to know is which conception of justice characterizes our considered judgements in reflective equilibrium and best serves as the public moral basis of society. Unless one maintains that this conception is given by the principle of utility, one is not a utilitarian.[11]

The advocate of utility can maintain, however, that this principle also gives a sense to the Kantian idea, namely, the sense provided by Bentham's formula 'everybody to count for one, nobody for more than one'. This means, as Mill remarks, that one person's happiness assumed to be equal in degree to another person's is to be counted exactly the same.[12] The weights in the additive function that represents the utility principle are identical for all individuals, and it is natural to take them as one. The principle of utility, one might say, treats persons both as ends and as means. It treats them as ends by assigning the same (positive) weight to the welfare of each; it treats them as means by allowing higher life prospects for some to counterbalance lower life prospects for others who are already less favourably situated. The two principles of justice give a stronger and more characteristic interpretation to Kant's idea. They rule out even the tendency to regard men as means to one another's welfare. In the design of the social system we must treat persons solely as ends and not in any way as means. The preceding arguments draw upon this more forceful interpretation.

I shall conclude this section by observing that the conditions of generality of principle, universality of application, and limited information as to natural and social status are not enough by themselves to characterize the original position of justice as fairness. The reasoning for the average principle of utility shows this. These conditions are necessary but not sufficient. The original position requires the parties to make a collective agreement, and therefore the restrictions on valid undertakings as well as the publicity and finality conditions are an essential part of the argument for the two principles. I have discussed the role of these constraints in connection with the strains of commitment and the problem of stability. Once these considerations are established the doubts about the reasoning for the average principle become more urgent.

The tentative conclusion, then, is that the balance of reasons clearly favours the two principles of justice over the principle of average utility, and assuming transitivity, over the classical doctrine as well. Insofar as the conception of the original position is used in the justification of principles in everyday life, the claim that one would agree to the two principles of justice is perfectly credible. There is no reason offhand to think that it is not sincere. In order for this profession to be convincing, it is not necessary that one should have actually given and honoured this undertaking. Thus it is able to serve as a conception of justice in the public acceptance of which persons can recognize one another's good faith.

Notes

1. As the text suggests, I shall regard Locke's *Second Treatise of Government*, Rousseau's *The Social Contract*, and Kant's ethical works beginning with *The Foundations of the Metaphysics of Morals* as definitive of the contract tradition. For all of its greatness, Hobbes's *Leviathan* raises special problems. A general historical survey is provided by J. W. Gough, *The Social Contract*, 2nd ed. (Oxford, The Clarendon Press, 1957), and Otto Gierke, *Natural Law and the Theory of Society*, trans. with an introduction by Ernest Barker (Cambridge, The University Press, 1934). A presentation of the contract view as primarily

an ethical theory is to be found in G. R. Grice, *The Grounds of Moral Judgment* (Cambridge, The University Press, 1967).

2. Kant is clear that the original agreement is hypothetical. See *The Metaphysics of Morals*, pt. I (*Rechtslehre*), especially §§ 47, 52; and pt. II of the essay 'Concerning the Common Saying: This May Be True in Theory but It Does Not Apply in Practice', in *Kant's Political Writings*, ed. Hans Reiss and trans. by H. B. Nisbet (Cambridge, The University Press, 1970), pp. 73–87. See Georges Vlachos, *La Pensée politique de Kant* (Paris, Presses Universitaires de France, 1962), pp. 326–35; and J. G. Murphy, *Kant: The Philosophy of Right* (London, Macmillan, 1970), pp. 109–12, 133–6, for a further discussion.

3. In section 25 of *A Theory of Justice*.

4. For the formulation of this intuitive idea I am indebted to Allan Gibbard.

5. The process of mutual adjustment of principles and considered judgements is not peculiar to moral philosophy. See Nelson Goodman, *Fact, Fiction, and Forecast* (Cambridge, Mass., Harvard University Press, 1955), pp. 65–8, for parallel remarks concerning the justification of the principles of deductive and inductive inference.

6. Henri Poincaré remarks: 'Il nous faut une faculté qui nous fasse voir le but de loin, et, cette faculté, c'est l'intuition.' *La Valeur de la science* (Paris, Flammarion, 1909), p. 27.

7. In the last of the three parts of *A Theory of Justice*, much attention is paid to another primary good, that of self-respect.

8. The argument is given in section 82 of *A Theory of Justice*.

9. *Utilitarianism*, ch. I, par. 5.

10. See *The Foundations of the Metaphysics of Morals*, pp. 427–30 of vol. IV of *Kants Gesammelten Schriften*, Preussische Academie der Wissenschaften (Berlin, 1913), where the second formulation of the categorical impeiative is introduced.

11. Thus while Brandt holds that a society's moral code is to be publicly recognized, and that the best code from a philosophical standpoint is the one that maximizes average utility, he does not maintain that the principle of utility must belong to the code itself. In fact, he denies that within the public morality the final court of appeal need be to utility. Thus by the definition in the text, his view is not utilitarian. See 'Some Merits of One Form of Rule Utilitarianism', *University of Colorado Studies* (Boulder, Colo., 1967), pp. 58f.

12. *Utilitarianism*, ch. V, par. 36.

Biographical Note

John Rawls has been Professor of Philosophy at Harvard University since 1962. Before then, he taught at the Massachusetts Institute of Technology, Cornell University and Princeton University. Before publication of *A Theory of Justice* (1971), he was known as the author of a number of essays on justice, in particular 'Justice as Fairness', which appeared in *Philosophy, Politics and Society* (2nd series, 1962) edited by Peter Laslett and W. G. Runciman.

Further Reading

Rawls's theory of justice, in an earlier form, is stated in his essay 'Justice as Fairness', *Philosophical Review* LVII (1958), reprinted in *Philosophy, Politics and Society*, 2nd Series (Oxford: Blackwell, 1962), edited by Peter Laslett and W. G. Runciman. Readers may also wish to consult his 'Distributive Justice' in *Philosophy, Politics and Society*, 3rd Series (Oxford: Blackwell, 1967) also edited by Laslett and Runciman.

Relevant books are J. W. Gough, *The Social Contract*, 2nd edition (Oxford: Clarendon Press, 1957); John Stuart Mill, *Utilitarianism* (many editions); Robert Nozick, *Anarchy, State and Utopia* (New York: Basic Books, and Oxford: Blackwell, 1974), especially Chapter 7, of which the first part is reprinted in the present volume. The second part is about Rawls.

A book on Rawls is Brian Barry, *The Liberal Theory of Justice: A Critical Examination of the Principal Doctrines in a Theory of Justice by John Rawls* (Oxford: Clarendon Press, 1973). There is a long and very critical review of *A Theory of Justice* by Professor R. M. Hare in *Philosophical Quarterly*, XXIII, 1973. It is reprinted in *Reading Rawls* (Oxford: Blackwell, 1975), along with other writings on *A Theory of Justice*.

Robert Nozick

Distributive Justice:
The Entitlement Theory

It is fair to say that the publication of Professor Robert Nozick's book, *Anarchy, State and Utopia*, raised some political philosophers and some economists out of certain unreflective habits into which they had fallen. Indeed it has been said, however fairly, that it roused them from dogmatic slumbers.

Consider first the procedure of the utilitarians and the utilitarian-egalitarians, as we may call them, in judging the comparative worth of societies or possible societies. It was their habit to proceed by ascertaining the total amount of utility or satisfaction in each society, in a more or less technical way, or else by ascertaining both the total and also the extent to which it was equally shared out. No more than such a table of quantities, or matrix, was taken to be needed in order to make a choice among the given societies. Sometimes only a given moment in a society was taken into account, and sometimes a period of time, perhaps as long as an average lifetime. In either case, members of societies were considered only as consumers of satisfactions, so to speak, and not at all in certain other ways. No attention was paid to what we can call *claims* to satisfactions or goods, the goods being such things as property and income, and hence sources of satisfaction. All that was taken into account was end-results of satisfaction and, necessarily, *certain* related natural qualities of individuals, such as their similar or different abilities to get satisfaction from various goods, or their common vulnerabilities, or their shared humanity.

A second and diverse group of thinkers, in judging the justice of a society, were accustomed to concern themselves with whether amounts of satisfaction, or the various goods, were distributed in accordance with other natural attributes of individuals: attributes taken to give rise to what we may call *natural claims*. (Natural claims include a man's deserts, but also more than that.) Were goods or satisfactions distributed in the society according to the pattern of productivity, with more productive workers or more productive classes getting better shares? Or, to choose another kind of natural claim, was the distribution according to the pattern of moral merit in the society? Or the pattern of usefulness to society? Or need, or effort, or services to others? Or was the distribution according to some chosen combination of these qualities, or all of them, perhaps with particular qualities counting for more?

The utilitarians and the utilitarian-egalitarians above all, but also some other thinkers, provide what Nozick calls *end-result* theories of justice. They do not take into account certain claims, natural or otherwise, to goods or satisfactions. Welfare economics comes in here as well, of course. Another possible end-result theory, although very different, is the theory that goods should be distributed according to I.Q. Still another end-result theory, different again, is that of John Rawls. It is the subject of the previous selection in the present volume.

The second group of thinkers mentioned above do take claims into account, if only natural claims, those having to do with productivity and the like. Their theories are therefore distinct from end-result theories. However, there is the fact of similarity that both types of theory proceed on the basis of natural attributes of persons. Both types of theory follow some pattern, regular or irregular, of such qualities. Nozick refers to all such theories as *patterned* theories.

There is a third and different way of approaching the question of how things ought to be. Unlike end-result theories, it *is* concerned with the claims of individuals. Nonetheless, it is also in a way unlike the theories about natural claims. It is concerned with claims of another kind, *entitlements*. A part of Nozick's achievement is that he provides a large reminder of this most common way of thinking about societies. His audaciously conservative view, for which he gives close arguments, is that a member of a society has the good things he ought to have if certain entitling conditions are satisfied, conditions having to do with the history of those goods. If theories about natural claims are also to be described as historical, they nevertheless do not depend on the history *of goods.*

One condition that must be satisfied, if a man has a good which he ought to have, is that the good in question was *justly acquired* by someone, in a special sense of the word 'acquired'. That is, something *which until then had been possessed by no one*, was justly taken into the possession of someone, quite likely not the man who now possesses it. A piece of land may provide the simplest example. In the opinion of John Locke, the land was acquired justly if, roughly, someone mixed his labour with it, and, after he took it over, there was 'enough and as good left in common for others'. Nozick depends on a related but less demanding criterion of what can be called justice in acquisition. There does not have to be as much and as good left for others.

The second condition which may be satisfied, if a member of a society has the holdings he ought to have, is that if he himself did not acquire them, in the sense of the word just noticed, then he possesses them as a result of just *transfers*. They were justly transferred to him, either from whoever acquired them, or as a result of two or more just transfers. The notion of a just transfer, like that of a just acquisition, requires close attention. At bottom, however, a just transfer is a transfer that is *chosen* or *agreed to* by both parties. Hence it is one exemplified by ordinary sales, gifts, inheritances, profits, interest on capital, and so on. A just transfer must not be thought to require anything more than the facts of mutual choice or agreement. It need not be just in any further sense.

It is right that I have whatever I have if both the first two conditions are in fact satisfied: what I have was justly acquired by someone, and, assuming that person was not myself, the thing has been justly transferred to me. (The conditions can *be* satisfied, of course, without their being *known* to be satisfied.) However, there is another possibility. It may be that a good was not justly acquired, in the special sense, or that it was at some point not justly transferred. Perhaps, in place of a just transfer at some point, there was a theft, a piece of fraud, or an enforced transfer, perhaps enforced by government. Here, principles of rectification are required. They are more difficult to formulate than the principles of acquisition and transfer, but there must be principles for putting right any injustices which are known, injustices as defined by way of the principles of acquisition and transfer. They will have to do, importantly, with what would have happened if there had not been an unjust acquisition or transfer. What we have, then, is that it is right that a man has whatever he gains by the operation of principles of rectification.

This, in brief outline, is the entitlement theory of distributive justice. It pays attention to the history of goods, and hence, one can say, to people as possessors. It does not advocate distributing or redistributing goods or satisfactions according to any natural qualities, including those which give rise to natural claims. Indeed, the entitlement theory does not advocate that there should be a *redistribution* or a *distribution* at all, in a certain sense. We are not to engage significantly in *any* central giving-out of things, however acceptable and necessary this may now seem. What is right is what has *come about* through just acquisition and just transfer, as defined, or just rectification. There is to be no depriving a man of what he rightly has, according to the given principles. Whatever may be done by him in charity, or not done, no man is under any obligation to act, perhaps to vote, on the maxim 'To each according his need', or the maxim 'From each according to his ability to give'. The different maxim of the entitlement theory appears at the end of Section 2 below.

Nozick's classification of theories of justice, a classification that is in several ways complex, may be summed up as follows.

	Theories about goods or satisfactions, and claims to them ('Historical' theories)	Theories about goods or satisfactions, but not claims to them ('End-Result' theories)
Theories concerned with natural qualities of individuals ('Patterned' theories)	Productivity Moral merit Usefulness to society Need Effort Services to others Etc. Combinations of the above natural claims	Utilitarianism Egalitarianism Utilitarianism–egalitarianism Welfare economics I.Q. Rawls's theory Etc.
Theories not concerned with natural qualities of individuals ('Unpatterned' theories)	Entitlement	

In Section 3 Nozick gives his 'Wilt Chamberlain' argument for his entitlement theory and against virtually any other theory of justice. It is, in part, that if there is a certain freedom in a society, people will upset the particular distribution of goods called for by virtually any theory of justice other than the entitlement theory. That theory alone calls for a distribution that does not have to be, in a certain sense, enforced. It alone is in accordance with what is called individual liberty. In another related part, the argument is that no defender of an alternative theory can object to the free departure of the society from his preferred distribution.

Section 4, which draws on an argument by Professor Amartya Sen, an economist, requires a bit of close attention. The nub of the argument is that if each member of a society has (i) a view on certain questions, and also (ii) a right to decide them, but, with respect to other questions, only a view as to how they should be decided, it may be impossible to arrive at a reasonable collective decision, or what is called a social ordering of preferences. The upshot, rather, may be a self-contradictory ranking of possible plans or policies or whatever. In terms of the example, the upshot may be that in the social ordering W is preferred to X, and X to Y, and Y to Z, and, sadly, Z to W. Nozick finds support for his entitlement theory in this state of affairs. His theory is to the effect that there ought not to be collective decisions or social orderings of the kind in question, since they infringe individual liberty. In particular, there ought not to be socially imposed distributions of goods based on some pattern of natural qualities, need or whatever.

Section 5 discusses various aspects of such 'patterned' distributions and their supporting theories, and also aspects of an entitlement distribution. There is the question of whether ordinary taxation on earnings from labour, which is involved in most redistribution of goods, is on a par with forced labour. If a government, partly in order to finance a national health service, imposes income tax of the ordinary kind, is this on a par with a policy of forced labour? Arguments for an affirmative answer are given. Sections 6 and 7 return to the matter of first acquisition, and difficulties that it raises for the entitlement theory. They are found not to be insuperable.

It may or may not be that the many thinkers about justice mentioned at the beginning of this introduction will change their ways. Nozick does give them reason to think about the question of doing so.

T.H.

Robert Nozick

Distributive Justice: The Entitlement Theory

From Chapter 7, 'Distributive Justice', in *Anarchy, State and Utopia* by
Robert Nozick © 1974 by Basic Books, Inc., Publishers, New York.
English edition by Basil Blackwell, Publisher, Oxford. Reprinted by
permission of the author and the publishers. Slight revisions by the
author for this reprinting.

The term 'distributive justice' is not a neutral one. Hearing the term
'distribution', most people presume that some thing or mechanism
uses some principle or criterion to give out a supply of things. Into
this process of distributing shares some error may have crept. So it is
an open question, at least, whether *re*distribution should take place;
whether we should do again what has already been done once, though
poorly. However, we are not in the position of children who have
been given portions of pie by someone who now makes last minute
adjustments to rectify careless cutting. There is no *central* distribution,
no person or group entitled to control all the resources, (jointly)
deciding how they are to be doled out. What each person gets, he
gets from others who give to him in exchange for something, or as a
gift. In a free society, diverse persons control different resources, and
new holdings arise out of the voluntary exchanges and actions of
persons. There is no more a distributing or distribution of shares than
there is a distributing of mates in a society in which persons choose
whom they shall marry. The total result is the product of many
individual decisions which the different individuals involved are
entitled to make. Some uses of the term 'distribution', it is true, do not
imply a previous distributing appropriately judged by some criterion
(e.g., 'probability distribution'); nevertheless, despite the title of this
essay, it would be best to use a terminology that clearly is neutral.
We shall speak of people's holdings; a principle of justice in holdings
describes (part of) what justice tells us (requires) about holdings.*

* The essay here differs only slightly from the first part of Chapter 7 of
Anarchy, State and Utopia. It will be helpful to the reader of this essay to know

The subject of justice in holdings consists of three major topics. The first is the *original acquisition of holdings*, the appropriation of unheld things. This includes the issues of how unheld things may come to be held, the process(es) by which unheld things may come to be held, the things that may come to be held by these processes, the extent of what comes to be held by a particular process, and so on. We shall refer to the complicated truth about this topic, which we shall not formulate here, as the principle of justice in acquisition. The second topic concerns the *transfer of holdings* from one person to another. By what processes may a person transfer holdings to another? How may a person acquire a holding from another who holds it? Under this topic come general descriptions of voluntary exchange, and gift, and (on the other hand) fraud, as well as reference to particular conventional details fixed upon a given society. The complicated truth about this subject (with placeholders for conventional details) we shall call the principle of justice in transfer. (And we shall suppose

---

its place in the book. The book's central concerns are the consequences for political philosophy of a far-reaching theory of individual rights; in particular, the question of what activities, if any, may be performed by the state or its agents without violating these rights. The first half of the book, 'State of Nature Theory, or How to Back into a State Without Really Trying', sets out the structure of these individual rights, and argues that a minimal state would arise from anarchy even though no one intended or tried to bring about that result, and argues that the 'invisible-hand process' by which the state would arise need not violate anyone's rights. The present essay opens the second part of the book, and functions there to *rebut* the possible claim that a state more extensive than the minimal one justified in the first half would be necessary or appropriate in order to achieve distributive justice.

This essay can stand alone. But it does not stand as solidly, I think, without the material of the book's first half that underlies it, the later material of Chapter 7, and of the second part of the book, which buttresses the essay by critically examining other reasons which purport to justify a state more extensive than the minimal one, and the book's last part on utopia and utopian theorizing, whose abstract model and whose discussion of filter devices, intertwine with it. I direct these remarks, of course, especially to the readers this essay will leave unbudged. Very rarely does someone protest against a favourable reaction to the only part of his work another has experienced, on the grounds that the work is an organic unity, no part of which can be judged in isolation.

it also includes principles governing how a person may divest himself of a holding, passing it into an unheld state.)

If the world were wholly just, the following inductive definition would exhaustively cover the subject of justice in holdings.

(1) A person who acquires a holding in accordance with the principle of justice in acquisition is entitled to that holding.

(2) A person who acquires a holding in accordance with the principle of justice in transfer, from someone else entitled to the holding, is entitled to the holding.

(3) No one is entitled to a holding except by (repeated) applications of (1) and (2).

The complete principle of distributive justice would say simply that a distribution is just if everyone is entitled to the holdings they possess under the distribution.

A distribution is just if it arises from another (just) distribution by legitimate means. The legitimate means of moving from one distribution to another are specified by the principle of justice in transfer. The legitimate first 'moves' are specified by the principle of justice in acquisition.[1] Whatever arises from a just situation by just steps is itself just. The means of change specified by the principle of justice in transfer, preserve justice. As correct rules of inference are truth preserving, and any conclusion deduced via repeated application of such rules from only true premises is itself true, so the means of transition from one situation to another specified by the principle of justice in transfer are justice preserving, and any situation actually arising from repeated transitions in accordance with the principle from a just situation is itself just. The parallel between justice-preserving transformations and truth-preserving transformations illuminates where it fails as well as where it holds. That a conclusion could have been deduced by truth-preserving means from premises that are true suffices to show its truth. That a situation *could* have arisen via justice-preserving means from a just situation does *not* suffice to show its justice. The fact that a thief's victims voluntarily *could* have presented him with gifts, does not entitle the thief to his ill-gotten gains. Justice in holdings is historical; it depends upon what actually has happened. We shall return to this point below.

Not all actual situations are generated in accordance with the two principles of justice in holdings: the principle of justice in acquisition and the principle of justice in transfer. Some people steal from others, or defraud them, or enslave them, seizing their product and preventing them from living as they choose, or forcibly exclude others from competing in exchanges. None of these are permissible modes of transition from one situation to another. And some persons acquire holdings by means not sanctioned by the principle of justice in acquisition. The existence of past injustice (previous violations of the first two principles of justice in holdings) raises the third major topic under justice in holdings: the rectification of injustice in holdings. If past injustice has shaped present holdings in various ways, some identifiable and some not, what now, if anything, ought to be done to rectify these injustices? What obligations are the performers of injustice under to their victims? What obligations do the beneficiaries of injustice have to those whose position is worse than it would have been had the injustice not been done? Or, than it would have been had compensation been paid promptly? How, if at all, do things change if the beneficiaries and those made worse off are not the direct parties in the act of injustice, but, for example, their descendants? Is an injustice done to someone whose holding was itself based upon an unrectified injustice? How far back must one go in wiping clean the historical slate of injustices? What may victims of injustice permissibly do in order to rectify the injustices being done to them, including the many injustices done by persons acting through their government? I do not know of a thorough or theoretically sophisticated treatment of such issues. Idealizing greatly, let us suppose theoretical investigation will produce a principle of rectification. This principle uses historical information about previous situations and injustices done in them (as defined by the first two principles of justice, and rights against interference), and information about the actual course of events that flowed from these injustices, up until the present, and it yields a description (or descriptions) of holdings in the society. The principle of rectification presumably will make use of (its best estimate of) subjunctive information about what would have occurred (or a probability distribution over what might have occurred, using the expected value) if the injustice had not taken place. If the actual description of holdings turns out not to be one of the descriptions yielded by the principle, then one of the descriptions yielded must be realized.[2]

The general outlines of the theory of justice in holdings are that the holdings of a person are just if he is entitled to them by the principles of justice in acquisition and transfer, or by the principle of rectification of injustice (as specified by the first two principles). If each person's holdings are just then the total set (distribution) of holdings is just. To turn these general outlines into a specific theory we would have to specify the details of each of the three principles of justice in holdings: the principle of acquisition of holdings, the principle of transfer of holdings, and the principle of rectification of violations of the first two principles. I shall not attempt that task here. (Locke's principle of justice in acquisition is discussed below.)

1. *Historical Principles and End-Result Principles.* The general outlines of the entitlement theory illuminate the nature and defects of other conceptions of distributive justice. The entitlement theory of justice in distribution is *historical*; whether a distribution is just depends upon how it came about. In contrast, *current time-slice principles* of justice hold that the justice of a distribution is determined by how things are distributed (who has what) as judged by some *structural* principle(s) of just distribution. A utilitarian who judges between any two distributions by seeing which has the greater sum of utility and, if these tie, who applies some fixed, equality criterion to choose the more equal distribution, would hold a current time-slice principle of justice. As would someone who had a fixed schedule of trade-offs between the sum of happiness and equality. All that needs to be looked at, in judging the justice of a distribution, according to a current time-slice principle, is who ends up with what; in comparing any two distributions one need look only at the matrix presenting the distributions. No further information need be fed into a principle of justice. It is a consequence of such principles of justice that any two structurally identical distributions are equally just. (Two distributions are structurally identical if they present the same profile, but [perhaps] have different persons occupying the particular slots. My having ten and your having five, and my having five and your having

ten are structurally identical distributions.) Welfare economics is the theory of current time-slice principles of justice. The subject is conceived as operating on matrices representing only current information about distribution. This, as well as some of the usual conditions (e.g., the choice of distribution is invariant under relabelling of columns), guarantees that welfare economics will be a current time-slice theory, with all of its inadequacies.

Most persons do not accept current time-slice principles as constituting the whole story about distributive shares. They think it relevant in assessing the justice of a situation to consider not only the distribution it embodies, but also how that distribution came about. If some persons are in prison for murder or war crimes, we do not say that to assess the justice of the distribution in the society we must look only at what this person has, and that person has, and that person has . . . at the current time. We think it relevant to ask whether someone did something so that he *deserved* to be punished, deserved to have a lower share. Most will agree to the relevance of further information with regard to punishments and penalties. Consider also desired things. One traditional socialist view is that workers are entitled to the product and full fruits of their labour; they have earned it; a distribution is unjust if it does not give the workers what they are entitled to. Such entitlements are based upon some past history. No socialist holding this view would find it comforting to be told that because the actual distribution A happens to coincide structurally with the one he desires D, A therefore is no less just than D; it differs only in that the 'parasitic' owners of capital receive under A what the workers are entitled to under D, and the workers receive under A what the owners are entitled to (under D), namely very little. Rightly in my view, this socialist holds onto the notions of earning, producing, entitlement, desert, etc. and he rejects (current time-slice) principles that look only to the structure of the resulting set of holdings. (The set of holdings resulting from what? Isn't it implausible that how holdings are produced and come to exist has no effect at all on who should hold what?) His mistake lies in his view of what entitlements arise out of what sorts of productive processes.

We construe the position we discuss too narrowly by speaking of *current* time-slice principles. Nothing is changed if structural principles operate upon a time sequence of current time-slice profiles and, for example, give someone more now to counterbalance the less he has had earlier. A utilitarian or an egalitarian or any mixture of the two over time will inherit the difficulties of his more myopic comrades. He is not helped by the fact that *some* of the information others consider relevant in assessing a distribution is reflected, unrecoverably, in past matrices. Henceforth, we shall refer to such unhistorical principles of distributive justice, including the current time-slice principles, as *end-result principles* or *end-state principles*.

In contrast to end-result principles of justice, *historical principles* of justice hold that past circumstances or actions of people can create differential entitlements or differential deserts to things. An injustice can be worked by moving from one distribution to another structurally identical one, for the second, in profile the same, may violate people's entitlements or deserts; it may not fit the actual history.

2. *Patterning*. The entitlement principles of justice in holdings that we have sketched are historical principles of justice. To better understand their precise character, we shall distinguish them from another subclass of the historical principles. Consider, as an example, the principle of distribution according to moral merit. This principle requires total distributive shares to vary directly with moral merit; no person should have a greater share than anyone whose moral merit is greater. (If moral merit could be not merely ordered but measured on an interval or ratio scale, stronger principles could be formulated.) Or consider the principle that results by substituting 'usefulness to society' for 'moral merit' in the previous principle. Or instead of 'distribute according to moral merit', or 'distribute according to usefulness to society', we might consider 'distribute according to the weighted sum of moral merit, usefulness to society, and need', with the weights of the different dimensions equal. Let us call a principle of distribution *patterned* if it specifies that a distribution is to vary along with some natural dimension, weighted sum of natural dimensions, or lexicographic ordering of natural dimensions. And let us say a distribution is patterned if it accords with some patterned principle. (I speak of natural dimensions, admittedly without a general criterion for them, because for any set of holdings some artificial dimensions

can be gimmicked up to vary along with the distribution of the set.) The principle of distribution in accordance with moral merit is a patterned historical principle, which specifies a patterned distribution. 'Distribute according to I.Q.' is a patterned principle that looks to information not contained in distributional matrices. It is not historical, however, in that it does not look to any past actions creating differential entitlements to evaluate a distribution; it requires only distributional matrices whose columns are labelled by I.Q. scores. The distribution in a society, however, may be composed of such simple patterned distributions, without itself being simply patterned. Different sectors may operate different patterns, or some combination of patterns may operate in different proportions across a society. A distribution composed in this manner, from a small number of patterned distributions, we also shall term patterned. And we extend the use of 'pattern' to include the overall designs put forth by combinations of end-state principles.

Almost every suggested principle of distributive justice is patterned: to each according to his moral merit, or needs, or marginal product, or how hard he tries, or the weighted sum of the foregoing, and so on. The principle of entitlement we have sketched is *not* patterned.[3] There is no one natural dimension or weighted sum or combination of (a small number of) natural dimensions that yields the distributions generated in accordance with the principle of entitlement. The set of holdings that results when some persons receive their marginal products, others win at gambling, others receive a share of their mate's income, others receive gifts from foundations, others receive interest on loans, others receive gifts from admirers, others receive returns on investment, others make for themselves much of what they have, others find things, and so on, will not be patterned. Heavy strands of patterns will run through it; significant portions of the variance in holdings will be accounted for by pattern variables. If most people most of the time choose to transfer some of their entitlements to others only in exchange for something from them, then a large part of what many people hold will vary with what they held that others wanted. More details are provided by the theory of marginal productivity. But gifts to relatives, charitable donations, bequests to children, and the like, are not best conceived, in the first instance, in this manner. Ignoring the strands of pattern, let us suppose for the moment that a distribution actually gotten by the operation of the principle of entitlement is random with respect to any pattern. Though the resulting set of holdings will be unpatterned, it will not be incomprehensible, for it can be seen as arising from the operation of a small number of principles. These principles specify how an initial distribution may arise (the principle of acquisition of holdings) and how distributions may be transformed into others (the principle of transfers of holdings). The process whereby the set of holdings is generated will be intelligible, though the set of holdings itself that results from this process will be unpatterned.

The writings of F. A. Hayek focus less than others' upon what patterning distributive justice requires. Hayek argues that we cannot know enough about each person's situation to distribute to each according to his moral merit (but would justice demand we do so if we did have this knowledge?); and he goes on to say, 'our objection is against all attempts to impress upon society a deliberately chosen pattern of distribution, whether it be an order of equality or of inequality'.[4] However, Hayek concludes that in a free society there will be distribution in accordance with value rather than (moral) merit; that is, in accordance with the perceived value of a person's actions and services to others. Despite his rejection of a patterned conception of distributive justice, Hayek himself suggests a pattern he thinks justifiable: distribution in accordance with the (perceived) benefits given to others, and so leaves room for the complaint that a free society does not realize exactly this pattern. Stating this patterned strand of a free capitalist society more precisely, we get: 'To each according to how much he benefits others who have the resources for benefiting those who benefit them.' This will seem arbitrary unless some acceptable initial set of holdings is specified, or unless it is held that the operation of the system over time washes out any significant effects from the initial set of holdings. As an example of the latter, if almost anyone would have bought a car from Henry Ford, the supposition that it was an arbitrary matter who held the money then (and so bought) would not place Henry Ford's earnings under a cloud. In any event, *his* coming to hold it is not arbitrary. Distribution according to benefits to others *is* a major patterned strand in a free capitalist society, as Hayek correctly points out, but it is only a strand and does *not* constitute the whole pattern of a system of entitlements (viz., inheritance, gifts for arbitrary reasons, charity, etc.) or a standard one should insist a society fit. Will people tolerate for long a system yielding distributions that (they believe) are unpatterned?[5] No doubt people will not long accept a distribution they believe is *unjust*. People want their society to be and to look just. But must the look of justice reside in a resulting pattern rather than in the underlying generating principles? We are in no position to conclude the inhabitants of a society embodying an entitlement conception of justice in holdings will find it unacceptable. Still, it must be granted that were people's reasons for transferring some of their holdings to others always irrational or arbitrary, we would find this disturbing. (Suppose people always determined what holdings they would transfer, and to whom, by using a random device.) We feel more comfortable upholding the justice of an entitlement system if most of the transfers under it are done for reasons. This does not mean necessarily that all deserve what holdings they receive. It means only that there is a purpose or point to someone's transferring a holding to one person rather than to another; that usually we can see what the transferrer thinks he's gaining, what cause he thinks he's serving, what goals he thinks he's helping to achieve, etc. Since often in a capitalist society people transfer holdings to others in accordance with how much they perceive these others benefiting them, the fabric constituted by the individual transactions and transfers is largely reasonable and intelligible. (Gifts to loved ones, bequests to children, charity to the needy also are nonarbitrary components of the fabric.) In stressing the large strand of distribution in accordance with benefit to others, Hayek shows the point of many transfers, and so shows that the system of transfer of entitlements is not just spinning its gears aimlessly. The system of entitlements is defensible when constituted by the individual aims of individual transactions. No overarching aim is needed, no distributional pattern is required.

To think that the task of a theory of distributive justice is to fill in the blank in 'to each according to his —————', is to be predisposed to search for a pattern; and the separate treatment of 'from each according to his —————', treats production and distribution as two separate and independent issues. On an entitlement view these are *not* two separate questions. Whoever makes something, having bought or contracted for all other held resources used in the process (transferring some of his holdings for these cooperating factors), is entitled to it. The situation is *not* one of something's getting made, and there being an open question of who is to get it. Things come into the world already attached to people having entitlements over them. From the point of view of the historical entitlement conception of justice in holdings, those who start afresh to complete 'to each according to his ——————', treat objects as if they appeared from nowhere, out of nothing. A complete theory of justice might cover this limit case as well; here perhaps is a use for the usual conceptions of distributive justice.[6]

So entrenched are maxims of the usual form that perhaps we should present the entitlement conception as a competitor. Ignoring acquisition and rectification, we might say:

From each according to what he chooses to do, to each according to what he makes for himself (perhaps with the contracted-for aid of others) and what others choose to do for him and choose to give him of what they've been given previously (under this maxim) and haven't yet expended or transferred.

This, the discerning reader will have noticed, has its defects as a slogan. So as a summary (and not as a maxim with any independent meaning) and great simplification we have:

From each as he chooses, to each as he is chosen.

3. *How Liberty Upsets Patterns.* It is not clear how those holding alternative conceptions of distributive justice can reject the entitlement conception of justice in holdings. For suppose a distribution favoured by one of these nonentitlement conceptions is realized. Let us suppose it is your favourite one and call this distribution D_1; perhaps everyone has an equal share, perhaps shares vary in accordance with some dimension you treasure. Now suppose that Wilt Chamberlain is greatly in demand by basketball teams, being a great gate-attraction. (Also suppose contracts run only for a year, with players being free agents.) He signs the following sort of contract with a team: In each

home game, twenty-five cents from the price of each ticket of admission goes to him. (We ignore the question of whether he is 'gouging' the owners, letting them look out for themselves.) The season starts, and people cheerfully attend his team's games; they buy their tickets, each time dropping a separate twenty-five cents of their admission price into a special box with Chamberlain's name on it. They are excited about seeing him play; it is worth the total admission price to them. Let us suppose that in one season one million persons attend his home games, and Wilt Chamberlain winds up with $250,000, a much larger sum than the average income and larger even than anyone else has. Is he entitled to this income? Is this new distribution D_2 unjust? If so, why? There is *no* question about whether each of the people was entitled to the control over the resources they held, in D_1, because that was the distribution (your favourite) that (for the purposes of argument) we assumed was acceptable. Each of these persons *chose* to give twenty-five cents of their money to Chamberlain. They could have spent it on going to the movies, or on candy bars, or on copies of *Dissent* magazine, or of *Monthly Review*. But they all, at least one million of them, converged on giving it to Wilt Chamberlain in exchange for watching him play basketball. If D_1 was a just distribution, and people voluntarily moved from it to D_2, transferring parts of their shares they were given under D_1 (what was it for if not to do something with?), isn't D_2 also just? If the people were entitled to dispose of the resources to which they were entitled (under D_1), didn't this include their being entitled to give it to, or exchange it with, Wilt Chamberlain? Can anyone else complain on grounds of justice? Each other person already has his legitimate share under D_1. Under D_1 there is nothing that anyone has that anyone else has a claim of justice against. After someone transfers something to Wilt Chamberlain, third parties *still* have their legitimate shares; *their* shares are not changed. By what process could such a transfer among two persons give rise to a legitimate claim of distributive justice on a portion of what was transferred, by a third party who had no claim of justice on any holding of the others *before* the transfer?[7] To cut off objections irrelevant here, we might imagine the exchanges occurring in a socialist society, after hours. After playing whatever basketball he does in his daily work, or doing whatever other daily work he does, Wilt

Chamberlain decides to put in *overtime* to earn additional money. (First his work quota is set; he works time over that.) Or imagine it is a skilled juggler people like to see, who puts on shows after hours.

Why might some people work overtime in a society in which it is assumed their needs are satisfied? Perhaps because they care about things other than needs. I like to write in books that I read, and to have easy access to books for browsing at odd hours. It would be very pleasant and convenient to have the resources of Widener Library in my back yard. No society, I assume, will provide such resources close to each person who would like them as part of his regular allotment (under D_1). Thus, persons either must do without some extra things that they want, or be allowed to do something extra to get (some of) these things. On what basis could the inequalities that would eventuate be forbidden? Notice also that small factories would spring up in a socialist society, unless forbidden. I melt down some of my personal possessions (under D_1) and build a machine out of the material. I offer you, and others, a philosophy lecture once a week in exchange for your cranking the handle on my machine, whose products I exchange for yet other things, and so on. (The raw materials used by the machine are given to me by others who possess them under D_1, in exchange for hearing lectures.) Each person might participate to gain things over and above their allotment under D_1. Some persons even might want to leave their job in socialist industry, and work full time in this private sector. I say something more about these issues elsewhere. Here I wish merely to note how private property, even in means of production, would occur in a socialist society that did not forbid people to use as they wished some of the resources they are given under the socialist distribution D_1.[8] The socialist society would have to forbid capitalist acts between consenting adults.

The general point illustrated by the Wilt Chamberlain example and the example of the entrepreneur in a socialist society is that no end-state principle or distributional pattern principle of justice can be continuously realized without continuous interference into people's lives. Any favoured pattern would be transformed into one unfavoured by the principle, by people choosing to act in various ways; e.g., by people exchanging goods and services with other people, or giving things to other people, things the transferrers are entitled to under the favoured distributional pattern. To maintain a pattern one must either continuously interfere to stop people from transferring resources as they wish to, or continually (or periodically) interfere to take from some persons resources that others for some reason chose to transfer to them. (But if some time limit is to be set on how long people may keep resources others voluntarily transfer to them, why let them keep these resources for *any* period of time? Why not have immediate confiscation?) It might be objected that all persons voluntarily will choose to refrain from actions which would upset the pattern. This presupposes unrealistically (a) that all will most want to maintain the pattern (are those who don't, to be 're-educated' or forced to undergo 'self-criticism'?); (b) that each can gather enough information about his own actions and the ongoing activities of others to discover which of his actions will upset the pattern; and (c) that diverse and farflung persons can coordinate their actions to dovetail into the pattern. Compare the manner in which the market is neutral among persons' desires, as it reflects and transmits widely scattered information via prices, and coordinates persons' activities.

It puts things perhaps a bit too strongly to say that every patterned (or end-state) principle is liable to be thwarted by the voluntary actions of the individual parties transferring some of their shares they receive under the principle. For perhaps some *very* weak patterns are not so thwarted.[9] Any distributional pattern with any egalitarian component is overturnable by the voluntary actions of individual persons over time; as is every patterned condition with sufficient content so as actually to have been proposed as presenting the central core of distributive justice. Still, given the possibility that some weak conditions or patterns may not be unstable in this way, it would be better to formulate an explicit description of the kind of (interesting and contentful) patterns under discussion, and to prove a theorem about their instability. Since the weaker the patterning, the more likely it is that the entitlement system itself satisfies it, a plausible conjecture is that any patterning either is unstable or is satisfied by the entitlement system.

4. *Sen's Argument.* Our conclusions are reinforced by considering a recent general argument of Amartya K. Sen.[10] Suppose individual

rights are interpreted as the right to choose which of two alternatives is to be more highly ranked in a social ordering of the alternatives. Add the weak condition that if one alternative unanimously is preferred to another then it is ranked higher by the social ordering. If there are two different individuals each with individual rights, interpreted as above, over different pairs of alternatives (having no members in common), then for some possible preference rankings of the alternatives by the individuals, there is no linear social ordering. For suppose that person I has the right to decide among (X, Y) and person II has the right to decide among (Z, W); and suppose their individual preferences are as follows (and that there are no other individuals). Person I prefers W to X to Y to Z, and person II prefers Y to Z to W to X. By the unanimity condition, in the social ordering W is preferred to X (since each individual prefers it to X), and Y is preferred to Z (since each individual prefers it to Z). Also in the social ordering, X is preferred to Y, by person I's right of choice among these two alternatives. Combining these three binary rankings, we get W preferred to X preferred to Y preferred to Z, in the social ordering. However, by person II's right of choice, Z must be preferred to W in the social ordering. There is no transitive social ordering satisfying all these conditions, and the social ordering, therefore, is nonlinear. Thus far, Sen.

The trouble stems from treating an individual's right to choose among alternatives as the right to determine the relative ordering of these alternatives within a social ordering. The system is no better that has individuals rank *pairs* of alternatives, and separately rank the individual alternatives; their ranking of pairs feeds into some method of amalgamating preferences to yield a social ordering of pairs; and the choice among the alternatives in the highest ranked pair in the social ordering is made by the individual with the right to decide between this pair. This system also has the result that an alternative may be selected although *everyone* prefers some other alternative; e.g., I selects X over Y, where (X, Y) somehow is the highest ranked *pair* in the social ordering of pairs, although everyone, including I, prefers W to X. (But the choice person I was given, however, was only between X and Y.)

A more appropriate view of individual rights is as follows. Individual rights are co-possible; each person may exercise his rights as he chooses. The exercise of these rights fixes some features of the world. Within the constraints of these fixed features, a choice may be made by a social choice mechanism based upon a social ordering, if there are any choices left to make! Rights do not determine a social ordering but instead set the constraints within which a social choice is to be made, by excluding certain alternatives, fixing others, and so on. (If I have a right to choose to live in New York or in Massachusetts, and I choose Massachusetts, then alternatives involving my living in New York are not appropriate objects to be entered in a social ordering.) Even if all possible alternatives are ordered first, apart from anyone's rights, the situation is not changed; for then the highest ranked alternative *that is not excluded by anyone's exercise of their rights* is instituted. Rights do not determine the position of an alternative or the relative position of two alternatives in a social ordering; they *operate upon* a social ordering to constrain the choice it can yield.

If entitlements to holdings are rights to dispose of them, then social choice must take place *within* the constraints of how people choose to exercise these rights. If any patterning is legitimate, it falls within the domain of social choice, and hence is constrained by people's rights. *How else can one cope with Sen's result?* The alternative of first having a social ranking with rights exercised within *its* constraints, is no alternative at all. Why not just select the top ranked alternative and forget about rights? If that top ranked alternative itself leaves some room for individual choice (and here is where 'rights' of choice is supposed to enter in) there must be something to stop these choices from transforming it into another alternative. Thus Sen's argument leads us again to the result that patterning requires continuous interference with individuals' actions and choices.[11]

5. *Redistribution and Property Rights.* Apparently patterned principles allow people to choose to expend upon themselves, but not upon others, those resources they are entitled to (or rather, receive) under some favoured distributional pattern D_1. For if each of several persons chooses to expend some of his D_1 resources upon one other person, then that other person will receive more than his D_1 share, disturbing the favoured distributional pattern. Maintaining a distributional pat-

tern is individualism with a vengeance! Patterned distributional principles do not give people what entitlement principles do, only better distributed. For they do not give the right to choose what to do with what one has; they do not give the right to choose to pursue an end involving (intrinsically, or as a means) the enhancement of another's position. To such views, families are disturbing; for within a family occur transfers that upset the favoured distributional pattern. Either families themselves become units to which distribution takes place, the column occupiers (on what rationale?), or loving behaviour is forbidden. We should note in passing the ambivalent position of radicals towards the family. Its loving relationships are seen as a model to be emulated and extended across the whole society, while it is denounced as a suffocating institution to be broken, and condemned as a focus of parochial concerns that interfere with achieving radical goals. Need we say that it is not appropriate to enforce across the wider society the relationships of love and care appropriate within a family, relationships which are voluntarily undertaken?[12] Incidentally, love is an interesting instance of another relationship that is historical, in that (like justice) it depends upon what actually occurred. An adult may come to love another because of the other's characteristics; but it is the other person, and not the characteristics, that is loved. The love is not transferable to someone else with the same characteristics, even to one who 'scores' higher for these characteristics. And the love endures through changes of the characteristics that gave rise to it. One loves the particular person one actually encountered. Why love is historical, attaching to persons in this way and not to characteristics, is an interesting and puzzling question.

Proponents of patterned principles of distributive justice focus upon criteria for determining who is to receive holdings; they consider the reasons for which someone should have something, and also the total picture of holdings. Whether or not it is better to give than to receive, proponents of patterned principles ignore giving altogether. In considering the distribution of goods, income, etc., their theories are theories of recipient-justice; they completely ignore any right a person might have to give something to someone. Even in exchanges where each party is simultaneously giver and recipient, patterned principles of justice focus only upon the recipient role and its supposed rights.

Thus discussions tend to focus on whether people (should) have a right to inherit, rather than on whether people (should) have a right to bequeath or on whether persons who have a right to hold also have a right to choose that others hold in their place. I lack a good explanation of why the usual theories of distributive justice are so recipient-oriented; ignoring givers and transferrers and their rights is of a piece with ignoring producers and their entitlements. But why is it *all* ignored?

Patterned principles of distributive justice necessitate *re*distributive activities. The likelihood is small that any actual freely arrived at set of holdings fits a given pattern; and the likelihood is nil that it will continue to fit the pattern as people exchange and give. From the point of view of an entitlement theory, redistribution is a serious matter indeed, involving, as it does, the violation of people's rights. (An exception is those takings that fall under the principle of the rectification of injustices.) From other points of view, also, it is serious.

Taxation of earnings from labour is on a par with forced labour.[13] Some persons find this claim obviously true: taking the earnings of *n* hours labour is like taking *n* hours from the person; it is like forcing the person to work *n* hours for another's purpose. Others find the claim absurd. But even these, *if* they object to forced labour, would oppose forcing unemployed hippies to work for the benefit of the needy.[14] And they also would object to forcing each person to work five extra hours each week for the benefit of the needy. But a system that takes five hours' wages in taxes does not seem to them like one that forces someone to work five hours, since it offers the forcee a wider range of choice in activities than does taxation in kind with the particular labour specified. (But we can imagine a gradation of systems of forced labour, from one that specifies a particular activity, to one that gives a choice among two activities, to . . .; and so on up.) Furthermore, people envisage a system with something like a proportional tax on everything above the amount necessary for basic needs. Some think this does not force someone to work extra hours, since there is no fixed number of extra hours he is forced to work, and since he can avoid the tax entirely by earning only enough to cover his basic needs. This is a very uncharacteristic view of forcing for those who *also* think people are forced to do something *whenever* the alternatives they face are considerably worse. However, *neither* view is correct. The fact that others intentionally intervene, in violation of a side-constraint against aggression, to threaten force to limit the alternatives, in this case to paying taxes or (presumably the worse alternative) bare subsistence, makes the taxation system one of forced labour, and distinguishes it from other cases of limited choices which are not forcings.[15]

The man who chooses to work longer to gain an income more than sufficient for his basic needs prefers some extra goods or services to the leisure and activities he could perform during the possible non-working hours; whereas the man who chooses not to work the extra time prefers the leisure activities to the extra goods or services he could acquire by working more. Given this, if it would be illegitimate for a tax system to seize some of a man's leisure (forced labour) for the purpose of serving the needy, how can it be legitimate for a tax system to seize some of a man's goods for that purpose? Why should we treat the man whose happiness requires certain material goods or services differently from the man whose preferences and desires make such goods unnecessary for his happiness? Why should the man who prefers seeing a movie (and who has to earn money for a ticket) be open to the required call to aid the needy, while the person who prefers looking at a sunset (and hence need earn no extra money) is not? Indeed, isn't it surprising that redistributionists choose to ignore the man whose pleasures are so easily attainable without extra labour, while adding yet another burden to the poor unfortunate who must work for his pleasures? If anything, one would have expected the reverse. Why is the person with the nonmaterial or nonconsumption desire allowed to proceed unimpeded to his most favoured feasible alternative, whereas the man whose pleasures or desires involve material things and who must work for extra money (thereby serving whoever considers his activities valuable enough to pay him) is constrained in what he can realize? Perhaps there is no difference in principle. And perhaps some think the answer concerns merely administrative convenience. (These questions and issues will not disturb those who think forced labour to serve the needy or realize some favoured end-state pattern acceptable.) In a fuller discussion we would have (and want) to extend our argument to include interest, entrepreneurial profits, etc. Those who doubt that this extension can be carried through, and who draw the line here at taxation of income from labour, will have to state rather complicated patterned *historical* principles of distributive justice; since end-state principles would not distinguish *sources* of income in any way. It is enough for now to get away from end-state principles and to make clear how various patterned principles are dependent upon particular views about the sources or the illegitimacy or the lesser legitimacy of profits, interest, etc.; which particular views may well be mistaken.

What sort of right over others does a legally institutionalized end-state pattern give one? The central core of the notion of a property right in X, relative to which other parts of the notion are to be explained, is the right to determine what shall be done with X; the right to choose which of the constrained set of options concerning X shall be realized or attempted.[16] The constraints are set by other principles or laws operating in the society; in our theory by the Lockean rights people possess (under the minimal state). My property rights in my knife allow me to leave it where I will, but not in your chest. I may choose which of the acceptable options involving the knife is to be realized. This notion of property helps us to understand why earlier theorists spoke of people as having property in themselves and their labour. They viewed each person as having a right to decide what would become of himself and what he would do, and as having a right to reap the benefits of what he did.

This right of selecting the alternative to be realized from the constrained set of alternatives may be held by an *individual* or by a *group* with some procedure for reaching a joint decision; or the right may be passed back and forth, so that one year I decide what's to become of X, and the next year you do (with the alternative of destruction, perhaps, being excluded). Or, during the same time period, some types of decisions about X may be made by me, and others by you. And so on. We lack an adequate, fruitful, analytical apparatus for classifying the *types* of constraints on the set of options among which choices are to be made, and the *types* of ways decision powers can be held, divided, and amalgamated. A *theory* of property would, among other things, contain such a classification of constraints and decision modes, and from a small number of principles would follow a host of interesting statements about the *consequences* and effects of certain combinations of constraints and modes of decision.

When end-result principles of distributive justice are built into the legal structure of a society, they (as do most patterned principles) give each citizen an enforcible claim to some portion of the total social product; that is, to some portion of the sum total of the individually and jointly made products. This total product is produced by individuals labouring, using means of production others have saved to bring into existence, by people organizing production or creating means to produce new things or things in a new way. It is on this batch of individual activities that patterned distributional principles give each individual an enforcible claim. Each person has a claim to the activities and the products of other persons, independently of whether the other persons enter into particular relationships that give rise to these claims, and independently of whether they voluntarily take these claims upon themselves, in charity or in exchange for something.

Whether it is done through taxation on wages or on wages over a certain amount, or through seizure of profits, or through there being a big *social pot* so that it's not clear what's coming from where and what's going where, patterned principles of distributive justice involve appropriating the actions of other persons. Seizing the results of someone's labour is equivalent to seizing hours from him and directing him to carry on various activities. If people force you to do certain work, or unrewarded work, for a certain period of time, they decide what you are to do and what purposes your work is to serve apart from your decision. This process whereby they take this decision from you makes them a *part owner* of you; it gives them a property right in you. Just as having such partial control and power of decision, by right, over an animal or inanimate object would be to have a property right in it.

End-state and most patterned principles of distributive justice institute (partial) ownership by others of people and their actions and labour. These principles involve a shift from the classical liberals' notion of self-ownership to a notion of (partial) property rights in *other* people.

Considerations such as these confront end-state and other patterned conceptions of justice with the question of whether the actions necessary to achieve the selected pattern don't themselves violate moral side-constraints. Any view holding that there are moral side-constraints on actions, that not all moral considerations can be built into end-states that are to be achieved,[17] must face the possibility that some of its goals are not achievable by any morally permissible available means. An entitlement theorist will face such conflicts in a society that deviates from the principles of justice for the generation of holdings, if and only if the only actions available to realize the principles themselves violate some moral constraints. Since deviation from the first two principles of justice (in acquisition and transfer) will involve other persons' direct and aggressive intervention to violate rights, and since moral constraints will not exclude defensive or retributive action in such cases, the entitlement theorist's problem rarely will be pressing. And whatever difficulties he has in applying the principle of rectification to persons who did not themselves violate the first two principles, are difficulties in balancing the conflicting considerations so as correctly to formulate the complex principle of rectification itself; he will not violate moral side-constraints by applying the principle. Proponents of patterned conceptions of justice, however, often will face head-on clashes (and poignant ones if they cherish each party to the clash) between moral side-constraints on how individuals may be treated on the one hand and, on the other, their patterned conception of justice that presents an end-state or other pattern that *must* be realized.

May a person emigrate from a nation that has institutionalized some end-state or patterned distributional principle? For some principles (e.g. Hayek's) emigration presents no theoretical problem. But for others it is a tricky matter. Consider a nation having a compulsory scheme of minimal social provision to aid the neediest (or one organized so as to maximize the position of the worst-off group); no one may opt out of participating in it. (None may say, 'don't compel me to contribute to others and don't provide for me via this compulsory mechanism if I am in need.') Everyone above a certain level is forced to contribute to aid the needy. But if emigration from the country were allowed, anyone could choose to move to another country that did not have compulsory social provision but otherwise was (as much as possible) identical. In such a case, the person's only motive for leaving would be to avoid participating in the compulsory scheme of social provision. And if he does leave, the needy in his initial country will receive no (compelled) help from him. What rationale yields the result that the person be permitted to emigrate, yet forbidden to stay and opt out of the compulsory scheme of social provision? If providing for the needy is of overriding importance, this does militate against allowing internal opting out; but it also speaks against allowing external emigration. (Would it also support, to some extent, the kidnapping of persons living in a place without compulsory social provision, who could be forced to make a contribution to the needy in your community?) Perhaps the crucial component of the position that allows emigration solely to avoid certain arrangements, while not allowing anyone internally to opt out of them, is a concern for fraternal feelings within the country. 'We don't want anyone here who doesn't contribute, who doesn't care enough about the others to contribute.' That concern, in this case, would have to be tied to the view that forced aiding tends to produce fraternal feelings between the aided and the aider (or perhaps merely to the view that the knowledge that someone or other voluntarily is not aiding produces fraternal feelings).

6. *Locke's Theory of Acquisition.* We must introduce an additional bit of complexity into the structure of the entitlement theory. This is best approached by considering Locke's attempt to specify a principle of justice in acquisition. Locke views property rights in an unowned object as originating through someone's mixing his labour with it. This gives rise to many questions. What are the boundaries of what labour is mixed with? If a private astronaut clears a place on Mars, has he mixed his labour with (so that he comes to own) the whole planet, the whole uninhabited universe, or just a particular plot? Which plot does an act bring under ownership? The minimal (possibly disconnected) area such that an act decreases entropy in that area, and not elsewhere? Can virgin land (for the purposes of ecological investigation by high flying airplanes) come under ownership by a Lockean process? Building a fence around a territory presumably would make one the owner of only the fence (and the land immediately underneath it).

Why does mixing one's labour with something make one the owner of it? Perhaps because one owns one's labour, and so one comes to own a previously unowned thing that becomes permeated with what one owns. Ownership seeps over into the rest. But why isn't mixing what I own with what I don't own a way of losing what I own rather than a way of gaining what I don't? If I own a can of tomato juice, and spill it in the sea so that its molecules (radioactive, so I can check this) mingle evenly throughout the sea, do I thereby come to own the sea, or have I foolishly dissipated my tomato juice? Perhaps the idea, instead, is that labouring on something improves it and makes it more valuable; and anyone is entitled to own a (thing whose) value he has created. (Reinforcing this, perhaps, is the view that labouring is unpleasant. If some people made things effortlessly, as the cartoon characters in *The Yellow Submarine* trail flowers in their wake, would they have lesser claim to their own products whose making didn't *cost* them anything?) Ignore the fact that labouring on something may make it less valuable (spraying pink enamel paint on a found piece of driftwood). Why should one's entitlement extend to the whole object rather than just to the *added value* one's labour has produced? (Such reference to value might also serve to delimit the extent of ownership; e.g., substitute 'increases the value of' for 'decreases entropy in' in the above entropy criterion.) No workable or coherent value-added property scheme has yet been devised, and any such scheme presumably would fall to objections (similar to those) that fell to the theory of Henry George.

It will be implausible to view improving an object as giving full ownership to it, if the stock of unowned objects that might be improved is limited. For an object's coming under one person's ownership changes the situation of all others. Whereas previously they were at liberty (in Hohfeld's sense) to use the object, they now no longer are. This change in the situation of others (by removing their liberty to act on a previously unowned object) need not worsen their situation. If I appropriate a grain of sand from Coney Island, no one else may now do as they will with *that* grain of sand. But there are plenty of others left for them to do the same with. Or if not grains of sand, then other things. Alternatively, the things I do with the grain of sand I appropriate might improve the position of others, counterbalancing their loss of the liberty to use that grain. The crucial point is whether appropriation of an unowned object worsens the situation of others.

Locke's proviso that there be 'enough and as good left in common for others' is meant to ensure that the situation of others is not worsened. (If this proviso is met, is there any motivation for his further condition of non-waste?) It is often said that this proviso once held but now no longer does. But there appears to be an argument for the conclusion that if the proviso no longer holds, then it cannot ever have held so as to yield permanent and inheritable property rights. Consider the first person, Z, for whom there is not enough and as good left to appropriate. The last person, Y, to appropriate, left Z without his previous liberty to act on an object, and so worsened Z's situation. So Y's appropriation is not allowed under Locke's proviso. Therefore the next-to-last person, X, to appropriate left Y in a worse position, for X's act ended permissible appropriation. Therefore X's appropriation wasn't permissible. But then the appropriator two from last, W, ended permissible appropriation and so, since it worsened X's position, W's appropriation wasn't permissible. And so on back to the first appropriator A of a permanent property right.

This argument, however, proceeds too quickly. Someone may be made worse off by another's appropriation in two ways: first, by losing the opportunity to improve his situation by a particular appropriation or any one; and second, by no longer being able to use freely (without appropriation) what he previously could. A *stringent* requirement that another not be made worse off by an appropriation would exclude the first way if nothing else counterbalances the diminution in opportunity, as well as the second. A *weaker* requirement would exclude the second way though not the first. With the weaker requirement, we cannot zip back so quickly from Z to A, as in the above argument; for though person Z can no longer *appropriate*, there may remain some for him to *use* as before. In this case Y's appropriation would not violate the weaker Lockean condition. (With less remaining that people are at liberty to use, users might face more inconvenience, crowding, etc; in that way the situation of others might be worsened, unless appropriation stopped far short of such a point.) It is arguable that no one legitimately can complain if the weaker provision is satisfied. However, since this is less clear than in the case of the more stringent proviso, Locke may have intended this stringent proviso by 'enough and as good' remaining, and perhaps he meant the non-waste condition to delay the end point from which the argument zips back.

Is the situation of persons who are unable to appropriate (there being no more accessible and useful unowned objects) worsened by a system allowing appropriation and permanent property? Here enter the various familiar social considerations favouring private property: it increases the social product by putting means of production in the hands of those who can use them most efficiently (profitably); experimentation is encouraged, because with separate persons controlling resources, there is no one person or small group whom someone with a new idea must convince to try it out; private property enables people to decide on the pattern and types of risks they wish to bear, leading to specialized types of risk bearing; private property protects future persons by leading some to hold back resources from current consumption for future markets; it provides alternate sources of employment for unpopular persons who don't have to convince any one person or small group to hire them, and so on. These considerations enter a Lockean theory to support the claim that appropriation of private property satisfies the intent behind the 'enough and as good left over' proviso, *not* as a utilitarian justification of property. They enter to rebut the claim that because the proviso is violated, no natural right to private property can arise by a Lockean process. The difficulty in working such an argument to show the proviso is satisfied is in fixing the appropriate baseline for comparison. Lockean appropriation makes people no worse off than they would be *how*?[18] This question of fixing the baseline needs more detailed investigation than we are able to give it here. It would be desirable to have an estimate of the general economic importance of original appropriation for a society, in order to see how much leeway there is for differing theories of appropriation and of the location of the baseline. Perhaps this importance can be measured by the percentage of all income that is based upon untransformed raw materials and given resources (rather than human actions), mainly rental income representing the unimproved value of the land, and the price of raw materials *in situ*, and by the percentage of current wealth that represents such income in the past.[19]

We should note that it is not only persons favouring *private* property who need a theory of how property rights legitimately originate. Those believing in collective property – for example, those believing that a group of persons living in an area jointly own the territory, or its mineral resources – also must provide a theory of how such property rights arise, of why the persons living there have rights to determine what is done with the land and resources there that persons living elsewhere don't have (with regard to the same land and resources).

7. *The Proviso.* Whether or not Locke's particular theory of appropriation can be spelled out so as to handle various difficulties, I assume that any adequate theory of justice in acquisition will contain a proviso similar to the weaker of the ones we have attributed to Locke. A process normally giving rise to a permanent bequeathable property right in a previously unowned thing, will not do so if the position of others no longer at liberty to use the thing is thereby worsened. It is important to specify *this* particular mode of worsening the situation of others, for the proviso does not encompass other modes. It does not include the worsening due to more limited opportunities to appropriate (the first way above, corresponding to the more stringent condition), and it does not include how I 'worsen' a seller's position if I appropriate materials to make some of what he is selling, and enter into competition with him. Someone whose appropriation (otherwise) would violate the proviso still may appropriate provided he compensates the others so that their situation is not thereby worsened; unless he does compensate these others, his appropriation will violate the (proviso of the) principle of justice in acquisition and will be an illegitimate one.[20] A theory of appropriation incorporating this Lockean proviso will handle correctly the cases (objections to the theory lacking the proviso) where someone appropriates the total supply of something necessary for life.[21]

A theory that includes this proviso in its principle of justice in acquisition, also must contain a more complex principle of justice in transfer. Some reflection of the proviso about appropriation constrains later actions. If my appropriating all of a certain substance violates the Lockean proviso, then so does my appropriating some and purchasing all the rest from others who obtained it without (otherwise) violating the Lockean proviso. If the proviso excludes someone's appropriating all the drinkable water in the world, it also excludes his purchasing it all. (More weakly, and messily, it may exclude his charging certain prices for some of his supply.) This proviso (almost?) never will come into effect; the more someone acquires of a scarce substance that others want, the higher the price of the rest will go, and the more difficult it will become for him to acquire it all. But still, we can imagine, at least, that something like this occurs: someone makes simultaneous secret bids to the separate owners of a substance, each of whom sells assuming he can easily purchase more from the other owners; or some natural catastrophe destroys all of the supply of something except that in one person's possession. The total supply could not be all permissibly appropriated by one person at the beginning. His later acquisition of it all does not show that the original appropriation violated the proviso (even by a reverse argument similar to the one above that tried to zip back from Z to A). Rather, it is the combination of the original appropriation *plus* all the later transfers and actions that violates the Lockean proviso.

Each owner's title to his holding includes the historical shadow of the Lockean proviso in appropriation. This excludes his transferring it into an agglomeration that does violate the Lockean proviso, and excludes his using it in a way, in coordination with others or independently of them, so as to violate the proviso by making the situation of others worse than their baseline situation. Once it is known that someone's ownership runs afoul of the Lockean proviso, there are stringent limits on what he may do with (what it is difficult any longer unreservedly to call) 'his property'. Thus a person may not appropriate the only water hole in a desert and charge what he will. Nor may he charge what he will if he possesses one, and unfortunately it chances that all the water holes in the desert dry up, except for his. This unfortunate circumstance, admittedly no fault of his, brings into operation the Lockean proviso and limits his property rights.[22] Similarly, an owner's property right in the only island in an area does not allow him to order a castaway from a shipwreck off his island as a trespasser, for this would violate the Lockean proviso.

Notice that the theory does not say that owners do have these rights but that the rights are overridden to avoid some catastrophe. (Overridden rights do not disappear; they leave a trace of a sort absent in the cases under discussion).[23] There is no such external (and *ad hoc*?) overriding. Considerations internal to the theory of property itself, to its theory of acquisition and appropriation, provide the means for handling such cases. The results, however, may be coextensive with some condition about catastrophe, since the baseline for comparison is so low as compared to the productiveness of a society with private appropriation, that the question of the Lockean proviso being violated arises only in the case of catastrophe (or a desert-island situation).

The fact that someone owns the total supply of something necessary for others to stay alive, does *not* entail that his (or anyone's) appropriation of anything left some people (immediately or later) in a situation worse than the baseline one. A medical researcher who synthesizes a new substance that effectively treats a certain disease and who refuses to sell except on his terms, does not worsen the situation of others by depriving them of whatever he has appropriated. The others (easily can) possess the same materials he appropriated; the researcher's appropriation or purchase of chemicals didn't make those chemicals scarce in a way so as to violate the Lockean proviso. Nor would someone else's purchasing the total supply of the synthesized substance from the medical researcher. The fact that the medical researcher uses easily available chemicals to synthesize the drug no more violates the Lockean proviso than does the fact that the only surgeon able to perform a particular operation eats easily obtainable food in order to stay alive and have the energy to work. This shows that the Lockean proviso is not an 'end-state principle'; it focuses on a particular way that appropriative acts affect others, and not on the structure of the situation that results.

Intermediate between someone who takes all of the public supply, and someone who makes the total supply out of easily obtainable substances, is someone who appropriates the total supply of something in a way that does not deprive the others of it. For example, someone finds a new substance in an out-of-the-way place. He discovers that it effectively treats a certain disease, and appropriates the total supply. He does not worsen the situation of others; if he did not stumble upon the substance no one else would have, and the others would remain without it. However, as time passes, the likelihood increases that others would have come across the substance; upon this fact might be based a limit to his property right in the substance so that others are not below their baseline position, e.g., its bequest might be limited. The theme of someone worsening another's situation by depriving him of something he otherwise would possess, may also illuminate the example of patents. An inventor's patent does not deprive others of an object which would not exist if not for the inventor. Yet patents would have this effect on others who independently invent the object. Therefore, these independent inventors, upon whom the burden of proving independent discovery may rest, should not be excluded from utilizing their own invention as they wish (including selling it to others). Furthermore, a known invention drastically lessens the chances of actual independent invention. For persons who know of an invention usually will not try to re-invent it, and the notion of independent discovery here would be murky at best. Yet we may assume that in the absence of the original invention, sometime later someone else would have come up with it. This suggests placing a time limit on patents, as a rough rule of thumb to approximate how long it would have taken, in the absence of knowledge of the invention, for independent discovery.

I believe that the free operation of a market system will not actually run afoul of the Lockean proviso. If this is correct, the proviso will not provide a significant opportunity for future state action. Indeed, were it not for the effects of previous *illegitimate* state action, people would not think the possibility of the proviso's being violated as of more interest than any other logical possibility. (Here I make an empirical historical claim; as does someone who disagrees with this.) This completes our indication of the complication in the entitlement theory introduced by the Lockean proviso.

Notes

1. Applications of the principle of justice in acquisition, may also occur as part of the move from one distribution to another. You may find an unheld thing now, and appropriate it. Acquisitions also are to be understood as included when, to simplify, I speak only of transitions by transfers.

2. If the principle of rectification of violations of the first two principles yields more than one description of holdings, then some choice must be made as to which of these is to be realized. Perhaps the sort of considerations about distributive justice and equality I argue against play a legitimate role in *this* subsidiary choice. Similarly, there may be room for such considerations in deciding which otherwise arbitrary features a statute will embody, when such features are unavoidable because other considerations do not specify a precise line, yet one must be drawn.

3. One might try to squeeze a patterned conception of distributive justice into the framework of the entitlement conception, by formulating a gimmicky obligatory 'principle of transfer' that would lead to the pattern. For example, the principle that if one has more than the mean income, one must transfer everything one holds above the mean to persons below the mean so as to bring them up to (but not over) the mean. We can formulate a criterion for a 'principle of transfer' to rule out such obligatory transfers, or we can say that no correct principle of transfer, no principle of transfer in a free society will be like this. The former is probably the better course, though the latter also is true.

Alternatively, one might think to make the entitlement conception instantiate a pattern, by using matrix entries that express the relative strength of a person's entitlements as measured by some real-valued function. But even if the limitation to natural dimensions failed to exclude this function, the resulting edifice would *not* capture our system of entitlements to *particular* things.

4. F. A. Hayek, *The Constitution of Liberty* (Chicago, 1972), Chapter 6, 'Equality, Value, and Merit', p. 87.

5. This question does not imply that they will tolerate any and every patterned distribution. In discussing Hayek's views, Irving Kristol has recently speculated that people will not long tolerate a system that yields distributions patterned in accordance with value rather than merit. (" "When Virtue Loses All Her Loveliness" – Some Reflections on Capitalism and "The Free Society" ', *The Public Interest* [Fall 1970], pp. 3–15.) Kristol, following some remarks of Hayek's, equates the latter with justice. Since some case can be made for the external standard of distribution in accordance with benefit to others, we ask about a weaker (and therefore more plausible) hypothesis.

6. Varying situations continuously from that limit situation to our own would force us to consider whether entitlement considerations lexicographically precede the considerations of the usual theories of distributive justice, so that the *slightest* strand of entitlement outweighs the considerations of the usual theories of distributive justice.

7. Might not a transfer have instrumental effects on a third party, changing his feasible options? (But what if the two parties to the transfer independently had used their holdings in this fashion?) I discuss this question elsewhere, but note here that this question concedes the point for distributions of ultimate intrinsic noninstrumental goods (pure utility experiences, so to speak) that are transferrable. It also might be objected that the transfer might make a third party more envious because it worsens his position relative to someone else. I find it incomprehensible how it can be thought that this involves a claim of justice. On envy, see *Anarchy, State, and Utopia*, Chapter 8.

Here and elsewhere in this essay, a theory which incorporates elements of pure procedural justice might find what I say acceptable, *if* kept in its proper place; that is, if background institutions exist to ensure the satisfaction of certain conditions on distributive shares. But if these institutions are not themselves the sum or invisible-hand result of people's voluntary (nonaggressive) actions, the constraints they impose require justification. At no point does *our* argument assume any background institutions more extensive than those of the minimal night watchman state, limited to protecting persons against murder, assault, theft, fraud, etc. .

8. See the selection from John Henry MacKay's novel, *The Anarchists*, reprinted in Leonard Krimmerman and Lewis Perry, eds., *Patterns of Anarchy* (New York, 1966), pp. 16–33, in which an individualist anarchist presses upon a communist anarchist the question: 'Would you, in the system of society which you call "free Communism" prevent individuals from exchanging their labour among themselves by means of their own medium of exchange? And further: Would you prevent them from occupying land for the purpose of personal use?' The novel continues: '[the] question was not to be escaped; if he answered "Yes!" he admitted that society had the right of control over the individual and threw overboard the autonomy of the individual which he had always zealously defended; if on the other hand, he answered "No!" he admitted the right of private property which he had just denied so emphatically ... Then he answered "In Anarchy any number of men must have the right of forming a voluntary association, and so realizing their ideas in practice. Nor can I understand how any one could justly be driven from the land and house which he uses and occupies ... every serious man must declare himself: for Socialism, and thereby for force and against liberty, or for Anarchism, and thereby for liberty and against force." ' In contrast, we find Noam Chomsky writing, 'Any consistent anarchist must oppose private ownership of the means of production' and 'the consistent anarchist then ... will be a socialist ... of a particular sort' (Introduction to Daniel Guerin, *Anarchism: From Theory to Practice* [New York, 1970], pp. xiii and xv).

9. Is the patterned principle stable that requires merely that a distribution be Pareto-optimal? One person might give another a gift or bequest that the second could exchange with a third to their mutual benefit. Before the second makes this exchange, there is not Pareto-optimality. Is a stable pattern pre-

sented by a principle choosing that among the Pareto-optimal positions that satisfies some further condition *C*? It may seem there cannot be a counter-example, for won't any voluntary exchange made away from a situation show that the first situation wasn't Pareto-optimal? (Ignore the implausibility of this last claim for the case of bequests.) But principles are to be satisfied over time, during which new possibilities arise. A distribution that at one time satisfies the criterion of Pareto-optimality might not do so when some new possibilities arise (Wilt Chamberlain grows up and starts playing basketball); and though people's activities will tend to move then to a new Pareto-optimal position, *this* new one need not satisfy the contentful condition *C*. Continued interference will be needed to ensure the continual satisfaction of *C*. (The theoretical possibility should be investigated of a pattern's being maintained by some invisible-hand process that brings it back to an equilibrium that fits the pattern when deviations occur.)

10. *Collective Choice and Social Welfare* (San Francisco, 1970), Chapters 6 and 6*.

11. Oppression will be less noticeable if the background institutions do not prohibit certain actions that upset the patterning (various exchanges or transfers of entitlement), but rather prevent them from being done, by nullifying them.

12. One indication of the stringency of Rawls's difference principle, which I attend to in the second part of Chapter 7 of *Anarchy, State and Utopia*, is its inappropriateness as a governing principle even within a family of individuals who love one another. Should a family devote its resources to maximizing the position of its least well-off and talented child, holding back the other children or using resources for their education and development only if they will follow a policy throughout their lifetimes of maximizing the position of their least fortunate sibling? Surely not. How then can this even be considered as the appropriate policy for enforcement in the wider society? (I discuss below what I think would be Rawls's reply: that some principles apply at the macro-level which do not apply to micro-situations.)

13. I am unsure as to whether the arguments I present below show that such taxation just *is* forced labour; so that 'is on a par with' means 'is one kind of'. Or alternatively, whether the arguments emphasize the great similarities between such taxation and forced labour, to show it is plausible and illuminating to view such taxation in the light of forced labour. This latter approach would remind one of how John Wisdom conceives of the claims of metaphysicians.

14. Nothing hangs on the fact that here and elsewhere I speak loosely of *needs*; since I go on, each time, to reject the criterion of justice which includes it. If, however, something did depend upon the notion, one would want to examine it more carefully. For a sceptical view, see Kenneth Minogue, *The Liberal Mind* (New York, 1963), pp. 103–12.

15. Further details that this statement should include are contained in my

essay, 'Coercion', in *Philosophy, Science, and Method*, eds. S. Morgenbesser, P. Suppes, and M. White (New York, 1969).

16. On the themes in this and the next paragraph, see the writings of Armen Alchian.

17. See *Anarchy, State, and Utopia*, Chapter 3.

18. Compare Section II of Robert Paul Wolff's 'A Refutation of Rawls' Theorem on Justice', *Journal of Philosophy* 63 (March 1966): 179–90. Wolff's criticism does not apply to Rawls's conception under which the baseline is fixed by the difference principle.

19. I have not seen a precise estimate. David Friedman discusses this issue (*The Machinery of Freedom* [Harper and Row, 1973], pp. xiv, xv) and suggests one twentieth (of national income) as an upper limit for the first two factors mentioned. However, he does not attempt to estimate the percentage of current wealth that is based upon such income in the past.

20. Fourier held that since the process of civilization had deprived the members of society of certain liberties (to gather, pasture, engage in the chase), a socially guaranteed minimum provision for persons was justified as compensation for the loss (Alexander Gray, *The Socialist Tradition* [New York, 1968], p. 188). But this puts the point too strongly. This compensation would be due those persons, if any, for whom the process of civilization was a *net loss*, for whom the benefits of civilization did not counterbalance being deprived of these particular liberties.

21. For example, Rashdall's case of someone who comes upon the only water in the desert several miles ahead of others who also will come to it, and appropriates it all. Hastings Rashdall, 'The Philosophical Theory of Property', in *Property, its Duties and Rights* (London, 1915).

22. The situation would be different if his water hole didn't dry up, due to special precautions he took to prevent this. Compare our discussion of the case in the text with Hayek's, *The Constitution of Liberty*, p. 136; and also with Ronald Hamowy's 'Hayek's Concept of Freedom; A Critique', *New Individualist Review* (April 1961): 28–31.

23. I discuss overriding and its moral traces in 'Moral Complications and Moral Structures', *Natural Law Forum* 13 (1968): 1–50.

Biographical Note

Robert Nozick has been Professor of Philosophy at Harvard University since 1969. Previously he taught at Rockefeller University and at Princeton. He was a fellow of the Center for Advanced Study in the Behavioral Sciences in 1971 and a Fullbright Scholar in Oxford in 1963. He has published a number of philosophical articles and some short stories. His book *Anarchy, State and Utopia* (a portion of which is reprinted in this book) won the National Book Award for 1975.

Further Reading

John Locke, *Second Treatise on Government*. F. A. Hayek, *The Constitution of Liberty* (London: Routledge and Kegan Paul, 1960) and *Law, Legislation and Liberty* (London: Routledge and Kegan Paul, 1973), Vol. II.

John Rawls, *A Theory of Justice* (Cambridge, Mass.: Harvard University Press, 1971; Oxford: Oxford University Press, 1972), of which an excerpt is reprinted in the present volume.

Richard Wollheim

Art as a Form of Life

It is a mark of good philosophy, as of any inquiry, that its questions are newly devised and so capture one's attention. That is not to say, of course, that they are merely ingeniously novel, that they bear no relation to what has gone before. At least in a subject where there is no ongoing production of further facts, as in some sciences, questions which bear no relation to what has gone before are unlikely to be even of interest. The right questions are not unconnected with the past, but rather are those which make a good and inventive use of it.

Aesthetics, in the view of some philosophers, has not always been distinguished by its questions. Many of these unapproving philosophers agree that there has been rather too much direct and single-minded attention to the grand conundrum, 'What is Art?' It is true, no doubt, that that question may be taken to sum up, or to serve as a kind of title for, the inquiry which is aesthetics. More interestingly, it may be that a question rather like it, as extremely general, could be well-devised in the sense indicated above. But it is more likely that any question which does make an acute use of preceding reflections will be particular rather than general in character.

It is one of the virtues of the following excerpt from Richard Wollheim's distinguished book, *Art and Its Objects* (as indeed it is a virtue of the book as a whole), that it asks particular questions which do engage one's attention. In this case, as often, it is the recent past which is drawn upon, and not only the recent past of philosophy itself.

Suppose that there is something seen in men which can be called the entrepreneurial impulse, or, something related but different, an instinct for business. It is clear enough that the very idea of the impulse or the instinct depends for its sense on certain practices and institutions: trade, markets, capital, and the like. There could not be anything rightly called the entrepreneurial impulse if we lacked the relevant practices and institutions. The sexual impulse is different. The idea of it does not have any similar dependence on related institutions and practices. There is also the aesthetic impulse or intention, by means of which we may try to explain the unitary character of all art. We come to the question, then, whether this impulse or intention, insofar as relevant institutions and practices are concerned, is like the entrepreneurial or the sexual impulse. Things are interestingly less clear here.

This first question is one which has to do with something presumed to be common to artists generally, and common to the makings or creations of different works of art by the same artist. Consider now a particular work of art, perhaps a painting. It is ordinarily supposed that it is the product of some *particular* intention or impulse of the artist. But what, on closer reflection, *is* this supposition? Suppose that someone says that *La Poudreuse* is the product of a particular impulse on the part of Seurat, or that *Westminster* is the product of a particular impulse on the part of Coldstream. Can 'particular impulse' be given more meaning than 'the impulse which led to *La Poudreuse*' or 'the impulse which led to *Westminster*'? Can the words have more descriptive content, what some might call really useful content? To express our second large question more generally, can we suppose that for each work of art there is an impulse which can be identified without, so to speak, just pointing at the work? If this is not so, is there nothing we can do in order to get someone to see what impulse is expressed by a painting? If it is so, if there *is* a kind of paraphrase, is the work of art of a lesser or indeed of no value, and why?

It may certainly be maintained that certain answers to our principal questions are correct: talk of the general and the particular aesthetic impulses is in a way or ways dependent on 'external' practices, institutions, processes and stuffs. There are implications here about the error of a traditional theory owed to Benedetto Croce and R. G. Collingwood. That theory finds apparently plausible reasons to locate works of art in the mind, and makes paintings, statues and the like into merely the public 'externalizations' of these works. It is in connection with this dependence on the external that Freud's comparison and distinction between the artistic and the neurotic personalities surely offers an illuminating insight into the nature of art.

Our two questions and their answers make a third question more pressing. Artistic impulses, we are supposing, are dependent on, among other things, certain stuffs: paint, constructed objects, certain sequences of sound and of words, and so on. Why *these*? Why is it that these things and not others play the role they do with respect to the aesthetic impulse? (They may seem no more fitted to these roles than the bits and pieces pressed into service by a mere 'handiman', as contrasted with the craftsman who requires and waits for what he takes to be the only right materials for the job to hand.) Again, in a phrase, why are these things and not others the vehicles of art?

The three main questions mentioned so far, particularly the first two, are related to the answer given to a fourth and somewhat more general one. It is an answer which stands behind all of the excerpted sections from *Art and Its Objects* (45–53, 57–9). The somewhat more general question, briefly put, is this: What are the significant similarities and differences between two fundamental human facts, art and language? The answer is that art and language may each be said to enter into, or indeed to *be*, a form of life. The conception of a form of life, which is owed to Ludwig Wittgenstein, is evocative and suggestive rather than precisely articulated.

What may be said here is that the phrase 'form of life' calls attention to the dependence of language on a complex of practices without which it could not operate, which practices in turn, however, cannot be identified without reference to linguistic activity itself. A form of life, this is to say, is not a sandwich consisting of language plus supporting practices, but a complex whole whose parts, features and aspects are interdependent. And the philosophical point of viewing language, or a particular part of language, in terms of the form of life it constitutes, is precisely to emphasize the interconnectedness of the various elements involved. To isolate one part or feature on its own, as aestheticians in particular have too often done, leads to distortion, exaggeration or indeed radical misunderstanding.

The reader will find that the view of art as related in the given general way to language is a fertile one. It gives rise to more questions than those already mentioned. It also gives to all these questions certain nuances and implications, many of which must be passed over in this introductory expression.

What is it to come to an *understanding* of a work of art? There will presumably be such a thing if art does stand in the suggested analogy with language. It is of relevance to this line of inquiry that a good deal of art is *iconic*. That is, it consists of that which actually resembles or matches something else. A portrait is iconic; a description of the sitter in words is not. The remark may bring to mind something else: if it is relevant to the matter of artistic understanding that much of art is iconic, it is also relevant that much is not. Much art *is* in fact language in the ordinary literal sense, since language is the medium in which it exists.

That of which art consists, however, is not exhaustively described in terms of iconic or non-iconic expression. If the analogy of art and language is enlivening and fertile, it must nevertheless not be allowed to constrain us. The section below which begins with a letter from Mozart to his father has to do with what might be called the independent and ongoing life of art itself. Art may be said to have an existence of its own, in a way that language does not. One can move from these metaphors into literalness by making use of certain conceptions of Freud. If one does so, one takes the independence of art to be something which brings it into relation with dreams and into close relation with the making of jokes.

What we have, then, in what follows, are good questions, and, partly as a result, answers which also engage one's attention. They are not humdrum answers. That they do engage one's attention is also partly to be explained by the fact that they are speculative. Perhaps it can be said that they result from a good policy for proceeding toward final answers, which is not to aim prematurely at them.

T.H.

Richard Wollheim

Art as a Form of Life

From *Art and Its Objects: An Introduction to Aesthetics* (New York: Harper & Row, 1968) copyright © 1968, 1971 by Richard Wollheim. Reprinted by permission. Text arranged and modified for this volume by the author.

In the mature expression of Wittgenstein's philosophy, the phrase 'form of life' (*Lebensform*) makes a frequent appearance. Art is, in Wittgenstein's sense, a form of life.

The phrase appears as descriptive or invocatory of the total context within which alone language can exist: the complex of habits, experiences, skills, with which language interlocks in that it could not be operated without them and, equally, they cannot be identified without reference to it. In particular Wittgenstein set himself against two false views of language. According to the first view, language consists essentially in names: names are connected unambiguously with objects, which they denote: and it is in virtue of this denoting relation that the words that we utter, whether to ourselves or out loud, are about things, that our speech and thought are 'of' the world. According to the second view, language in itself is a set of inert marks: in order to acquire a reference to things, what is needed are certain characteristic experiences on the part of the potential language-users, notably the experiences of meaning and (to a lesser degree) of understanding: it is in virtue of these experiences that what we utter, aloud or to ourselves, is about the world. There are obviously considerable differences between these two views. In a way they are diametrically opposite, in that one regards language as totally adherent for its distinctive character on certain experiences, the other regards it as altogether complete prior to them. Nevertheless, the two views also have something in common. For both presuppose that these experiences exist, and can be identified, quite separately from language;

that is, both from language as a whole, and also from any piece of language that directly refers to them. (This last distinction is useful, but it would be wrong to press it too hard.) The characterization of language (alternatively, of this or that sublanguage) as 'a form of life' is intended to dispute the separation on either level.

The characterization of art too as a form of life has certain parallel implications.

The first implication would be that we should not think that there is something which we call the artistic impulse or intention, and which can be identified quite independently of and prior to the institutions of art.

An attempt is sometimes made to explain artistic creativity (and, therefore, ultimately art itself) in terms of an artistic instinct, conceived, presumably, on the analogy of the sexual instinct or hunger. But if we pursue the analogy, it fails us. For there is no way in which we can ascribe manifestations to this artistic instinct until there are already established in society certain practices recognized as artistic: the sexual instinct, on the other hand, manifests itself in certain activities, whether or not society recognizes them as sexual – indeed, in many cases, society actively denies their true character. To put the matter the other way round: If the sexual instincts are indulged, then certain sexual activities follow; we cannot, however, regard the arts as though we were observing in them the consequences that follow when the artistic instinct is indulged. Either way round the point is the same: in the case of sexuality, the connexion between the instinct and its satisfaction in the world is immediate, in the case of art it is mediated by a practice or institution. (If it is not always true that the sexual instinct manifests itself directly, at least the mediation is through privately determined thoughts or phantasies, not through a public institution: the parallel in the sexual sphere to talking of an artistic instinct would be to postulate a 'matrimonial' instinct.)

Nor does the more fashionable kind of analogy between the artistic instinct and disordered mental functioning, e.g. an obsession, fare any better. For, once again, there is an immediate connexion between the obsession and the compulsive behaviour in which it is discharged, to which we find no parallel in art. There may, of course, be an obsessional element in much artistic activity, but the choice by the artist of certain activities, which in point of fact happen to be artistic activities, need not be obsessional. To put it in a way that may seem paradoxical, the kind of activity in which the artist engages need not be for him, as the compulsive behaviour is of necessity for the obsessional, 'meaningful': for on one level at any rate, the obsessional wants to do what he does, and in consequence the analysis of his obsession consists in tracing this wish to another and earlier wish, of which it is a symptom. It was just to distinguish art from this kind of case that Freud classed it as sublimation, where 'sublimation' means the discharge of energy in socially acceptable channels.

Of course, this is not to deny that art is connected with instinctual movements, or that it could exist away from their vicissitudes. There are, indeed, certain psychic forces, such as the reparative drive or the desire to establish whole objects, without which the general forms that art takes, as well as its value, would be barely comprehensible. In much the same way, religious belief would be barely comprehensible without an understanding of early attitudes to parents: but it would miss the distinctive character of such beliefs to analyse them without remainder, in the case of each individual, into the personal motivation that leads him to embrace them.

The error against which this section has been directed is that of thinking that there is an artistic impulse that can be identified independently of the institutions of art. It does not follow that there is no such thing as an artistic impulse. On the contrary, there is, where this means the impulse to produce something as a work of art: an impulse which, as we have seen, constitutes, on the artist's side, the match to the aesthetic attitude, where this means the attitude of seeing something as a work of art. Indeed, reference to this impulse is necessary in order to escape from an error implicit in a certain approach to art, which, in addition to its natural appeal, has been reinforced by certain anti-generalizing tendencies in recent philosophy: that of seeing art as an unordered set of disjoined activities or products. For what gives art its unity is that the objects that centrally belong to it have been produced under the concept of art.

After considering the first implication of the idea of art as a form of life, I shall for this section digress, and consider briefly what I call the *bricoleur* problem.

The term itself I owe to the striking comparison made by Levi-Strauss of human culture to a *bricoleur* or handiman, who improvises only partly useful objects out of old junk, and I use it to focus our attention on the fact that the media of art are seemingly arbitrarily identified stuffs or processes.

The *bricoleur* problem here acquires a new urgency. For, if it is true that artistic creativity can occur only in so far as certain processes or stuffs are already accredited as the vehicles of art, then it becomes important to know how and why these accreditations are made. More specifically, are these accreditations in fact arbitrary – arbitrary in, for instance, the sense in which it is arbitrary that, out of the stock of articulated sounds, some and not others have been appropriated by the various natural languages as their phonetic representations? Furthermore, if they are arbitrary, does this mean that the artist is dominated by whoever is responsible for the accreditations – let us for the moment identify him with the spectator – and that the picture we have of the artist as a free agent is erroneous?

I shall begin with the second question: I shall concede that there is a way in which the spectator is supreme over the artist: and I shall then try to take away the air of paradox that attaches to this truth. In the first place, we are wrong to contrast the artist and the spectator as though we were dealing here with different classes of people. For in reality what we have are two different roles, which can be filled by the same person. Indeed, it seems a necessary fact that, though not all spectators are also artists, all artists are spectators. This truth has many applications, not the least of which relates to the present problem of the social determination of art forms or art vehicles. Secondly, it is unnecessarily dramatic to speak here of 'domination': even if we do think that the accreditation of art forms is arbitrary. For we might go back for a moment to the example by reference to which I introduced the notion of arbitrariness: I did so by reference to language. Now, do we think that the native speaker of a language is 'dominated' in what he says by his predecessors and his contemporaries, in whose mouths his language has evolved to become what it now is?

We may now take up the first question and ask, Is it in fact arbitrary that certain processes and stuffs, and not others, have been accredited as the vehicles of art? It is obvious that we can make any single artistic process, e.g. placing pigment on canvas, *seem* arbitrary by stripping away from it, in our minds, anything that gives it any air of familiarity or naturalness. But all that this shows is that, when we raise questions about the arbitrariness or otherwise of a certain process, we need to specify the context in relation to which they are asked. If we indicate – as we did just now in asking about painting – a quite 'open', or zero, context, the accreditation will clearly seem arbitrary. But it does not follow from this that it will seem arbitrary for all contexts or even for a large range of contexts.

Perhaps we can see this more clearly by going back, once again, to the phonetic problem. If we take a natural language in the abstract, it is obviously arbitrary that certain articulated sounds, not others, were chosen to be its phonemes: where this means little more than that there are others that could have been chosen. If we fill in the historical background, including the development of language, the arbitrariness diminishes. If we complete the context and include such facts as that native speakers of one language will barely be able to form some of the phonemes of another, any suggestion of arbitrariness that a particular man living in a particular society might think attaches to the sounds that he employs quite vanishes. In such a situation a man can scarcely think of his language other than as, in Hamann's phrase, 'his wedded wife'.

In the case of art a natural context in which to determine the arbitrariness or otherwise of the vehicles of art is provided by certain very general principles which have historically been advanced concerning the essential characteristics of a work of art. Examples would be: that the object must be enduring, or at least that it must survive (not be consumed in) appreciation; that it must be apprehended by the 'theoretical' senses of sight and hearing; that it must exhibit internal differentiation, or be capable of being ordered; that it must not be inherently valuable, etc. Each of these principles can, of course, be questioned, and certainly as they stand none seems irreproachable. But that is not the point here: for I have introduced these principles solely to show the kind of context in which alone we can ask whether it is arbitrary that a certain stuff or process has become an accredited vehicle of art.

A second implication of the point that art is a form of life would be that we do wrong to postulate, of each work of art, a particular aesthetic intention or impulse which both accounts for that work and can be identified independently of it. For though there could be such a thing, there need not be.

In the *Brown Book* Wittgenstein notes an interesting ambiguity in the usage of words such as 'particular' and 'peculiar', which he thinks it is characteristic of philosophy to misunderstand. If we take the word 'particular' the ambiguity might be brought out by considering the phrase 'the particular way in which A enters a room'. For this phrase might be used in such a way that we could then ask the question, 'Which way?' and expect some such answer as 'Oh, he sticks his head into the room first'. Alternatively, it might be used in such a way as to eliminate the question or if, nevertheless, the question is raised, as to make appropriate the answer 'The way he does'. In the first usage – the 'transitive' use – the phrase stands in for a description by which it is altogether replaceable. In the second usage – the 'intransitive' use – there need be no description in the background, and the phrase is then employed exclusively to draw attention to or emphasise some feature of whatever it is.

Wittgenstein's distinction might be invoked in aesthetics to make clear something about the way philosophers of art have often thought about the 'aesthetic attitude'. If they have thought about it as 'a particular attitude', the attitude has been thought to be particular only in the intransitive sense. There is no commitment to a generally true description of what the attitude is. However, another and more immediately relevant invocation of the distinction would be so as to make a point about expression: a point, that is, about the expressiveness not of art in general but of individual works of art. When we say that a work of art expresses a particular state of mind, or even we say of it that it expresses a particular state of mind with great intensity or poignancy, the word 'particular' is very often used in its intransitive sense.

But in invoking Wittgenstein's distinction, we must also pay attention to the misunderstanding that he points to as often surrounding it. If a work of art is said or thought to express a particular state of mind in the intransitive sense of that phrase, there is nevertheless some state of mind that it does express: and this conclusion holds, even if it is only in this sense of the phrase that we can talk of the work of art as expressive. Just because we do not, or even if we cannot, describe the state of mind that the work of art expresses, it does not follow that all we have is weak or generalized expression, even less that we do not have expression at all. Though this is just how Edouard Hanslick would appear to have argued when he concluded from the fact that music doesn't express definite feelings like piety, love, joy, sadness, that it isn't an art of expression. A corrective to this misunderstanding might be to consider, momentarily, the work of art itself as a description of the state of mind expressed, and then to recognize in a view like that of Hanslick's the unwarranted demand that the state of mind should be further, or additionally, describable.

The point that needs to be emphasized is that the difference between the two usages of 'This expresses a particular state' does not necessarily correspond to any difference in the expressiveness of the work, in the sense either of what is expressed or of how it is expressed. The difference lies simply in the way in which we refer to the inner state: whether we describe it, or whether we simply draw attention to or gesture towards it.

When we say L'Embarquement pour l'Île de Cythère or the second section of En Blanc et Noir expresses a particular feeling, and we mean this intransitively, we are misunderstood if we are then asked 'What feeling?' Nevertheless, if someone tells us that to him the painting or the piece of music means nothing, there are many resources we have at our disposal for trying to get him to see what is expressed. In the case of the music, we could play it in a certain way, we could compare it with other music, we could appeal to the desolate circumstances of its composition, we could ask him to think why he should be blind to this specific piece: in the case of the painting, we could read to him A Prince of Court Painters, pausing, say, on the sentence 'The evening will be a wet one', we could show him other paintings by Watteau, we could point to the fragility of the resolutions in the picture. It almost looks as though in such cases we can compensate for how little we are able to say by how much we are able to do. Art rests on the fact that deep feelings pattern themselves in a coherent way all over our life and behaviour.

The appeal of the view that a work of art expresses nothing unless what it expresses can be put into (other) words, can be effectively reduced by setting beside it another view, no less well entrenched in the theory of art, to the effect that a work of art has no value if what it expresses, or more generally says, can be put into (other) words.

Now, if this view had been advanced solely with reference to the nonverbal arts, it would have been of dubious significance. Or it might have been countered that the reason why a work of art not in words should not be expressible in words is just that it was not originally in words, i.e. the view reflects on the media of art, not on art itself. However, it is a significant fact that the view has been canvassed most heavily, precisely in that area of art where its cutting-edge is sharpest: in literature. For if the literature is in a language rich enough to exhibit synonymy, the view would seem to assert something about art.

Within the so-called 'New Criticism' it has been a characteristic tenet that there is a 'heresy of paraphrase'. It is, of course, conceded that we can try to formulate what a poem says. But what we produce can never be more than approximate; moreover, it does not lead us to the poem itself. For 'the paraphrase is not the real core of meaning which constitutes the essence of the poem' (Cleanth Brooks).

This view would appear to have a number of different sources. One, which is of little aesthetic interest, is that sometimes in poetry, language of such simplicity or directness is used (e.g. the Lucy poems, *Romances sans Paroles*) that it is hard to see where we would start if we tried to say the same thing in other words. But not all poetry employs such language: nor, moreover, is the employment of such language peculiar to poetry. In consequence, the heresy of paraphrase, in so far as it bases itself on this consideration, is an instance of faulty generalization. Another source is that even when the poetry is in a kind of language that admits of paraphrase – metaphor would be the supreme example here – any elucidation of what the poem says would have to contain, in addition to a paraphrase of the metaphors, an account of why these particular metaphors were used.

A third source is that often in poetry there is such a high degree of concentration or superimposition of content that it is not reasonable to expect that we could separate out the various thoughts and feelings ('meanings', as they are sometimes called by critics) that are afforded expression in the work.

It is impossible in this essay to pursue these last two points, though they relate to very general and important features of art which cannot be ignored in a full understanding of the subject. One is the importance of the mode of presentation in art: a phrase which naturally changes its application somewhat as we move from medium to medium but includes very different things like brushwork, choice of imagery, interrelation of plot and sub-plots, etc. The other is the condensation characteristic of art.

In the light of the preceding discussion, we might turn to the so-called Croce–Collingwood theory of art and the artistic process. For we are now in a position to see this theory, which lays itself open to a number of detailed criticisms, as fundamentally an instance of a very general error: and seen thus the theory acquires a new interest.

For the equation, central to that theory, first of the work of art with an internally elaborated image or 'intuition', and then of the artistic gift with the capacity to elaborate and refine images in this way, is just another attempt, though perhaps a peculiarly plausible one, to conceive of art in a way that makes no allusion to a form of life. For, on this theory, not only can the artist create a particular work of art without in point of fact ever externalizing it, but his capacity in general to create works of art, or his attainment as an artist (as we might put it), may flourish quite independently of there being in existence any means of externalization. The artist is an artist solely in virtue of his inner life: where 'inner life', it will be appreciated, is understood narrowly so as not to include any thoughts or feelings that contain an explicit reference to art.

The analogy with language, which the phrase 'form of life' suggests, should help us to see what is wrong here. For parallel to the conception of the artist as the man whose head is crammed with intuitions though he may know of no medium in which to externalize them would be the conception of the thinker as a man with his head full of ideas though he possesses no language (taken even in the broadest sense) in which to express them. The second conception is evidently absurd. And if we do not always recognize the absurdity of the first conception too, this is because we do not allow the parallel. For we might rather think that the true parallel to the Crocean artist is, in the domain of language, the man who thinks to himself. But this would be wrong: for three reasons.

In the first place, the man who thinks to himself has already acquired a medium, or language. The peculiarity is in the way he employs it: that is, always internally. Secondly, it is a distinctive characteristic of language, to which there is no analogue in art (with the possible exception of the literary arts), that it has this internal employment. We can talk to ourselves, but we cannot (with the possible exception just noted) make works of art to ourselves. Thirdly, we must appreciate that it is an essential feature of the Croce–Collingwood thesis that not only can the artist make works of art to himself, but he may be in the situation in which he can make works of art only to himself: in other words, it is possible that he could have the intuitions and there be no way in the society of externalizing them. But there is no parallel to this in the case of thought. For if we have language which we employ internally, then we always can, physical defects apart, also employ it externally: though in point of fact we may never do so. There could not be a language that it was impossible for someone who knew it to speak. Accordingly, the proper analogue to the artist, conceived according to the Croce–Collingwood theory, is not the thinker who has a medium of thought which he uses only to himself but the thinker who has no medium of thought, which, I have maintained, is an absurdity.

Freud, in several places, tried to approach the problem of the artistic personality by means of a comparison he proposed between the artist and the neurotic. For both the artist and the neurotic are people who, under the pressure of certain clamorous instincts, turn away from reality and lead a large part of their lives in the world of phantasy. But the artist differs from the neurotic in that he succeeds in finding 'a path back to reality'. Freud's thinking at this point is highly condensed. He would appear to have had a number of ideas in mind in using this phrase. But one of the ideas, perhaps the central one, is that the artist refuses to remain in that hallucinated condition to which the neurotic regresses, where the wish and the fulfilment of the wish are one. For the artist, unlike the neurotic, the phantasy is a starting point, not the culmination, of his activity. The energies which have initially driven him away from reality, he manages to harness to the process of making, out of the material of his wishes, an object that can then become a source of shared pleasure and consolation. For it is distinctive of the work of art, in contrast, that is, to the daydream, that it is free of the excessively personal or the utterly alien elements that at once disfigure and impoverish the life of phantasy. By means of his achievement the artist can open to others unconscious sources of pleasure which hitherto they had been denied: and so, as Freud sanguinely puts it, the artist wins through his phantasy what the neurotic can win only in his phantasy: honour, power, and the love of women.

It will be apparent that on this account all art involves renunciation: renunciation, that is, of the immediate gratifications of phantasy. This feature is not peculiar to art, though it may be peculiarly powerful in art: it is shared with any activity in which there is a systematic abandonment of the pleasure principle in favour of the testing of wish and thought in reality. In the case of art this testing occurs twice over: first, in the confrontation of the artist and his medium, and then again in the confrontation of the artist and his society. On both occasions it is characteristic that the artist surrenders something that he cherishes in response to the stringencies of something that he recognizes as external to, and hence independent of, himself.

Now it is precisely this feature of art, art as renunciation – a feature which accounts in some measure for the pathos of art, certainly of all great art, for the sense of loss so precariously balanced against the riches and grandeur of achievement – that the theory we have been considering totally denies. The Croce–Collingwood theory of the artist is, it might be said, a testimony to the omnipotent thinking from which, in point of fact, it is the mission of art to release us.

Hitherto in presenting art as a form of life, I have discussed it from the artist's point of view, not the spectator's: though, of course, the two discussions overlap, as do (as I have argued) the points of view themselves. Indeed, that they do is largely what warrants the phrase 'form of life'. However, within the form of life there is a distinctive function that accrues to the spectator: I now turn to it.

For guidance we must once again appeal to the analogy with language. What distinguishes the hearer of a language who knows it from one who doesn't is not that he reacts to it, whereas the other doesn't: for the other could, just as, say, a dog responds to his master's call. The difference is that the man who knows the language replaces an associative link, which might or might not be conditioned, with understanding. The man who does not know the language might associate to the words – or rather noises as they will be for him. In this way he might even come to know as much about the speaker as the man who shares a language with him: but the distinctive feature is that his coming to know about the speaker and the speaker's revealing it will be two independent events, whereas the man who knows the language can't but find out what he is told.

However, how are we to use the analogy? Are we to say bluntly that it is distinctive of the spectator versed in art that he understands the work of art? Or are we to use the analogy more tentatively and say of the spectator that he characteristically replaces mere association to the work with a response that stands to art as understanding does to language?

Around the answer to this question whole theories of art (e.g. cognitive, subjective, contemplative) have been constructed. Their internecine conflict, which constitutes a large part of aesthetics, is sufficiently barren as to suggest that something has gone wrong in their initial formation. What appears to happen in most cases is this: Something is found in our characteristic reactions to art that corresponds to *a* use of a particular word: this word is then adopted as *the* word for the spectator's attitude: but when this happens, it is the whole of the use of the word, or its use in all contexts, that is collected: and the spectator's attitude is then pronounced to be all those things which are covered by this word. A theory is established, and an insight obscured. An example is provided by Tolstoy's theory of Art. Tolstoy, recognizing that there is an element of communication in all art, or that all art is, in *some* sense of the word, communication, then said that art *was* communication, then turned his back on the original recognition by insisting that art was, or was properly, communication in some further sense of the word than that in which it had originally forced itself upon him.

What I shall do is to retain the word 'understand' to characterize the spectator's attitude, try not to import alien associations, and see what can be said about what is characteristically involved in this kind of understanding.

There are two points of a general character that it will be profitable to bear in mind throughout any such examination. I mention them here, though I shall not be able to elaborate more than a fraction of what they suggest.

The first is this: that for it to be in any way in order to talk of understanding apropos of art, there must be some kind of match or correspondence between the artist's activity and the spectator's reaction. There is reason enough to think that in the domain of art the match will never be complete. The spectator will always understand more than the artist intended, and the artist will always have intended more than any single spectator understands – to put it paradoxically. Nor, moreover, is it clear whether the match must be with what the artist actually did on the specific occasion of producing this particular work, or whether it has only to be with, say, the kind of thing that the artist does. Is the spectator's understanding to be directed upon the historical intention of the artist, or upon something more general or idealized? And if this element of uncertainty seems to put the understanding of art in jeopardy, we should appreciate that this is not a situation altogether peculiar to art. It is present in many cases where (as we say) we understand fully, or only too well, what someone really did or said.

Secondly, I suggest that, when we look round for examples on which to test any hypotheses that we might form about the spectator's attitude, it would be instructive to take cases where there is something which is a work of art, which is habitually not regarded as one, and which we then at a certain moment come to see as one. Works of architecture that we pass daily in city streets unthinkingly are likely to provide fruitful instances. And it is significant what a very different view we are likely to get of the spectator's attitude from considering these cases rather than those which we are conventionally invited to consider in aesthetics. So Kant cites the con-

templation of a rose and Edward Bullough, more elaborately, contrasts the various attitudes that might be adopted towards a fog at sea:
ranging across the various practical attitudes from annoyance through
anxiety to terror, and then setting against these the aesthetic attitude
in which the various features of the phenomenon – the veil that has
the opaqueness of milk, the weird carrying power of the air, the curious creamy smoothness of the water – are distanced and viewed in a
way that is abstracted from all practical concerns.

It is not possible to read far in aesthetics without encountering a
traditional view which ascribes to art in its expressive function a kind
of translucency. The view is sometimes put by saying that, if expression
is not natural, but works through signs – and this is indeed hard to
resist – it may still be insisted upon that the signs through which art
works are iconic. We might think that we now have an elucidation
of this rather cryptic view in the idea that it is characteristic of the
spectator's attitude to art that he replaces association by understanding. For, it might be argued, the difference between iconic and
noniconic signs, which is generally treated as though it were a difference in the relations in which the signs stand to the referent, is really
a difference in the relations in which we stand to the sign: to call a
sign iconic is just to say of it that it is part of a well-entrenched or
familiar system. The naturalness of a sign is a function of how natural
we are with it. Now, to talk of replacing association by understanding is just to talk of a greater familiarity with the signs we use.
Therefore, if we understand a sign, we can regard it as iconic, and in
this way we have an overall explanation of the iconic character of signs
in art.

It would certainly seem to be true that we distinguish the cases
where we 'read off' certain information from a diagram from the
cases where we just see it, largely on considerations of how entrenched
the medium of communications is in our life and habits. We read off
the coloured picture from the black-and-white diagram, we read off
the profile of the hill from the contour lines, just because these
methods are so tangential to the processes by which we ordinarily
acquire and distribute knowledge. However, we cannot conclude
from this that *any* sign-system that we regularly operate is for us

iconic. Familiarity may be a necessary, but it is not a sufficient, condition of being iconic, otherwise we should have to regard any language of which we are native speakers as *eo ipso* iconic.

If, therefore, the suggestion before us has some plausibility, this is only because the traditional view under discussion contains one distinction too few. For it seems part of that view that the distinction between cases where we 'read off' information and cases where the information is conveyed iconically is exhaustive. But this is absurd. For instance, we do not *read off* something when we *read* it.

However, even if we cannot account for the distinction between iconic and noniconic signs entirely in terms of a particular relation in which we stand to the signs, i.e. our familiarity in handling them, some advantage can be obtained from looking at it in this way if only because it attenuates the distinction. Intervening cases suggest themselves, and the peculiarity of an iconic sign is thus reduced.

Furthermore, even if we cannot analyse the distinction entirely in terms of this *one* attitude of ours toward signs, there may be *another* attitude of ours in terms of which the analysis can be completed: and in this way the original character, if not the detail, of the analysis may be preserved. Let us say that every (token) sign that we use has a cluster of properties. Ordinarily the degree of our attention to these properties varies greatly over their range: with spoken words, for instance, we pay great attention to the pitch, little to the speed. Now it may happen that, for some reason or other, we extend, or increase the scope of, our attention either intensively or extensively: we consider more properties, or the same properties more carefully. Now, my suggestion is that it is as, and when, signs become for us in this way 'fuller' objects that we may also come to feel that they have a greater appropriateness to their referent. (As a deep explanation we might want to correlate the seeing of a sign as iconic with a regression, or partial regression, to the 'concrete thinking' of earliest infancy.) Of course, the adoption of this attitude on our part will not automatically bring it about that we see the sign as iconic, for the properties of the sign may themselves be recalcitrant: but it can be contributory towards it. However, once we have seen the sign as iconic through an increasing sensitivity to its many properties, we then tend to disguise this by talking as though there were just one very special property of the sign, that of being iconic, of which we had now become aware. We think that the sign is tied to its referent by one special link, whereas in point of fact there are merely many associations.

(I have, it will be observed, followed the convention whereby an iconic sign is thought of as matching, or resembling, or being congruent with, its *referent*: but why referent or reference, rather than *sense*, is left unexamined – as, for reasons of space, it will be here.)

I want to complete the present discussion by suggesting that it is part of the spectator's attitude to art that he should adopt this attitude towards the work: that he should make it the object of an everincreasing or deepening attention. Here we have the mediating link between art and the iconicity of signs. Most significantly, we have here further confirmation for the view, which to my mind is independently compelling, that the properties of a work of art cannot be demarcated: for, as our attention spreads over the object, more and more of its properties may become incorporated into its aesthetic nature. It was some such thought as this that we may believe Walter Pater to have intended when he appropriated the famous phrase that all art 'aspires to the condition of music'.

Mozart – his father: Vienna, 26 September 1781.

... As Osmin's rage gradually increases, there comes (just when the aria seems to be at an end) the *allegro assai*, which is in a totally different tempo and in a different key: this is bound to be very effective. For just as a man in such a towering rage oversteps all the bounds of order, moderation and propriety and completely forgets himself, so must the music too forget itself. But since passions, whether violent or not, must never be expressed to the point of exciting disgust, and as music, even in the most terrible situations, must never offend the ear, but must please the listener, or in other words must never cease to be *music*, so I have not chosen a key remote from F (in which the aria is written) but one related to it – not the nearest, D minor, but the more remote A minor.

There is here, not far below the surface, a clue to something which we have perhaps ignored, or at any rate underestimated, in connexion with the problems raised in the last section: more generally, in connexion with expression. For what Mozart's letter brings out is the way in which the attribution of expressive value or significance to a work of art presupposes an autonomous activity, carried out over time, which consists in the building up, in the modifying, in the decomposing, of things which we may think of as unities or structures. A precondition of the expressiveness of art is – to appropriate the title of a famous work in general art history – the 'life of forms in art'. This phrase should not lead us, as perhaps it did Henri Foçillon, who coined it, to assign a kind of impetus or quasi-evolutionary efficacy to the forms themselves, distinct from human agency. On the contrary, it is always the artist who, consciously or unconsciously, shapes the forms that bear his name. (Indeed, nothing less than that would suit my point.) Nevertheless the artist does not conjure these forms out of nothing: nor do we have to maintain that he does so in order to attribute agency to him. In creating his forms the artist is operating inside a continuing activity or enterprise, and this enterprise has its own repertoire, imposes its own stringencies, offers its own opportunities, and thereby provides occasions, inconceivable outside it, for invention and audacity.

A parallel suggests itself. In recent years our knowledge of the emotional life and development of children – and hence of adults in so far as we all retain infantile residues – has increased beyond anything believed feasible forty or fifty years ago, through the exploitation of an obvious enough resource: the play of children. By observing and then interpreting how children play it has proved possible to trace back certain dominant anxieties, and the defences that are characteristically invoked against them, to the earliest months of infancy. But such observation has in turn proved possible only because of the inherent structure that games possess and that the child twists and turns to his own needs. There is, we may say, a 'life of forms in play'.

So, for instance, we say that play is inhibited when the child's interest in a doll consists solely in dressing and undressing it, or when the only game it can play with toy trains or cars consists in accidents or collisions, just because we are aware that these games admit of further possibilities, which the child is unable to utilize. Or, again, we argue that the child is anxious when it moves continuously from playing with water, to cutting out in paper, to drawing with crayon, and back again, just because these activities have already been identified as different games. If the structure of play is not explicitly referred to in psychoanalytic writing, this can only be because it seems such an obvious fact. Yet it is in virtue of it that we are enabled to assign to the child such a vast range of feelings and beliefs – frustration, envy of the mother, jealousy, guilt, and the drive to make reparation.

I am not saying that art is, or is a form of, play. There is a view to this effect, deriving from Schiller and then lost in vulgarization in the last century. Here I compare art and play, only to make a point about art analogous to that I have been asserting about play: namely, that art must first have a life of its own, before it can then become all the other things that it is.

This point, about the priority or autonomy of art's own procedures, was made by the psychoanalyst Ernst Kris, and in a way which allows us a further insight into its significance. Kris put it by saying that in the creation of a work of art the relations of the primary and the secondary processes are reversed from those revealed in the study of the dream. The terms need explication. In *The Interpretation of Dreams*, Freud was driven to conclude that two fundamentally different types of psychical process can be discriminated in the formation of dreams. One of these, which also accounts for our ordinary thinking, issues in rational trains of thought. The other process, which is the survival of our earliest mental apparatus, seizes hold of this train of thought and operates upon it in certain characteristic ways: the ways which Freud singled out for scrutiny are condensation, displacement, and the casting of thought into a visually representable form. The more primitive of the two processes Freud called the primary process: the other, the process of rationality, he called the secondary process: and as to their interrelations, Freud formed the hypothesis that a train of thought, which is the product of the secondary process, is subjected to the operations of the primary process when and only when there has been transferred on to it a wish to which expression is denied. The result of these interrelations, or the dream, is a kind of picture-puzzle, unintelligible in itself, in which the various latent thoughts constituting the wish are represented in a pictographic script, to be deciphered only after the most careful analysis.

The work of art has this in common with the dream: that it draws upon powerful unconscious sources. But it is unlike the dream in that even at its freest it exhibits a vastly greater measure of control, and Kris' suggestion is that if we want an analogue for artistic creation we should find it in the formation not of dreams but of jokes. For in *Jokes and the Unconscious* Freud had proposed a somewhat different relation as holding between the primary and the secondary processes when a joke is formed. Freud expressed this by saying that a joke comes into being when a preconscious thought is 'given over for a moment' to unconscious revision. Jokes, like dreams, have some of the characteristics of our earliest mode of thinking. (It was, Freud pointed out, no coincidence that many people, confronted for the first time with the analysis of a dream, find it funny or in the nature of a joke.) At the same time, whereas a dream is asocial, private and eludes understanding, a joke is social, public and aims at intelligibility. And the explanation of these differences – along with what the two phenomena have in common – lies in the relative influence of the two psychic processes. A dream remains *au fond* an unconscious wish that makes use of the secondary process in order to escape detection and to avoid unpleasure: a joke is a thought which takes advantage of the primary process to gain elaboration and to produce pleasure. On this level, the work of art resembles the joke, not the dream.

It is not necessary to accept the precise way in which Kris goes on to demarcate the primary and secondary processes in order to benefit from his suggestion. For what it permits us to see is the necessity, for art's expressiveness, indeed for its achievements in general, that there should be certain accredited activities with stringencies of their own, recognized as leading to works of art, upon which the secondary process operates. We could not make jokes unless there was, in general, language; more particularly, something that we had to say in that language. By contrast, dreams lack such presuppositions.

But the comparison between jokes as Freud explained them and works of art allows us to see more than this. It allows us to see yet another thing that is wrong in the Croce–Collingwood theory: and that is the extent to which the theory distorts or disguises what occurs at the moment of 'externalization'. For that is the moment at which, in Freud's words, the thought, or the project that lies behind the work of art, is 'dipped in the unconscious'. Without such an immersion, the elaboration that makes for much of the depth of the work of art would be missing.

Again, the assimilation of works of art to jokes rather than to dreams restores to its proper place in aesthetic theory the element of making or agency appropriate to the artist. For, as Freud points out, we 'make' jokes. Of course we do not – as he goes on to say – make jokes in the sense in which we make a judgement or make an objection. We cannot, for instance, decide to make a joke, nor can we make a joke to order. Similarly, as Shelley pointed out, 'a man cannot say "I will compose poetry" ': but it does not follow from this that the poet does not compose poetry. In a clear sense he does. There is, however, no sense at all in which we can say that we make our dreams.

I have been trying to elucidate the notion of art as a form of life by pursuing the analogy that the phrase itself intimates: that with language. However a point is reached at which the analogy runs out. I want in this and the subsequent section to touch on two important limitations that must be set upon it.

But, first, an objection to the analogy as such, which I mention solely in order to get it out of the way. It might be argued that art cannot be compared to language in that the two differ radically in function: for the function of language is to communicate ideas, whereas the function of art is something quite different, e.g. to arouse, express, evoke emotions, etc. Alternatively, it is the function of *one* of the two uses of language, i.e. the scientific, to communicate ideas, though it is the function of the other use, i.e. the poetic, to express emotion, and the analogy is therefore ambiguous in a significant respect, in that it does not state which of the two uses of language is intended. But the theory that language is essentially concerned with the communication of ideas is a dogmatic notion, which does not even take account of the variety of ways in which ideas are communicated. However, the theory of the two uses of language (as in the critical theory of I. A. Richards) constitutes no real improvement on it, incorporating as it does the original error: for it would never have been necessary to postulate the poetic use if the account of the scientific use had not been taken over unexamined from the theory of the single use.

However, a related point constitutes the first of the genuine limitations to the analogy. To compare art to language runs into the difficulty that some works of art, more generally some kinds of work of art, e.g. poems, plays, novels, are actually in language. In the case of the literary arts, does the analogy simply collapse into identity? Or are we to observe here a difference in level, and say that literary works of art at one and the same time are like linguistic structures and also have as their components linguistic structures?

There certainly seems no easy way of deciding whether it is fruitful to persist in the analogy over the range of the literary arts. In view of the way we have been using the analogy, it looks as though the crucial question to ask would be, Is there a special sense in which we could be said to understand a poem or a novel over and above our understanding of the words, phrases, sentences, that occur in it? But it remains unclear how this question is to be decided. For instance: If it is asserted, as it is in the New Criticism, that understanding poetry is grasping a certain structure of metaphors, is this tantamount to giving an affirmative answer to this question?

The second limitation that must be placed on the analogy between art and language is more pervasive, in that it operates across the whole range of the arts: and that is, the far higher degree of tolerance or permissibility that exists in art. In language, for instance, we can recognize degrees of grammaticality, or we distinguish between those statements to which a semantic interpretation is assigned, those where one may be imposed, and those where no such interpretation is feasible. It is evident that, though works of art can become incoherent, it is impossible to construct a set of rules or a theory by reference to which this could be exhibited.

At the risk of obviousness it must be emphasized that what we have encountered here is a defect in a certain analogy between art and something else, not a defect in art itself. It would be wrong, for instance, to think that art exhibits to a high degree something that language tolerates only to a low degree, i.e. what we might think of as 'vagueness'. To counteract this temptation we need to see the positive side to the indeterminacy possessed by art: more specifically, how this indeterminacy accommodates, or brings to a convergence, demands characteristically made of art by the spectator and demands characteristically made of art by the artist. There is a variety of material that bears upon this.

From the spectator's point it is required that he should be able to structure or interpret the work of art in more ways than one. The freedom in perception and understanding that this allows him is one of the recognized values that art possesses. But this freedom is acceptable only if it is not gained at the expense of the artist: it must, therefore, be congruent with some requirement of his.

To identify this requirement, we need to realize that, at any rate over a great deal of art, the artist is characteristically operating at the intersection of more than one intention. It would, therefore, be quite alien to his purposes if there were rules in art which allowed him to construct works which could be unambiguously correlated with a 'meaning': whether this meaning is envisaged as an inner state or a message. For it would be of no interest to him to construct such works: or, to put it another way, his distinctive problem would always consist in the fusion or condensation of works constructed in this way.

A misleading way of putting the preceding point would be to say that all (or most) art is 'ambiguous'. Misleading: because it suggests that the intentions whose point of intersection is a work of art are of the same type or order: for instance, that they are all meanings. But it needs to be appreciated that very often the confluence will occur between a meaning and, say, a purely 'formal' intention. By a formal intention I mean something like the desire to assert the materiality or physical properties of the medium: alternatively, an intention connected with the tradition, in the sense of wanting to modify it, or to realize it, or to comment upon it.

It is instructive to reflect how little any of these considerations arise in an area that is often in philosophy bracketed with art, i.e. morality. Once this is appreciated to the full it should cause little surprise that, whereas morality is rule-dependent, art isn't.

In the last section the word 'incoherent' was introduced in connexion with defective works of art, and it might be thought an error that this was not taken up, since it would have provided us with a means towards the solution of our problem. For do we not have here a concept for characterizing deviation in the domain of art, analogous to that of ungrammaticality or nonsense as applied to language?

The suggestion is attractive: incorporating, as it does, an ancient idea, at least as old as Aristotle, that the peculiar virtue of a work of art consists in its unity, or the relation of parts to whole. There are, however, certain difficulties that emerge in the course of working out this suggestion, which somewhat detract from its *prima facie* utility.

The appeal of the suggestion lies in the idea that we can straightforwardly equate the coherence demanded of works of art with some clear-cut concept of order as this has been systematically developed in some adjacent theory: for instance, with mathematical concepts of symmetry or ratio, alternatively with the concept of *Gestalt* as this occurs in experimental psychology. The trouble, however, is that any such equation yields us at best a characterization of certain versions, or historical variants, of the coherence demand: it does not give us a universal account. It allows, for instance, for the Renaissance notion of *concinnitas*, which was, significantly enough, developed with a mathematical model explicitly in mind: it will not, however, allow for the types of order that we find exemplified in many of the great Romanesque sculptural ensembles or, again, in the work of late Monet or Pollock.

There are a number of considerations that account for this inadequacy. In the first place, the coherence that we look for in a work of art is always relative to the elements that the artist is required to assemble within it. (The requirement may, of course, originate either externally or internally to the artist.) In this way all judgements of coherence are comparative: that is to say, the work of art is pronounced to be more coherent than it might otherwise have been, given its elements, alternatively more coherent than some other arrangement of those same elements.

Secondly, there are likely to be considerable differences in weighting between the different elements, so that whereas some elements are treated as highly malleable and can be adjusted at will to fit the demands of composition, other elements are comparatively intractable and their original characteristics must be safeguarded. An example of a somewhat superficial kind comes from the *Madonna della Sedia* where, it has been pointed out, Raphael, confronted by the possibility of having two adjacent circular shapes on his canvas, preferred to flatten out the knob of the chair back rather than distort the eye of the Infant Christ: in acting thus he was implicitly accepting a certain evaluation concerning the integrity of his elements. It is arguable that the schedules of hand, ear, finger, worked out for each artist, or traced from his existing autograph works, by the great Italian art-historian, Giovanni Morelli, in the interests of putting attribution or connoisseurship on a firm scientific basis, are inadequate to this task just because they fail to recognize the existence of such con-straints upon the artist.

Thirdly, the elements themselves will not always be homogeneous as to type or matter. For instance, in certain Braque still-lifes from 1912 onwards the elements to be ordered will include the profiles of the various objects that constitute the still life and also the materiality of the picture surface. It is, indeed, necessary to appreciate the very wide range of elements that are characteristically assembled in works of art, if we are to see why there always is a problem of order in art. Equally, this enables us to see why the argument, which originates with Plotinus, that beauty cannot consist in organization because, if it did, we would not be able to predicate beauty of totally simple ob-jects, is vacuous in its application to art. For within art there will be no such cases.

The foregoing considerations alone would account for the very limited utility of introducing strict or systematic notions of order or regularity in the explication of artistic order. But to them we can add another consideration, whose consequences are far-reaching indeed. And that is that in many instances, the kind of order that is sought by the artist depends from historical precedents: that is, he will assemble his elements in ways that self-consciously react against, or overtly presuppose, arrangements that have already been tried out within the tradition. We might call such forms of order 'elliptical', in that the work of art does not, in its manifest properties, present us with enough evidence to comprehend the order it exhibits. This is, of course, something to be met with more at certain historical periods than others. It is no coincidence that the art-historical term which we use to characterize a period when this phenomenon was most in evidence, 'mannerism', has a twofold meaning: it connotes at once erudition concerning the past, and a deep preoccupation with style.

Biographical Note

Richard Wollheim has been Grote Professor of the Philosophy of Mind and Logic at University College London since 1963, before which he was Lecturer and then Reader in the college. His books, other than *Art and Its Objects*, are *F. H. Bradley* (1959), *A Family Romance* (1969), which is a novel, *Freud* (1971), and *On Art and the Mind* (1973). He is a Fellow of the British Academy.

Further Reading

Ludwig Wittgenstein, *Philosophical Investigations* (Oxford: Blackwell, 1953) and *The Blue and Brown Books* (Oxford: Blackwell, 1958); R. G. Colling-wood, *The Principles of Art* (London: Oxford University Press, 1938); Edward Bullough, *Aesthetics* ed. Elizabeth Wilkinson (London: Bowes, 1957); Stanley Cavell, *Must We Mean What We Say?* (New York: Scribners, 1969); Nelson Goodman, *Languages of Art* (Indianapolis and New York: Bobbs-Merrill, 1968); Richard Wollheim, *On Art and the Mind* (London: Allen Lane, 1973); E. H. Gombrich, *Art and Illusion* (London: Phaidon, 1960) and *Meditations on a Hobby-Horse* (London: Phaidon, 1963); Adrian Stokes, *The Invitation in Art* (London: Tavistock, 1965).

Gabriele Taylor

Love

The subject of love has been very little discussed within analytic philosophy. It was one of the great themes of classical philosophy – both Plato and Aristotle took for granted that a comprehensive view of man must include an account of the nature of love – and it is, very obviously, central to the contribution of Christianity to the values of our culture. But while analytic philosophy has had a considerable interest in the emotions in general, this has usually been in connection with wider issues in the philosophy of mind and moral philosophy. Individual emotions, love among them, have seldom been singled out as worth understanding for their own sake. Gabriele Taylor's paper on love brings the subject back into contemporary philosophy and shows that there are questions to be asked about love which require a specifically philosophical approach.

Mrs Taylor's question is whether love can ever be justified, and if it can, what kinds of consideration are involved in the justification. She sets up the problem, in Section I of the paper, with the help of certain characteristic features of a class of emotions which undoubtedly do admit of justification in the sense that concerns her. The features she describes are not only necessary conditions for experiencing the relevant emotions; they also provide a structure in terms of which questions of justification are raised and answered. She then goes on to consider, in Sections II and III, whether love exhibits structural features of the same kind or whether it is an altogether different sort of emotion, to which questions of justification are simply not appropriate. Readers will want to decide for themselves how far they agree with her eventual answer (which is not a straight 'Yes' or 'No'), but to follow her argument it is essential to appreciate her strategy in Section I.

Questions of justification are questions about reasons and reasonableness. Where do reasons find a place in the experiencing of an emotion?

Answer: in connection with beliefs on which the emotion is based. Suppose we take as an example a relatively straightforward emotion such as fear. Fear involves belief at two levels: a person who fears something believes (i) it is dangerous, and he believes this *because* he believes (ii) that it has some more determinate property such as sharp claws or a malicious temperament which makes it dangerous.

To achieve a more general and precise account we may introduce some terminology: each emotion of the class we are interested in is directed to an *object*. (The object, in this sense, of fear is *what* a man fears, the object of anger is whom he is angry *with*, of anxiety what he is anxious *about*, and so on.) The emotion is directed to an object, in the first place, because the object is believed to have a certain *determinable* quality, which in the case of fear is dangerousness. Dangerousness is called a determinable quality, because anything that is dangerous is so in virtue of one or more of a number of different *determinate* qualities (sharp claws, malicious temperament, etc.). Thus anything a man fears he believes to be dangerous, but the determinate qualities in virtue of which he believes it dangerous will vary with different objects of his fear. The point can be generalized. There is a whole class of emotions which are like fear in that each involves believing that an object has some determinable quality (the ϕ quality in Mrs Taylor's notation), the same for every object of the emotion in question, and each involves believing the object has the determinable quality *because* it has some determinate quality or qualities ψ, which may vary from case to case of the emotion.

Now that term 'because' is the sign of a reason. It points to a dimension in which a man's emotion can be assessed as reasonable or unreasonable. Perhaps the thing's having a malicious temperament is not a good reason for him to think it dangerous; that is one case in which his fear may be held to be unreasonable. A different possibility is that he may be unreasonable in believing it malicious at all. In either of these cases, his fear is unjustified.

This is only the beginning of Mrs Taylor's account, but it sets the framework for what is to follow in Sections II and III. A divergence between love and the type of emotion we have been considering so far emerges as soon as we look for a determinable quality common to all objects of love (an analogue to dangerousness in the case of fear). Surely there is none. The structure of love in relation to belief is unlike that of fear, where the various qualities which induce fear are all seen as making the object dangerous. The various determinate qualities which inspire love are not in this way seen as contributing to some common feature of persons loved. We have the term 'lovable', but Mrs Taylor argues that it does not serve to pick out a determinable quality under which all objects of love are seen; it is true that x may be said to *find* y lovable, but that is too subjective a description of x to indicate a range of qualities he is responding to in y. Accordingly, we cannot expect to explain x loving y in terms of x believing that y has certain qualities in virtue of which x further believes that y is lovable. Hence, finally, we cannot assess the reasonableness or unreasonableness of x's love for y in terms of the reasonableness or unreasonableness of the grounds for believing that y is lovable.

At this point some readers may feel that the whole project of finding reason in love misconceived. What has love, an emotion, to do with reason and reasonableness? Part of the answer, as we have already seen, is that reason does enter into emotions like fear; the overworked antithesis between emotion and reason finds no purchase there. The rest of the answer can be put as a challenge: in the specific case of love, no doubt love is sometimes 'blind', irrational, but don't we need to distinguish that phenomenon, which is infatuation, from the love which has a more or less clear-eyed perception of the qualities of the person loved? And Mrs Taylor's suggestion is that to make the distinction we shall need to refer to the different relations of feeling to belief in the two cases.

She argues that, while we cannot say that x loves y because x believes y to have certain qualities which make him lovable, we can say that if x loves y, x entertains a variety of *wants* in relation to y: to be with him, to benefit and cherish him, to be benefited and cherished in return, and so on. And why does x want these things? If it is infatuation, there may be no answer, or none that is at all reasonable – and that is the sense of saying that infatuation is 'blind' and irrational. If it is not infatuation, however, we may explain why x has these wants in relation to y by reference to things that x believes about y: y is kindly, good company, or whatever. These are simple examples to illustrate the pattern of explanation: it is no part of Mrs Taylor's case that the relevant beliefs should all be readily accessible to x himself or easy to formulate. But once the place of belief has been located in the structure of love, it offers a dimension in which assessments of reasonableness and unreasonableness can be brought to bear.

It turns out to be a complex and interesting dimension of assessment. The reader who has followed Mrs Taylor's argument so far is rewarded when the results are applied to a range of cases drawn from the literature of love. The peculiarities and complexities of love, and of different types of love, receive fruitful discussion under Mrs Taylor's account. To pick just one example, she has suggestive things to say about the way in which a man's virtues and weaknesses enter into the kind of love he is capable of offering. All this, it should be emphasized, presupposes and draws upon the more abstract, logical considerations about the structure of love advanced earlier in the paper. It is, perhaps, a peculiarly philosophical achievement to have made such difficult and personal matters amenable to orderly discussion.

M.F.B.

Gabriele Taylor

Love [1]

Reprinted from *Proceedings of the Aristotelian Society* LXXVI (1975/76), pp. 147–64 © 1975/76 The Aristotelian Society with the permission of the author and by courtesy of the Editor of the Aristotelian Society.

I

There is a class of emotions the members of which share the following characteristics:

1. If a man x feels one of these emotions then it will always be possible for him to specify, however vaguely, what the emotion is 'about'. What it is about, the 'object' of the emotion, will normally be the thing, person, event or situation indicated by the grammatical object-phrase in sentence-forms of the kind 'x Es y', 'x is E with/of/about y'. This very loose characterization of 'object' is simply meant to exclude from consideration those cases where such an object-phrase is not in place, or where 'y' can be replaced by 'everything' or 'nothing in particular'; as for example if 'E' stands for 'feeling depressed', 'feeling happy', or 'experiencing nameless fears'.

2. If x feels the emotion, and if y is the object, then x will believe y to have a specific property or set of properties, Depending on which emotion he feels he will believe, for example, that y is dangerous, that y has done him an injury or a good turn. Put more formally,* this requirement reads: for any member of this class of the emotions there is a quality or set of qualities ϕ that for all x and all y, if x feels the emotion towards y then x believes y to be ϕ, i.e. $[(\exists\phi)(x)(y)(Exy \rightarrow Bx\phi y)]$.[2]

The quality ϕ cannot, of course, tell us much about the object y, or much about how y appears to x. As the same quality is supposed to belong to *any* object of fear, or *any* object of anger or gratitude, it

---

* The formula which follows and that in the next section are in each case preceded by an ordinary language paraphrase. – Edd.

can hardly give us much information, and I shall call such qualities 'determinable qualities'.

Evidently, it may be in virtue of very many different determinate qualities that a man may believe y to be dangerous or to be an injury or a good to him.

3. x will therefore also believe, and normally be able to articulate, that y has certain determinate qualities ψ, and further he will believe that it has the determinable quality ϕ because it has the determinate quality ψ: the thing is dangerous, say, because it is aggressive and has sharp claws, or again because it is malicious and powerful. So we have the further requirement, that if x feels the emotion in question towards some object y then x believes y to have some determinate quality, which normally but not necessarily he will be able to specify, i.e. $[(x)(y)(\exists \psi)(Exy \rightarrow Bx\psi y)]$.

But although the determinate quality which x believes y to have may vary widely from case to case, it is clear that some restraint must be put on x's belief if he is to feel a particular emotion. He cannot fear y, be angry with or grateful to y in virtue of *any* quality he cares to mention. The necessary constraints are, however, not far to seek, for they are given by the relevant determinable quality: if x, for example, fears y, then the determinate qualities of y he picks out must be such that they explain why x believes y to be dangerous. The relation between the two requirements is therefore that the first requirement, concerning determinable qualities, entails the second requirement concerning determinate qualities: if x believes that y is dangerous then he must believe that y is dangerous because it has certain determinate characteristics, even if he is not able to name these. The second requirement does not entail the first; x may believe that y is powerful and malicious and yet not believe that y is dangerous. But if x is to count as feeling the emotion in question towards y, then it must be possible for him to see the determinate qualities as falling under the relevant determinable one. So what we substitute for ϕ in the first formula will impose limiting conditions on what is substituted for ψ in the second.

4. The features set out under 1 to 3 are offered as necessary conditions for feeling one of the emotions belonging to the class under

discussion. They are not, of course, meant to be sufficient. It is at least one further necessary condition that x will have certain wants and consequently tendencies to behave in certain ways towards y: he may want to run away from y, to hit y, or do him a good turn. He will have these wants just because, at least in his view, y has certain qualities. If then he is to count as experiencing a specific emotion such as fear it must be possible to explain his wants as a response to his belief that the situation is dangerous, so that again the determinable quality imposes constraints: just as x cannot cite any determinate quality of y's in explanation of his fear so he cannot produce any want he likes as relevant. To be so relevant, it must be causally related to his view of the situation, or at least by him believed to be so related. This is of course not a complete characterization of wants involved in fear, for x when confronted by a dangerous situation may have other wants which, though causally related to it, have nothing to do with fear.

With these conditions in hand we have a basis on which to decide whether experiencing some emotion on this or that occasion is justified or not: x may or may not be justified in believing that y is ψ, or that given y is ψ it is also ϕ. If either or both of these beliefs are irrational then x can hardly be justified in experiencing an emotional reaction based on them. The converse of this proposition may however appear to be more doubtful, for surely it is possible for a man's beliefs to be perfectly well-founded and yet it might be better if he had not felt the emotion at all. So for instance it could be argued that however rational the beliefs involved in a man's envy, jealousy or hatred, such emotions are highly undesirable, and if so it would be odd to regard their occurrence as ever justified.[3] So there appears to be a lack of symmetry here: while it is sufficient for an emotional reaction to be unjustified if the beliefs involved are irrational, the rationality of such beliefs is not enough for the occurrence of the emotion to be justified.

But this objection ignores the complexity of the relevant beliefs. They all involve an assessment of the situation which will often rely on an appeal to norms of various kinds or to previously formed moral views, so that in judging them true or false, rational or irrational, we have to take these views into account as well. It is therefore quite possible to hold that the beliefs involved in some of the emotions are based on views which themselves are irrational, or at least unjustifiable in the sense that no good reason can be given for them. For example, if x envies y then he believes (roughly) that y possesses some good which he wants for himself, that y is an unworthy possessor of it whereas x would not be, and that consequently the good should be removed from y, or at any rate to restore the balance some harm should befall y. On some occasions x may of course be mistaken in believing that y possesses such a good at all, or indeed that he is unworthy of it. But even if these beliefs are correct it may be possible to argue that these cannot by themselves be grounds for justifying the further belief that therefore y is harm-deserving. The view that they are such grounds may well involve quite unfounded beliefs concerning one's own role in life as opposed to that of one's neighbour. Fully justifying the feeling of this or other emotions on some occasion will therefore often be a difficult and troublesome undertaking as it is likely to include a defence of one's moral values. How complex this may be can only be shown by an investigation of individual emotions when the relevant beliefs are spelt out. If it is correct to say that appeal to norms, standards and values is often involved then it is not surprising to find that whether a man does or does not have a particular emotional response on some occasion may tell us something about his moral views. Emotional reactions may then be based on defensible or indefensible beliefs of various kinds, and so may the lack of such reactions. In particular, it is possible to show that if on some occasion where a man would be justified in experiencing a certain emotion but he does not do so this may be due to an attitude of his which we should regard as morally objectionable in some way. Obvious and extreme examples would be a man who does not feel pity because he never spends enough thought on others to realize that they may find themselves in a painful situation, or one who does not feel remorse because he cannot conceive of himself as ever doing wrong.[4]

With so much said by way of preamble, I can now turn to the main business of this paper.

II

The question I want to discuss here is whether love belongs to the class of emotions characterized by the conditions set out above and can therefore be judged to be on occasion justified or otherwise. We tend to think of love as so great a good that it seems sacrilegious to raise the possibility of it being unjustified under some circumstances, but on my account love being always justified would entail that the beliefs involved in it are always well-founded, and that would be a very strange state of affairs. But of course love may turn out to be so different from other emotions that the various moves appropriate to them simply do not apply.

There is at least no trouble at all about the preliminary step, viz., that if love is to fit the scheme at all it has to have an object. One always loves something or somebody, and if there is any embarrassment here then it is that the objects of love can be of such limitless variety. One can love very many different sorts of things without being thought conceptually muddled, though one may of course be thought to be very eccentric. Many of such objects can be ignored for present purposes, and I shall concentrate solely on that love which has another person as its object. I also need the further restriction, that the other person not be the object merely of a man's 'practical love'.[5] In Kant's sense of this term anybody qualifies for this sort of love, and what one's own particular feelings are towards this neighbour is neither here nor there; it is sufficient that he is one's neighbour. It can therefore hardly qualify as an emotion at all, and this is indeed Kant's point when he distinguishes it from 'pathological love'.

We are left, then, with personal love, and even this may well be thought to be more than should be brought under one common denominator which will have to suit among others romantic love, passionate love, a mother's or a friend's love. But I hope that given a general starting-point the necessary additions and qualifications can be introduced in order to distinguish between different kinds of love.

If x loves y, can it be said that x believes y to have a determinable quality ϕ comparable to 'dangerous' in the case of fear or 'caused an injury' in that of anger? The most suitable candidate would seem to be 'lovable' (or perhaps 'attractive') so that if x loves y then x believes y to be lovable. But this will hardly do. There are after all criteria for settling, at least in the paradigm cases, whether or not a person is lovable, just as there are criteria for settling by and large what sorts of situations are dangerous. If this were not so it would be impossible to decide whether a man's belief that a situation has certain particular features can be related to his belief that it is dangerous and whether the belief is well-founded or not. It is of course true that what is a danger to one man need not be one to another, or again what seems dangerous to some may not seem so to others. Taking a lovable person to be one who is outgoing, friendly and open to affection, then similarly apparently unlovable people may not be so to the lover, or not to him appear to be so. But there is no reason to suppose that this must always be the case; there seems to be no contradiction in saying that x loves y although he does not believe y to be lovable in the accepted sense, as there is a contradiction in saying that x fears y and yet does not believe y to be dangerous in some respect. If this is so, and if a no more suitable candidate than 'lovable' (or 'attractive') can be found, then we have here no determinable quality as we do in the case of the other emotions. We therefore lack a guide as to what sorts of determinate qualities we are to look for in the object of love and so what substance to give to the love-beliefs. This is of course reflected in our occasional inability to deny that x loves y in spite of our total failure to understand why he does. Maybe x can still be said to *find* y lovable. This description, unlike the one in terms of beliefs, applies to matters of taste and does not imply that x believes y to have some recognizably attractive characteristics. But if all that can be said is that if x loves y he finds y lovable, then although this may tell us something about x and his tastes it can tell us nothing whatever about what qualities to look for in y, and in this sense love could be said to be more subjective than other emotions. No wonder then that this formulation is more vacuous than that applying to other emotions, and no wonder that it cannot be used to put constraints upon the ψ qualities which x may believe y to have.

We are left with two possibilities: either something analogous to ϕ qualities will have to be found to which beliefs that y is ψ can be related and so shown to be beliefs relevant to love; or love does not lend itself at all to treatment in terms of belief. No doubt there are cases where all that can be said of x is that he just finds y attractive or lovable. But on the other hand, it seems true and even trivial that very often at least if x loves y then he does so in virtue of certain determinate qualities which he believes y to have, even though such qualities may vary greatly for different persons, and even though the lover may find it difficult to be articulate about them. But though choice and variety may be great, not just any description of such beliefs will do if x is to love y. Some constraints upon them can perhaps be derived from the original restriction, that the love in question be of a particular person; this allows us to rule out such features as are universally possessed by any normal person. But this is hardly good enough. Additional constraints can however be found when we consider that a man experiencing an emotion will have wants as well as beliefs. The beliefs and wants are interrelated in that a man will have certain wants because he has certain beliefs, so that an explanation of why he has such-and-such a want will refer to his beliefs. Conversely, given his wants, some beliefs will account for them, others will not. If therefore we can find a set of wants which are typically involved in the case where x loves y then this will put a constraint upon the beliefs concerning particular qualities in virtue of which x can love y, and allow us to dismiss those which can in no way be seen as explanatory of the wants in question.

We view love as a give-and-take relationship, so the essential wants will have to reflect this feature. If x loves y we have on the one hand x's wants to benefit and cherish y, on the other his wants to be with y, to communicate with y, to have y take an interest in him, to be benefited and cherished by y. Such wants allow us to impose constraints on x's beliefs in that only those are now relevant which can explain his wants. This, quite properly, leaves a wide choice of ψ properties at x's disposal in virtue of which he may have these wants. It is indeed difficult to give an example of an irrelevant belief, for we can hardly say *a priori* of any quality ψ that it could not feature in a sufficiently complex causal story which could quite plausibly explain that x loves y because he believes y has just this ψ. Presumably, though, there are some descriptions of x's belief which x himself cannot subscribe to, as for example 'y is such a *deadly* bore'.

The description I have given of the wants involved in love is a rough-and-ready one and will need qualifications and refinements. One of these arises out of the possibility mentioned earlier that after all beliefs may not be central to love at all, that the wants enumerated can perhaps be sufficiently accounted for by the simple fact that x finds y attractive. Whatever form a further description may take, it need not be in terms of x's beliefs. This possibility is not, I think, a threat to an account of love in terms of beliefs as well as wants; it does on the contrary enable us to draw a worth-while distinction between what is to count as love and what as mere infatuation, a phenomenon sometimes identified with love and sometimes contrasted with it. Lack of clarity in this area is natural enough, for infatuated x and loving x may well have the same wants in the sense of wanting the same sorts of things. If so, then *what* x wants offers no clue for a distinction. But it may still be the case that such wants are differently based in that love proper requires certain beliefs and infatuation does not. This at any rate would conform to our view of infatuation as a state which we do not even attempt to link with anything that is accessible to rational, or for that matter, moral evaluation. It is otherwise with love, which has traditionally been regarded as capable of being rational and as admitting of degrees of moral excellence.[6] Such considerations are not enough to justify the proposed distinction between love and infatuation, but they are hints which can be exploited and given a theoretical backing if we accept that there are (at least) two very different kinds of want.[7] The crucial difference between these is that wants of one kind do and of the other do not involve some form of evaluation of what is wanted. If a man wants to have or do a in the former sense then he believes it is worth while to do or have it, although he may not believe it to be the most worth-while thing to do or have, given the alternatives. But he cannot regard doing or having a as being of no value whatever, for his wanting a is based on the thought that a is of some value to do or have. If on the other hand he simply desires a, i.e. has a want of the second kind, then there are a number of possibilities: he may not evaluate a at all; or he may think that no value or even that a disvalue attaches to doing or having a; and finally he may think it worth while to do or have a, but if so then not because a as such is worth doing or having, but because he thinks it worth while to satisfy his desires, either on this occasion or as a general policy.

My tentative suggestion is that while infatuated x and loving x may have the same wants in the sense of wanting the same sorts of things, their wants are different in the sense just indicated. If x loves y then at least some of his wants will be based on the thought that it is worth while e.g., to be with and cherish y, while the wants of his infatuation have no such base. Such a distinction is a highly theoretical one, and not only because in practice the two types of wants are no doubt untidily mixed up, or because what started as infatuation may turn into love, and the other way about. In many cases it would seem impossible for either x himself or anyone else to decide which of the two states applies to him: does he attach value to, say, y as a companion or merely to the satisfaction of his desire to be with y? It may be somewhat easier to settle the question if x does not value y's company at all and perhaps even deliberately sets out to satisfy his want to be with y as a step towards eliminating it. But again in practice this may not always be clearly distinguishable from the case where x, while believing it worth while to be in y's company, nevertheless rates it low in his hierarchy of values. For these reasons it is also difficult to produce a clear-cut example of infatuation as opposed to love. A possibly uncontroversial case is Count Muffat's passion for Nana, which so conflicts with his values as a man of religious convictions.[8] By contrast, Swann's complex thoughts about Odette and his 'appreciation of her based on the sure foundation of his aesthetic principles' make his feeling for her a more likely candidate for love.[9] Practical difficulties of this sort do not, however undermine the distinction; it rather helps to explain why we have such troubles in this area. Moreover, infatuation, being thought of as a blind passion, is very suitably linked with a type of desire which may lead a man to act against his better judgement, while the type of want ascribed to love accounts for the view that the lover tends to value what he loves. Such an assessment on the lover's part would hardly be possible if he did not believe that y had certain characteristics in virtue of which it would be worth while to have his wants satisfied, indeed he will think this if what he values is being with y, cherishing y etc., and not just the satisfaction of his desires. So a distinction between love and infatuation in terms of different kinds of wants leads back to the point that if x is to love y, x must believe y to have certain properties in virtue of which x has the wants specified.

The infatuated man may want to use the satisfaction of his wants as a means towards a further end, viz., to eliminate desires which are a source of discomfort to him. This at least seems a clear case of x's not loving y, and one which can be used to introduce a more general restriction: if x loves y then the satisfaction of the relevant wants taken collectively cannot by x be seen as a means towards some other end. So x cannot be said to love y if he regards benefiting and being with y solely as a means towards, say, obtaining social status and wealth.

To summarize: if x loves y then x wants to benefit and be with y etc., and he has these wants (or at least some of them) because he believes y has some determinate characteristics ψ in virtue of which he thinks it worth while to benefit and be with y. He regards satisfaction of these wants as an end and not as a means towards some other end.

Given these ingredients it is possible, as in the case of other emotions, to assess a man's love favourably or unfavourably on the basis of a number of considerations:

i. First and most obviously, the belief that y is ψ may be well- or ill-founded.

ii. Another type of belief is involved if we accept that one distinction between wants and mere idle wishes is that necessarily, if a man wants something and not just wishes for it then he believes there is a real possibility that he can obtain whatever it may be. He may then have more or less good grounds for the belief that his wants can be satisfied, or even cling to it in the face of contrary evidence.

iii. Finally there is also the possibility of a man's being mistaken in attaching the value he does to what he wants. This of course is not only more difficult to assess than the justification of the other beliefs mentioned, but also raises the question of what is here to count as the criterion. The happiness or unhappiness of the lover can be no more than an indication, for happiness may be blind and unhappiness due to different sources, so that the problem of a criterion reappears when we try to eliminate irrelevant types of unhappiness. Maybe it can be said that a man is mistaken in valuing, or in valuing so greatly, what he wants if the satisfaction of this want frustrates the satisfaction of some other more important want. But how then is one to settle the relative importance of different wants? I am not sure that anything generally useful can be said on this point, except perhaps that we should doubtlessly count as at least among the most important wants those arising out of human needs. The most basic and universal needs are presumably those which have to be met if a man is to stay alive, and among the wants that arise out of these is the want to avoid that which threatens his existence or capacity to exercise a certain amount of control over the situations in which he finds himself. Perhaps no more controversial is the human need for contact with other human beings and social inter-relationships. The want to be with y etc., may interfere with wants stemming from such basic needs and from that point of view one may think the value the lover attaches to what he wants mistaken. But the criterion is a crude one and will hardly do as it stands, for in the event of a clash between wants arising from need and from love respectively we should not always and necessarily wish to say that a man was mistaken in putting the latter first. But where a third person may be uncertain and suspend judgement it is at least possible for the lover himself to see or come to see that something has gone wrong with his evaluations.

Cases of love irrationally based in any of these ways are of course plentiful in literature. George Eliot's Dorothea, for example, is an extreme case of a person's wants to be with y and to benefit y being based on quite irrational beliefs, for Casaubon does not possess the characteristics she ascribes to him, and she would not have ascribed them to him had she applied a little more common sense to the situation.[10] Misguided beliefs of the third type are naturally a popular theme as they are almost inevitably fatal to the lover. In the ballad we have Lord Randal explaining to his mother that he has just been with his true love and then promptly dying of the poison his true love had administered to him. Venus, in Wagner's *Tannhäuser*, harms her lover not quite so drastically but poisons him by draining his energy so that he no longer has the will to lead an active life. If one can speak of a person's need for some freedom of action and a certain degree of richness in his life then she is fatal to this particular need. Proust allots a similar role to Odette in her relation to Swann. His life is emptier in many ways than it would have been had he not loved her, and he is indeed aware of this:

> he realized, too, that Odette's qualities were not such as to justify his setting so high a value on the hours he spent in her company. And often, when the cold government of reason stood unchallenged, he would readily have ceased to sacrifice so many of his intellectual and social interests to this imaginary pleasure.[11]

Not only does the attempt to satisfy some of his wants interfere with the satisfaction of perhaps more fundamental ones, but Swann can also be said to have unjustified beliefs of the second type. Odette herself is quite incapable of loving or giving anything, and Swann should have realized that even his rather low-pitched expectations were unlikely to be satisfied. The three types of ill-founded beliefs are naturally dependent on each other in that both a mistaken evaluation and the unjustified belief that one's wants can be satisfied are very likely based on misguided views about the nature of the object loved. So Swann's mistakes at least partly stem from his rather Berkeleyan conception of Odette as existing only when perceived by him.[12]

In these ways, then, love may involve ill-founded beliefs. But more than that may go wrong, for love has a dimension which to a large extent at least other emotions lack. This complicating factor may be called the 'nature' of a man's love; it consists of the form taken by the individual beliefs and various wants, and their relation to each other. What x sees as satisfying his want for y's company will of course vary in different cases, as will what he understands by 'benefiting y', which may range from the simple and mundane to such a complex one as making y aware of being valued as the person he is. Again, the wants in the two groups may vary very much in intensity, so x's want to have y take an interest in him may be much stronger than his want to benefit y, or the other way about. He may also put a higher value on the satisfaction of one set of wants than on the other, irrespective of their intensity. The sorts of beliefs he holds here as well as the focus and intensity of his wants will indicate the kind of love he feels, whether it is relatively disinterested or possessive, sentimental or passionate.

I do not intend to offer conditions under which the various elements of the nature of love come out 'right' and are properly balanced. But something can be done with the conditions already available: what is seen by the lover as satisfying his various wants will often be connected with his belief that y has certain characteristics, his evaluation of these, and his estimate of his success. If these latter beliefs are irrational then very likely something will be wrong with the former ones as well. So for example, as a consequence of ill-founded beliefs about Casaubon's character, Dorothea's notion of how to benefit him is quite mistaken and certainly does not meet with his approval. Similarly, Helmer, in Ibsen's *A Doll's House*, benefits and cherishes his wife, Nora, according to his lights, but he is concerned with her desires as a charming plaything, not at all with her needs as a person. His knowledge of Nora is defective, but his case is different from that of Dorothea in that he does not ascribe characteristics to her which she does not possess. Nora is, as he believes, gay, affectionate and eager to please. His fault is rather that he regards only these qualities as important and ignores any others she may possess. His expectations of how he himself will benefit by their relationship are therefore not as unfounded as Dorothea's corresponding beliefs, but they are totally lop-sided and tailored to fit his ideal of domestic life. Helmer's way of benefiting Nora in the way he does, seems, therefore, a means towards obtaining from her just the kinds of benefits he requires, viz., those bestowed by his 'featherbrain', as he sometimes calls her, and not those which a responsible person like Nora is capable of giving. Where x's view of what constitutes a benefit to y is so entirely coloured by considerations of his own interests, his wants concerning y will be correspondingly 'unbalanced' in that he is more concerned with taking than giving, and the demands he makes on y will tend to be unreasonable.

III

I made two claims for the emotions described in section I of this paper:

1. There are two sets of conditions, the first to be satisfied if x is to feel the relevant emotion at all, and the second to be satisfied if x is justified in feeling the emotion in question.

2. As the beliefs very often include what might roughly be described as 'moral beliefs' the justification conditions are more substantial and complex than may at first appear. For where the experiencing of an emotion on some occasion is based on an ill-founded belief of this type, or conversely where the lack of emotional response on some occasion is due to an ill-founded belief, then either the emotional experience or the lack of it may indicate some failing or short-coming in the agent.

In the case of love I have tried to set out both sets of conditions. Here, too, we have beliefs which may or may not be well-founded, and so it seems that we have reason to think of it, too, as justified or otherwise. But to speak of an emotion as being on this or that occasion unjustified implies that it would have been better not to have felt it, and we tend to think of love as such a good in itself that it may be better to have loved irrationally than not to have loved at all. Although we may agree that love may indeed be defective, 'unjustified' seems hardly an appropriate term. Such reluctance on our part may of course be no more than romantic prejudice, but some of the features of love itself go some way towards explaining the difficulty we have in moving from the irrational to the unjustified:

1. Unlike other emotions, love is not 'occasional': while it is appropriate to speak of an occasion for being angry, afraid, grateful etc., we can hardly talk in this way of love. This is partly so because to link love with particular occasions would leave open the possibility of its being very short-lived indeed, and this we are not prepared to do. More importantly, the beliefs and wants involved are too varied to be tied to one particular occasion. The emotional states in virtue of which we say that x loves y may, when each is taken in isolation, lack that complexity which is a feature of love itself. While particular experiences of fear and anger will differ from each other merely in degree of intensity, particular experiences of love may differ also in kind. Not only may x on some occasion have just this or that desire involved in love, but more than any other emotion it may be responsible for his finding himself in almost any emotional state we can think of, covering the whole range from bliss to despair, or hope to jealousy. This feature makes love far more difficult to assess than other emotions, and if there are no particular occasions for

feeling love then of course we cannot ask whether a man is justified or not in feeling love on this or that occasion.

2. But it is not only the lack of occasions which makes this question such a strange one; the nature of love further complicates the matter. For a man's anger or fear to be unjustified it is sufficient that his beliefs about the situation are irrational, but in the case of love we should also want to know what sort of love he is offering. It is after all only very likely but by no means necessary that if x's beliefs about y are ill-founded then the nature of his love is in some way defective; his want to benefit may be wholly generous and indeed result in benefiting y. So the nature of x's love may well compensate for any mistaken beliefs about y. Even if his view that such-and-such would benefit y is quite unfounded we may still not want to judge the love adversely. We may for example still admire the feeling of the mother which prompts her to part with her son in the belief that this is in his best interest, although we think her quite wrong-headed in taking this to be the best course for the child.

The complexity of the matter is therefore such that it may well prevent us from speaking of love as unjustified. But that is not all there is to it. Love is thought of as somehow enriching to the lover as well as the person loved, and there seems something sad or even sinister about the man who never loves at all. Given the various wants and beliefs involved in love it is of course not difficult to enumerate possible failings and shortcomings of the man who does not love at all: most obviously, he may be so utterly preoccupied with his own concerns that no other interest can compete, and so he may never want to benefit and cherish another, or may want to do so only with an eye to the return. If not too self-absorbed he may be too mean ever to think of giving anything, or he may be too arrogant to think that other people can possibly possess characteristics in virtue of which it would be worth his while to seek their company and take an interest in them. Or again he may be too indolent to take the trouble involved in caring for another person, or to make the effort to get to know him. So sloth may be at the root of his lack of love. Equally, it may be cowardice: the want to be with and communicate with y, and to be to y an object of interest and attention commits x to wanting some form of intimacy with y, and he may not have such wants because he lacks the courage to face the risks involved. He may wish to avoid not only being hurt through or by a person loved, but also letting himself be known by y, which he could hardly avoid if there is to be some intimacy between them. He may dislike to reveal his weaknesses or just be afraid of what there may be to reveal. Casaubon largely fails in love because he cannot afford to let Dorothea know what he is really like. He cannot afford this not only because he would run the risk of losing her respect when, after all, her role was specifically that of the admiring wife, but particularly also because such revelation might force him to look at himself and so perhaps for him destroy the fiction that he is a creative man of immaculate integrity.

Selfishness, avarice, arrogance, sloth and cowardice are at any rate among the major failings a man may possess if he lacks this or that belief or want essential to the lover. But it cannot be said without further ado that the man who loves will lack these failings, or that he will have the corresponding virtues. It seems that this can be said only of the 'good' lover whose beliefs are well-based and whose wants well-balanced. So there lurks the Aristotelian thought that only the good man can offer a love which is not defective. The bad lover, on the other hand, may have much the same defects as the non-lover. Maybe it can be said that he cannot have these to quite the same degree, for there must at least be some involvement with another person. And perhaps here we come to the crux of the matter. It may be the case that the good lover must have many virtues, but on the other hand a man may have many virtues and not love at all. Like Kant's man of moral worth he may do much for others from a sense of duty, and he may indeed be very admirable. On many occasions his treatment of his neighbour may do very well: in our various roles we do not on the whole expect more than is 'due' to us. But such roles, we think, are not exhaustive. What we value about love is no doubt the spontaneous appreciation of another person, and maybe it can be said that even in its most defective form it involves a trust in another which is spontaneous in that it is not backed by any rights or conventions. From that point of view x's wants to be with y etc., are as important as his wants to benefit etc. y; not because such wants indicate any kind of virtue in him, but because they express appreciation of the other person, for whatever reason. Maybe this is why we do not like to commit ourselves to the unqualified judgement that it would have been better if *x* had not loved *y* at all.

My question was whether love in its structure is sufficiently like other emotions to be thought of as justified or unjustified. My answer is that there is no structure common to all the emotions, but love is not so unlike paradigmatic emotions that the question of justification does not arise: in the form of questions of deficiency and of propriety it does. This may not be a conclusion to please the tidy-minded, but untidiness is unavoidable where it reflects the complexity of the phenomena involved.

Notes

1. I should like to thank the many people who have made helpful suggestions, in particular Kathleen Lennon and Anthony Savile.

2. I deliberately abstract from the notorious difficulties of quantifying into intentional contents. They are not relevant here. My two formulae are not meant to display logical form; they are merely offered as visual aids.

3. It is of course a different matter whether or not it would be prudent to *express* the emotion.

4. For a more detailed account of this see my paper 'Justifying the Emotions' in *Mind* LXXXIV (1975), pp. 390–402.

5. Kant: *Grundlegung zur Metaphysik der Sitten*, Ch. 1 [English translation by H. J. Paton: *The Moral Law* (London: Hutchinson, 3rd ed. 1956)].

6. The moral status of love is of course much discussed by philosophers, poets and novelists. Its intellectual standing is less often explicitly mentioned, but e.g., Aquinas speaks of some of its manifestations as 'intellectual and rational' (*Summa Theologica*, *Prima Secundae*, Question 26, Article 1) and Dante's love for Beatrice is ruled by the 'faithful council of reason' (*La Vita Nuova* II).

7. The distinction is made and defended in Gary Watson's paper 'Free Agency', *Journal of Philosophy*, 72 (1975), pp. 205–20.

8. Zola: *Nana*, esp. Chapter 13.

9. Proust: *Remembrance of things past. Swann's Way*, II p. 8 in the Chatto and Windus uniform edition. But Vlastos takes a different view of the case in his paper 'The Individual as Object of Love in Plato': Gregory Vlastos, *Platonic Studies* (Princeton: Princeton University Press, 1973) pp. 7 and 30.

10. George Eliot: *Middlemarch*, esp. Books I and III.

11. *Swann's Way*, Pt. II, p. 26.

12. It may be thought that these conditions ignore those cases where it is a

feature of the love in question that the object is unattainable, as e.g., described in some of the poetry of *amour courtois*. On my account the 'courtly lover' is not irrational as he holds no unfounded beliefs about the satisfiability of certain wants. He may be worshipping an ideal and so not count as exemplifying personal love. Where the love is personal it is thought to be ennobling and so a means of narrowing the gulf between lover and beloved. Here the lover has wants which may be well- or ill-founded, though it may be that my descriptions of the wants will need some qualification to meet his case.

Biographical Note

Gabriele Taylor has taught in the Australian National University at Canberra and since 1962 has been Fellow of St Anne's College, Oxford. She has written articles on subjects in the philosophy of mind and moral philosophy. She is at present working on a book on the emotions.

Further Reading

On emotion in general: Anthony Kenny, *Action, Emotion and Will* (London: Routledge & Kegan Paul, 1963), chaps. 1–5; Bernard Williams, 'Morality and the Emotions', Inaugural Lecture, Bedford College, London 1965; repr. in Bernard Williams, *Problems of the Self* (Cambridge: Cambridge University Press, 1973), pp. 207–29; Gabriele Taylor, 'Justifying the Emotions', *Mind* LXXXIV (1975), pp. 390–402.

On love: Gregory Vlastos, 'The Individual as Object of Love in Plato', in Gregory Vlastos: *Platonic Studies* (Princeton: Princeton University Press, 1973), pp. 3–34; David L. Norton and Mary F. Kille, *Philosophies of Love* (San Francisco, London, Toronto: Chandler Publishing Co., 1971).

Derek Parfit

Personal Identity

The phrase 'personal identity' has both a popular and a philosophical use. The popular use is the one employed when people speak of going through a crisis of personal identity. A man in such a crisis is said not to know who he is, not in the sense that he could not give his name, relate facts of his history and the like, but in the sense that he is uncertain of the fundamental values and aims of his life. His conception of his own self is wavering. By contrast, when philosophers talk of personal identity they have in mind the rather more precise notion involved in questions of the form 'Is X the same person as Y?' – for example, 'Is the man we saw her with yesterday the man who met us at Land's End last year?'

Since Locke there has been a keen debate about the conditions under which this question may be answered in the affirmative. Is it enough that X have the same human body as Y or must X have, in addition, memories of Y's doings? Is it necessary to have the same body or could a person change bodies and preserve his identity by virtue of having memories of actions done in the previous body? Is there such a thing as the self over and above sameness of body and/or sameness of personality, memory, etc.? These questions are asking whether continuity of body or continuity of memory, or perhaps some combination of the two, constitute the grounds for deciding that X is the same person as Y. In Derek Parfit's view, however, cases can be described which such grounds do not cover: cases in which no plausible decision can be made as to whether X is the same person as Y. It is not that there is an answer, only we cannot decide what it is. Rather, our concept of personal identity is not such as to admit of any reasonable answer being found.

This can be an unsettling thought. How am I to come to terms with the idea that there may be no way of deciding whether some future person is (the same person as) me? Parfit replies, in effect, that only the popular notion of personal identity is important. It contains everything that matters to one's sense of one's self. In some measure, therefore, what Parfit proposes is an end to the philosophical debate about personal identity. But the argument he gives on behalf of the proposal is, of course, a strictly philosophical one.

He describes an imaginary but logically possible case of brain transplantation. My brain is divided and each half is put into a new body, with the result that there are now *two* people with my character and apparent memories of my earlier life. It is not plausible to say that I am identical with just one of the two, but equally it will not do to say I am identical with both at once. Nevertheless, in some sense I surely do survive. But if I do survive, yet without being clearly identical with either or both of the two people now alive who apparently remember the things I did and experienced, we must distinguish the question 'Do I survive?' from the question 'Is there some person alive who is identical with me?'. For in the case described, the first question has a definite answer – in the affirmative – but the second has not. Therefore, they are not the same question.

This separation of the question of survival from the question of identity is the key move in Parfit's discussion. He invites us to accept the novel idea that I might survive as two people without being (the same as or identical with) either or both of them. Identity, as he notes, is a one–one relation (a relation requiring only two terms), but survival need not be; it may be a one–many relation, holding between one original and several successors. Parfit is then free to argue that the concerns important to one's sense of one's self can perfectly well be secured by survival without identity; and, moreover, that whereas identity is an all-or-nothing affair, in that either X is identical with Y or X and Y are completely distinct, most of what matters in survival are relations of degree. I can survive to a greater or a less extent. The operative concepts here are q-memory and q-intention – concepts so defined as to remove the implication, which is normally part of what we understand by memory and intention, that the person who has a memory or an intention is one and the same with the person who had the remembered experience or the person who will perform the intended act. With the aid of these specially constructed counterparts of memory and intention Parfit ingeniously describes several logically conceivable forms of survival in which identity in the strict sense is lost but the beings who survive can, to varying degrees, enjoy a sense of themselves continuing through time in terms of their q-memories and q-intentions.

Parfit concludes with a moral. If what matters in the continued exist-

ence of a person are, for the most part, relations of degree, someone
who recognizes this should be less biased in favour of his own interests
than most of us are inclined to be. To the extent that the argument has
succeeded in weakening the hold of the idea that all a man's future interests, however distant, are equally *his* interests, to that extent it ought
to weaken his present attachment to those concerns as against the interests of other persons now and to come. A good question for the
reader to ask himself is whether such a diminution of self-concern seems
feasible. If it does, Parfit's argument has gone home. If it does not, the
strict notion of personal identity retains its hold.

M.F.B.

Derek Parfit

Personal Identity [1]

Reprinted by permission of the author and publisher from *The Philosophical Review* LXXX (1971), pp. 3–27.

We can, I think, describe cases in which, though we know the answer to every other question, we have no idea how to answer a question about personal identity. These cases are not covered by the criteria of personal identity that we actually use.

Do they present a problem?

It might be thought that they do not, because they could never occur. I suspect that some of them could. (Some, for instance, might become scientifically possible.) But I shall claim that even if they did they would present no problem.

My targets are two beliefs: one about the nature of personal identity, the other about its importance.

The first is that in these cases the question about identity must have an answer.

No one thinks this about, say, nations or machines. Our criteria for the identity of these do not cover certain cases. No one thinks that in these cases the questions 'Is it the same nation?' or 'Is it the same machine?' must have answers.

Some people believe that in this respect they are different. They agree that our criteria of personal identity do not cover certain cases, but they believe that the nature of their own identity through time is, somehow, such as to guarantee that in these cases questions about their identity must have answers. This belief might be expressed as follows: 'Whatever happens between now and any future time, either I shall still exist, or I shall not. Any future experience will either be *my* experience, or it will not.'

This first belief – in the special nature of personal identity – has, I think, certain effects. It makes people assume that the principle of self-interest is more rationally compelling than any moral principle. And it makes them more depressed by the thought of ageing and of death.

I cannot see how to disprove this first belief. I shall describe a problem case. But this can only make it seem implausible.

Another approach might be this. We might suggest that one cause of the belief is the projection of our emotions. When we imagine ourselves in a problem case, we do feel that the question 'Would it be me?' must have an answer. But what we take to be a bafflement about a further fact may be only the bafflement of our concern.

I shall not pursue this suggestion here. But one cause of our concern is the belief which is my second target. This is that unless the question about identity has an answer, we cannot answer certain important questions (questions about such matters as survival, memory, and responsibility).

Against this second belief my claim will be this. Certain important questions do presuppose a question about personal identity. But they can be freed of this presupposition. And when they are, the question about identity has no importance.

I

We can start by considering the much-discussed case of the man who, like an amoeba, divides.[2]

Wiggins has recently dramatized this case.[3] He first referred to the operation imagined by Shoemaker.[4] We suppose that my brain is transplanted into someone else's (brainless) body, and that the resulting person has my character and apparent memories of my life. Most of us would agree, after thought, that the resulting person is me. I shall here assume such agreement.[5]

Wiggins then imagined his own operation. My brain is divided, and each half is housed in a new body. Both resulting people have my character and apparent memories of my life.

What happens to me? There seem only three possibilities: (1) I do not survive; (2) I survive as one of the two people; (3) I survive as both.

The trouble with (1) is this. We agreed that I could survive if my brain were successfully transplanted. And people have in fact survived with half their brains destroyed. It seems to follow that I could survive if half my brain were successfully transplanted and the other half were destroyed. But if this is so, how could I *not* survive if the other half were also successfully transplanted? How could a double success be a failure?

We can move to the second description. Perhaps one success is the maximum score. Perhaps I shall be one of the resulting people.

The trouble here is that in Wiggins's case each half of my brain is exactly similar, and so, to start with, is each resulting person. So how can I survive as only one of the two people? What can make me one of them rather than the other?

It seems clear that both of these descriptions – that I do not survive, and that I survive as one of the people – are highly implausible. Those who have accepted them must have assumed that they were the only possible descriptions.

What about our third description: that I survive as both people?

It might be said, 'If "survive" implies identity, this description makes no sense – you cannot be two people. If it does not, the description is irrelevant to a problem about identity.'

I shall later deny the second of these remarks. But there are ways of denying the first. We might say, 'What we have called "the two resulting people" are not two people. They are one person. I do survive Wiggins's operation. Its effect is to give me two bodies and a divided mind.'

It would shorten my argument if this were absurd. But I do not think it is. It is worth showing why.

We can, I suggest, imagine a divided mind. We can imagine a man having two simultaneous experiences, in having each of which he is unaware of having the other.

We may not even need to imagine this. Certain actual cases, to which Wiggins referred, seem to be best described in these terms. These involve the cutting of the bridge between the hemispheres of the brain. The aim was to cure epilepsy. But the result appears to be, in the surgeon's words, the creation of 'two separate spheres of consciousness',[6] each of which controls one half of the patient's body. What is experienced in each is, presumably, experienced by the patient.

There are certain complications in these actual cases. So let us imagine a simpler case.

Suppose that the bridge between my hemispheres is brought under my voluntary control. This would enable me to disconnect my hemispheres as easily as if I were blinking. By doing this I would divide my mind. And we can suppose that when my mind is divided I can, in each half, bring about reunion.

This ability would have obvious uses. To give an example: I am near the end of a maths exam, and see two ways of tackling the last problem. I decide to divide my mind, to work, with each half, at one of two calculations, and then to reunite my mind and write a fair copy of the best result.

What shall I experience?

When I disconnect my hemispheres, my consciousness divides into two streams. But this division is not something that I experience. Each of my two streams of consciousness seems to have been straight-forwardly continuous with my one stream of consciousness up to the moment of division. The only changes in each stream are the disappearance of half my visual field and the loss of sensation in, and control over, half my body.

Consider my experiences in what we can call my 'right-handed' stream. I remember that I assigned my right hand to the longer calculation. This I now begin. In working at this calculation I can see, from the movements of my left hand, that I am also working at the other. But I am not aware of working at the other. So I might, in my right-handed stream, wonder how, in my left-handed stream, I am getting on.

My work is now over. I am about to reunite my mind. What should I, in each stream, expect? Simply that I shall suddenly seem to remember just having thought out two calculations, in thinking out each of which I was not aware of thinking out the other. This, I submit, we can imagine. And if my mind was divided, these memories are correct.

In describing this episode, I assumed that there were two series of thoughts, and that they were both mine. If my two hands visibly wrote out two calculations, and if I claimed to remember two corresponding series of thoughts, this is surely what we should want to say.

If it is, then a person's mental history need not be like a canal, with only one channel. It could be like a river, with islands, and with separate streams.

To apply this to Wiggins's operation: we mentioned the view that it gives me two bodies and a divided mind. We cannot now call this absurd. But it is, I think, unsatisfactory.

There were two features of the case of the exam that made us want to say that only one person was involved. The mind was soon reunited, and there was only one body. If a mind was permanently divided and its halves developed in different ways, the point of speaking of one person would start to disappear. Wiggins's case, where there are also two bodies, seems to be over the borderline. After I have had his operation, the two 'products' each have all the attributes of a person. They could live at opposite ends of the earth. (If they later met, they might even fail to recognize each other.) It would become intolerable to deny that they were different people.

Suppose we admit that they are different people. Could we still claim that I survived as both, using 'survive' to imply identity?

We could. For we might suggest that two people could compose a third. We might say, 'I do survive Wiggins's operation as two people. They can be different people, and yet be me, in just the way in which the Pope's three crowns are one crown.'[7]

This is a possible way of giving sense to the claim that I survive as two different people, using 'survive' to imply identity. But it keeps the language of identity only by changing the concept of a person. And there are obvious objections to this change.[8]

The alternative, for which I shall argue, is to give up the language of identity. We can suggest that I survive as two different people without implying that I am these people.

When I first mentioned this alternative, I mentioned this objection: 'If your new way of talking does not imply identity, it cannot solve our problem. For that is about identity. The problem is that all the possible answers to the question about identity are highly implausible.'

We can now answer this objection.

We can start by reminding ourselves that this is an objection only if we have one or both of the beliefs which I mentioned at the start of this paper.

The first was the belief that to any question about personal identity, in any describable case, there must be a true answer. For those with this belief, Wiggins's case is doubly perplexing. If all the possible answers are implausible, it is hard to decide which of them is true, and hard even to keep the belief that one of them must be true. If we give up this belief, as I think we should, these problems disappear. We shall then regard the case as like many others in which, for quite unpuzzling reasons, there *is* no answer to a question about identity. (Consider 'Was England the same nation after 1066?')

Wiggins's case makes the first belief implausible. It also makes it trivial. For it undermines the second belief. This was the belief that important questions turn upon the question about identity. (It is worth pointing out that those who have only this second belief do not think that there must *be* an answer to this question, but rather that we must decide upon an answer.)

Against this second belief my claim is this. Certain questions do presuppose a question about personal identity. And because these questions *are* important, Wiggins's case does present a problem. But we cannot solve this problem by answering the question about identity. We can solve this problem only by taking these important questions and prizing them apart from the question about identity. After we have done this, the question about identity (though we might for the sake of neatness decide it) has no further interest.

Because there are several questions which presuppose identity, this claim will take some time to fill out.

We can first return to the question of survival. This is a special case, for survival does not so much presuppose the retaining of identity as seem equivalent to it. It is thus the general relation which we need to prize apart from identity. We can then consider particular relations, such as those involved in memory and intention.

'Will I survive?' seems, I said, equivalent to 'Will there be some person alive who is the same person as me?'

If we treat these questions as equivalent, then the least unsatisfactory description of Wiggins's case is, I think, that I survive with two bodies and a divided mind.

Several writers have chosen to say that I am neither of the resulting people. Given our equivalence, this implies that I do not survive, and hence, presumably, that even if Wiggins's operation is not literally death, I ought, since I will not survive it, to regard it *as* death. But this seemed absurd.

It is worth repeating why. An emotion or attitude can be criticized for resting on a false belief, or for being inconsistent. A man who regarded Wiggins's operation as death must, I suggest, be open to one of these criticisms.

He might believe that his relation to each of the resulting people fails to contain some element which is contained in survival. But how can this be true? We agreed that he *would* survive if he stood in this very same relation to only *one* of the resulting people. So it cannot be the nature of this relation which makes it fail, in Wiggins's case, to be survival. It can only be its duplication.

Suppose that our man accepts this, but still regards division as death. His reaction would now seem wildly inconsistent. He would be like a man who, when told of a drug that could double his years of life, regarded the taking of this drug as death. The only difference in the case of division is that the extra years are to run concurrently. This is an interesting difference. But it cannot mean that there are *no* years to run.

I have argued this for those who think that there must, in Wiggins's case, be a true answer to the question about identity. For them, we might add, 'Perhaps the original person does lose his identity. But there may be other ways to do this than to die. One other way might be to multiply. To regard these as the same is to confuse nought with two.'

For those who think that the question of identity is up for decision, it would be clearly absurd to regard Wiggins's operation as death. These people would have to think, 'We could have chosen to say that I should be one of the resulting people. If we had, I should not have regarded it as death. But since we have chosen to say that I am neither person, I *do*.' This is hard even to understand.[9]

My first conclusion, then, is this. The relation of the original person to each of the resulting people contains all that interests us – all that matters – in any ordinary case of survival. This is why we need a sense in which one person can survive as two.[10]

One of my aims in the rest of this paper will be to suggest such a sense. But we can first make some general remarks.

II

Identity is a one–one relation. Wiggins's case serves to show that what matters in survival need not be one–one.

Wiggins's case is of course unlikely to occur. The relations which matter are, in fact, one–one. It is because they are that we can imply the holding of these relations by using the language of identity.

This use of language is convenient. But it can lead us astray. We may assume that what matters *is* identity and, hence, has the properties of identity.

In the case of the property of being one–one, this mistake is not serious. For what matters is in fact one–one. But in the case of another property, the mistake *is* serious. Identity is all-or-nothing. Most of the relations which matter in survival are, in fact, relations of degree. If we ignore this, we shall be led into quite ill-grounded attitudes and beliefs.

The claim that I have just made – that most of what matters are relations of degree – I have yet to support. Wiggins's case shows only that these relations need not be one–one. The merit of the case is not that it shows this in particular, but that it makes the first break between what matters and identity. The belief that identity *is* what matters is hard to overcome. This is shown in most discussions of the problem cases which actually occur: cases, say, of amnesia or of brain damage. Once Wiggins's case has made one breach in this belief, the rest should be easier to remove.[11]

To turn to a recent debate: most of the relations which matter can be provisionally referred to under the heading 'psychological continuity' (which includes causal continuity). My claim is thus that we use the language of personal identity in order to imply such continuity. This is close to the view that psychological continuity provides a criterion of identity.

Williams has attacked this view with the following argument. Identity is a one–one relation. So any criterion of identity must appeal to a relation which is logically one–one. Psychological continuity is not logically one–one. So it cannot provide a criterion.[12]

Some writers have replied that it is enough if the relation appealed to is always in fact one–one.[13]

I suggest a slightly different reply. Psychological continuity is a ground for speaking of identity when it is one–one.

If psychological continuity took a one–many or branching form, we should need, I have argued, to abandon the language of identity. So this possibility would not count against his view.

We can make a stronger claim. This possibility would count in its favour.

The view might be defended as follows. Judgements of personal identity have great importance. What gives them their importance is the fact that they imply psychological continuity. This is why, whenever there is such continuity, we ought, if we can, to imply it by making a judgement of identity.

If psychological continuity took a branching form, no coherent set of judgements of identity could correspond to, and thus be used to imply, the branching form of this relation. But what we ought to do, in such a case, is take the importance which would attach to a judgement of identity and attach this importance directly to each limb of the branching relation. So this case helps to show that judgements of personal identity do derive their importance from the fact that they imply psychological continuity. It helps to show that when we can, usefully, speak of identity, this relation is our ground.

This argument appeals to a principle which Williams put forward.[14] The principle is that an important judgement should be asserted and denied only on importantly different grounds.

Williams applied this principle to a case in which one man is psychologically continuous with the dead Guy Fawkes, and a case in which two men are. His argument was this. If we treat psychological continuity as a sufficient ground for speaking of identity, we shall say that the one man is Guy Fawkes. But we could not say that the two men are, although we should have the same ground. This disobeys the principle. The remedy is to deny that the one man is Guy Fawkes, to insist that sameness of the body is necessary for identity.

Williams's principle can yield a different answer. Suppose we regard psychological continuity as more important than sameness of the body.[15] And suppose that the one man really is psychologically (and causally) continuous with Guy Fawkes. If he is, it would disobey the principle to deny that he is Guy Fawkes, for we have the same important ground as in a normal case of identity. In the case of the two men, we again have the same important ground. So we ought to take the importance from the judgement of identity and attach it directly to this ground. We ought to say, as in Wiggins's case, that each limb of the branching relation is as good as survival. This obeys the principle.

To sum up these remarks: even if psychological continuity is neither logically, nor always in fact, one–one, it can provide a criterion of identity. For this can appeal to the relation of *non-branching* psychological continuity, which is logically one–one.[16]

The criterion might be sketched as follows. 'X and Y are the same person if they are psychologically continuous and there is no person who is contemporary with either and psychologically continuous with the other.' We should need to explain what we mean by 'psychologically continuous' and say how much continuity the criterion requires. We should then, I think, have described a sufficient condition for speaking of identity.[17]

We need to say something more. If we admit that psychological continuity might not be one–one, we need to say what we ought to do if it were not one–one. Otherwise our account would be open to the objections that it is incomplete and arbitrary.[18]

I have suggested that if psychological continuity took a branching form, we ought to speak in a new way, regarding what we describe as having the same significance as identity. This answers these objections.[19]

We can now return to our discussion. We have three remaining aims. One is to suggest a sense of 'survive' which does not imply identity. Another is to show that most of what matters in survival are relations of degree. A third is to show that none of these relations needs to be described in a way that presupposes identity.

We can take these aims in the reverse order.

III

The most important particular relation is that involved in memory. This is because it is so easy to believe that its description must refer to identity.[20] This belief about memory is an important cause of the view that personal identity has a special nature. But it has been well discussed by Shoemaker[21] and by Wiggins.[22] So we can be brief.

It may be a logical truth that we can only remember our own experiences. But we can frame a new concept for which this is not a logical truth. Let us call this 'q-memory'.

To sketch a definition.[23] I am q-remembering an experience if (1) I have a belief about a past experience which seems in itself like a memory belief, (2) someone did have such an experience, and (3) my belief is dependent upon this experience in the same way (whatever that is) in which a memory of an experience is dependent upon it.

According to (1) q-memories seem like memories. So I q-remember *having* experiences.

This may seem to make q-memory presuppose identity. One might say, 'My apparent memory of *having* an experience is an apparent memory of *my* having an experience. So how could I q-remember my having other people's experiences?'

This objection rests on a mistake. When I seem to remember an experience, I do indeed seem to remember *having* it.[24] But it cannot be a part of what I seem to remember about this experience that I, the person who now seems to remember it, am the person who had this experience.[25] That I am is something that I automatically assume. (My apparent memories sometimes come to me simply as the belief that *I* had a certain experience.) But it is something that I am justified in assuming only because I do not in fact have q-memories of other people's experiences.

Suppose that I did start to have such q-memories. If I did, I should cease to assume that my apparent memories must be about my own experiences. I should come to assess an apparent memory by asking two questions: (1) Does it tell me about a past experience? (2) If so, whose?

Moreover (and this is a crucial point) my apparent memories

would now come to me *as* q-memories. Consider those of my apparent memories which do come to me simply as beliefs about my past: for example, 'I did that.' If I knew that I could q-remember other people's experiences, these beliefs would come to me in a more guarded form: for example, 'Someone – probably I – did that.' I might have to work out who it was.

I have suggested that the concept of q-memory is coherent. Wiggins's case provides an illustration. The resulting people, in his case, both have apparent memories of living the life of the original person. If they agree that they are not this person, they will have to regard these as only q-memories. And when they are asked a question like 'Have you heard this music before?' they might have to answer 'I am sure that I q-remember hearing it. But I am not sure whether I remember hearing it. I am not sure whether it was I who heard it, or the original person.'

We can next point out that on our definition every memory is also a q-memory. Memories are, simply, q-memories of one's own experiences. Since this is so, we could afford now to drop the concept of memory and use in its place the wider concept q-memory. If we did, we should describe the relation between an experience and what we now call a 'memory' of this experience in a way which does not presuppose that they are had by the same person.[26]

This way of describing this relation has certain merits. It vindicates the 'memory criterion' of personal identity against the charge of circularity.[27] And it might, I think, help with the problem of other minds.

But we must move on. We can next take the relation between an intention and a later action. It may be a logical truth that we can intend to perform only our own actions. But intentions can be redescribed as q-intentions. And one person could q-intend to perform another person's actions.

Wiggins's case again provides the illustration. We are supposing that neither of the resulting people is the original person. If so, we shall have to agree that the original person can, before the operation, q-intend to perform their actions. He might, for example, q-intend, as one of them, to continue his present career, and, as the other, to try something new.[28] (I say 'q-intend *as* one of them' because the phrase '*q*-intend that one of them' would not convey the directness of the relation which is involved. If I intend that someone else should do something, I cannot get him to do it simply by forming this intention. But if I am the original person, and he is one of the resulting people, I can.)

The phrase '*q*-intend *as* one of them' reminds us that we need a sense in which one person can survive as two. But we can first point out that the concepts of *q*-memory and *q*-intention give us our model for the others that we need: thus, a man who can *q*-remember could *q*-recognize, and be a *q*-witness of, what he has never seen; and a man who can *q*-intend could have *q*-ambitions, make *q*-promises, and be *q*-responsible for.

To put this claim in general terms: many different relations are included within, or are a consequence of, psychological continuity. We describe these relations in ways which presuppose the continued existence of one person. But we could describe them in new ways which do not.

This suggests a bolder claim. It might be possible to think of experiences in a wholly 'impersonal' way. I shall not develop this claim here. What I shall try to describe is a way of thinking of our own identity through time which is more flexible, and less misleading, than the way in which we now think.

This way of thinking will allow for a sense in which one person can survive as two. A more important feature is that it treats survival as a matter of degree.

IV

We must first show the need for this second feature. I shall use two imaginary examples.

The first is the converse of Wiggins's case: fusion. Just as division serves to show that what matters in survival need not be one–one, so fusion serves to show that it can be a question of degree.

Physically, fusion is easy to describe. Two people come together. While they are unconscious, their two bodies grow into one. One person then wakes up.

The psychology of fusion is more complex. One detail we have already dealt with in the case of the exam. When my mind was reunited, I remembered just having thought out two calculations. The one person who results from a fusion can, similarly, q-remember living the lives of the two original people. None of their q-memories need be lost.

But some things must be lost. For any two people who fuse together will have different characteristics, different desires, and different intentions. How can these be combined?

We might suggest the following. Some of these will be compatible. These can coexist in the one resulting person. Some will be incompatible. These, if of equal strength, can cancel out, and if of different strengths, the stronger can be made weaker. And all these effects might be predictable.

To give examples – first, of compatibility: I like Palladio and intend to visit Venice. I am about to fuse with a person who likes Giotto and intends to visit Padua. I can know that the one person we shall become will have both tastes and both intentions. Second, of incompatibility: I hate red hair, and always vote Labour. The other person loves red hair, and always votes Conservative. I can know that the one person we shall become will be indifferent to red hair, and a floating voter.

If we were about to undergo a fusion of this kind, would we regard it as death?

Some of us might. This is less absurd than regarding division as death. For after my division the two resulting people will be in every way like me, while after my fusion the one resulting person will not be wholly similar. This makes it easier to say, when faced with fusion, 'I shall not survive', thus continuing to regard survival as a matter of all-or-nothing.

This reaction is less absurd. But here are two analogies which tell against it.

First, fusion would involve the changing of some of our characteristics and some of our desires. But only the very self-satisfied would think of this as death. Many people welcome treatments with these effects.

Second, someone who is about to fuse can have, beforehand, just as much 'intentional control' over the actions of the resulting individual as someone who is about to marry can have, beforehand, over the actions of the resulting couple. And the choice of a partner for fusion can be just as well considered as the choice of a marriage partner. The two original people can make sure (perhaps by 'trial fusion') that they do have compatible characters, desires, and intentions.

I have suggested that fusion, while not clearly survival, is not clearly failure to survive, and hence that what matters in survival can have degrees.

To reinforce this claim we can now turn to a second example. This is provided by certain imaginary beings. These beings are just like ourselves except that they reproduce by a process of natural division.

We can illustrate the histories of these imagined beings with the aid of a diagram. The lines on the diagram represent the spatio-temporal paths which would be traced out by the bodies of these beings. We can call each single line (like the doubled line) a 'branch'; and we can call the whole structure a 'tree'. And let us suppose that each 'branch' corresponds to what is thought of as the life of one

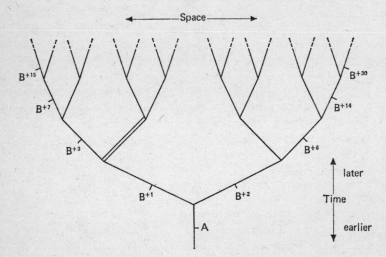

individual. These individuals are referred to as 'A', 'B + 1', and so forth.

Now, each single division is an instance of Wiggins's case. So A's relation to both B + 1 and B + 2 is just as good as survival. But what of A's relation to B + 30?

I said earlier that what matters in survival could be provisionally referred to as 'psychological continuity'. I must now distinguish this relation from another, which I shall call 'psychological connectedness'.

Let us say that the relation between a q-memory and the experience q-remembered is a 'direct' relation. Another 'direct' relation is that which holds between a q-intention and the q-intended action. A third is that which holds between different expressions of some lasting q-characteristic.

'Psychological connectedness', as I define it, requires the holding of these direct psychological relations. 'Connectedness' is not transitive, since these relations are not transitive. Thus, if X q-remembers most of Y's life, and Y q-remembers most of Z's life, it does not follow that X q-remembers most of Z's life. And if X carries out the q-intentions of Y, and Y carries out the q-intentions of Z, it does not follow that X carries out the q-intentions of Z.

'Psychological continuity', in contrast, only requires overlapping chains of direct psychological relations. So 'continuity' is transitive.

To return to our diagram. A is psychologically continuous with B + 30. There are between the two continuous chains of overlapping relations. Thus, A has q-intentional control over B + 2, B + 2 has q-intentional control over B + 6, and so on up to B + 30. Or B + 30 can q-remember the life of B + 14, B + 14 can q-remember the life of B + 6, and so on back to A.[29]

A, however, need *not* be psychologically connected to B + 30. Connectedness requires direct relations. And if these beings are like us, A cannot stand in such relations to every individual in his indefinitely long 'tree'. Q-memories will weaken with the passage of time, and then fade away. Q-ambitions, once fulfilled, will be replaced by others. Q-characteristics will gradually change. In general, A stands in fewer and fewer direct psychological relations to an individual in his 'tree' the more remote that individual is. And if the individual is (like B + 30) sufficiently remote, there may be between the two *no* direct psychological relations.

Now that we have distinguished the general relations of psychological continuity and psychological connectedness, I suggest that connectedness is a more important element in survival. As a claim about our own survival, this would need more arguments than I have space to give. But it seems clearly true for my imagined beings. A is as close psychologically to B + 1 as I today am to myself tomorrow. A is as distant from B + 30 as I am from my great-great-grandson.

Even if connectedness is not more important than continuity, the fact that one of these is a relation of degree is enough to show that what matters in survival can have degrees. And in any case the two relations are quite different. So our imagined beings would need a way of thinking in which this difference is recognized.

V

What I propose is this.

First, A can think of any individual, anywhere in his 'tree', as 'a descendant self'. This phrase implies psychological continuity. Similarly, any later individual can think of any earlier individual on the single path[30] which connects him to A as 'an ancestral self'.

Since psychological continuity is transitive, 'being an ancestral self of' and 'being a descendant self of' are also transitive.

To imply psychological connectedness I suggest the phrases 'one of my future selves' and 'one of my past selves'.

These are the phrases with which we can describe Wiggins's case. For having past and future selves is, what we needed, a way of continuing to exist which does not imply identity through time. The original person does, in this sense, survive Wiggins's operation: the two resulting people are his later selves. And they can each refer to him as 'my past self'. (They can share a past self without being the same self as each other.)

Since psychological connectedness is not transitive, and is a matter of degree, the relations 'being a past self of' and 'being a future self of' should themselves be treated as relations of degree. We allow for this series of descriptions: 'my most recent self', 'one of my earlier selves', 'one of my distant selves', 'hardly one of *my* past selves (I can only *q*-remember a few of his experiences)', and, finally, 'not in any way one of *my* past selves – just an ancestral self'.

This way of thinking would clearly suit our first imagined beings. But let us now turn to a second kind of being. These reproduce by fusion as well as by division.[31] And let us suppose that they fuse every autumn and divide every spring. This yields the following diagram:

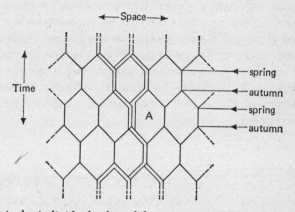

If A is the individual whose life is represented by the three-lined 'branch', the two-lined 'tree' represents those lives which are psychologically continuous with A's life. (It can be seen that each individual has his own 'tree', which overlaps with many others.)

For the imagined beings in this second world, the phrases 'an ancestral self' and 'a descendant self' would cover too much to be of much use. (There may well be pairs of dates such that every individual who ever lived before the first date was an ancestral self of every individual who ever will live after the second date.) Conversely, since the lives of each individual last for only half a year, the word 'I' would cover too little to do all of the work which it does for us. So part of this work would have to be done, for these second beings, by talk about past and future selves.

We can now point out a theoretical flaw in our proposed way of thinking. The phrase 'a past self of' implies psychological connectedness. Being a past self of is treated as a relation of degree, so that this phrase can be used to imply the varying degrees of psychological connectedness. But this phrase can imply only the degrees of connectedness between different lives. It cannot be used within a single life. And our way of delimiting successive lines does not refer to the degrees of psychological connectedness. Hence there is no guarantee that this phrase, 'a past self of ', could be used whenever it was needed. There is no guarantee that psychological connectedness will not vary in degree within a single life.

This flaw would not concern our imagined beings. For they divide and unite so frequently, and their lives are in consequence so short, that within a single life psychological connectedness would always stand at a maximum.

But let us look, finally, at a third kind of being.

In this world there is neither division nor union. There are a number of everlasting bodies, which gradually change in appearance. And direct psychological relations, as before, hold only over limited periods of time. This can be illustrated with a third diagram (which is found below). In this diagram the two shadings represent the degrees of psychological connectedness to their two central points.

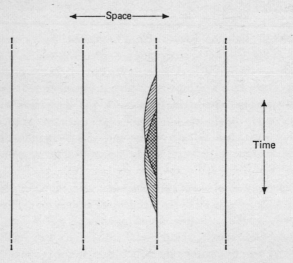

These beings could not use the way of thinking that we have proposed. Since there is no branching of psychological continuity, they would have to regard themselves as immortal. It might be said that this is what they are. But there is, I suggest, a better description.

Our beings would have one reason for thinking of themselves as immortal. The parts of each 'line' are all psychologically continuous.

But the parts of each 'line' are not all psychologically connected. Direct psychological relations hold only between those parts which are close to each other in time. This gives our beings a reason for *not* thinking of each 'line' as corresponding to one single life. For if they did, they would have no way of implying these direct relations. When a speaker says, for example, 'I spent a period doing such and such', his hearers would not be entitled to assume that the speaker has any memories of this period, that his character then and now are in any way similar, that he is now carrying out any of the plans or intentions which he then had, and so forth. Because the word 'I' would carry none of these implications, it would not have for these 'immortal' beings the usefulness which it has for us.[32]

To gain a better way of thinking, we must revise the way of thinking that we proposed above. The revision is this. The distinction between successive selves can be made by reference, not to the branching of psychological continuity, but to the degrees of psychological connectedness. Since this connectedness is a matter of degree, the drawing of these distinctions can be left to the choice of the speaker and be allowed to vary from context to context.

On this way of thinking, the word 'I' can be used to imply the greatest degree of psychological connectedness. When the connections are reduced, when there has been any marked change of character or style of life, or any marked loss of memory, our imagined beings would say, 'It was not I who did that, but an earlier self.' They could then describe in what ways, and to what degree, they are related to this earlier self.

This revised way of thinking would suit not only our 'immortal' beings. It is also the way in which we ourselves could think about our lives. And it is, I suggest, surprisingly natural.

One of its features, the distinction between successive selves, has already been used by several writers. To give an example, from Proust: 'we are incapable, while we are in love, of acting as fit predecessors of the next persons who, when we are in love no longer, we shall presently have become. . . .'[33]

Although Proust distinguished between successive selves, he still thought of one person as being these different selves. This we would not do on the way of thinking that I propose. If I say, 'It will not be me, but one of my future selves', I do not imply that I will be that future self. He is one of my later selves, and I am one of his earlier selves. There is no underlying person who we both are.

To point out another feature of this way of thinking. When I say, 'There is no person who we both are', I am only giving my decision. Another person could say, 'It will be you', thus deciding differently. There is no question of either of these decisions being a mistake. Whether to say 'I', or 'one of my future selves', or 'a descendant self' is entirely a matter of choice. The matter of fact, which must be agreed, is only whether the disjunction applies. (The question 'Are X and Y the same person?' thus becomes 'Is X *at least* an ancestral [or descendant] self of Y?')

VI

I have tried to show that what matters in the continued existence of a person are, for the most part, relations of degree. And I have proposed a way of thinking in which this would be recognized.

I shall end by suggesting two consequences and asking one question.

It is sometimes thought to be especially rational to act in our own best interests. But I suggest that the principle of self-interest has no force. There are only two genuine competitors in this particular field. One is the principle of biased rationality: do what will best achieve what you actually want. The other is the principle of impartiality: do what is in the best interests of everyone concerned.

The apparent force of the principle of self-interest derives, I think, from these two other principles.

The principle of self-interest is normally supported by the principle of biased rationality. This is because most people care about their own future interests.

Suppose that this prop is lacking. Suppose that a man does not care what happens to him in, say, the more distant future. To such a man, the principle of self-interest can only be propped up by an appeal to the principle of impartiality. We must say, 'Even if you don't care, you ought to take what happens to you then equally into account.' But for this, as a special claim, there seem to me no good arguments.

It can only be supported as part of the general claim, 'You ought to take what happens to everyone equally into account.'[34]

The special claim tells a man to grant an *equal* weight to all the parts of his future. The argument for this can only be that all the parts of his future are *equally* parts of *his* future. This is true. But it is a truth too superficial to bear the weight of the argument. (To give an analogy: The unity of a nation is, in its nature, a matter of degree. It is therefore only a superficial truth that all of a man's compatriots are *equally* his compatriots. This truth cannot support a good argument for nationalism.)[35]

I have suggested that the principle of self-interest has no strength of its own. If this is so, there is no special problem in the fact that what we ought to do can be against our interests. There is only the general problem that it may not be what we want to do.

The second consequence which I shall mention is implied in the first Egoism, the fear not of near but of distant death, the regret that so much of one's *only* life should have gone by – these are not, I think, wholly natural or instinctive. They are all strengthened by the beliefs about personal identity which I have been attacking. If we give up these beliefs, they should be weakened.

My final question is this. These emotions are bad, and if we weaken them we gain. But can we achieve this gain without, say, also weakening loyalty to, or love of, other particular selves? As Hume warned, the 'refined reflections which philosophy suggests ... cannot diminish ... our vicious passions ... without diminishing ... such as are virtuous. They are ... applicable to all our affections. In vain do we hope to direct their influence only to one side.'[36]

That hope *is* vain. But Hume had another: that more of what is bad depends upon false belief. This is also my hope.

Notes

1. I have been helped in writing this by D. Wiggins, D. F. Pears, P. F. Strawson, A. J. Ayer, M. Woods, N. Newman, and (through his publications) S. Shoemaker.

2. Implicit in John Locke, *Essay Concerning Human Understanding*, ed. by John W. Yolton, vol. 2, chap. 27, sec. 18 (London, 1961) and discussed by (among others) A. N. Prior in 'Opposite Number', *Review of Metaphysics*, 11

(1957–8), 196–201, and 'Time, Existence and Identity', *Proceedings of the Aristotelian Society* LVII (1965–6), 183–92; J. Bennett in 'The Simplicity of the Soul', *Journal of Philosophy* LXIV (1967), 648–60; and R. Chisholm and S. Shoemaker in 'The Loose and Popular and the Strict and the Philosophical Senses of Identity', in *Perception and Personal Identity: Proceedings of the 1967 Oberlin Colloquium in Philosophy*, ed. Norman Care and Robert H. Grimm (Cleveland, 1967).

3. David Wiggins, *Identity and Spatio-Temporal Continuity* (Oxford, 1967), p. 50.

4. Sydney S. Shoemaker, *Self-Knowledge and Self-Identity* (Ithaca, N.Y., 1963), p. 22.

5. Those who would disagree are not making a mistake. For them my argument would need a different case. There must be some multiple transplant, faced with which these people would both find it hard to believe that there must be an answer to the question about personal identity, and be able to be shown that nothing of importance turns upon this question.

6. R. W. Sperry, in *Brain and Conscious Experience*, ed. J. C. Eccles (New York, 1966), p. 299.

7. Cf. David Wiggins, op. cit., p. 40.

8. Suppose the resulting people fight a duel. Are there three people fighting, one on each side, and one on both? And suppose one of the bullets kills. Are there two acts, one murder and one suicide? How many people are left alive? One? Two? (We could hardly say, 'One and a half.') We could talk in this way. But instead of saying that the resulting people are the original person – so that the pair is a trio – it would be far simpler to treat them as a pair, and describe their relation to the original person in some new way. (I owe this suggested way of talking, and the objections to it, to Michael Woods.)

9. Cf. Sydney Shoemaker, in *Perception and Personal Identity*, p. 54.

10. Cf. David Wiggins, op. cit.

11. Bernard Williams's 'The Self and the Future', *Philosophical Review*, 79 (1970), 161–80, is relevant here. He asks the question 'Shall I survive?' in a range of problem cases, and he shows how natural it is to believe (1) that this question must have an answer, (2) that the answer must be all-or-nothing, and (3) that there is a 'risk' of our reaching the wrong answer. Because these beliefs are so natural, we should need in undermining them to discuss their causes. These, I think, can be found in the ways in which we misinterpret what it is to remember (cf. Sec. III below) and to anticipate (cf. Williams's 'Imagination and the Self', *Proceedings of the British Academy*, 52 [1966], 105–24); and also in the way in which certain features of our egoistic concern – e.g., that it is simple, and applies to all imaginable cases – are 'projected' onto its object. (For another relevant discussion, see Terence Penelhum's *Survival and Disembodied Existence* [London, 1970], final chapters.)

12. 'Personal Identity and Individuation', *Proceedings of the Aristotelian Society*, LVII (1956–7), 229–53; also *Analysis*, XXI (1960–61), 43–8.

13. J. M. Shorter, 'More about Bodily Continuity and Personal Identity', *Analysis* XXII (1961–2), 79–85; and Mrs J. M. R. Jack (unpublished), who requires that this truth be embedded in a causal theory.

14. *Analysis* XXI (1960–61), 44.

15. For the reasons given by A. M. Quinton in 'The Soul', *Journal of Philosophy* LIX (1962), 393–409.

16. Cf. S. Shoemaker, 'Persons and Their Pasts', *American Philosophical Quarterly*, 7 (1970), 269; and 'Wiggins on Identity', *Philosophical Review* LXXIX (1970), 542.

17. But not a necessary condition, for in the absence of psychological continuity bodily identity might be sufficient.

18. Cf. Bernard Williams, 'Personal Identity and Individuation', *Proceedings of the Aristotelian Society* LVII (1956–7), 240–41, and *Analysis* XXI (1960–61), 44; and also Wiggins, op. cit., p. 38: 'if coincidence under [the concept] *f* is to be *genuinely* sufficient we must not withhold identity . . . simply because transitivity is threatened'.

19. Williams produced another objection to the 'psychological criterion', that it makes it hard to explain the difference between the concepts of identity and exact similarity (*Analysis* XXI [1960–61], 48). But if we include the requirement of causal continuity we avoid this objection (and one of those produced by Wiggins in his note 47).

20. Those philosophers who have held this belief, from Butler onward, are too numerous to cite.

21. Op. cit.

22. 'Locke, Butler and the Stream of Consiousness: and Men of a Natural Kind', *Philosophy*, 51 (1976), pp. 131–57.

23. I here follow Shoemaker's 'quasi-memory'. Cf. also Penelhum's 'retro-cognition', in his article on 'Personal Identity', in the *Encyclopedia of Philosophy*, ed. Paul Edwards.

24. As Shoemaker put it, I seem to remember the experience 'from the inside' (op. cit.).

25. This is what so many writers have overlooked. Cf. Thomas Reid: 'My memory testifies not only that this was done, but that it was done by me who now remember it' ('Of Identity', in *Essays on the Intellectual Powers of Man*, ed. A. D. Woozley [London, 1941], p. 203). This mistake is discussed by A. B. Palma in 'Memory and Personal Identity', *Australasian Journal of Philosophy* XLII (1964), 57.

26. It is not logically necessary that we only *q*-remember our own experiences. But it might be necessary on other grounds. This possibility is intriguingly explored by Shoemaker in his 'Persons and Their Pasts' (op. cit.). He shows that *q*-memories can provide a knowledge of the world only if the observations which are *q*-remembered trace out fairly continuous spatiotemporal paths. If the observations which are *q*-remembered traced out a network of frequently interlocking paths, they could not, I think, be usefully

ascribed to persisting observers, but would have to be referred to in some more complex way. But in fact the observations which are q-remembered trace out single and separate paths; so we can ascribe them to ourselves. In other words, it is epistemologically necessary that the observations which are q-remembered should satisfy a certain general condition, one particular form of which allows them to be usefully self-ascribed.

27. Cf. Wiggins's paper cited in n. 22.

28. There are complications here. He could form *divergent* q-intentions only if he could distinguish, in advance, between the resulting people (e.g., as 'the left-hander' and 'the right-hander'). And he could be confident that such divergent q-intentions would be carried out only if he had reason to believe that neither of the resulting people would change their (inherited) mind. Suppose he was torn between duty and desire. He could not solve this dilemma by q-intending, as one of the resulting people, to do his duty, and, as the other, to do what he desires. For the one he q-intended to do his duty would face the same dilemma.

29. The chain of continuity must run in one direction of time. $B + 2$ is not, in the sense I intend, psychologically continuous with $B + 1$.

30. Cf. David Wiggins, op. cit.

31. Cf. Sydney Shoemaker in 'Persons and Their Pasts', op. cit.

32. Cf. Austin Duncan Jones, 'Man's Mortality', *Analysis* XXVIII (1967-8), 65-70.

33. *Within a Budding Grove* (London, 1949), I, 226 (my own translation).

34. Cf. Thomas Nagel's *The Possibility of Altruism* (Oxford, 1970), in which the special claim is in effect defended as part of the general claim.

35. The unity of a nation we seldom take for more than what it is. This is partly because we often think of nations, not as units, but in a more complex way. If we thought of ourselves in the way that I proposed, we might be less likely to take our own identity for more than what it is. We are, for example, sometimes told, 'It is irrational to act against your own interests. After all, it will be you who will regret it.' To this we could reply, 'No, not me. Not even one of my future selves. Just a descendant self.'

36. 'The Sceptic', in 'Essays Moral, Political and Literary', *Hume's Moral and Political Philosophy* (New York, 1959), p. 349.

Postscript, 1976

Of the many things which I now regret in this paper, I shall briefly mention three. (1) Talk about 'successive selves' is only a *façon de parler*; taken as anything more it can be misleading. (2) I should not have claimed that connectedness was more important than continuity. I now think that neither relation can be shown to be more important than the other. (3) The real issue seems to me now this. Does personal identity just consist in bodily and psychological continuity, or is it a further fact, independent of the facts about these continuities? Our reactions to the 'problem cases' show, I think, that we believe the latter. And we seem inclined to believe that this further fact is peculiarly deep, and is all-or-nothing – we believe that in any describable case it must hold either completely or not at all. My main claim is *the denial of this further fact*. This is what may make a difference. (No one needs to be told that psychological continuity is, in part, a matter of degree.) For some further remarks, see 'On "The Importance of Self-Identity"', *Journal of Philosophy*, 21 October 1971, 'Later Selves and Moral Principles', in *Philosophy and Personal Relations*, ed. Alan Montefiore (Routledge & Kegan Paul, 1973) and 'Lewis, Perry, and What Matters', in *The Identities of Persons*, ed. Amélie Rorty (University of California Press, 1976).

Biographical Note

Derek Parfit is Fellow of All Souls College, Oxford, and has contributed a number of papers to philosophical journals. He has held visiting appointments at Princeton and elsewhere.

Further Reading

Derek Parfit's notes give references to a good deal of the recent literature on personal identity. We would especially recommend Bernard Williams's papers on the subject, now conveniently collected in his book *Problems of the Self* (Cambridge: Cambridge University Press, 1973), and Sydney Shoemaker's *Self-Knowledge and Self-Identity* (Ithaca, N.Y.: Cornell University Press, 1963). The classics in the field are John Locke, *Essay Concerning Human Understanding*, Book II, Chap. XXVII, and Bishop Butler, *Analogy of Religion*, Dissertation I. A useful selection from this material is available in John Perry (ed.), *Personal Identity* (Berkeley, Los Angeles, London: University of California Press, 1975). Another recent collection, devoted to recent discussion and reflecting the stimulus of Parfit's views, is Amélie Rorty (ed.), *The Identities of Persons* (Berkeley, Los Angeles, London: University of California Press, 1976).

Donald Davidson

Mental Events

Among philosophy's principal and recalcitrant problems are those of determinism and of the fundamental nature of mind. What is the truth of the idea that our decisions and choices and indeed all mental events are determined by natural law, that when a person votes for the Labour Party, say, he could no more vote against it than water could freeze at the temperature which in fact makes it boil? As for the fundamental nature of mind, can we in these neurophysiological days continue in our conviction that thoughts and feelings, decisions and choices – again, all mental events – are strange things strangely connected to the physical events which occur in the brain, and are not identical with those very events? In Professor Donald Davidson's remarkable essay, these two questions come together, and an answer to the first one of them is shown to be an argument for a new answer to the other.

To begin with the problem of determinism, there are three firm propositions. One, which is so firm as to be beyond denial, is that there are causal connections between mental events and physical events. A desire or want played a causal role in a later physical event, a movement or turning of a page of this book, and that physical event was causally related to certain subsequent mental events involved in your seeing of the page.

The second proposition is that the relationship between an effect and what caused it is nomological, a matter of natural law or natural necessity. That is, there is a generalization that events like the effect go with events like the one that caused it, and this generalization is lawlike or indeed a law. A generalization that events of type S are followed by events of type T is a lawlike generalization to the extent that it implies that any event of type S would be accompanied by an event of type T, and hence that it is not just an accidental fact about all the S-events there actually are that a T-event occurs in conjunction with them.

The third proposition, which seems forced upon us by our experience, and fundamental to our view of ourselves as persons, is that our decisions and choices, to speak only of those mental events, are *not* a matter of iron law or necessitation, in the sense just explained. What is true, rather, is that we are free – not merely in the sense that we often act as we decide, without obstruction, but free in another sense. Our decisions are not unalterably law-governed but rather, in Davidson's word, are 'anomalous'. A man's decision to campaign against more one-way streets in London does not stand to its antecedents as the water's boiling stands to its being raised to a certain temperature, whatever the similarities between the decision and the boiling.

These are *firm* propositions, but the first two appear to run head-on into the third. The first of them, the 'principle of causal interaction', together with the second, the 'principle of the nomological character of causality', collide with the third, the 'principle of the anomalism of the mental'. It seems that one of the first two principles, or the third, must be given up.

To turn briefly to the recent history of the problem of the nature of mind, it has very often consisted in the controversy mentioned at the beginning, as to whether a dualistic or a monistic account of mental events is correct. When I noticed the Post Office Tower a moment ago, were there *two* things in question: a mental happening, and a physical happening in my brain? (That there *was* a complex physical happening, something which falls into the province of neurophysiology, is beyond question.) Or, was there but *one* thing in question? There certainly are reasons for thinking that some proposition about there being only one thing is true. One reason is the correlation between mental facts and physical facts, facts about the brain. Clearly, they go together, so neatly as to suggest that each pair of facts are really facts about a single thing.

Those philosophers who have defended the latter answer, monism, now often called the identity theory, have for the most part supposed of any particular mental event, M_1, that it was not an accident that it was also the physical event, P_1. That is, to speak of processes rather than events, they have supposed, or would have supposed if the matter arose, that it is a matter of natural law that each instance of a man's thinking of his father in a certain way, say, is identical with an instance of just one kind of brain-process. It is a matter of necessity, that is, that each and every instance of one kind of thing, the man's thinking of his father, is identical with precisely a physical process of the kind P and not a physical process of kind Q or any other kind. (The situation is not much different if the preferred view is that each mental event is taken to be identical with a physical event which is an instance of one of a certain number of kinds and not any other.)

The basic argument of Davidson's paper is as follows. We must not give up, as have many philosophers concerned with determinism and freedom, either one of the first two of our principles, or the third. There is too much to be said for each of them. We must then see how it is that they are consistent, which they must be if each is true. By the principle of causal interaction and the principle of the nomological character of causality, at least some mental events are law-governed; let us take as an example my thinking of a street, Flask Walk, in a certain way today. But, by the principle of the anomalism of the mental, nothing mental can be law-governed. *All* that can be law-governed is what is physical. We can emerge from this conflict, it is argued, only by concluding that the bit of thinking is law-governed *as* something else: a physical event or process. It must then *be* that other thing – physical – as well as being mental. We are driven to the identity theory.

The argument presupposes what Davidson also accepts: that to say some event, E_1, caused another, E_2, is not necessarily to say that it was as E_1 and E_2 that the two events were, as they had to be, in lawlike connection. All that is required is that there be *some* descriptions such that events so-described are in lawlike connection.

Having denied that mental events fall under *any* laws, enter into *any* law-governed relations, we also have a further conclusion. It is not only that today's bit of thinking of Flask Walk is not law-governed in its relations with antecedent and consequent things, but also that its actually being a particular physical happening is not law-governed. It is not a matter of law that if I think of Flask Walk in just that way again tomorrow, my thinking will be identical with an instance of precisely the same kind of physical happening again. What we have now got, by label, is 'anomalous monism'.

In solving the problem of determinism, if we have, we have also solved the problem of the nature of mind, or at any rate come upon a new argument for one quite new solution, anomalous monism. It is a striking argument. It is a challenge to certain intuitive convictions. For example, it seems that to say something is law-governed *as* this, but not *as* that, is to say that one of its properties (or a set) is law-governed, but another property (or another set) is not. But then we may feel that there is a case for saying that there are *two* things in question, not one. A second and different conviction follows on the supposition that there is but one thing. We can accept that it does not follow from its being of the kind P that it is, as a matter of law, of the kind M. Still, if this thing, P_1, is subject to law, and if P_1 is M_1, even as a matter of pure chance, can it really be true to say that M_1 can escape being subject to law? Davidson, of course, is not without things to say about such convictions as these two.

Let us turn briefly to the arrangement of his paper, which is not quite the arrangement suggested by the main argument.

The introductory part sets out the seeming contradiction of the three principles. Section I, which follows, has partly to do with a prior question: 'What does it mean to say that an event is mental or physical?' Here one encounters the idea, roughly, that what is mental is what is characterized by a mental verb, with a mental verb being one such that the truth-value of a statement may change when a certain reasonable substitution is made. (The statement is 'nonextensional'.) Take the true statement, 'He intended to propose to the queen'. If the queen, unknown to him, was his mother, and one substitutes 'his mother' for 'the queen', the resulting statement seems to be false. Not so when one substitutes in 'The queen weighed a lot'.

There follows, also in Section I, a discussion of what might be called the old identity theory, where a bit of my dream's being identical with a certain physical event is law-governed, and the new identity theory, where the identity is not a matter of law. There is also in Section I a certain moderation introduced in connection with the principle of the anomalism of the mental. The mental is not claimed to be quite so 'free' as might have been understood.

Section II is given over to a discussion of the principle just mentioned and a defence of it. There is the question of whether the truth of the principle is something to be decided by scientists, not philosophers. There is also the prior question of what it is for a general statement to be one which states a natural law. We have already noticed how the difference can be characterized, but problems remain. What, more fundamentally, is the difference between 'All the men in this room are mortal', which is a matter of natural law, and 'All the men in this room have suits on'?

Finally, in Section II, there are the considerations put forward in defence of the principle of the anomalism of the mental. Partly because of economy in expression, they do not come together into an easy read. That there are no psycho-physical laws whatever may be taken to be suggested by the fact that there seem to be no such laws of a certain kind. That is, there seem to be no laws which link mental events and outward behaviour. Secondly, laws bring together terms that were 'made for each other', and this is not true of mental and physical terms. A third and large consideration is that it makes no sense to suppose of a man, for example, that he is angry at someone's being a poor neighbour, without being prepared to attribute to him a vast panoply of beliefs, attitudes and so on. It could not be that a man had some *single* idea connected with the term 'neighbour' and that was pretty well all. For a start he would have to have ideas of human relationship and of certain expectations. Given all this, and what follows from it, the claim that there *are* psycho-physical laws is at least obscure. These three considerations, and related ones, are not to be grasped easily. More is said of them in Davidson's other writings mentioned in the bibliography and in footnotes 13, 14 and 15.

Section III brings together what has gone before, and so we have the basic argument of the essay, the one sketched above. *It*, certainly, is made very clear. By coming to a particular view about determinism, one which may give us both determinism *and* freedom, we also have the added extra of anomalous monism. It is not, of course, an optional extra.

T.H.

Donald Davidson

Mental Events

Mental events such as perceivings, rememberings, decisions, and actions resist capture in the nomological net of physical theory.[1] How can this fact be reconciled with the causal role of mental events in the physical world? Reconciling freedom with causal determinism is a special case of the problem if we suppose that causal determinism entails capture in, and freedom requires escape from, the nomological net. But the broader issue can remain alive even for someone who believes a correct analysis of free action reveals no conflict with determinism. *Autonomy* (freedom, self-rule) may or may not clash with determinism; *anomaly* (failure to fall under a law) is, it would seem, another matter.

I start from the assumption that both the causal dependence, and the anomalousness, of mental events are undeniable facts. My aim is therefore to explain, in the face of apparent difficulties, how this can be. I am in sympathy with Kant when he says,

it is as impossible for the subtlest philosophy as for the commonest reasoning to argue freedom away. Philosophy must therefore assume that no true contradiction will be found between freedom and natural necessity in the same human actions, for it cannot give up the idea of nature any more than that of freedom. Hence even if we should never be able to conceive how freedom is possible, at least this apparent contradiction must be convincingly eradicated. For if the thought of freedom contradicts itself or nature . . . it would have to be surrendered in competition with natural necessity.[2]

Generalize human actions to mental events, substitute anomaly for freedom, and this is a description of my problem. And of course the connection is closer, since Kant believed freedom entails anomaly.

Now let me try to formulate a little more carefully the 'apparent contradiction' about mental events that I want to discuss and finally dissipate. It may be seen as stemming from three principles.

The first principle asserts that at least some mental events interact causally with physical events. (We could call this the principle of causal interaction.) Thus for example if someone sank the *Bismarck*, then various mental events such as perceivings, notings, calculations, judgements, decisions, intentional actions and changes of belief played a causal role in the sinking of the *Bismarck*. In particular, I would urge that the fact that someone sank the *Bismarck* entails that he moved his body in a way that was caused by mental events of certain sorts, and that his bodily movement in turn caused the *Bismarck* to sink.[3] Perception illustrates how causality may run from the physical to the mental: if a man perceives that a ship is approaching, then a ship approaching must have caused him to come to believe that a ship is approaching. (Nothing depends on accepting these as examples of causal interaction.)

Though perception and action provide the most obvious cases where mental and physical events interact causally, I think reasons could be given for the view that all mental events ultimately, perhaps through causal relations with other mental events, have causal intercourse with physical events. But if there are mental events that have no physical events as causes or effects, the argument will not touch them.

The second principle is that where there is causality, there must be a law: events related as cause and effect fall under strict deterministic laws. (We may term this the principle of the nomological character of causality.) This principle, like the first, will be treated here as an assumption, though I shall say something by way of interpretation.[4]

The third principle is that there are no strict deterministic laws on the basis of which mental events can be predicted and explained (the anomalism of the mental).

The paradox I wish to discuss arises for someone who is inclined to accept these three assumptions or principles, and who thinks they are inconsistent with one another. The inconsistency is not, of course, formal unless more premises are added. Nevertheless it is natural to reason that the first two principles, that of causal interaction, and that of the nomological character of causality, together imply that at least some mental events can be predicted and explained on the basis of laws, while the principle of the anomalism of the mental denies this. Many philosophers have accepted, with or without argument, the view that the three principles do lead to a contradiction. It seems to me, however, that all three principles are true, so that what must be done is to explain away the appearance of contradiction; essentially the Kantian line.

The rest of this paper falls into three parts. The first part describes a version of the identity theory of the mental and the physical that shows how the three principles may be reconciled. The second part argues that there cannot be strict psychophysical laws; this is not quite the principle of the anomalism of the mental, but on reasonable assumptions entails it. The last part tries to show that from the fact that there can be no strict psychophysical laws, and our other two principles, we can infer the truth of a version of the identity theory, that is, a theory that identifies at least some mental events with physical events. It is clear that this 'proof' of the identity theory will be at best conditional, since two of its premises are unsupported, and the argument for the third may be found less than conclusive. But even someone unpersuaded of the truth of the premises may be interested to learn how they may be reconciled and that they serve to establish a version of the identity theory of the mental. Finally, if the argument is a good one, it should lay to rest the view, common to many friends and some foes of identity theories, that support for such theories can come only from the discovery of psychophysical laws.

I

The three principles will be shown consistent with one another by describing a view of the mental and the physical that contains no inner contradiction and that entails the three principles. According to this view, mental events are identical with physical events. Events are taken to be unrepeatable, dated individuals such as the particular eruption of a volcano, the (first) birth or death of a person, the playing of the 1968 World Series, or the historic utterance of the words, 'You may fire when ready, Gridley'. We can easily frame identity statements about individual events; examples (true or false) might be:

The death of Scott = the death of the author of *Waverley*;
The assassination of the Archduke Ferdinand = the event that started the First World War;
The eruption of Vesuvius in A.D. 79 = the cause of the destruction of Pompeii.

The theory under discussion is silent about processes, states, and attributes if these differ from individual events.

What does it mean to say that an event is mental or physical? One natural answer is that an event is physical if it is describable in a purely physical vocabulary, mental if describable in mental terms. But if this is taken to suggest that an event is physical, say, if some physical predicate is true of it, then there is the following difficulty. Assume that the predicate 'x took place at Noosa Head' belongs to the physical vocabulary; then so also must the predicate 'x did not take place at Noosa Head' belong to the physical vocabulary. But the predicate 'x did or did not take place at Noosa Head' is true of every event, whether mental or physical.[5] We might rule out predicates that are tautologically true of every event, but this will not help since every event is truly describable either by 'x took place at Noosa Head' or by 'x did not take place at Noosa Head'. A different approach is needed.[6]

We may call those verbs mental that express propositional attitudes like believing, intending, desiring, hoping, knowing, perceiving, noticing, remembering, and so on. Such verbs are characterized by the fact that they sometimes feature in sentences with subjects that refer to persons, and are completed by embedded sentences in which the usual rules of substitution appear to break down. This criterion is not precise, since I do not want to include these verbs when they occur in contexts that are fully extensional ('He knows Paris', 'He perceives the moon' may be cases), nor exclude them whenever they are not followed by embedded sentences. An alternative characterization of the desired class of mental verbs might be that they are psychological verbs as used when they create apparently nonextensional contexts.

Let us call a description of the form 'the event that is M' or an open sentence of the form 'event x is M' a *mental description* or a *mental open sentence* if and only if the expression that replaces 'M' contains at least one mental verb essentially. (Essentially, so as to rule out cases where the description or open sentence is logically equivalent to one not containing mental vocabulary.) Now we may say that an event is mental if and only if it has a mental description, or (the description operator not being primitive) if there is a mental open sentence true of that event alone. Physical events are those picked out by descriptions or open sentences that contain only the physical vocabulary essentially. It is less important to characterize a physical vocabulary because relative to the mental it is, so to speak, recessive in determining whether a description is mental or physical. (There will be some comments presently on the nature of a physical vocabulary, but these comments will fall far short of providing a criterion.)

On the proposed test of the mental, the distinguishing feature of the mental is not that it is private, subjective, or immaterial, but that it exhibits what Brentano called intentionality. Thus intentional actions are clearly included in the realm of the mental along with thoughts, hopes, and regrets (or the events tied to these). What may seem doubtful is whether the criterion will include events that have often been considered paradigmatic of the mental. Is it obvious, for example, that feeling a pain or seeing an after-image will count as mental? Sentences that report such events seem free from taint of non-extensionality, and the same should be true of reports of raw feels, sense data, and other uninterpreted sensations, if there are any.

However, the criterion actually covers not only the havings of pains and after-images, but much more besides. Take some event one would intuitively accept as physical, let's say the collision of two stars in distant space. There must be a purely physical predicate 'Px' true of this collision, and of others, but true of only this one at the time it occurred. This particular time, though, may be pinpointed as the same time that Jones notices that a pencil starts to roll across his desk. The distant stellar collision is thus *the* event x such that Px and x is simultaneous with Jones's noticing that a pencil starts to roll across his desk. The collision has now been picked out by a mental description and must be counted as a mental event.

This strategy will probably work to show every event to be

mental; we have obviously failed to capture the intuitive concept of the mental. It would be instructive to try to mend this trouble, but it is not necessary for present purposes. We can afford Spinozistic extravagance with the mental since accidental inclusions can only strengthen the hypothesis that all mental events are identical with physical events. What would matter would be failure to include bona fide mental events, but of this there seems to be no danger.

I want to describe, and presently to argue for, a version of the identity theory that denies that there can be strict laws connecting the mental and the physical. The very possibility of such a theory is easily obscured by the way in which identity theories are commonly defended and attacked. Charles Taylor, for example, agrees with protagonists of identity theories that the sole 'ground' for accepting such theories is the supposition that correlations or laws can be established linking events described as mental with events described as physical. He says, 'It is easy to see why this is so: unless a given mental event is invariably accompanied by a given, say, brain process, there is no ground for even mooting a general identity between the two.'[7] Taylor goes on (correctly, I think) to allow that there may be identity without correlating laws, but my present interest is in noticing the invitation to confusion in the statement just quoted. What can 'a given mental event' mean here? Not a particular, dated, event, for it would not make sense to speak of an individual event being 'invariably accompanied' by another. Taylor is evidently thinking of events of a given *kind*. But if the only identities are of kinds of events, the identity theory presupposes correlating laws.

One finds the same tendency to build laws into the statement of the identity theory in these typical remarks:

When I say that a sensation is a brain process or that lightning is an electrical discharge, I am using 'is' in the sense of strict identity . . . there are not two things: a flash of lightning and an electrical discharge. There is one thing, a flash of lightning, which is described scientifically as an electrical discharge to the earth from a cloud of ionized water molecules.[8]

The last sentence of this quotation is perhaps to be understood as saying that for every lightning flash there exists an electrical discharge to the earth from a cloud of ionized water molecules with which it is identical. Here we have an honest ontology of individual events and can make literal sense of identity. We can also see how there could be identities without correlating laws. It is possible, however, to have an ontology of events with the conditions of individuation specified in such a way that any identity implies a correlating law. Kim, for example, suggests that Fa and Gb 'describe or refer to the same event' if and only if $a = b$ and the property of being F = the property of being G.* The identity of the properties in turn entails that (x) $(Fx \longleftrightarrow Gx)$.[9] No wonder Kim says:

> If pain is identical with brain state B, there must be a concomitance between occurrences of pain and occurrences of brain state B . . . Thus, a necessary condition of the pain–brain state B identity is that the two expressions 'being in pain' and 'being in brain state B' have the same extension . . . There is no conceivable observation that would confirm or refute the identity but not the associated correlation.[10]

It may make the situation clearer to give a fourfold classification of theories of the relation between mental and physical events that emphasizes the independence of claims about laws and claims of identity. On the one hand there are those who asssert, and those who deny, the existence of psychophysical laws; on the other hand there are those who say mental events are identical with physical and those who deny this. Theories are thus divided into four sorts: *Nomological monism*, which affirms that there are correlating laws and that the events correlated are one (materialists belong in this category); *nomological dualism*, which comprises various forms of parallelism, interactionism, and epiphenomenalism; *anomalous dualism*, which combines ontological dualism with the general failure of laws correlating the mental and the physical (Cartesianism). And finally there is *anomalous monism*, which classifies the position I wish to occupy.[11]

Anomalous monism resembles materialism in its claim that all events are physical, but rejects the thesis, usually considered essential to materialism, that mental phenomena can be given purely physical

---

* The formulae 'Fa' and 'Gb' can be read as 'a thing a has the property F' and 'a thing b has the property G', or simply 'a is F' and 'b is G'. The formula '$a = b$' is of course 'a is identical with b'. The formula '$(x)(Fx \longleftrightarrow Gx)$' is 'Anything that is F is G, and anything that is G is F'.

explanations. Anomalous monism shows an ontological bias only in that it allows the possibility that not all events are mental, while insisting that all events are physical. Such a bland monism, un-buttressed by correlating laws or conceptual economies, does not seem to merit the term 'reductionism'; in any case it is not apt to inspire the nothing-but reflex ('Conceiving the *Art of the Fugue* was nothing but a complex neural event', and so forth).

Although the position I describe denies there are psychophysical laws, it is consistent with the view that mental characteristics are in some sense dependent, or supervenient, on physical characteristics. Such supervenience might be taken to mean that there cannot be two events alike in all physical respects but differing in some mental respect, or that an object cannot alter in some mental respect without altering in some physical respect. Dependence or supervenience of this kind does not entail reducibility through law or definition: if it did, we could reduce moral properties to descriptive, and this there is good reason to *believe* cannot be done; and we might be able to reduce truth in a formal system to syntactical properties, and this we *know* cannot in general be done.

This last example is in useful analogy with the sort of lawless monism under consideration. Think of the physical vocabulary as the entire vocabulary of some language L with resources adequate to express a certain amount of mathematics, and its own syntax. L′ is L augmented with the truth predicate 'true-in-L', which is 'mental'. In L (and hence L′) it is possible to pick out, with a definite description or open sentence, each sentence in the extension of the truth predicate, but if L is consistent there exists no predicate of syntax (of the 'physical' vocabulary), no matter how complex, that applies to all and only the true sentences of L. There can be no 'psychophysical law' in the form of a biconditional, '(x) (x is true-in-L if and only if x is ϕ)' where 'ϕ' is replaced by a 'physical' predicate (a predicate of L). Similarly, we can pick out each mental event using the physical vocabulary alone, but no purely physical predicate, no matter how complex, has, as a matter of law, the same extension as a mental predicate.

It should now be evident how anomalous monism reconciles the three original principles. Causality and identity are relations between individual events no matter how described. But laws are linguistic;

and so events can instantiate laws, and hence be explained or predicted in the light of laws, only as those events are described in one or another way. The principle of causal interaction deals with events in extension and is therefore blind to the mental–physical dichotomy. The principle of the anomalism of the mental concerns events described as mental, for events are mental only as described. The principle of the nomological character of causality must be read carefully: it says that when events are related as cause and effect, they have descriptions that instantiate a law. It does not say that every true singular statement of causality instantiates a law.[12]

II

The analogy just bruited, between the place of the mental amid the physical, and the place of the semantical in a world of syntax, should not be strained. Tarski proved that a consistent language cannot (under some natural assumptions) contain an open sentence 'Fx' true of all and only the true sentences of that language.* If our analogy were pressed, then we would expect a proof that there can be no physical open sentence 'Px' true of all and only the events having some mental property. In fact, however, nothing I can say about the irreducibility of the mental deserves to be called a proof; and the kind of irreducibility is different. For if anomalous monism is correct, not only can every mental event be uniquely singled out using only Physical concepts, but since the number of events that falls under each mental predicate may, for all we know, be finite, there may well exist a physical open sentence coextensive with each mental predicate, though to construct it might involve the tedium of a lengthy and uninstructive alternation. Indeed, even if finitude is not assumed, there seems no compelling reason to deny that there could be coextensive predicates, one mental and one physical.

The thesis is rather that the mental is nomologically irreducible: there may be *true* general statements relating the mental and the physi-

---

* 'Fx' might be read as 'it is F'. The point is that there is not some property F which is had by each of the true sentences of the language. And, as Davidson continues, it can be argued that there is no physical property P which is had by each of the mental events of a certain kind.

cal, statements that have the logical form of a law; but they are not *lawlike* (in a strong sense to be described). If by absurdly remote chance we were to stumble on a nonstochastic true psychophysical generalization, we would have no reason to believe it more than roughly true.

Do we, by declaring that there are no (strict) psychophysical laws, poach on the empirical preserves of science – a form of *hubris* against which philosophers are often warned? Of course, to judge a statement lawlike or illegal is not to decide its truth outright; relative to the acceptance of a general statement on the basis of instances, ruling it lawlike must be *a priori*. But such relative apriorism does not in itself justify philosophy, for in general the grounds for deciding to trust a statement on the basis of its instances will in turn be governed by theoretical and empirical concerns not to be distinguished from those of science. If the case of supposed laws linking the mental and the physical is different, it can only be because to allow the possibility of such laws would amount to changing the subject. By changing the subject I mean here: deciding not to accept the criterion of the mental in terms of the vocabulary of the propositional attitudes. This short answer cannot prevent further ramifications of the problem, however, for there is no clear line between changing the subject and changing what one says on an old subject, which is to admit, in the present context at least, that there is no clear line between philosophy and science. Where there are no fixed boundaries only the timid never risk trespass.

It will sharpen our appreciation of the anomological character of mental-physical generalizations to consider a related matter, the failure of definitional behaviourism. Why are we willing (as I assume we are) to abandon the attempt to give explicit definitions of mental concepts in terms of behavioural ones? Not, surely, just because all actual tries are conspicuously inadequate. Rather it is because we are persuaded, as we are in the case of so many other forms of definitional reductionism (naturalism in ethics, instrumentalism and operationalism in the sciences, the causal theory of meaning, phenomenalism, and so on – the catalogue of philosophy's defeats), that there is system in the failures. Suppose we try to say, not using any mental concepts, what it is for a man to believe there is life on Mars. One line we could take is this: when a certain sound is produced in the man's presence ('Is there life on Mars?') he produces another ('Yes'). But of course this shows he believes there is life on Mars only if he understands English, his production of the sound was intentional, and was a response to the sounds as meaning something in English; and so on. For each discovered deficiency, we add a new proviso. Yet no matter how we patch and fit the non-mental conditions, we always find the need for an additional condition (provided he *notices, understands,* etc.) that is mental in character.[13]

A striking feature of attempts at definitional reduction is how little seems to hinge on the question of synonymy between definiens and definiendum. Of course, by imagining counterexamples we do discredit claims of synonymy. But the pattern of failure prompts a stronger conclusion: if we were to find an open sentence couched in behavioural terms and exactly coextensive with some mental predicate, nothing could reasonably persuade us that we had found it. We know too much about thought and behaviour to trust exact and universal statements linking them. Beliefs and desires issue in behaviour only as modified and mediated by further beliefs and desires, attitudes and attendings, without limit. Clearly this holism of the mental realm is a clue both to the autonomy and to the anomalous character of the mental.

These remarks apropos definitional behaviourism provide at best hints of why we should not expect nomological connections between the mental and the physical. The central case invites further consideration.

Lawlike statements are general statements that support counterfactual and subjunctive claims, and are supported by their instances. There is (in my view) no nonquestion-begging criterion of the lawlike, which is not to say there are no reasons in particular cases for a judgement. Lawlikeness is a matter of degree, which is not to deny that there may be cases beyond debate. And within limits set by the conditions of communication, there is room for much variation between individuals in the pattern of statements to which various degrees of nomologicality are assigned. In all respects, nomologicality is much like analyticity, as one might expect since both are linked to meaning.

'All emeralds are green' is lawlike in that its instances confirm it, but 'all emeralds are grue' is not, for 'grue' means 'observed before time t and green, otherwise blue', and if our observations were all made before t and uniformly revealed green emeralds, this would not be a reason to expect other emeralds to be blue. Nelson Goodman has suggested that this shows that some predicates, 'grue' for example, are unsuited to laws (and thus a criterion of suitable predicates could lead to a criterion of the lawlike). But it seems to me the anomalous character of 'All emeralds are grue' shows only that the predicates 'is an emerald' and 'is grue' are not suited to one another: grueness is not an inductive property of emeralds. Grueness *is* however an inductive property of entities of other sorts, for instance of emerires. (Something is an emerire if it is examined before t and is an emerald, and otherwise is a sapphire.) Not only is 'All emerires are grue' entailed by the conjunction of the lawlike statements 'All emeralds are green' and 'All sapphires are blue', but there is no reason, as far as I can see, to reject the deliverance of intuition, that it is itself lawlike.[14] Nomological statements bring together predicates that we know *a priori* are made for each other – know, that is, independently of knowing whether the evidence supports a connection between them. 'Blue', 'red', and 'green' are made for emeralds, sapphires, and roses; 'grue', 'bleen', and 'gred' are made for sapphalds, emerires, and emeroses.

The direction in which the discussion seems headed is this: mental and physical predicates are not made for one another. In point of lawlikeness, psychophysical statements are more like 'All emeralds are grue' than like 'All emeralds are green'.

Before this claim is plausible, it must be seriously modified. The fact that emeralds examined before t are grue not only is no reason to believe all emeralds are grue; it is not even a reason (if we know the time) to believe *any* unobserved emeralds are grue. But if an event of a certain mental sort has usually been accompanied by an event of a certain physical sort, this often is a good reason to expect other cases to follow suit roughly in proportion. The generalizations that embody such practical wisdom are assumed to be only roughly true, or they are explicitly stated in probabilistic terms, or they are insulated from counterexample by generous escape clauses. Their importance lies mainly in the support they lend singular causal claims and related explanations of particular events. The support derives from the fact that such a generalization, however crude and vague, may provide good reason to believe that underlying the particular case there is a regularity that could be formulated sharply and without caveat.

In our daily traffic with events and actions that must be foreseen or understood, we perforce make use of the sketchy summary generalization, for we do not know a more accurate law, or if we do, we lack a description of the particular events in which we are interested that would show the relevance of the law. But there is an important distinction to be made within the category of the rude rule of thumb. On the one hand, there are generalizations whose positive instances give us reason to believe the generalization itself could be improved by adding further provisos and conditions stated in the same general vocabulary as the original generalization. Such a generalization points to the form and vocabulary of the finished law: we may say that it is a *homonomic* generalization. On the other hand there are generalizations which when instantiated may give us reason to believe there is a precise law at work, but one that can be stated only by shifting to a different vocabulary. We may call such generalizations *heteronomic*.

I suppose most of our practical lore (and science) is heteronomic. This is because a law can hope to be precise, explicit, and as exceptionless as possible only if it draws its concepts from a comprehensive closed theory. This ideal theory may or may not be deterministic, but it is if any true theory is. Within the physical sciences we do find homonomic generalizations, generalizations such that if the evidence supports them, we then have reason to believe they may be sharpened indefinitely by drawing upon further physical concepts: there is a theoretical asymptote of perfect coherence with all the evidence, perfect predictability (under the terms of the system), total explanation (again under the terms of the system). Or perhaps the ultimate theory is probabilistic, and the asymptote is less than perfection; but in that case there will be no better to be had.

Confidence that a statement is homonomic, correctible within its own conceptual domain, demands that it draw its concepts from a theory with strong constitutive elements. Here is the simplest possible illustration; if the lesson carries, it will be obvious that the simplification could be mended.

The measurement of length, weight, temperature, or time depends (among many other things, of course) on the existence in each case of a two-place relation that is transitive and asymmetric: warmer than, later than, heavier than, and so forth. Let us take the relation *longer than* as our example. The law or postulate of transitivity is this:

$$(\text{L}) \quad \text{L}(x, y) \text{ and } \text{L}(y, z) \rightarrow \text{L}(x, z)^\star$$

Unless this law (or some sophisticated variant) holds, we cannot easily make sense of the concept of length. There will be no way of assigning numbers to register even so much as ranking in length, let alone the more powerful demands of measurement on a ratio scale. And this remark goes not only for any three items directly involved in an intransitivity: it is easy to show (given a few more assumptions essential to measurement of length) that there is no consistent assignment of a ranking to any item unless (L) holds in full generality.

Clearly (L) alone cannot exhaust the import of 'longer than' – otherwise it would not differ from 'warmer than' or 'later than'. We must suppose there is some empirical content, however difficult to formulate in the available vocabulary, that distinguishes 'longer than' from the other two-place transitive predicates of measurement and on the basis of which we may assert that one thing is longer than another. Imagine this empirical content to be partly given by the predicate '$\text{O}(x, y)$'. So we have this 'meaning postulate':

$$(\text{M}) \quad \text{O}(x, y) \rightarrow \text{L}(x, y)$$

that partly interprets (L). But now (L) and (M) together yield an empirical theory of great strength, for together they entail that there do not exist three objects a, b, and c such that $\text{O}(a, b)$, $\text{O}(b, c)$, and $\text{O}(c, a)$. Yet what is to prevent this happening if $\text{O}(x, y)$ is a predicate we can ever, with confidence, apply? Suppose we *think* we observe an intransitive triad; what do we say? We could count (L) false, but then we would have no application for the concept of length. We could say (M)

$\star$ The formula (L) can be read as 'If x is related in way L to y (or, simply, if x is L to y) and Y is related in way L to z, then x is related in way L to z'. The formula (M) below, then, can be read as 'If x is related in way O to y, then x is related in way L to y'. The formula '$\text{O}(a, b)$' is of course 'a is related in way O to b' – and not 'b is related in way O to a'.

gives a wrong test for length; but then it is unclear what we thought was the *content* of the idea of one thing being longer than another. Or we could say that the objects under observation are not, as the theory requires, *rigid* objects. It is a mistake to think we are forced to accept some one of these answers. Concepts such as that of length are sustained in equilibrium by a number of conceptual pressures, and theories of fundamental measurement are distorted if we force the decision, among such principles as (L) and (M): analytic or synthetic. It is better to say the whole set of axioms, laws, or postulates for the measurement of length is partly constitutive of the idea of a system of macroscopic, rigid, physical objects. I suggest that the existence of lawlike statements in physical science depends upon the existence of constitutive (or synthetic *a priori*) laws like those of the measurement of length within the same conceptual domain.

Just as we cannot intelligibly assign a length to any object unless a comprehensive theory holds of objects of that sort, we cannot intelligibly attribute any propositional attitude to an agent except within the framework of a viable theory of his beliefs, intentions, and decisions.

There is no assigning beliefs to a person one by one on the basis of his verbal behaviour, his choices, or other local signs no matter how plain and evident, for we make sense of particular beliefs only as they cohere with other beliefs, with preferences, with intentions, hopes, fears, expectations, and the rest. It is not merely, as with the measurement of length, that each case tests a theory and depends upon it, but that the content of a propositional attitude derives from its place n the pattern.

Crediting people with a large degree of consistency cannot be counted mere charity: it is unavoidable if we are to be in a position to accuse them meaningfully of error and some degree of irrationality. Global confusion, like universal mistake, is unthinkable, not because imagination boggles, but because too much confusion leaves nothing to be confused about and massive error erodes the background of true belief against which alone failure can be construed. To appreciate the limits to the kind and amount of blunder and bad thinking we can intelligibly pin on others is to see once more the inseparability of the question what concepts a person commands and the question what he does with those concepts in the way of belief, desire, and intention. To the extent that we fail to discover a coherent and plausible pattern in the attitudes and actions of others we simply forego the chance of treating them as persons.

The problem is not bypassed but given centre stage by appeal to explicit speech behaviour. For we could not begin to decode a man's sayings if we could not make out his attitudes towards his sentences, such as holding, wishing, or wanting them to be true. Beginning from these attitudes, we must work out a theory of what he means, thus simultaneously giving content to his attitudes and to his words. In our need to make him make sense, we will try for a theory that finds him consistent, a believer of truths, and a lover of the good (all by our own lights, it goes without saying). Life being what it is, there will be no simple theory that fully meets these demands. Many theories will effect a more or less acceptable compromise, and between these theories there may be no objective grounds for choice.

The heteronomic character of general statements linking the mental and the physical traces back to this central role of translation in the description of all propositional attitudes, and to the indeterminacy of translation.[15] There are no strict psychophysical laws because of the disparate commitments of the mental and physical schemes. It is a feature of physical reality that physical change can be explained by laws that connect it with other changes and conditions physically described. It is a feature of the mental that the attribution of mental phenomena must be responsible to the background of reasons, beliefs, and intentions of the individual. There cannot be tight connections between the realms if each is to retain allegiance to its proper source of evidence. The nomological irreducibility of the mental does not derive merely from the seamless nature of the world of thought, preference and intention, for such interdependence is common to physical theory, and is compatible with there being a single right way of interpreting a man's attitudes without relativization to a scheme of translation. Nor is the irreducibility due simply to the possibility of many equally eligible schemes, for this is compatible with an arbitrary choice of one scheme relative to which assignments of mental traits are made. The point is rather that when we use the concepts of belief, desire and the rest, we must stand prepared, as the evidence accumulates, to adjust our theory in the light of considerations of overall cogency: the constitutive ideal of rationality partly controls each phase in the evolution of what must be an evolving theory. An arbitrary choice of translation scheme would preclude such opportunistic tempering of theory; put differently, a right arbitrary choice of a translation manual would be of a manual acceptable in the light of all possible evidence, and this is a choice we cannot make. We must conclude, I think, that nomological slack between the mental and the physical is essential as long as we conceive of man as a rational animal.

III

The gist of the foregoing discussion, as well as its conclusion, will be familiar. That there is a categorial difference between the mental and the physical is a commonplace. It may seem odd that I say nothing of the supposed privacy of the mental, or the special authority an agent has with respect to his own propositional attitudes, but this appearance of novelty would fade if we were to investigate in more detail the grounds for accepting a scheme of translation. The step from the categorial difference between the mental and the physical to the impossibility of strict laws relating them is less common, but certainly not new. If there is a surprise, then, it will be to find the lawlessness of the mental serving to help establish the identity of the mental with that paradigm of the lawlike, the physical.

The reasoning is this. We are assuming, under the principle of the causal dependence of the mental, that some mental events at least are causes or effects of physical events; the argument applies only to these. A second principle (of the nomological character of causality) says that each true singular causal statement is backed by a strict law connecting events of kinds to which the events mentioned as cause and effect belong. Where there are rough, but homonomic, laws, there are laws drawing on concepts from the same conceptual domain and upon which there is no improving in point of precision and comprehensiveness. We urged in the last section that such laws occur in the physical sciences. Physical theory promises to provide a comprehensive closed system guaranteed to yield a standardized description of every physical event couched in a vocabulary amenable to law.

It is not plausible that mental concepts alone can provide such a framework, simply because the mental does not, by our first principle, constitute a closed system. Too much happens to affect the mental that is not itself a systematic part of the mental. But if we combine this observation with the conclusion that no psychophysical statement is, or can be built into, a strict law, we have the principle of the anomalism of the mental: there are no strict laws at all on the basis of which we can predict and explain mental phenomena.

The demonstration of identity follows easily. Suppose *m*, a mental event, caused *p*, a physical event; then under some description *m* and *p* instantiate a strict law. This law can only be physical, according to the previous paragraph. But if *m* falls under a physical law, it has a physical description; which is to say it is a physical event. An analogous argument works when a physical event causes a mental event. So every mental event that is causally related to a physical event is a physical event. In order to establish anomalous monism in full generality it would be sufficient to show that every mental event is cause or effect of some physical event; I shall not attempt this.

If one event causes another, there is a strict law which those events instantiate when properly described. But it is possible (and typical) to know of the singular causal relation without knowing the law or the relevant descriptions. Knowledge requires reasons, but these are available in the form of rough heteronomic generalizations, which are lawlike in that instances make it reasonable to expect other instances to follow suit without being lawlike in the sense of being indefinitely refinable. Applying these facts to knowledge of identities, we see that it is possible to know that a mental event is identical with some physical event without knowing which one (in the sense of being able to give it a unique physical description that brings it under a relevant law). Even if someone knew the entire physical history of the world, and every mental event were identical with a physical, it would not follow that he could predict or explain a single mental event (so described, of course).

Two features of mental events in their relation to the physical – causal dependence and nomological independence – combine, then, to dissolve what has often seemed a paradox, the efficacy of thought and purpose in the material world, and their freedom from law. When we portray events as perceivings, rememberings, decisions and actions, we necessarily locate them amid physical happenings through the relation of cause and effect; but that same mode of portrayal insulates mental events, as long as we do not change the idiom, from the strict laws that can in principle be called upon to explain and predict physical phenomena.

Mental events as a class cannot be explained by physical science; particular mental events can when we know particular identities. But the explanations of mental events in which we are typically interested relate them to other mental events and conditions. We explain a man's free actions, for example, by appeal to his desires, habits, knowledge and perceptions. Such accounts of intentional behaviour operate in a conceptual framework removed from the direct reach of physical law by describing both cause and effect, reason and action, as aspects of a portrait of a human agent. The anomalism of the mental is thus a necessary condition for viewing action as autonomous. I conclude with a second passage from Kant:

It is an indispensable problem of speculative philosophy to show that its illusion respecting the contradiction rests on this, that we think of man in a different sense and relation when we call him free, and when we regard him as subject to the laws of nature ... It must therefore show that not only can both of these very well co-exist, but that both must be thought *as necessarily united* in the same subject ...[16]

Notes

1. I was helped and influenced by Daniel Bennett, Sue Larson, and Richard Rorty, who are not responsible for the result. My research was supported by the National Science Foundation and the Center for Advanced Study in the Behavioral Sciences.

2. *Fundamental Principles of the Metaphysics of Morals*, trans. T. K. Abbott (London, 1909), pp. 75–6.

3. These claims are defended in my 'Actions, Reasons and Causes', *The Journal of Philosophy*, LX (1963), pp. 685–700 and in 'Agency', in *Agent, Action and Reason*, ed. Robert Binkley (Toronto and Oxford, 1971).

4. In 'Causal Relations', *The Journal of Philosophy*, LXIV (1967), pp. 691–703,

I elaborate on the view of causality assumed here. The stipulation that the laws be deterministic is stronger than required by the reasoning, and will be relaxed.

5. The point depends on assuming that mental events may intelligibly be said to have a location; but it is an assumption that must be true if an identity theory is, and here I am not trying to prove the theory but to formulate it.

6. I am indebted to Lee Bowie for emphasizing this difficulty.

7. Charles Taylor, 'Mind–Body Identity, a Side Issue?', *The Philosophical Review*, LXXVI (1967), p. 202.

8. J. J. C. Smart, 'Sensations and Brain Processes', *The Philosophical Review*, LXVIII (1959), pp. 141–56. The quoted passages are on pp. 163–5 of the reprinted version in *The Philosophy of Mind*, ed. V. C. Chappell (Englewood Cliffs, N.J., 1962). For another example, see David K. Lewis, 'An Argument for the Identity Theory', *The Journal of Philosophy*, LXIII (1966), pp. 17–25. Here the assumption is made explicit when Lewis takes events as universals (p. 17, footnotes 1 and 2). I do not suggest that Smart and Lewis are confused, only that their way of stating the identity theory tends to obscure the distinction between particular events and kinds of events on which the formulation of my theory depends.

9. Jaegwon Kim, 'On the Psycho–Physical Identity Theory', *American Philosophical Quarterly*, III (1966), p. 231.

10. Ibid., pp. 227–8. Richard Brandt and Jaegwon Kim propose roughly the same criterion in 'The Logic of the Identity Theory', *The Journal of Philosophy* LIV (1967), pp. 515–37. They remark that on their conception of event identity, the identity theory 'makes a stronger claim than merely that there is a pervasive phenomenal-physical correlation' (p. 518). I do not discuss the stronger claim.

11. Anomalous monism is more or less explicitly recognized as a possible position by Herbert Feigl 'The "Mental" and the "Physical"', in *Concepts, Theories and the Mind–Body Problem*, vol. II, *Minnesota Studies in the Philosophy of Science* (Minneapolis, 1958); Sydney Shoemaker, 'Ziff's Other Minds', *The Journal of Philosophy*, LXII (1965), p. 589; David Randall Luce, 'Mind–Body Identity and Psycho-Physical Correlation', *Philosophical Studies*, XVII (1966), pp. 1–7; Charles Taylor, op. cit., p. 207. Something like my position is tentatively accepted by Thomas Nagel, 'Physicalism', *The Philosophical Review*, LXXIV (1965), pp. 339–56, and briefly endorsed by P. F. Strawson in *Freedom and the Will*, ed. D. F. Pears (London, 1963), pp. 63–7.

12. The point that substitutivity of identity fails in the context of explanation is made in connection with the present subject by Norman Malcolm, 'Scientific Materialism and the Identity Theory', *Dialogue*, III (1964–5), pp. 123–4. See also my 'Actions, Reasons and Causes', *The Journal of Philosophy*, LX (1963), pp. 696–9 and 'The Individuation of Events' in *Essays in Honor of Carl G. Hempel*, ed. N. Rescher et al. (Dordrecht, 1969).

13. The theme is developed in Roderick Chisholm, *Perceiving* (Ithaca, New York, 1957), chap. 11.

14. This view is accepted by Richard C. Jeffrey, 'Goodman's Query', *The Journal of Philosophy*, LXII (1966), p. 286 ff., John R. Wallace, 'Goodman, Logic, Induction', same journal and issue, p. 318, and John M. Vickers, 'Characteristics of Projectible Predicates', *The Journal of Philosophy*, LXIV (1967), p. 285. On pp. 328–9 and 286–7 of these journal issues respectively Goodman disputes the lawlikeness of statements like 'All emerires are grue'. I cannot see, however, that he meets the point of my 'Emeroses by Other Names', *The Journal of Philosophy*, LXIII (1966), pp. 778–80.

15. The influence of W. V. Quine's doctrine of the indeterminacy of translation, as in Chapter 2 of *Word and Object* (Cambridge, Mass., 1960), is, I hope, obvious. In §45 Quine develops the connection between translation and the propositional attitudes, and remarks that 'Brentano's thesis of the irreducibility of intentional idioms is of a piece with the thesis of indeterminacy of translation' (p. 221).

16. Op. cit., p. 76.

Biographical Note

Donald Davidson is University Professor of Philosophy at the University of Chicago. He has in the past been a Professor at Rockefeller University and also taught at Princeton and Stanford Universities and at Queen's College. He has been a Visiting Professor at Tokyo, Adelaide and elsewhere, and has given the John Locke lectures in Oxford. He is the author, with Patrick Suppes, of *Decision Making: An Experimental Approach* (1957). He has also written many articles, and is co-editor of a number of books, *Words and Objections* (1969), *Semantics for Natural Language* (1970) and *The Logic of Grammar* (1975).

Further Reading

Readers may wish to consult Davidson's 'Psychology as Philosophy', in *Philosophy of Psychology* (London: Macmillan, 1974), edited by S. C. Brown, reprinted in *The Philosophy of Mind* (Oxford: University Press, 1976) edited by Jonathan Glover, and 'The Material Mind' in *Philosophy of Science IV* (Amsterdam: North Holland Publishing Co., 1973) edited by P. Suppes et al., both of which essays are along some of the lines of 'Mental Events'. Also relevant are Davidson's essays mentioned in notes 3, 4 and 12 above, and also: 'Truth and Meaning', *Synthese* XVII (1967); 'On the Very Idea of a Conceptual Scheme', in *Proceedings and Addresses of the American Philosophical Association*, 47 (1974); 'Radical Interpretation', *Dialectica* XVII (1973); 'Thought and Talk', in *Mind and Language* (Oxford: Clarendon Press, 1975), edited by Samuel Guttenplan; 'Freedom to Act', in *Essays on Freedom of Action* (London: Routledge & Kegan Paul, 1973) edited by Ted Honderich.

Ted Honderich

One Determinism

'Determinism' is a name for a family of doctrines which some philosophers have professed to find too obscure to merit really serious concern, while some others have supposed they understood them well enough to be sure they must be false. Many philosophers, some inclined to take a side and some uncertain whether all the doctrines are true or false, have agreed on this, that doctrines of determinism are intolerable. The essay below, in answer, sets out to supply a single clear doctrine of determinism, and to say why it is true, and to suggest why it will come to be tolerable.

The essay thus has a feature which would be unremarkable, save for its being mentioned, to many who are not philosophers. That is, it does deal with the question of the truth of determinism, to the small extent that this can be done within the compass of an essay. It goes beyond conceptual clarification and takes up the issue of fact. Until recently this would have been held to be a trespass outside the boundaries of philosophy. One mark of the opening up of broader philosophical perspectives in recent years is that such self-confinement within the conceptual domain is no longer so much practised.

The determinism sketched in the essay consists of three premises and several conclusions, the latter being closely related to one another. The first section of the essay expounds the premise with which it is most convenient to begin, although it is most naturally listed as the second. The correlation thesis is to the effect that it is not chance or mere probability that when a certain purely physical process is occurring in a man's brain, he is thinking or feeling or deciding or doing a certain thing, and not something else. Matter and mind, or rather mind and *some* matter, go together. They go together as a result of natural or scientific law. They are connected or correlated in the way, say, that the heating and the expansion of a metal coin are connected or correlated, or the temperature and the pressure of a gas. This is not to say that the mind *is* the brain, that conscious occurrents *are* electrochemical processes, whatever those puzzling utterances about identity may come to.

It is maintained that the correlation thesis should no longer be a matter of controversy. This is so, according to the essay, for the reason of the existence of the science of neurophysiology. There may be nothing in it that will *refute*, neatly and once and for all, the idea that there exist what might be called 'free-floating' conscious occurrents. (Such inconclusive states of affairs are far from unknown in science.) However, all the evidence is against occurrents with no physical correlates, and it is very pertinent that of many philosophers anxious to preserve 'the freedom of the will', few have chosen to oppose the correlation thesis.

The second section of the essay also has to do with brain processes, and, more particularly, with the states which comprise these processes. Each brain state, according to another premise of the given determinism, was an effect of a previous set of physical conditions, some of them being brain states themselves. This set of conditions was sufficient for the brain state. Furthermore, each of the conditions in the set was itself such an effect of a prior set and so on back.

To say a brain state is the effect of sufficient or necessitating conditions is to say that it stands to those conditions in the way that the lighting of a match stands to some set of conditions which includes the match's being struck, its being dry, there being oxygen present, and so on. As one would ordinarily say, the lighting of the match *had to happen* or was *necessary*, once all the conditions obtained. Many philosophers have supposed that this connection amounts to an instance of a 'constant conjunction'. That is, they have supposed that to say an event *E* was made necessary by a condition-set *C* is to say that condition-sets like *C* are constantly or always conjoined with or followed by *E*-like events.

The first two premises taken together are in conflict with the traditional doctrine of libertarianism or freewill. That doctrine, in one form, is that some or all of a person's choices are creations of the self or the will, which creations, whatever else may be said of them, are not *caused* to happen. The essay maintains that enough can be said to confirm the two premises and hence to disconfirm libertarianism. If we accept the two premises, further, we must give up something else. We must give up certain traditional philosophical accounts of the relationship of mind and matter, but, it is said, this does not count as a penalty. The positions that remain open to us are in any case the most plausible. We *may* choose a *certain* identity theory as best satisfying, consistently with the two theses, our conviction that it is thoughts and feelings, to speak only of those occurrents, and not something *separate*, brain processes, which give rise to other thoughts and feelings.

The third section of the essay is concerned with the third premise, that our actions are necessitated by sets of conditions which include brain states. An action is taken to be just a bodily movement, or sequence of movements, although one related to an intention. An action is not something more encompassing, as has been supposed by some philosophers.

To bring together the three premises into a single example of a certain kind, we have this: each state of a particular brain process *BP* was the effect of a sufficient physical condition, and hence of a physical sequence going back in time to before the birth of the person; *BP* inevitably was accompanied by a certain correlate, the man's thinking that he would vote for the Labour Party; finally, and roughly speaking, his act of reporting this thought to his wife was a sequence of movements each one the effect of sufficient physical conditions, some of these conditions comprising or being part of process *BP*.

The remaining sections of the essay have to do with what follows from the three premises. It may come as a surprise to some that many philosophers would answer that what follows from the premises is nothing much. They would say that it does *not* follow that we cannot decide or act otherwise than we do, or that we are not free or not responsible for our actions.

It all depends on what meanings are given to the words 'cannot', 'free' and 'responsible'. It is one burden of the last sections of the essay that if we persist in certain natural and relevant meanings for these key words, the meanings called for by certain fundamental interests we have, it follows that we cannot decide or act otherwise than we do, that we are not free, and that we are not responsible for our actions. This needs some argument, and some is given. It has to do with explanation and individuality.

For many, no doubt, these are intolerably dark conclusions. It has been said, in fact, that they go against the possibility of any recognizably human existence. However, we cannot *decide*, simply in order to make life tolerable, that one proposition does or does not follow from another. Belief is involuntary rather than a matter of decision. This fact does not depend at all on determinism and is certainly recognized by others than determinists. There does exist something or other called self-deception, to be sure, but it does not obscure the fact that one cannot choose to believe what one wants. This is not a matter of principle nor of honour. It would indeed be a silliness to suppose that we have an obligation to believe what we find to be true. We cannot do otherwise; if we find something to be true, we are stuck with it.

Still, that is not quite all. The essay ends with remarks about the seeming darkness of the conclusions. Despair is not required, it is suggested, and the idea that it may nevertheless be in place will in time disappear.

T.H.

Ted Honderich

One Determinism

From *Essays on Freedom of Action* edited by Ted Honderich © Routledge & Kegan Paul Ltd, 1973. Reprinted by permission of the author and publisher. Revised for this printing.

States of the brain are in the first place *effects*, the effects of other physical states, including other states of the brain. Many states of the brain, secondly, make up *correlates*. Hence a particular sequence of states, making up a brain process, accompanied my experience the other moment of thinking about having walked a lot on Hampstead Heath, and any identical brain process in the future will be accompanied by a like bit of thinking about having walked a lot on Hampstead Heath. States of the brain, thirdly, are *causes*, both of other states of the brain, as already remarked, and of certain movements of one's body. The latter are actions. Some of these are relatively simple while others, such as speech-acts and bits of ritual, depend on settings of convention and have complex histories. Simple or complex, however, all actions are movements, or stillnesses, caused by states of the brain. It follows from these three premises, about states of the brain as effects, as correlates, and as causes, that on every occasion when we decide or choose, we can only decide or choose as in fact we do. So with our actions. The ones we actually do are the only ones that we can do. It follows too that we are not responsible for our decisions, choices or actions, and, what is most fundamental, that we do not possess selves of a certain character.

Determinism, one version of determinism,[1] can be expressed in these sentences, the latter of which contain belaboured terms, notably 'can' and 'responsible', which can also be put to other uses. The excessively simple and schematic diagram below represents the three premises of this determinism. It may be useful in forestalling certain misunderstandings, although at the risk of giving rise to others.

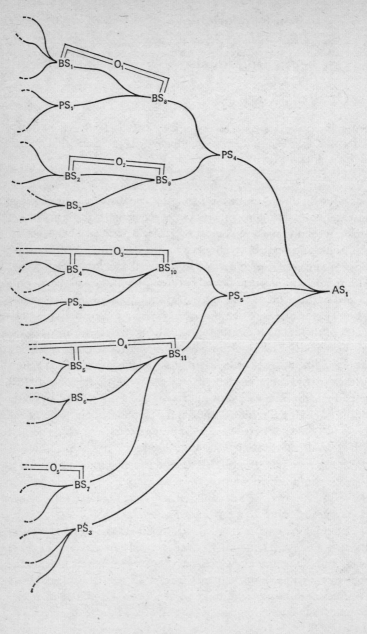

AS_1 is a particular physical state, one of a sequence of states which comprised a particular action, perhaps your turning the page a few moments ago, or saying a word to someone. AS_1 may be regarded as an initial state of the process or movement which was the action. In order to simplify the diagram it is the only action-state shown, and hence only a first bit of the whole action is shown. AS_1 is given in the diagram as the effect of three prior physical states, PS_4, PS_5 and PS_3, which together make up a causally sufficient or necessitating condition for it. Each of these three states it itself the effect of an earlier sufficient condition. PS_4 is thus the effect of BS_8 and BS_9, which are brain states. The brain process which consists of the brain states BS_1 and BS_8 has as a simultaneous correlate a conscious experience or occurrent O_1, perhaps a momentary perception. The diagram represents the very last bit, an exceedingly tiny bit, of the causal sequence which issued in action state AS_1. The earliest states shown, BS_1 and those in a line underneath it, must of course be regarded as effects of earlier sufficient conditions, also of a physical kind, and so on back. AS_1, on the other hand, will of course be taken as causing a later state of the action of which it was a part.

In what follows, incidentally, I shall speak in an ordinary way of causes. That is, a cause will be taken to be a chosen member of some set of conditions which is sufficient to produce an event or state. To say of a state that it had a cause is to imply, rather than assert, that the state was the effect of some sufficient set of conditions. It will make no substantial difference if one understands sufficiency in terms of constant conjunction or in terms of some stronger notion. The latter course is taken when one understands the statement, say, that a particular brain state caused an action-state, in some such way as this: the brain state occurred, as did the action-state, and the action-state would still have followed the brain state and the other conditions, whatever logically consistent circumstances had obtained.[2] The sufficiency relation, somehow understood, enters into lawlike connections or relations generally, of course, and not just those where the terms are an effect and its set of conditions. It is worth adding that in all such connections the terms must in a fundamental sense comprise two things rather than one. Without two independent entities, there cannot be the required kind of relationship. This will be of some significance in what follows.

The sketched conception of determinism, when it has been set out more fully, will go some way toward meeting the supposition that determinism is not in need of serious attention because it is irredeemably obscure or indeed incoherent.[3] It will also be clearer in the end how determinism, or anyway one determinism, is related to certain traditional philosophical pictures of mind, and clear that it does not rest on certain notions which are at least controversial, such as those of Freudian psychology. My other particular intentions in this essay, insofar as clarification is in question, have to do with movement and action, the word 'can', and the idea of responsibility.

Arguments for the truth of the determinism in question are not to be construed as anything else, and in particular not as urgings of a kind of primacy or of fundamentality. Determinism is but one characterization of human existence. There are many others, and they are as enlightening or more enlightening. With respect to the determinist characterization, it is a travesty of empiricism to declare, as do some who have been too taken by a kind of science, that when all is said and done, or at bottom, men are merely homeostatic machines. Appearances are otherwise, and here at least we may side with Oscar Wilde in the proposition that it is only shallow people who do not judge things by their appearances.

I The Correlation Thesis

It may be best to begin with the middle one of our three premises, which we may call the correlation thesis. It is to the effect that there exists, for each conscious occurrent, a simultaneous, theoretically discriminable brain correlate. An occurrent is simply anything that a person can discriminate in consciousness, however simple or complex. Some examples are my awareness, a moment ago, that the wall is blue, my thinking of being at home in England, feeling puzzled or warm or angry, wanting something, deciding something. Occurrents are dateable particulars, owned by particular persons. They are not types, but rather instances of types. An instance is not identified by the fact that it falls under a certain ordinary description. Despite certain reasonable presumptions, it is not necessarily true, of two occasions when I truly report that I feel puzzled about what my father said, that the two occurrents are identical, of the same type. Nor is it necessary, of course, that two occurrents are of the same type when two persons truly report, for example, that they feel warm. Two occurrents *are* of the same type when the person in question cannot distinguish between them qualitatively, or when they are such that if a single person owned them, he could not distinguish between them qualitatively.

A neurophysiologist's version of the correlation thesis would be a large affair. Brain injuries and also a good deal of research have established that the normal brain possesses redundant capability. A particular function which ordinarily is that of one part of the brain can be taken over by another part. For these and other reasons, even an amateur's version of the correlation thesis must allow the possibility that not just one type of brain process, but rather some set of process-types related to each type of occurrent. This is certainly not to say that any mentioned type of brain process is related to a set of types of occurrents. The relation between types of occurrents and types of brain processes is never many–one, but often one–many.

Ordinary brain function, further, is in a certain sense diffuse. There is no question of the entire physical correlate of, say, one thought being found in one micro-locale of the brain. The correlation thesis should not be taken to imply any such thing. A developed version of the thesis would take into account the true complication. Again, it seems likely that further description of brain activity will require something other than an atomistic or reductionist model. What I have in mind here is only that the further description will not be of elements all of which exist at some one level. There are, no doubt, different properties at different levels. This too, if it is not too vague, would be represented in the correlation thesis as stated by a neurophysiologist.[4]

It is perhaps a touch contentious to label the physical correlates as states or processes of a part or the whole of *the brain*. Given certain propositions in contemporary neurophysiology, and an inclination to caution, we might better talk of states and processes of the central nervous system. The term *part*, in any case, as used of the brain, is no more than a stand-in for other more adequate descriptions. Nothing substantial hangs on these points and so I shall persist in a traditional usage. Finally, by way of caveats, or rather examples of caveats, it is true enough that there are old problems of several kinds concerning the individuation of conscious occurrents, and the truth conditions for statements about them. To my mind these problems are not impediments to us, and I shall not discuss them in this essay.

The correlation thesis can be stated, then, as this:

Any type of occurrent obtains in the conscious life of an individual if and only if one of a set of types of processes obtains in his brain.

This allows the possibility that a dream image may be accompanied by any of three or indeed thirty processes on different occasions, although not by any process. Since a set may have only one member, it also allows the possibility that an occurrent-type is accompanied by only one type of process. It does not allow something else, that any particular process of the set may be accompanied on different occasions by different occurrents, say different dream images.

It is essential, of course, that we take the words 'if and only if' in the statement of the correlation thesis as having a particular meaning. They are not to be taken as meaning that there is a logical or conceptual connection between occurrent and processes. The words 'if and only if' signify just this: that there is some lawlike connection between occurrents and processes. The connection is a matter of natural or scientific law. The thesis might less comfortably but more accurately be called the thesis of lawlike correlation.

The correlation thesis is of course consistent with certain traditional dualistic pictures of mind. The first is epiphenomenalism, roughly the proposition that brain processes cause simultaneous conscious occurrents. The second, sometimes called mentalism, is roughly the proposition that occurrents cause simultaneous brain processes. The third, as shop-worn and obscure as the others, is that there is interaction. Some brain processes cause some occurrents, and some occurrents cause some processes. The correlation thesis is consistent, too, with one thing that might be called a monistic theory of mind, or an identity theory, but certainly not consistent with something else that might be so-called. There is more to be said of these various pictures of mind, but I shall put it off for a time.

To pass on to the truth of the correlation thesis, one can imagine a very stern objector who demands a confirmation beginning with a physical description of a really decent brain process: one correlated, say, with someone's liking Bertorelli's Restaurant, or one for a man's deciding not to pay taxes to a government waging an unjust war. Such demands, of course, cannot be met. Nor, even in the future states of neurophysiology that can now be anticipated, are they likely to be met. This does not matter much. What is to be confirmed is that for each occurrent there is a correlate.[5] What is to be confirmed is that there exists, for each discriminable type of conscious occurrent, a theoretically discriminable physical correlate, a certain set of types of brain processes. This generalization can be confirmed without each or even many of its instances being confirmed.

On the basis of evidence of several kinds, one can extrapolate to the conclusion that there exists, for each and every occurrent-type, a set of types of brain processes. It would indeed be jejune to suppose that either the data we can have, or the principles of non-deductive inference, are capable of such precise formulation that propositions of this character can be 'proved'. What one can say is that the evidence is all one way and that an acceptance of the proposition in question is unavoidable. Since some will disagree, I shall sketch a part of the evidence.

One does not need neurophysiology in order to find in oneself a rational inclination towards belief in the correlation thesis. We share the conviction, almost all of us, that all consciousness, whatever more may be said of it, is correlated with the existence of a functioning brain. That is, roughly, we do not get what can decently be described as consciousness without a functioning brain, and vice versa. It requires no audacity to assert that all the evidence we have, here below, is in favour of this proposition. It hardly needs adding that the correlation is a correlation of natural law, not of accident or of mere probability, however high.

Secondly, we accept many correlations of a more particular kind, or at any rate, we will accept them after a bit of reflection. Suppose that two people are well placed to see the Empire State Building.

One reports that he does see it, and the other reports that he does not see anything at all of the sort. After a certain amount of inquiry we may accept that the capabilities of the second man, his perceptual capabilities, are in some way impaired, and that if they were corrected, so as to be put back more or less in line with those of the first man, he would see something of a certain sort. If we regard the claim that for the man to exercise the capabilities in question is for some physical sequence to occur, one which includes light transmission, events in the retina, and subsequent events in the central nervous system, we are led to the conclusion that processes of the brain are correlated with a certain occurrent, the having of certain visual experience. We are led toward the conclusion that it is in general true of persons that certain brain processes obtain if and only if they are having certain visual experience.

Facts of this kind, and the previous fact about consciousness generally, cannot but lead one towards the correlation thesis. So long as it is sharply distinguished from certain implausibilities, such as that identical occurrents obtain whenever we speak in an ordinary way of having the same experience, the thesis has the support of what might be called reflective common sense.

There is also neurophysiology, whose recent textbooks will have to go without recapitulation.[6] To have a reasonable grasp of the evidence, one must have some understanding of neurophysiology's breadth and richness. I shall, as a poor substitute, give several unrelated instances in order to indicate that some physical description of some correlates of consciousness is available. It is to be allowed, of course, that neurophysiology is a changing and progressing inquiry. It is no more a corpus of settled truths, no more devoid of dispute and speculation, than any other live science. However, if it would be absurd to see it as some finished work of indubitable truths, it would be equally absurd to regard it as a congeries of possibilities, some suitable for use no matter which way the mind of a philosopher may turn. Many of the propositions of neurophysiology are beyond question and certainly what might be called the philosophical consequence of neurophysiology is clear.

(1) It is possible, even in the present stage of research, to provide a considerable physical description of a physical process which obtains

if the owner of the brain does satisfy the description of *being conscious*. If an individual is conscious what is labelled as the reticular activating system is in a certain ongoing condition, one that is open to physical description. What we have is something close to a locatable site of consciousness and an account of what electrochemical states must obtain in this part of the brain for the person to be conscious. The system in question is the subject of many unanswered questions, and of many uneasinesses that are not yet clear questions. In this, I suppose, it is not unlike those other sources of mystery, physical states generally, not only those in neurophysiology.

(2) It was supposed of early experiments in the electro-stimulation of the hypothalamus in lower animals that all that was produced was 'sham' emotion. That is, implanted electrodes were thought to produce only what are taken to be, under ordinary conditions, the *behavioural manifestations* of emotion. Such resistance is no longer possible. Further investigation of lower animals, much of it morally offensive, has produced very considerable findings. Also, treatment of mentally ill persons has resulted in the identification of what are often called, if too loosely, the centres of pleasure and pain in the human brain. Electrical stimulation at various points produces satisfaction, relaxation, restlessness, fright and other discriminable emotional states. What we have, then, is something like an adequate identification of brain processes correlated with certain states of consciousness.

(3) There are also Penfield's results having to do with the eliciting of past experiences.[7] Again as a result of exact electro-stimulation, subjects have experiences which are related to ordinary remembering but of a greatly more vivid nature. These are experiences which have precise conceptual content. As long as stimulation continues, thereby producing a certain electrical state, there occurs a sequential 're-experiencing' of a previously forgotten period of ordinary life. The 're-experiencing' ends with the ending of stimulation. It may begin again, where it began in the first instance of stimulation, if stimulation is begun again.

(4) Finally, there is absolutely no evidence to be found in neurophysiology that goes against the correlation thesis.

Despite all that can be said of this character, it remains a possibility for someone to maintain that the thesis is false, that there are *certain* occurrents that lack physical correlates. In the past, even the recent past, candidates would have been drawn from moral experience, perhaps the experience of resolving a conflict of duty and desire. Today, some may be inclined to take a similar line with higher kinds of intellectual performance, or judgements that depend for their sense on institutions of a culture. It seems that a rational persistence in such a view is impossible. Who can believe, to take one consequence of denying the thesis, that one's judgement on some occasion, of *whatever* character, might have been different in some respect without one's brain having been in a different state? Since this is on a par with a belief in ghosts, I am inclined to feel that I have already offended against Hume's dictum that next to the ridicule of denying an evident truth is the ridicule of taking much pains to defend it.

II   The Causation of Brain States

We have so far looked at one premise of the determinism being advanced. Another, to which we now turn, is the proposition that brain states are themselves the effects of other physical states. This is unlikely to be confused with other things and it is not, in itself, about consciousness. For these reasons we may proceed a bit more briskly. I shall take it, as might have been mentioned above, that a physical state is one, roughly, which has location in space. (Consciousness is to be conceived in terms of what can be called relational existence; very roughly, it is that which exists *to* or *for*, or has to-ness or for-ness.)

Those states which are causes of brain states fall into whole ranges of useful classifications. Let us notice only a taxonomy of three broad groupings. There are those causal states that are members of sets of conditions sufficient for the generation of a person with a functioning brain. Second, there are causal states of such a person, not brain states themselves, which contribute to the ongoing sequence of brain states. Third, there are those causal states which are themselves brain states.

Examples of states of the first grouping, to begin at the beginning, can be had from a single human cell, whose structure is open to physical descriptions of different specificity and different degrees of confirmation. A particular effect already mentioned is that particular brain state correlated with consciousness generally, a state of the reticular activating system. An example of a state in the second grouping, or examples of several such states, can be had from an ordinary sequence beginning with a touch-receptor. Pressure on hair results in a change of orientation of appendages, the production of an electrical potential, and, in the end, certain events in the brain. These events are correlated with tactile awareness. There are a great many known connections of this kind. An example of a causal state in the third grouping (those which are themselves brain states) is a state of the cortex, one which cannot be described except in the higher technicalities of neurophysiology and is correlated with learning. The effects in question are brain states correlated with certain performances.

We do not know what causal connections hold between physical states and the brain states that are correlated with very specific higher mental events, such events as noticing the date or speculating that America is a plutocracy. The general thesis that each brain state is the effect of some set of sufficient conditions is the result of extrapolatory argument of several kinds. The premises for the extrapolation come from ordinary belief, which is not to be disdained, and, as we have just seen, from neurophysiology. There are also premises of a certain character to be had from the history of the life-sciences, including such episodes as the defeat of vitalism. These premises, indeed, are of great importance. We may also add something that might have been included in the discussion of the correlation thesis, research in the mechanical simulation of intelligence. It is of considerable importance to our present concern, given our ignorance of the brain, which must not be minimized, and in particular our ignorance of the causal relations between brain states. The central point is that complex and sophisticated problem-solving, of a kind once thought to be exclusively a matter of competences associated with consciousness, is a function of physical states which indubitably are the effects of other physical states.

The thesis that all brain states are the effects of other physical conditions, unlike the thesis about correlation, runs up against a certain amount of philosophical and indeed quite ordinary inclination and conviction. It is here that one encounters both libertarianism and also something much more substantial, a good deal of less-clear doctrine held by both philosophers and others. Certainly, we assign efficacy of some kind to conscious occurrents. We are wont to believe that thoughts and feelings, somehow or other, produce other thoughts and feelings.

There are several responses open to anyone who accepts both correlation and the thesis that brain states are effects of other physical states. It may be argued, first, that while kinds of relations between different occurrents are undeniable, there is no point in assigning *efficacy* to occurrents. We already have all we need of efficacy, and efficacy that can be understood. That is, we may explain that it is *as if* one thought gives rise to another because the brain process correlated with the first thought stands in ordinary causal relations with the brain process correlated with the second thought. There is the appearance of efficacy because of correlation with that which is causally connected. It is worth adding, to make this epiphenomenalism more tolerable, that while we as persons do ordinarily identify with our thoughts, we can also identify with our brain processes. It is not as if persons as agents were being ushered off the scene.

This response can be added to, and so become a kind of monistic theory of mind. On this theory, there is one thing, A, that has certain electrochemical properties and also has properties that are in question when we say, for example, that a man is thinking of a glass of wine. What is A? One can describe it, partially, as electrochemical activity in the brain. One can also describe it, partially, as thinking of a glass of wine. There is no more to it than properties that are brought in by these two descriptions. We need not inquire further into the rationale of speaking of A as one thing. To do so, obviously, must be to do something consistent with the first set of properties being different in number from the second, since lawlike relation is in question.

There is also a different response, perhaps that one which is most uncomfortable. A determinist can allow the possibility of over-determination, in some enlarged sense, of the brain states correlated with occurrents. That is, it can be allowed that these states are not only the effects of sufficient physical conditions but also in some sense the products of occurrents. There are problems about the very conception of over-determination, admittedly, and still more severe difficulties about the present use of the conception. We are offered the supposition that a certain physical state, a brain state, is the effect of a set of sufficient conditions of a physical nature and also has some other sufficient genesis in consciousness. The first of these propositions, by comparison, is a paradigm of clarity. The second is a matter of mystery, that same mystery that shrouds the three dualist pictures of mind mentioned above.

The main point upon which I wish to insist is that there is one ground rule in all of this. One must take it as true that brain states are effects of sufficient physical conditions. This second thesis of our determinism is not an attractive proposition, but a denial of it is quixotic. It is well confirmed, and, as I have indicated, it is in accord with whole bodies of established theory. I mean, of course, bodies of theory of the physical world and of persons as physical systems. The thesis that brain states are effects of a certain kind is as well supported as the correlation thesis. It is no surprise that many contemporary philosophers wishing to break a lance for responsibility have done so in another field. Even in the absence of decently articulated premises of determinism, they have chosen to offer resistance elsewhere instead, in the matter of conceptions of action and responsibility, to which we shall come. *If* our theses about correlation and causation gave us *no* possibility of explaining the seeming efficacy of conscious states, the theses would be vulnerable. That there are possibilities of explanation, however uncomfortable, allows the theses to remain what they are: incontrovertible on the evidence that we have.

The correlation thesis, to recall, leaves open to us certain traditional pictures of mind. The addition of the second thesis excludes two of these pictures, at any rate if they are given clear edges. One picture that must go is mentalism, construed as the conjunctive proposition that conscious occurrents have efficacy with respect to brain states *and* those brain states lack sufficient conditions of a physical nature. This loss, I take it, is not alarming. Our other loss, if it is such, is interactionism, construed in part as the proposition that *some* brain states derive from occurrents and are not effects of sufficient physical conditions. This picture derives, no doubt, from the fact that some occurrents are customarily talked of as causes while others are talked of as effects. My deciding to avoid 42nd Street makes me think of other routes, but my seeing stars is made to happen by my bumping my head. One is tempted to feel that this particular picture is no more than an unnecessary state of philosophical dither, produced by paying too much attention to what we customarily say. A discontinuity of the supposed kind flies in the face of factual consistency. It is unthinkable that some occurrents should derive from occurrents and others from causes wholly different in kind.

What is also closed to us, in this case by the correlation thesis itself, is another kind of monistic theory of mind. To proceed in terms of the example of a moment ago, this identity theory is to the effect that the electrochemical properties *are* the mental properties in question when we say the man is thinking of a glass of wine. This theory, whatever else is to be said of it, or more likely against it,[8] does not allow for lawlike connection between the property-sets. Lawlike connection requires two things. If the theory were tolerable, of course, it would explain very simply our feelings about the efficacy of occurrents. That efficacy would be identifiable with the causal powers of brain states.

We now have an idea of how our determinism stands to certain traditional pictures of mind. This is a matter of its first two premises. It is arguable that it leaves open the only possibilities that on independent grounds are worth considering.

III   Actions as Effects of Brain States

There remains to be considered the third and last premise, that brain states cause certain body movements and stillnesses. They cause, to speak more particularly, each of the states which comprise such movements and stillnesses. Let us stick to movements. It is not true, obviously, even if we restrict ourselves to externally visible movements, that all of them are caused by brain states. This is so for several reasons. For example, it is well known that the nervous system includes what are called reflex arcs. Movements of the limbs, which usually have a different genesis, are sometimes 'reflexes': consequences of a sequence that begins in a receptor mechanism, ends in musculature, and does not get there by way of the usual brain functions.

It is equally certain that many movements, for example those of my fingers in typing this essay, are the effects of brain states. Any such assertion, at any rate in an essay on determinism, is bound to call up an anticipatory retort. It is commonplace to find it admitted that body movements of the kind in question are effects, products of sufficient conditions whose nature is left unclear. We are told, however, that this admission is of no use to the determinist. It is of no use because it itself is not, and it does not entail, the proposition that *actions* are caused. Determinism, it is supposed, requires the latter proposition. What I wish to suggest is that if certain movements are caused, then actions are caused, because the movements *are* the actions.

Why is it supposed that movements cannot be actions? One main reason can be brought out by noticing that *the same movement*, in one sense of those words, may occur both in the knee-jerk reflex and in the action of moving one's lower leg. Therefore, it is supposed, since there is no action at all in the first case but only a movement, it cannot be that the same movement which occurs in the second case is the action. All that needs to be said about this is that there is a perfectly clear sense in which *the same movement* does *not* occur in the two cases. It may be that the two movements are identical, that they are instances of the same movement-type, in that they would leave the same record on the film of a movie camera. They are not identical or instances of the same movement-type, in that one does not *derive from intention* and one does. We need not pursue the analyses of what it is to *have an intention* and what it is for a movement to *derive from intention*. Having an intention appears to be a matter of wants and beliefs, including beliefs of several kinds. A movement, if it derives from an intention, falls under some description that is related to a description of an intention. Neither of these comments is near to being adequate. Still, what we do need, and what we certainly have, is a grasp of ordinary truth-conditions governing the ascription of intentions and the description of movements as deriving from intention. We distinguish actions from those movements which are not actions.

The main point, that there is no difficulty in regarding actions as movements, can be made with respect to slightly more familiar examples. In one sense, *the same movement* can enter into these four actions: switching on the floor lamp, switching it from dim to medium, switching it from medium to bright, switching it off. The camera will record the same flick of the fingers on each occasion. These are, none the less, four different movements in the sense that each derives from a different intention. That it also makes sense to say they are not different movements does not affect the issue. That two 1967 Dodge Coronet station-wagons are not different as cars does not prevent us from distinguishing them. They can be distinguished as the one that is yours and the one that is mine.

It can certainly be granted that it would be mistaken to identify the class of actions with any class of movements whose selection did not bring in intention. It would be equally mistaken, obviously, to suppose that one could conclude, from such properties of a particular movement as those that might appear on film, that it was a particular action. This is nothing to the point.

What I wish to maintain, then, is that actions, which are certain movements, are caused by brain states. They are caused by states which enter into the brain processes, correlated with intentions to perform the actions. Given the amount of consternation about action in the philosophy of mind, it will be as well to rule out some possible confusions. (1) It is not being maintained, certainly, that we ordinarily individuate actions by first picking out movements and then by finding out if they are effects of brain states. It can be granted that we never individuate actions in such a way. Nor, obviously, is any such thing required for the argument. (2) Nor is it important that in order to provide evidence for the contention that actions are effects of brain states, a neurophysiologist must begin by picking out actions in the ordinary way. This is not denied. Having done so, he can proceed to establish that the movements in question, while in some way intentional, are also effects of states of the brain. (3) It is not being supposed, either, that the determinist argues in this way: movement M, identified only by such as its film properties, has a cause, and therefore action A is caused. If only because of the one–many relation between movements with those film properties, on the one hand, and actions, this would be difficult. All that is supposed is that there are movements which derive from certain intentions, and are individuated in this way, and that they have certain causes.[9]

As for the truth of the causal claim about actions, what we have is an evidence situation very much of the kind mentioned in connection with previous propositions. Again, we lack knowledge of precisely what particular conditions give rise to particular actions, such actions as giving a hopeful answer, buying a ticket, pressing the button to explode the charge. The evidence we do have, which is of several kinds, is sufficient for a general conclusion. Neurophysiology, as many will be aware, has passed well beyond the stage of the familiar maps of the brain which assign kinds of motor function to particular parts. I take it that no serious question can be raised about the truth of our third premise. Each and every action is a movement, or a still-ness, or of course a sequence of movements or stillnesses, caused by states of the brain.

None the less, this discussion of action may be taken by some to be paradoxical. Surely, it may be said, it is eccentric to reduce the com-plexity of action to the simplicity of movement, eccentric to reduce the *experiential* character of action, which is inescapable, to the facts of matter in motion. Signing a contract, uttering a supplication, making love, putting on the brakes, committing an offence – surely it must be distortion to see these actions and activities merely as mat-ters of movement. It must then be entirely mistaken to conclude from the premise of caused movements that actions too are caused.

The correct response is that it would be more than eccentric to reduce action and its character to the simplicity of matter in motion. Nothing of the sort has been attempted. It can certainly be granted that one could give only the most impoverished account of human existence, or that existence of which action is a part, if one fastened on only such features of certain movements as those which turn up on film. These movements have their place in our attitudes by virtue of what precedes and accompanies them, and does not turn up on film: the complex processes of consciousness, the correlates of certain physical states. A determinist, furthermore, if he were to content himself with the proposition that actions are effects, would fail to direct his guiding principle to that which is of greatest importance. He would fail, indeed, to state a determinism. This would be so for the reason that it would remain possible to give something other than a deterministic account of the occurrence of the *causes* of action.

The determinism that has been advanced here is not in this way incomplete. (1) Actions are movements caused by states of the brain. (2) These latter, the physical correlates of consciousness, are themselves the effects of other physical states, many of which are likely to be correlates themselves. The propositions expressed in these two sentences have as their subject-matter the whole of human experience. They do not pertain only to a reduced subject-matter. To think that they do, at this point, can only be the consequence of fixing attention on the first proposition to the exclusion of the second.

IV 'Can'

Let us turn to what follows from the premises we have. The first conclusion, if it is rightly so called, is that whenever we decide or act, we can only decide or act as we do. Initially, let us consider actions alone. There are, certainly, uses of 'can' such that it does *not* follow from the premises that one can only act as one does. What I wish to assert at this juncture, if only for purposes of clarification, is that there is one use of 'can' such that it does follow from the premises that one can only act as one actually does.

The relevant use is bound up with causation, and it is 'cannot', rather than 'can', that is of the greater pertinence. To say that something, A, cannot happen in a given situation is to say that something else, not-A, is caused to happen. To say something, B, can happen in a given situation is to say that something else, not-B, is not caused to happen. It is to be noticed that in asserting that B can happen in a given situation we are not asserting that B is caused to happen. We may indeed believe just that, but it is not a part of our assertion. If we do assert our further belief, that B is caused to happen, then it follows that what can happen is what does happen. It follows, in a related sense of the word 'possible', that what is possible is only what becomes actual.

We can enlarge on these accounts of 'cannot' and 'can' in several ways. We may write in either of the two accounts of causation mentioned at the beginning of this essay. Let us take the stronger one, where to say that one thing caused another is to say that the second thing would have happened, given the first and its accompanying conditions, whatever other logically consistent circumstances had obtained. The second enlargement of our accounts has to do with what may be called the scope of 'cannot' and 'can'. What *cannot* happen, given attention to a part of a sequence of events, is something that *can* happen, given attention to more of the sequence. Suppose that *not-G* is the effect of F. We may say that G cannot happen. The statement takes into its scope, in so far as causal antecedents are concerned, only F. Suppose, however, that we go further back prior to F, and accept that F was not caused to happen. We may then say, despite the fact that *not-G* is the effect of F, that G can happen. Alternatively, if we believe that F was caused to happen, we may again say G cannot happen, in this case taking into account the longer sequence.

Consider, then, a man's action of signing a petition on a particular occasion, and the claim that he cannot do other than sign it. The claim contains or presupposes two propositions. (1) Given certain brain states which are correlated with occurrents related to his action, and certain other conditions, he would have signed it as he did whatever other consistent circumstances had obtained. (2) Given certain earlier physical states, the mentioned brain states would have obtained whatever other consistent conditions had obtained. The assertion that he can do other than sign it, if the assertion is made, means or presupposes the falsehood of (1) or (2) or both.

The determinism that has been advanced includes generalizations of the two propositions. These generalizations are, respectively the third and the first theses. It follows from these two theses, then, that a man cannot ever do otherwise than he does. It would be patently mistaken, of course, to suppose that the given usage of 'cannot' and 'can' are our only usages. We sometimes say that B can happen in a certain situation and mean, essentially, that B will happen if some further condition is satisfied. This is not, as in the first usage, a denial that *not-B* will be caused to happen. Indeed, something that *cannot* happen, in the first usage, will be something that *can* happen, in the second usage.

It is not only that our chosen usage of 'cannot' and 'can' is not the only one. It may well be that it is not *all* of *any* ordinary usage. It is a part, however, of one very ordinary usage of the words when persons are under discussion. When we say that a man can do G we mean or presuppose, I think, that he is not compelled to do *not-G* and also that he is not caused to do *not-G*. If he is caused to do *not-G*, then he cannot do G. These contentions, or contentions of this general character, have often been opposed by philosophers, notably those of the British empirical tradition. It is denied that our chosen usage of 'cannot' and 'can' enters into *any* ordinary usage. I shall in effect take up oppositions of this kind at a later stage, in connection with responsibility.

It may be thought at this point, reasonably enough, that nothing much has been gained by giving only this much attention to 'cannot' and 'can' as used of actions. The propositions expressed by the sentence that we cannot act otherwise than we do, with 'cannot' used in the given way, are no more than the first and third theses. It is misleading, in fact, to talk of a conclusion being derived from premises. I have in fact included what has been said about 'cannot' and 'can' only to make clear what I am *not* claiming. What I am not claiming, of course, is that the premises of our determinism generate conclusions about what one cannot and can do, where these are understood in any but the given way. A number of philosophers have paid enough attention to 'cannot' and 'can' to make a certain caution irresistible.

For the same reason, I should like to look briefly at the pair of terms as used of decisions and choices. When they are so used, for obvious reasons, a different account must be given. What is to be understood, to go over to the past tense, by the claim that I *could not* have decided to look at something else in the gallery yesterday, when in fact I decided to look at pictures by Seurat? Our determinism, it will be remembered, does not assert that such occurrents as my deciding to look at Seurat are caused. We cannot take it, then, that to say I could not have decided to look at something else is to be understood, even in part, as the proposition that my deciding to look at Seurat was caused to happen. What is to be remembered, however, is that our determinism asserts of my deciding to look at Seurat that it was an occurrent in lawlike correlation with a certain brain process, each state of which was the effect of previous physical states. The obvious idea, then, is that we assign to this statement, 'He could not have decided to look at something else', this force: the different decision he did make was a lawlike correlate of a brain process, each state of which was the effect of previous physical states.

It may be objected that while 'cannot' is capacious, it is not so capacious as all that. Its meaning, it may be objected, does not allow for any ordinary use which is near to, or includes, the use that has just been made of it. I think that an opposing case can be made out, but I shall not try to do so. Let me say only that ordinary users of English, whatever definition can be attached to their use of 'cannot', would say, if they accepted the correlation thesis and the prior thesis about causation, that we cannot decide in ways other than we do. My concern at the moment, as in the case of actions, is only to make clear all that is to be understood by the claim that a man cannot decide in ways other than he does. Neither the statement that we cannot *do* other than we do, nor the statement that we cannot *decide* other than we do decide, is needed for what follows. These are, in fact, no more than expressions of the premises that have been set out.

V Responsibility

At this point, we might attempt to establish that it follows from these premises that our actions are never free or voluntary. The argument would have to do, centrally, with accounts of voluntariness or freedom. As may be anticipated, I think we could succeed in this argument. A second option is to consider instead whether it is true, given the three premises, that we are ever responsible for our actions. The two questions are intimately related, and I am inclined to think that the second takes one more directly to the answer to both.

What we must do is settle on the truth or falsity of several propositions, and, quite as important, fix their place in human life. Precisely what propositions these are is a matter of some difficulty. What is clear enough is that they can be expressed by this sentence: 'We are sometimes responsible for our actions'. The determinist will assert that one proposition that can be expressed by the sentence is false. He will assert, too, that the proposition and its falsehood are not irrelevant to our attitudes and concerns. Certainly there are other propositions that can be expressed by the sentence, propositions whose truth is not put in jeopardy by the theses that have been advanced.

It has been maintained of these propositions about responsibility that they are, in effect, the only ones which need be paid attention by anyone with a grasp of the real world. Only these are important to our ordinary attitudes and concerns.

I shall not attempt to supply anything like an exhaustive survey of the many notions of responsibility, each of which gives rise to one of the propositions that can be expressed by the sentence given above. All of these notions, I think, can be separated into two categories. The categories can be indicated by reference to two uses of ordinary forms of speech. We often speak, with a particular intention, of persons *being responsible* for this or that. We also speak of *holding persons responsible* for this or that. In the second class of cases it is often natural to talk of a man's liability. Although we can use these two labels, it must be admitted that there are no sure-fire linguistic criteria which enable us to distinguish these two classes of ascriptions of responsibility. It is ordinary to talk of someone's being responsible for something and to mean what would be expressed more consistently by saying that he is being held responsible.

This does not prevent us from making the distinction. Let us first consider ascriptions where it is most natural to speak of *holding someone responsible*. Three categories of such ascriptions come to mind.

(a) We may begin with a divide in the law. For the most part, statutes require for conviction that it be established that a man intended to perform a prohibited action or at least was negligent about avoiding it. Other statutes, notably those which are interpreted as imposing what is called strict liability, do not require for conviction that it be established that a man intended to perform a prohibited action or even that he was negligent. It is enough that he did the thing. It is enough in order to establish his responsibility, so-called, that he did perform an action which falls under a certain description. One such action, briefly described, is the selling of whisky to a man who is already intoxicated. It is ascriptions of responsibility of this second kind, where it is enough to have done a certain action, to which I wish to draw attention.

(b) In the history of philosophical reflection on the freedom of the will, secondly, one can find a related characterization. Its simplest version is to the effect that a man is responsible for an action if his future behaviour can be affected by punishment. Proponents of the view typically have it in mind that a man is responsible for an action if punishment will make it probable that he will not repeat the action. Those who are not responsible for their actions are those whose future conduct cannot be affected in this way. It is notable, to say nothing else, that one abuses language if one wishes to convey only that a man may effectively be punished, and one attempts to do so by saying, merely, that he is or was responsible for some action. Not even a description of the man as *being held responsible* for the action is tolerable. Still, we may admit this as a stipulated usage.

(c) There are related conceptions of responsibility, considerably more suited to the name, which fasten on those conditions of persons which may be thought to make punishment reasonable. Some, but certainly not all, have had an inception in a concern with punishment. Here, a man may be described as responsible for an action if his performance of it was uncompelled. That is, the action was in accordance with his desires or intentions and these were not forced upon him. A man is not responsible for an action if its performance was compelled: if, that is, it was in some way in conflict with his desires, his intentions or indeed his true personality. Conceptions of this kind, which have a beginning with Aristotle, have been usefully developed in several ways.

What is to be noticed now is that we have three uses of 'responsible', strained or otherwise, such that it does *not* follow from the determinist premises that there are no actions for which a man may be held responsible. More precisely, that an action of mine was in a certain way an effect does not entail, given the rules of strict liability, that I cannot be held in a sense legally responsible for it. That an action of mine was in this way an effect does not entail that I cannot be held responsible, where that means something about the efficacy of punishment. It is not entailed, finally, by the fact that my action was in a certain way an effect, that I cannot be held responsible for it, where that means, roughly, that it was not in accord with my own uncoerced intentions.

So much for one category of notions of responsibility, those that may be labelled as notions of a person's *being held responsible*. They give rise to propositions, all of them open to expression by the sentence, 'We are sometimes responsible for our actions'. These propositions are not falsified by the three theses. The determinist must admit the existence of such notions of responsibility, and this he will do without reluctance. In fact, he will regard at least the last of the three notions as of great consequence. If his enterprise is successful, it will be first among the admissible notions of responsibility.

What seems to me to be our ordinary conception of responsibility falls into the other category and pretty well exhausts it. It is here that we can most naturally speak of a man *being*, rather than being held, responsible. It is a requisite that if a man is responsible for his action in this way he has not been forced into it. It is in accordance with his uncoerced intentions. This is the requisite which provides the whole of the limited conception just mentioned. However, our ordinary conception includes another feature as well. I shall look at this conception in several of its most familiar settings. What I shall consider are not those occasions, perhaps mercifully rare, when we do in fact declare that someone is responsible for this or that, using the very word.

If a man to whom I am talking is persisting, as I think, in a refusal to recognize a distinction that he does in fact see, I may feel a certain irritation. I am irritated, too, if my chosen projects are frustrated because the car does not accelerate properly, or the elevator ignores my signal and does not stop at the right floor, or the corkscrew does not draw the cork cleanly. One can be irritated, however, in different ways. I may, to choose one of several locutions, *hold it against* the man that he is being mulish. I do not hold it against the corkscrew that it obstructed me, or against the car, or the elevator. If I do find such a feeling in myself, I am sufficiently aware that it is out of place. It is, at best, a kind of self-indulgence. If, to take another example, someone passes lightly over one of my mistakes, or takes a special care to remember my vulnerabilities, my response may be one of relief or pleasure. I may also be pleased to discover that the record-player now works adequately or that the typewriter doesn't skip. I shall not, however, *be grateful to* either machine. So with certain other related responses.

All of them are in place only as responses to persons, and they rest on tacit ascriptions of a responsibility. To ascribe this responsibility is to have certain beliefs about persons. I wish for the moment to single out one of these beliefs and to describe it in an introductory way. I cannot hold it against the corkscrew that it did what it did, because that was all it could have done. There was, from the point of view of its contribution, no other possibility. That is, its not drawing the cork cleanly was a simple effect of forces applied to it. I can hold it against the man that he refused to recognize the distinction if I believe, among other things, that he had a certain possibility of doing so. If I believe that his action was an effect of such a causal sequence as the one we have sketched, I cannot hold it against him. At best, I can enter into a kind of feigning. So with gratefulness. I can be grateful to a man for a particular action only if some other action was possible. In general the involved ascriptions of responsibility depend on the assumption, which is very nearly universal, that the actions which evoke them are not the only possibilities.

What is true of responses of this kind to other persons is also true of certain moral attitudes, of certain related practices, and of certain attitudes to oneself. However, I shall not consider any of these.

VI Responsibility and Explanation

All of this, predictably, will call up agreement and disagreement. There are those, surely a majority, who will readily accept that their conception of responsibility is of the kind that I have just described and called our ordinary one. They will have no doubt that the theses of determinism that have been advanced are incompatible with the existence of this responsibility. They will resist any suggestion that one can accept the theses while persisting in holding things against people and being grateful to people in the way we are. They will not mean that a psychological obstruction to certain responses is raised up by the claim that actions are effects of a certain kind. Rather they will suppose that there exists an inconsistency in accepting the claim that actions are such effects and also persisting in tacit ascriptions of responsibility of the kind involved.

There are others, surely a minority, who will maintain that *their* distinction between responsible and non-responsible actions, the distinction that enters into such responses as gratefulness, is only a distinction between actions of different causal ancestries. They may accept as true that actions are effects of a certain kind, and conjoin with that view an account of responsibility (c) mentioned above. That is, they may say that responsible actions are those caused by brain states with which there are correlated certain uncoerced intentions or desires. This, they will say, is entirely sufficient. Causality and correlation, by themselves, are in no way inconsistent with the existence of such actions. It will be maintained that gratitude and the other responses are in no way put in question by the fact that actions are in a certain way effects.

It would seem absurd for members of the majority party to deny the existence of conceptions of responsibility which are thought to be (as indeed they are) consistent with the premises of our determinism. It would seem as mistaken for members of the minority party to deny the existence of conceptions of responsibility rightly thought to be inconsistent with the premises. This amounts to the denial that there are any significant number of people who actually possess a belief which is fundamental to such of their attitudes as gratitude and which they take to be inconsistent with the premises. The denial is no more than a piece of audacity, owed in the main to Hume. It is falsified, even, by the relevant part of the written history of philosophy, which does not falsify very much. The belief in question, as must be admitted despite my attempt at general description, is in an essential respect obscure. That philosophers and many others *have had it* is a truism.

There are two other responses that may be made by the members of the minority party, and both are more interesting. They are inclined to believe that what I have called the ordinary conception of responsibility is a mess. They would say, I think, that the conception is such that it cannot possibly be *shown* that there exists an inconsistency between the relevant ascriptions of responsibility and the given theses. They would maintain that this statement, 'You have reason for gratefulness to him on account of his action', cannot be shown to be inconsistent with the statement that his action was an effect of a certain kind.

I am inclined to agree, in a way, that the inconsistency cannot be made perspicuous. More precisely, it seems impossible first to give a characterization of the responsibility in question which is independent of the statement about the action's being an effect, and then to proceed to display an inconsistency with that statement. Rather, a characterization of the responsibility in question *is* essentially a characterization of something as inconsistent with actions being effects. In the end the responsibility is described as that which cannot exist given certain causal sequences. Still, it may be that something can be done to make things clearer.

What is wrong with what I have called our ordinary conception of responsibility is that it contains what some of its defenders have called a primitive or irreducible element. It contains, one might better say, a blank where an essential element ought to appear. It is not a matter of importance, but it is worth notice that to accept determinism is not to be deprived of a satisfactorily articulated conception of responsibility. The blank occurs at that point where one should have an account of the non-causal agency that is ordinarily supposed to enter into responsible action. No one has ever offered more, by way of explanation, than a certain amount of dubious machinery, notably the 'creative self'. It is pretty hard to maintain the required suspension of disbelief in such items, or rather, it is hard to see what it is that one is trying not to disbelieve.

Despite this unintelligibility, let us make the attempt to shed some light on the conflict between the given conception of responsibility and the theses of determinism. Suppose that Tom Green performs an action and we accept that it was the effect of a set S of antecedent physical conditions, some of them being brain states correlated with certain choices or decisions. We accept, furthermore, that all of these conditions were themselves effects of earlier sets of sufficient physical conditions. Let us call the group of sets R. What is implied by this, whatever tolerable analysis of causation one takes up, is that *all* R-like groups of conditions are followed by S-like sets of conditions. And, similarly, *all* S-like sets are followed by actions like that one performed by Tom Green. It does not matter that as a matter of fact neither S nor R are likely to recur. It is true, of course, that subsets of both R and S do in fact recur.

The central point is that *anyone* in an R-like state would come to be in an S-like state, and, furthermore, would perform an action like

Tom Green's. Our propositions, then, imply a denial of individuality. This claim can certainly be understood in such ways as to make it plainly false. What I have in mind is only this, that what Tom Green did is *explained*, if one accepts the causal propositions, by something that is not individual to, or peculiar to, Tom Green. More precisely, it is explained by properties of his, which no matter who else had them, would issue in an action like his.

The point is the simple one that causal explanations of particular conditions or events are implicitly general in that they rest on invariable connections. Certainly it is true that to explain *B* by the proposition that *A* caused it is to cite some feature of *A*. The feature does any work in the account, however, only in virtue of being an instance of a type. The same point, incidentally, can be made about statistical explanations, as distinct from traditional causal explanations.

What remains to be said can be anticipated. To regard a man as responsible for an action, in the ordinary sense, *is* to make an ascription of individuality. It is to take the position that the action has not got a general explanation. I do not intend, of course, the truth that anyone who says that Tom Green was responsible for his action has in mind intentions or whatever which were those of Tom Green and nobody else. This *is* a truth, and is one condition that must be satisfied if Tom is to be regarded as responsible for the action. What I do intend is that anyone who says he was responsible, in the given sense, takes it that his action *cannot* be explained in such a way that all of his features cited in the explanation are explanatory in virtue of being instances of a type.

There is, I feel, no more than that to be said about what might be called individual explanation, and thus about the ordinary conception of responsibility. Any attempt to give a fuller account of the actions which have such explanations, if they can be called such, will result in vagaries about the self or the will, or in more ordinary talk which has even less utility. These melancholy facts, it seems, do not put in question what I wish to maintain. An ordinary ascription of responsibility, tacit or otherwise, rests on a belief or an attitude to the effect that an action cannot be explained in an essentially general way. It is unimportant that this belief or attitude is rarely articulated, even to the extent that it can be, but rather is a matter of unreflective commitment.

One can take different views of this state of affairs. It is a mistake, first of all, to suppose that the given conception of responsibility is not even coherent. What *is* true of it is that it is exceedingly thin. In a word, responsible action is characterized by what it is not. This is not to say that it is not characterized at all. If one is asked to display the inconsistency of such action and causation, it is not as if one had *nothing* of a literal character to offer. Such action is that which is inconsistent with causation.

There are, I suggested, two responses of interest that may be made by the minority whose conception of responsibility is not in conflict with the theses of determinism, and who wish to question the alternative conception. We have looked at one response, to the effect that the alternative majority conception is a matter of confusion or obscurity. The other response has as its burden that a general acceptance of the theses could not possibly issue in the disappearance of fundamental human attitudes. It could not possibly issue in the disappearance of such attitudes as are claimed to enter into the majority party's conception of responsibility. These attitudes, one of which is gratitude, are constitutive of any recognizably human existence. They constitute, anyway, what is a large part of human existence, interpersonal relationships.[10]

One thing to be said about this is that it rests on overstatement. This is not the place for a general survey of human attitudes but surely it is clear that many of one's attitudes to others which are the substance of relationship are *not* attitudes which depend on ordinary ascriptions of responsibility. None the less, it must be granted that many of our present attitudes of relationship do depend on such ascriptions. Can it be that all of these must go, given the coming of a new Enlightenment produced by the determinist?

The answer is far from easy. Let us concern ourselves for a moment with gratitude alone. When we feel it, we feel several things. There is, typically, the satisfaction which derives from a happy event, an event of benefit. This satisfaction is not necessarily connected with the actions of others, let alone assumptions about the nature of such actions. If I need money, then a loan, a win in the lottery or my own successful counterfeiting will all do something for my state of mind. Second, gratitude certainly involves a less contingent satisfaction, that satisfaction which derives from an awareness of the goodwill of another person. Beyond any doubt, this is something that is at the foundation of the experience of gratitude. Third, when I am grateful for an act, it appears that I take satisfaction from the supposition that the person to whom I feel grateful could have done something else, and did not. I take satisfaction, if that is not too crude a description, from a belief in responsibility or individual explanation, a belief which conflicts with the theses of our determinism.

There is no reason to think, obviously, that an acceptance of the theses would undermine the first two satisfactions or perhaps others. To accept them *would* undermine the third satisfaction. Because of this loss, or, more precisely, because of the accompanying change in belief about persons, one's state of feeling could not be described as gratitude. That is, it would fail to satisfy one condition which governs our present concept of gratitude, that condition which has to do with individual explanation or responsibility. To say this, obviously, is not to admit that a general conversion to determinism would leave nothing where gratitude was before.

In the history of reflection on our problem, both too little and too much have been made of the fact of causation. One can make too little of it by supposing, as did Hume, that it has consequences only for the fantasies of metaphysicians and divines. It has, on the contrary, consequences for beliefs and attitudes which are very general and which enter into small and large practices. We have seen one way in which too much can be made of the fact of causation. A general acceptance of it would not be so destructive of attitudes as to transform human life. In the past there have been revisions of attitude of as substantial a nature.

There is, as always, more to be said, but I shall finish with three remarks.

(1) A good deal has been suggested about responsibility and action, but nothing about responsibility and decisions or choices. If it is accepted that actions have the character that has been claimed for them, and that there cannot be a certain responsibility for them, the matter of decisions and responsibility will have little interest. An assertion of responsibility for decisions and choices, whatever it might amount to, would not secure that reassurance to which proponents of freewill

aspire. They wish, principally, to have the reassurance that men are responsible for their actions. They have in mind that responsibility that I have denied. It should be clear enough, in any case, that the correlation thesis, together with the thesis about the physical causation of physical correlates, issues in a denial of responsibility for decisions. Again, this is the responsibility which is a matter of individual explanation. The argument is much the same as with actions, and I shall not set it out.

(2) That it is actions that are important, given the view that has been advanced, may give rise to the question of why I have given attention to the correlation thesis. It may appear, that is, that the conclusion of my reflections, that we are in one way not responsible for our actions, might have been derived from just the two theses that physical states are sufficient conditions of brain states and that these latter states, with other conditions, are sufficient for actions. It is essential, however, to any determinism of a forceful kind, that it give an account of the place of decision, choice, and consciousness generally. It is these that have been in the forefront of both philosophical and ordinary reflection on our subject.

There is also a better reason. It is impossible to escape the conviction that choices and decisions, and also intentions and a good deal else, are in some way bound up with the genesis of action. Any account of the genesis of action that is not in line with this conviction will certainly fail. If, in the given account, the brain states that are said to cause actions were not intimately connected with choices and decisions and the rest, hardly any amount of empirical evidence would bring us to accept the causal claim. The correlation thesis, then, is essential to the determinism that has been advanced. It is essential to an acceptance of the truth, if it is such, that actions are effects of a certain kind. As we saw earlier, it is also essential to one explanation of the relation of efficacy that seems to hold between mental events.

(3) Finally, a word on our view of ourselves. That view, which seems doomed always to be inchoate, is closely connected with the given conception of responsibility and hence the individual explanation of actions and also decisions, reflections and the like. If it is accepted that these have the character that has been claimed for them, that they are not open to individual explanation, then we must revise

our view of ourselves. It seems evident that it is here that the theses of determinism may have the greatest consequence for our attitudes. Again, however, it is far from being a consequence that is unthinkable.[11]

Notes

1. I have succumbed to the inclination to amend my essay for its reprinting in this book. The account of determinism given here, then, is significantly different from the account given in the essay as it appeared in the original and the paperback editions of *Essays on Freedom of Action*. The changes are in the formulation of the premises, and in what is said of monistic pictures of mind. The conclusions are the same.

2. The stronger notion of a causally sufficient condition is set out in my essay, 'Causes and Causal Circumstances as Necessitating', *Proceedings of the Aristotelian Society*, 1977–8.

3. J. L. Austin was 'inclined to think that determinism ... is a name for nothing clear', and that it 'has been argued for only incoherently' ('Ifs and Cans', *Proceedings of the British Academy*, 1956). P. F. Strawson aligns himself with 'the party of those who do not know what the thesis of determinism is', although, as he says, he has 'some inkling – some notion of what sort of thing is being talked about' ('Freedom and Resentment', *Proceedings of the British Academy*, 1962). It is noteworthy that both of these distinguished essays arrive at substantial conclusions about what was thought to be unclear. A good many subsequent essays have made something like the same assumption about the condition of determinism.

4. Any 'emergent' properties will, of course, be physical properties. I do not have in mind unrestrained speculations that emerge from time to time about properties of a non-physical nature. Cf. R. W. Sperry, 'A Modified Concept of Consciousness', *Psychological Review*, 1969.

5. Following the usual procedure in talking of types and their instances, 'correlate' is used both for an occurrent and for that type of occurrent. It is also used for a set of types of brain processes and for a type of brain process and for an instance of a type.

6. A very useful layman's guide to neurophysiology is given by Dean E. Wooldridge, *The Machinery of the Brain* (New York, 1963). See also, for example, Peter M. Milner, *Physiological Psychology* (New York, 1970); Sidney Ochs, *Elements of Neurophysiology* (New York, 1965); Peter Nathan, *The Nervous System* (Philadelphia, 1969); J. Z. Young, *A Model of the Brain* (Oxford, 1964); A. R. Luria, *Higher Cortical Functions in Man* (London, 1966); J. C. Eccles, *The Neurological Basis of Mind* (Oxford, 1953).

7. Wilder Penfield and Lamar Roberts, *Speech and Brain Mechanisms* (Princeton, 1959).

8. It seems to me that there is an insuperable argument against this identity theory, now popular partly because it seems to allow for 'real' mental efficacy. Take 'Brain process BP_1 was identical with conscious occurrent O_1.' The only acceptable meaning for 'was identical with', roughly, is 'had all and only the features of'. BP_1, presumably, had only physical features; so, therefore, did O_1. Or, if the quoted proposition is read from right to left, so to speak, we have the conclusion that BP_1 had only features of consciousness. This identity theory, then, amounts to an absolute denial of the existence of consciousness, which is a splendid non-starter, or a denial of the physicality of certain brain processes, also a splendid non-starter. Either a flat materialism or a species of 'local idealism'. If it is now presumed instead that BP_1 had *both* physical and conscious features, we have a dualism of features, and simply the kind of so-called monism mentioned on p. 254. This does not allow for 'real' mental efficacy.

9. Some further reflections on action and movement, germane to the foregoing discussion, and also an argument about movement and responsibility, may be found in my essay, 'A Conspectus of Determinism', *Proceedings of the Aristotelian Society*, Supplementary Volume, 1970.

10. Cf. P. F. Strawson, 'Freedom and Resentment' op. cit.

11. My thanks for comments on this essay are due to Myles Burnyeat, G. A. Cohen, A. R. Jonckheere, John Odling-Smee, Timothy Shallice, John Watling, J. Z. Young, and philosophers to whom it was read at University College London, Princeton, Columbia, Yale, Pennsylvania, Connecticut, and Swansea. None I think, has agreed with all of it.

Further Reading

Donald Davidson's 'Mental Events' reprinted in the present volume (and the first two items of further reading in connection with 'Mental Events') in effect include discussions and rejections of the correlation thesis. See also, for Wittgenstein, *Philosophical Investigations* (Oxford: Blackwell, 1958), section 611 ff., and *Zettel* (Oxford: Blackwell, 1967), sections 575 ff., 608 ff. With respect to causation, see J. L. Mackie's contribution to the present volume and the essay mentioned in note 2 above. About actions and their antecedents, *The Philosophy of Action* (Oxford: University Press, 1968) edited by Alan R. White. Works in neurophysiology are mentioned in note 6 above. See also *Content and Consciousness* (London: Routledge & Kegan Paul, 1969) by D. C. Dennett. With respect to responsibility see *Responsibility* (London: Routledge & Kegan Paul, 1970), by Jonathan Glover, and P. F. Strawson's essay mentioned in note 3 above. For general discussions of determinism see the essay mentioned in note 8 above and also Honderich (ed.), *Essays on Freedom of Action* (London: Routledge & Kegan Paul, 1973).

Stuart Hampshire

Some Difficulties in Knowing

There is a common picture of knowledge as always and essentially consisting in a reliable grasp of a reality which is independent of the knowing. What is to be known is fixed by its own causes and the cognitive task is to use a reliable method to ascertain what it is. Stuart Hampshire's concern in 'Some Difficulties in Knowing' is to show that, in the case of some *self*-knowledge, knowledge of some of our own present and future psychological states, the picture is a distortion of what actually happens and, in consequence, an obstacle to the proper understanding of the complexities involved in an important dimension of human freedom.

The connection with freedom and determinism can be introduced as follows. There is a kind of uncertainty expressed by the questions 'Do I want this?' and 'What is my attitude to that?'. Could someone else answer these questions for me, someone in possession of a psychological theory giving knowledge of the causes of my attitudes and desires, on the basis of which he could infer what my attitudes and desires must be even where I am myself uncertain? There would seem to be no reason, in principle, why someone should not use a theory to infer what I want if my wanting something is a fact that obtains, as the picture suggests, independently of my knowing it. Yet most of us would feel our freedom threatened by the prospect. It would seem to take away from us a decision which is ours and ours alone to make – or so we might obscurely feel. And it is one of the characteristic tasks of philosophy to translate a presentiment or intuition of this kind into clear argument.

Hampshire's argument is based on a careful examination of different kinds of uncertainty that may arise in the area of self-knowledge. The possibility of uncertainty comes from the possibility of a negative answer to the question 'Are you sure that you are right?', which is a question that may be raised in regard to any claim to knowledge, about anything whatever. By contrast, epistemology has more usually (and quite properly) been interested in the question 'How do you know?', which asks about the source of a knowledge-claim – how, or by the use of what method, the speaker is in a position to know. But while this question is always admissible in regard to knowledge-claims about external reality, the case is different with claims about one's own psychological states. There the speaker, as the person whose states of mind are at issue, is very often in the best position possible to know what they are. His authority in the matter is not open to challenge. Nevertheless, he may still be asked, or ask himself, whether he is sure he is right in what he says about them. On reflection he may decide that he is not certain that he is.

But this uncertainty amounts to different things in different cases. When it is a sensation – say, a pain of some kind – which he is currently experiencing, the uncertainty is indeed an uncertainty about the nature of an established independent reality. The question is one of finding the right words to match the sensation as it already is. Hampshire calls this 'semantic uncertainty', and he contrasts it with the 'intentional uncertainty' which arises when a man is uncertain whether, for example, he wants to go to Italy. Here he may be uncertain, not because there is a desire already formed and he is unclear what it is or how to describe it, but rather because there is not yet a clear and determinate desire to report. Some desires – hunger, sexual lust – may simply come to consciousness, in the manner of sensations, already formed; but often the formation of a desire is through a process of thought, and until that process has been completed there is not yet a fully specifiable desire to report.

Intentional uncertainty, then, is the uncertainty of the man who cannot say whether he wants to go to Italy because he has not yet done the thinking which alone will make it the case that he definitely does, or definitely does not, desire to take the trip. When he comes to know whether he does or does not desire it, and thus resolves his uncertainty, this will typically be by deliberation, the weighing of reasons for and against the trip, terminating in a decision: a quite different procedure from that of accumulating evidence about himself and the state of his desires. It will be coming to know, not what his desire already is, but what it *is to be*, starting from now. His coming to know what he wants initiates and is partly constitutive of his wanting it. It is not the recognition of a fact concerning himself which obtains in virtue of its own causes independently of his knowing it.

Yet, to add a complication, that latter thing can happen too. A man may discover, perhaps by inference from the evidence of his own behaviour, or the pattern of his thought, that he does in fact want a certain thing. He may say, 'I must want this', where the 'must' marks the conclusion of an inference bringing him to recognize a desire which until now he has been unaware of. But the point here is that now the desire is conscious, it is a question whether he will endorse it: the question, namely, whether he really wants (whether from now on he is to want) that which until now he has (must have) wanted. And this question, once posed, is a question for deliberation, not for discovery; the uncertainty is intentional, not semantic.

We have concentrated on sensations and desires as the most perspicuous examples by which to illustrate Hampshire's central distinction between the two types of uncertainty. In fact, however, his thesis is of wider scope. There are subtle variations to be observed when questions about uncertainty and self-knowledge are raised in connection with beliefs, attitudes, emotions, actions, even perception. These variations on the main theme the reader can discover for himself, being enabled to do so by the paper's masterly demonstration that philosophy may be true to complexity without loss of clarity. We conclude our introduction by returning briefly to the topic of freedom.

Recall the troubling suggestion that someone else might use a psychological theory and causal inference to tell me what my desires or attitudes must be. We can now see that, if Hampshire is right, this would not eliminate uncertainty of the intentional kind; it would not cut out all scope for deliberation and the weighing of reasons. On the contrary, inferential knowledge about my desires or attitudes, whether the inference is my own or communicated to me by another, brings with it potential uncertainty. Any fully formed fact about myself will have its causes, which common sense or psychological theory may be able to explain, but knowing the fact or its causes confronts me with the question, how to respond to the knowledge. Do I wish the fact to be otherwise? Is it caused by what I can approve as good reasons? I must now consider reasons for and against the desire or attitude which has come into question. Such reflection already alters the psychological reality which from now on exists to be known and explained. This is so even if I conclude that, much as I would wish to, I cannot change myself in the relevant respect. For either I have endorsed the attitude and the reasons for it, which is itself a change, or I have not; if I have not, but the attitude or desire persists, it does so in conflict with my higher-order desire that I should not feel what I do, which again is a change in my overall state of mind. In sum, according to Hampshire's view, from now on I am a participant, willing or reluctant, but in any event self-aware, in these states of mind. I have contributed by my own power of reflection and deliberation to determining what they are to be. In this sense self-knowledge is, as it has traditionally been conceived to be, a liberating and not a restricting possession.

M.F.B.

Stuart Hampshire

Some Difficulties in Knowing

Reprinted from *Philosophy, Science and Method* edited by Sidney Morgenbesser, Patrick Suppes and Morton White (New York: St Martin's Press, Inc.; London and Basingstoke: Macmillan, 1969), pp. 26–47. With permission of the author and publishers. Minor revisions by the author.

I

There are at least three distinct kinds of challenge to, or rebuttals of, a claim to knowledge: The first is the simple rebuttal – 'What you claim to know to be true is not true'; the second is a challenge which questions the source of the knowledge or the method by which the alleged knowledge has been obtained. This challenge is commonly expressed in the words 'How do you know?' When such a question is put as a challenge, it is implied that the claim to genuine knowledge is not acceptable unless a reliable source, or a reliable method, has been used in the particular case. A claim to knowledge is not to be respected unless the knowledge claimed has a respectable origin; the speaker may be required to show that he is an *authority* on the particular issue, as he has implicitly claimed to be. He must be able to show that he is in a position to know that which he claims to know. Otherwise he is exposed to the rebuttal: 'What you say may be true – but *you* cannot now possibly know that it is'. A third and different challenge, or different kind of challenge, may be phrased in various ways, but is commonly expressed in the words 'Are you sure?' Human beings are apt to err: a liability to mistake attends all their performances, not excluding their search for knowledge. They make mere mistakes, as it seems, by chance, or perhaps even inexplicably. They use words carelessly, inaccurately. They forget things. They overlook things. They write down the wrong number for no reason at all, or for no reason that they can give. They often have a reliable source and a reliable method; they have been asked the time; they have a watch; but then they misread the figure on the dial carelessly.

A machine may misread the figure on the dial, but not carelessly; for it does not employ, or need to employ, care in reading it correctly. But human beings do. They are not instruments: or, if they are instruments, they are instruments that use themselves, and they may misuse themselves. They need to be careful in order finally to be sure, because they may go wrong without anyone having a reliable method of finding out why they have gone wrong. 'Are you sure?' unlike 'How do you know?' asks, among other things, whether you have on this occasion been careful, or careful enough, in using a generally reliable method. Of course you can also make a machine check its results; but this is not the same as asking it whether it is sure that it has not made a mistake. A claim to knowledge is certainly not to be respected unless the knowledge claimed has a respectable origin. But more than this can properly be asked: 'Are you sure that you have not just made a mistake?'

I am just mentioning well-known facts here. These well-known facts are of the first importance in understanding the notion of knowledge, and perhaps also the concept of following a rule. I check the proof to be sure that I have not made a mere mistake, just a slip, somewhere in the derivation, I look at my watch again when the small boy who has asked me the time says 'Are you sure?' This kind of fallibility, or corrigibility, is always in the background, and with some of us, on some topics, it has to be in the foreground when we claim to know. I may be in the best possible position to know that something is the case, and yet I may throw away my advantage, inadvertently, carelessly, incompetently, for no reason at all. This is why I can be asked 'Are you sure that you are right?' when I have claimed to know something on occasions when it would be absurd to ask me *how* I know. I may be reminded of one kind of fallibility even when the other kind of fallibility – fallibility in respect of source or method – is not in question.

There notoriously are occasions when the question 'How do you know?' would be at least absurd, and perhaps unintelligible, as a question. These are the same occasions on which a statement shows, in virtue of its grammatical form and its topic, these two taken together, that the speaker is in the best possible position to claim to know that it is true. For example, he who reports that he is currently experiencing a certain sensation cannot intelligibly be asked how he knows that he is; it is already shown, in the grammar and vocabulary of the statement itself, that he is in the best possible position to claim to know that his statement is true. The grammar and vocabulary show that he is the authority on this matter, that he is in the optimum position for making that statement. But he can intelligibly be asked whether he is sure that his report is correct; doctors often do put just this question, and it is sometimes, and in abnormal conditions, difficult to answer it; on the other hand, it is often, and in normal conditions, very easy indeed to answer it – e.g., when the description is not a very specific one or when the sensation is a familiar one. Of the first person, present tense reports of sensations, one may say that it is evident that the speaker is the authority. But he is also a fallible authority, particularly if he attempts a very specific description, or a description that is in some other way ambitious and highly informative, or when he describes a sensation that is very unfamiliar.

We may therefore, as a preliminary, divide statements about states of mind, attitudes, and desires into two classes: first, those statements which admit the challenge 'How do you know?' when a claim to knowledge has been made, as well as the less specific challenge 'Are you sure?' In the second class, we have those statements which show, in their grammar and vocabulary, that the speaker is in the best possible position for claiming to know that the statement is true, that he is the authority, and that no question about the *source* of his knowledge arises; then only the less specific challenge 'Are you sure?' is in place, a challenge that requires the speaker to think again about the statement in case he has been careless in making it and has not on this occasion taken due precautions against mistake. This latter challenge is appropriate to *any* claim to knowledge of *any* kind, whatever the grammar and the vocabulary of the statement may be. But it will be especially appropriate when the topic is complex, or when for some reason it requires a careful use of words or careful matching of a specific description, or when there is evidence that the speaker has been hasty or careless or that he has been unreliable in the past. We all know, for example, how difficult it may be to describe sensations when they constitute symptoms to a doctor; there is the difficulty of not exaggerating or understating, of distinguishing between that which is more correctly called pain and that which is more correctly called discomfort. And if we are asked 'What kind of pain?' or 'What is the pain like?' we know how difficult it may be to give a more specific description and to avoid error in matching the right description to the phenomenon.

With this kind of possibility of mistake, I may hesitate, be doubtful, and need to stop to think before answering a question, even though I am clearly in the best position for claiming to know the correct answer; the grammar and vocabulary of the question alone may show that, if I do claim to know the answer, no question would arise of how I know or what the source of my knowledge is. Yet I hesitate, am doubtful, and do not know what the correct answer is. Someone else may think that he knows what the correct answer is, and his belief may prove correct, even though I, the authority, do not yet know. The doctor may know: he has seen lots of cases like mine; perhaps he has had the disease himself, or he has heard lots of reports, and he is thoroughly familiar with the appropriate vocabulary. He has used a reliable method of inference; and I may subsequently confirm that his conclusion was correct. He had arrived at a conclusion that turns out to be correct by an argument that establishes that so-and-so must be true or is likely to be true. If after careful attention to the phenomenon and to the description, I confirm his conclusion, I do not present the conclusion of an argument; I report what I claim to know, or what I believe, without benefit of argument. In the old-fashioned, much abused phrase, I now either know, or I think I know, directly.

Because of the possibility of carelessness of different kinds and the possibility of inaccuracy in the use of words or symbols, it is never an offence against the proper use of language for someone to argue that he who is in the best possible position for making a certain statement is probably, in a particular case, mistaken. It may, in the circumstances of a particular case, be irrational and silly so to argue; but it will not be an offence against the proper use of language, as it would be to ask 'How do you know that you are in great pain?' as opposed to 'Are you sure that "great pain" is not an overstatement and untrue?' Because of this kind of corrigibility, an inductive argument may be relevant to establishing the truth or falsity of a statement which the speaker himself was in a position to claim to know to be true without any appeal to evidence or argument. From the fact that we may sometimes have good inductive reasons to believe that a man is probably mistaken in the report that he gives, for example, of his sensations, we must not conclude that such statements *require* inductive evidence as their support when a claim to knowledge is made. They do not require inductive support when the speaker is also the designated subject of the statement; but an inductive inference may on occasion lead us to the conclusion that such a statement, made on the best authority, by a man trying to be truthful, is probably false, or even, in some cases, that it *must* be false, where the 'must' is the sign of an inference.

II

In the case of sensations, then the subject's difficulty, if he has one, will typically be one of matching the right description to the phenomenon experienced. If he hesitates and is unsure about the right reply to a question about a present sensation, he may be uncertain about what to call the sensation or how to classify it. Since truth has always been represented as an agreement between a statement and that to which it refers, the subject has a doubt which is a pure case of doubt about the truth of the various possible descriptions that suggest themselves to him. This is one particular kind of doubt among others, and a particular kind of difficulty in achieving a true statement. He needs to be accurate, or exact, to find words that fit perfectly and that are not just approximately right; and it may be difficult to get an exact fit in words. On the one side is the phenomenon, the reality to be described, which is in no way concealed from him, and is, so to speak, transparent when he attends to it; he therefore does not *need* to investigate further, or to prove or to experiment or to approach the phenomenon from another angle. On the other side, requiring to be matched, is the commonplace vocabulary in use from which he has to make a fitting selection. If he is not sure whether a particular description that suggests itself would be a truthful description, this would not normally be accounted a case of ignorance; it is not exactly that kind of lack of knowledge from which he suffers, unless it is some ignorance of the standard use of the relevant words. It is an uncertainty of another kind. Let us call it the semantic uncertainty. It is in some respects very like the uncertainty that a man may feel when trying to discern whether one pattern exactly matches another pattern in a different medium. It is uncertainty about matching possible descriptions with an independent reality. This kind of uncertainty, which might occur in connection with almost any kind of empirical statement, is often at its most acute when a man is trying to find the most fitting and accurate description of his own sensations. Every kind of statement has its own kind of liability to error, and this matching of descriptions to the phenomena becomes more crucial when other liabilities to error have dropped away. Then one may resolve his uncertainty but by inductive inference. – 'This description is probably the right one.' Then he may tell you, by reconstructing the inference, why he believes that this must be the correct description; but he will not tell you how he knows; for his belief evidently falls short of the ideal case and therefore does not constitute knowledge. He was indeed in a position to know, but he was unsure; therefore he had to use an eccentric, and not the standard, method of arriving at his statement. In a parallel case, a man was in a position to know what was said at a meeting because he was present and heard the speeches, but he happens not to be sure. He may fill the gap by inferring what must have been said. If he is asked 'Do you *know* that this is a true account?' he will have to indicate that he is not claiming the authority of a witness. He can tell you why (using what evidence) he believes that this is a true account.

III

Consider next another type of case in which a man is asked a question about himself, in respect of which he is in the best position to know the answer; and yet he does not know and admits that he is uncertain about it. He is asked whether he wants, or would like, to go to Italy with a certain group of people or not; let us suppose that it is certain that his emotions are strongly engaged by the prospect, and that he is far from being indifferent about it. He is not being asked whether he will go; that is, he is not being asked to decide an immediate practical question. Let us suppose that the inquirer is intensely curious about the subject's state of mind, as it concerns this question, and that there is no practical possibility immediately in view at the time of the inquiry. The questioner wants the subject to reflect and to tell him what his desires are; the questioner might even ask how he feels about going to Italy. The request is a request for information.

The subject reflects and replies: 'I do not know whether I want to go or not. I can't tell you yet; you must allow me to think about it further.' We are very often uncertain about what we want to do in a specific matter which is very far from indifferent to us. 'I don't know what I want to do about it: I am not sure whether I want to or not' is a form of words often used when, for example, a man has a divided mind about the project; perhaps there are features of it that are attractive to him and features that are repugnant. Or perhaps he feels that he has not thought about it enough, or perhaps he is confused about it. Or again there is a wide range of different types of cases where 'I am not sure what I want' may express an uncertainty in specifying precisely the nature of the object wanted rather than an uncertainty about the balance of desirability in an already fully specified object. Or the uncertainty may be an unsureness in focusing my desire on its proper object and in eliminating alternatives. Or the subject may be vacillating and in a state of turmoil about the matter. Anyone who (in delineating the notion of knowledge) respects the actual uses of language will admit that uncertainties of this general kind are as genuine as any other cases of uncertainty. They are genuine cases of not knowing. As I may be uncertain about the real properties of some object before me, and as I may be uncertain both about the truth of some highly specific statement about my sensations, so I may be uncertain again when asked to make some statement about my desires or my aims, ambitions, hopes, attitudes, sentiments.

When I am not sure what I want to do or want to have, because my desires are confused or inchoate or because they conflict or because they are not clearly formed, I may try to end the uncertainty; for someone requires the information about myself which only I can give him authoritatively. When in this situation I stop to think, my problem is not generally, typically, that of matching words to an independently recognized reality; my uncertainty is not usually a semantic uncertainty, although it could be that, or it could be that as well. In the journey-to-Italy situation I would naturally consider the merits of the proposed courses of action. In determining what I want to do when I am in a state of uncertainty and am not sure and do not know, I attend to the features of the possible courses of action. If after careful reflection, I announce my conclusion in the words 'I now know the answer to your question: I now know what I want', I would normally be able to give my reasons, the considerations that have led me to the conclusion; now I can say 'I now know what I want'. The reasons would be reasons for wanting, and they would not naturally be counted as evidence that a certain account of my already existing wants is true.

For these reasons some typical cases of 'I do not know what I want' may be assimilated to some typical cases of 'I do not know what I shall do', in respect of the kind of knowledge involved. And it is not surprising that making up one's mind, or coming to know, what one wants to do is often very like the formation of an intention: very like, in that the required precautions against error are very often precautions against misguidedness or incorrectness in the desire and the intention rather than precautions against incorrectness in the statement of the desire or intention, taken as something already independently formed.

There are contrasting cases when a man notices and reports his desires, cravings, and impulses as phenomena of experience, exactly as he may report his sensations; he notices that he wants a drink or finds that, being hungry, he wants to eat. In such a situation a man may be uncertain about the correct characterization (or the name) of the thing that he wants, although there is an acceptable sense in which he does know what he wants; for he may know that he would unhesitatingly and unerringly recognize the particular thing, or the kind of thing, that he wants if it were produced before him. In such cases his knowledge of what he wants, when attained, is knowledge of a fact about himself, closely parallel with the fact that he has such-and-such a sensation in his leg. He may often be surprised to discover, or to notice, that at this moment he has an impulse, or desire, which he had not expected that he would have. In such cases he would not be said to have formed the desire, even less to have formed it as the conclusion of a process of thought; rather he has come across it, as a fact of his consciousness. The desire occurred and emerged in his consciousness, independently of any calculations. The word 'lust', for example, particularly if it has a sexual connotation, is almost, but not quite, the name of a sensation. There is a whole spectrum of cases between the felt bodily craving, which approximates to a sensation in respect of the kind of knowledge that we have of it, and the reflective desire or interest that is formed as the outcome of a process of thought. A man may, for example, be led to recognize that he has at this time (already) a desire which he had not known that he had and which a friend had inferred from the evidence of his behaviour. The desire was not something that he had felt; nor was it a desire that he had formed; he had not come to know of its existence in either of these ways. Prompted by his friend, he had originally inferred its existence from his behaviour – 'This must be what I have been wanting to do'.

But here I want to concentrate on the case of the man who does not know whether he wants to go to Italy and who has to stop to think whether he does. If from this initial state of uncertainty he moves to a conclusion which amounts to his now knowing what he wants, or to his now knowing what his attitude is, his process of thought is properly characterized as deliberation. Deliberation is a process of thought that begins with uncertainty and that is aimed at some conclusion, accepted by the subject, of the form 'This is to be true of me'. The uncertainty from which the process of thought started was not an uncertainty about the matching of a statement with an independent reality. The uncertainty that leads to deliberation is always an uncertainty about what is to be the case and not about what is or was the case. It is an uncertainty about the future, conceived as alterable, one way or the other, by removing the uncertainty.

Formation of a present belief, desire, intention, attitude, or sentiment is a case of coming to know what my belief, desire, intention, attitude, or sentiment *is to be*, starting from now, and not of coming to know what it already is. Coming to know or to be sure what my attitudes and sentiments about something are counts as a decision, insofar as the subject has aimed, in reaching his conclusion, at some kind of appropriateness in attitudes or sentiments taken in relation with their object. Perhaps one can distinguish this intentional self-knowledge and intentional uncertainty from semantic uncertainty in this way: if the subject is still uncertain and is wondering whether he has a certain aim or ambition or not, then an observer cannot know either that he does have the aim or ambition or that he does not, and any knowledge that an observer possesses on this topic must be knowledge of the future. An observer may believe that the subject has *had* an aim or ambition, perhaps an unconscious one, which can be inferred from his past behaviour. But if the subject is still doubtful about his *present* aims, the observer will not claim to know that the subject still has this aim, definitely and without qualification, unless and until the subject's uncertainty ends. A doctor may know what I am now feeling and that a statement about my present sensations is true, even when I am myself still uncertain what the correct account of my sensations is. In respect of aims and ambitions, and that which I want to achieve, an uncertainty in giving a correct account, whether for my own benefit or for the benefit of others, usually amounts to an uncertainty of aim. The opposite case would be the situation in which I am uncertain of the right words to describe my objective. The verb 'believe', being (like 'try') a strongly intentional verb, scarcely admits of this opposite case. But there are many situations in which I do not know which of two things I believe about something, and therefore no one else can know what I believe until I make up my mind and thereby come to know what I believe. An observer can only predict that I *will* make up my mind in a particular way. And he, no less than I, may infer from my behaviour and from other evidence that I must *have* believed so-and-so before now, but not that I must now believe so-and-so when I myself am doubtful. So I may say of my friend – 'He cannot know what I want to do, because I do not yet know myself.' He can only use his psychological knowledge to predict what I *will* want to do.

IV

It seems that if I am still uncertain about what I want to do, I do not, as my friend might, use the scientific knowledge of causes that I may happen to possess to settle the question of what I now want to do by

some kind of inductive inference. There does seem to be a real difference between on the one hand self-knowledge, in the sense of contemporary knowledge of one's own mind at the present time, and, on
the other, knowledge of the desires, beliefs, and sentiments of others,
or knowledge of one's own past, of the history of one's desires,
beliefs, and sentiments, which one may regard exactly as one regards
the history of another person. Referring to one's own past, one may
try to explain why the sequence of desires and attitudes was what it
was. This might be a standard causal type of explanation, because the
facts to be explained can be established prior to, and independently
of, the explanation of them.

Consider two different questions: (1) 'What *do* I now want to do?'
and (2) 'What *will* I want to do?' A man who has an adequate psychological theory may in many cases use his knowledge of causal connections to predict what he will want to do, if and when certain
sufficient conditions are satisfied. He knows that he will want to eat
later in the day. He knows from experience that he will want to laugh
when he meets his old friend, or that he will want to run away when
he meets his enemy. But it does not follow that he can use his knowledge of causes to discover what his wants are in cases where he is
doubtful and does not already know what he wants to do. If he finds
that he does actually feel certain desires, he will then use his psychological knowledge to explain why his present desires are as he finds
them to be. Suppose a man believes that if he knew the relevant
covering laws, and if he knew that the initial conditions stated were
satisfied, he would know that it *must* be true that he *will* want to do
so-and-so. It must be true that he will want to eat before six o'clock.
But could he settle his uncertainty about what he *now* wants to do
by a similar inductive inference? If he could, then the conclusion of
the inference could be expressed in the words 'Given that such-and-
such sufficient conditions have occurred, I must want so-and-so':
or, more plausibly, 'So-and-so must be what I want'. But then it
seems that he will naturally ask – 'But is it?' He will look for an en-
dorsement of this conclusion. He will ask himself whether he finally
does want what he has inferred that he must want. An observer might
have said to him, 'I know all about you and about people in your
condition: so-and-so must be what you want.' But he will wait for

the subject's confirmation; for while the subject is still doubtful whether the so-and-so is what he wants, his desire is still inchoate and unformed.

There is a typical use of the word 'must' which will, I think, serve to mark the distinction between the two kinds of knowledge which I am pursuing; this is the 'must' that marks an inference from evidence that compels one to draw a certain conclusion. This is the use of 'must' in such statements as 'This must be my hat' or 'Your hat must be upstairs since it is not here' or 'He must have been very unhappy when he heard the news'. It may be useful to interpolate something about this use of 'must' in claims to knowledge of matters of fact.

It has sometimes been said, mistakenly, that this use of the modal form makes a stronger statement of fact than the corresponding plain indicative statements – 'This *is* your hat' and 'Your hat *is* upstairs' and 'He *is* very unhappy'. If by a 'stronger statement' is meant a statement which claims a greater degree of certainty, this is surely not true. The flat assertion 'This is your hat' would commonly be taken to imply a greater degree of certainty than the more tentative 'This must be your hat', if any implications at all about certainty can be drawn from the wording of these statements alone. The function of 'must' in such cases as these is to imply that the assertion about the hat is the conclusion of an inference, when the statement might have been known to be true directly and without the aid of inference. In a well-known short story by Saki, a woman, descending from a train at a country station, is accosted by a stranger who says, – 'You must be the new governess'. The woman replies, 'Well, if I must, I must', and the story proceeds from there, from this wilful confusion of two kinds of necessity. Had the stranger simply said, 'You are the new governess', she might simply have denied it. The necessity in 'You must be the new governess' is contrasted with the possibility represented by the weaker form of modal statement 'You may be the new governess'; both show something of the weight of evidence for the conclusion, in the one case compelling evidence, in the other not. Because 'It must have been X' and 'It must be X' indicate the conclusion of an inference, they often do not make such a strong claim, in respect of certainty, as the unmodified 'It was X' and 'It is X'. The man who says, 'It must have rained' makes no stronger claim, in respect of certainty, than the man who says, 'It was raining'; the former is typically the man who has seen the wet pavements, the latter the man who remembers the rain coming down.

So much is true of putative statements of fact about the present and the past. But the situation in respect of statements about the future course of events is quite different. Here the contrast between statements which are the conclusions of an inference and statements known to be true non-inferentially is at least far from obvious. If I am considering the future course of events, nothing corresponds to my just seeing my hat and recognizing it, or my having seen the rain and having remembered it. For this reason we may be inclined to say that all statements about the future course of events, other than statements of intention, are known to be true, if known at all, by some kind of inference. 'Fascism will not happen here', no less than 'Fascism cannot happen here', will be supported by some inference; 'It will happen' no less than 'It must happen' will be supported, in face of the challenge 'How do you know that it will?' by an appeal to some evidence that it will, or to some method of inference, and not by any claim to the authority of direct knowledge, parallel to 'I can see it' or 'I remember it'. For this reason there is a definite sense in which 'It must happen' is normally stronger than 'It will happen'. 'It must happen' here has a greater logical force, because it says both that it will happen and that there is compelling evidence that it will. 'This horse, Ajax, must win the race' says more than 'This horse, Ajax, will win': namely, that there is no possibility of its losing; and this cannot be a correct thing to say if the evidence does not exclude the possibility of its losing. The possibility is typically excluded, and the 'must' is justified, when a contrary outcome is incompatible with some well-confirmed general proposition.

Let us then try to transfer this idiom of 'must', marking the conclusion of an inference that compels assent, into the present tense. A man may say 'I must be in love' or 'I must be jealous' because he has noticed features of his own behaviour that amount to compelling evidence that he is. In respect of these passions, revealed by their typical symptoms, he here speaks of himself as he might speak of another or of his own past. These are the facts that he has discovered about himself, and he can tell you how he knows and of the evidence that has led him to this conclusion. Such an inference is not unusual. On the other hand, only in very peculiar circumstances would a man intelligibly say 'I must be in pain', or 'I think I must be in pain'; he scarcely ever infers that he is in pain, and there is not normally any question of him telling you *how* he has discovered that he is in pain, or of his giving you the source of his knowledge. Least of all would he say 'I must be in pain because such-and-such has happened, which, as you know, causes pain.' There are exceptional circumstances in which the modal idiom has a use: a man might reasonably say to a doctor – 'I suppose you are right when you infer, on the basis of your experience and medical knowledge, that I *cannot* be in great pain, only in some acute discomfort; perhaps I am exaggerating.' He infers that the doctor's description is likely to be, or even must be, the correct one and that he must be misdescribing; what he is calling great pain is not what is ordinarily called great pain. He resolves the semantic doubt (exceptional for the unspecific description 'pain', less so for 'great pain') by an inductive inference.

But one cannot naturally say of oneself 'I must believe p', although one may say 'I must have believed p at that time'. 'I must believe p', representing an inference from the evidence of behaviour, is a way of saying 'I must have believed p up to now', the moment of realization. I may infer from signs and behavioural indications what my past beliefs were – 'I must have believed him' – as I may infer the present beliefs of another. But one cannot infer what one's beliefs are to be, starting from now. Either one already knows, or one has to answer a normative question, to form a belief on the evidences of truth, as one takes them to be. I may in exceptional circumstances infer what my beliefs will be in the future. For example, I might say 'I know from experience that when I see him I shall fall under his influence, and that I will believe what he tells me, even in defiance of the evidence.' The implication here is that I shall no longer know, remember, or realize, when I am in his presence, that my beliefs are formed under his influence and only under his influence. I will not have in mind the correct explanation, as I now suppose, of my having the belief. I cannot transfer this melancholy self-knowledge into the present without incoherence – 'I only believe this story because I am under his influence'. This is not the expression of a contemporary belief but a kind of irony; for a declared belief is normally endorsed by the subject as to be explained, at least in part, by his reasons, and as not to be explained wholly by external causes which are not taken to be evidence of truth. He who can truly claim to believe p to be true normally intends his favourable attitude to p to be alterable by evidences of error. For this is how believing that p is true is distinguished from cognate propositional attitudes – e.g., hoping that p is true, liking to imagine that p is true, wishing p to be true, and many others. So it would be absurd to arrange an experiment to determine the causes of beliefs of a certain kind, and to ask the cooperation of the subjects: 'The experimenter will apply certain stimuli and change your environment in various ways, and you are to report the change in your beliefs that are the effects of these external changes.' There would be a conceptual impossibility in carrying out these instructions. Some apparent psychological effects could be reported – e.g., a changing inclination to believe a certain proposition. But the subjects, in the circumstance of the experiment, would not call these noticeable psychological effects changes in belief. Nor can a man under posthypnotic suggestion say 'I only believe this because I have been hypnotized to believe it'.

My declared beliefs are not facts about myself that I may discover after a preliminary uncertainty, as I may discover, after a preliminary uncertainty, that I must be in the grip of some passion because I exhibit the symptoms. For the same reason I cannot intelligibly say 'I must intend to do so-and-so', although I can intelligibly say 'I must have intended to post the letter and then forgotten it'. On the other hand, I could intelligibly say, using the concept of purpose, and the present tense, 'I see now: this must be my ultimate aim or purpose in doing this although I had not known that it was'. I may infer what my more or less unconscious aim or purpose has been *up to now* from signs in my overt behaviour. But now I have to endorse or repudiate the purpose; what is to be my purpose, starting from now? Perhaps I do not know the answer to this question; perhaps I do not know, in respect of some activity in which I am engaged, what my aim or purpose really is. In removing this uncertainty, I fix my aim. Similarly with the two-faced concept of desire: While I make up my mind what I now want, there are no knowable facts to be expressed in the words 'I want to do so-and-so'. If I infer that I must already really want so-and-so, or that I must already have such-and-such an unconscious desire, it is still an open question whether I dissociate myself from this desire, now brought to consciousness. The 'openness' resides in the reference to the immediate future, to 'now' as meaning 'starting from now' as opposed to 'up to now'. Given that I have discovered, perhaps as the conclusion of an inference from my previous behaviour, that I do have the desire, do I want to get rid of this desire, if I can, or do I now endorse it? Does it now persist as a conscious desire? The fact that I have learned is a fact about the immediate past, leading into the present. Starting from now, and from this fact, I may think again about what is to be desired. In this uncertainty there is room for deliberation, that is, for determining what is to be true of me.

Suppose that I am doubtful about what I want, and suppose that, under the influence of an adequate and tested psychological theory, I think that it must be possible to infer what I now want, just as I infer what another man now wants on the basis of a theory – 'Given so-and-so that has happened, he *must* want so-and-so'; for the relevant initial conditions, and causal factors are known; so I conclude that I *must* now want so-and-so, given that so-and-so has occurred. Is this odd and unusual? I think it is: but is it odd and unusual for the same reason that it would be odd for a doctor to conclude by a parallel argument that he, the doctor, *must* be in pain because he has a disease which is always painful? Surely not – the oddity has a different source. Of the doctor and his pain, one would merely say that if he already has a pain, he must know directly that he has. 'Am I in pain?' is an unusual question for which a particular context of semantic uncertainty must be imagined: the context, already mentioned, in which the speaker is doubtful whether he would be exaggerating if he described his condition as pain rather than, e.g., discomfort. But the question 'Do I want so-and-so?' is far from unusual and is intelligible in a very ordinary context. That I should not be sure what I want is entirely normal. One would not appeal to the principle that if a man has a desire he must generally, and except in odd circumstances, know directly that he has; for the very range of cases under consideration shows that no such principle operates. It is an intrinsic feature of desires, aims, ambitions, purposes, attitudes, that they may be uncertain, unfocused, confused, inchoate. It was one of the strengths of Aristotle's *Ethics* to have recognized this, as against those empiricists who have taken desires as invariably given facts of consciousness.

The oddity of saying 'Applying a reliable psychological theory, I have come to the conclusion that I must now want this' resides in the kind of knowledge claimed, which does not match the original uncertainty, expressed as 'I do not know what I want'. Admittedly there are cases in which a man may infer that he must really want to do so-and-so, although he had not realized this until his attention was drawn to the evidence. But in coming to know this, he has not removed the kind of uncertainty which he might have expressed in the words 'I do not know whether I now want to do X or not'. If he had been asked 'Do you want X?' he might have answered 'I do not know', and then be convinced that he had been wanting X. But he still has the immediate future, starting from now, to determine. The man who does not know what he now wants in a matter that deeply concerns him, and who also does not know whether he admires an action or not, normally has a question for decision. Just because he has a question for decision, it seems that he cannot settle his doubt by a factual inference, which could only lead him to a conclusion about what *must have* already been true before this doubt arose. In removing this present uncertainty, he has to consider the features of X that make it desirable for him and the features of Y that make it admirable. In confessing his uncertainty, he has confessed that his desire for X and his admiration of Y are still mere possibilities, to be endorsed or eliminated by him. An observer, may infer, applying a theory, that he *will* make up his mind in a particular way and that he *will* emerge from his deliberations with a particular desire and a particular attitude. But the subject will not now remove his uncertainty in this way. If therefore someone were to say to him, in this situation of uncertainty, 'You must want X' and 'You must admire Y', he would normally take this 'must' as prescriptive, as an imperative of rationality or perhaps even of morality – perhaps as meaning 'You have compelling *reasons* for wanting X and for admiring Y'. There would be an implied allusion to some standard of correctness – for example, 'You must, on pain of being inconsistent' or 'You must, on pain of being utterly misguided in your desires and admirations'. The 'must' would not naturally be taken as 'It must be the case that you do in fact want X and admire Y'.

Suppose I say to you: 'You must want to save your friend.' I may intend this to be taken as 'It must be true that you do. No human being could be so unfeeling.' But you would not express agreement with this proposition in the words 'All right, I must'. This would be Saki's governess again. You would say 'Strangely enough, I don't' or 'I do'. Either you know whether you do or do not, or it is not yet true either that you do or you do not, just because you are still uncertain about it, after the question has been put to you. Even if the inference to the desire had been correct, and the desire was an unconscious desire unrecognized by the subject, it still would not be true that you simply want now to help your friend if, at the conscious level, you are now doubtful. However, 'You must *have* wanted X and admired Y' would be construed as 'It must be the case that you did'. 'I must have wanted X and admired Y' would in similar fashion be construed as meaning 'It must be the case that I did'. On the other hand 'I suppose I must still want X' would often be interpreted as 'I suppose I must if I am to be consistent and rational'. I might be committed, logically or otherwise, to wanting X by my other desires and admirations. If the 'must' is expanded as 'I must, on the pain of being inconsistent or irrational', then it is not misleading, I think, to characterize the statement as normative. It is normative in the same way as 'I must accept the conclusion of this argument' or 'This cannot be doubted', which does not normally represent a psychological impossibility. But 'I suppose I must still want X' might represent the discovery and acknowledgement of a desire, particularly a long-range, or so-called dispositional, desire, which has existed up to now; so a man might say 'I suppose I must still want to please him', acknowledging this fact about himself. And then the question arises – 'Given that it is an inferred fact that I have this desire, do I want to get rid of it or not?' He has discovered and acknowledged that he has wanted to please up to now; but does this desire, once recognized, disappear, and if it does not, but rather lingers, does he wish that it would disappear? In either case his state of mind and its explanation have become more complex.

I view the history of my past states of mind and attitudes from the standpoint of an observer; that I am writing an autobiography rather than a biography imposes no limits upon the inferences that I may make about my desires and attitudes, as they have existed up to now, or upon the explanations that I may give of them. The settlement of any doubts that I may have about what these states of mind actually were does not modify the states of mind themselves; in recognizing them for what they were, I do not endorse them. But while I do not yet know what I want and am still uncertain what to aim at, the adequate psychological theory cannot be applied, just because uncertainty exists in my mind, and uncertainty of a particular kind, the kind of uncertainty which is neither ignorance, nor a semantic uncertainty, but rather an intentional uncertainty, which raises, at least in part, a normative question. Imagine a man who believed that he had an adequate psychological theory which would never leave him uncertain about his future conscious desires, aims, ambitions, and attitudes. He would expect to find himself, as it were, saddled with desires, aims, ambitions, with states and attitudes, which he had all along expected to occur in the foreseen conditions of his particular case. He would expect all his own desires, aims, ambitions, and attitudes to occur, just as the ordinary man now expects that, after a long fast, he will want to eat, or that under certain conditions he will have a craving for sugar, or for alcohol, or a longing to fall asleep. Such a psychological theorist would expect to find himself, under foreseeable conditions, acquiring a certain ambition or falling into an attitude of admiration, as the ordinary man expects to find himself, under foreseeable conditions, becoming angry or frightened or jealous, or having an impulse to run away, or becoming depressed about something.

There are indeed desires, emotions, moods, which I know will descend upon me under certain conditions; I can often infer and then observe their occurrence in myself no less than in other people. There is nothing in the characterization of such desires, emotions, moods which excludes the possibility of my being the passive and helpless observer of them, and my knowing of their existence in this way. I may, without contradiction, be said to observe myself 'falling into' these states or being subject to these impulses; I can see myself in these respects as a specimen. I know that I will want this or fear that or be disappointed by the other. But then further uncertainty occurs at a higher level, which by itself introduces a new complexity into my state of mind. For there is always the question of the attitude that I am now to adopt to these presumed facts or presumed probabilities about myself: do I want them to be otherwise or not? The 'doubling' of my references to myself is unavoidable, as long as I have the means to infer and to notice these facts about myself.

As soon as we develop this hypothesis of the man who applies a psychological theory in self-prediction, we see that he might be led to discard many of the idioms that a man now uses to talk about himself, about his aims, ambitions, interests, hopes, and attitudes. The state into which the 'psychological theorist' might expect himself to fall, a state in some respects like the attitude of admiration, still might not *be* admiration. The state into which the man falls might be like admiration in, for example, the behaviour that accompanies it. It would not *be* admiration unless the predictor was ready to ask himself whether he thought that the action or person admired was in some respects admirable; having 'fallen into' the state that resembles admiration, he would not be said to admire unless he thought that his state was to some degree appropriate to its object. Even if he admires only reluctantly or unwillingly, he still must think of the object as in *some* way admirable. If this thought that the object is in some way admirable is predicted by him, the prediction will be justified, at least in part, by reference to the predicted features of the object that will explain his thinking the object admirable. Will this thought be uncontrollable?

I labour these points because, through the empiricist tradition, we have received an idea of knowledge, and therefore of self-knowledge, as essentially and in all cases, knowledge of something that has an independent existence, independent, that is, of the knowing. The tradition therefore has difficulty in admitting that the very same process of thought may be *both* a coming to be sure or to know, that something is to be the case and a process of making it the case. The reasoning that makes me sure that something is true of me is sometimes also the reasoning that makes it true of me – e.g., I have to admit that I want X, or that I am trying to do X. The empiricist tradition freely admits that a man has genuine knowledge of his own given sensations and impressions, which are kinds of transparent objects that we encounter in our experience. Sensations are taken within the tradition to differ from external physical objects in that we see right through them, and that we do not need to investigate them from different points of view in order to know what they are; they are presented all at once and in their entirety, and there is no distance between the observer and the object, which needs to be judged in determining what the object really is. There is no difference between their surface and their substance.

In recent years it has been widely admitted that the more complex states of mind, passions, and emotions do often need to be investigated by the subject, and the elements and aspects seen as a pattern, before a man can be sure what they are, even though they are his own states of mind. It is sometimes also admitted that the subject's knowledge of their proper characterization may be essential to the states being characterized in a particular way, and therefore that self-knowledge makes the states of mind different, and more complex, from what they would otherwise be. It is recognized that there are states of mind – for example, the state of being indignant about something or of being embarrassed by it – which are of their nature fully intentional states, just because this kind of self-knowledge is constitutive of them. Someone – for example, a very young child – who does not possess any of the concepts which would enable him to discriminate his state as one of indignation, as opposed, for example, to anger, could not in fact be indignant, although he could be angry. This is the feature of self-knowledge on which I am insisting because I think that, following this path, one can come to see what is peculiar to intentional knowledge, merely as a kind of knowledge.

One difference between being made to feel uncomfortable by something that someone has just said and being embarrassed by his remark is that in the latter case the subject believes or knows that the remark is part of the explanation of his feeling; his knowledge of the explanation of his feeling distinctly modifies the state of mind. A remark may have the effect, or consequence, that he feels uncomfortable, without his recognizing that his feeling is caused by, or is the consequence of, just that remark. If he does come to believe, or to know, that his feeling is the effect of that remark, then a further question arises for him – 'Is there anything about the remark that is embarrassing? Was it an embarrassing remark?' That is, was there ground or good reason for embarrassment? Certainly he may recognize that he is embarrassed by it, while admitting that this is to some degree an inappropriate, or even a ridiculous, feeling for him to have about it. But he must believe that his feeling has *some* minimum appropriateness, if it is to count as a case of embarrassment. Of a child, it may be true that he is feeling uncomfortable and ill at ease, and that this is the effect of a cause, namely, a remark made which touched off certain associations in his mind. But it might be false, and in some cases absurd, to say that he was embarrassed at or by the remark, and, even more absurd, to say that he found the remark embarrassing. The reflexive self-knowledge is essential in converting a case of being made uncomfortable by it, where this is an instance of correlation between stimulus and effect, into a case of being embarrassed by it or ashamed of it or guilty about it, where these are typical intentional relations constituted and distinguished from each other by the accompanying knowledge of, or belief about, the partial explanation of the feeling.

The knowledge is arrived at by considering the properties of the object which constitute reasons for being embarrassed, ashamed, or guilty. I am embarrassed, ashamed, or guilty *because* the object seems to me to have certain properties, and I would mention my noticing of these properties, or my belief that the object has these properties, in giving a partial explanation of why I am embarrassed, ashamed, or guilty. Each of these states has a standard target, or paradigm case. There is something that it is normal to be ashamed of, embarrassed by, guilty about. This is part of the sense, of Aristotle's doctrine of the mean in respect of the passions: that there is, built into the concept of any one of the passions, a norm of appropriateness in the object of the passion. If I have not been sure whether I am embarrassed by something or not, then my becoming sure is often the outcome of my being sure that there is something normally embarrassing about it, and that there is something in the object to explain the embarrassment as not altogether inappropriate. I can usually say why I am embarrassed by it, even if I admit that the reasons are insufficient; giving my reasons for the attitude or feeling is in such cases more like giving my reasons for a present or future action than it is like finding a causal explanation of a state of mind which I have independently identified. If the state of mind is the outcome of reflection or deliberation, I have not identified it as existing independently of the reasons that I now take to be the partial explanation of it. In the case imagined, when I ask myself the question 'Is this uneasy feeling that I have embarrassment about so-and-so?' I look for an explanation of the feeling, and, as a result of this search for an explanation, my state of mind may cease to be what it was before. Originally it was only true that I felt uneasy; and then, with my recognition of the source of this feeling as a normal one, it became true that I was embarrassed by the object, e.g. a remark made.

The situation is very like that in which a man's attention is drawn to something that he is doing without his being distinctly aware that he is doing it. His action acquires a new character in virtue of his knowledge that he is doing it; new descriptions are applicable to his performances in virtue of the fact that they are no longer unintentional in these respects. Previously there *was* a cause: now there is room for a reason, and for an explanation of his doing it, known to him, which, in virtue of this knowledge, changes the character of the action.

The difference between 'He is breaking the box', where this is the causal judgement that he is the cause of its breaking, and 'He is breaking the box' in a stronger sense, including the intention to break it, is very like the difference between 'He is made uncomfortable by it' and 'He is embarrassed by it'. In virtue of his knowing what he is doing, the subject will normally be in a position to explain his action by some reason that he has for doing it, or at least authoritatively to reject other explanations that are suggested. He can give *some* explanation of why he is doing it, however rough and vague and incomplete.

To summarize: 'I do not know what I shall now do', 'I do not know what I want', 'I do not know what I feel about it', 'I do not know what my attitude to it is', typically confess uncertainty, not about what is already true, but about what is to be true of me, starting from now. This requires a process of reflection, akin to deliberation, which is aimed at the kind of knowledge or certainty which has as its outcome that I do now intend to do so-and-so, want so-and-so, feel so-and-so, have such-and-such an attitude, or sentiment. If I start from an uncertainty about myself of this kind – about what is to be true of me in these respects – I will not infer from a statement of initial conditions together with some general psychological proposition what must be true of me, starting from now, as I may infer what must have been true of me up to now. If deliberation ends with the conclusion that I *must*, starting now, want so-and-so, feel so-and-so, have such-and-such an attitude, the 'must' will allude to some standard of rationality or morality: so to a kind of correctness, which is not truth.

A present tense question put to me as a request for information – 'Do you want?' 'What is your attitude to this?' – places me in an ambiguous position, a position of facing both ways; I am confronted with the need to report the facts, as they already are, and with the need to make a decision; for I may dissociate myself, with a second-level desire or attitude, from the desire or attitude which I find that I already have. The request for information forces me into this position of active self-consciousness; and the asking of the question may change the facts just by engendering this selfconsciousness. In response to the question, I may for the first time recognize that I in fact have a desire or attitude that I now wish that I did not have. The movement from knowledge of the facts about oneself, about one's desires and attitudes up to this moment, to a knowledge of that which is to be true of me is a continuous movement of consciousness; it is so pervasive that it is easily overlooked. Present-tense avowals of desires and attitudes have been found baffling in their logic, partly because they mark this movement from the one kind of knowledge to the other. 'I want X' is open to a two-faced challenge, when the question 'Are you sure that you want X?' is asked; the first face of the challange calls on the autobiographer not to disregard any evidence, perhaps of behaviour, that suggests that the facts are not yet as he reports; the second challenge calls on him not to disregard any reasons there may be for not desiring X. The contrast between evidence and reasons here is a contrast between steps that lead to, and are taken to justify, a conclusion which is a belief about already wanting X, and steps that lead to, and are taken to justify, wanting X; justification of both kinds might be needed because the belief that X is already wanted might be a mistake, and wanting X might be a mistake. The observer, considering the desires of the subject, would hold these possibilities of mistake apart; he would know from which point of view he was considering the desires. But the subject would normally not separate the factual from the deliberative question. This is part of the asymmetry, stressed in the controversy about knowledge of other minds, between first-person, present-tense statements and other statements about states of mind, or at least about desires and attitudes.

It is plain that this distinction between two kinds of uncertainty and of knowledge touches the issue of freedom and determinism – but at what point and with what consequences? I will state the minimum consequence first. Whatever facts a man may learn about his present desires and attitudes, he always has the higher-order question of his desires and attitudes in the face of these facts – does he want them to be otherwise? He may sometimes find that he is powerless to change his passionate attitude toward something, although he wishes to, and that he cannot control or suppress a desire that he already has. He is then left in a state of conflict. He might know the explanation of his original desire and understand its causes; he might have been in a position to predict, accurately and with confidence, that he would have just this desire; and he might have known that he would be powerless to prevent himself feeling this desire, although he had wanted not to feel it. Experimental knowledge of the explanation of his states, the kind of knowledge that is stressed by a determinist, is knowledge of the conditions under which he would be able to prevent something being true of him, if he wanted to prevent it. The 'if he wanted to' states a condition which always arises no matter what scientific explanation of desires is available. If a man had known that under stated conditions he would want X and also that he would want not to want X, he has before him the further question, which arises in virtue of this knowledge, of whether he wishes this conflict not to occur. Even if he foresees accurately the sequence of his desires and moods, and also his conflicts of desire, he would still adopt an attitude and have wishes in respect of this sequence and of the various elements in it. My argument is that any knowledge which a man acquires from experiment and observation about his own present and future states presents him with another potential uncertainty and with the need of knowledge of another kind, and that this is a feature of knowledge itself.

This feature of knowledge could as well be illustrated by reference to perceptual knowledge as by knowledge of mental states and attitudes. Suppose that a man comes to know, for the first time, about some physiological mechanism of perception; using this knowledge, he is able to predict what his perceptions will be when a stimulus of a very specific type is provided; the stimulus is a sufficient condition of a certain physical state, which is in turn a sufficient condition of his perceiving something – for example, a certain pattern of colours on the ceiling; he may still be uncertain, when the perception occurs, whether the perception is veridical or not, whether his inclination to believe that there is a pattern of colours on the ceiling is to be endorsed or not. He must then find reasons to accept or reject the belief, and must actively inquire whether the explanation of his perception is of the kind that allow it to be a veridical one. As one learns about the causes and conditions upon which one's perceptions depend, one is in a position to apply this knowledge of causes in distinguishing veridical from deceiving perceptions; and applying the knowledge includes actively performing tests – e.g., by changing the perspective or angle of vision or by performing some simple interference experiments. I can legitimately regard myself, with my sensory equipment, as an instrument that records the presence of objects in the environment; but I am an instrument which deliberately employs itself to find the answers to questions which I have raised. When I find myself inclined to believe that there is a certain pattern of colours on the ceiling, and not as the conclusion of an inference, I may still suspend belief until I have performed tests and found good reasons for believing. I am normally free, and not powerless, to question any of my beliefs, whether they arise directly from perception or not. In the setting of questioning an inclination to believe, or of resolving uncertainty, that which causes me to believe is called a reason for believing; in a setting in which a perceptual belief has formed without any active inquiry, or even the shadow of an uncertainty, there must still be an ascertainable cause of the belief, but it may not be called a reason. If I am altogether ignorant of the psychology of perception, I will not know which perceptual clues make me form certain beliefs, e.g., about the distance between visible objects. I will not know how I know, and I will say that I know directly, in cases where there has been no uncertainty resolved by inquiry and where my belief is true. When I am uncertain and actively investigate, my final belief has an explanation which includes a reason, the evidence from which I have inferred. Sometimes my reason may only be the belief that my first inclinations to believe (my first impressions of distance) almost always are confirmed, that is, that I am a reliable instrument in this matter; this is a reason for endorsing my first impression of distance on a particular occasion. But the further question – 'Am I sure that there is nothing abnormal in the circumstances in which this perceptual belief was formed?' – is never an absurd question. I do not wish to deny, but rather to stress, the many differences between knowledge of the external world and the knowledge that a man may have of his own states of mind, desires, and attitudes. But the corrigibility in principle of any empirical knowledge claim, apparent in perceptual claims, has an often neglected consequence in claims to self-knowledge. Suppose that a man knows what he will want to do when certain sufficient conditions obtain, which he knows will occur very soon. When the anticipated desire occurs under the foreseen conditions, he can still raise the question 'But am I sure that I do want to do this? Are there good reasons why I should want this?' Of course he knows that he does now want it, that this primary desire exists, and, in the case supposed, he knows why it exists. He is so far like the man who sees the pattern of colours on the ceiling, and who knows that this is a possible correct description of what he sees, but is still not sure whether there is in fact a pattern of colours on the ceiling.

The mere raising of the reflective question has already changed his state of mind; and this distinguishes self-knowledge of this kind from knowledge of the external world. For there is now a sense in which he knows what he wants to do and a sense in which he does not know what he wants to do. Recognizing this primary desire and knowing the conditions (perhaps a physical state) that have produced it, he may still be hesitant and uncertain, and any conclusion of the uncertainty will have a reason as at least part of its explanation. The uncertainty in this case of desire amounts to a kind of conflict, and will be plainly a conflict of desire if the outcome is that he does not want, on reflection, to do that which he also feels a desire to do. Similarly with attitudes of mind: I may find myself predictably feeling admiration for someone and being inclined to act correspondingly, while on reflection I am uncertain about my attitude to him, because I am uncertain whether there is anything admirable about him. I have therefore a divided and uncertain attitude, which may be continuously modified as I continue to reflect upon what my attitude is.

The transition, in self-knowledge, from knowledge of psychological fact, and of the causes that explain my desires and attitudes, to a reflection on these facts, which introduces causes that are reasons, depends, firstly, on a feature of knowledge itself: that a claim to empirical knowledge is always challengeable by the question 'Am I sure that this is so?' This challenge to reflect upon desires and states of mind, when it is contemporary with these states, leads to the consideration of reasons. Insofar as a desire that is to be in part explained by reasons differs from a previous desire that was independent of these reasons, the reflection by itself brings about a change.

This conclusion obviously leaves many of the traditional issues associated with a thesis of determinism untouched. But it is incompatible with a particular picture that is often associated with a thesis of determinism: namely, the picture of advancing psychological knowledge gradually displacing the kind of uncertainty that is expressed by the questions 'Do I want to do this?' and 'What is my attitude to this?' when these questions call for a decision. Any additions to our systematic knowledge in psychology, and thus to our power of calculating exactly what we will or would feel under specifiable conditions, will always leave a place open for this kind of uncertainty.

Biographical Note

Stuart Hampshire is Warden of Wadham College, Oxford and was Grote Professor of Mind and Logic at University College London and then Professor of Philosophy at Princeton University. He has written *Thought and Action* (1959), *Freedom of the Individual* (1965), *Modern Writers and other Essays* (1969), *Freedom of Mind* (1972) and *Two Theories of Morality* (1977).

Further Reading

Hampshire's remarks in the present paper are connected with views he has elaborated in his books *Thought and Action* (London: Chatto & Windus, 1959) and *Freedom of the Individual* (New Edition, London: Chatto & Windus, 1975). His account of predicting and deciding, which is related to the theme of intentional uncertainty in the present paper, has received a lot of discussion: see the discussion on 'Freedom and Knowledge' in D. F. Pears (ed.), *Freedom of the Will* (London: Macmillan, 1963) and David Pears, *Questions in the Philosophy of Mind* (London: Duckworth, 1975) Chapter 1, 'Predicting and Deciding'. For a critical discussion, see John Watling, 'Hampshire on Freedom', in *Essays on Freedom of Action* (London: Routledge & Kegan Paul, 1973), edited by Ted Honderich.

A. J. Ayer

Construction of Our Theory of the Physical World

From the beginning, philosophers have been taken up with the nature of reality, some of them coolly and many of them with feeling, often of a spiritual kind. David Hume, perhaps the finest of cool philosophers in recent centuries, was in no doubt that our ordinary beliefs about the nature of the world and its objects are somehow true. At any rate, he found it impossible to give them up. An ordinary physical object is a single thing which can be experienced by more than one person, and by way of more than one sense, and which continues to exist when it is not being experienced by anyone or anything. When we both see a book the main fact about the episode is that there is a single thing in question, not two things, each private to its respective perceiver. Nor is the thing which is seen one thing, and the thing which is touched another. Nor need we follow Bishop Berkeley in requiring God's awareness of the book in order to keep it in existence when the rest of us are otherwise engaged. *Nonetheless*, Hume maintained, the experience of our senses does not seem to give us adequate reason for our ordinary beliefs. That is for him the problem of reality. It is too, at bottom, the problem of reality for Professor Sir Alfred Ayer, who has a place in Hume's tradition and is of a like temper and style. His response, however, is different from Hume's.

The problem, in one large part, is not about the nature of the physical world but about our sense-experience, or our sense-experience *in itself*. How is it to be characterized? Of exactly what does it consist? The problem in another large part, to state it generally, is that of the connection between this experience and our ordinary beliefs about reality. Finally, despite the conviction carried by these ordinary beliefs, are they to be put in question, or at any rate amended, as a result of what is said in connection with the first two issues?

In the first sections below from Ayer's *The Central Questions of*

Philosophy, an account of our sense-experience is given and defended. It has been maintained by 'realists' that ordinary things are within our direct experience. We see the book itself, and thus we are to accept no substitutes, no private entities, when we turn to philosophical reflection on our experience. Furthermore, we need not suppose that any serious philosophical question about reality arises if we take up this position. It is essentially this last contention which Ayer opposes. Eschewing certain older forms of argument, he presses the claims that we do not *see* or otherwise *sense* that a thing is public (accessible to other observers) or that it is accessible to different senses. We may indeed infer or gather this from what we sense, but that is another matter. If we are concerned with the evidential basis for our beliefs about the physical world, we must look to what is given us straight off by that world, not to what we subsequently make of it. To clinch the point by reference to our third condition on ordinary physical objects, it is very clear that we do not *see* or otherwise *sense* that something goes on existing when it is not being perceived. Yet this continued existence is fundamental to our belief about it.

However, to proceed in this way is to say what our sense-experience is not, or does not include, rather than what it is. A succession of philosophers have described our sense-experience as consisting in, or being of, sensible qualities, impressions, what were called ideas, representations, sense-data and so on. These items, for the most part, have been taken to be something other than physical things or their parts. That is to say, fundamentally, that the items have not been taken to be public, open to more than one sense, and such as to exist unperceived. For Hume they were 'fleeting and perishing impressions'.

Ayer speaks of *qualia*, which can be described as sensible qualities, or, in the way of some philosophers, as universals. They include, if we stick to visual experience, blueness, roundness and largeness. However, visual *qualia* also include what may be called patterns, of which examples are a leaf-pattern or a spoon-pattern. A visual leaf-pattern is simply any of the patterns of visual items which would typically lead a person to think he was seeing a leaf. What we can call a *visual field* consists in visual *qualia* of the several kinds. However, it may also be characterized in another way. *Qualia*, being such qualities as blueness, and also those *qualia* which are patterns, are in some way general. What one is in touch with, in experiencing blueness, is nonetheless a particular. It is constituted by the universal *quale* of blueness being instantiated at a particular place and time. Such a particular is a *percept*. We can then correctly speak of a person's visual field as consisting of visual percepts.

This account of sense-experience is given in section two below. The most immediate question it raises is likely to be whether percepts are objective or subjective. Are they of the nature of physical objects or of the nature of mental images? The question, using the same three criteria as before, is whether percepts are or are not public, whether they are open to more than one sense or to one alone, whether they persist or not when unperceived. The answer in each case is that neither alternative is to be adopted. Percepts are not to be taken as being of the nature of things, and they are not to be taken as being of the nature of images. At this point, rather, we are contemplating the stuff of experience, and this stuff is to be conceived without its being assigned to either of the two categories. Percepts are in this respect neutral.

Let us take a moment to exemplify these propositions. Imagine an infant who, as we would ordinarily say, is entirely attracted by the slowly rolling orange marble, the only thing on the table at which he sits. His visual experience in itself consists of a succession of visual fields, each of which pretty well amounts to a percept which is orange, round and of a certain size. Each of these is a numerically different percept, and none is connected by the infant with any other percept. He does not have any idea of a persisting thing, the marble. (For this reason, incidentally, his percepts, like percepts generally, can be described as *appearances* only in a special sense of the word – one which does not carry the implication that they are appearances *of* something.) It is not important whether in fact an infant's experience is ever correctly described in the given way. It may be that what we have been calling sense-experience in itself comes with some accompaniment, having to do with persisting objects, from the beginning. Still, we can isolate this experience in itself. It is also clear that it is our access to the physical world.

Before turning to the second large part of the problem, there is an objection to be considered. It is owed to Wittgenstein and in its original form it had to do with the supposition that a person might have a private language. That is, he might be able to conceptualize or have names or terms for wholly private experiences, such as pains may seem to be, or visual experiences considered in themselves. The essential idea of the objection was that any language or conceptualization requires rules, and rules involve independent checks to make sure that words and concepts are being used correctly; if there is no guarantee that words or concepts are effectively governed by rules, there is no reason to accept that they are being used with clear and settled meaning. The difficulty about a supposed private language, according to the objection, is that independent checks seem to be out of the question if the things designated are not available to anyone but the user of the language. The objection can also be raised, clearly enough, against the idea that one might conceptualize that which is not said to be public, as distinct from that which is said to be private. Accordingly, in section three below, Ayer confronts the question of privacy and sets out his reply. He also deals with other related objections to his enterprise.

We have a conception of sense-experience as consisting in the presentation of percepts, then, and we have our ordinary conception of the physical world, a conception of a world made up of physical objects as already characterized. Our problem now is the connection between the two. The physical world as we conceive it, clearly enough, is much more than a succession of sense-fields, a succession of sets of percepts as defined.

Various possibilities arise. It might be maintained that our conception of the physical world is such that it cannot come from sense-experience as we have characterized it; that the conception does nevertheless depend on sense-experience; and that therefore we have characterized sense-experience mistakenly, and in fact it consists of more than the presentation of percepts. Alternatively, but similarly, it might be argued that our world-conception cannot come from sense-experience as characterized; that sense experience in itself *is* as characterized; and that therefore it cannot be that our world-conception comes from sense-experience alone. There is, thirdly, the response of the sceptic. Sense-experience and our world-conception are both as described, and the second can be based only on the first; nonetheless, the first is not sufficient to sustain the second, and therefore our ordinary beliefs about the world lack rational warrant.

In order to avoid all these three possibilities, we can try to analyse our conception of the world, to break it down into elements, and to see if these elements are in fact no more than percepts, or at any rate are intimately connected with percepts alone. We can also make an approach to this same answer by working in the other direction. That is, we begin with experience as conceived, and attempt to see if it can be worked upon so as to yield our conception of the world. We can attempt to *construct* our picture of the world from the material of percepts.

By way of analogy, consider human groups, say crowds, mobs or nations, of which it has sometimes been thought that they are more than the sums of their parts. It has been thought, for example, that a mob may have passions which are not wholly to be explained in terms of the psychology of the individuals who make it up. One might test this hypothesis, supposing it to be clear enough, and worth the trouble, either by seeing if one could break down the supposed group-fact into facts about the individuals, or by seeing if facts about the individuals could be assembled together and built up into an adequate account of the supposed group-fact.

In a somewhat similar way, in the fourth section below, Ayer undertakes to construct out of percepts our ordinary conception of the physical world. His argument in its essential idea, expressed in an exceedingly simple way, is that from the imagined infant's succession of marble-percepts, or visual fields, and from other such sequences, some of them produced by the infant's moving his head rather than by the movement of something in his environment, he could come in the end to our conception of the physical world. He would not need other materials than percepts.

This involves his making an escape, so to speak, from the current sense-field. It involves, in terms of the example, establishing relations between successive sense-fields, and hence taking a number of round orange percepts to count as *one* of something. However, there is no possibility of quickly anticipating the course of Ayer's argument. It includes the notion of *visual continuants*, and *visuo-tactual continuants*, and in the end the distinction between the objective and the subjective. Until this last stage the construction has proceeded in terms of percepts, or fundamentally so. At this stage, but not before, they come to be characterized as subjective, and to be given a role in the theory subordinate to the role of something else, *physical objects* as we ordinarily conceive them. The latter are regarded as causally responsible for percepts.

This last transition rests on the *positing* of physical objects and involves a kind of imagination. There is at least a partial analogy to this transition in the development of science, and in particular of physics, out of an ordinary view of the world. Some philosophers and physicists begin with things in the ordinary sense, and then downgrade them in terms of reality, giving pride of place instead to particles and forces with no perceptible qualities. If it seems odd to regard the issue of what fundamentally exists as a matter for decision, in some sense, rather than discovery, it can be argued that there is no other possibility.

In the fifth section below, the sophisticated realism to which we have come is contrasted with phenomenalism. The latter is taken to be the doctrine that statements about physical objects essentially are statements about percepts. The connection we have is not of this kind. It is not that object-statements can be neatly translated into percept-statements. The subject of the sixth and last section has already been mentioned, in the analogy of a moment ago. The question is whether we must now follow the mentioned physicists and philosophers, and conceive of physical objects in a certain way. Are objects to be taken, in the very end, as consisting in particles and forces which are wholly outside of sense experience? There is another alternative, a compromise by which Ayer neatly completes a formidable solution to a large and recalcitrant problem.

T.H.

A. J. Ayer

Construction of Our Theory of the Physical World

Reprinted from *The Central Questions of Philosophy* by A. J. Ayer, copyright © A. J. Ayer, 1973. Published by Weidenfeld and Nicolson. Reprinted by permission of the author and publisher. Slight revisions by the author for this reprinting.

1. What Do We Perceive?

How does a philosopher come to assert that the access to physical objects which we believe that we obtain from the exercise of sight and touch is not direct? In the normal way, if someone were to say that he was seeing a table indirectly, one would probably construe his statement as a rather eccentric way of saying that he was seeing it reflected, in an ordinary mirror, perhaps, or through a periscope: if he said that he was touching it indirectly, one might take him to mean that he was in contact with it through some instrument, but clearly this is not what the philosopher has in mind, since these cases are exceptional, whereas he is contending that our perception of physical objects can only be indirect. What he is asserting is not, as in these construes, that one physical object is perceived through the medium of another, but rather that every physical object is perceived, if at all, through the medium of something else: an entity of a different sort. Our first task, then, is to make clear what he takes these other entities to be.

The view that our perception of physical objects is mediated in this way holds a very respectable place in the history of philosophy. It has given a foothold to sceptics who have raised the question whether one can be rationally justified in believing in the existence of a physical world to which one's experience gives one no direct access, but it has also been held by many philosophers who were not primarily sceptics, or even not sceptics at all. Thus, Descartes maintained that physical objects were perceived not directly but through the medium of what he called ideas. Locke, under Descartes's influence, referred to the objects by which he thought that perception was mediated, as simple ideas of sensation. Berkeley, following Locke, spoke indifferently of our perceiving ideas and perceiving sensible qualities. Hume took the same position, but substituted the word 'impression' for Berkeley's 'idea', reserving the word 'idea' for images or concepts. Kant, whose *Critique of Pure Reason* was a response to Hume's scepticism, spoke similarly of 'Vorstellungen' of which the favoured English rendering is 'representations'. John Stuart Mill took perception to consist in having sensations, and used the word 'sensation' to refer not only to such perceptual acts as those of seeing or hearing but also to what was seen or heard or otherwise sensed. In more recent times, philosophers who have wished to make a clear distinction between what they called acts of sensing, or states of acquaintance or awareness, and their immediate objects, have commonly followed Moore and Russell in characterizing these objects as sense-data. There have, however, been other locutions. Russell himself, regarding the notion of sense-data as being tied to that of mental acts, in the existence of which he came to disbelieve, preferred in his later works to use the term 'percepts' to refer to the data of the outer senses. In one of his early essays, Moore used the term 'sense-content' as an alternative to 'sense-datum', and I also used it, in my *Language, Truth and Logic*, in a way corresponding to Russell's use of 'percept'. The Cambridge philosopher, C. D. Broad, advancing the theory that 'Whenever I truly judge that [a physical object] x appears to me to have the sensible quality q, what happens is that I am directly aware of a certain object y which (a) really does have the quality q and (b) stands in some peculiarly intimate relation, yet to be determined, to x',[1] used the term 'sensa' to designate the objects which fulfilled the function of y. This way of introducing sensa was also employed by Moore and Russell to introduce sense-data. More recently still, the American philosophers, C. I. Lewis and Nelson Goodman, have used the term '*qualia*', in a way that is reminiscent of Berkeley's reference to sensible qualities.

While there is a large measure of agreement in the ways in which these various terms have been used, they are not in all cases exactly interchangeable. It is not even true of them severally that they have been given a wholly consistent use. Thus, Locke employed the term 'idea' to refer to particular objects, to general characteristics and to concepts. The examples that he gave of simple ideas of sense were general characteristics, but he seems in fact to have conceived of the immediate data of perception as particular objects in which these characteristics inhered. For Berkeley, on the other hand, the things which we sense were complexes of qualities, though he thought of these complexes as constituting particulars. Moore began by using the term 'sense-datum' to refer indiscriminately to general characteristics and to the particular objects which exemplified them, but ended by confining its extension to particulars. Russell thought of sense-data as particulars but came to represent percepts as complexes of qualities. Since it is arguable that particulars can anyhow be constructed out of qualities and their relations, this divergence may not be very important, but it can have a bearing on the status which is assigned to the immediate data of perception.

One question which has been thought to arise concerning their status is whether or not they exist objectively, and here again there has been a divergence of opinion. Thus, as their choice of the term 'idea' indicates, Descartes, Locke and Berkeley agreed in making them subjective, in the sense that they denied them all three of the pervasive properties which common sense attributes to physical objects, including the two which are attributed to most of the other things that the ordinary man might say that he perceived. They took it to be necessarily true of ideas, in this usage, that they were not accessible to more than one sense, that they were not individually presented to more than one observer, and that they did not exist independently of being perceived. On the other hand, Moore and Russell, while they thought of sense-data as being, like Berkeley's ideas, the objects of acts of sensing, did not regard this as being incompatible with their existing unsensed. Unlike Moore, who wished to keep open the possibility of identifying some sense-data with the surfaces, or parts of the surfaces, of physical objects, Russell did confine each of them to a single mode of sensing and to a single observer, but his reason for this was that they were causally dependent upon the bodily state of the observer. That he did not regard them as constitutionally incapable of existing independently is shown by the fact that he did attribute independent existence to the objects to which he gave the name of 'sensibilia', describing them as objects 'of the same metaphysical and physical status as sense-data',[2] with the difference that they were not actually sensed. The same must have applied to the percepts which he substituted for sense-data, since he ended by identifying them with states of the observer's brain. Even so, he assumed that in their character as percepts, they were private to the observer whose mind they helped to constitute. In the same way, Hume thought of impressions as entering into mutually exclusive series, each of which constituted a different person, and held it to follow from their nature that they were 'fleeting and perishing'.[3] This cannot, indeed, be true of qualia, if they are treated as general characteristics; for it is in the nature of a general characteristic or, as philosophers now mostly say, a universal, that it can occur at many places and at many times. Nevertheless, the grouping of qualia which has been thought to furnish a perceptual datum has also been thought to be contained within the limits of a single sense-experience.

From this it appears that, for all the differences in detail, there has been a widespread agreement that the immediate data of perception do not enjoy what Hume called ' a continued and distinct existence'.[4] The suggestion is that when I look, or at any rate believe myself to be looking, at the table in front of me, what I primarily see is not the table at all but something else, which has the impermanence and perhaps also the subjectivity of a mental image. In general, this view has been advanced as if it were an empirical discovery, with the implication that the naive realist who thinks that he does see the table is simply mistaken on a question of empirical fact. Thus, Professor Prichard, who thought it correct to say that we see colours, is supposed to have remarked of the ordinary man that when he sees a colour he 'straight off mistakes it for a body'.[5] In this way, all our ordinary judgements of perception are assimilated to the cases in which we misidentify what we perceive. It is as if we were constantly like the Eskimos who when they were first shown Flaherty's film about their lives rushed to harpoon the seals which they saw on the screen. But surely this is not a fair analogy. In the ordinary way, the ground for thinking that an object has been misidentified is that one's identification of it is not borne out by further observations. The Eskimos soon discovered that they were not destroying animals but defacing images. But what experience could reveal that we had constantly been mistaking colours, or ideas, or sense-data, for bodies? If bodies are not directly perceptible, there can be no chance for our senses to detect the masquerade. It follows that if the ordinary man is making any mistake at all when he thinks that he perceives physical objects without the mediation of other entities, it is a mistake of a different kind; a purely theoretical error. He must be misinterpreting not just some particular item but the general character of his perceptual experiences. But then what grounds do we have for thinking that this is so?

The issue here may be brought out more clearly if we examine Russell's claim that ordinary judgements of perception like 'This is a table' entail an inference, reserving for the moment the question what sort of inference it is: the suggestion then will be that we need to provide ourselves with the means of formulating the premises on which such inferences are based. In Russell's case, the claim was supported, in traditional fashion, by the argument from illusion,[6] but there is, I believe, a simpler and more effective way of establishing it. We need only consider the range of the assumptions which our ordinary judgements of perception carry. To begin with, there are the assumptions which we have seen to be involved in characterizing anything as a physical object like a table. It has to be accessible to more than one sense and to more than one observer and it has to be capable of existing unperceived. In addition, it has to occupy a position or series of positions in three-dimensional space and to endure throughout a period of time. It may, indeed, be argued that these are not straightforwardly empirical assumptions, but postulates of a conceptual system. They set the framework into which the results of our observations are mostly made to fit. The fact remains, however, that in particular instances they can fail to be satisfied. The Eskimos discovered that the images which they had mistaken for seals were not tangible; the presence of the snakes which the drunkard thinks he sees is not corroborated by other observers, and the fact that it is not so corroborated is taken as evidence that these visionary snakes do not have the capacity of existing unperceived. Similarly, we may discover in the course of further experience that what we had taken to be a physical object has not the requisite location in physical space or persistence through time. Part of the point of the argument from illusion is, indeed, that it calls attention to the fact that such mistakes are possible.

Neither is it only a question of the validity of these general assumptions. Our perceptual judgements are seldom indefinite, in the sense that we claim only to perceive a physical object of some sort or other. In the normal way, we identify it as a thing of some specific kind, and this brings in further assumptions, as, for example, that the object is solid, or flexible, or that it is not hollow. These further assumptions may relate to the purposes which the object serves, as when we identify something as a pen-knife, or a telephone; they may relate to its physical constitution as in the identification of an object as an orange or an apple, which denies its being made of wax. They may presume on the deliverances of other senses, as when our description of an object which we believe ourselves to be seeing or touching carries implications about the way in which it tastes or sounds or smells.

But now can it seriously be maintained that all this can fall within the content of a single act of perception? Can my present view of the table, considered purely in itself as a fleeting visual experience, conceivably guarantee that I am seeing something that is also tangible, or visible to other observers? Can it guarantee even that I am seeing something which exists at any other time than this, let alone something that is made of such-and-such materials, or endowed with such-and-such causal properties, or serving such-and-such a purpose? I think it evident that it cannot. But if these conclusions are not logically guaranteed by the content of my present visual experience, one is surely entitled to say that they go beyond it, and just this is what I take to be meant by saying that my judgement that this is a table embodies an inference. It embodies an inference, not in the sense that it results from any conscious process of reasoning, but just in the sense that it affirms more than can logically be entailed by any strict account of the experience on which it is based. What I mean here by a strict account is one that is tailored to the experience, in that it describes the quality of what is sensibly presented, without carrying any further implication of any sort. In the normal way, we do not formulate such propositions because we are interested not in the data as such, but in the interpretations which we have learned to put upon them. I cannot, however, see any logical reason why they should not be formulable. The question is how these experiential propositions, as I shall call them, should be formulated.

2. The Elements

This is a question on which we have already touched, in talking about the use which philosophers have made of terms like 'idea' or 'sense-datum', and we have seen that there has been some disagreement about the way in which it should be answered. Part of the reason for the difficulties which have arisen is that we normally do not attend to the character of our sensory experiences to any greater extent than is necessary for us to be able to interpret them successfully. In the ordinary way it is enough for us to be able to identify the object at which we are looking as a tree, or a book, or a match-box, or whatever it may be: we make no precise assessment of its size or shape or even of its colour; we may notice that the surface of the match-box is predominantly yellow, but most probably do not observe what shade of yellow it is. Thus, while it is possible to hold that my visual field at any given moment consists of nothing more than an array of colours it has to be admitted that I do not see these colours merely *as* colours, and to the extent that I do see them as colours, I do not discriminate them very finely.

Are we then to say that I am actually presented with the shades of colour which I do not consciously distinguish? The argument in favour of saying this is that it is logically necessary that any colour should be of some specific shade. The fact that I do not notice the difference in shade between two separate occurrences of the colour yellow in my present visual field does not entail that the difference does not exist. It may even be maintained that there have to be differences which I am incapable of detecting. For instance, it may happen that I cannot distinguish the colour of A from that of B, or the colour of B from that of C, but that I can distinguish the colour of A from that of C. It is then held to follow that the colour of B must really be different from that of both A and C, although the difference is too fine in either case for me to be able to observe it.

The objection to this realistic way of talking about appearances is that if we do not take what we notice, however cursorily, as a criterion for what appears to us, it is not clear what other criterion is available. We could try to appeal to physiology, but apart from the objection that we have first to decide what the appearances are before we can discover what states of our nervous systems are correlated with them, this would not yield a set of rules that we could practically apply. A better course might be to assess the visual data in terms of the judgements of colour, size and shape, that the observer would make if he fully exercised his powers of discrimination, together with any further refinements which these judgements might logically be considered to entail. This would, indeed, leave us for the most part in some doubt as to what the appearances really were, but it might be argued that this did not matter, since the doubt is one that generally exists.

I think that this course is feasible, so long as one is not pursuing it in the context of the theory of knowledge. If one is interested merely in constructing a language which will serve for the description of appearances, without claiming any priority for it over a language in which terms that refer to physical objects are allowed to be primitive, one is entitled to take whatever steps will enable one to deal most satisfactorily with the technical problems. An excellent example of this is supplied by Nelson Goodman in his book *The Structure of Appearance*, where he develops a system of which the basic elements are *qualia* of colour, *qualia* of place, and *qualia* of time. The places, as one would expect, are places in a visual field, and the times those that furnish the temporal order of experiences rather than the dating of physical events. Concrete particulars are constituted by a relation of togetherness which holds between *qualia* of these different types, and between *qualia* of one type and combinations of *qualia* of the other two. Thus a particular item in my present visual field may be characterized alternatively as a colour together with a place-time, or a colour-spot together with a time, or a colour-moment together with a place. The qualities of size and shape, which characterize these particulars, are then defined, and the ordering of colours and of places is achieved on the basis of a relation of matching by a method which could also be applied to data of other sorts, such as sounds. In this way the framework is set for a systematic description of visual appearances. To what extent, if any, a description of the physical world could be fitted into this framework, or into an extension of it which admitted the data of the other senses, is left an open question.

There are two reasons why I shall follow a different procedure. In the first place, I am mainly concerned not to organize appearances into a system but rather to show how they are capable of sustaining the interpretations which we put upon them. Secondly, I propose to make it necessary for anything to be an appearance that it be something of which the observer at least implicitly takes notice, and this induces me to treat as primitive a number of concepts which, from a purely logical point of view, it might be thought preferable to construct. Beginning also with the visual field, I add to the *qualia* of colour, not only *qualia* of size and shape, but also a set of patterns of which the description may be borrowed from that of the physical objects with which they come to be identified. Thus I shall speak of a visual chair-pattern, a visual leaf-pattern, a visual cat-pattern, and so forth, and I shall construe these terms as applying to any members of the range of visual patterns which would typically lead the observer to think that he was seeing the corresponding physical object. This is not to say that the character of the visual pattern is wholly determined by the identity of the physical object which it actually presents. If the object is camouflaged the pattern may be one that is associated with a different object: in the case of a puzzle-picture one and the same object may be responsible for patterns of different types; if the observer is undergoing an hallucination there may be no object which the pattern presents. Neither is it to say that the observer characterizes these patterns *as* patterns. He notices them implicitly, in the sense that it is his registering of them that governs his identification of the physical objects which he thinks he sees. They provide the main visual clues on which our everyday judgements of perception are based.

Both spatial and temporal relations hold between these patterns and between them and *qualia* of other sorts. Thus, a face-pattern encloses a nose-pattern; a cat-pattern may be spatially coincident with a *quale* of black; a bird-pattern may appear at successive moments at different points in a visual field. Spatial relations hold only between data of the same sense which are partners in the same sense-field, but temporal relations may hold between data of different senses. For instance, a visual bird-pattern may precede or follow an occurrence of a bird-note. It must be made clear that these descriptions are intended to be purely qualitative. The reference to a bird-note should not be understood as implying that the sound is caused by a bird. It serves only to characterize a sound of a distinctive type.

It has been argued, notably by Berkeley,[7] that the visual field is originally two-dimensional and that we come to see things in depth only through the association of sight with touch. Against this, psychologists like William James have maintained that depth is as much an intrinsic property of our visual fields as are length and breadth.[8] Since the arguments on which Berkeley relies are drawn from optics, whereas James takes his stand upon the way things actually seem, the issue between them is not a straightforward question of fact, but rather a disagreement over what is to count as primitive. Since we have chosen to adopt a psychological rather than a physiological criterion for determining what appearances are, we can side on this point with William James. This means that we can conceive of the spatial relations between *qualia* in three dimensions as being presented with the same immediacy as the *qualia* themselves. In the same way, I take the temporal relations of simultaneity and precedence to be directly given, with the consequence that the time at which a sense-field occurs is treated as having some duration. In both psychological and physical terms, this duration is likely to be short, but no general measure can be set. It is for the observer to judge in any given instance at what point an earlier datum passes out of the content of his present experience and into the domain of memory. In many cases the distinction will not be sharp.

At the most elementary stage, a *quale* is particularized simply by the recording of its occurrence. The primitive language-game, if I may so call it, consists merely in designating presented *qualia*, together, perhaps, with their spatio-temporal relations. It is these relations that set the limits of the sense-field in which the *qualia* occur. Indeed, since at this stage spatio-temporal relations do not extend beyond the presented field, except in so far as temporal relations may serve to correlate the data of different senses, we can actually define a visual or tactual sense-field as consisting of anything to which some designated *quale* is both spatially and temporally related. This makes the particular identity of the sense-field, and of the items in it, dependent on the context. We cannot exclude the possibility that the same configuration of *qualia* is presented on various occasions, but there can be only one such assemblage with which the observer is actually confronted when he records the occurrence of the items he picks out. If we wish to particularize *qualia* in a purely descriptive way, we have to proceed to a further stage at which we are able to conceive of sense-fields as having predecessors and successors. We can then take advantage of the empirical fact that complete repetition occurs only in short stretches of anyone's experience, and identify a sense-field by reference not only to its own character but also to that of its neighbours, and if necessary to that of their neighbours, and so on until we obtain a complex which is in fact unique. This method is not foolproof. It fails, for example, in the case where two different periods of unconsciousness are each interrupted briefly by qualitatively identical experiences. Such exceptional cases can, however, be provisionally disregarded. They will not be found to impede the progress of the argument. The resources which are needed to deal with them will become available to us only when we have constructed a physical system into which we can then reinterpret the elements on which it was based. I intend to show later how this is done.

3. The Question of Privacy

When *qualia* are turned into particulars, whether by being located demonstratively or descriptively, I shall usually refer to them as percepts. In this I follow Russell, who also came to think of percepts as constituted out of qualities, and the term was used in much the same way before him by the pragmatists, Peirce and William James. There is, however, one important point in which I differ from Russell.

Unlike him, I do not characterize percepts from the outset as private entities. It is obvious that *qualia* are not private entities, since they are universals which can be exemplified in anyone's experience. It might, however, be thought that privacy accrued to them when they were turned into percepts, in as much as their particularization has been made to depend on their location in sense-fields which are presented to a single observer. But the answer to this is that while the reference to a particular observer may occur in our explanation of the way that percepts come into being, it does not, and indeed cannot, occur in the primitive designation of percepts themselves. As I have tried to make clear, this is simply a matter of recording the presence of a set of patterns. Since persons do not yet come into the picture, there is no implication that the patterns occur in the experience of any particular observer, nor, therefore, that their concretion into percepts gives any one person a monopoly of them.

Not only, then, is it not necessary to characterize percepts as private from the outset; it would not be legitimate. The antithesis between what is private and what is public, in the sense which is here in question, comes into play only at a level where we have the means both of referring to different persons and of distinguishing between their inner experiences and the external objects which they perceive in common. I shall try to show later how this stage can be attained. At the level at which we are now operating, the question of privacy or publicity simply does not arise.

Nevertheless, our experiential propositions do possess a feature which is the main target of the objections which Wittgenstein has raised against the possibility of what he calls a private language. The only criterion for determining the truth of these propositions is the observer's recognition of the patterns which he picks out. But what guarantee is there that he recognizes them correctly? He can appeal to his memory of previous occasions on which the same pattern, or what he assumes to be the same pattern, was presented to him. But how can he be sure that his memory is not playing him false? The answer is that he can at this stage have no better reason than his feeling sure. If he is satisfied with his judgement, that is all that can be asked for. As Goodman puts it, the identification of a presented *quale* is settled by the observer's decree.[9]

The objection then is that for anything to qualify as a language, it must consist of signs which are employed in accordance with rules, and that this condition is not satisfied if the speaker is able simply to decree what is right: his decrees must be subject to some independent check. My answer is just to deny that this is a good enough reason for saying that the condition is not satisfied. The speaker of our primitive language can be assumed to have his habits of classi- fication and these will constitute the rules. At the most primitive level there are indeed no checks, but they too can be supplied as soon as the observer starts to associate percepts over a wider range. He then may find that different decrees which he is disposed to issue come into conflict and consequently decide to rescind one of them. The decree which he rescinds may then be said to have constituted the infringement of a rule. Admittedly, he will still not be able to dis- tinguish between the case in which he has been false to his habitual method of classification and that in which his experience is deviant, but this is a distinction for which there is no use at this stage. To make it, we should need the resources of the theory which we are engaged in developing.

This answer may appear more convincing, when it is shown that in this matter the speakers of what is deemed to be a public language are essentially in the same position. For, as I have argued elsewhere,[10] we too are obliged in the end to rely simply on our powers of recognition. When we are referring to what we conceive to be persistent objects, we may indeed have other specimens at hand by which to check our usage. Even when this is not possible, we may be able to compare our verdict with that of other speakers. But then the specimens must themselves be recognized. When other speakers are consulted, their signs or gestures have to be identified, if any- thing is to be learned from them. In the end we must simply decide that this is an instance of such-and-such a word or such-and-such another type of object. We do, indeed, have the advantage over the players of the primitive language-game that we command a much wider area within which our decisions can be cross-checked, but this is only a difference of degree. Even though we do not, as a rule, explicitly characterize the percepts which alone permit us to recognize physical objects or to receive any information from other people, our power to apply our language to the world depends on their being implicitly identified. Unless the primitive language-game were possible, our more sophisticated language-game could not be played.

A similar and equally unsound objection to our procedure is that the use of sentences which refer to percepts could not be understood by anyone who did not already understand the use of sentences which refer to physical objects. From this it is thought to follow that we are already pre-supposing the system which we are professing to construct. This objection gains some plausibility from the fact that I introduced percepts by whittling down our ordinary judgements of perception, and from the fact that my designations of *qualia* were largely borrowed from those of the physical objects which they are ordinarily taken to present. Nevertheless this plausibility is only superficial. In explaining, as opposed to defining, the use of unfamiliar terms, one is free to use any means to make oneself intelligible, and in devising a technical vocabulary, one is free to take account of the purposes which it is intended to serve. The objection would hold good only if I had so contrived my references to percepts that they logically entailed the assumption of the existence of physical objects, and this we have seen not to be the case.

But, it may be argued, even if the reference to percepts does not have this logical consequence, still our power to identify percepts does logically depend on our power to identify physical, or anyhow public, objects, and this is equally objectionable. The argument is that the *qualia* out of which percepts are constituted are supposed to be defined ostensively and that only what is public is ostensively definable. It is true that I have taken care not to characterize percepts as private entities, but equally I have not characterized them as public. The point that matters here is that I am allowing their character to be determined by the verdict of a single observer, independently of the way things seem to anybody else.

But why should it be thought that an object has to be public to be ostensively definable? If the reason is just that any use of language has to conform to some public standard of correctness, we are brought back to the previous objection, which I have already met. If it is rather that only a public object can be pointed to, in the way that I can point to my physical possessions but not to my thoughts, the simple answer is that to suppose that ostensive definitions require pointing is to take the word 'ostensive' much too literally. Not only that, but the view of the distinction between what is public and what is private which underlies this argument is altogether too naive. Objects are not given as either public or private. The distinction comes into operation only under the auspices of a theory in which a sense is attached to saying that different persons see and touch the same chairs and tables, books and trees and stars, see the same pictures in the cinema, even hear the same sounds, taste the same tastes and smell the same smells, but no sense is attached to saying that they similarly inspect one another's thoughts and feelings and sensations. I shall attempt later on to show how this distinction is arrived at.[11] For the present, I wish only to remark that it has no essential bearing on the way in which one learns to characterize the different parties to it. When we teach someone ostensively the name of what is classed in the theory as a public object we bring him into a situation in which we assume that he will have, let us say, a visual experience which is similar to our own, and that he will come to put a similar interpretation on it. If he subsequently seems to us to repeat the word that we have taught him in a way that we find appropriate, we infer that he has learned his lesson. When we teach someone the name of what is classed in the theory as a private sensation, we again rely on discovering him in a situation where we assume that he is having an experience similar to that which we should have under similar conditions, and we expect him to put a similar interpretation on it; for instance, sooner or later not to regard it, in the way small children are said to do, as a property of the stimulus, but rather as a state of his own. In this case also we infer that he has learned his lesson if he seems to us to repeat the word in a way that we find appropriate to our own experience; not indeed, normally, our experience of a similar sensation, but our observation of conditions in which it seems to us that the use of the word is called for. In either case there is the problem of drawing his attention to the right item in his experience. When it is a question of his having to select a percept from his visual field, the effect of our making a gesture may, indeed, be helpful, but even then it is not indispensable.

I deal elsewhere with the problem of our right to attribute experiences to others.[12] The point that I now wish to make is that if there is a difficulty here, it arises just as much with respect to the perception of what are deemed to be public objects and events, as with respect to so-called inner states and processes. Those who maintain that inner processes stand in need of outward criteria are justified in the sense that we need some observable evidence on which to base our belief that some other person is having such and such thoughts or feelings or sensations, but equally we need some observable evidence on which to base the belief that some other person is perceiving any physical object. If I have any philosophical reason for doubting whether another person has feelings similar to mine, or indeed any feelings at all, it will equally be a reason for doubting whether he perceives physical objects in the same way as I do, or indeed whether he perceives anything at all. The insistence on outward criteria does not avoid this problem, and the choice of percepts as a basis for the construction of the physical world does not worsen it.

The mistake which philosophers who have followed this procedure have too commonly made is that of assuming that if they start with percepts, they must also start with a percipient, to whom the percepts are exclusively attributed. Not only is this illegitimate for the reasons which I have already given, but it leads to insuperable difficulties. If the percipient is just the philosopher himself, which alone would seem to be warranted, he will be hard put to escape the conclusion reached by the German Idealist, Fichte, that 'the world is my idea': a proposition which is simply false if taken as referring only to the speaker and contradictory if it is generalized.[13] If he tries, inconsistently, to assemble the data of a number of percipients, he falls foul of the objection that no one can be in a position to perform this synthesis. These difficulties are avoided by making percepts neutral, which is not to be confused with making them common. I shall, indeed, represent the theory out of which the physical world is constituted as being developed by a single observer. This Robinson Crusoe approach is not meant to be historical, but only to do justice to the fact that any knowledge of the world which anyone acquires is bound to be based upon his own experiences. It might seem, at first sight, as if this is to take the idealist position which

I have just been condemning, but there are two vital points of difference. The first and most important is that the observer is not permitted to conceive of the data with which he works as private to himself. We shall see that this is eventually possible, but only when the theory has been developed and is allowed to transform its own origins. The second is that the observer is not identified either with myself or with any other person. If I am asked who is then supposed to carry out the construction, my answer is that we can think of it as being carried out by anyone who disposes of the necessary percepts.

4. Outline of the Construction

It is obvious that our observer can make no progress so long as we confine his attention to the contents of a single visual field. We may for the present continue to restrict his data to those provided by the sense of sight, but we need now to credit him with both memories and expectations. He is not, of course, in a position to prove that his memories are correct, but it is not required that he should be. It is not even necessary to postulate that his memories are in fact correct, but only that he holds the appropriate beliefs about his past experiences. If it is asked how these memories and expectations could be generated, a sufficient answer, except that he speaks of thoughts instead of percepts, has been given by William James. 'If the present thought is of ABCDEFG, the next one will be of BCDEFGH, and the one after that of CDEFGHI – the lingerings of the past dropping successively away, and the incomings of the future making up the loss. These lingerings of old objects, these incomings of new, are the germs of memory and expectation, the retrospective and the prospective sense of time. They give that continuity to consciousness without which it could not be called a stream.' [14] The implication is that sense-fields overlap in their contents, and that this makes it natural for the relation of temporal precedence, which is originally given as holding between members of a single sense-field, to be projected on to its neighbours on either side. If this relation is then conceived to hold between the members of these sense-fields and members of their neighbours, and if the exercise of memory endows it also with the power to bridge gaps in consciousness, one can come to conceive of the domain of temporal relations as being, if not infinitely, at least indefinitely extended. In the case of the past, this need not go so far as an actual belief in the existence of percepts that precede the earliest that are remembered. It is enough that this be treated as an open possibility.

The overlapping of sense-fields can also be regarded as facilitating the projection of spatial relations beyond the limits in which they are originally given. Thus a percept which appears at the right-hand edge of one visual field may in succeeding fields appear at the centre and finally at the left-hand edge; the percepts on the left of the original field are not found in its successors, and fresh percepts appear upon the right. At the same time, the observer remembers that the percepts which have disappeared from view bore the same spatial relation to the surviving percept as it now seems to bear to the new arrivals. Accordingly, he comes to think of these successive sense-fields as spatially adjacent. The result, here again, is that any given visual field can come to be regarded as indefinitely extensible.

An important empirical fact, without which, indeed, the development of our theory would not be possible, is that the observer inhabits a predominantly stable world. What I mean by this, in physical terms, is that although things may change their perceptible qualities, they mostly do so gradually and very often by stages between which there is no perceptible difference, and although they may change their relative positions they mostly stay put, in the sense that there are many other things to which they bear constant spatial relations over fairly long periods of time. One result of this is that the process by which a percept appears at different positions in successive fields is often found to be reversible. Percepts similar to those that appeared on the former run occur in the same spatial relations as their predecessors stood to one another. From different angles of approach the members of the various series appear in different orders, but their qualities remain very similar, and the spatial relations within the series remain constant. This makes it natural for the observer to adopt a new measure of identity, according to which the corresponding percepts in these different series are not merely similar but identical. Not only that, but the fact that these percepts are recoverable, after longer lapses of time, and are then found to have much the same qualities, to stand in much the same spatial relations to one another, and to appear in much the same wider environment, leads him to think of them as having persisted throughout the interval. In this way, percepts which appear to him successively are conceived to exist simultaneously and to occupy permanent positions in an indefinitely extended three-dimensional visual space.

At this point the objection may be raised that we are assuming a greater degree of constancy among our observer's percepts than is justified by the facts of our experience. Even if we assume, in physical terms, that the objects in his environment are relatively static, and that their real qualities do not noticeably change, still they are going to look different to him, according as he sees them in different lights, or from different distances, or from different angles, or according as his own condition varies. How then can he naturally come to conceive of any single percept as persisting in each case?

To a considerable extent, I have already provided against this objection by the degree of generality which I have allowed into the original designations of *qualia*. The characterization of a *quale* as, say, a cat-pattern, leaves room for appreciable differences among the presentations which answer to it; in some cases, indeed, these differences will be greater than is consonant with ascribing identity to the percepts that display them. A more specific designation will then be needed. This will still allow for some variation in the percepts to which it applies, but not so much as to destroy the constancy of the pattern. The percept which is conceived to persist may be said to be standardized, in the sense that it constitutes a model which the actual percepts match more or less closely. From now on, I shall speak of these standardized percepts as visual continuants. There is then no reason why a visual continuant should not be regarded as subject to change. For instance, it may be spatially coincident with a *quale* of black at one time and with a *quale* of grey at another. It is to be noted that for our observer all changes are objective. He is not yet in a position to distinguish between the variations in appearances which are due to changes in the object and those which are due to changes in the environment, or in his spatial relation to the object, or in himself: indeed, he cannot as yet be credited with any conception of himself.

The next step is to allow for the possibility of movement. For this, we have to think of the observer as abstracting from the other qualities of percepts and considering only their extension. Then, since the extension of a percept is equivalent to the amount of space which it occupies, it becomes possible for him to think of places in detachment from their occupants. Not only the visual continuant, but also the place where it is, come to be regarded as permanently there. Since the place has to be identified as the meeting-point of a number of sensory routes, which are themselves sufficiently constant to be re-identifiable, the constituents of the observer's world have still to be predominantly static. Nevertheless a certain amount of movement can now be admitted. If a number of very similar percepts appear successively at neighbouring places, they may be deprived of their separate identities and treated as a single percept in motion. In the case where, as we should say, only the result of the displacement is observed, and not the actual process, it can be held either that the visual continuant has moved, or that it has ceased to exist and another one, closely resembling it, has come into existence at another place. The first of these hypotheses is the more likely to be adopted if the continuant is one of a kind that has frequently been observed to move. In other cases, the observer has no reasons for deciding the question one way or the other. He will acquire them only when he commands a much richer theory, in which causes are assigned for things coming into existence or ceasing to exist.

Among the visual continuants which the observer comes to posit there are some that are constructed on a different principle from the rest. The percepts which enter into their constitution do not regularly appear in a similar environment, except in so far as the visual continuants in question are seen to stand in constant spatial relations to one another. The peculiarity of these percepts consists first in their tendency to occupy similar positions in the sense-fields in which they figure and, secondly, in their pervasiveness; the *qualia* which they particularize are found in an unusually high proportion of sense-fields. It is on this account that they are transformed into persistent objects. These visual continuants are, in physical terms, those parts of the observer's body that he customarily sees. The acquisition of the concept of this body as a whole depends upon a fusion of visual with tactual and kinaesthetic data, and both accompanies and facilitates the identification of visual with tactual space.

Although the same general method serves for the construction of tactual as of visual space, there is the important difference that the tactual field is normally much less extensive than the visual, so that if our observer lacked the sense of sight, he would need to associate tactual *qualia* with kinaesthetic *qualia* of movement, and perhaps also with auditory *qualia*, in order to arrive at the conception of tactual places as permanently accessible. For one who is not so handicapped, we can take visual space to be primary, and then consider how it can be made to accommodate the data of touch. For this purpose we can take advantage of the double aspect of tactual percepts; in physical terms, the fact that they are felt both in the object which is being touched and, say, in the fingers which are touching it. Accordingly, the tactual percept comes to be located at the point of temporary coincidence of these different visual continuants. Since the visual percepts belonging to the observer's body are a relatively constant factor, the variations in the tactual *qualia* are ascribed to the differences in the other visual percepts. By this means the visual continuants of which they are members become endowed with tactual qualities. Once the association of visual with tactual qualities has been established in the cases where, as we should say, an object is both touched and seen, it is easily extended to the cases where the object is touched but not seen, and also to the cases where it is seen but not touched. The possibility of this last step depends on the fact that tactual, like visual, *qualia* are found to be reinstatable at the junction of relatively constant visual and tactual routes.

The association of visual with tactual qualities also permits the observer to round out the concept of his body. The parts of his body which he sees only in reflection are thought to be adjacent to the directly visible parts, rather than located separately in the place where the reflection is seen, because of their contiguity to them in tactual space. It is because of this contiguity and also because it is observed to be maintained when, as we should say, the body is displaced, that the various parts, which can still be represented as different visuo-tactual continuants, are also thought to constitute a single whole.

In speaking of the way in which our observer develops the concept of his own body, I do not mean to imply that he already conceives of it as his own. We have not yet given him any reason for distinguishing himself from the objects which he perceives. So far as he is concerned, at this stage, his body is just one among other visuo-tactual continuants. If it comes to assume a special importance for him, it is partly because it is the locus of kinaesthetic data, in a way the other continuants are not, but mainly because it is distinguished from the others by being what Peirce called the central body. Not only is it exceptionally pervasive, in the way we have already noted, but it supplies, as it were, the view-point from which the world appears to him.

At this stage we may suppose that the observer begins to make some simple causal correlations. He incorporates sounds and smells and tastes into his world-picture by tracing them to their apparent sources, this being partly a matter of locating the places of their maximum intensity, and partly one of noting the visuo-tactual conditions under which they are produced; and he also associates changes in the position or quality of one continuant with changes in the position or quality of another. In this way, the status of the central body is still further enhanced, because of the extent to which it is associated with changes in other things. In particular, it comes to be presented as the instrument through which the observer's desires for change are realized.

Having thus acquired some notion of the way in which the world works, the observer is at last able to take the first step towards drawing a distinction between his own experiences and the things which he perceives. The great majority of his percepts are interpreted objectively. The *qualia* which they particularize and the relations in which they stand are treated as qualities and relations of the rudimentary physical objects into which they have grown. There may, however, be some experiences which cannot be fitted into the general pattern. They are, perhaps, visual hallucinations, or dreams which the observer may be supposed to recollect, or even his day-dreams if these are sufficiently vivid to be mistakable for percepts. From his point of view, there is nothing amiss with these experiences as such. It is just that they do not noticeably concur with one another, nor do they fit into the general picture of the world which he has developed. He therefore distinguishes the various subsidiary accounts of the way things are, which these untoward experiences would lead him to give, from what we may call the main or central account, which is based on the general run of his experiences.

This is about as far as our Robinson Crusoe can be expected to go without a Man Friday to assist him. As an object of perception, Man Friday is just another visuo-tactual continuant. His importance to Crusoe and that of the other observers, whom we may now admit on to the scene, is that they also make sounds or marks or movements which Crusoe is able to interpret as signs. They share this capacity with the central body. What they do not share, so far as our original observer is concerned is the centrality of this body or its use as an instrument to realize his wishes.

In communicating with these other observers, our Crusoe finds that they appear to be giving information which very largely tallies with the course of his experience. In particular, he judges that it regularly corroborates his main account of the world. He also finds, however, that these people tell subsidiary stories which fit in neither with his main account, nor with his subsidiary accounts. In this way he acquires the idea of himself not only as an object represented by the central body, which figures in a main account of the world that the other makers of signs accept, but also as a teller of stories that they do not corroborate. From this he infers that the events which these subsidiary stories describe are events that exist only for him and correspondingly that the events which occur in the subsidiary stories that the others tell are events that exist only for them. The making of the private-public distinction thus goes together with the acquisition of self-consciousness and the attribution of consciousness to others.

In the final stage the private-public distinction is taken a great deal further. What happens is that the theory which I have been calling the main account of the world predominates over its origins. The objects to which I have been referring as visuo-tactual continuants are cut loose from their moorings. The possibility, which has already been accorded them, of existing at times when they are not perceived is extended to the point where it is unnecessary to their existence that they ever should be perceived, or even that there should be any observers to perceive them. Since the theory also requires that these objects do not change their perceptible qualities except as a result of some physical alteration in themselves, they come to be contrasted with the fluctuating impressions that different observers have of them. In this way the objects are severed from the actual percepts from which they have been abstracted and are even regarded as being causally responsible for them. A distinction is drawn between the main account of the world, as it is in itself, and any particular relation of it, with the result that all the observer's experiences, not only those that furnish the subsidiary accounts, but even those that furnish the main account are taken to be subjective. Thus the percepts out of which the theory grew are re-interpreted into it, and given a subordinate status. So far from being the only things that there are thought to be, they may be denied any independent existence, and treated merely as states of the observer. Whether they can be transmuted to the extent of being identified with physical states is a more doubtful question into which I shall not enter here. The point which now concerns us is that once the theory of the physical world has been developed, whether or not it has to allow room for objects or properties which are not classified as physical, we are entitled to let it take command, in the sense that it determines what there is. The fact that in doing so it downgrades its starting-point, in much the same way as a self-made man may repudiate his humble origins, is not a logical objection to this procedure. It may have a parallel, as we shall see, in the surgery which physics may be thought to practise upon commonsense.

5. Phenomenalism

As I said before, my account of the way in which the common-sense theory of the physical world is developed is not meant to be historical. Young children, who very quickly assume the theory, do not elaborate it on their own; they are taught a language which already embodies it, and whatever may be logically possible, it is factually improbable that they would arrive at it otherwise. I have told a fictitious story, the purpose of which has been to highlight the general features of our experience that make it possible for each of us to employ the theory successfully. It is in order to throw these features into stronger relief that I have represented what is in effect a process of analysis as a process of construction. In its general outline, my description of this process has been very similar to Hume's.[15] The main difference is that whereas he found in the relations of 'constancy and coherence', which our 'perceptions' exhibit, a means of explaining how we are deceived into treating them as persistent objects, I have represented these relations not as accounting for a deception but as justifying an acceptable theory.

It is to be noted that while the position which I have taken has some affinity with Mill's view that things are permanent possibilities of sensation, it is not a phenomenalist position, in the sense in which this term is usually understood. I am not suggesting that physical objects are reducible to percepts, if this is taken to mean that all the statements that we make about physical objects, even at the common-sense level, can be adequately translated into statements which refer only to percepts. If the demand for an adequate translation requires that the statements referring to percepts set out necessary and sufficient conditions for the truth of the statements about a physical object which they are meant to replace, I think it unlikely that it can be satisfied. For the conditions to be necessary it would have to be the case that the statement referring to the physical object could not be true unless they obtained, and for the conditions to be sufficient it would have to be the case that the statement referring to the physical object could not be false if they did obtain. But here there is, on the one hand, the difficulty that a visuo-tactual continuant may be represented by an indefinite variety of percepts in an equal variety of contexts, so that if the percepts in question had not occurred, some others would have done as well, and, on the other hand, the objection that any description of a particular set of percepts will be bound to leave open at least the logical possibility that the observer is undergoing some illusion.[16] But even if these difficulties could be met, there is another reason why I do not wish to adopt this position. The actual percepts that are presented to any observer, or even to the totality of observers at all times, are too scanty to answer to our conception of the physical world. It was for this reason that Berkeley required an ever-vigilant deity to keep the world under observation, at times when other spirits were not being supplied with the necessary ideas. But apart from any other objections that there may be to the introduction of this *deus ex machina*, it takes us outside the boundaries of phenomenalism. If the phenomenalist thesis is to be at all plausible, it has to draw on possible as well as actual percepts, with the result that most of the propositions which render its account of the world will take the form of unfulfilled conditionals. They will state that if such and such conditions, which are not in fact realized, were to be so, then such and such percepts would occur. But apart from the obvious difficulty of giving a sufficient description of the conditions in purely sensory terms, I no longer think that such conditional statements are suitable to play this part. I believe that conditional statements of this sort are best understood as belonging to a secondary system, which has an explanatory function with respect to a primary system of purely factual propositions: and from this it follows that they are not themselves equipped to function as primary statements of fact.[17]

In the scheme which I have outlined, the need to have recourse to conditional statements is avoided by our treating the passage from percepts to physical objects, not strictly as a process of logical construction, but rather, in Hume's way, as an exercise of the imagination. The continued and distinct existence, not of percepts, but of the objects into which they are transmuted, is simply posited. Consequently, we are able to forsake phenomenalism for a sophisticated form of realism. Under the dominion of the theory which is erected on the basis of our primitive experiential propositions, the existence of visuo-tactual continuants becomes a matter of objective fact. If, as I shall advocate, we adopt this standpoint for judging what there is, these objects become the elements of our primary system.

A list might be given of the different ways in which philosophers have tried to meet the argument by which the sceptic professes to show, at various levels, that our claims to knowledge, or even to rational belief, cannot be justified. The course which we have followed is a variant of what I have called the scientific approach. It would, indeed, be somewhat misleading to say that we are represesenting the existence of physical objects as a probable hypothesis, since this description would ordinarily be taken to apply to propositions that lie within the framework of our general theory, rather than to the principles of the theory itself. Nevertheless, the difference is only a difference of degree. The theory is vindicated not indeed by any special set of observations but by the general features of our experience on which it is founded, and since these features are contingent, it could conceivably be falsified, in the sense that our experiences might in general be such that it failed to account for them.

6. Common Sense and Physics

We have seen how the objects of perception come to be detached from any actual percepts and made causally responsible for them. The question which we have now to consider is whether this process can be carried further, to the point where these objects are stripped of all their perceptible qualities and left only with the properties which the science of the day attributes to physical particles. This step is certainly not forced on us, as some philosophers have taken it to be, by our having to reckon with the causal process of perception, since this can be taken to imply no more than that the states of different entities, which are alike generated out of percepts, can be systematically correlated. There may, however, be other reasons in favour of taking it. The unprocessed object, the thing as it is in itself, if we are to have any concept of it at all, is bound to be a creature of theory: the question is only what theory this should be.

To obtain a satisfactory answer, we have to try to get clear about the relation between the scientific view of the nature of physical objects and that which can be attributed to common sense. Were Russell and Eddington right in thinking that they are incompatible? It has been argued that they were wrong on the ground that the two views relate to different subjects. Thus Ryle has suggested that they are no more incompatible than an artist's picture of a landscape is incompatible with a geologist's description of the same area, or than the annual report of the activities of a college is incompatible with the entries relating to the same activities which appear in the college's accounts.[18] What is implied by these analogies is that physics differs from common sense only in being concerned with different aspects of the same things, but even if this is true it needs further explanation.

For instance, it would be hard to say what aspect of a physical object can be taken to exhaust a physicist's interests in the way that an accountant's interest in the activities which he records is limited to their cost. The other analogy may come nearer the mark, in that the geologist is concerned with the physical composition of the objects which the artist paints. But then the question remains whether their having this physical composition is indeed consistent with their really being as the artist pictures them.

This question would present no difficulty if it could be shown that the statements which enter into scientific theories were logically equivalent to statements describing the observable states of affairs by which these theories would be verified; but there are good reasons for concluding that this is not the case.[19] There is, however, a weaker thesis which for our present purposes would achieve the same result. It could be maintained that the factual content of a scientific theory consisted only in those propositions of our primary system that actually supported it, and that the theory itself belonged to a secondary system, the function of which would be purely explanatory. The entities which figured in any such secondary system, to the extent that they could not be identified with objects of the primary system, would be thought of simply as conceptual tools which served for the arrangement of the primary facts.

The distinction between primary and secondary systems is one that needs to be made on other grounds. It does not, however, strictly require that the boundaries of the actual world be drawn so narrowly as I have now proposed. It could be consistent with a realistic view of the status of physical particles. The main argument in favour of adopting such a view would be that it is more consonant with the outlook of physicists themselves.

If one does hold a realistic view, there would appear to be just two forms that it could take, both of which go back in a way to Locke. The first of them consists in transferring all the perceptible qualities of things to the observer's account, leaving things, as they are in themselves, to be represented by the necessarily imperceptible objects of physical theory. The objection to this procedure is that these imperceptible objects, having been moved into the territory which the perceptible objects have been forced to abandon, are located in perceptible space, and it is not easy to understand how spatial relations can be thought to persist when their terms have been taken away from them. The second course would be to conceive of physical particles as being what Locke called the minute parts of perceptible objects, in which case their being imperceptible would not be a necessary part of their nature, but simply an empirical consequence of their being so minute. On this view, it has just to be accepted as an empirical fact that particles which are individually colourless compose coloured objects when enough of them come together, and since these particles are conceived to be in relative motion, it also has to be conceded that we are actually in error when we believe that the surfaces of physical objects are continuous. It is just that the gaps between their minute parts are too small for us to notice. These consequences make this position less agreeable to common sense, but do not, I think, prevent it from being tenable.

It may seem strange that I have represented the question as to what there physically is as being so much a question for decision. Why should not the opposition between a realist and a pragmatic view of the status of physical particles be taken to relate to an objective matter of fact? The answer is that if the problem were treated in that way, we should have no procedure for solving it. Questions as to what there is can be treated as empirical only within the framework of a theory which supplies criteria for answering them. When, as in the present case, there is the threat of conflict between two different theories both of which we are inclined to accept, we must either find a way of blending them coherently, or else remove the competition by treating only one of them as determining the character of fact and the other as purely explanatory. If I have a slight preference for the compromise which is effected by the second form of Lockean realism, it is because it makes some concession to scientific orthodoxy, without doing any great violence to the more simple theory which is naturally developed out of our experiences.

Notes

1. C. D. Broad. *Scientific Thought*, p. 239.
2. Bertrand Russell. *Mysticism and Logic*, p. 148.
3. David Hume. *A Treatise of Human Nature*, Book I, Part IV, Section 2.
4. *Ibid.*
5. See H. H. Price. 'Obituary of Harold Arthur Prichard', *Proceedings of the British Academy* XXXIII.
6. See *The Central Questions of Philosophy* (Pelican edition), pp. 73–80.
7. George Berkeley. *A New Theory of Vision*.
8. William James. *The Principles of Psychology*, Vol. II, Ch. XX.
9. Nelson Goodman. *The Structure of Appearance*, p. 134.
10. See my *The Concept of a Person*, pp. 41–3.
11. See below, pp. 338–40.
12. See *The Central Questions of Philosophy*, pp. 132–5.
13. See *The Central Questions of Philosophy*, pp. 126–7.
14. William James. *The Principles of Psychology*, Vol. I, pp. 606–7.
15. See *The Central Questions of Philosophy*, pp. 61–3.
16. See my essay on Phenomenalism. *Philosophical Essays*, Ch. VI.
17. See *The Central Questions of Philosophy*, pp. 151–2.
18. See G. Ryle. *Dilemmas*, pp. 75–81.
19. See *The Central Questions of Philosophy*, pp. 31–3.

Biographical Note

Professor Sir Alfred Ayer was Wykeham Professor of Logic in the University of Oxford from 1959 to 1978, before which he was Grote Professor of Mind and Logic at University College London, Fellow of Wadham College, and Lecturer and Student in Philosophy at Christ Church. His books, other than *The Central Questions of Philosophy*, include *Language, Truth and Logic* (1936), *Foundations of Empirical Knowledge* (1940), *Philosophical Essays* (1954), *The Problem of Knowledge* (1956), *The Concept of a Person and other Essays* (1963), *The Origins of Pragmatism* (1968), *Metaphysics and Common Sense* (1969), *Russell and Moore: The Analytical Heritage* (1971) and *Probability and Evidence* (1972). He is a Fellow of the British Academy and was knighted in 1970.

Further Reading

Readers may wish to consult three other pieces of writing by Professor Ayer: 'Has Austin Refuted the Sense-Datum Theory?', which is an essay reprinted in his book *Metaphysics and Common Sense* (London: Macmillan, 1969); section C of his comments on William James in *The Origins of Pragmatism* (London: Macmillan, 1968); and 'The Causal Theory of Perception', *Supplementary Proceedings of the Aristotelian Society*, 1977. Other relevant writings include David Hume, *A Treatise of Human Nature*, Book 1, Part IV, section 2 and also the appendix to the *Treatise*; Bertrand Russell, *The Problems of Philosophy* (London: Williams and Northgate, 1912, and other editions), and *Our Knowledge of the External World* (London: Allen and Unwin, 1926); H. H. Price, *Perception* (London: Methuen, 1932); and Nelson Goodman, *The Structure of Appearance* (New York: Bobbs-Merrill, 1951). The subject of Ayer's first-mentioned essay is J. L. Austin's *Sense and Sensibilia* (Oxford: Clarendon Press, 1962). Also relevant is Ludwig Wittgenstein, 'Notes for Lectures on "Private Experience" and "Sense Data"' (1935-6) edited with a note by Rush Rhees, *Philosophical Review* LXXVII (1968) pp. 271-320.

Hilary Putnam

The 'Corroboration' of Theories

No survey of contemporary philosophy would be complete if it did not include some recognition of the continuing importance of the work of Sir Karl Popper. Popper set forth his views on the nature and methods and problems of science as long ago as 1934 in his book *Logik der Forschung* (translated into English as *The Logic of Scientific Discovery* in 1959) and has been developing and defending them formidably ever since. His ideas have become widely known outside philosophy – a distinction not often granted to philosophical doctrines – and, even if they have not wholly ousted from currency what is sometimes called Baconian inductivism, the view they were aimed against, some of them are now securely part of the public domain.

Most notably is this true of the idea that a scientific hypothesis must be falsifiable, which for the Popperian is not only a key to the understanding of science but also a polemical weapon to discredit as unscientific Marxist theories of society and psychoanalytic theories of the human mind, and not only these. Such theories, it is said, are so formulated as to be immune from falsification; it is not allowed that any evidence would show them to be incorrect; and a theory which is not open to refutation cannot be genuinely explanatory of anything. It is not a mark of a true science that there is or seems to be a mass of evidence showing it to be true. The mark of a true science, roughly, is that it is clear what facts would show it to be false.

One of the distinctions of Hilary Putnam's paper 'The "Corroboration" of Theories' is the lucidity with which he shows that the idea of the falsifiability of scientific hypotheses is by no means a straightforward tool of analysis and criticism. It is not in question, of course, that a scientific theory must be answerable to experience. The issue is the manner in which the relation to experience is to be conceived.

The experience which is relevant in this connection is that which is recorded in statements giving the results of a scientist's observations, laboratory tests, etc. The technical term for these statements is 'observation sentences'. Putnam's target is any view according to which observation sentences are always directly deducible from theories. If the relation were one of direct deducibility, we would have:

Theory $\rightarrow O_1, O_2, O_3, \ldots$

where $O_1, O_2, O_3, \ldots$ are the observation sentences expressing the various observational consequences implied or predicted by the theory – in short, its predictions. The traditional inductivist view maintains that if, subject to certain supplementary conditions, $O_1, O_2, O_3, \ldots$ turn out to be true, the theory is so far confirmed. Also, confirming evidence establishes that the theory is scientific. The falsificationist (deductivist) view lays the emphasis on the negative case, where one of $O_1, O_2, O_3, \ldots$ turns out false. That is, we have:

Theory $\rightarrow O_1, O_2, O_3, \ldots$
But O_2 is not the case,

from which we can deduce that the theory is false. We have a refutation of the theory. For simple logic tells us that a sentence which implies a falsehood must itself be false.

Now, on this view, for a theory to be scientific it must be possible clearly to envisage such a negative case – although not, of course, necessary that there *be* one. If no such case has been found, after serious and varied efforts to find one, the theory is thus far 'corroborated'; it enjoys a degree of 'corroboration' proportionate to the severity and variety of tests it has withstood. This is the 'corroboration' of Putnam's title. The Popperian claim is that corroboration is to be distinguished from the traditional inductivist notion of confirmation because, while confirming a hypothesis or theory is usually conceived to be a process of getting closer to establishing that it is *true* or *probable*, no such claim is envisaged in connection with corroboration. The hypothesis or theory is a 'conjecture', and remains such. It becomes corroborated merely in the sense and to the degree that, by withstanding severe and varied tests, it proves its fitness to survive as the best conjecture science has so far achieved.

As the reader will discover (section 11), there are certain qualifications to be included in Popper's version of the falsificationist schema. But the aim of Putnam's critique is to strike at the idea of a direct link between theory and prediction on which both the deductivist and the inductivist, in their different ways, rely. Putnam argues: in many cases *a theory implies no observational predictions whatever.* It is only when certain auxiliary assumptions are brought in that the link to experience can be effected. Hence, logically speaking, what is falsified if one of $O_1, O_2, O_3, \ldots$ turns out false is not the theory but rather the conjunction of the theory with the statement of these auxiliary assumptions (A.S.). Thus:

(Theory & A.S.) $\rightarrow O_1, O_2, O_3, \ldots$
But not, say, O_2.
Therefore not (Theory & A.S.),

which is to say no more than that *either* the theory *or* the auxiliary assumptions need to be revised. And often, according to Putnam, it is more likely to be the latter.

In essence, the point is simple, and it has been made before in the philosophy of science. But in Putnam's discussion what begins as a simple logical point comes to have fascinating and far-reaching implications for our understanding of scientific method. Additionally, in the course of discussion Putnam contributes an illuminating perspective on an important controversy which began when Popperian philosophy of science was challenged by the radically antifalsificationist ideas of Thomas Kuhn's book, *The Structure of Scientific Revolutions* (1962). The final upshot is a picture of science and scientific method which makes it harder to dismiss as intellectually disreputable such theories as those of Marx and Freud. In this sense, the paper illustrates how clear, creative thinking in philosophy can be of relevance to the wider culture of our society.

That said by way of introduction, it is necessary to add that in the volume where the foregoing paper originally appeared it was the subject of a strongly worded reply by Sir Karl Popper (see bibliography). This reply was entitled 'Putnam on "Auxiliary Sentences", Called by Me "Initial Conditions"'. It addressed certain exegical questions concerning the correct reading of Popper's philosophy of science and the logical question of what types of prediction, if any, can be derived from a theory.

Popper states, first, that he has always held that one type of prediction ('basic statements') is not derivable from a theory without a statement of initial conditions, while another type of prediction ('instantial statements') is so derivable. (For simplicity let our 'theory' be the statement 'All swans are white'. Then the distinctions just mentioned can be illustrated as follows: basic statement – 'There is a white swan at space-time region R'; instantial statement – 'There is no non-white swan at R' or 'If there is a swan at R, there is a white swan at R'. Initial conditions are singular statements specifying, for example, the position of the moon and the earth at a particular time; the present illustration casts 'There is a swan at R' in an analogous logical role.) Popper states, further, that he was correct to hold this view, since there could be circumstances in which Newton's theory of universal gravitation was directly refuted via an instantial statement *without* the use of initial conditions or any kind of auxiliary assumption.

In this last claim there is a head-on clash with Putnam's account of Newton's theory and of scientific theories generally – a clash which is independent of the exegetical problems which arise in reading Popper. The philosophical issue is important in its own right, not least in view of the simplified versions of falsificationism which are current in public debate about Marx and Freud. It is to that issue that we would direct the reader's attention, recommending him to investigate Popper's philosophy of science for himself later when he has grasped what is at stake in the controversy.

Meanwhile, we have given Professor Putnam the opportunity to clarify his position on these matters. His reply to Popper's reply will be found in a Retrospective Note following the paper.

M.F.B.

Hilary Putnam

The 'Corroboration' of Theories

Reprinted with permission of the author and publisher from *The Philosophy of Karl Popper*, edited by Paul Arthur Schilpp (La Salle, Illinois: Open Court, 1974), pp. 221–40. Additional note by the author for this reprinting.

Sir Karl Popper is a philosopher whose work has influenced and stimulated that of virtually every student in the philosophy of science. In part this influence is explainable on the basis of the healthy-mindedness of some of Sir Karl's fundamental attitudes: 'There is no method peculiar to philosophy'. 'The growth of knowledge can be studied best by studying the growth of scientific knowledge.'

Philosophers should not be specialists. For myself, I am interested in science and in philosophy only because I want to learn something about the riddle of the world in which we live, and the riddle of man's knowledge of that world. And I believe that only a revival of interest in these riddles can save the sciences and philosophy from an obscurantist faith in the expert's special skill and in his personal knowledge and authority.

These attitudes are perhaps a little narrow (can the growth of knowledge be studied without also studying nonscientific knowledge? Are the problems Popper mentions of merely theoretical interest – just 'riddles'?), but much less narrow than those of many philosophers; and the 'obscurantist faith' Popper warns against is a real danger. In part this influence stems from Popper's realism, his refusal to accept the peculiar meaning-theories of the positivists, and his separation of the problems of scientific methodology from the various problems about the 'interpretation of scientific theories' which are internal to the meaning-theories of the positivists and which positivistic philosophers of science have continued to wrangle about.[1]

In this paper I want to examine his views about scientific methodology – about what is generally called 'induction', although Popper rejects the concept – and, in particular, to criticize assumptions that Popper has in common with received philosophy of science, rather than assumptions that are peculiar to Popper. For I think that there are a number of such common assumptions, and that they represent a mistaken way of looking at science.

1. Popper's View of 'Induction'

Popper himself uses the term 'induction' to refer to any method for verifying or showing to be true (or even probable) general laws on the basis of observational or experimental data (what he calls 'basic statements'). His views are radically Humean: no such method exists or can exist. A principle of induction would have to be either synthetic *a priori* (a possibility that Popper rejects) or justified by a higher-level principle. But the latter course necessarily leads to an infinite regress.

What is novel is that Popper concludes neither that empirical science is impossible nor that empirical science rests upon principles that are themselves incapable of justification. Rather, his position is that empirical science does not really rely upon a principle of induction!

Popper does not deny that scientists state general laws, nor that they test these general laws against observational data. What he says is that when a scientist 'corroborates' a general law, that scientist does not thereby assert that law to be true or even probable. 'I have corroborated this law to a high degree' only means 'I have subjected this law to severe tests and it has withstood them'. Scientific laws are *falsifiable*, not verifiable. Since scientists are not even trying to *verify* laws, but only to falsify them, Hume's problem does not arise for empirical scientists.

2. A Brief Criticism of Popper's View

It is a remarkable fact about Popper's book, *The Logic of Scientific Discovery* that it contains but a half-dozen brief references to the *application* of scientific theories and laws; and then all that is said is that application is yet another *test* of the laws. 'My view is that . . . the theorist is interested in explanations as such, that is to say, in testable explanatory theories: applications and predictions interest him only for theoretical reasons – because they may be used as *tests* of theories' (*Logic of Scientific Discovery*, p. 59).

When a scientist accepts a law, he is recommending to other men that they rely on it – rely on it, often, in practical contexts. Only by wrenching science altogether out of the context in which it really arises – the context of men trying to change and control the world – can Popper even put forward his peculiar view on induction. Ideas are not *just* ideas; they are guides to action. Our notions of 'knowledge', 'probability', 'certainty', etc., are all linked to and frequently used in contexts in which action is at issue: may I confidently rely upon a certain idea? Shall I rely upon it tentatively, with a certain caution? Is it necessary to check on it?

If 'this law is highly corroborated', 'this law is scientifically accepted', and like locutions merely meant 'this law has withstood severe tests' – and there were no suggestion at all that a law which has withstood severe tests is likely to withstand further tests, such as the tests involved in an application or attempted application, then Popper would be right; but then science would be a wholly unimportant activity. It would be practically unimportant, because scientists would never tell us that any law or theory is safe to rely upon for practical purposes; and it would be unimportant for the purpose of understanding, since on Popper's view, scientists never tell us that any law or theory is true or even probable. Knowing that certain 'conjectures' (according to Popper all scientific laws are 'provisional conjectures') have not yet been refuted is *not understanding anything*.

Since the application of scientific laws does involve the anticipation of future successes, Popper is not right in maintaining that induction is unnecessary. Even if scientists do not inductively anticipate the future (and, of course, they do), men who apply scientific laws and theories do so. And 'don't make inductions' is hardly reasonable advice to give these men.

The advice to regard all knowledge as 'provisional conjectures' is also not reasonable. Consider men striking against sweat-shop conditions. Should they say 'it is only a provisional conjecture that the boss is a bastard. Let us call off our strike and try appealing to his better nature'. The distinction between *knowledge* and *conjecture* does real work in our lives; Popper can maintain his extreme scepticism only because of his extreme tendency to regard theory as an end for itself.

3. Popper's View of Corroboration

Although scientists, on Popper's view, do not make inductions, they do 'corroborate' scientific theories. And although the statement that a theory is highly corroborated does not mean, according to Popper, that the theory may be accepted as true, or even as approximately true,[2] or even as probably approximately true, still, there is no doubt that most readers of Popper read his account of corroboration as an account of something like the verification of theories, in spite of his protests. In this sense, Popper has, *contre lui* a theory of induction. And it is this theory, or certain presuppositions of this theory, that I shall criticize in the body of this paper.

Popper's reaction to this way of reading him is as follows:

My reaction to this reply would be regret at my continued failure to explain my main point with sufficient clarity. For the sole purpose of the elimination advocated by all these inductivists was to *establish as firmly as possible the surviving theory* which, they thought, must be the *true* one (or, perhaps, only a *highly probable* one, in so far as we may not have fully succeeded in eliminating every theory except the true one).

As against this, I do not think that we can ever seriously reduce by elimination, the number of the competing theories, since this number remains always infinite. What we do – or should do – is to *hold on, for the time being, to the most improbable of the surviving theories* or, more precisely, to the one that can be most severely tested. We tentatively '*accept*' this theory – but only in the sense that we select it as worthy to be subjected to further criticism, and to the severest tests we can design.

On the positive side, we may be entitled to add that the surviving theory is the best theory – and the best tested theory – of which we know. (*Logic of Scientific Discovery*, p. 419)

If we leave out the last sentence, we have the doctrine we have been criticizing in pure form: when a scientist 'accepts' a theory, he does not assert that it is probable. In fact, he 'selects' it as most improbable!

In the last sentence, however, am I mistaken, or do I detect an inductivist quaver? What does 'best theory' mean? Surely Popper cannot mean 'most likely'?

4. The Scientific Method – The Received Schema

Standard 'inductivist' accounts of the confirmation[3] of scientific theories go somewhat like this: Theory implies prediction (basic sentence, or observation sentence); if prediction is false, theory is falsified; if sufficiently many predictions are true, theory is confirmed. For all his attack on inductivism, Popper's schema is not *so* different: Theory implies prediction (basic sentence); if prediction is false, theory is falsified; if sufficiently many predictions are true, and certain further conditions are fulfilled, theory is highly corroborated.

Moreover, this reading of Popper does have certain support. Popper does say that the 'surviving theory' is *accepted* – his account is, therefore, an account of the logic of accepting theories. We must separate two questions: is Popper right about what the scientist means – or should mean – when he speaks of a theory as 'accepted'; and is Popper right about the methodology involved in according a theory that status? What I am urging is that his account of that methodology fits the received schema, even if his interpretation of the status is very different.

To be sure there are some important conditions that Popper adds. Predictions that one could have made on the basis of background knowledge do not test a theory; it is only predictions that are *improbable* relative to background knowledge that test a theory. And a theory is not corroborated, according to Popper, unless we make sincere attempts to derive false predictions from it. Popper regards these further conditions as anti-Bayesian;[4] but this seems to me to be a confusion, at least in part. A theory which implies an improbable prediction is improbable, that is true, but it may be the most probable of all theories which imply that prediction. If so, and the prediction turns out true, then Bayes's theorem itself explains why the theory receives a high probability. Popper says that we select the most improbable of the *surviving* theories – i.e., the accepted theory is most improbable even *after* the prediction has turned out true; but, of course, this depends on using 'probable' in a way no other philosopher of science would accept. And a Bayesian is not committed to the view that *any* true prediction significantly confirms a theory. I share Popper's view that quantitative measures of the probability of theories are not a hopeful venture in the philosophy of science;[5] but that does not mean that Bayes's theorem does not have a certain *qualitative* rightness, at least in many situations.

Be all this as it may, the heart of Popper's schema is the theory-prediction link. It is because theories imply basic sentences in the sense of 'imply' associated with deductive logic – because basic sentences are *deducible* from theories – that, according to Popper, theories and general laws can be falsifiable by basic sentences. And this same link is the heart of the 'inductivist' schema. Both schemes say: *look at the predictions that a theory implies; see if those predictions are true.*

My criticism is going to be a criticism of this link, of this one point on which Popper and the 'inductivists' agree. I claim: in a great many important cases, scientific theories do not imply predictions at all. In the remainder of this paper I want to elaborate this point, and show its significance for the philosophy of science.

5. The Theory of Universal Gravitation

The theory that I will use to illustrate my points is one that the reader will be familiar with: it is Newton's theory of universal gravitation. The theory consists of the law that every body a exerts on every other body b a force F_{ab} whose direction is towards a and whose magnitude is a universal constant g times $M_a M_b / d^2$, together with Newton's three laws. The choice of this particular theory is not essential to my case: Maxwell's theory, or Mendel's, or Darwin's would have done just as well. But this one has the advantage of familiarity.

Note that this theory does not imply a single basic sentence! Indeed, any motions whatsoever are compatible with this theory, since the theory says nothing about what forces other than gravitations may be present. The forces F_{ab} are not themselves directly measurable; consequently not a single *prediction* can be deduced from the theory.

What do we do, then, when we apply this theory to an astronomical situation? Typically we make certain simplifying assumptions.

For example, if we are deducing the orbit of the earth we might assume as a first approximation:

(I) No bodies exist except the sun and the earth.
(II) The sun and the earth exist in a hard vacuum.
(III) The sun and the earth are subject to no forces except mutually induced gravitational forces.

From the conjunction of the theory of universal gravitation (U.G.) and these auxiliary statements (A.S.) we can, indeed, deduce certain predictions – e.g., Kepler's laws. By making (I), (II), (III) more 'realistic' – i.e., incorporating further bodies in our model solar system – we can obtain better predictions. But it is important to note that these predictions do not come from the theory alone, but from the conjunction of the theory with A.S. As scientists actually use the term 'theory', the statements A.S. are hardly part of the 'theory' of gravitation.

6. Is the Point Terminological?

I am not interested in making a merely *terminological* point, however. The point is not just that scientists don't use the term 'theory' to refer to the conjunction of U.G. with A.S., but that such a usage would obscure profound methodological issues. A *theory*, as the term is actually used, is a set of *laws*. Laws are statements that we hope to be *true*; they are supposed to be true by the nature of things, and not just by accident. None of the statements (I), (II), (III) has this character. We do not really believe that *no* bodies except the sun and the earth exist, for example, but only that all other bodies exert forces small enough to be neglected. This statement is not supposed to be a law of nature: it is a statement about the 'boundary conditions' which obtain as a matter of fact in a particular system. To blur the difference between A.S. and U.G. is to blur the difference between *laws* and *accidental statements*, between statements the scientist wishes to establish as *true* (the laws), and statements he already knows to be false (the oversimplifications (I), (II), (III)).

7. Uranus, Mercury, 'Dark Companions'

Although the statements A.S. *could* be more carefully worded to avoid the objection that they are known to be false, it is striking that they are not in practice. In fact, they are not 'worded' at all. Newton's calculation of Kepler's laws makes the assumptions (I), (II), (III) without more than a casual indication that this is what is done. One of the most striking indications of the difference between a theory (such as U.G.) and a set of A.S. is the great care which scientists use in stating the theory, as contrasted with the careless way in which they introduce the various assumptions which make up A.S.

The A.S. are also far more subject to revision than the theory. For over two hundred years the law of universal gravitation was accepted as unquestionably true, and used as a premise in countless scientific arguments. If the standard kind of A.S. had not led to successful prediction in that period, they would have been modified, not the theory. In fact, we have an example of this. When the predictions about the orbit of Uranus that were made on the basis of the theory of universal gravitation and the assumption that the known planets were all there were turned out to be wrong, Leverrier in France and Adams in England simultaneously predicted that there must be another planet. In fact, this planet was discovered – it was Neptune. Had this modification of the A.S. not been successful, still others might have been tried – e.g., postulating a medium through which the planets are moving, instead of a hard vacuum, or postulating significant nongravitational forces.

It may be argued that it was crucial that the new planet should itself be observable. But this is not so. Certain stars, for example, exhibit irregular behaviour. This has been explained by postulating companions. When those companions are not visible through a telescope, this is handled by suggesting that the stars have *dark companions* – companions which cannot be seen through a telescope. The fact is that many of the assumptions made in the sciences cannot be directly tested – there are many 'dark companions' in scientific theory.

Lastly, of course, there is the case of Mercury. The orbit of this planet can almost but not quite be successfully explained by Newton's theory. Does this show that Newton's theory is wrong? *In the light of an alternative theory*, say the General Theory of Relativity, one answers 'yes'. But, in the absence of such a theory, the orbit of Mercury is just a slight anomaly, cause: unknown.

What I am urging is that all this is perfectly good scientific practice. The fact that any one of the statements A.S. may be false – indeed, they are false, as stated, and even more careful and guarded statements might well be false – is important. We do not know for sure all the bodies in the solar system; we do not know for sure that the medium through which they move is (to a sufficiently high degree of approximation in all cases) a hard vacuum; we do not know that non-gravitational forces can be neglected in all cases. Given the overwhelming success of the Law of Universal Gravitation in almost all cases, one or two anomalies are not reason to reject it. It is more *likely* that the A.S. are false than that the theory is false, at least when no alternative theory has seriously been put forward.

8. The Effect on Popper's Doctrine

The effect of this fact on Popper's doctrine is immediate. The Law of Universal Gravitation is *not* strongly falsifiable at all; yet it is surely a paradigm of a scientific theory. Scientists for over two hundred years did not derive predictions from U.G. in order to falsify U.G.; they derived predictions from U.G. in order to explain various astronomical facts. If a fact proved recalcitrant to this sort of explanation it was put aside as an anomaly (the case of Mercury). Popper's doctrine gives a correct account of neither the nature of the scientific theory nor of the practice of the scientific community in this case.

Popper might reply that he is not describing what scientists do, but what they *should* do. Should scientists then not have put forward U.G.? Was Newton a bad scientist? Scientists did not try to falsify U.G. because they could not try to falsify it; laboratory tests were excluded by the technology of the time and the weakness of the gravitational interactions. Scientists were thus limited to astronomical data for a long time. And, even in the astronomical cases, the problem arises that one cannot be absolutely sure that no nongravitational force is relevant in a given situation (or that one has summed *all* the gravitational forces). It is for this reason that astronomical data can *support*

U.G., but they can hardly *falsify* it. It would have been incorrect to reject U.G. because of the deviancy of the orbit of Mercury; given that U.G. predicted the other orbits, to the limits of measurement error, the possibility could not be excluded that the deviancy in this one case was due to an unknown force, gravitational or nongravitational, and in putting the case aside as one they could neither explain nor attach systematic significance to, scientists *were* acting as they 'should'.[6]

So far we have said that (1) theories do not imply predictions; it is only the conjunction of a theory with certain 'auxiliary statements' (A.S.) that, in general, implies a prediction. (2) The A.S. are frequently suppositions about boundary conditions (including initial conditions as a special case of 'boundary conditions'), and highly risky suppositions at that. (3) Since we are very unsure of the A.S., we cannot regard a false prediction as definitively falsifying a theory; theories are *not* strongly falsifiable.

All this is not to deny that scientists do sometimes derive predictions from theories and A.S. in order to test the theories. If Newton had not been able to derive Kepler's laws, for example, he would not have even put forward U.G. But even if the predictions Newton had obtained from U.G. had been wildly wrong, U.G. might still have been true: the A.S. might have been wrong. Thus, even if a theory is 'knocked out' by an experimental test, the theory may still be right, and the theory may come back in at a later stage when it is discovered the A.S. were not useful approximations to the true situation. As has previously been pointed out,[7] falsification in science is no more conclusive than verification.

All this refutes Popper's view that what the scientist does is to put forward 'highly falsifiable' theories, derive predictions from them, and then attempt to falsify the theories by falsifying the predictions. But it does not refute the standard view (what Popper calls the 'inductivist' view) that scientists try to *confirm* theories *and* A.S. by deriving predictions from them and verifying the predictions. There is the objection that (in the case of U.G.) the A.S. were known to be false, so scientists could hardly have been trying to confirm them; but this could be met by saying that the A.S. could, in principle, have been formulated in a more guarded way, and would not have been false if sufficiently guarded.[8] I think that, in fact, there is some truth in the 'inductivist' view: scientific theories are shown to be correct by their successes, just as all human ideas are shown to be correct, to the extent that they are, by their successes in practice. But the inductivist schema is still inadequate, except as a picture of one aspect of scientific procedure. In the next sections, I shall try to show that scientific activity cannot, in general, be thought of as a matter of deriving predictions from the conjunction of theories and A.S., whether for the purpose of confirmation or for the purpose of falsification.

9. Kuhn's View of Science

Recently a number of philosophers have begun to put forward a rather new view of scientific activity. I believe that I anticipated this view about ten years ago when I urged that some scientific theories cannot be overthrown by experiments and observations *alone*, but only by alternative theories.[9] The view is also anticipated by Hanson,[10] but it reaches its sharpest expression in the writings of Thomas Kuhn[11] and Louis Althusser.[12] I believe that both of these philosophers commit errors; but I also believe that the tendency they represent (and that I also represent, for that matter) is a needed corrective to the deductivism we have been examining. In this section, I shall present some of Kuhn's views, and then try to advance on them in the direction of a sharper formulation.

The heart of Kuhn's account is the notion of a *paradigm*. Kuhn has been legitimately criticized for some inconsistencies and unclarities in the use of this notion; but at least one of his explanations of the notion seems to me to be quite clear and suitable for his purposes. On this explanation, a paradigm is simply a scientific theory together with an example of a successful and striking application. It is important that the application – say, a successful explanation of some fact, or a successful and novel prediction – be *striking*; what this means is that the success is sufficiently impressive that scientists – especially young scientists choosing a career – are led to try to emulate that success by seeking further explanations, predictions, or whatever on the same model. For example, once U.G. had been put forward and one had the example of Newton's derivation of Kepler's laws together with the example of the derivation of, say, a planetary orbit or two, then one had a paradigm. The most important paradigms are the ones that generate scientific fields; the field generated by the Newtonian para· digm was, in the first instance, the entire field of celestial mechanics. (Of course, this field was only a part of the larger field of Newtonian mechanics, and the paradigm on which celestial mechanics is based is only one of a number of paradigms which collectively structure Newtonian mechanics.)

Kuhn maintains that the paradigm that structures a field is highly immune to falsification – in particular, it can only be overthrown by a new paradigm. In one sense, this is an exaggeration: Newtonian physics would probably have been abandoned, even in the absence of a new paradigm, if the world had started to act in a markedly non-Newtonian way. (Although even then – would we have concluded that Newtonian physics was false, or just that we didn't know what the devil was going on?) But then even the old successes, the successes which were paradigmatic for Newtonian physics, would have ceased to be available. What is true, I believe, is that in the absence of such a drastic and unprecedented change in the world, and in the absence of its turning out that the paradigmatic successes had something 'phony' about them (e.g., the data were faked, or there was a mistake in the deductions), a theory which is paradigmatic is not given up because of observational and experimental results by themselves, but only because and when a better theory is available.

Once a paradigm has been set up, and a scientific field has grown up around that paradigm, we get an interval of what Kuhn calls 'normal science'. The activity of scientists during such an interval is described by Kuhn as 'puzzle solving' – a notion I shall return to.

In general, the interval of normal science continues even though not all the puzzles of the field can be successfully solved (after all, it is only human experience that some problems are too hard to solve), and even though some of the solutions may look *ad hoc*. What finally terminates the interval is the introduction of a new paradigm which manages to supersede the old.

Kuhn's most controversial assertions have to do with the process whereby a new paradigm supplants an older paradigm. Here he tends to be radically subjectivistic (overly so, in my opinion): data, in the usual sense, cannot establish the superiority of one paradigm over another because data themselves are perceived through the spectacles of one paradigm or another. Changing from one paradigm to another requires a 'Gestalt switch'. The history and methodology of science get rewritten when there are major paradigm changes; so there are no 'neutral' historical and methodological canons to which to appeal. Kuhn also holds views on meaning and truth which are relativistic and, on my view, incorrect; but I do not wish to discuss these here.

What I want to explore is the interval which Kuhn calls 'normal science'. The term 'puzzle solving' is unfortunately trivializing; searching for explanations of phenomena and for ways to harness nature is too important a part of human life to be demeaned (here Kuhn shows the same tendency that leads Popper to call the problem of the nature of knowledge a 'riddle'). But the term is also striking: clearly, Kuhn sees normal science as neither an activity of trying to falsify one's paradigm nor as an activity of trying to confirm it, but as something else. I want to try to advance on Kuhn by presenting a schema for normal science, or rather for one aspect of normal science; a schema which may indicate why a major philosopher and historian of science would use the metaphor of solving puzzles in the way Kuhn does.

10. Schemata for Scientific Problems

Consider the following two schemata:

SCHEMA I
_____

THEORY
AUXILIARY STATEMENTS
_____

PREDICTION – TRUE OR FALSE?
_____

SCHEMA II
_____

THEORY
???????????????
_____

FACT TO BE EXPLAINED

These are both schemata for scientific problems. In the first type of problem we have a theory, we have some A.S., we have derived a prediction, and our problem is to see if the prediction is true or false: the situation emphasized by standard philosophy of science. The second type of problem is quite different. In this type of problem we have a theory, we have a fact to be explained, but the A.S. are missing: the problem is to find A.S., if we can, which are true, or approximately true (i.e., useful oversimplifications of the truth), and which have to be conjoined to the theory to get an explanation of the fact.

We might, in passing, mention also a third schema which is neglected by standard philosophy of science:

SCHEMA III
_____

THEORY
AUXILIARY STATEMENTS

_____

??????????????????????

This represents the type of problem in which we have a theory, we have some A.S., and we want to know what consequences we can derive. This type of problem is neglected because the problem is 'purely mathematical'. But knowing whether a set of statements has testable consequences at all depends upon the solution to this type of problem, and the problem is frequently of great difficulty – e.g., little is known to this day concerning just what the physical consequences of Einstein's 'unified field theory' are, precisely because the mathematical problem of deriving those consequences is too difficult. Philosophers of science frequently write as if it is *clear*, given a set of statements, just what consequences those statements do and do not have.

Let us, however, return to Schema II. Given the known facts concerning the orbit of Uranus, and given the known facts (prior to 1846) concerning what bodies make up the solar system, and the standard A.S. that those bodies are moving in a hard vacuum, subject only to mutual gravitational forces, etc., it was clear that there was a problem: the orbit of Uranus could not be successfully calculated if we assumed that Mercury, Venus, Earth, Mars, Saturn, Jupiter, and Uranus were all the planets there are, and that these planets together with the sun make up the whole solar system. Let S_1 be the conjunction of the various A.S. we just mentioned, including the statement that the solar system consists of at least, but not necessarily of only, the bodies mentioned. Then we have the following problem:

> Theory: U.G.
> A.S.: S_1
> Further A.S.: ????????
>
> _____
>
> *Explanandum:* The orbit of Uranus

– note that the problem is not to find further explanatory laws (although sometimes it may be, in a problem of the form of Schema II); it is to find further assumptions about the initial and boundary conditions governing the solar system which, together with the Law of Universal Gravitation and the other laws which make up U.G. (i.e., the laws of Newtonian mechanics) will enable one to explain the orbit of Uranus. If one does not require that the missing statements be true, or approximately true, then there are an infinite number of solutions, mathematically speaking. Even if one includes in S_1 that no nongravitational forces are acting on the planets or the sun, there are still an infinite number of solutions. But one tries first the simplest assumption, namely:

(S_2) There is one and only one planet in the solar system in addition to the planets mentioned in S_1.

Now one considers the following problem:

> Theory: U.G.
> A.S.: S_1, S_2
>
> _____
>
> Consequence ??? – turns out to be that the unknown planet must have a certain orbit O.

This problem is a mathematical problem – the one Leverrier and

Adams both solved (an instance of Schema III). Now one considers the following empirical problem:

> Theory: U.G.
> A.S.: S_1, S_2
>
> ───────────────────────
>
> Prediction: A planet exists moving
> in orbit O – TRUE OR FALSE?

– this problem is an instance of Schema I – an instance one would not normally consider, because one of the A.S., namely the statement S_2, is not at all known to be true. S_2 is, in fact, functioning as a low-level hypothesis which we wish to test. But the test is not an inductive one in the usual sense, because a verification of the prediction is also a verification of S_2 – or rather, of the approximate truth of S_2 (which is all that is of interest in this context) – Neptune was not the only planet unknown in 1846; there was also Pluto to be later discovered. The fact is that we are interested in the above problem in 1846, because we know that if the prediction turns out to be true, then that prediction is precisely the statement S_3 that we need for the following deduction:

> Theory: U.G.
> A.S.: S_1, S_2, S_3
>
> ───────────────────────
>
> *Explanandum:* the orbit of Uranus

– i.e., the statement S_3 (that the planet mentioned in S_2 has precisely the orbit O) [13] is the solution to the problem with which we started. In this case we started with a problem of the Schema II type: we introduced the assumption S_2 as a simplifying assumption in the hope of solving the original problem thereby more easily; and we had the good luck to be able to deduce S_3 – the solution to the original problem – from U.G. together with S_1, S_2, and the more important good luck that S_3 turned out to be true when the Berlin Observatory looked. Problems of the Schema II-type are sometimes mentioned by philosophers of science when the missing A.S. are *laws*; but the case just examined, in which the missing A.S. was just a further contingent fact about the particular system is almost never discussed. I want to suggest that Schema II exhibits the logical form of what Kuhn calls a 'puzzle'.

If we examine Schema II, we can see why the term 'puzzle' is so appropriate. When one has a problem of this sort one is looking for something to fill a 'hole' – often a thing of rather under-specified sort – and that *is* a sort of *puzzle*. Moreover, this sort of problem is extremely widespread in science. Suppose one wants to explain the fact that water is a liquid (under the standard conditions), and one is given the laws of physics; the fact is that the problem is extremely hard. In fact, quantum mechanical laws are needed. But that does not mean that from classical physics one can deduce that water is *not* a liquid; rather the classical physicist would give up this problem at a certain point as 'too hard' – i.e., he would conclude that he could not find the right A.S.

The fact that Schema II is the logical form of the 'puzzles' of normal science explains a number of facts. When one is tackling a Schema II-type problem there is no question of deriving a prediction from U.G. plus given A.S., the whole problem is to find the A.S. The theory – U.G., or whichever – is *unfalsifiable in the context*. It is also not up for 'confirmation' any more than for 'falsification'; *it is not functioning in a hypothetical role*. Failures do not falsify a theory, because the failure is not a false prediction from a theory together with known and trusted facts, but a failure to *find* something – in fact, a failure to find an A.S. Theories, during their tenure of office, are highly immune to falsification; that tenure of office is ended by the appearance on the scene of a better theory (or a whole new explanatory technique), not by a basic sentence. And successes do not 'confirm' a theory, once it has become paradigmatic, because the theory is not a 'hypothesis' in need of confirmation, but the basis of a whole explanatory and predictive technique, and possibly of a technology as well.

To sum up: I have suggested that standard philosophy of science, both 'Popperian' and non-Popperian, has fixated on the situation in which we derive predictions from a theory, and test those predictions in order to falsify or confirm the theory – i.e., on the situation represented by Schema I. I have suggested that, by way of contrast, we see the 'puzzles' of 'normal science' as exhibiting the pattern represented by Schema II – the pattern in which we take a theory as fixed, take the fact to be explained as fixed, and seek further facts – frequently contingent[14] facts about the particular system – which will enable us to fill out the explanation of the particular fact on the basis of the theory. I suggest that adopting this point of view will enable us better to appreciate both the relative unfalsifiability of theories which have attained paradigm status, and the fact that the 'predictions' of physical theory are frequently facts which were known beforehand, and not things which are surprising relative to background knowledge.

To take Schema II as describing everything that goes on between the introduction of a paradigm and its eventual replacement by a better paradigm would be a gross error in the opposite direction, however. The fact is that normal science exhibits a dialectic between two conflicting (at any rate, potentially conflicting) but interdependent tendencies, and that it is the conflict of these tendencies that drives normal science forward. The desire to solve a Schema II-type problem – explain the orbit of Uranus – led to a new hypothesis (albeit a very low-level one): namely, S_2. Testing S_2 involved deriving S_3 from it, and testing S_3 – a Schema I-type situation. S_3 in turn served as the solution to the original problem. This illustrates the two tendencies, and also the way in which they are interdependent and the way in which their interaction drives science forward.

The tendency represented by Schema I is the *critical* tendency. Popper is right to emphasize the importance of this tendency, and doing this is certainly a contribution on his part – one that has influenced many philosophers. Scientists do want to know if their ideas are wrong, and they try to find out if their ideas are wrong by deriving predictions from them, and testing those predictions – that is, they do this *when they can*. The tendency represented by Schema II is the *explanatory* tendency. The element of conflict arises because in a Schema II-type situation one tends to regard the given theory as something *known*, whereas in a Schema I-type situation one tends to regard it as *problematic*. The interdependence is obvious: the theory which serves as the major premise in Schema II *may* itself have been the survivor of a Popperian test (although it need not have been – U.G. was accepted on the basis of its explanatory successes, not on the basis of its surviving attempted falsifications). And the solution to a

Schema II-type problem must itself be confirmed, frequently by a Schema I-type test. If the solution is a general law, rather than a singular statement, that law may itself become a paradigm, leading to new Schema II-type problems. In short, attempted falsifications do 'corroborate' theories – not just in Popper's sense, in which this is a tautology, but in the sense he denies, of showing that they are true, or partly true – and explanations on the basis of laws which are regarded as *known* frequently require the introduction of *hypotheses*. In this way, the tension between the attitudes of explanation and criticism drives science to progress.

11. Kuhn versus Popper

As might be expected, there are substantial differences between Kuhn and Popper on the issue of the falsifiability of scientific theories. Kuhn stresses the way in which a scientific theory may be immune from falsification, whereas Popper stresses falsifiability as the *sine qua non* of a scientific theory. Popper's answers to Kuhn depend upon two notions which must now be examined: the notion of an auxiliary hypothesis and the notion of a *conventionalist stratagem*.

Popper recognizes that the derivation of a prediction from a theory may require the use of auxiliary hypotheses (though the term 'hypothesis' is perhaps misleading, in suggesting something like putative laws, rather than assumptions about, say, boundary conditions). But he regards these as part of the total 'system' under test. A 'conventionalist stratagem' is to save a theory from a contrary experimental result by making an *ad hoc* change in the auxiliary hypotheses. And Popper takes it as a fundamental methodological rule of the empirical method to avoid conventionalist stratagems.

Does this do as a reply to Kuhn's objections? Does it contravene our own objections, in the first part of this paper? It does not. In the first place, the 'auxiliary hypotheses' A.S. are not fixed, in the case of U.G., but depend upon the context. One simply cannot think of U.G. as part of a fixed 'system' whose other part is a fixed set of auxiliary hypotheses whose function is to render U.G. 'highly testable'.

In the second place, an alteration in one's beliefs, may be *ad hoc* without being unreasonable. '*Ad hoc*' merely means 'to this specific purpose'. Of course, 'ad hoc' has acquired the connotation of 'unreasonable' – but that is a different thing. The assumption that certain stars have dark companions is *ad hoc* in the literal sense: the assumption is made for the specific purpose of accounting for the fact that no companion is visible. It is also highly reasonable.

It has already been pointed out that the A.S. are not only context-dependent but highly uncertain, in the case of U.G. and in many other cases. So, changing the A.S., or even saying in a particular context 'we don't know what the right A.S. are' may be *ad hoc* in the literal sense just noted, but is not 'ad hoc' in the extended sense of 'unreasonable'.

12. Paradigm Change

How does a paradigm come to be accepted in the first place? Popper's view is that a theory becomes corroborated by passing severe tests: a prediction (whose truth value is not antecedently known) must be derived from the theory and the truth or falsity of that prediction must be ascertained. The severity of the test depends upon the set of basic sentences excluded by the theory, and also upon the improbability of the prediction relative to background knowledge. The ideal case is one in which a theory which rules out a great many basic sentences implies a prediction which is very improbable relative to background knowledge.

Popper points out that the notion of the number of basic sentences ruled out by a theory cannot be understood in the sense of cardinality; he proposes rather to measure it by means of concepts of *improbability* or *content*. It does not appear true to me that improbability (in the sense of logical [im]probability)[15] measures falsifiability, in Popper's sense: U.G. excludes *no* basic sentences, for example, but has logical probability *zero*, on any standard metric. And it certainly is not true that the scientist always selects 'the most improbable of the surviving hypotheses' on *any* measure of probability, except in the trivial sense that all strictly universal laws have probability zero. But my concern here is not with the technical details of Popper's scheme, but with the leading idea.

To appraise this idea, let us see how U.G. came to be accepted.

Newton first derived Kepler's Laws from U.G. and the A.S. we mentioned at the outset: this was not a 'test', in Popper's sense, because Kepler's Laws were already known to be true. Then he showed that U.G. would account for the tides on the basis of the gravitational pull of the moon: this also was not a 'test', in Popper's sense, because the tides were already known. Then he spent many years showing that small perturbations (which were already known) in the orbits of the planets could be accounted for by U.G. By this time the whole civilized world had accepted – and, indeed, acclaimed – U.G.; but it had not been 'corroborated' at all in Popper's sense!

If we look for a Popperian 'test' of U.G. – a derivation of a new prediction, one risky relative to background knowledge – we do not get one until the Cavendish experiment of 1781 – roughly a hundred years after the theory had been introduced! The prediction of S_3 (the orbit of Neptune) from U.G. and the auxiliary statements S_1 and S_2 can also be regarded as a confirmation of U.G. (in 1846!); although it is difficult to regard it as a severe test of U.G. in view of the fact that the assumption S_2 had a more tentative status than U.G.

It is easy to see what has gone wrong. A theory is not accepted unless it has real explanatory successes. Although a theory may legitimately be preserved by changes in the A.S. which are, in a sense, 'ad hoc' (although not *unreasonable*), its *successes* must not be *ad hoc*. Popper requires that the predictions of a theory must not be antecedently known to be true in order to rule out *ad hoc* 'successes'; but the condition is too strong.

Popper is right in thinking that a theory runs a risk during the period of its establishment. In the case of U.G., the risk was not a risk of definite falsification; it was the risk that Newton would not find reasonable A.S. with the aid of which he could obtain real (non- *ad hoc*) explanatory successes for U.G. A failure to explain the tides by the gravitational pull of the moon alone would not, for example, have falsified U.G.; but the success did strongly support U.G.

In sum, a theory is only accepted if the theory has substantial, non- *ad hoc*, explanatory successes. This is in accordance with Popper; unfortunately, it is in even better accordance with the 'inductivist' accounts that Popper rejects, since these stress *support* rather than *falsification*.

13. On Practice

Popper's mistake here is no small isolated failing. What Popper consistently fails to see is that *practice is primary*: ideas are not just an end in themselves (although they are *partly* an end in themselves), nor is the selection of ideas to 'criticize' just an end in itself. The primary importance of ideas is that they guide practice, that they structure whole forms of life. Scientific ideas guide practice in science, in technology, and sometimes in public and private life. We are concerned in science with trying to discover correct ideas: Popper to the contrary, this is not *obscurantism* but *responsibility*. We obtain our ideas – our correct ones, and many of our incorrect ones – by close study of the world. Popper denies that the accumulation of perceptual experience leads to theories: he is right that it does not lead to theories in a mechanical or algorithmic sense; but it does lead to theories in the sense that it is a regularity of methodological significance that (1) lack of experience with phenomena and with previous knowledge about phenomena decreases the probability of correct ideas in a marked fashion; and (2) extensive experience increases the probability of correct, or partially correct, ideas in a marked fashion. 'There is no logic of discovery' – in that sense, there is no logic of *testing*, either; all the formal algorithms proposed for testing, by Carnap, by Popper, by Chomsky, etc., are, to speak impolitely, *ridiculous*; if you don't believe this, program a computer to employ one of these algorithms and see how well it does at testing theories! There are *maxims* for discovery and maxims for testing: the idea that correct ideas just come from the sky, while the methods for testing them are highly rigid and predetermined, is one of the worst legacies of the Vienna Circle.

But the correctness of an idea is not certified by the fact that it came from close and concrete study of the relevant aspects of the world; in this sense, Popper is right. We judge the correctness of our ideas by applying them and seeing if they succeed; in general, and in the long run, correct ideas lead to success, and ideas lead to failures where and insofar as they are incorrect. Failure to see the importance of practice leads directly to failure to see the importance of success.

Failure to see the primacy of practice also leads Popper to the idea of a sharp 'demarcation' between science, on the one hand, and political, philosophical, and ethical ideas, on the other. This 'demarcation' is pernicious, in my view; fundamentally, it corresponds to Popper's separation of theory from practice, and his related separation of the critical tendency in science from the explanatory tendency in science. Finally, the failure to see the primacy of practice leads Popper to some rather reactionary political conclusions. Marxists believe that there are laws of society; that these laws can be known; and that men can and should act on this knowledge. It is not my purpose here to argue that this Marxist view is correct; but surely any view that rules this out *a priori* is reactionary. Yet this is precisely what Popper does – and in the name of an anti-*a priori* philosophy of knowledge!

In general, and in the long run, true ideas are the ones that succeed – how do we know this? This statement too is a statement about the world; a statement we have come to from experience of the world; and we believe in the practice to which this idea corresponds, and in the idea as informing that kind of practice, on the basis that we believe in any good idea – it has proved successful! In this sense 'induction is circular'. But of course it is! Induction has no deductive justification; induction is not deduction. Circular justifications need not be totally self-protecting nor need they be totally uninformative:[16] the past success of 'induction' increases our confidence in it, and its past failure tempers that confidence. The fact that a justification is circular only means that that justification has no power to serve as a *reason*, unless the person to whom it is given as a reason already has some propensity to accept the conclusion. We do have a propensity – an *a priori* propensity, if you like – to reason 'inductively', and the past success of 'induction' increases that propensity.

The method of testing ideas in practice and relying on the ones that prove successful (for that is what 'induction' is) is not unjustified. That is an *empirical* statement. The method does not have a 'justification' – if by a justification is meant a proof from eternal and formal principles that justifies reliance on the method. But then, nothing does – not even, in my opinion, pure mathematics and formal logic. Practice is primary.

Notes

1. I have discussed positivistic meaning theory in 'What Theories Are Not', published in *Logic, Methodology, and Philosophy of Science*, ed. by A. Tarski, E. Nagel, and P. Suppes (Stanford: Stanford University Press, 1962), pp. 240–51, and also in 'How Not to Talk about Meaning', published in *Boston Studies in the Philosophy of Science*, Vol. II, ed. by R. S. Cohen and M. W. Wartofsky (New York: Humanities Press, 1965), pp. 205–22.

2. For a discussion of 'approximate truth', see the second of the papers mentioned in the preceding note.

3. 'Confirmation' is the term in standard use for *support* a positive experimental or observational result gives to a hypothesis; Popper uses the term 'corroboration' instead, as a rule, because he objects to the connotations of 'showing to be true' (or at least probable) which he sees as attaching to the former term.

4. *Bayes's theorem* asserts, roughly, that the probability of a hypothesis H on given evidence E is directly proportional to the probability of E on the hypothesis H, and also directly proportional to the antecedent probability of H – i.e., the probability of H if one doesn't know that E. The theorem also asserts that the probability of H on the evidence E is less, other things being equal, if the probability of E on the assumption – (*not*-H) is greater. Today probability theorists are divided between those who accept the notion of 'antecedent probability of a hypothesis', which is crucial to the theorem, and those who reject this notion, and therefore the notion of the probability of a hypothesis on given evidence. The former school are called 'Bayesians'; the latter 'anti-Bayesians'.

5. Cf. my paper '"Degree of Confirmation" and Inductive Logic', in *The Philosophy of Rudolf Carnap* (The Library of Living Philosophers, Vol. 11), ed. by Paul A. Schilpp (La Salle, Ill.: Open Court Publishing Co., 1963), pp. 761–84.

6. Popper's reply to this sort of criticism is discussed below in the section titled 'Kuhn versus Popper'.

7. This point is made by many authors. The point that is often missed is that, in cases such as the one discussed, the auxiliary statements are much less certain than the theory under test; without this remark, the criticism that one *might* preserve a theory by revising the A.S. looks like a bit of formal logic, without real relation to scientific practice. (See below, 'Kuhn versus Popper'.)

8. I have in mind saying 'the planets exert forces on each other which are more than ·999 (or whatever) gravitational', rather than 'the planets exert *no* non-gravitational forces on each other'. Similar changes in the other A.S. could presumably turn them into true statements – though it is not methodologically unimportant that no scientist, to my knowledge, has bothered to calculate exactly what changes in the A.S. would render them true while preserving their usefulness.

9. Hilary Putnam, 'The Analytic and the Synthetic', in *Minnesota Studies in*

the Philosophy of Science, Vol. III, ed. by H. Feigl and G. Maxwell (Minneapolis: University of Minnesota Press, 1962), pp. 358–97.

10. N. R. Hanson, in Patterns of Discovery (Cambridge: Cambridge University Press, 1958).

11. Thomas S. Kuhn, The Structure of Scientific Revolutions, Vol. II, No. 2 of International Encyclopedia of Unified Science (Chicago: University of Chicago Press, 1962).

12. Louis Althusser, Pour Marx and Lire le Capital (Paris: Maspero, 1965).

13. I use 'orbit' in the sense of space-time trajectory, not just spatial path.

14. By 'contingent' I mean not physically necessary.

15. 'Logical probability' is probability assigning equal weight (in some sense) to logically possible worlds.

16. This has been emphasized by Professor Max Black in a number of papers: e.g. 'Self-supporting Inductive Arguments', Journal of Philosophy 55 (1958), pp. 718–25; reprinted in Richard Swinburne (ed.), The Justification of Induction (Oxford Readings in Philosophy, Oxford University Press, 1974).

Retrospective Note (1978): A Critic Replies to his Philosopher

Popper's reply[1] to my criticism consists of two main charges: (1) that I misrepresent him to such an extent that I must not have read his main book, The Logic of Scientific Discovery; and (2) that I commit an outright logical blunder. Both of these charges are false and unfounded.

The Charge of Textual Misrepresentation

The charge that I misrepresented Popper's doctrine itself rests on two claims: that I say of Popper that he neglects the need for auxiliary statements; and that Popper in fact talked about auxiliary statements at length (under the name 'initial conditions') in The Logic of Scientific Discovery.

The first claim is false: nowhere in my essay does there appear one sentence which says Popper denies the existence of, ignores, or neglects auxiliary statements. In fact, my section on the Kuhn–Popper debate talks explicitly about Popper's treatment of auxiliary hypotheses (which is (1) that they are part of 'the total system' under test;

and (2) that one must not preserve the total system by *adjusting* this part – to do so is a 'conventionalist stratagem' and *bad*). What I *did* say is that Popper *blurs the distinction* between auxiliary statements and theory, and this, I still maintain, is true.

The second claim is also false. The auxiliary statements I was talking about, the ones I was taking as examples and on which my argument turned, were *not* 'initial conditions'.

'Initial Conditions', in Popper's sense, are *singular* statements (as he stresses again and again in *The Logic of Scientific Discovery*). Moreover, whenever he treats the question of their testability, he treats them as *verifiable* ('true basic statements', in his terminology).

The auxiliary statements I gave as examples were:

(1) The solar system consists of *only* the following bodies (list).

(2) *No* non-gravitational forces (or gravitational forces from outside the solar system) are acting on the solar system (to a certain small ϵ of accuracy).

Both of these statements are *universal* statements, not singular statements. Neither can be verified as a basic statement can – indeed, to verify the second one would *already* have to know the true theory of gravitation! Popper's charge of textual misrepresentation is unfounded, and, in fact, I was very careful to present his doctrine *accurately*.[2]

The Charge of Logical Blunder

What I contended in my criticism is that as scientists actually use the term 'theory' (and, as I argued, they *should* use it), Newton's theory of universal gravitation is *not* falsifiable: only its conjunction with the two auxiliary statements just listed is falsifiable.

Popper claims that this is a logical blunder. His proof that this is a logical blunder – that U.G. is falsifiable *without* A.S. (auxiliary statements) – *is a quotation from me* – a quotation in which I say we would give up U.G. if the world started acting in a 'markedly non-Newtonian manner'.

Now the logical situation is precisely this: *any trajectories whatsoever of all the observed bodies are compatible with U.G. without A.S.* Moreover, this is so for a number of reasons:

(1) U.G. without A.S. says nothing at all about what *non*-gravitational forces there might be! By assuming non-gravitational forces perturbing the system, we can account for any trajectories at all, even if U.G. is true.

(2) Even if we assume the system is acted on only by *gravitational* forces, we can still account for any trajectories at all, to any finite degree of accuracy, by assuming gravitational fields *in addition* to the ones caused by the observed bodies (e.g. there might be bodies too small and too rapid to be observed which are so massive that they give rise to significant fields).

Of course, such *ad hoc* assumptions as would be required to preserve U.G. if the trajectories did 'crazy' things (e.g. if we got *square* orbits), would be enormously *inductively implausible* – which is why we would give up U.G. in such a case. But I was not conceding that square orbits (or whatever) would *deductively* falsify U.G. – which is what Popper takes me to be conceding. The logical blunder is his, not mine.

The Main Point

Since the reader has my article available, I do not have to expand on what I actually said there. The main points are two: that Popper's prohibition on saving a successful theory by modifying the A.S. is *bad methodological advice* (as Imre Lakatos and others also pointed out); and that successful predictions *can* confirm a theory plus A.S. even when they are not potential falsifiers in Popper's sense. My distinction between a theory in the canonical sense and A.S. is not the same as Popper's distinction between theory and initial conditions, as has already been pointed out, but it is closely related to, if not quite the same as, Lakatos's distinction between a 'theory core' and a 'protective belt'. The importance of such a distinction has become widely recognized in recent years.

Notes

1. See Introduction, p. 351 – Edd.
2. For example, I say that Popper says that a 'theory' implies predictions. 'Predictions' is a non-technical word which covers what Popper himself calls

instantial sentences (conditionals whose antecedent and consequent are both basic sentences) as well as basic sentences, and the claim that a theory by itself implies instantial sentences occurs in many places in *The Logic of Scientific Discovery*. I did, unfortunately, write 'basic sentence' instead of 'instantial sentence' in the article in a number of places.

Biographical Note

Hilary Putnam is Professor of Philosophy at Harvard University. He is the author of *Philosophy of Logic* (1971), and his collected papers were published by the Cambridge University Press in 1975: *Mathematics, Matter and Method* (vol. 1) and *Mind, Language and Reality* (vol. 2).

Further Reading

Karl Popper: *The Logic of Scientific Discovery*, 3rd ed., revised and enlarged (London: Hutchinson, 1972); *Conjectures and Refutations*, 4th ed., revised and enlarged (London: Routledge & Kegan Paul, 1972). Thomas S. Kuhn: *The Structure of Scientific Revolutions*, 2nd ed., enlarged (Chicago: Univ. of Chicago Press, 1972). Louis Althusser: *For Marx*, English translation by Ben Brewster (London: Allen Lane, 1969), esp. Chaps. II and IV; *Reading Capital*, English translation by Ben Brewster (London: New Left Books, 1970). Paul Arthur Schilpp (ed.): *The Philosophy of Karl Popper*, 2 vols. (La Salle, Illinois: Open Court, 1974.) This contains Popper's 'Intellectual Autobiography' and a number of essays on different aspects of his philosophy. Particularly relevant to the issues under discussion in Putnam's paper from the same collection are the following: Imre Lakatos: 'Popper on Demarcation and Induction'; Grover Maxwell: 'Corroboration without Demarcation'; Thomas S. Kuhn: 'Logic of Discovery or Psychology of Research'. Part III of the Schilpp collection contains Popper's 'Replies to My Critics' and here may be found his reply to Putnam: 'Putnam on "Auxiliary Sentences", Called by Me "Initial Conditions"'.

J. L. Mackie

A Conditional Analysis of the Concept of Causation

One of the really fundamental facts about the universe, along with its being spatial and in time, and having things in it, is that most or all of the things in it are causes and effects. It is no surprise, then, that the relation of cause and effect holding between two things enters into so much of language, or, as some philosophers more grandly say, into so much of our conceptual scheme. We are speaking of causation not only when we use 'cause', 'effect' and related words, but also, most importantly, when we use many of our commonest verbs: for example when we say that one thing pushed another, or pulled, held back, broke, warmed, lit up, made something happen to, changed, or indeed cheered up, another. It is not too much to say, as John Mackie does (making use of a phrase from David Hume) that causation is the cement of the universe.

Causation is also puzzling and complex. The philosophical controversy about it is mainly about the analysis of our concept or concepts of causation. What, on reflection, do we mean by our causal talk? What do we take, truly or falsely, to be the distinguishing features of causal connection between things, or, as some call it, necessary connection between things? Our own concepts may indeed fit the facts, since it is not too much to say that that is where they come from, but a question about the actual nature of reality, about what the facts are, is a separate one. Unlike the analytical question, it is perhaps not primarily one for philosophers. The analytical question is the main concern of the chapter we reprint here from Mackie's admirable book about causation, *The Cement of the Universe*. The answer is cogent, methodical, detailed and complete. It requires close attention, and certainly repays it. This introduction follows roughly the course of the chapter.

Suppose we believe that hitting a chestnut with a hammer flattened it, or, as we can also say, caused it to be flatter. What do we mean? An answer derived from Hume, and with variations still defended by many philosophers, is essentially this: 'Such hammer-blows in such circumstances are always followed by such chestnut-flattenings, and such chestnut-flattenings in such circumstances are always preceded by such hammer-blows'. This is the first of several different things that can be meant by saying that the hammer-blow in the circumstances was *sufficient* for the flattening, and also in the circumstances *necessary* to the flattening.

As Mackie remarks (p. 388), we can if we want also express this Humean answer by the use of *if-then* or conditional sentences understood in a special way defined for the purposes of formal logic. This is their understanding as what logicians call *material conditionals*. (The contrast between this logician's understanding of conditional sentences and other understandings also comes up in other connections in what follows.) For convenience, let us use 'b' for any hammer-blow of the given kind, 'c' for any such circumstance and 'f' for any such chestnut-flattening. Then the essence of the Humean analysis of the given causal statement can be put in this way: 'Always, if there is a b in c, then there is an f; and always, if there is an f in c, then there is a b', where that is understood as merely denying that b ever occurs in c without f, and denying that f ever occurs in c without b. To put the point slightly differently, *all* that is needed to make the conditional true on this understanding is that there are no cases of b in c without f and no cases of f in c without b.

What is specifically left out here is the idea that there is a certain *connection* between the state of affairs mentioned in the antecedent of each conditional sentence and the state of affairs mentioned in the consequent. What is left out is the idea, as some describe it, that the second state of affairs is in some way a *consequence* of the first. As a result, two entirely 'unconnected' states of affairs can result in perfectly true *if-then* sentences so long as these are understood as material conditionals. 'If men dream, then there are daisies' is an example.

Mackie does not offer a Humean analysis of causation, although his answer does involve conditional sentences. To say that hitting the chestnut with the hammer caused it to be flatter is to say that in the circumstances if the hammer had not hit the chestnut, it would not have become flatter, or that in the circumstances since the chestnut did become flatter, it was hit by the hammer. The first way of putting it presents the antecedent – the proposition that the hammer did *not* hit the chestnut – as false. Conditionals with this feature are often referred to as 'contrary-to-fact' conditionals or 'counterfactuals'. The main thing about such conditionals, of which more of a positive kind will be said shortly, is that they are *not* to be understood in the 'material' way. The first essential idea in Mackie's analysis of causation, then, is that causal statements are to be seen as conditional statements of a certain kind.

Are *all* events which are related in this way cause and effect? To express the same question differently, we can ask if each event which is in this way necessary to another is a cause of the other. (We here have a second sense in which one event can be said to be necessary to another.) It seems that the answer to the question is no. To take one example (p. 391), if we have two events which are both effects of a common cause, such as James's being pleased and John's being saddened, then if one had not happened the other would not have happened. Each event is necessary to the other, in the given sense, but they are not cause and effect.

Mackie's way of dealing with this (p. 391, p. 408) has to do in part with our practice of conceiving or imagining things to have been or to be in various ways different from what they were or they are – our conceiving different 'possible worlds'. It also has to do, more importantly, with the idea (the second essential idea in his analysis of causation) that the world has 'a way of running on' from one change or event to another. There is a direction in things, or, as we can say, one change or event is *prior* to another, where this does not mean prior in time. Rather, the priority in question has to do with a number of facts. One of these involves there being a time when one thing is fixed and unalterable and the other not. Another involves our being able to do one thing (such as strike a match) in order to bring about another (the match's lighting) but not the other way round. The direction of things in the case of our troublesome example, to return to it for a moment, is from the common cause to James's being pleased and also from the cause to John's being saddened. The direction is *not* from James's being pleased to John's being saddened or vice versa. Causes, then, may seem to be necessary conditions of their effects and also in the given sense prior to them.

However, there is yet a third thing to be added. It will be brought to mind by the fact that the chestnut would not have been made flatter, although it was struck by the hammer, if circumstances had been different – if, for example, it had been lying on a soft and very deep cushion. That it was lying on another sort of surface instead was *also* a necessary and prior condition of the flattening. But we would usually consider it to be merely a condition, not also a cause of the flattening; still less would we count it as *the* cause of that event.

Mackie gives a careful account (pp. 391 f.) of the features of a condition which lead us to pick it out as the cause. Its being an event rather than a standing condition may be important (as in the chestnut example), or its being in some way abnormal rather than normal. Also, if we take some feature as being part of the causal field, that is, of the background against which we see the causal process as going on, it is thereby made ineligible for the role of cause.

What we have in the end, in bare outline, is this: to say one thing caused another is to say (i) that if the first thing had not happened, the second would not have – the first is in a particular sense necessary to the second; and (ii) that the first was in the special sense prior to the second; and (iii) that the first thing was different in one of a number of ways from other conditions also necessary to and prior to the effect.

It is the first part of this analysis which gets most attention in the chapter. One large question raised by it is this: Do we not take causes to be not only necessary but also sufficient or ensuring or necessitating conditions? (It will be recalled that the Humean view involves both necessity and sufficiency, although very differently understood.) Take the same statement as before, that hitting the chestnut with the hammer caused it to be flatter. We have already found it to mean (a) that in the circumstances if the hammer had not hit it, the chestnut would not have become flatter, but does it not also mean (b) that in the circumstance if the chestnut had not been going to get flatter, the hammer would not have hit it?

To many philosophers it would seem that the answer is yes. Our concept of cause is indeed of something that is necessary and also in a related way sufficient. A cause involves sufficiency in the non-material or what can be called the strong sense. Mackie thinks otherwise, and argues for his position mainly by way of his three shilling-in-the-slot machines (p. 398). The most important one is such that when it does work, there nonetheless is no such sufficient condition for the coming-out of the bar of chocolate. Even so, it seems, there is a cause of that event.

Subsequently Mackie considers certain examples which seem to threaten his thesis and, perhaps, to support an alternative one, that causes are *just* sufficient conditions. The causes in these examples do not seem to be necessary conditions. It is here that we encounter the unfortunate traveller who died in the desert. He had two enemies, one of whom had put a deadly poison in his reserve can of drinking water and the other of whom had made a hole in the bottom of the can. Neither of these things, it seems, was necessary to his death. Mackie argues that the example, and others like it, do not in fact refute his thesis that we take causes to be necessary conditions and not either just sufficient conditions or necessary-plus-sufficient conditions. There are some different considerations (pp. 405–6) that do lead to some amendment of his thesis but not to its abandonment.

We finally come to a positive account of the meaning or nature of non-material conditional statements (p. 410). They themselves have long been a matter of philosophical disagreement. They are a good deal more complex than conditional statements understood in the material way. One view, as already remarked, is that statements of the form 'if p, then q', as ordinarily understood, assert that the state of affairs described by q is a *consequence* of the state of affairs described by p, or that the latter is a *ground* of the former.

Mackie's own view (p. 410) is that such conditionals are best described in a related way. Some of them are condensed or telescoped arguments. To make a conditional statement may be, in effect, to run through an argument of the form: 'Suppose . . ., then . . .'. More generally, conditionals are said to involve our supposing something (the antecedent) and then asserting something (the consequent) on the basis of, or within the scope of, that supposition. As a result, a conditional statement says something like this: 'In the possible situation that . . ., such and such also holds'. Given this novel view, some conditionals – those in which the antecedent is not fulfilled, in which the possible situation is not realized – are neither true nor false. There is the further consequence that the causal statements into which they enter are not all true or false. Mackie does not take this further consequence to raise a serious question about his analysis of causation.

Some questions which arise in the course of this chapter are treated more fully elsewhere in the book from which it comes. Chapter 10 is concerned with the question (p. 391) of whether causal statements are extensional statements: that is, whether they remain true when one takes out a particular description of a thing and puts in a different description referring to the same thing. A view of causation as functional dependence (p. 401) is considered in Chapter 6. Whether causes are events or facts or what – the ontological question which is referred to in passing (p. 403) – is also taken up in Chapter 10.

The question (p. 407) of whether causal statements are implicitly but essentially general, referring to all like events, as suggested by the Humean analysis given above, is considered more fully in Chapter 13. Hume's analysis of causation is examined in Chapter 1, and Kant's in Chapter 4. The use of causal concepts and statements in legal decisions – the subject of the excellent book *Causation in the Law*, by Hart and Honoré – is touched upon in Chapter 5. Statistical or probabilistic laws (p. 407), as distinct from deterministic and exceptionless causal laws, are discussed in Chapter 9. Causal priority is the subject of Chapter 7. The general question of non-material conditional statements, and Mackie's own analysis of them, as telescoped arguments, is fully discussed in Chapter 3 of another of his books, *Truth, Probability and Paradox*.

T.H.

J. L. Mackie

A Conditional Analysis of the Concept of Causation

What is our concept of causal as opposed to non-causal sequences? What do we (rightly or wrongly) take to be their distinguishing feature? The obvious, naïve, way of tackling this question would be to compare two otherwise similar sequences, only one of which we recognize as causal, and see what distinctive comment we should make about the causal one. Let us, then, compare the following sequences *A* and *B*.

A: A chestnut is stationary on a flat stone. I swing a hammer down so that it strikes the chestnut directly from above. The chestnut becomes distinctly flatter than before.

B: A chestnut is stationary on a hot sheet of iron. I swing a hammer down so that it strikes the chestnut directly from above. At the very instant that the hammer touches it, the chestnut explodes with a loud pop and its fragments are scattered around.

I assume that we know or perceive enough about sequences *A* and *B* to be able to say that the chestnut's becoming flatter in *A* was caused by its being hit with the hammer, but that its exploding in *B* was not caused by its being hit with the hammer. (Among other things, the explosion was not due to the hammer's pushing the chestnut into closer contact with the hot metal, or anything like that.) I am not concerned, at the moment, with how we know this, but merely with what we mean, what we are *saying* when we say that the blow-flattening sequence was causal but that the blow–exploding sequence was not.

I suggest that the obvious answer, the one that pretty well any intelligent but unprejudiced person would give to this question, is that in *A* the chestnut would not have become flatter if the hammer had not struck it, whereas in *B* it would have exploded even if the hammer had not struck it. It is tempting to say, then, that the contrast between these two contrary-to-fact conditionals is at least an initial indication of what we mean by calling the one sequence causal and the other not: it is to assert such a contrary-to-fact conditional as the former. As Mill says, 'if a person eats of a particular dish, and dies in consequence, that is, would not have died if he had not eaten of it, people would be apt to say that eating of that dish was the cause of his death'.[1] They would indeed.

Curiously enough, Hume says this too. In the *Enquiry*, after giving the regularity definition ('we may define a cause to be an *object, followed by another, and where all objects similar to the first are followed by objects similar to the second*'), he adds 'or in other words *where, if the first object had not been, the second never had existed*'.[2] Now of course this variant is *not* the regularity definition in other words. (It does not even follow from the regularity definition as given here, though on a certain interpretation of the conditional it might be held to follow from, and even to be equivalent to, a different regularity statement, namely 'where all the objects similar to the second are preceded by objects similar to the first'.) But I shall not spend time on the questions of why Hume asserted this implausible equivalence, or of why he did not realize that this was a much better answer than the one he had given in all his previous discussion to the question 'What is our *idea* of necessary connection?', but consider directly the merits and the defects of this suggestion.

To simplify matters, I shall for the present be considering only singular causal statements, especially statements about individual event sequences, such as 'The hammer's striking the chestnut caused the flattening of the chestnut'. I shall speak of causes and effects (or results) as events, but 'event' is just a general term that stands in for such items as 'the hammer's striking the chestnut'. (Anxieties about the exact ontology of causation may be postponed for later consideration.[3]) Such phrases are nominalizations of singular event-sentences or event-clauses; e.g. 'the flattening of the chestnut' is a nominalization of 'the chestnut became flatter'. The present suggestion, then, is that a statement of the form '*X* caused *Y*' means '*X* occurred and *Y* occurred and *Y* would not have occurred if *X* had not', it being understood that when we instantiate '*X*' and '*Y*' with particular event descriptions we can express the suggested meaning most neatly by going back from the nominalizations to the corresponding clauses or their negations: e.g. 'the striking of the match caused the appearance of the flame' would, on this suggestion, mean 'the match was struck and the flame appeared and the flame would not have appeared if the match had not been struck'.

But is the suggestion correct?

First, are there cases where we would say that *X* caused *Y* but would not say what is proposed above as the meaning of this claim? Well, clearly we cannot say that *X* caused *Y* unless both *X* and *Y* occurred, provided that we take 'occurred' in a fairly broad sense, to include the presence or persistence of standing conditions. But what about the counterfactual conditional? Might we not say that the striking of the match caused the appearance of the flame and yet admit that even if the match had not been struck the flame would have appeared if, say, this match had been touched by a red-hot poker? Certainly we might, so the suggestion needs some modification at least: let us insert 'in the circumstances', reading '. . . and in the circumstances the flame would not have appeared if the match had not been struck'. 'The circumstances' can be taken to include the fact that this match was not in fact touched by a red-hot poker at the critical time. And in general we can modify our suggestion to read '. . . in the circumstances *Y* would not have occurred if *X* had not', the qualifying phrase being interpreted in the sort of way indicated by our example.

An objector, however, might say, 'But what if, for example, the match really was touched by a red-hot poker at the same instant that it was struck? Then even *in the circumstances* the flame would have appeared even if the match had not been struck.' True, but it is not clear whether in this case we would say that the striking of the match caused the appearance of the flame. What we would or should say in such cases of causal over-determination, of fail-safe causes, will be considered later: for the moment we need not take them as falsifying our modified suggestion.

Secondly, and more awkwardly, are there cases where we would *not* say that *X* caused *Y* but would say that *X* and *Y* both occurred and that in the circumstances Y would not have occurred if X had not? Would we not have to say the latter, trivially, if X and Y were identical? Provided that X occurred, we must admit that X occurred and X occurred and in the circumstances X would not have occurred if X had not. But events, unlike Spinoza's God, are not commonly said to cause themselves. Equally, the penny would not have fallen heads-up if it had not fallen tails-down; but we would not say that its falling tails-down caused its falling heads-up. Again, the driver would not in the circumstances have broken the law if he had not exceeded the speed limit; but we would not say that his exceeding the speed limit caused his breaking of the law. To exclude all such counter-examples, we must say that, in addition to the meaning suggested above, 'X caused Y' presupposes that X and Y are distinct events, and, as the last two examples show, this must be taken in a stronger sense than merely that 'X' and 'Y' are logically or conceptually independent descriptions. Indeed, it is not even necessary, any more than it is sufficient for this purpose, that these should be logically independent descriptions. It is legitimate, though trivial, to say that X caused every effect of X; again I can say that my meeting Tom on Monday caused my remembering, on Tuesday, my meeting Tom on Monday. And so on. Logically independent descriptions, then, are not called for; what is required is that the cause and the effect should be, as Hume says, distinct existences. It may be objected that this requirement is vague or obscure, but it is not, I think, necessary for me to aim at any great precision here. I am discussing only what causal statements mean, and for this purpose it is sufficient to say that someone will not be willing to say that X caused Y unless *he* regards X and Y as distinct existences.

But are there really no limits to the possible descriptions of X and Y? What about *irrelevant* descriptions, ones that have, as we would say, nothing to do with the causal relationship? Some seem acceptable: 'the incident in the tennis court advanced the French Revolution'. But consider 'Jane's eating fishpaste in the pantry caused her feeling ill' and the corresponding suggested expansion 'Jane ate fishpaste in the pantry and felt ill and in the circumstances she wouldn't have felt ill if she hadn't eaten fishpaste in the pantry'. We are inclined to comment that she felt ill either because she ate too much fishpaste or because the fishpaste was bad, and in either case it wouldn't have mattered where she ate it. This raises a question[4] about the extensionality of causal statements. For the present it is enough to say that the issue is in doubt: we might want to reject or deny both the proposed singular causal statement and its expansion, or we might want to say that so long as it was eating the fishpaste that made Jane ill, and it was in the pantry that she ate it, they are both true but merely misleading. But it seems that whatever we decide to say, we can say about both the singular causal statement and its proposed expansion, so that examples of this sort do not tell against the suggestion that the latter shows what the former means.

Cases where X and Y are collateral effects of a common cause create a more serious difficulty. Labour's defeat at the election pleases James but saddens John, who, as it happens, are quite unknown to each other. Then James's being pleased does not cause John's being sad, and yet we might well say that in the circumstances John would not have been sad if James had not been pleased. Yet there is a way of handling the words 'if' and 'in the circumstances' that will defeat this supposed counter-example. Construct a 'possible world' in the following way: take something that is just like the actual world up to the point where, in the actual world, James is pleased; keep out, from your possible world, James's being pleased, but otherwise let your possible world run on in the same manner as the actual world; only if John does not become sad in your possible world can you say 'in the circumstances John would not have been sad if James had not been pleased'. And if you *can* say this, then you can also say that James's being pleased caused John's being sad (in the actual world). But this special way of handling 'if in the circumstances' runs a grave risk of circularity if we want to use this conditional as an analysis of causal statements, since in explaining this handling we have had to use the notion of letting the possible world run on. Yet without this special interpretation of the counterfactual conditional, it seems that while it may be required for the truth of the corresponding causal statement, it is not sufficient for this.

Another difficulty is concerned with the distinction which we are inclined to draw between conditions and causes. There may be a set of factors which were, in the circumstances, jointly sufficient and severally necessary for a certain result, and which all occurred, as, consequently, did the result. Then we can say of each of these factors that if in the circumstances it had not occurred the result would not; but we may not be so willing to say of each of them that it caused the result. Perhaps we *ought* to say this, since they are all logically related to the result in the same way: the situation as described is symmetrical with respect to all the factors. But at present we are discussing not what we ought to say but what our causal statements mean. And there is no doubt that we tend to be a bit selective, to be more ready to call some kinds of factors causes than others. There are no firm rules governing this selection, but there are some fairly systematic tendencies.

Thus we are more ready to say that an event caused a certain effect than that a standing condition did: it was the spark rather than the presence of inflammable material that caused the fire. Even among events ones which are seen as intrusive are picked as causes in preference to ones which occur within some going concern: it was the severing of the artery rather than the pumping of the heart that caused the loss of blood. This preference shades into one governed by moral and legal assumptions: what is normal, right, and proper is not so readily called a cause as is something abnormal or wrong. This third tendency may conflict with and override the first. Since it is normal for people to be striking matches and lighting cigarettes in a residential flat, but a gas leak is abnormal and should not occur, we may well say that the explosion which wrecked this block of flats was caused by the presence of a quantity of gas rather than that it was caused by Jones lighting his cigarette.

These matters may be clarified to some extent if we realize that causal statements are commonly made in some context, against a background which includes the assumption of some *causal field*.[5] A causal statement will be the answer to a causal question, and the question 'What caused this explosion?' can be expanded into 'What made the difference between those times, or those cases, within a certain range, in which no such explosion occurred, and this case in which an explosion did occur?' Both cause and effect are seen as differences within a field; anything that is part of the assumed (but commonly unstated) description of the field itself will, then, be automatically ruled out as a candidate for the role of cause. Consequently if we take the field as being *this block of flats as normally used and lived in*, we must take Jones's striking a match to light his cigarette as part of the field, and therefore not as the cause of, or even a cause of, or as causing, the explosion. What caused the explosion must be a difference in relation to the field, and the gas leak, or the presence of the gas that had leaked out, is the obvious candidate.

What is said to be caused, then, is not just an event, but an event-in-a-certain-field, and some 'conditions' can be set aside as not causing this-event-in-this-field simply because they are part of the chosen field, though if a different field were chosen, in other words if a different causal question were being asked, one of those conditions might well be said to cause this-event-in-that-other-field. Any part of the chosen field is decisively ruled out as a cause; a more elusive point is that among factors not so ruled out which are still severally necessary for the effect, we still show some degree of preference on the grounds indicated above. But I think that this can be taken as reflecting not the meaning of causal statements but rather their conversational point, the sorts of use to which they are likely to be put. We often want to know what caused some event with a view to saying how it could, and perhaps should, have been prevented: pointing to the spark rather than to the presence of inflammable material indicates what would have been the last chance of preventing the fire. But it might be conceded that the statement that the presence of this material caused the fire would be as true as the statement that the spark caused it, and merely in some ways less interesting. We can and do indeed distinguish between triggering causes and predisposing causes, which shows that standing conditions are not prevented from being causes by the mere meaning of the noun, or of the verb, 'cause'. Similarly we may agree that the collision was caused just as much by Smith's driving straight ahead as by Brown's deviating to his right without warning, but say that it is more important, for moral and legal purposes, to draw attention to the second of the two causal relationships.

The supposed distinction between conditions and causes can be adequately accounted for in these two ways: an alleged condition which is not called a cause, although if in the circumstances it had not occurred the result would not, either is part of the field presupposed in the view taken by the speaker of the result (and so is not a cause in relation to this field) or is a cause, but mention of this fact happens to be irrelevant, or less relevant than mention of some other cause of the same result, to some current purpose.

There is admittedly some logical redundancy in the two treatments offered here of conditions which we are reluctant to call causes. We should get a neater account if, say, we assigned all such conditions to the assumed causal field, and said that anyone who withheld the title of cause from what he admitted to be one of a set of severally necessary and jointly sufficient conditions for some result was implicitly taking that condition to be part of the field. Again, we should get a neater account if we discarded the notion of a field, and interpreted the withholding of the title of cause from any such necessary factor as reflecting some conversational or other purpose of the speaker. But at present my object is not so much to give a logically neat account as to analyse our ordinary thinking about causal sequences, and I believe that this does contain the two separate elements I have tried to describe. On the one hand there is the implicit question, 'What caused such-and-such?', where 'such-and-such' is already thought of as a change in a certain material or background state of affairs; on the other hand, even among *differentiae* within this background, we tend to downgrade some and at least initially deny that they caused the result, though we might reluctantly concede, if pressed, that they helped to cause it.

Another sort of apparent counter-example is easily disposed of in the same way. It can be truly said of anyone now dead that if he had not been born he would not have died, and although it would here be pointless to insert 'in the circumstances', such an insertion would not make the statement false. Yet we would not say that being born caused his death – that is, not ordinarily: with sufficient ingenuity one can construct a case for saying this. But the reason is merely that when we look for a cause of someone's death, the event, this person's death, is a change in a field which centrally includes this person's being alive for a while, and hence (in the ordinary course of nature) his having been born. As before, his being born is part of the field, and therefore cannot be the cause of his death.

The suggested meaning for 'X caused Y' which we have been considering is 'X occurred and Y occurred and in the circumstances, Y would not have occurred if X had not'. A slightly different formula would run '. . . and there were circumstances such that in them Y would not have occurred if X had not'. To see the difference, suppose that the effect is that a certain part of a certain house catches fire, that the presence of oxygen, the absence of any extinguishing device, etc., are taken as parts of the field, and that in relation to this field the following three conditions, which were all present on the occasion in question, were severally necessary and jointly sufficient for the effect: an electric current in a certain wire (A), decayed insulation at a point on that wire (B), and inflammable material near that point (C). Then there were circumstances, namely B and C, such that in them the fire would not have occurred if the current, A, had not; equally there were circumstances, namely A and C, such that in them the fire would not have occurred if the faulty insulation, B, had not, and again circumstances, namely A and B, such that in them the fire would not have occurred if the inflammable material, C, had not. So by our modified formula, A, B, and C would each equally count as causing the fire. But someone who says that, for example, the faulty insulation, B, caused the fire, may be thinking of A and C as 'the circumstances', may be presupposing them rather than saying *that there are* circumstances in relation to which B was necessary. Before he will agree that A caused the fire, he will have to make a switch of presuppositions, and take B and C, rather than A and C, as 'the circumstances'. So whereas with our modified formula there is no conflict at all between the three statements that A caused the fire, that B did so, and that C did so – since the three existential statements are entirely compatible – there is, with our first formula, using the phrase 'in the circumstances', a contrast of approach and presupposition between those who assert these three statements, although no outright disagreement. And this surely is the case. If three speakers put forward these three alternative causal statements, they would be conscious of such a contrast of approach. I think, therefore, that our first formula is the better for catching the force of a causal statement in use. The modified formula might be said to yield more clearly marked truth conditions for causal statements; but I shall argue that what it yields are not, strictly speaking, truth (or falsity) conditions. Still, it may be conceded that the modi-fied formula represents a perhaps desirable tidying up of the meaning of causal statements, whereas the original formula comes closer to displaying the meaning they actually have.

There is, however, something surprising in our suggestion that 'X caused Y' means, even mainly, that X was *necessary* in the circum-stances for Y. Would it not be at least as plausible to suggest that it means that X was *sufficient* in the circumstances for Y? Or perhaps that it was both necessary and sufficient in the circumstances? After all, it is tempting to paraphrase 'X caused Y' with 'X necessitated Y' or 'X ensured Y', and this would chime in with some of the thought behind the phrase 'necessary connection'. But if 'X necessitated Y' is taken literally, it says that Y was made necessary by X or became necessary in view of X, and this would mean that X was sufficient rather than necessary for Y. Of course, an X which in ordinary dis-course is said to cause a Y is practically never *in itself* sufficient for that Y, or even believed to be so; as before, we must add the qualification 'in the circumstances'. And then the suggested description seems to fit what we recognize as causes. Taking our last example again, and letting the circumstances include the electric current and the inflam-mable material, we can say that the faulty insulation (which on these assumptions caused the fire) was sufficient in the circumstances for it. And similarly in sequence A in our earlier example the hammer-blow was sufficient in the circumstances for the chestnut's becoming flatter. But is sufficiency sufficient, or is necessity necessary as well? Can we explain the fact that in sequence B the hammer-blow did not cause the explosion on the ground that it was not sufficient for it in the cir-cumstances? In fact the circumstances in themselves, without the hammer-blow, were sufficient: does it not follow that the hammer-blow was trivially and automatically sufficient in the circumstances, since anything at all, or nothing, would have been so, provided that the relevant circumstances were not tampered with? If we argued that what is only thus trivially sufficient in the circumstances cannot be properly so described, and that that is why it cannot be said to cause the result, are we not covertly reintroducing the requirement that a cause should be necessary in the circumstances rather than sufficient?

What there is any point in mentioning as sufficient in the circumstances will be necessary in the circumstances as well.

This point seems to be confirmed if we try to expand the phrase 'sufficient in the circumstances' into a conditional statement. 'X will be sufficient in the circumstances for Y' may be taken as saying 'Given the circumstances, if X occurs then Y will', and even as a non-material conditional this will count as true provided that the circumstances do not change, X occurs, and Y occurs also.[6] And then 'X was sufficient in the circumstances for Y' will be equivalent to 'Given the circumstances, if X occurred, then Y did', and provided that the circumstances referred to are the actual ones this will automatically be true of any sequence in which X and Y actually occurred. Sufficiency in the circumstances is, then, of no use for our present purpose of finding the distinguishing feature of causal sequences; every cause is sufficient in the circumstances for its effect, but so are many non-causes for events which are not their effects.

But this is a weak sense of 'sufficient in the circumstances'. Can we find also a strong, counterfactual sense which will not apply to the antecedent in every actual sequence? This would be that, given the circumstances, if Y had not been going to occur, X would not have occurred. This is a possible sense, and what we recognize as causes are in general sufficient in the circumstances in this strong sense as well as in the weak one. In the appropriate possible world in which the circumstances are the same as in sequence A, but the chestnut does not become flatter, the hammer-blow has not occurred. (In constructing this possible world, we are, of course, taking over laws of working from the actual world.) And we cannot say the corresponding thing about the non-causal sequence B. The statement 'If in the circumstances of sequence B the explosion had not been going to occur, the hammer-blow would not have occurred' is not true or even acceptable. The supposition implicit in its antecedent cannot be coherently considered in the light of the actual world's laws of working, for, given these laws, in the circumstances of sequence B the explosion was going to occur. And if we take the antecedent as inviting us to consider some change in those laws of working, there is still no reason why we should not combine, with whatever coherent interpretation we place on this supposition, the view that the hammer-blow still occurred. It looks, then, as if the strong counterfactual sense of 'sufficient in the circumstances' will distinguish causal from non-causal sequences, though the weak sense does not.

But granted that causes are in general sufficient in the circumstances, in this strong sense, as well as necessary in the circumstances, for their effects, while neither relation holds in non-causal sequences, we can still ask whether in calling something a cause we require both of these features or only one, and if so which.

To clear up this problem, let us consider three different shilling-in-the-slot machines, K, L, and M. Each of them professes to supply bars of chocolate; also each of them has a glass front, so that its internal mechanism is visible. But in other respects the three are different. K is deterministic, and conforms to our ordinary expectations about slot-machines. It does not always produce a bar of chocolate when a shilling is put in the slot, but if it does not there is some in principle discoverable fault in or interference with the mechanism. Again, it can be induced to emit a bar of chocolate without a shilling's being inserted, for example by the use of some different object which sufficiently resembles a shilling, or perhaps by poking at the mechanism with pieces of wire. Inserting a shilling is neither absolutely necessary nor absolutely sufficient for the appearance of a bar of chocolate, but in normal circumstances it is both necessary and sufficient for this. ('Necessary' and 'sufficient' are here being used with reference to the machine's laws of working, they describe general relations rather than relations between single occurrences. But it will be a consequence of these general relations that if on a particular occasion, in normal circumstances, a shilling is inserted, a bar of chocolate will come out, and further that the inserting of a shilling on this particular occasion was both necessary in the circumstances and sufficient in the circumstances in the strong sense for this result.) L, on the other hand, is an indeterministic machine. It will not, indeed, in normal circumstances produce a bar of chocolate unless a shilling is inserted, but it may fail to produce a bar even when this is done. And such failure is a matter of pure chance. L's failures, unlike K's, are not open to individual explanation even in principle, though they may be open to statistical explanation. With L, in normal circumstances, putting a shilling in the slot is necessary, but not sufficient, for the appearance of a bar of chocolate. *M* is another indeterministic machine, but its vagaries are opposite to *L*'s. *M* will, in ordinary circumstances, produce a bar of chocolate whenever a shilling is inserted; but occasionally, for no reason that is discoverable even in principle, the mechanism begins to operate even though nothing has been inserted, and a bar of chocolate comes out. With *M*, in normal circumstances, putting a shilling in the slot is sufficient, but not necessary, for the appearance of a bar of chocolate.

Now on some occasion I put a shilling into *K* and a bar of chocolate comes out. As I have said, putting in the shilling was, in the circumstances, both sufficient in the strong sense and necessary for this result, and we have no hesitation in saying that it caused this result.

Again, I put a shilling into *L* and receive a bar of chocolate. Putting in the shilling was, in the circumstances, necessary for this result. It was also sufficient in the circumstances in the weak sense, but not in the strong, counterfactual, sense. A possible world, with the same laws of working as the actual world, can contain the same circumstances, can lack the result, and yet still contain the inserting of the shilling. The statement, 'Given the circumstances, if the chocolate had not been going to appear, the shilling would not have been inserted' is not now acceptable. But would we say in this case that the inserting of the shilling caused the appearance of the bar of chocolate? I think we would. Our ordinary causal concept seems to require that where the shilling is put in, the mechanism operates, and a bar of chocolate appears, and would not have appeared if the shilling had not been inserted, the insertion of the shilling caused the appearance of the chocolate despite the fact that in the circumstances even given that the shilling was inserted, the chocolate might not have appeared.

Similarly, I put a shilling into *M* and receive a bar of chocolate. Putting in the shilling was this time sufficient in the circumstances, in the strong sense as well as in the weak sense, for this result. In an appropriate possible world in which the chocolate did not appear, the shilling would not have been put in. But putting in the shilling was not, it seems, necessary in the circumstances. Not only generally but also on this particular occasion the chocolate might have appeared even if no shilling, or anything else, had been put in. But there is room for dispute here. Perhaps, it might be argued, the insertion of the shilling may have been necessary in the circumstances on this particular occasion, though not generally; it may be that on this occasion the mechanism would not have operated if the shilling had not been put in. Moreover, it may be possible to settle this issue. We can, by hypothesis, see the works of the machine. If on this occasion only the later stages of the mechanism operated, not those earlier ones which are normally actuated directly by the shilling, we can decide that the chocolate would have come out anyway, that the insertion of the shilling was not necessary in the circumstances. But if the whole mechanism operated, the issue cannot be settled. Since M is, by hypothesis, indeterministic, there is in principle no discoverable answer to the question whether the chocolate would on this occasion have come out if the shilling had not been put in, or, therefore, to the question whether the insertion of the shilling was on this occasion necessary in the circumstances for the result. And yet, it seems to me, it is just this question that we need to have answered before we can say whether the insertion of the shilling caused the result. If the chocolate would not have come out if the shilling had not been put in, then the insertion of the shilling caused the result. But if it would have come out anyway, the insertion of the shilling did not cause this. (This last ruling prejudges a question about causal over-determination that has still to be considered; but we shall reach an answer to this question which agrees with the present ruling.) And, consequently, if it is in principle undecidable whether the chocolate would on this particular occasion have come out if the shilling had not been put in, it is equally undecidable whether the putting in of the shilling caused the appearance of the chocolate.

The contrast between the comments we have made about the two indeterministic slot-machines L and M seem to show that 'X caused Y' entails 'X was necessary in the circumstances for Y' and also, trivially, 'X was sufficient in the circumstances for Y' in the weak sense, but *not* the latter in the strong counterfactual sense. This is not required, though in general it holds for what we recognize as causes, at least in the physical sphere. Indeterministic machines are pretty rare.

This conclusion is confirmed by what we are prepared to say about human beings without prejudging the question whether they are wholly deterministic or not. 'Tom's saying what he did caused Bill to hit Tom' is acceptable even if we suppose that Bill had free will, that in the circumstances even after Tom's remark Bill might have controlled himself, provided that we believe that in the circumstances Bill would not have hit Tom if Tom had not said what he did. In this respect we treat Bill in the way I have proposed to treat slot-machine L.

There are, however, several possible objections to the thesis that 'X caused Y' entails 'X was necessary in the circumstances for Y'.

The first of these concerns what we may call quantitative over-determination. In sequence A, the hammer-blow caused the chestnut's becoming flatter. But the whole of the blow was not necessary for this result, though it was more than sufficient: a somewhat lighter blow would have sufficed. Even if part of the hammer-head had been absent, this result would still have come about. And so on. But this difficulty is easily overcome. It is possible to go on to a functional dependence view of causation, which would relate exact quantities on the cause side with exact quantities on the effect side.[7] But for the present we are dealing only with a fairly primitive causal concept, which treats events, states, and occurrences, as ordinarily recognized and described, as causes and effects. From this point of view we regard the hammer-blow as a unit, and simply do not consider parts or subdivisions of it or quantitative alterations to it. The alternatives considered are that I strike the chestnut in the way described and that I do not. In constructing possible worlds, in considering what might or would have happened, we either plug in the hammer-blow as a whole or leave it out as a whole. Reducing it a little bit is simply not an option at present under consideration. From this point of view the hammer-blow was necessary in the circumstances: leave it out as a whole from your possible world, and the chestnut remains round.

A much more serious objection concerns what we may call, by contrast, alternative over-determination, or what have been called fail-safe causes. Let us list some examples, some of which are favourites with writers on moral and legal responsibility.

(i) A man is shot dead by a firing squad, at least two bullets entering his heart at once, either of which would have been immediately fatal.

(ii) Lightning strikes a barn in which straw is stored, and a tramp throws a burning cigarette butt into the straw at the same place and at the same time: the straw catches fire.

(iii) '... conditions (perhaps unusual excitement plus constitutional inadequacies) [are] present at 4.0 p.m. that guarantee a stroke at 4.55 p.m. and consequent death at 5.0 p.m.; but an entirely unrelated heart attack at 4.50 p.m. is still correctly called the cause of death, which, as it happens, does occur at 5.0 p.m.'

(iv) Smith and Jones commit a crime, but if they had not done so the head of the criminal organization would have sent other members to perform it in their stead, and so it would have been committed anyway.

(v) A man sets out on a trip across the desert. He has two enemies. One of them puts a deadly poison in his reserve can of drinking water. The other (not knowing this) makes a hole in the bottom of the can. The poisoned water all leaks out before the traveller needs to resort to this reserve can; the traveller dies of thirst.[8]

In each of these five cases, we cannot say of either of the candidates for the role of cause that it was necessary in the circumstances for the effect. If either of the two bullets had not been fired, the man would still have died. If the lightning had not struck, the straw would still have caught fire; and equally if the tramp had not thrown the butt away. If Smith and Jones had suddenly abandoned a life of crime, the same crime would still have been committed by the other members of the gang; but equally if those other members had not been ready to act, the crime would still have been committed, as it was, by Smith and Jones. If the heart attack had not occurred, the stroke would have carried the man off at 5.0 p.m.; but if the conditions for the stroke had been absent, the heart attack would still have killed him as and when it did. If the can had not been punctured, the traveller would have died of poison, perhaps even sooner than he actually died of thirst; but if it had not been poisoned, he would have died just as and when he did.

But though they have this common feature, these examples fall into two groups. In (iii) and (iv) we have no hesitation in making specific causal statements, that the heart attack caused the man's death, and that the actions of Smith and Jones brought about the criminal result. In (v) also it seems clear to me that the puncturing of the can caused the traveller's death, but as Hart and Honoré say that 'it is impossible to give a satisfactory answer to this question in terms of either *B* or *C* or both causing *A*'s death', and that 'their mutual frustration of each other's plan precludes us from saying that either caused *A*'s death', I need to explain and defend my view of this case.

Where we have no hesitation in making causal statements we can tell some more detailed causal story: we can say how the heart attack caused the man's death, how Smith and Jones committed the crime. But the rival story about the alternative or reserve cause cannot be completed. The conditions for the stroke did not actually lead to a stroke, and since there was no stroke, no stroke led to death. The reserve members of the gang remained in reserve. What we accept as causing each result, though not necessary in the circumstances for that result described in some broad way, was necessary in the circumstances for the result *as it came about*.

This matter can be thoroughly clarified if we introduce here a distinction[9] between *facts* and *events* both as causes and as results or effects. In (v) the puncturing of the can brought it about that the traveller died of thirst, that is, it caused his dying of thirst (though it prevented his dying of poison). But we cannot say that the puncturing of the can brought it about that he died, or caused his dying – since he would have died anyway, if it had not been punctured. *That he died*, and *that he died of thirst*, are distinguishable facts, and hence distinguishable results. So, as long as we are dealing with fact-results, it is not surprising that the puncturing of the can should have brought about the second of these but not the first. But if we think of an effect as a concrete event, then the event which was the traveller's death was also his death from thirst, and we must say that the puncturing of the can caused it, while the poisoning did not. For a concrete event effect, we require a cause, or causal chain, that leads to it, and it is the chain puncturing-lack-of-water-thirst-death that was realized, whereas the rival chain that starts with poison-in-can was not completed. In this way I would defend my judgement that the traveller's death – that is, the concrete event – was caused by the puncturing of the can, but at the same time explain the doubts felt by lawyers (and others) about this case as due to the equally correct judgement that his dying – that is, the fact that he died on this journey – was not caused by the puncturing of the can.

These distinctions vindicate our general thesis that 'X caused Y' entails 'X was necessary in the circumstances for Y': apparently conflicting answers arise from some uncertainty or equivocation about what is to count as Y, whether it is a concrete event or a fact, and if so, which fact. If Y is the fact that the traveller died of thirst, then the puncturing of the can both caused and was necessary in the circumstances for Y. If Y is the fact that the traveller died on this journey, then the puncturing of the can neither caused Y nor was necessary in the circumstances for Y. If Y is the traveller's death *qua* concrete event, which was, among other things, a death from thirst, the puncturing of the can both caused and was necessary in the circumstances for Y.

In the dubious cases of alternative over-determination, such as (i) and (ii), it is natural to reject such statements as 'This bullet caused his death' and 'The lightning caused the fire'. In these cases even a detailed causal story fails to discriminate between the rival candidates for the role of cause, we cannot say that one rather than the other was necessary in the circumstances even for the effect *as it came about*. Even if we take the effect as a concrete event all that was clearly necessary for it in the circumstances was in (i) the volley and in (ii) the lightning/cigarette-butt cluster of events, and it is such clusters that we can confidently take as causing these effects. 'But which item in the cluster really caused (or "brought about") this effect (or "result")?' is a sensible question in so far as it asks for a discrimination between the alternative 'causes' by way of the filling in of a more detailed account. But if no more detailed correct account would provide the desired discrimination, this question has no answer.

For instance, if, as in an example mentioned earlier, a match is struck and touched with a red-hot poker at the same time, and a flame appears, we can say that the striking and the touching together caused the flame to appear, since if neither of them had occurred in the circumstances no flame would have appeared, but if the match was affected in both these ways simultaneously, we cannot say that either by itself caused this. Our ruling in these cases agrees with what we said about slot-machine M, where a shilling was put in and a bar of chocolate came out, but the bar might have come out even if no shilling had been put in: if on this particular occasion a bar of chocolate *would* (not merely *might*) have come out anyway, then the insertion of the shilling did not cause its appearance. This is a strange case of causal over-determination, because one of the rival factors is a null one: the bar would, on the present hypothesis, have come out spontaneously. But even a null alternative in a case of alternative over-determination is enough to prevent the other alternative from causing the result.

So far, then, we can defend the conclusion reached earlier: the statement that X caused Y entails that X was necessary in the circumstances for Y, but it does not entail that X was in the strong sense sufficient in the circumstances for Y. But the latter often holds as well.

Something very like this is the main negative thesis of Professor Anscombe's Inaugural Lecture: contrary to a long dominant philosophical tradition, causes need not be 'sufficient' for their effects, need not 'necessitate' them. Raymond Martin also has defended a 'necessity thesis' while criticizing a 'sufficiency thesis' which he finds in an earlier work of mine.[10]

But is there anything still to be said for the sufficiency thesis? A corollary of its rejection is that causal consequence is *not* formally analogous to logical consequence, legal consequence, and so on. If Q is a logical consequence of P, then P is logically sufficient for Q. If, given R, Q is a logical consequence of P, then, given R, P is logically sufficient for Q. Similarly if Q is a legal consequence of P, then P is, in the circumstances, legally sufficient for Q. And this holds in general for other sorts of consequences. But by our present account, Q may be a causal consequence of P without P being causally sufficient for Q even in the circumstances. This is strange, and yet it seems correct. There being a radon atom here now is a causal consequence of there having been a radium atom here a little earlier, but if radioactive decay is a non-deterministic process there are no circumstances such that in them the earlier presence of the radium atom was sufficient (in the strong, counterfactual sense) for the radon atom's being here now: the former might not have decayed, and even if it had the latter might also have decayed already. Similarly if Jim, who is colour-blind, and his wife Alice, who carries no gene for colour-blindness, have a daughter, Jane, who has a son, Tom, and Tom is colour-blind, then Tom's being colour-blind is a causal consequence of Jim's being colour-blind; but the latter gave only a fifty-fifty chance that any son of Jane would be colour-blind.

On the other hand, if P caused Q, we can surely say that Q occurred because P did; the latter is practically equivalent to 'Since P occurred, Q occurred'; a since-statement can be fairly aptly described, in Goodman's terms, as a factual conditional, that is, as adding to the open non-material conditional 'If P occurred, Q occurred' the presupposition that P did occur (and hence that Q did so too). Putting these steps together, we seem compelled to take 'P caused Q' as entailing the non-material conditional 'If P occurred, Q occurred', which would commit its user to the counterfactual 'If Q had not been going to occur, P would not have occurred', that is to the strong counterfactual sufficiency of P for Q.

Another argument on the same side is that a future causal statement 'P will cause Q' or 'P would cause Q' seems to claim that P is sufficient in the circumstances for Q, that if P occurs, Q will occur also, and that if Q is not going to occur, neither is P. Even if we were right in saying that a past-tense, singular, causal statement entails only that the cause was necessary, not also sufficient, in the circumstances for the effect, this may be characteristic of past-tense uses rather than of causal statements in general.

It seems, then, that the analysis of a tenseless, singular, causal statement 'P causes Q' should include both the non-material conditionals 'If P occurs, Q occurs' and 'If P does not occur, Q does not occur', and therefore also their contrapositives, each of which will change into a counterfactual if the speaker takes its antecedent not to be fulfilled. But different parts of this concept will be stressed in different settings. When P and Q are both known to have occurred, it is natural to lay stress on the counterfactual form of the second conditional; but if their occurrence is problematic, it is natural to emphasize the open form of the first conditional, though the second is also in force. The general notion of a cause is of something which is both necessary and sufficient in the circumstances for its effect, but where the cause and the effect have both actually occurred we do not require that the cause should be sufficient in the strong counterfactual sense.

Some writers who have recognized that causes need not be sufficient for their effects have drawn the further conclusion that our ordinary concept is primarily probabilistic. Thus Patrick Suppes[11] argues that 'the everyday concept of causality is not sharply deterministic' from the evidence that we may say 'His reckless driving is bound to lead to an accident', where ' "lead to" conveys the causal relation between the reckless driving and the predicted accident' and yet ' "is bound to" means [only] that the probability is high'. But this is a confusion. Saying that A is likely to cause B does not put likelihood into the causing itself: it could (though it does not) mean that A is likely to necessitate B, and I think it does mean that A is likely to be, in some particular case, necessary in the circumstances for B. What will fulfil this probabilistic prediction is an actual crash for which the man's reckless driving was necessary in the circumstances. Similarly Suppes is right in claiming that a mother who says that her child is afraid of thunder does not mean that a state of fright ensues whenever the child hears thunder, but rather that there is a fairly high probability of this; but when the child is actually frightened by thunder, the thunder is necessary in the circumstances for its state of fright.

Thus it may often happen that the only fully explicit causal generalization that a speaker is prepared to make is a probabilistic one, and yet he may still be taking it that the causal relation in any particular case that fulfils it is one of necessity, and perhaps also sufficiency, in the circumstances. To go straight from this evidence to a probabilistic theory is a mistake, and one that results from holding on to the Humean doctrine that causation is essentially general while admitting that causal claims need not involve *universal* generalizations.[12]

These points seriously undermine Suppes's project of analysing causation as a whole in terms of probabilities. We can admit, none the less, that there may be probabilistic or statistical laws, and singular sequences of events which in some sense fulfil them, and that both of these can be called causal in a broad sense. These need to be discussed with particular reference to problems about the form and content of statistical laws and the interpretation of the 'probabilities' associated with them – problems which Suppes does not bring out or resolve.[13]

For the present, however, we can affirm that a cause is ordinarily taken to be necessary in the circumstances for its effect, and perhaps sufficient in the circumstances as well.

We cannot, however, conclude that necessity-in-the-circumstances is *the* distinguishing feature of a cause. As we saw, one collateral effect may be necessary in the circumstances for another, but it is not said to cause the other. Also, if X caused Y, we have seen that X may be in the strong sense sufficient in the circumstances for Y. If it is, then Y will be necessary in the circumstances for X; but we shall not say that Y caused X.

Such counter-examples show that another relation, which we may call *causal priority*, is thought of as being required, along with necessity-in-the-circumstances, for causing. Of a pair of collateral effects, neither is causally prior to the other, and in our other example since X caused Y, X was causally prior to Y, and Y was therefore not causally prior to X. But it seems that if any X is both necessary in the circumstances for and causally prior to Y, we shall say that X caused Y; also, wherever we are prepared to say that X caused Y we are prepared to say that X was necessary in the circumstances for and causally prior to Y. The distinguishing feature of causal sequence is the conjunction of necessity-in-the-circumstances with causal priority.[14]

The core of the notion of causal priority is that the world has some way of running on from one change to another. But we can speak with any accuracy only when we associate causal priority with some kind of sufficiency or necessity. Thus X is sufficient in the circumstances in the weak sense for and causally prior to Y provided that if X is put into the world in the circumstances referred to and the world runs on from there, Y will occur. Similarly X is necessary in the circumstances for and causally prior to Y provided that if X were kept out of the world in the circumstances referred to and the world ran on from there, Y would not occur. And X is sufficient in the circumstances in the strong sense for and causally prior to Y provided that if X were put into the world in the circumstances referred to and the world ran on from there, Y would occur. Sufficiency-in-the-weak-sense plus causal priority is shown by an experiment on the actual world; but necessity and sufficiency-in-the-strong-sense plus causal priority involve counterfactual claims, and therefore involve assertions about how the world would have run on if something different had been done: they involve thought about the independent running of a merely possible world.

We have already illustrated this in suggesting a way out of the difficulty about collateral effects. We thought of constructing a possible world which was just like the actual world up to the point where, in the actual world, the proposed antecedent occurs, of excluding this antecedent from the possible world and then letting that world run on: if and only if the result did not occur in that possible world were we prepared to say that the antecedent was *in the special sense* necessary in the circumstances for the result. That 'special sense' of 'necessary in the circumstances' is what we now recognize as the conjunction 'necessary in the circumstances for and causally prior to'.

But this account needs some adjustment to make it generally applicable. Our proposal to make the possible world just like the actual one up to the point of time at which the proposed antecedent X occurs in the actual world would have the undesired result of making temporal priority necessary, though not sufficient, for causal priority. For if Y had occurred before X in the actual world, it would already have been included, by the above proposal, in the possible world: we should have left no chance that the exclusion of X from the possible world might, as that world ran on, exclude Y also. But temporal priority is not conceptually necessary for causal priority. We can coherently consider the possibility of backwards or time-reversed causation.

To leave room for this, we must modify the suggested account. We must think of somehow excluding an X from a possible world at a time t_3 (where X occurred in the actual world at t_3) without prejudice to the question whether a Y occurred in that possible world (as it did in the actual one) at an earlier time t_2. But to combine this with the notion of letting the possible world run on, we must think of excluding X indirectly, by excluding some other possible event W which actually occurred at a still earlier time t_1 and which is believed to be necessary in the circumstances for X. Our possible world is to have the same *circumstances* as the actual world, but to diverge from it by the exclusion of W at t_1; from there on it is allowed to run on by whatever laws of working the actual world obeys. This leaves open the possibility that there should be among these laws a backward causal one such that this indirect exclusion of X would carry with it the non-occurrence of Y. If Y does occur in our possible world at t_2, then X is not necessary in the circumstances for and causally prior to it; but if Y does not occur in our possible world at t_2, X may be so, though there are other possibilities which it is not easy to exclude.

The notion of necessity-in-the-circumstances-plus-causal-priority, then, involves the thought of what would happen when a possible world, constructed by some appropriate alteration from the actual world, was allowed to run on. It presupposes that the actual world has some laws of working – not necessarily strictly deterministic ones – which can be carried over to the possible world. But it does not require that in order to use this notion we should know what those laws of working are.

I have explicitly added the notion of causal priority to that of being necessary in the circumstances. But I must admit that the terms 'necessary' and 'sufficient' are often so used as to include a suggestion of causal priority: even where a cause is sufficient in the circumstances in the strong sense for its effect we find it strange to say that the effect is necessary in the circumstances for the cause, just because the effect is not causally prior to the cause. However, there are senses of 'necessary' and 'sufficient' which do not include causal priority and which are exhausted by the appropriate conditional analyses, and I think it makes things clearer if we use 'necessary' and 'sufficient' in these simpler senses, and introduce causal priority as a further element.

In so far as we have used conditionals, especially counterfactual ones, in our analysis of the concept of causation, that analysis is incomplete until these conditionals have themselves been explained. A view of conditionals has probably been implicit in what I have already said; to make it explicit I want simply to take over conclusions that I have reached elsewhere.[15] A non-material conditional statement introduces a supposition (the antecedent) and asserts something (the consequent) within the scope of that supposition. The conditional 'If P, Q' can be paraphrased by 'Suppose that P; on that supposition, Q'; or again by 'In the possible situation that P, Q also'. This account holds for all non-material conditionals; a counterfactual adds to this the suggestion that the antecedent does not hold in the actual world. If so, there is liable to be a certain arbitrariness in the choice of 'the possible situation that P', or in other words of the particular possible world of which the consequent is being asserted. It is a consequence of this analysis that only some conditionals are capable of being true or false. A conditional whose antecedent is fulfilled will be true if its consequent is true and false if its consequent is false. But if the antecedent of a counterfactual is, as its user believes, unfulfilled, it cannot be true or false in this way. A counterfactual whose antecedent entails its consequent can be allowed to count as true. But most counterfactuals cannot achieve truth in this way either, and will be neither true nor false, though they may be acceptable or unacceptable, well or poorly supported, and so on.

We are led, then, towards two conclusions which are similar to Hume's. Statements of singular causal sequence involve in their analysis counterfactual conditionals which on the present showing are not capable of being true; so the singular causal statements cannot be true either.[16] (They can still be false in rather obvious ways: 'X caused Y' will be false, for example, if either X or Y did not occur.) Also, whether they can be true or not, these counterfactual conditionals describe possible situations or possible worlds, they are concerned with suppositions and their consequences or accompaniments, they do not describe what actually occurred, let alone what was observed to occur, in the actual individual sequence. They state what would have happened, not what did happen. Causal necessity, then, in the sense in which this is the distinguishing feature of causal sequences, is not something that can be observed in any of those sequences. Consequently a question analogous to one of Hume's arises here: how do we acquire the idea of this causal necessity, since we do not derive it from anything we observe in the individual causal sequences to which we apply it? It looks as if a psychological account is called for. Perhaps Hume's resort to psychology was not wrong in principle.

But the item for which we must seek a psychological explanation is not, as Hume thought, the idea of a support for a priori inferences from one distinct existence to another, but the sort of thinking that is expressed by the counterfactual conditional, 'If in these circumstances X had not occurred, Y would not have occurred either', coupled with the notion of X's causal priority to Y, the thought that the actual world ran on from X to Y, and that the appropriate possible world would run on from the exclusion of X to the non-occurrence of Y. Let us take the counterfactual first, leaving aside the priority. It can be paraphrased as 'Suppose that in these circumstances X did not occur; then Y did not occur either' or 'Given these circumstances, in the possible situation that X did not occur, Y did not occur'. For the general capacity and tendency to make suppositions, to consider possibilities that appear not to be realized, I can offer no explanation beyond the obvious evolutionary one; this capacity and tendency are of some value to their possessors and could have been fostered by the ordinary processes of natural selection. But it is worth stressing here that although we express this kind of thinking in words, its development need not have waited for the development of language. It is not essentially tied to verbal expression, and there is some reason to suppose that other, non-verbal, animals share this capacity with us. Possibilities can be literally envisaged rather than described.[17]

But, given that we have this general tendency, can we explain the particular ways in which we employ it? That is, can we explain how, having supposed X not to have occurred in these circumstances, we decide what else to assert within the scope of this supposition, or how to fill out our picture of this merely possible situation? We can distinguish a sophisticated and a primitive way of doing this.

The sophisticated way uses general propositions which we take to be confirmed by observations of the actual world, but which we feel justified in extending beyond the instances in which they are confirmed not only to other actual instances but to merely possible ones which are related to the confirming instances in the same way that other actual instances would be.[18] These are combined with the supposition, and consequences drawn by deductive reasoning from the combination are asserted within the scope of the supposition. This sophisticated way of developing a supposition anticipates a well-known procedure of 'natural deduction'.

The primitive way of doing the same job relies not on this combination of inductive and deductive reasoning, but on imagination and analogy. I have observed another situation very like the present one, in which (unlike the present one) no event of the X type occurred. I borrow features from that other situation to fill out my imaginative picture of the possible situation that in the present circumstances X did not occur. In particular, if no event of the Y type occurred in that other situation, I see the possible situation that X did not occur in the present circumstances as continuing without the occurrence of Y. The sort of observation that can be immediately used in this imaginative analogizing is that prescribed for Mill's Method of Difference: two otherwise very similar instances, in one of which both the 'cause' and the 'effect' occur, and in the other of which neither of these occurs. Such a pair of instances may be found in a number of different ways, but the most obvious, and presumably the most fruitful original source of the causal concept, is provided by the 'before and after' observation. In an otherwise apparently static situation, one striking change (X) occurs, followed shortly afterwards by another (Y). The situation before X occurred, when equally Y did not occur, provides the control case or negative instance, while the later situation, in which both X and Y occurred, provides the experimental case or positive instance. And in a quite primitive and unsophisticated way we can transfer the non-occurrence of Y from the before situation to a *supposed* later situation in which, similarly, X did not occur, and form the thought which is expressed by the statement 'If X had not occurred, Y would not have occurred', or, in other words, 'X was necessary in the circumstances for Y'.

But this is only one part of our ordinary idea of necessary connection. We have also to account for the other element, the causal priority. It seems undeniable that this notion arises from our experience of our own active interventions in the world. If I *introduce* the change X into an apparently static situation and then the other change Y occurs, I not only see X as in the weak sense sufficient in the circumstances for Y, but also see X as causally prior to Y. I see the actual world as running on from my introduction of X to the occurrence of Y. If, further, I think (for the reasons just outlined) of X as necessary in the circumstances for Y, I see the *possible* world in which I do *not* introduce X as running on without Y's occurring. I seem then to have introduced into the actual world not only X, but the whole X–Y sequence; but I seem to have done so by operating on the X end of it. The notion of the actual world's running on *from* – not *to* – X, and of a possible world's similarly running on from not-X, is derived from this complex experience of intervening and then waiting for results. Rightly or wrongly, I see myself as a free agent in introducing X, and therefore rule out the possibility that anything else in the objective situation is causally prior to X, that the world ran on to X; I therefore rule out also both the possibility that X and Y should be collateral effects of some common cause and the possibility that Y should have caused X, even if I see Y, as I well may, as being necessary in the circumstances for X.

We can, then, find natural and presumably instinctive ways of thinking which would be expressed by the counterfactual conditionals and assertions of causal priority which we have given as the analysis of the distinguishing feature of causal sequence. But our account of the psychological mechanism involved is different from Hume's. The key item is a picture of what *would* have happened if things had been otherwise, and this is borrowed from some experience where things *were* otherwise. It is a contrast case rather than the repetition of like instances that contributes most to our primitive concept of causation.

My main concern has been to analyse our actual concept of causing, to formulate what we commonly take to be the distinguishing mark of causal sequences, and then, since this has turned out not to be an observed feature of those sequences, to sketch an explanation of our thinking in this way. In this analysis the major item is that a cause is thought to be both necessary and sufficient in the circumstances for its effect, but that the sufficiency is less firmly required than the necessity, particularly where the sequence is known to have occurred. But whatever our actual concept may be, it is obvious that we can construct causal concepts as we wish, which may be useful for particular purposes. We can speak, if we like, of *necessary causes*, and make it explicit that sufficiency is not required. Or we can speak of *sufficient causes*, and make it explicit that necessity is not required. Or we can make it plain that we are requiring both necessity and sufficiency in the circumstances. But the general pattern on which such concepts are constructed is that we combine the appropriate non-material conditional(s) with the notion of causal priority.

My aim here has been only to analyse the *concept* of causation with the help of non-material conditionals. This merely begins and does not complete the analysis of causation. There are further questions about what constitutes causation as it is in reality, in the objects, and about our knowledge of it – questions of factual and epistemic, rather than conceptual, analysis. In particular we should inquire what further backing there may be for such conditional statements, further relations in the objects that may encourage us to speak and think in these ways.

Notes

1. *System of Logic*, Book III, Ch. 5, Sect. 3. Conditional analyses of causal statements are defended and discussed by Ardon Lyon in 'Causality', *British Journal for the Philosophy of Science*, xviii (1967), 1–20.

2. *Enquiry*, Sect. VII, Pt. II, Selby-Bigge, p. 76.

3. See below, p. 403. The question is discussed more fully in Chapter 10 of *The Cement of the Universe*.

4. It is discussed in Chapter 10 of *The Cement of the Universe*.

5. This notion of a causal field was introduced by John Anderson in 'The Problem of Causality', *Australasian Journal of Psychology and Philosophy*, xvi (1938), reprinted in his *Studies in Empirical Philosophy*, and used to resolve difficulties in Mill's account of causation. I also used it in 'Responsibility and Language', *Australasian Journal of Philosophy*, xxxiii (1955), 143–59, to deal with problems of moral and legal responsibility.

6. I have discussed non-material conditionals, both open and counterfactual, and their truth conditions, in Chapter 3 of *Truth, Probability, and Paradox*.

7. The matter is considered in Chapter 6 of *The Cement of the Universe*.

8. I touched on this problem in 'Causes and Conditions', *American Philosophical Quarterly*, ii (1965), 245–64, esp. 250–2. Examples (ii) and (iv) are borrowed from K. Marc-Wogau, 'On Historical Explanation', *Theoria*, xxviii (1962), 213–33, the latter coming originally from P. Gardiner, *The Nature of Historical Explanation*, p. 101. Example (iii) is quoted from M. Scriven, review of E. Nagel, *The Structure of Science*, in *Review of Metaphysics* (1964). Example (v) is based on a modification by Hart and Honoré (*Causation in the Law*, pp. 219–20) of a hypothetical case devised by J. A. McLaughlin, *Harvard Law Review*, xxxix (1925–6), 149, 155 n. 25.

9. It is fully discussed in Chapter 10 of *The Cement of the Universe*.

10. G. E. M. Anscombe, *Causality and Determination*; Raymond Martin, 'The Sufficiency Thesis', *Philosophical Studies*, xxiii (1972), 205–11; Martin, who criticizes my 'Causes and Conditions', *American Philosophical Quarterly*, ii (1965), 245–64, sent me an earlier version of his paper in 1969.

11. *A Probabilistic Theory of Causality*, p. 7.

12. Chapter 3 of *The Cement of the Universe* contains arguments for the primacy of singular as opposed to general causal statements.

13. Chapter 9 contains a discussion of these matters.

14. Chapter 7 contains a full discussion of causal priority.

15. In Chapter 3 of *Truth, Probability, and Paradox*.

16. A similar conclusion is reached by A. J. Ayer, *Probability and Evidence*, pp. 132–9. But for me this is only a tentative conclusion, which is qualified at the end of Chapter 8 of *The Cement of the Universe*.

17. Cf. *Truth, Probability, and Paradox*, p. 100.

18. Cf. *Truth, Probability, and Paradox*, pp. 117–18, and Chapter 8 of *The Cement of the Universe*.

Biographical Note

John Mackie became a Fellow in Philosophy at University College, Oxford, in 1967. Before then he was Professor of Philosophy at the University of Otago (1955–9), the University of Sydney (1959–63), and the University of York (1963–7). He is the author of *Truth, Probability and Paradox* (1973), which has to do with fundamental questions in logical theory, and *The Cement of the Universe: A Study of Causation* (1974), whose second chapter is reprinted in the present book. He is also the author of *Problems from Locke* (1976), which deals mainly with the theory of knowledge, and of *Ethics: Inventing Right and Wrong* (1977). He has also published many articles in various branches of philosophy, including the philosophy of science and the philosophy of religion.

Further Reading

Other chapters of *The Cement of the Universe* contain full discussions of a number of the topics which come up in the chapter reprinted here, as already mentioned. Mr Mackie's full account of conditional statements appears in his book, *Truth, Probability and Paradox* (Oxford: Clarendon Press, 1973). Readers may also wish to look at his earlier essay on causation, 'Causes and Conditions', which appears in the *American Philosophical Quarterly*, 2 (1965), and also in *Causation and Conditionals* (Oxford: University Press, 1975), edited by Ernest Sosa. Relevant writings on causation by other authors include the other articles in Sosa's collection, and works referred to in footnotes in this chapter, particularly those by Lyon, Hart and Honoré, and Anscombe. Classical discussions include those of Hume, in Book I, Part 3, of his *Treatise of Human Nature*, and of Kant in the Second Analogy in his *Critique of Pure Reason*.

Alvin Plantinga

God, Possible Worlds and the Problem of Evil

If God exists, and if he is perfectly good, supremely powerful and all-knowing, how does it come about that there is evil in the world? How can the three divine attributes be reconciled with the wrongfulness, suffering and other evils we see about us? This problem, traditionally known as the problem of evil, is likely to be familiar to the reader, whether he considers himself a believer, an agnostic or an atheist.

It is a problem that may be deeply felt in an agony of faith and conscience. It has often been a source of scepticism and disbelief. It is also a problem to engage the intellect: attributes such as omnipotence, omniscience and perfect goodness require all our resources for clear, logical thinking if we are to have a reasoned answer to the question whether their combination in the divine nature can be reconciled with the existence of evil. Here is where the philosopher's analytic skills and logical techniques have much to contribute.

The special contribution of Alvin Plantinga's discussion of the problem of evil is the interesting use he makes of the notion of possible worlds, together with certain techniques for handling that notion which have recently been developed in quite another context, the semantics of modal logic. With the aid of these new devices Plantinga proposes to vindicate the essential coherence of the theist's position, and to defeat the supposition that the existence of evil disproves the existence of God. Whether the reader is convinced or not, he will discover that an old problem has been transformed by the new approach which Plantinga brings to it.

The problem can be stated, as Plantinga states it on p. 423, in this way: If we begin with the proposition that God is omniscient, omnipotent and wholly good, can we find another proposition from which it follows that there is evil but which is, nevertheless, consistent with the first proposition about the attributes of God? There is a partial answer to be had in the idea that there may be evils which are necessarily presupposed by or contained within a greater good. An example might be moral heroism, which presupposes adversity or suffering. In some such cases at least, the world might, on balance, be worse if the evil were eliminated, since the cost would be the loss of a greater good. And making the world worse would not be compatible with God's perfect benevolence. We thus come to see that possibly God has good reason to permit some, if not all, of the evil present in the world. It is the rest that poses the harder problem. More particularly, it would not be at all plausible to try to excuse all *moral* evil – evil due to the immorality of human agents – on the grounds that it is the inevitable concomitant of some greater good.

Perhaps, however, moral evil is something that has to be accepted as the price for our having the capacity for moral good. One traditional reply to the problem of moral evil has been to say that God wished his creatures to be capable of moral good, and for this he had to give us free will. An essential feature of moral good is that it is good arising from action which the agent is free to do or not to do. Moral good presupposes that the agent is free to act for good *or* for ill. The capacity for one is necessarily at the same time a capacity for the other. God in his omniscience may know that some of his creatures will use their freedom to commit evil. But he cannot both grant the freedom and prevent the evil he knows will result from it, since creatures who are prevented from doing evil are not in the relevant sense free agents. Assuming, then, that moral freedom is a great good both in itself and in many of its results, God may be found to have good reason to create a world containing evil.

This traditional argument, which was propounded, for example, by Saint Augustine, is the argument that Plantinga proposes to restate, clarify and vindicate in modern terms – with one important difference. He does not claim that the proposition:

(a) 'God creates a world containing evil and has good reason for doing so'

is true; merely that it is *possible* for it to be true. The nub of what Plantinga calls the 'free will defence' is the claim that proposition (a) is consistent with the proposition we began from:

(b) 'God is omniscient, omnipotent and wholly good'.

And what it means for two propositions to be consistent is that it is *possible* for them to be true together. That is why it is not necessary for Plantinga to claim, as Saint Augustine did, that (a) is actually true. It is enough for his purposes if (a) is possible, if it might be true, and might be true together with (b). If (a) and (b) *could* be true together, that means it is *possible* for there to be a state of affairs in which God is omnipotent, omniscient and perfectly good and yet at the same time evil exists. To show that this state of affairs is possible (that the propositions are consistent) is to show that the existence of evil in the world is compatible with the divine attributes.

We are concerned, then, with one particular reason God might have to create a world such as ours which contains evil. He might wish there to be free agents, beings capable both of moral good and moral evil and hence beings who will do evil if they so choose. More precisely, if God creates free agents he *has to* permit them to do evil if they so choose. The question now is whether this is compatible with his omnipotence and perfect benevolence.

The objection that it is not compatible is forcibly stated in the quotation from J. L. Mackie on p. 425. The point at issue is the following. Nearly every philosopher who has considered the attribute of omnipotence has agreed that logical limitations do not count. It is no limitation on God's omnipotence that he should be unable to create a square circle: there is no consistent sense in the idea that he might do so. But there is nothing inconsistent in the idea of free agents who invariably choose to do good, even though they could choose evil. (Indeed, according to Saint Augustine, there are angels who have free will but never sin.) Such agents are logically possible. If, therefore, God's omnipotence means that he can create anything which is not logically impossible, he ought to be able to create free agents who invariably choose the good. If he does not, either he is not, after all, omnipotent or he is not a perfectly benevolent being who would wish no evil on the world which he could prevent.

This objection is the first main concern of Plantinga's essay. It is in order to formulate a precise and convincing reply that he develops the apparatus of possible worlds in the second section below. But it may help the reader if we sum up the result he will argue for in more familiar terms. In effect, Plantinga agrees that there is no logical impossibility in the idea of agents who (i) are free and (ii) invariably choose the good, but he points out that this is a different idea from that of agents who (i) are free, (ii) invariably choose the good, and (iii) *are caused by God to do so*. This latter idea, he claims, does involve a logical impossibility, since clause (i) and clause (iii) are inconsistent with each other. (There is a controversial presupposition here that freedom of choice is incompatible with causation by antecedent conditions, or at any rate incompatible with causation by antecedent conditions arranged by an all powerful creator God. See Plantinga's remarks on p. 424 and his further discussion cited in note 3.) But it appears to be exactly this second, inconsistent idea that Mackie's objection requires God to bring about. Indeed, he cannot create such agents because it would be logically impossible to do so. But if it is *logically* impossible, it does not count (as has already been agreed) against God's omnipotence and goodness. If it is logically impossible, that merely shows that God cannot do something it would make no consistent sense to suppose him doing.

On, then, to possible worlds. Plantinga's account of this notion in the second section below is one of the clearest available, and there would be little to be gained from trying to recapitulate it here. Suffice it to say that the question 'Is it possible for there to be free agents who do no wrong?' becomes the question 'Are there possible worlds containing agents who are free but do no wrong?' (answer: Yes), and the question 'Could God create free agents who do no wrong?' becomes the question 'Are there possible worlds such that (i) they contain free agents who do no wrong and (ii) God could make one of them actual?' This last question brings out one of the advantages of translation into the jargon of possible worlds. For it is evidently a special case of the more general question 'Are there possible worlds which God could not actualize?' To which Plantinga's answer is 'Yes' – for a start, any possible world in which God does not exist is one that, for obvious reasons, he could not make actual. Plantinga's statement of this point on p. 431 prepares us to face the fact that, just because something is a possible world, it need not follow that God could actualize it. Even if the world itself is a possible one, there may be a logical impossibility in the idea of God's actualizing it. It is a mistake to think that an omnipotent God can actualize any possible world he pleases, the mistake which (for reasons given on pp. 426 and 435) Plantinga calls 'Leibniz's lapse'.

We are now ready to apply these results to the case of free agents. The essential thought in a long and quite difficult argument is that a possible world which contains free agents is a world in which some part of the course of events is left to those agents to determine. God cannot – logically cannot – both leave them free to decide their own actions and bring it about that all their actions are good rather than evil. It is not that there is any contradiction in the idea of free agents who commit no evil. That is to say, there are possible worlds blessed with such beings. There are even possible worlds in which the most notorious villains known to our world do no wrong. But whether God could bring it about that such a world was actual depends on what those villains would choose to do if they existed in the actual world. God must leave it up to them if they are to be free agents; and if in actual fact they would choose to commit evil, God cannot actualize any of the admittedly possible worlds in which they behave blamelessly.

We here meet the engaging characteristic which Plantinga calls 'transworld depravity' (formally defined on pp. 438–9). The villains just mentioned suffer from it, as does any person who, if he actually existed, would go wrong with respect to at least one action. And to simplify a subtle argument, it is possible that every free agent suffers from transworld depravity. Although there are innumerable possible worlds in which the actual persons of our world are perfectly virtuous, and others containing different agents from those of our world, all of flawless character and conduct, yet it may still be that if those agents actually existed they would go wrong with respect to at least one action. If that is so, if all free agents suffer from transworld depravity, God could not actualize any of the possible worlds in which they do no wrong. But it is certainly possible that all free agents do suffer from transworld depravity. Hence it is possible that God, omnipotent as he is, could not actualize a world containing moral good but no moral evil. Hence, finally, he may possibly have good reason to allow moral evil: for possibly he has to allow it if moral good is also to be present in the world. Thus our two propositions (a) and (b) are consistent with each other. That is to say, the existence of evil in our world is not inconsistent with the divine attributes of omnipotence, omniscience and perfect goodness.

This completes the argument of the free will defence. The reader may wish to consult Plantinga's book, *God, Freedom and Evil*, to see how he goes on to argue, along similar lines, first that the divine attributes are not inconsistent with the world containing as much moral evil as it actually does contain, and second that they are not inconsistent with the existence of natural (non-moral) evils such as earthquakes and pestilence. If the reader has worked his way successfully through the quite complex details of Plantinga's argument, he will not only have become acquainted with an interesting new view of a fundamental problem of religious belief, but he will also have acquired some feeling for one of the key notions of contemporary philosophy, the idea of possible worlds.

M.F.B.

Alvin Plantinga

Possible Worlds

From *God, Freedom and Evil* (New York: Harper & Row, 1974; London: George Allen & Unwin, 1975), pp. 29–55. Copyright © 1974 by Alvin Plantinga. Reprinted by permission.

1. The free will defence

In what follows I shall focus attention upon the free will defence. I shall examine it more closely, state it more exactly, and consider objections to it; and I shall argue that in the end it is successful. Earlier we saw that among good states of affairs there are some that not even God can bring about without bringing about evil: those goods, namely, that *entail* or *include* evil states of affairs. The free will defence can be looked upon as an effort to show that there may be a very different kind of good that God can't bring about without permitting evil. These are good states of affairs that don't include evil; they do not entail the existence of any evil whatever; nonetheless God himself can't bring them about without permitting evil.

So how does the free will defence work? And what does the free will defender mean when he says that people are or may be free? What is relevant to the free will defence is the idea of *being free with respect to an action*. If a person is free with respect to a given action, then he is free to perform that action and free to refrain from performing it; no antecedent conditions and/or causal laws determine that he will perform the action, or that he won't. It is within his power, at the time in question, to take or perform the action and within his power to refrain from it. Freedom so conceived is not to be confused with unpredictability. You might be able to predict what you will do in a given situation even if you are free, in that situation, to do something else. If I know you well, I may be able to predict what action you will take in response to a certain set of conditions; it does not follow that you are not free with respect to that action.

Secondly, I shall say that an action is *morally significant*, for a given person, if it would be wrong for him to perform the action but right to refrain or vice versa. Keeping a promise, for example, would ordinarily be morally significant for a person, as would refusing induction into the army. On the other hand, having Cheerios for breakfast (instead of Wheaties) would not normally be morally significant. Further, suppose we say that a person is *significantly free*, on a given occasion, if he is then free with respect to a morally significant action. And finally we must distinguish between *moral evil* and *natural evil*. The former is evil that results from free human activity; natural evil is any other kind of evil.[1]

Given these definitions and distinctions, we can make a preliminary statement of the free will defence as follows. A world containing creatures who are significantly free (and freely perform more good than evil actions) is more valuable, all else being equal, than a world containing no free creatures at all. Now God can create free creatures, but he can't *cause* or *determine* them to do only what is right. For if he does so, then they aren't significantly free after all; they do not do what is right *freely*. To create creatures capable of *moral good*, therefore, he must create creatures capable of moral evil; and he can't give these creatures the freedom to perform evil and at the same time prevent them from doing so. As it turned out, sadly enough, some of the free creatures God created went wrong in the exercise of their freedom; this is the source of moral evil. The fact that free creatures sometimes go wrong, however, counts neither against God's omnipotence nor against his goodness; for he could have forestalled the occurrence of moral evil only by removing the possibility of moral good.

I said earlier that the free will defender tries to find a proposition that is consistent with

(1) God is omniscient, omnipotent, and wholly good

and together with (1) entails that there is evil. According to the free will defence, we must find this proposition somewhere in the above story. The heart of the free will defence is the claim that it is *possible* that God could not have created a universe containing moral good (or as much moral good as this world contains) without creating one that also contained moral evil. And if so, then it is possible that God has a good reason for creating a world containing evil.

Now this defence has met with several kinds of objections. For example, some philosophers say that *causal determinism* and *freedom*, contrary to what we might have thought, are not really incompatible.[2] But if so, then God could have created free creatures who were free, and free to do what is wrong, but nevertheless were causally determined to do only what is right. Thus he could have created creatures who were free to do what was wrong, while nevertheless preventing them from ever performing any wrong actions – simply by seeing to it that they were causally determined to do only what is right. Of course this contradicts the free will defence, according to which there is inconsistency in supposing that God determines free creatures to do only what is right. But is it really possible that all of a person's actions are causally determined while some of them are free? How could that be so? According to one version of the doctrine in question, to say that George acts freely on a given occasion is to say only this: *if George had chosen to do otherwise, he would have done otherwise*. Now George's action A is causally determined if some event E – some event beyond his control – has already occurred, where the state of affairs consisting in E's occurrence conjoined with George's *refraining* from performing A, is a causally impossible state of affairs. Then one can consistently hold both that all of a man's actions are causally determined and that some of them are free in the above sense. For suppose that all of a man's actions are causally determined and that he *couldn't*, on any occasion, have made any choice or performed any action different from the ones he did make and perform. It could still be true that if he *had* chosen to do otherwise, he would have done otherwise. Granted, he couldn't have chosen to do otherwise; but this is consistent with saying that *if* he had, things would have gone differently.

This objection to the free will defence seems utterly implausible. One might as well claim that being in jail doesn't really limit one's freedom on the grounds that if one were *not* in jail, he'd be free to come and go as he pleased. So I shall say no more about this objection here.[3]

A second objection is more formidable. In essence it goes like this. Surely it is possible to do only what is right, even if one is free to do wrong. It is *possible*, in that broadly logical sense, that there be a world containing free creatures who always do what is right. There is certainly no *contradiction* or *inconsistency* in this idea. But God is omnipotent; his power has no nonlogical limitations. So if it's possible that there be a world containing creatures who are free to do what is wrong but never in fact do so, then it follows that an omnipotent God could create such a world. If so, however, the free will defence must be mistaken in its insistence upon the possibility that God is omnipotent but unable to create a world containing moral good without permitting moral evil. J. L. Mackie states this objection:

> If God has made men such that in their free choices they sometimes prefer what is good and sometimes what is evil, why could he not have made men such that they always freely choose the good? If there is no logical impossibility in a man's freely choosing the good on one, or on several occasions, there cannot be a logical impossibility in his freely choosing the good on every occasion. God was not, then, faced with a choice between making innocent automata and making beings who, in acting freely, would sometimes go wrong; there was open to him the obviously better possibility of making beings who would act freely but always go right. Clearly, his failure to avail himself of this possibility is inconsistent with his being both omnipotent and wholly good.[4]

Now what, exactly, is Mackie's point here? This. According to the free will defence, it is possible both that God is omnipotent and that he was unable to create a world containing moral good without creating one containing moral evil. But, replies Mackie, this limitation on his power to create is inconsistent with God's omnipotence. For surely it's *possible* that there be a world containing perfectly virtuous persons – persons who are significantly free but always do what is right. Surely there are *possible worlds* that contain moral good but no moral evil. But God, if he is omnipotent, can create any possible world he chooses. So it is *not* possible, contrary to the free will defence, both that God is omnipotent and that he could create a world containing moral good only by creating one containing moral evil. If he is omnipotent, the only limitations of his power are *logical* limitations; in which case there are no possible worlds he could not have created.

This is a subtle and important point. According to the great

German philosopher G. W. Leibniz, *this* world, the actual world, must be the best of all possible worlds. His reasoning goes as follows. Before God created anything at all, he was confronted with an enormous range of choices; he could create or bring into actuality any of the myriads of different possible worlds. Being perfectly good, he must have chosen to create the best world he could; being omnipotent, he was able to create any possible world he pleased. He must, therefore, have chosen the best of all possible worlds; and hence *this* world, the one he did create, must be the best possible. Now Mackie, of course, agrees with Leibniz that God, if omnipotent, could have created any world he pleased and would have created the best world he could. But while Leibniz draws the conclusion that this world, despite appearances, must be the best possible, Mackie concludes instead that there is no omnipotent, wholly good God. For, he says, it is obvious enough that this present world is not the best of all possible worlds.

The free will defender disagrees with both Leibniz and Mackie. In the first place, he might say, what is the reason for supposing that *there is* such a thing as the best of all possible worlds? No matter how marvellous a world is – containing no matter how many persons enjoying unalloyed bliss – isn't it possible that there be an even better world containing even more persons enjoying even more unalloyed bliss? But what is really characteristic and central to the free will defence is the claim that God, though omnipotent, could not have actualized just any possible world he pleased.

2. Was it within God's power to create any possible world he pleased?

This is indeed the crucial question for the free will defence. If we wish to discuss it with insight and authority, we shall have to look into the idea of *possible worlds*. And a sensible first question is this: what sort of thing is a possible world? The basic idea is that a possible world is a *way things could have been*; it is a *state of affairs* of some kind. Earlier we spoke of states of affairs, in particular of good and evil states of affairs. Suppose we look at this idea in more detail. What sort of thing is a state of affairs? The following would be examples:

Nixon's having won the 1972 election
7 + 5's being equal to 12
All men's being mortal

and

Gary, Indiana's, having a really nasty pollution problem.

These are *actual* states of affairs: states of affairs that do in fact *obtain*. And corresponding to each such actual state of affairs there is a true proposition – in the above cases, the corresponding propositions would be *Nixon won the 1972 presidential election, 7 + 5 is equal to 12, all men are mortal*, and *Gary, Indiana, has a really nasty pollution problem.* A proposition *p corresponds* to a state of affairs *s*, in this sense, if it is impossible that *p* be true and *s* fail to obtain and impossible that *s* obtain and *p* fail to be true.

But just as there are false propositions, so there are states of affairs that do *not* obtain or are *not* actual. *Kissinger's having swum the Atlantic* and *Hubert Horatio Humphrey's having run a mile in four minutes* would be examples. Some states of affairs that do not obtain are *impossible*: e.g., *Hubert's having drawn a square circle, 7 + 5's being equal to 75*, and *Agnew's having a brother who was an only child*. The propositions corresponding to these states of affairs, of course, are necessarily false. So there are states of affairs that *obtain* or *are actual* and also states of affairs that don't obtain. Among the latter some are *impossible* and others are *possible*. And a possible world is a possible state of affairs. Of course not every possible state of affairs is a possible world; *Hubert's having run a mile in four minutes* is a possible state of affairs but not a possible world. No doubt it is an *element* of many possible worlds, but it isn't itself inclusive enough to be one. To be a possible world, a state of affairs must be very large – so large as to be *complete* or *maximal*.

To get at this idea of completeness we need a couple of definitions. A state of affairs *A includes* a state of affairs *B* if it is not possible that *A* obtain and *B* not obtain or if the conjunctive state of affairs *A but not B* – the state of affairs that obtains if and only if *A* obtains and *B* does not – is not possible. For example, *Jim Whittaker's being the first American to climb Mt Everest* includes *Jim Whittaker's being an American*. It also includes *Mt Everest's being climbed, something's being climbed, no*

American having climbed Everest before Whittaker did, and the like. *Inclusion* among states of affairs is like *entailment* among propositions; and where a state of affairs *A* includes a state of affairs *B*, the proposition corresponding to *A* entails the one corresponding to *B*. Accordingly, *Jim Whittaker is the first American to climb Everest* entails *Mt Everest has been climbed*, *something has been climbed*, and *no American climbed Everest before Whittaker did*. Now suppose we say further that a state of affairs *A precludes* a state of affairs *B* if it is not possible that *both* obtain, or if the conjunctive state of affairs *A and B* is impossible. Thus *Whittaker's being the first American to climb Mt Everest* precludes *Luther Jerstad's being the first American to climb Everest*, as well as *Whittaker's never having climbed any mountains*. If *A* precludes *B*, then *A*'s corresponding proposition entails the denial of the one corresponding to *B*. Still further, let's say that the *complement* of a state of affairs is the state of affairs that obtains just in case *A* does not obtain. (Or we might say that the complement (call it *Ā*) of *A* is the state of affairs corresponding to the *denial* or *negation* of the proposition corresponding to *A*.) Given these definitions, we can say what it is for a state of affairs to be *complete*: *A* is a complete state of affairs if and only if for every state of affairs *B*, either *A includes B or A precludes B*. (We could express the same thing by saying that if *A* is a complete state of affairs, then for every state of affairs *B*, either *A* includes *B* or *A* includes *B̄*, the complement of *B*.) And now we are able to say what a possible world is: a possible world is any possible state of affairs that is complete. If *A* is a possible world, then it says something about everything; every state of affairs *S* is either included in or precluded by it.

Corresponding to each possible world *W*, furthermore, there is a set of propositions that I'll call *the book on W*. A proposition is in the book on *W* just in case the state of affairs to which it corresponds is included in *W*. Or we might express it like this. Suppose we say that a proposition *P* is *true in a world W* if and only if *P would have been true if W had been actual* – if and only if, that is, it is not possible that *W* be actual and *P* be false. Then the book on *W* is the set of propositions true in *W*. Like possible worlds, books are *complete*; if *B* is a book, then for any proposition *P*, either *P* or the denial of *P* will be a member of *B*. A book is a *maximal consistent set* of propositions; it is so large that the addition of another proposition to it always yields an explicitly inconsistent set.

Of course, for each possible world there is exactly one book corresponding to it (that is, for a given world W there is just one book B such that each member of B is true in W); and for each book there is just one world to which it corresponds. So every world has its book.

It should be obvious that exactly one possible world is actual. At *least* one must be, since the set of true propositions is a maximal consistent set and hence a book. But then it corresponds to a possible world, and the possible world corresponding to this set of propositions (since it's the set of *true* propositions) will be actual. On the other hand there is at *most* one actual world. For suppose there were two: W and W'. These worlds cannot include all the very same states of affairs; if they did, they would be the very same world. So there must be at least one state of affairs S such that W includes S and W' does not. But a possible world is maximal; W', therefore, includes the complement $\bar{S}$ of S. So if both W and W' were actual, as we have supposed, then both S and $\bar{S}$ would be actual – which is impossible. So there can't be more than one possible world that is actual.

Leibniz pointed out that a proposition p is necessary if it is true in every possible world. We may add that p is possible if it is true in at least one world and impossible if true in none. Furthermore, *p entails q* if there is no possible world in which p is true and q is false; and *p is consistent with q* if there is at least one world in which both p and q are true.

A further feature of possible worlds is that people (and other things) *exist* in them. Each of us exists in the actual world, obviously; but a person also exists in many worlds distinct from the actual world. It would be a mistake, of course, to think of all of these worlds as somehow 'going on' at the same time, with the same person reduplicated through these worlds and actually existing in a lot of different ways. This is not what is meant by saying that the same person exists in different possible worlds. What is meant, instead, is this: a person Paul exists in each of those possible worlds W which is such that, if W *had been actual*, Paul would have existed – actually existed. Suppose Paul had been an inch taller than he is, or a better tennis player. Then the world that does in fact obtain would not have been actual; some other world – W', let's say – would have obtained instead. If W' had been actual, Paul would have existed; so Paul exists in W'. (Of course there are still other possible worlds in which Paul does not exist – worlds, for example, in which there are no people at all.) Accordingly, when we say that Paul exists in a world W, what we mean is that Paul *would have* existed had W been actual. Or we could put it like this: Paul exists in each world W that includes the state of affairs consisting in Paul's existence. We can put this still more simply by saying that Paul exists in those worlds whose books contain the proposition *Paul exists*.

But isn't there a problem here? *Many* people are named 'Paul': Paul the apostle, Paul J. Zwier, John Paul Jones, and many other famous Pauls. So who goes with 'Paul exists'? Which Paul? The answer has to do with the fact that books contain *propositions* – not sentences. They contain the sort of thing sentences are used to express and assert. And the same sentence – 'Aristotle is wise', for example – can be used to express many different propositions. When Plato used it, he asserted a proposition predicating wisdom of his famous pupil; when Jackie Onassis used it, she asserted a proposition predicating wisdom of her wealthy husband. These are distinct propositions (and might even differ in truth value); but they are expressed by the same sentence. Normally (but not always) we don't have much trouble determining which of the several propositions expressed by a given sentence is relevant in the context at hand. So in this case a given person, Paul, exists in a world W if and only if W's book contains the proposition that says that *he* – that particular person – exists. The fact that the sentence we use to express this proposition can also be used to express *other* propositions is not relevant.

After this excursion into the nature of books and worlds we can return to our question. Could God have created just any world he chose? Before addressing the question, however, we must note that God does not, strictly speaking, *create* any possible worlds or states of affairs at all. What he creates are the heavens and the earth and all that they contain. But he has not created states of affairs. There are, for example, the state of affairs consisting in God's existence and the state of affairs consisting in his nonexistence. That is, there is such a thing as the state of affairs consisting in the existence of God, and there is also such a thing as the state of affairs consisting in the nonexistence of God, just as there are the two propositions *God exists* and *God does not exist*. The theist believes that the first state of affairs is actual and the first proposition true; the atheist believes that the second state of affairs is actual and the second proposition true. But, of course, both propositions *exist*, even though just one is true. Similarly, there are two states of affairs here, just one of which is actual. So both states of affairs *exist*, but only one *obtains*. And God has not created either one of them since there never was a time at which either did not exist. Nor has he created the state of affairs consisting in the earth's existence; there was a time when *the earth* did not exist, but none when the state of affairs consisting in the earth's existence didn't exist. Indeed, God did not bring into existence any states of affairs at all. What he did was to perform actions of a certain sort – creating the heavens and the earth, for example – which resulted in the *actuality* of certain states of affairs. God *actualizes* states of affairs. He actualizes the possible world that does in fact obtain; he does not create it. And while he has created Socrates, he did not create the state of affairs consisting in Socrates' existence.[5]

Bearing this in mind, let's finally return to our question. Is the atheologian right in holding that if God is omnipotent, then he could have actualized or created any possible world he pleased? Not obviously. First, we must ask ourselves whether God is a *necessary* or a *contingent* being. A *necessary* being is one that exists in every possible world – one that would have existed no matter which possible world had been actual; a contingent being exists only in some possible worlds. Now if God is not a necessary being (and many, perhaps most, theists think that he is not), then clearly enough there will be many possible worlds he could not have actualized – all those, for example, in which he does not exist. Clearly, God could not have created a world in which he doesn't even exist.

So, if God is a contingent being then there are many possible worlds beyond his power to create. But this is really irrelevant to our present concerns. For perhaps the atheologian can maintain his case if he revises his claim to avoid this difficulty; perhaps he will say something like this: if God is omnipotent, then he could have actualized any of those possible worlds *in which he exists*. So if he exists and is omnipotent, he could have actualized (contrary to the free will defence) any of those possible worlds in which he exists and in which there exist free creatures who do no wrong. He could have actualized worlds containing moral good but no moral evil. Is this correct?

Let's begin with a trivial example. You and Paul have just returned to the United States from an Australian hunting expedition: your quarry was the elusive double-wattled cassowary. Paul captured an aardvark, mistaking it for a cassowary. The creature's disarming ways win it a place in Paul's heart; he is deeply attached to it. Upon your return to the States you offer Paul $500 for his aardvark, only to be rudely turned down. Later you ask yourself, 'What would he have done if I'd offered him $700?' Now what is it, exactly, that you are asking? What you're really asking in a way is whether, under a *specific set of conditions*, Paul would have sold it. These conditions include your having offered him $700 rather than $500 for the aardvark, everything else being as much as possible like the conditions that did in fact obtain. Let S' be this set of conditions or state of affairs. S' includes the state of affairs consisting in your offering Paul $700 (instead of the $500 you did offer him); of course it does not include his *accepting* your offer, and it does not include his *rejecting* it; for the rest, the conditions it includes are just like the ones that did obtain in the actual world. So, for example, S' includes Paul's being free to accept the offer and free to refrain; and if in fact the going rate for an aardvark was $650, then S' includes the state of affairs consisting in the going rate's being $650. So we might put your question by asking which of the following conditionals is true:

(2) If the state of affairs S' had obtained, Paul would have accepted the offer

(3) If the state of affairs S' had obtained, Paul would not have accepted the offer.

It seems clear that at least one of these conditionals is true, but naturally they can't both be; so exactly one is.

Now since S' includes neither Paul's accepting the offer nor his rejecting it, the antecedent of (2) and (3) does not entail the consequent of either. That is,

(4) S' obtains

does not entail either

(5) Paul accepts the offer

or

(6) Paul does not accept the offer.

So there are possible worlds in which both (4) and (5) are true, and other possible worlds in which both (4) and (6) are true.

We are now in a position to grasp an important fact. Either (2) or (3) is in fact true; and either way there are possible worlds God could not have actualized. Suppose, first of all, that (2) is true. Then it was beyond the power of God to create a world in which (A) Paul is free to sell his aardvark and free to refrain, and in which the other states of affairs included in S' obtain, and (B) Paul does not sell. That is, it was beyond God's power to create a world in which (4) and (6) are both true. There is at least one possible world like this, but God, despite his omnipotence, could not have brought about its actuality. For let W be such a world. To actualize W, God must bring it about that Paul is free with respect to this action, and that the other states of affairs included in S' obtain. But (2), as we are supposing, is true; so if God had actualized S' and left Paul *free* with respect to this action, he would have sold: in which case W would not have been actual. If, on the other hand, God had *brought it about* that Paul didn't sell or had *caused him* to refrain from selling, then Paul would not have been free with respect to this action; then S' would not have been actual (since S' includes Paul's being free with respect to it), and W would not have been actual since W includes S'.

Of course if it is (3) rather than (2) that is true, then another class of worlds was beyond God's power to actualize – those, namely, in which S' obtains and Paul *sells* his aardvark. These are the worlds in which both (4) and (5) are true. But either (2) or (3) is true. Therefore, there are possible worlds God could not have actualized. If we consider whether or not God could have created a world in which, let's say, both (4) and (5) are true, we see that the answer depends upon a peculiar kind of fact; it depends upon what Paul would have freely chosen to do in a certain situation. So there are any number of possible worlds such that it is partly up to Paul whether God can create them.[6]

That was a past tense example. Perhaps it would be useful to consider a future tense case, since this might seem to correspond more closely to God's situation in choosing a possible world to actualize. At some time *t* in the near future Maurice will be free with respect to some insignificant action – having freeze-dried oatmeal for breakfast, let's say. That is, at time *t* Maurice will be free to have oatmeal but also free to take something else – shredded wheat, perhaps. Next, suppose we consider *S'*, a state of affairs that is included in the actual world and includes Maurice's being free with respect to taking oatmeal at time *t*. That is, *S'* includes Maurice's being free at time *t* to take oatmeal and free to reject it. *S'* does not include Maurice's taking oatmeal, however; nor does it include his rejecting it. For the rest *S'* is as much as possible like the actual world. In particular there are many conditions that do in fact hold at time *t* and are *relevant* to his choice – such conditions, for example, as the fact that he hasn't had oatmeal lately, that his wife will be annoyed if he rejects it, and the like; and *S'* includes each of these conditions. Now God no doubt knows what Maurice will do at time *t*, if *S* obtains; he knows which action Maurice would freely perform if *S* were to be actual. That is, God knows that one of the following conditionals is true:

(7) If *S'* were to obtain, Maurice will freely take the oatmeal

or

(8) If *S'* were to obtain, Maurice will freely reject it.

We may not know which of these is true, and Maurice himself may not know; but presumably God does.

So either God knows that (7) is true, or else he knows that (8) is. Let's suppose it is (7). Then there is a possible world that God, though omnipotent, cannot create. For consider a possible world *W'* that shares *S'* with the actual world (which for ease of reference I'll name 'Kronos') and in which Maurice does *not* take oatmeal. (We know there *is* such a world, since *S'* does not include Maurice's taking the oatmeal.) *S'* obtains in *W'* just as it does in Kronos. Indeed, everything in *W'* is just as it is in Kronos up to time *t*. But whereas in Kronos Maurice takes oatmeal at time *t*, in *W'* he does not. Now *W'* is a perfectly possible world; but it is not within God's power to create it or bring about its actuality. For to do so he must actualize S'. But (7) is in fact true. So if God actualizes S' (as he must to create W') and leaves Maurice free with respect to the action in question, then he will take the oatmeal; and then, of course, W' will not be actual. If, on the other hand, God causes Maurice to *refrain* from taking the oatmeal, then he is not *free* to take it. That means, once again, that W' is not actual; for in W' Maurice is free to take the oatmeal (even if he doesn't do so). So if (7) is true, then this world W' is one that God can't actualize; it is not within his power to actualize it even though he is omnipotent and it is a possible world.

Of course, if it is (8) that is true, we get a similar result; then too there are possible worlds that God can't actualize. These would be worlds which share S' with Kronos and in which Maurice *does* take oatmeal. But either (7) or (8) *is* true; so either way there is a possible world that God can't create. If we consider a world in which S' obtains and in which Maurice freely chooses oatmeal at time t, we see that whether or not it is within God's power to actualize it depends upon what Maurice would do if he were free in a certain situation. Accordingly, there are any number of possible worlds such that it is partly up to Maurice whether or not God can actualize them. It is, of course, up to God whether or not to create Maurice and also up to God whether or not to make him free with respect to the action of taking oatmeal at time t. (God could, if he chose, cause him to succumb to the dreaded *equine obsession*, a condition shared by some people and most horses, whose victims find it *psychologically impossible* to refuse oats or oat products.) But if he creates Maurice and creates him free with respect to this action, then whether or not he actually performs the action is up to Maurice – not God.[7]

Now we can return to the free will defence and the problem of evil. The free will defender, you recall, insists on the possibility that it is not within God's power to create a world containing moral good without creating one containing moral evil. His atheological opponent – Mackie, for example – agrees with Leibniz in insisting that *if* (as the theist holds) God is omnipotent, then it *follows* that he could have created any possible world he pleased. We now see that this contention – call it 'Leibniz's lapse' – is a mistake. The atheologian is right in holding that there are many possible worlds containing moral good but no moral evil; his mistake lies in endorsing Leibniz's lapse. So one of his premises – that God, if omnipotent, could have actualized just any world he pleased – is false.

3. Could God have created a world containing moral good but no moral evil?

Now suppose we recapitulate the logic of the situation. The free will defender claims that the following is possible:

(9) God is omnipotent, and it was not within his power to create a world containing moral good but no moral evil.

By way of retort the atheologian insists that there are possible worlds containing moral good but no moral evil. He adds that an omnipotent being could have actualized any possible world he chose. So if God is omnipotent, it follows that he could have actualized a world containing moral good but no moral evil; hence (9), contrary to the free will defender's claim, is not possible. What we have seen so far is that his second premise – Leibniz's lapse – is false.

Of course, this does not settle the issue in the free will defender's favour. Leibniz's lapse (appropriately enough for a lapse) is false; but this doesn't show that (9) is possible. To show this latter we must demonstrate the possibility that among the worlds God could not have actualized are all the worlds containing moral good but no moral evil. How can we approach this question?

Instead of choosing oatmeal for breakfast or selling an aardvark, suppose we think about a morally significant action such as taking a bribe. Curley Smith, the mayor of Boston, is opposed to the proposed freeway route; it would require destruction of the Old North Church along with some other antiquated and structurally unsound buildings. L. B. Smedes, the director of highways, asks him whether he'd drop his opposition for $1 million. 'Of course,' he replies. 'Would you do it for $2?' asks Smedes. 'What do you take me for?' comes the indignant reply. 'That's already established,' smirks Smedes; 'all that remains is to nail down your price.' Smedes then offers him a bribe of $35,000; unwilling to break with the fine old traditions of Bay State politics, Curley accepts. Smedes then spends a sleepless night wondering whether he could have bought Curley for $20,000.

Now suppose we assume that Curley was free with respect to the action of taking the bribe – free to take it and free to refuse. And suppose, furthermore, that he would have taken it. That is, let us suppose that

(10) If Smedes had offered Curley a bribe of $20,000, he would have accepted it.

If (10) is true, then there is a state of affairs S' that (1) includes Curley's being offered a bribe of $20,000; (2) does not include either his accepting the bribe or his rejecting it; and (3) is otherwise as much as possible like the actual world. Just to make sure S' includes every relevant circumstance, let us suppose that it is a *maximal world segment*. That is, add to S' any state of affairs compatible with but not included in it, and the result will be an entire possible world. We could think of it roughly like this: S' is included in at least one word W in which Curley takes the bribe and in at least one world W' in which he rejects it. If S' is a maximal world segment, then S' is what remains of W when *Curley's taking the bribe* is deleted; it is also what remains of W' when *Curley's rejecting the bribe* is deleted. More exactly, if S' is a maximal world segment, then every possible state of affairs that includes S', but isn't included by S', is a possible world. So if (10) is true, then there is a maximal world segment S' that (1) includes Curley's being offered a bribe of $20,000; (2) does not include either his accepting the bribe or his rejecting it; (3) is otherwise as much as possible like the actual world – in particular, it includes Curley's being free with respect to the bribe; and (4) is such that if it were actual then Curley would have taken the bribe. That is,

(11) If S' were actual, Curley would have accepted the bribe

is true.

Now, of course, there is at least one possible world W' in which S' is actual and Curley does not take the bribe. But God could not have created W'; to do so, he would have been obliged to actualize S', leaving Curley free with respect to the action of taking the bribe. But under these conditions Curley, as (11) assures us, would have accepted the bribe, so that the world thus created would not have been S'.

Curley, as we see, is not above a bit of Watergating. But there may be worse to come. Of course, there are possible worlds in which he is significantly free (i.e., free with respect to a morally significant action) and never does what is wrong. But the sad truth about Curley may be this. Consider W', any of these worlds: in W' Curley is significantly free, so in W' there are some actions that are morally significant for him and with respect to which he is free. But at least one of these actions – call it A – has the following peculiar property. There is a maximal world segment S' that obtains in W' and is such that (1) S' includes Curley's being free *re* A but neither his performing A nor his refraining from A; (2) S' is otherwise as much as possible like W'; and (3) if S' had been actual, Curley would have gone wrong with respect to A.[8] (Notice that this third condition holds in fact, in the actual world; it does not hold in that world W'.)

This means, of course, that God could not have actualized W'. For to do so he'd have been obliged to bring it about that S' is actual; but then Curley would go wrong with respect to A. Since in W' he always does what is right, the world thus actualized would not be W'. On the other hand, if God *causes* Curley to go right with respect to A or *brings it about that* he does so, then Curley isn't free with respect to A; and so once more it isn't W' that is actual. Accordingly God cannot create W'. But W' was just any of the worlds in which Curley is significantly free but always does only what is right. It therefore follows that it was not within God's power to create a world in which Curley produces moral good but no moral evil. Every world God can actualize is such that if Curley is significantly free in it, he takes at least one wrong action.

Obviously Curley is in serious trouble. I shall call the malady from which he suffers *transworld depravity*. (I leave as homework the problem of comparing transworld depravity with what Calvinists call 'total depravity'.) By way of explicit definition:

(12) A person P *suffers from transworld depravity* if and only if the following holds: for every world W such that P is significantly free in W and P does only what is right in W, there is an action A and a maximal world segment S' such that
(1) S' includes A's being morally significant for P
(2) S' includes P's being free with respect to A

(3) S' is included in W and includes neither P's performing A nor P's refraining from performing A

and

(4) If S' were actual, P would go wrong with respect to A.

(In thinking about this definition, remember that (4) is to be true in fact, in the actual world – not in that world W.)

What is important about the idea of transworld depravity is that if a person suffers from it, then it wasn't within God's power to actualize any world in which that person is significantly free but does no wrong – that is, a world in which he produces moral good but no moral evil.

We have been considering a crucial contention of the free will defender: the contention, namely, that

(9) God is omnipotent, and it was not within his power to create a world containing moral good but no moral evil.

How is transworld depravity relevant to this? As follows. Obviously it is possible that there be persons who suffer from transworld depravity. More generally, it is possible that *everybody* suffers from it. And if this possibility were actual, then God, though omnipotent, could not have created any of the possible worlds containing just the persons who do in fact exist, and containing moral good but no moral evil. For to do so he'd have to create persons who were significantly free (otherwise there would be no moral good) but suffered from transworld depravity. Such persons go wrong with respect to at least one action in any world God could have actualized and in which they are free with respect to morally significant actions; so the price for creating a world in which they produce moral good is creating one in which they also produce moral evil.

4. Transworld depravity and essence

Now we might think this settles the question in favour of the free will defender. But the fact is it doesn't. For suppose all the people that exist in Kronos, the actual world, suffer from transworld depravity; it doesn't follow that God could not have created a world containing moral good without creating one containing moral evil. God could have created *other people*. Instead of creating us, i.e., the people that exist in Kronos, he could have created a world containing people, but not containing any of us – or perhaps a world containing some of us along with some others who do not exist in Kronos. And perhaps if he'd done that, he could have created a world containing moral good but no moral evil.

Perhaps. But then again, perhaps not. Suppose we look into the matter a little further. Let W be a world distinct from Kronos that contains a significantly free person x who does not exist in Kronos. Let us suppose that this person x does only what is right. I can see no reason to doubt that there *are* such worlds; but what reason do we have for supposing that God could have created any of them? How do we know that he can? To investigate this question, we must look into the idea of an *individual nature* or *essence*. I said earlier (p. 429) that the same individual – Socrates, for example – exists in many different possible worlds. In some of these he has properties quite different from those he has in Kronos, the actual world. But some of his properties are ones he has in every world in which he exists; these are his *essential* properties.[9] Among them would be some that are *trivially* essential – such properties as *being unmarried if a bachelor, being either six feet tall or else not six feet tall, being self-identical*, and the like. Another and more interesting kind of essential property can be explained as follows. Socrates has the property of being snubnosed. This property, presumably, is not essential to him; he could have had some other kind of nose. So there are possible worlds in which he is not snubnosed. Let W' be any such world. If W' had been actual, Socrates would not have been snubnosed; that is to say, Socrates has the property *being nonsnubnosed in W'*. For to say that an object x has a property of this sort – the property of having P in W, where P is a property and W is a possible world – is to say simply that x *would have had P if W had been actual*. Properties of this sort are *world-indexed* properties.[10] Socrates has the world-indexed property *being nonsnubnosed in W'*. He has this property in Kronos, the actual world. On the other hand, in W' Socrates has the property *being snubnosed in Kronos*. For suppose W' had been actual: then, while Socrates would not have been snubnosed, it would have been true that if *Kronos* had been actual, Socrates would have been snubnosed.

It is evident, I take it, that if indeed Socrates *is* snubnosed in Kronos, the actual world, then it is true in every world that Socrates is *snubnosed in Kronos*.[11] So he has the property *being snubnosed in Kronos* in every world in which he exists. This property, therefore, is essential to him; there is no world in which he exists and lacks it. Indeed, it is easy to see, I think, that every world-indexed property he has will be essential to him; and every world-indexed property he *lacks* will be such that its complement is essential to him.

But how many world-indexed properties does he have? Quite a few. We should note that for any world W and property P, there is the world-indexed property *has P in W*; and for any such world-indexed property, either Socrates has it or he has its complement – the property of *not* having P in W. For any world W and property P, either Socrates would have had P, had W been actual, or it's false that Socrates would have had P under that condition. So each world-indexed property P is such that either Socrates has P essentially, or else its complement $\bar{P}$ is essential to him.

Now suppose we define Socrates' *essence* as the set of properties essential to him. His essence is a set of properties, each of which is essential to him; and this set contains all his world-indexed properties, together with some others. But furthermore, it is evident, I think, that no *other* person has all of these properties in this set. Another person might have *some* of the same world-indexed properties as Socrates: he might be *snubnosed in Kronos* for example. But he couldn't have *all* of Socrates' world-indexed properties for then he would just *be* Socrates. So there is no person who shares Socrates' essence with him. But we can say something even stronger: there *couldn't* be any such person. For such a person would just be Socrates and hence not *another* person. The essence of Socrates, therefore, is a set of properties each of which he has essentially. Furthermore, there neither is nor could be another person distinct from Socrates that has all of the properties in this set. And finally, Socrates' essence contains a *complete* set of world-indexed properties – that is, if P is world-indexed, then either P is a member of Socrates' essence or else $\bar{P}$ is.[12]

Returning to Curley, we recall that he suffers from transworld depravity. This fact implies something interesting about Curleyhood, Curley's essence. Take those worlds W such that *is significantly free in*

W and never does what is wrong in W are contained in Curley's essence. Each of these worlds has an important property if Curley suffers from transworld depravity; each is such that God could not have created or actualized it. We can see this as follows. Suppose W' is some world such that Curley's essence contains the property *is significantly free in W' but never does what is wrong in W'*. That is, W' is a world in which Curley is significantly free but always does what is right. But, of course, Curley suffers from transworld depravity. This means that there is an action A and a maximal world segment S' such that

(1) S' includes A's being morally significant for Curley

(2) S' includes Curley's being free with respect to A

(3) S' is included in W' but includes neither Curley's performing A nor his refraining from A

and

(4) If S' had been actual, Curley would have gone wrong with respect to A.

But then (by the argument of p. 438) God could not have created or instantiated W'. For to do so he would have had to bring it about that S' obtain; and then Curley would have gone wrong with respect to A. Since in W' he always does what is right, W' would not have been actual. So if Curley suffers from transworld depravity, then Curley's essence has this property: God could not have created any world W such that Curleyhood contains the properties *is significantly free in W* and *always does what is right in W*.

We can use this connection between Curley's transworld depravity and his essence as the basis for a definition of transworld depravity as applied to essences rather than persons. We should note first that if E is a person's essence, then that person is the *instantiation* of E; he is the thing that has (or exemplifies) every property in E. To instantiate an essence, God creates a person who has that essence; and in creating a person he instantiates an essence. Now we can say that

(13) An essence E *suffers from transworld depravity* if and only if for every world W such that E contains the properties *is significantly free in W* and *always does what is right in W*, there is an action A and a maximal world segment S' such that

(1) *S'* includes *E's being instantiated* and *E's instantiation's being free with respect to A* and *A's being morally significant for E's instantiation*,

(2) *S'* is included in *W* but includes neither *E's instantiation's performing A* nor *E's instantiation's refraining from A*

and

(3) if *S'* were actual, then the instantiation of *E* would have gone wrong with respect to *A*.

By now it is evident, I take it, that if an essence *E* suffers from transworld depravity, then it was not within God's power to actualize a possible world *W* such that *E* contains the properties *is significantly free in W* and *always does what is right in W*. Hence it was not within God's power to create a world in which *E* is instantiated and in which its instantiation is significantly free but always does what is right.

And the interesting fact here is this: it is possible that every creaturely essence – every essence including the property of being created by God – suffers from transworld depravity. But now suppose this is true. Now God can create a world containing moral good only by creating significantly free persons. And, since every person is the instantiation of an essence, he can create significantly free persons only by instantiating some essences. But if every essence suffers from transworld depravity, then no matter which essences God instantiates, the resulting persons, if free with respect to morally significant actions, would always perform at least some wrong actions. If every essence suffers from transworld depravity, then it was beyond the power of God himself to create a world containing moral good but no moral evil. He might have been able to create worlds in which moral evil is very considerably outweighed by moral good; but it was not within his power to create worlds containing moral good but no moral evil – and this despite the fact that he is omnipotent. Under these conditions God could have created a world containing no moral evil only by creating one without significantly free persons. But it is possible that every essence suffers from transworld depravity; so it's possible that God could not have created a world containing moral good but no moral evil.

5. The free will defence vindicated

Put formally, you remember, the free will defender's project was to show that

(1) God is omniscient, omnipotent, and wholly good

is consistent with

(14) There is evil.

What we have just seen is that

(15) It was not within God's power to create a world containing moral good but no moral evil

is possible and consistent with God's omnipotence and omniscience. But then it is clearly consistent with (1). So we can use it to show that (1) is consistent with (14). For consider

(1) God is omnipotent, omniscient, and wholly good
(15) It was not within God's power to create a world containing moral good without creating one containing moral evil

and

(16) God created a world containing moral good.

These propositions are evidently consistent – i.e., their conjunction is a possible proposition. But taken together they entail

(14) There is evil.

For (16) says that God created a world containing moral good; this together with (15) entails that he created one containing moral evil. But if it contains moral evil, then it contains evil. So (1), (15), and (16) are jointly consistent and entail (14); hence (1) is consistent with (14). Remember: to serve in this argument (15) and (16) need not be known to be true, or likely on our evidence, or anything of the sort; they need only be consistent with (1). Since they are, there is no contradiction in the conjunction of (1) with (14); so the free will defence appears to be successful.

Notes

1. This distinction is not very precise (how, exactly, are we to construe 'results from'?); but perhaps it will serve our present purposes.

2. See, for example, A. Flew, 'Divine Omnipotence and Human Freedom', in *New Essays in Philosophical Theology*, eds. A. Flew and A. MacIntyre (London: SCM, 1955), pp. 150–53.

3. For further discussion of it see Plantinga, *God and Other Minds* (Ithaca: Cornell University Press, 1967), pp. 132–5.

4. J. L. Mackie, 'Evil and Omnipotence' in *The Philosophy of Religion*, ed. Basil Mitchell (London: Oxford University Press, 1971) pp. 100–101.

5. Strict accuracy demands, therefore, that we speak of God as *actualizing* rather than creating possible worlds. I shall continue to use both locutions, thus sacrificing accuracy to familiarity. For more about possible worlds see my book *The Nature of Necessity* (Oxford: The Clarendon Press, 1974), chapters 4–8.

6. For a fuller statement of this argument see *The Nature of Necessity*, Chapter 9, Sections 4–6.

7. For a more complete and more exact statement of this argument see *The Nature of Necessity*, Chapter 9, Sections 4–6.

8. A person goes wrong with respect to an action if he either wrongfully performs it or wrongfully fails to perform it.

9. For a discussion of essential properties see *The Nature of Necessity*, Chapters 2–4.

10. For more about world-indexed properties see *The Nature of Necessity*, Chapter 4, Section 11.

11. For argument see *The Nature of Necessity*, Chapter 4, Section 11.

12. For more discussion of essences see *The Nature of Necessity*, Chapter 5.

Biographical Note

Alvin Plantinga is Professor of Philosophy at Calvin College, Michigan; he is also a Professor at Notre Dame University and has been Visiting Professor at a number of American universities. He is the author of *God and Other Minds* (1967), *The Nature of Necessity* (1974) and *God, Freedom and Evil* (1975).

Further Reading

The classic discussion of the problem of evil is David Hume's *Dialogues concerning Natural Religion*. J. L. Mackie's challenge may be found in his article 'Evil and Omnipotence', *Mind* 64 (1955), pp. 200–212, reprinted (along with an earlier version of Plantinga's free will defence) in Basil Mitchell (ed.), *The*

Philosophy of Religion (Oxford Readings in Philosophy, Oxford University Press, 1971). Mention may also be made of Nelson Pike (ed.), *God and Evil: Readings on the Theological Problem of Evil* (London: Prentice-Hall, 1964).

The reader may also consult two larger works by Alvin Plantinga: *God and Other Minds* (Ithaca: Cornell University Press, 1967) and, for more on possible worlds and the problem of evil, *The Nature of Necessity* (Oxford: Clarendon Press, 1974).

For a vigorous attack on the free will defence, see Antony Flew, 'Divine Omniscience and Human Freedom', in Antony Flew and Alasdair MacIntyre (edd.), *New Essays in Philosophical Theology* (London: SCM Press, 1955), pp. 144–69.

Robert C. Stalnaker

Possible Worlds

The idea of possible worlds came into philosophy through Leibniz. It is Leibniz also who is generally credited with the idea that the important notion of necessary truth may be explained by saying that a necessarily true proposition is one that is true in all possible worlds. But it was the twentieth century which first developed formal logical systems to study the logic of the modal notions of necessity and possibility. As logic is concerned with inference in general, so modal logic is concerned with inference involving necessity and possibility. For example, one simple but fundamental principle of modal logic is this:

$$\Box(p \to q) \to (\Box p \to \Box q)$$

which means: if it is necessary that *if p, then q*, then if *p* itself is necessary, so is *q*.

Now with any formal logical system it is desirable, and to prove certain kinds of result it is necessary, to have a *semantics* for the system: roughly, a theoretical account of the conditions under which formulae of the system are true. The peculiarities of the concepts of necessity and possibility made this a difficult technical problem. It was not solved until, within the past two decades, Kripke and others applied to the task the Leibnizian notion of possible worlds.

The initial idea is that a statement of the form 'It is necessary that *p*' can be said to be true just in case '*p*' is true in all possible worlds, while 'It is possible that *p*' can be said to be true just in case '*p*' is true in at least one possible world. But, as the reader of the chapter by Plantinga in the present volume will have begun to realize (see especially pp. 426–30), a good deal of technical expertise goes into providing a determinate way of specifying the set of possible worlds and then interpreting into them not only simple and complex sentences or formulae but also names of individuals and predicates.

Our concern here will not be with technical details but with the notion of possible worlds itself. It often happens that a notion which has proved strikingly fruitful in one particular field of inquiry takes on a life of its own; it becomes common coin, in use over a range of problems other than that for which it was first minted. In the present volume possible worlds feature in the contributions of Kripke, Plantinga and Mackie – three very different contexts of inquiry in which the use made of possible worlds is by no means uniform. The starting point for Robert Stalnaker's examination of possible worlds is different again.

In his book *Counterfactuals* David Lewis made a notable adaptation of the notion of possible worlds to give an analysis of counterfactual conditionals. Counterfactual conditionals, which enter importantly into our thinking about causation, laws of nature, and other things, are statements of the form 'If it were the case that p, then it would be the case that q' (where 'p' is usually assumed false). Lewis's analysis of this form of statement is, in outline, as follows: in certain possible worlds where 'p' is true, 'q' is true also. And Lewis combined this analytical thesis with a defence of the metaphysical claim that the possible worlds referred to in his analysis really do exist no less than the actual world we inhabit.

Thus it is not too much to say that the notion of possible worlds, starting out from the strictly technical formulation of a semantics for modal logic, has come to assume a central place in the contemporary philosophical repertoire. At the same time – and this is highly characteristic of the way philosophy develops – it has become itself a problem for philosophy. That is, besides the question whether this problem or that (causation, counterfactuals, the theological problem of evil) will finally yield to solution in terms of possible worlds, there is now a major metaphysical issue: What are possible worlds? Do they exist, as Lewis holds, or should we follow the view of more sceptically-tempered philosophers that talk of possible worlds is a heuristically useful but mythical device which it would be misleading to take too realistically? That is the question to which Stalnaker's paper is addressed.

To focus the issue Stalnaker sets out (pp. 456–7) four theses on possible worlds stated by Lewis. We will comment briefly on the first three, which are not technical, and then turn to the more technical matters raised by the fourth.

Thesis (1): *Possible worlds exist.* It is Lewis's contention that we all believe this already, inasmuch as we believe that there are many ways things could have been besides the way they actually are. A possible world, then, is to be understood simply as one of 'the ways things could have been'. Thus far Stalnaker agrees – on condition, however, that talk of 'the ways things could have been' is understood in a particular fashion, in strict parallel to 'the way things are'. The proper construal of this latter phrase is that it signifies things being thus and so, i.e. a state or property of the (actual) world and the things in it, not the world itself or its contents. Compare the difference between 'the way people are' and 'people'. On such a construal 'the ways things could have been' ought to signify things being able to have been thus or so, i.e. modal states or properties of the (actual) world and the things in it, not this or any other *world* as such. Compare, again, 'the ways people could have been'. Thus understood, thesis (1) 'Possible worlds exist' means no more than: there really are many ways that things – the things of our actual world – could have been. And this, Stalnaker argues, by no means entails the second thesis on the list. Indeed, it may even be incompatible with this second thesis.

Thesis (2): *Other possible worlds are things of the same sort as the actual world – 'I and all my surroundings'*. It is this thesis that invites the caricature picture of vast numbers of possible worlds laid out in space like the raisins in a pudding (p. 454). The trouble is that the postulation of more worlds just like ours sounds all too much like the speculation of someone who says that somewhere in the actual universe there may be other planets like ours, with living creatures like us and a history like ours. But, of course, it is not meant to be that sort of speculation at all. Another possible world would be a *total* universe *alternative* to the actual one, with a history alternative to ours. Where Stalnaker and Lewis part company is over the question whether we have any respectable reason to pass from saying (a) there are possible worlds in the sense that there are alternative ways the (actual) universe might have developed, to saying (b) there are possible worlds in the sense that there are alternative possible universes existing alongside the actual one. Compare: 'There are many ways people could have been, alternative to the way they actually are' *versus* 'Besides ourselves, the actual people, there are alternative possible people'.

Stalnaker next seeks (p. 458) to undermine the support that thesis (2) may appear to gain from thesis (3): *The indexical analysis of the adjective 'actual' is the correct analysis*. What is meant by an indexical analysis is this: just as the word 'here' refers to the place at which it is uttered, and thus to different places in different utterances, so the adjective 'actual' (as in 'the actual universe', 'actual people') refers to the world in which it is uttered; if it is uttered in our world, it refers to our world, if in another possible world, to that other world in turn. Each world may be spoken of, within that world itself, as actual. Thus far Stalnaker agrees – but, as before, he demands care about what one is committed to by agreeing.

Thesis (3) may seem to have the consequence that the only difference between our world and any other world which may speak of itself as actual is that we inhabit this one; we are here, not there. Actuality is just like home: each of us may speak of our own house as home, so home is simply the house we ourselves happen to live in. No, replies Stalnaker, actuality is not like that, as may be seen by taking the case of the worlds of fiction. 'Actual' does refer in our world to our world and in fictional worlds to the fictional world it is uttered in, but the point of view which entitles fictional characters to speak of their own world as actual is itself fictional. Actuality is *everything* that is the case, including its being the case that fictional worlds are fictional and not real. Put differently, the point is that, while a possible world is a world such that it is *possible* for it to be actual, the question whether it *is* actual or not is one to be settled from an absolute standpoint: the standpoint of those people (ourselves) who really exist in a universe (world) whose history is the history of everything that has really happened.

We now have before us a position of moderate realism about possible worlds. Theses (1) and (3) have been found acceptable, given an appropriate understanding of what they assert; thesis (2), which leads to the extreme realism of David Lewis, has been rejected. In sum, possible worlds exist, but they are no more – but also no less – than *ways things might have been*. The remainder of Stalnaker's paper (from p. 459) may be regarded as an argument in defence of the claim that this is a perfectly satisfactory position at which to rest.

The discussion centres on thesis (4): *Possible worlds cannot be reduced to something more basic.* More specifically, the question is: Should possible worlds be reduced to propositions or propositions to possible worlds? Now when philosophers talk of reducing one thing to another they usually envisage a certain technical exercise undertaken as a means to an end which is not in itself technical at all. Given a theory or set of statements mentioning the one type of thing (e.g. possible worlds), the exercise is to find an equivalent theory or set of statements mentioning only the other type of thing (e.g. propositions) with which to translate or replace the first. This is the reduction. The particular reduction which Stalnaker discusses is one due to Robert Adams which reduces possible worlds to propositions, with propositions understood to be abstract entities or what may be called thought-contents. (We all have some sense of what it is for two utterances, perhaps in different words or indeed in different languages, to say the same thing or express the same thought. That 'same thing' is what the notion of a proposition, as contrasted with the sentences which express it, is designed to capture; but exactly *when* two sentences express the same proposition is one of the questions a theory of propositions has to settle.) Adams's reduction of possible worlds to propositions replaces sets of statements about possible worlds by sets of statements about world-stories, where a world-story is itself a certain specifiable set of propositions (the reader may compare here Plantinga's notion of the book on world W, this volume p. 428). Considerable technical sophistication may be required to carry out the reduction, but the exercise only takes on philosophical significance when it is conjoined with a further claim, to the effect that the feasibility of the reduction shows that possible worlds may be analysed or explained in terms of propositions, or that it is acceptable to believe in possible worlds because that is simply believing certain things about propositions. This is the non-technical purpose of reduction: to explain a problematic sort of thing in terms of another sort of thing which is thought to be clearer or less problematic.

That being the nature and the aim of reduction, what are we to do when confronted, on the one hand, with a reduction of possible worlds to propositions, and on the other with a reverse reduction, such as Stalnaker himself has proposed elsewhere, which construes propositions in terms of possible worlds? On Stalnaker's reduction, a proposition is that set of possible worlds (= that set of ways things might have been) in which the sentence expressing the proposition takes the value true. This analysis encapsulates the thought that to understand what proposition a sentence expresses is to know what possible states of affairs (possible worlds) would make it true. The rival analysis presses the thought that to know that such and such is a possible state of affairs is ultimately to know that certain propositions could possibly all be true together. Both analyses have philosophically plausible motivation and appeal. So which direction should we take? And what sorts of consideration are available to extricate us from the unprofitable situation in which, assuming that the reduction can, from a technical point of view, be effected either way, the two sides are left each insisting that their own favoured notion is the clearer and the more basic?

Stalnaker offers to break the deadlock in a manner that is fairly technical and compressed in execution, but the final upshot on p. 464

can be grasped and appreciated by the reader who follows only the general drift of the intervening argument. First, the competing reductions are not, as they stand, equivalent; Stalnaker's possible-worlds analysis of propositions entails consequences – the two consequences labelled (I) and (C) on p. 462 – which Adams's world-story analysis of possible worlds does not entail. But, Stalnaker claims, these two consequences are ones that his opponent ought to try to secure.

Anyone ought to accept that, in respect of any set of propositions, there is the proposition about the set *that* every member of it is true, which proposition is true if and only if every member of the given set is true – that is thesis (C). Thesis (I), that necessarily equivalent propositions are identical, comes to this: if it is necessary that *if p then q*, and also necessary that *if q then p*, then *p* is identical with or the same proposition as *q*. Thesis (I) is highly controversial and demands fuller defence, which may be found elsewhere, in Stalnaker's paper on 'Propositions' mentioned in the bibliography. In that paper, to give a very rough indication of a complex discussion, Stalnaker argues that we should consider propositions from the point of view of the theory of rational action. So considering them, he maintains that if '*p*' and '*q*' are necessarily equivalent, a belief or desire that *p* necessarily functions exactly like a belief or desire that *q* in the determination of any rational action; functionally, the beliefs or desires are the same, so their propositional objects should be taken to be the same. This, in outline, is his defence of thesis (I). Conditionally on that defence proving satisfactory, Stalnaker argues that the world-story analysis of possible worlds needs to be enriched to include (C) and (I), and when this is done it is equivalent to the possible-worlds analysis of propositions. Then the notion of proposition is itself reduced by Stalnaker, on behalf of the world-story theorist, to the notion of a certain set of what he calls basic propositions – propositions each of which is a member of just one world-story. The result is that propositions are now defined in terms of sets of world-stories, which is tantamount to Stalnaker's own analysis of propositions as sets of possible worlds. The competing theories, when fully developed, turn out to be the same theory.

There is, coming out of this technical manoeuvring, a substantive philosophical conclusion. It is a controversial conclusion, and one that demands further clarification and examination by proponents and critics alike, but it gives substance to the metaphysical problem of possible worlds. It is that if we start by thinking of propositions as things people express in the propositional acts of statement-making, promise-giving, etc., and as the objects of the propositional attitudes (they are what people believe, doubt, hope, etc., to be true), and then pursue thoroughly what is required of the notion of a proposition if it is to serve the purposes of a general account of propositional acts and attitudes, we shall find ourselves in the end speaking of objects which have all the properties that the possible-worlds theory attributes to possible worlds. In other words, we shall be speaking of possible worlds. In this sense, Stalnaker concludes, possible worlds are no metaphysical fancy but a basic concept in a true account of the way we represent the world in our propositional acts and attitudes.

M.F.B.

Robert C. Stalnaker

Possible Worlds

Reprinted by permission of the author and of the editor of *Noûs*, X (1976): pp. 65–75.

According to Leibniz, the universe – the actual world – is one of an infinite number of possible worlds existing in the mind of God. God created the universe by actualizing one of these possible worlds – the best one. It is a striking image, this picture of an infinite swarm of total universes, each by its natural inclination for existence striving for a position that can be occupied by only one, with God, in his infinite wisdom and benevolence, settling the competition by selecting the most worthy candidate. But in these enlightened times, we find it difficult to take this metaphysical myth any more seriously than the other less abstract creation stories told by our primitive ancestors. Even the more recent expurgated versions of the story, leaving out God and the notoriously chauvinistic thesis that our world is better than all the rest, are generally regarded, at best, as fanciful metaphors for a more sober reality. J. L. Mackie, for example, writes '. . . talk of possible worlds . . . cries out for further analysis. There *are* no possible worlds except the actual one; so what are we up to when we talk about them?' ([3]: 90).* Lawrence Powers puts the point more bluntly: 'The whole idea of possible worlds (perhaps laid out in space like raisins in a pudding) seems ludicrous.' ([4]).

These expressions of scepticism and calls for further analysis are of course not directed at Leibniz but at recent uses of parts of his metaphysical myth to motivate and give content to formal semantics for modal logics. In both formal and philosophical discussions of modality, the concept of a possible world has shown itself to have considerable heuristic power. But, critics have argued, a heuristic device

---

* A key to the works cited can be found at the end of this piece.

should not be confused with an explanation. If analyses of modal concepts (or of the concept of a proposition) in terms of possible worlds are to be more than heuristic aids in mapping the relationships among the formulae of a modal logic, the concept of a possible world itself must be explained and justified.

Although it is commonly taken to be an obvious truth that there really are no such things as possible worlds – that the myth, whether illuminating or misleading, explanatory or obfuscating, is nevertheless a myth – this common opinion can be challenged. That is, one might respond to the possible-worlds sceptic not by explaining the metaphor but by taking the story to be the literal truth. David Lewis responds in this way, and he cites common opinion and ordinary language on his side:

> I believe there are possible worlds other than the one we happen to inhabit. If an argument is wanted, it is this: It is uncontroversially true that things might have been otherwise than they are. I believe, and so do you, that things could have been different in countless ways. But what does this mean? Ordinary language permits the paraphrase: there are many ways things could have been besides the way that they actually are. On the face of it, this sentence is an existential quantification. It says that there exist many entities of a certain description, to wit, 'ways things could have been'. I believe things could have been different in countless ways. I believe permissible paraphrases of what I believe; taking the paraphrase at its face value, I therefore believe in the existence of entities which might be called 'ways things could have been'. I prefer to call them 'possible worlds'. ([2]: 84.)

Lewis does not intend this as a knockdown argument. It is only a presumption that the sentences of ordinary language be taken at face value, and the presumption can be defeated if the naïve reading of the sentences leads to problems which can be avoided by an alternative analysis. The aim of the argument is to shift the burden to the sceptic who, if he is to defeat the argument, must point to the problems which commitment to possible worlds creates, and the alternative analysis which avoids those problems. Lewis does not think the sceptic can do either.

The rhetorical force of Lewis's argument is in the suggestion that possible worlds are really not such alien entities as the metaphysical flavour of this name seems to imply. The argument suggests not that ordinary language and our common beliefs commit us to a weighty metaphysical theory, but rather that what appears to be a weighty metaphysical theory is really just some ordinary beliefs by another name. Believing in possible worlds is like speaking prose. We have been doing it all our lives.

But for this to be convincing, the shift from 'ways things might have been' to 'possible worlds' must be an innocent terminological substitution, and I do not believe that, as Lewis develops the concept of a possible world, it is. To argue this point I will state four theses about possible worlds, all defended by Lewis. Together they constitute a doctrine which I will call extreme realism about possible worlds. It is this doctrine against which the sceptic is reacting, and against which, I shall argue, he is justified in reacting. I believe the doctrine is false, but I also believe that one need not accept or reject the theses as a package. The main burden of my argument will be to show the independence of the more plausible parts of the package, and so to defend the coherence of a more moderate form of realism about possible worlds – one that might be justified by our common modal opinions and defended as a foundation for a theory about the activities of rational agents.

Here are Lewis's four theses:

(1) *Possible worlds exist.* Other possible worlds are just as real as the actual world. They may not *actually* exist, since to actually exist is to exist in the actual world, but they do, nevertheless, exist.

(2) *Other possible worlds are things of the same sort as the actual world –* '*I and all my surroundings*' ([2]: 86). They differ 'not in kind, but only in what goes on at them. Our actual world is only one world among others. We call it alone actual not because it differs in kind from all the rest, but because it is the world we inhabit' ([2]: 85).

(3) *The indexical analysis of the adjective 'actual' is the correct analysis.* 'The inhabitants of other worlds may truly call their own world actual if they mean by "actual" what we do; for the meaning we give to "actual" is such that it refers at any world *i* to that world *i* itself. "Actual" is indexical, like "I" or "here" or "now": it depends for

its reference on the circumstances of utterance, to wit, the world where the utterance is located' ([2]: 85–6).

(4) *Possible worlds cannot be reduced to something more basic.* 'Possible worlds are what they are and not another thing.' It would be a mistake to identify them with some allegedly more respectable entity, for example a set of sentences of some language. Possible worlds are 'respectable entities in their own right' ([2]: 85).

The first thesis, by itself, is compatible with Lewis's soothing claim that believing in possible worlds is doing no more than believing that things might have been different in various ways. What is claimed to exist are things which ordinary language calls 'ways things might have been', things that truth is defined relative to, things that our modal idioms may be understood as quantifiers over. But the first thesis says nothing about the nature of the entities that play these roles. It is the second thesis which gives realism about possible worlds its metaphysical bite, since it implies that possible worlds are not shadowy ways things could be, but concrete particulars, or at least entities which are made up of concrete particulars and events. The actual world is 'I and my surroundings'. Other possible worlds are more things like that. Even a philosopher who had no qualms about abstract objects such as numbers, properties, states and kinds, might balk at this proliferation of fullblooded universes which seem less real to us than our own only because we have never been there.

The argument Lewis gives for thesis one, identifying possible worlds with ways things might have been, seems even to be incompatible with his explanation of possible worlds as more things of the same kind as I and all my surroundings. If possible worlds are ways things might have been, then the actual world ought to be *the way things are* rather than *I and all my surroundings*. *The way things are* is a property or a state of the world, not the world itself. The statement that the world is the way it is, is true in a sense, but not when read as an identity statement (Compare: 'the way the world is, is the world'). This is important, since if properties can exist uninstantiated, then *the way the world is* could exist even if a world that is that way did not. One could accept thesis one – that there really are many ways that things could have been – while denying that there exists anything else that is like the actual world.

Does the force of thesis two rest, then, on a simple equivocation between 'the actual world', in the sense that is roughly captured in the paraphrase 'I and all my surroundings', and the sense in which it is equivalent to 'the way things are'? In part, I think, but it also has a deeper motivation. One might argue from thesis three – the indexical analysis of actuality – to the conclusion that the essential difference between our world and the others is that we are here, and not there.

Thesis three seems to imply that the actuality of the actual world – the attribute in virtue of which it is actual – is a world-relative attribute. It is an attribute which our world has relative to itself, but which all the other worlds have relative to themselves too; so the *concept* of actuality does not distinguish, from an absolute standpoint, the actual world from the others. But if there is no absolute property of actuality, does this not mean that, looking at things from an objective point of view, merely possible people and their surroundings are just as real as we and ours?

The mistake in this reasoning, I think, is in the assumption that the absolute standpoint is a neutral one, distinct from the view from within any possible world. The problem is avoided when one recognizes that the standpoint of the actual world *is* the absolute standpoint, and that it is part of the concept of actuality that this should be so. We can grant that fictional characters are as right, from their point of view, to affirm their fullblooded reality as we are to affirm ours. But their point of view is fictional, and so what is right from it makes no difference as far as reality is concerned.

My point is that the *semantical* thesis that the indexical analysis of 'actual' is correct can be separated from the metaphysical thesis that the actuality of the actual world is nothing more than a relation between it and things existing in it. Just as one could accept the indexical analysis of personal pronouns and be a solipsist, and accept the indexical analysis of tenses and believe that the past exists only as memory and the future only as anticipation, one can accept the indexical analysis of actuality while excluding from one's ontology any universes that *are* the way things might have been.

In fact, I want to argue, one must exclude those analogues of our universe from one's ontology. The thesis that the actual world alone is real is superficially analogous to solipsism – the thesis that I alone am real – but solipsism has content, and can be coherently denied, because it says something substantive about what alone is real. In effect, solipsism says that the actual world is a person, or a mind. But the thesis that the actual world alone is real has content only if 'the actual world' means something other than the totality of everything there is, and I do not believe that it does. The thesis that there is no room in reality for other things than the actual world is not, like solipsism, based on a restrictive theory of what there is room for in reality, but rather on the metaphysically neutral belief that 'the actual world' is just another name for reality.

So the moderate realism whose coherence I am trying to defend accepts theses one and three, and rejects thesis two. What about thesis four? If we identify possible worlds with ways things might have been, can we still hold that they are 'respectable entities in their own right', irreducible to anything more fundamental? Robert Adams has argued that to avoid extreme realism we must find an eliminative reduction of possible worlds. 'If there are any true statements in which there are said to be non-actual possible worlds,' he argues, 'they must be reducible to statements in which the only things there are said to be are things which are in the actual world, and which are not identical with non-actual possibles' ([1]: 224). Unless the reminder that by 'possible world' we mean nothing more than 'way things might have been' counts as such a reduction, I do not see why this should be necessary. Why cannot *ways things might have been* be elements of the actual world, as they are?

Two problems need to be separated: the first is the general worry that the notion of a possible world is a very obscure notion. How can explanations in terms of possible worlds help us to understand anything unless we are told what possible worlds are, and told in terms which are independent of the notions which possible worlds are intended to explain? The second problem is the specific problem that believing in possible worlds and in the indexical analysis of actuality seems to commit one to extreme realism, which (many believe) is obviously false. Now to point to the difference between a way our world might have been and a world which *is* the way our world might have been, and to make clear that the possible worlds whose existence the theory is committed to are the former kind of thing and not the latter, is to do nothing to solve the first problem; in fact it makes it more acute since it uses a modal operator to say what a possible world is. But this simple distinction does, I think, dissolve the second problem which was the motivation for Adams's demand for an analysis.

Not only is an eliminative reduction of possible worlds not necessary to solve the second problem, it also may not be sufficient to solve the first. I shall argue that the particular reduction that Adams proposes – a reduction of possible worlds to propositions – by itself says nothing that answers the critic who finds the concept of a possible world obscure. His reduction says no more, and in fact says less, about propositions and possible worlds than the reverse analysis that I would defend – the analysis of propositions in terms of possible worlds.

Adams's analysis is this: 'Let us say that a *world-story* is a maximal consistent set of propositions. That is, it is a set which has as its members one member of every pair of mutually contradictory propositions, and which is such that it is possible for all of its members to be true together. The notion of a possible world can be given a contextual analysis in terms of world-stories' ([1]: 225). For a proposition to be true in some or all possible worlds is for it to be a member of some or all world-stories. Other statements that seem to be about possible worlds are to be replaced in a similar way by statements about world-stories.

There are three undefined notions used in Adams's reduction of possible worlds: *proposition*, *possibility*, and *contradictory*. What are propositions? Adams leaves this question open for further discussion; he suggests that it might be answered in various ways. Little is said about them except that they are to be thought of as language independent abstract objects, presumably the potential objects of speech acts and propositional attitudes.

What is possibility? The notion used in the definition of world-story is a property of *sets* of propositions. Intuitively, a set of propositions is possible if all its members can be true together. This notion cannot, of course, be defined in terms of possible worlds, or world-stories, without circularity, but it should be a consequence of the theory that a set of propositions is possible if and only if its members are simultaneously true in some possible world (are all members of some world-story). Presumably, an explicit formulation of the world-story theory would contain postulates sufficient to ensure this.

What is a contradictory? This relation between propositions might be defined in terms of possibility as follows: A and B are contradictories if and only if $\{A, B\}$ is not possible, and for every possible set of propositions Γ either $\Gamma \cup \{A\}$ or $\Gamma \cup \{B\}$ is possible.* The theory tacitly assumes that every proposition has a contradictory; in an explicit formulation, this would be an additional postulate.

These definitions and postulates yield a minimal world-story theory. It is minimal in that it imposes no structure on the basic elements of the theory except what is required to justify what Adams calls the 'intuitively very plausible thesis that possibility is holistic rather than atomistic, in the sense that what is possible is possible only as part of a possible completely determinate world' ([1]: 225). But the theory justifies this thesis only by postulating it.

It will be useful to compare this reduction of possible worlds to propositions with the competing reduction of propositions to possible worlds. What is at stake in choosing which of these two notions to define in terms of the other? Adams refers to the 'not unfamiliar trade-off between non-actual possibles and intensions (such as propositions); given either, we may be able to construct the other, or do the work that was supposed to be done by talking about the other' ([1]: 228). But the two proposals are not equivalent. Part of what distinguishes them is an elusive question of conceptual priority, but there are also more substantive differences, both in the structure imposed on propositions and possible worlds and in the questions left to be answered by further developments of the respective theories.

---

* This definition may be understood as follows: 'A and B are contradictories if and only if (i) the set consisting of propositions A and B is not possible (sc. they cannot be true together, as explained in the previous paragraph), and (ii) for every set of propositions Γ which is possible in the sense explained, either the set containing the members of Γ plus A is possible or the set containing the members of Γ plus B is possible.' The effect of clause (i) is to ensure that A and B cannot both be true; the effect of clause (ii) is to ensure that one of them will fit compatibly into any possible story you like to tell, including any true story you tell. (Edd.)

If we set aside questions of conceptual priority – of which concepts and principles should be primitive and which defined or derived – what is the difference between the two analyses? The world-story theory is weaker, leaving open questions which are settled by the possible-worlds analysis of propositions. The following two theses are consequences of the possible-worlds analysis, but not of the world-story theory; the first concerns identity conditions; the second is a closure condition:

(I) Necessarily equivalent propositions are identical.
(C) For every set of propositions, there is a proposition which, necessarily, is true if and only if every member of the set is true.

Are these consequences of the possible-worlds analysis welcome or not? I believe that thesis (I) can be defended independently of the possible-worlds analysis of propositions, but that is a long story for another occasion. The thesis does have some notoriously problematic consequences, but I believe, first, that it is implied by a widely held and plausible assumption about the nature of propositional attitudes – the assumption that attitudes like belief and desire are dispositions of agents displayed in their rational behaviour – and second, that the apparently paradoxical consequences of the thesis can be explained away. But for now let me just point out that the possible-worlds analysis has this substantive consequence, and leave the part of my argument which depends on it conditional on the assumption that this consequence is welcome. The thesis is not implied by the minimal world-story theory, but it is compatible with it, so the world-story theorist who agrees with me about thesis (I) can add it to his theory as an additional postulate.

Thesis (C) seems reasonable on almost any theory of propositions and propositional attitudes. Whatever propositions are, if there are propositions at all then there are sets of them, and for any set of propositions, it is something determinately true or false that all the members of the set are true. If one is willing to talk of propositions at all, one will surely conclude that that something is a proposition. It may not be possible to express all such propositions since it may not be possible, in any actual language, to refer to all such sets; it may not be humanly possible to believe or disbelieve some such propositions, since it may not be humanly possible to grasp them. But if this is so, it is surely a contingent human limitation which should not restrict the range of potential objects of propositional attitudes. So I will assume that the world-story theorist will want to add thesis (C) to his theory.

If (I) and (C) are added as postulates to the minimal world-story theory, then it becomes equivalent to the possible-worlds analysis with respect to the structure it imposes on the set of propositions, and on the relation between propositions and possible worlds. The sole difference that remains between the two theories is that one takes as primitive what the other defines. And even this difference will be eliminated if we make one more change in response to a question about the further development of the world-story theory.

The next question for the world-story theorist is this: can he say more about his fundamental concept, the concept of a proposition? In particular, are there some *basic* propositions out of which all the rest can be constructed? The usual way to answer this question is to model basic propositions on the atomic sentences of a first order language; propositions are constructed out of individuals and primitive properties and relations in the same way that sentences are constructed out of names and predicates. But this strategy requires building further structure into the theory. There is another way to answer the question which needs no further assumption. We can deduce from what has already been built into the world-story theory that there is a set of propositions of which all propositions are truth-functions: this is the set of strongest contingent propositions – those propositions which are members of just one world-story. It is thus a harmless change, a matter of giving the theory a more economical formulation, to take these to be the basic propositions. (This change does not foreclose a further reduction of what are here called basic propositions. Any alternative reduction could be expressed as a further reduction; this is why the move is harmless.) We can then define propositions generally as sets of basic propositions (or, for a neater formulation, call the basic elements *propositional elements* and let their unit sets be the basic propositions). A non-basic proposition will be true just in case one of its members is true. This reduction has the added advantage that it allows us to define the previously primitive property of possibility, and to derive all of the postulates. With these primitive notions and assumptions eliminated, the world-story theory looks as good as the theory that takes possible worlds as primitive and defines propositions. This is, of course, because it is exactly the same theory.

I have gone through this exercise of changing the world-story theory into the possible-worlds analysis of propositions in order to make the following point: first, the minimal world-story theory with which I began is indeed a minimal theory of propositions, a theory that assumes nothing about them except that they have truth values and are related to each other by the standard propositional relations (entailment, compatibility, and so forth). But second, every step in the metamorphosis of this minimal theory into the possible-worlds analysis is motivated by independently plausible assumptions about propositions or by theory-neutral considerations of economy of formulation. If this is right, then the possible-worlds analysis is not just one theory which makes the assumptions about propositions that I have made. More than this, it is the whole content of that analysis to impose the minimal structure on propositions which is appropriate to a theory which understands propositions in this way. Anyone who believes that there are objects of propositional attitudes, and who accepts the assumptions about the formal properties of the set of these objects, must accept that there are things which have all the properties that the possible-worlds theory attributes to possible worlds, and that propositions can be reduced to these things.

Is the form of realism about possible worlds that I want to defend really realism? It is in the sense that it claims that the concept of a possible world is a basic concept in a true account of the way we represent the world in our propositional acts and attitudes. A full defence of this kind of realism would require a development and defence of such an account. All I have tried to do here is show that there is a coherent thesis about possible worlds which rejects extreme realism, but which takes possible worlds seriously as irreducible entities, a thesis that treats possible worlds as more than a convenient myth or a notational shortcut, but less than universes that resemble our own.

Notes

1. Robert Merrihew Adams, 'Theories of Actuality', *Noûs*, xvii (1974): 211-31.

2. David Lewis, *Counterfactuals* (Cambridge, Mass.: Harvard University Press, 1973).

3. J. L. Mackie, *Truth, Probability and Paradox* (Oxford: Clarendon Press, 1973).

4. Lawrence Powers, 'Comments' on R. Stalnaker, 'Propositions', *Issues in the Philosophy of Language*, Proceedings of the 1972 Oberlin Colloquium in Philosophy, edd. Alfred F. MacKay and Daniel D. Merrill (New Haven: Yale University Press, 1976), pp. 93-103.

Acknowledgement

I am indebted to the John Simon Guggenheim Memorial Foundation for support during the time when this paper was written.

Biographical Note

Robert Stalnaker is Professor of Philosophy at Cornell University; he previously taught at Yale University and at the University of Illinois at Urbana. He has published a number of articles in the areas of logical theory and the philosophy of language.

Further Reading

Besides the references listed at the end of the paper, mention may be made of two articles: R. H. Thomason, 'Modal Logic and Metaphysics', in *The Logical Way of Doing Things*, ed. Karel Lambert (New Haven: Yale University Press, 1969), pp. 119-46; Dana Scott, 'Advice on Modal Logic', in *Philosophical Problems in Logic*, ed. Karel Lambert (Dordrecht: Reidel, 1970), pp. 143-73.

Stalnaker's paper on 'Propositions', mentioned in the Introduction, may be found in *Issues in the Philosophy of Language*, Proceedings of the 1972 Oberlin Colloquium in Philosophy, edd. Alfred F. MacKay and Daniel D. Merrill (New Haven: Yale University Press, 1976), pp. 79-91, where it is followed by 'Comments' by Lawrence Powers.

The reader who wants to find out about modal logic may consult G. E. Hughes and M. J. Cresswell, *An Introduction to Modal Logic* (London: Methuen, 1968).

Saul Kripke

Identity and Necessity

The paper now before us, Saul Kripke's 'Identity and Necessity', is a shorter and simpler version of one of the most widely discussed contributions to recent philosophy: Kripke's essay on 'Naming and Necessity' (see bibliography). The topics mentioned in these titles – identity, names, necessity – belong to logical theory and the philosophy of language, but Kripke's treatment of them has far-reaching implications for other areas of philosophy. One bonus of the shorter and more manageable paper we print here is that these implications stand out more clearly.

Even in the shorter version the argument is a lengthy one. The reader has to familiarize himself with some radically new ideas in logical theory and the philosophy of language and then be ready to apply them to problems in the philosophy of science and the philosophy of mind. We believe that the argument is worth the sustained attention it demands, not only for the intrinsic interest of its results, but also for the way it illuminates the commanding position occupied by logical theory and the philosophy of language with respect to other areas of philosophy. Problems in these latter areas typically turn out to involve highly general notions such as identity and necessity, which are the special province of the former. New theories of identity and necessity, therefore, bring with them new views about other things: for example, a changed perspective on the age-old problem of the relation of mind and body.

To set the scene for the argument ahead we need briefly to introduce two of the most hallowed distinctions in philosophy: the distinction between necessary and contingent and that between *a priori* and *a posteriori*. We may follow the elucidation Kripke himself gives on p. 493, which takes the distinctions as they apply to truths or true statements.

A necessary truth is simply a true statement which could not have been false; the statement is necessarily true because it is impossible for it not to be true. A statement, on the other hand, which is in fact true but might not have been – the world could have been such as to make it false – is contingently true. For example, '2 + 2 = 4' states a necessary truth, 'Elephants have long memories' a contingent one – here it is easy to see that elephants might not have had long memories, and equally easy to see that there is no possibility at all of 2 + 2 not amounting to 4. The classification of a truth as necessary or contingent is not always so straightforward as it is in these cases, but it is best to come to the distinction through a perspicuous example of it. (Readers familiar with the once common philosophical claim that necessarily true statements are *analytic,* true by virtue solely of their meaning, should be warned that as Kripke understands necessity it has nothing to do with analyticity. For the purpose of grasping his argument, thoughts or preconceptions about the highly problematic and controversial analytic/synthetic distinction are best shelved; they may be pursued later with some of the material mentioned in the bibliography.)

Next, the distinction between *a priori* and *a posteriori.* This has to do with knowledge, specifically with whether or not a statement can be known to be true independently of our having experience of the world. A statement is *a posteriori* if it can only be known to be true on the basis of observation or, more generally, experience of the world as it actually is. An example of a type which will concern us below is the statement 'The Morning Star is identical with the Evening Star', or 'Phosphorus is identical with Hesperus', a truth whose discovery in early times required both observation and reflection. By contrast, no reference to facts of observation or experience is needed to establish the truth of the trivial identity 'The Morning Star is identical with the Morning Star', or 'Phosphorus is identical with Phosphorus'. This then, is *a priori*, and so also is the less trivial statement '2 + 2 = 4' which earlier served us as an example of necessary truth. That too is clearly a statement which can be known to be true without reference to facts of observation and experience, while our contingent statement 'Elephants have long memories' is *a posteriori.*

Now it has been a common belief among philosophers that, just as '2 + 2 = 4' is both necessary and *a priori* and 'Elephants have long memories' is both contingent and *a posteriori,* so, more generally, *any* true statement can be classified either as necessary and *a priori* or as contingent and *a posteriori.* That is to say, the two distinctions coincide.

Kripke does not share this view, and one major purpose of his paper is to argue against it. The two distinctions, he maintains, 'belong to different domains of philosophy. One of them has something to do with *knowledge*, with what can be known in certain ways about the actual world. The other has to do with *metaphysics*, with how the world *could* have been' (p. 494). In particular, Kripke argues for the existence of a class of identity statements which are necessary but yet *a posteriori* rather than *a priori*.

What this means is that there are identity statements which are true and necessarily so – they could not have failed to be true – but which we can only *know* to be true on the basis of observation and experience of the actual world. One example we have already met: 'The Morning Star is identical with the Evening Star'. Not only is this statement, as already noted, *a posteriori*; it is also, Kripke argues, a necessary truth. And this realignment of traditional categories turns out to have quite radical consequences. Kripke suggests, for example, that it will help us to prove that the identity theory of mind and body is false. But before we can follow him into the broader reaches of metaphysics, we need to retrace our steps and get a sense of the logical problems surrounding statements of identity.

Philosophical discussion of statements of identity has typically been oriented towards the question 'How are *contingent* statements of identity possible?', the classic example of such a statement being 'The Morning Star is identical with the Evening Star'. This has been taken to be a contingent statement because it is undoubtedly (as already explained) *a posteriori* and relatively few philosophers have been able to resist the idea that the distinction between necessary and contingent and the distinction between *a priori* and *a posteriori* coincide; if a statement is *a posteriori* they conclude it is also contingent. But for Kripke, for whom 'The Morning Star is identical with the Evening Star' is necessary, even though it is *a posteriori*, the problem of identity statements takes a rather different form. The difference shows itself in his response to the line of reasoning he sets out on pp. 478–9, a line of reasoning which has usually been regarded as presenting a difficulty for the possibility of contingent identity statements, and hence a difficulty to be circumvented or resolved. Kripke, however, regards it as a valid argument from true premises to a perfectly acceptable conclusion.

The argument, which in the text is formally expressed in symbolic notation, can be read as follows.

(1) Take any objects x and y such that x is identical with y: then, if x has a certain property F, y also has F.

(2) Take any object x whatsoever: necessarily, x is identical with x.

(3) Take, as in (1), any objects x and y such that x is identical with y, and let F be the property of necessarily being identical with x: applying premise (1), we see that if x has this property, y has it too.

But, (2) tells us that any object x has the property of necessarily being identical with x.

Hence (4), given any objects x and y such that x is identical with y, not only does x have the property of necessarily being identical with x [by (2)] but y has it also [by (3)]. That is, *any* object y which is identical with x is necessarily identical with x.

Some terminology. Premise (1), which Kripke calls the law of the substitutivity of identity, states the indiscernibility of identicals – things identical with each other have all their properties in common – and is often regarded as conveying an essential part of the meaning of identity. What it implies is that the identity of x and y is a licence to take any truth about x, such as that x has the property F, as equally a truth about y: y may be interchanged for x without loss of truth.

Premise (2) derives from the law of identity, which states that every object is identical with itself or *self-identical*. It appears here with the *modal operator* 'necessarily', so as to say that every object is *necessarily* identical with itself. ('Necessarily' is symbolized '$\Box$', which may also be read 'it is necessary that ...'; the symbol for possibility, which appears in some of the notes, is '$\Diamond$'.)

Step (3) is the indiscernibility of identicals again but applied to a specific property: the *modal property* of necessarily-being-identical-with-x. (Modal operator and modal property are so called because necessity and possibility are known as *modalities*.) This modal property is taken *de re* (the phrase is first used on p. 480), which means: the property is taken to belong to the actual object x in exactly the same way as any ordinary property like being yellow or having a long memory, and regardless of how x is picked out or designated in language. Not all philosophers would agree that it is legitimate to understand modal properties in this way. Some hold that modal properties belong to things only as these are picked out or designated in a particular way; this is known as the *de dicto* interpretation of modality. The classic example is Quine's: the number 9, so designated, has the property of necessarily being greater than 7, but that same number designated (correctly enough) as the number of the planets does not. It makes all the difference how the number is picked out: '9 is greater than 7' is a necessary truth, 'The number of the planets is greater than 7' is a contingent one, since it is only a contingent truth, which might have been otherwise, that our solar system contains as many as 9 planets. Thus on the *de dicto* interpretation, modality belongs rather to language, to the way we speak about things, than to the actual things we speak about. But nothing is said in (1)–(4) about picking out x and y by one designation rather than another. The argument takes x and y as they are and concludes that if x and y (however designated) are the same object, it is necessary that they be so. This, then, is necessity *de re*, necessity attributed to the things themselves.

We are now ready for the question how best to respond to the line of reasoning set forth and explained above. How does it bear on the possibility of contingent identity statements? Kripke's first point (p. 480) is that the argument does not bear directly on that issue at all. Since the argument deals throughout with necessity *de re*, its conclusion (4) says nothing about language, about statements as such. It does not deny that contingent identity statements are possible. Nevertheless, since (4) does say that if x and y are the same object, it is necessary that x and y are the same object, the question remains whether (4) is compatible with the existence of contingent identity statements, and if it is, how to make the compatibility perspicuous.

Kripke replies to this question by taking different types of identity statement one by one. We may distinguish three types.

(A) Identity statements which join two individuating descriptions: 'The first Postmaster General of the United States is identical with the inventor of bifocals' (in note 4 this type is symbolized '$\imath x Gx = \imath x Hx$', which may be read: 'The x which is G is identical with the x which is H').

(B) Identity statements which join two proper names: 'Cicero is Tully' (in symbols, '$a = b$').

(C) Theoretical identifications: 'Heat is the motion of molecules' or, more controversially, 'Pain is a certain state of the brain'.

It is Kripke's contention that type (A) alone supplies examples of contingent identity statements. Identity statements of types (B) and (C) are, if true, necessarily true; and the same holds, as we shall see, of certain examples from type (A). His task, therefore, is first to show how the contingency of the contingent cases from type (A) may be reconciled with his acceptance of (4), and second to defend his account of types (B) and (C).

The first point is quickly settled on pp. 481–2 by invoking a distinction, due to Bertrand Russell, having to do with the notion of the scope of a description. This distinction can be grasped intuitively, without entering into technical details, by reflecting on the difference between

(A)′ Just one thing x was the first Postmaster General of the United States and just one thing y was the inventor of bifocals and it is necessary that $x = y$

and

(A)″ It is necessary that just one thing x was the first Postmaster General of the United States and just one thing y was the inventor of bifocals and $x = y$.

Notice the different positions of the modal operator 'it is necessary that . . .' in the two sentences. In the second sentence (A)″, it is so placed as to say or imply that the statement 'The first Postmaster General of the United States is identical with the inventor of bifocals' is necessary. The upshot of (A)″ is that the two descriptions *necessarily* designate one and the same thing. Not so (A)′: all that tells us is, first, that a certain thing x is, as a matter of fact, designated by the description 'The first Postmaster General' and a certain thing y is, as a matter of fact, designated by the description 'The inventor of bifocals', and second, that x and y themselves are necessarily identical with one another. What is said to be necessary here is the identity of x and y; it is not said to be necessary that the first Postmaster General is identical with the inventor of bifocals. So (A)′ is compatible with the claim that the latter identity is contingent. It obviously is contingent that the first Postmaster General should be the same man as the inventor of bifocals. But this is quite compatible with the argument (1)–(4) because, given that the first Postmaster General is, in fact, the same as the inventor of bifocals, what the argument then allows us to infer is the unobjectionable consequence (A)′, not the contingency-denying proposition (A)″. (In technical terms, the descriptions in (A)″ have small scope and are governed by the modal operator, in (A)′ they have large scope, over the whole sentence, for they occur in front of the modal operator and are not governed by it.)

To come now to identity statements of types (B) and (C). Some standard arguments are rehearsed on pp. 484–7 for supposing that various examples of these two types are contingently true, but the arguments all rest on the (perfectly correct) claim that the discovery of the relevant identities was empirical, a matter of observation and experience; this establishes that the identities are *a posteriori*, but in the light of the sharp cleavage Kripke is going to make between being *a posteriori* and being contingent, it is obviously not enough to show that they are contingent. There is thus room for Kripke to argue that they are in fact necessary.

At this point we need one more distinction, a distinction of Kripke's own between *rigid* and *nonrigid designators*. Consider the two questions, 'Might someone else have been the inventor of bifocals – someone other than the man who in fact was the inventor of bifocals?' and 'Might someone else have been Richard Nixon – someone other than the man who in fact is Richard Nixon?' The answer to the first question is clearly 'Yes'. The answer to the second question, on the other hand, is 'No'. (Someone who doubts this may be confusing it with the quite different question 'Might Richard Nixon have been another *sort* of person from the person he in fact is?'.) The affirmative answer to the first question tells us that the expression 'The inventor of bifocals' is a nonrigid designator, meaning that it might have designated something other than it actually designates, and this not in the trivial sense in which *any* linguistic expression might have been differently used and might consequently have meant something different, but in the substantive sense that the *world* might have been such that a different object answered to the description 'The inventor of bifocals' as that is presently used in our language. This is because a description like 'The inventor of bifocals' means '*whoever* it is that invented bifocals', and it depends on the contingent course of events who that turns out to be. It is not, on the other hand, contingent but necessary that 5 is the number which is the square root of 25 – this could not be otherwise – so the description 'The square root of 25' is a rigid designator; and in 'Naming and Necessity' Kripke envisages further, more controversial examples such as 'The father of Elizabeth the Second'.

This is the explanation of the point alluded to earlier, that some type (A) identity statements are necessary. 'The square root of 25 is the cube root of 125' joins two individuating descriptions, so it is of type (A); but these descriptions are rigid designators, so the statement is necessarily true if it is true at all. A non-mathematical example (involving controversial views about the necessity of a thing's having the origin it has which Kripke develops in 'Naming and Necessity' and touches on here pp. 495 ff) would be 'The mother of Hamlet is the same person as the mother of Ophelia'. Given that it is necessary that Hamlet had the mother he had (it would not have been 'Hamlet' had a person exactly like him been born to different parents), and similarly for Ophelia, the descriptions 'the mother of Hamlet' and 'the mother of Ophelia' are rigid designators. So the type (A) identity statement 'The mother of Hamlet is the same person as the mother of Ophelia', if it is true, is necessarily true.

Turning now to proper names, it is Kripke's view that a proper name does not mean 'whoever has such and such properties' (see on this point pp. 500–502; in 'Naming and Necessity' he argues at length against theories which hold that a proper name is equivalent to a set of descriptions). A proper name refers directly to the thing it has been assigned to. Hence to ask whether the world might have been such that a different object answered to the name 'Richard Nixon' *as that is presently used in our language*, is to ask whether someone or something else might have been Richard Nixon; it is to ask whether Richard Nixon might have failed to be himself, and that is impossible. So 'Richard Nixon', and proper names generally, are rigid designators. No matter how different the world might have been, it could not have been different in such a way that someone else was Richard Nixon and therefore was rightly called 'Richard Nixon'. Or, to put the same point in the jargon of possible worlds: there is no possible world in which 'Richard Nixon' designates someone other than he who is actually Richard Nixon. There may be possible worlds (possible conditions of the actual world) in which 'Richard Nixon' does not designate anything because Richard Nixon does not exist. But if he exists, it is he and no one else who is Richard Nixon and who is therefore picked out by the name 'Richard Nixon' as we now use it. No other object could answer to the name, which is thus a rigid designator; it designates the same thing in all possible worlds in which it designates at all.

Now let 'a' and 'b' be rigid designators as thus defined. As rigid designators, 'a' designates the same object in all possible worlds and so does 'b'. If it is one and the same object which they both designate, they both designate it in all possible worlds in which they designate at all. Thus the identity statement '$a = b$', if it is true, is true in all possible worlds (sc. all possible worlds in which a – that is, b – exists). There is no possible world, i.e. there could be no condition of the actual world, in which $a \neq b$. Hence, if '$a = b$' is true, it is necessarily true.

It is important to grasp that this conclusion follows directly from the characterization of rigid designators. Given the distinction between rigid and nonrigid designators as Kripke expounds it, it is true, as he claims on p. 498, that there can be no question but that identity statements which join rigid designators are, if true, necessary. The substantive question is whether ordinary proper names, on the one hand, and the terms involved in theoretical identifications on the other, are rigid designators. Kripke holds that they are, and he defends that claim at greater length in 'Naming and Necessity'. But it is a perfectly proper test of the claim to consider whether one is willing to be persuaded of its consequence, that true identity statements of type (B), joining proper names, and of type (C), making theoretical identifications, are necessary. It is this consequence which Kripke goes on to defend and clarify, on pp. 498–502 for type (B) identities, and on pp. 502–5 for type (C).

Essentially, the argument is a challenge. An opponent who is tempted to think that Cicero might not have been Tully, or that heat might not have been molecular motion, is challenged to imagine and describe such a possibility in terms which are consistent with the designators involved retaining their present use. And the crux of the argument is Kripke's contention that – to take the type (C) example – it will not suffice to sketch a story in which sentient humans get *the sensation of heat* (the particular qualitative sensation we now call 'the sensation of heat') from something other than molecular motion, or perhaps from nothing at all. No doubt we identify heat via the sensation we get from it, and it certainly is contingent that molecular motion should be the thing which gives us this sensation. (Kripke imagines some Martians differently constituted from us, who might get the very sensation we call 'the sensation of heat' from things we experience as cold, and philosophers of the sceptical tradition used to illustrate the variety of actual human experience by citing the case of Demophon, butler to Alexander the Great, who would shiver in the sun or a hot bath, but felt warm in the shade.) But none of this means it is contingent that molecular motion is heat. To suppose otherwise is to overlook the important point (first made on pp. 500–501 for the type (B) case) that to use a nonrigidly designating description such as 'the thing which produces such and such a sensation in normal humans' *to fix the reference* of a name (rigid designator) such as 'heat' is simply to identify, via one of its contingent properties, the object which the name is to designate. It is not to make the name synonymous with the description, with the result that 'heat' then *means* 'whatever produces such and such a sensation in normal humans'. If that were so, then indeed it would be contingent that molecular motion is heat, since it is undoubtedly contingent that molecular motion is the thing which produces that particular qualitative sensation in us. But if the fact that molecular motion produces this sensation is merely used to fix the reference of 'heat', and once attached to its object 'heat' is a rigid designator, then it is necessary, not contingent, that heat is molecular motion. The illusion of contingency arises from confusing this identity with the distinct and genuinely contingent fact that molecular motion is what produces a particular qualitative sensation in normal humans.

We are now equipped, at last, to deal with the more controversial identities involved in the mind–body problem (pp. 505–7). In recent years a number of theorists have taken the view that one is well on the way to solving the traditional mind–body problem if one regards statements to the effect that pain (in general) is a certain state (perhaps a very complex state) of the brain or nervous system, or to the effect that some particular pain is a certain particular state of a particular brain or nervous system – statements whose truth, it is supposed, science has or will one day have established – as identity statements. The appeal of this solution is its economy. It dispenses with the mental as an ontological category additional to physical things. It is readily conceded that the identities are not necessary. Pain could have been some other state or event than science finds it to be. But that is no objection, says the identity theorist, for the identity is a contingent one, as the identities which science discovers commonly are – and here he appeals to the model of type (C) statements such as 'Heat is molecular motion', taking these to be contingent.

Kripke's counter-argument is simple (it is conveniently summarized in note 18), but it has the whole weight of the preceding discussion behind it. He agrees that theoretical identifications of type (C) are the right model for the mind–body case, but, as we have seen, about these he holds that when they are true, they are necessarily true. Hence, he argues, if the identity theorist's identification of pain with a certain bodily state was true, it would have to be necessarily true. But it is not necessarily true. (This the identity theorist has accepted all along, and Kripke reinforces the point with further argument, to prevent his opponent changing tack and suggesting that the identity is necessary after all – pp. 505–7.) Therefore, the identity is not true at all. Construed as an identity statement, 'Pain is a certain state of the brain or nervous system' is false. Alternatively, if the sentence expresses a truth which science has or will one day have discovered, it is not an identity. Either way, it is argued, the identity theorist's solution to the mind–body problem collapses.

M.F.B.

Saul Kripke

Identity and Necessity[1]

A problem which has arisen frequently in contemporary philosophy is: 'How are *contingent* identity statements possible?' This question is phrased by analogy with the way Kant phrased his question 'How are synthetic *a priori* judgements possible?' In both cases, it has usually been taken for granted, in the one case by Kant that synthetic *a priori* judgements were possible, and in the other case in contemporary philosophical literature, that contingent statements of identity are possible. I do not intend to deal with the Kantian question except to mention this analogy: After a rather thick book was written trying to answer the question how synthetic *a priori* judgements were possible, others came along later who claimed that the solution to the problem was that synthetic *a priori* judgements were, of course, impossible and that a book trying to show otherwise was written in vain. I will not discuss who was right on the possibility of synthetic *a priori* judgements. But in the case of contingent statements of identity, most philosophers have felt that the notion of a contingent identity statement ran into something like the following paradox. An argument like the following can be given against the possibility of contingent identity statements:

First, the law of the substitutivity of identity says that, for any objects x and y, if x is identical to y, then if x has a certain property F, so does y:

(1) $(x)(y) [(x = y) \supset (Fx \supset Fy)]$

On the other hand, every object surely is necessarily self-identical:

(2) $(x) \square (x = x)$

But

(3) $(x)(y) (x = y) \supset [\Box (x = x) \supset \Box (x = y)]$

is a substitution instance of (1), the substitutivity law. From (2) and (3), we can conclude that, for every x and y, if x equals y, then, it is necessary that x equals y:

(4) $(x)(y) ((x = y) \supset \Box (x = y))$

This is because the clause $\Box (x = x)$ of the conditional drops out because it is known to be true.

This is an argument which has been stated many times in recent philosophy. Its conclusion, however, has often been regarded as highly paradoxical. For example, David Wiggins, in his paper, 'Identity-Statements', says,

> Now there undoubtedly exist contingent identity-statements. Let $a = b$ be one of them. From its simple truth and (5) [= (4) above] we can derive '$\Box(a = b)$'. But how then can there be any contingent identity statements?[2]

He then says that five various reactions to this argument are possible, and rejects all of these reactions, and reacts himself. I do not want to discuss all the possible reactions to this statement, except to mention the second of those Wiggins rejects. This says,

> We might accept the result and plead that provided 'a' and 'b' are proper names nothing is amiss. The consequence of this is that no contingent identity-statements can be made by means of proper names.

And then he says that he is discontented with this solution and many other philosophers have been discontented with this solution, too, while still others have advocated it.

What makes the statement (4) seem surprising? It says, for any objects x and y, if x is y, then it is necessary that x is y. I have already mentioned that someone might object to this argument on the grounds that premise (2) is already false, that it is not the case that everything is necessarily self-identical. Well, for example, am I myself necessarily self-identical? Someone might argue that in some situations which we can imagine I would not even have existed and there-fore the statement 'Saul Kripke is Saul Kripke' would have been false or it would not be the case that I was self-identical. Perhaps, it would have been neither true nor false, in such a world, to say that Saul Kripke is self-identical. Well, that may be so, but really it depends on one's philosophical view of a topic that I will not discuss, that is, what is to be said about truth values of statements mentioning objects that do not exist in the actual world or any given possible world or counterfactual situation. Let us interpret necessity here weakly. We can count statements as necessary if whenever the objects mentioned therein exist, the statement would be true. If we wished to be very careful about this, we would have to go into the question of existence as a predicate and ask if the statement can be reformulated in the form: For every x it is necessary that, if x exists, then x is self-identical. I will not go into this particular form of subtlety here because it is not going to be relevant to my main theme. Nor am I really going to consider formula (4). Anyone who believes formula (2) is, in my opinion, committed to formula (4). If x and y are the same things and we can talk about modal properties of an object at all, that is, in the usual parlance, we can speak of modality *de re* and an object *necessarily* having certain properties as such, then formula (1), I think, has to hold. Where x is any property at all, including a property involving modal operators, and if x and y are the same object and x had a certain property F, then y has to have the same property F. And this is so even if the property F is itself of the form of necessarily having some other property G, in particular that of necessarily being identical to a certain object. Well, I will not discuss the formula (4) itself because by itself it does not assert, of any particular true statement of identity, that it is necessary. It does not say anything about *statements* at all. It says for every *object* x and *object* y, if x and y are the same object, then it is necessary that x and y are the same object. And this, I think, if we think about it (anyway, if someone does not think so, I will not argue for it here), really amounts to something very little different from the statement (2). Since x, by definition of identity, is the only object identical with x, '$(y)(y = x \supset Fy)$' seems to me to be little more than a garrulous way of saying 'Fx', and thus $(x)\,(y)(y = x \supset Fx)$ says the same as $(x)Fx$ no matter what 'F' is – in particular, even if 'F' stands for the property of necessary identity with x.* So if x has this property (of necessary identity with x), trivially everything identical with x has it, as (4) asserts. But, from statement (4) one may apparently be able to deduce various particular statements of identity must be necessary and this is then supposed to be a very paradoxical consequence.

Wiggins says, 'Now there undoubtedly exist contingent identity statements.' One example of a contingent identity statement is the statement that the first Postmaster General of the United States is identical with the inventor of bifocals, or that both of these are identical with the man claimed by the *Saturday Evening Post* as its founder (*falsely* claimed, I gather, by the way). Now some such statements are plainly contingent. It plainly is a contingent fact that one and the same man both invented bifocals and took on the job of Postmaster General of the United States. How can we reconcile this with the truth of statement (4)? Well, that, too, is an issue I do not want to go into in detail except to be very dogmatic about it. It was I think settled quite well by Bertrand Russell in his notion of the scope of a description. According to Russell, one can, for example, say with propriety that the author of *Hamlet* might not have written '*Hamlet*', or even that the author of *Hamlet* might not have been the author of '*Hamlet*'. Now here, of course, we do not deny the necessity of the identity of an object with itself; but we say it is true concerning a certain man that he in fact was the unique person to have written '*Hamlet*' and secondly that the man, who in fact was the man who wrote '*Hamlet*', might not have written '*Hamlet*'. In other words, if Shakespeare had decided not to write tragedies, he might not have written '*Hamlet*'. Under these circumstances, the man who in fact wrote '*Hamlet*' would not have written '*Hamlet*'. Russell brings this out by saying that in such a statement, the first occurrence of the description 'the author of "*Hamlet*"' has large scope.[3] That is, we say 'The author of "*Hamlet*" has the following property: that he

---

* The foregoing sentence can be paraphrased as follows: 'Since x, by definition of identity, is the only object identical with x, "Any object y which is identical with x has the property F" seems to me to be little more than a garrulous way of saying "x has the property F", and thus "Take any object x: any object y which is identical with x has the property F" says the same as "Any object x has the property F" no matter what "F" is – in particular, even if "F" stands for the property of necessary identity with x' (Edd.).

might not have written "*Hamlet*"'. We *do not* assert that the following statement might have been the case, namely that the author of '*Hamlet*' did not write '*Hamlet*', for that is not true. That would be to say that it might have been the case that someone wrote '*Hamlet*' and yet did not write '*Hamlet*', which would be a contradiction. Now, aside from the details of Russell's particular formulation of it, which depends on his theory of descriptions, this seems to be the distinction that any theory of descriptions has to make. For example, if someone were to meet the President of Harvard and take him to be a Teaching Fellow, he might say: 'I took the President of Harvard for a Teaching Fellow'. By this he does not mean that he took the proposition 'The President of Harvard is a Teaching Fellow' to be true. He could have meant this, for example, had he believed that some sort of democratic system had gone so far at Harvard that the President of it decided to take on the task of being a Teaching Fellow. But that probably is not what he means. What he means instead, as Russell points out, is 'Someone is President of Harvard and I took him to be a Teaching Fellow'. In one of Russell's examples someone says, 'I thought your yacht is much larger than it is'. And the other man replies, 'No, my yacht is not much larger than it is'.

Provided that the notion of modality *de re*, and thus of quantifying into modal contexts, makes any sense at all, we have quite an adequate solution to the problem of avoiding paradoxes if we substitute descriptions for the universal quantifiers in (4) because the only consequence we will draw,[4] for example, in the bifocals case, is that there is a man who both happened to have invented bifocals and happened to have been the first Postmaster General of the United States, and is necessarily self-identical. There is an object x such that x invented bifocals, and as a matter of contingent fact an object y, such that y is the first Postmaster General of the United States, and finally, it is necessary, that x is y. What are x and y here? Here, x and y are both Benjamin Franklin, and it can certainly be necessary that Benjamin Franklin is identical with himself. So, there is no problem in the case of descriptions if we accept Russell's notion of scope.[5] And I just dogmatically want to drop that question here and go on to the question about names which Wiggins raises. And Wiggins says he might accept the result and plead that, provided *a* and *b* are proper names, nothing is amiss. And then he rejects this.

Now what is the special problem about proper names? At least if one is not familiar with the philosophical literature about this matter, one naïvely feels something like the following about proper names. First, if someone says 'Cicero was an orator', then he uses the name 'Cicero' in that statement simply to pick out a certain object and then to ascribe a certain property to the object, namely, in this case, he ascribes to a certain man the property of having been an orator. If someone else uses another name, such as say 'Tully', he is still speaking about the same man. One ascribes the same property, if one says 'Tully is an orator', to the same man. So to speak, the fact, or state of affairs, represented by the statement is the same whether one says 'Cicero is an orator' or one says 'Tully is an orator'. It would, therefore, seem that the function of names is *simply* to refer, and not to describe the objects so named by such properties as 'being the inventor of bifocals' or 'being the first Postmaster General'. It would seem that Leibniz's law and the law (1) should not only hold in the universally quantified form, but also in the form 'if $a = b$ and Fa, then Fb', wherever '*a*' and '*b*' stand in place of names and '*F*' stands in place of a predicate expressing a genuine property of the object:

$$(a = b \cdot Fa) \supset Fb\star$$

We can run the same argument through again to obtain the conclusion where '*a*' and '*b*' replace any names, 'if $a = b$, then necessarily $a = b$'. And so, we could venture this conclusion: that whenever '*a*' and '*b*' are proper names, if *a* is *b*, that it is necessary that *a* is *b*. Identity statements between proper names have to be necessary if they are going to be true at all. This view in fact has been advocated, for example, by Ruth Barcan Marcus in a paper of hers on the philosophical interpretation of modal logic.[6] According to this view, whenever, for example, someone makes a correct statement of identity between two names, such as, for example, that Cicero is Tully, his statement has to be necessary if it is true. But such a conclusion

★ The formula can be read thus: 'If *a* is identical with *b* and *a* has the property *F*, then *b* has the property *F*' (Edd.).

seems plainly to be false. (I, like other philosophers, have a habit of understatement in which 'it seems plainly false' means 'it is plainly false'. Actually, I think the view is true, though not quite in the form defended by Mrs Marcus.) At any rate, it seems plainly false. One example was given by Professor Quine in his reply to Professor Marcus at the symposium: 'I think I see trouble anyway in the contrast between proper names and descriptions as Professor Marcus draws it. The paradigm of the assigning of proper names is tagging. We may tag the planet Venus some fine evening with the proper name "Hesperus". We may tag the same planet again someday before sunrise with the proper name "Phosphorus".' (Quine thinks that something like that actually was done once.) 'When, at last, we discover that we have tagged the same planet twice, our discovery is empirical, and not because the proper names were descriptions.' According to what we are told, the planet Venus seen in the morning was originally thought to be a star and was called 'the Morning Star', or (to get rid of any question of using a description) was called 'Phosphorus'. One and the same planet, when seen in the evening, was thought to be another star, the Evening Star, and was called 'Hesperus'. Later on, astronomers discovered that Phosphorus and Hesperus were one and the same. Surely no amount of *a priori* ratiocination on their part could conceivably have made it possible for them to deduce that Phosphorus is Hesperus. In fact, given the information they had, it might have turned out the other way. Therefore, it is argued, the statement 'Hesperus is Phosphorus' has to be an ordinary contingent, empirical truth, one which might have come out otherwise, and so the view that true identity statements between names are necessary has to be false. Another example which Quine gives in *Word and Object* is taken from Professor Schrödinger, the famous pioneer of quantum mechanics: A certain mountain can be seen from both Tibet and Nepal. When seen from one direction it was called 'Gaurisanker'; when seen from another direction, it was called 'Everest'; and then, later on, the empirical discovery was made that Gaurisanker *is* Everest. (Quine further says that he gathers the example is actually geographically incorrect. I guess one should not rely on physicists for geographical information.)

Of course, one possible reaction to this argument is to deny that names like 'Cicero', 'Tully', 'Gaurisanker', and 'Everest' really are proper names. Look, someone might say (someone has said it: his name was 'Bertrand Russell'), just because statements like 'Hesperus is Phosphorus' and 'Gaurisanker is Everest' are contingent, we can see that the names in question are not really purely referential. You are not, in Mrs Marcus's phrase, just 'tagging' an object; you are actually describing it. What does the contingent fact that Hesperus is Phosphorus amount to? Well, it amounts to the fact that *the* star in a certain portion of the sky in the evening is *the* star in a certain portion of the sky in the morning. Similarly, the contingent fact that Gaurisanker is Everest amounts to the fact that the mountain viewed from such and such an angle in Nepal is the mountain viewed from such and such another angle in Tibet. Therefore, such names as 'Hesperus' and 'Phosphorus' can only be abbreviations for descriptions. The term 'Phosphorus' *has* to mean 'the star seen . . .', or (let us be cautious because it actually turned out not to be a star), 'the *heavenly body* seen from such and such a position at such and such a time in the morning', and the name 'Hesperus' has to mean 'the heavenly body seen in such and such a position at such and such a time in the evening'. So, Russell concludes, if we want to reserve the term 'name' for things which really just name an object without describing it, the only real proper names we can have are names of our own immediate sense data, objects of our own 'immediate acquaintance'. The only such names which occur in language are demonstratives like 'this' and 'that'. And it is easy to see that this requirement of necessity of identity, understood as exempting identities between names from all imaginable doubt, can indeed be guaranteed only for demonstrative names of immediate sense data; for only in such cases can an identity statement between two different names have a general immunity from Cartesian doubt. There are some other things Russell has sometimes allowed as objects of acquaintance, such as one's self; we need not go into details here. Other philosophers (for example, Mrs Marcus in her reply, at least in the verbal discussion as I remember it – I do not know if this got into print, so perhaps this should not be 'tagged' on her[7]) have said, 'If names are really just tags, genuine tags, then a good dictionary should be able to tell us that they are names of the same object.' You have an object *a* and an object *b* with names 'John' and 'Joe'. Then, according to Mrs Marcus, a dictionary should be able to tell you whether or not 'John' and 'Joe' are names of the same object. Of course, I do not know what ideal dictionaries should do, but ordinary proper names do not seem to satisfy this requirement. You certainly *can*, in the case of ordinary proper names, make quite empirical discoveries that, let's say, Hesperus is Phosphorus, though we thought otherwise. We can be in doubt as to whether Gaurisanker is Everest or Cicero is in fact Tully. Even now, we could conceivably discover that we were wrong in supposing that Hesperus was Phosphorus. Maybe the astronomers made an error. So it seems that this view is wrong and that if by a name we do not mean some artificial notion of names such as Russell's, but a proper name in the ordinary sense, then there can be contingent identity statements using proper names, and the view to the contrary seems plainly wrong.

In recent philosophy a large number of other identity statements have been emphasized as examples of contingent identity statements, different, perhaps, from either of the types I have mentioned before. One of them is, for example, the statement 'Heat is the motion of molecules'. First, science is supposed to have discovered this. Empirical scientists in their investigations have been supposed to discover (and, I suppose, they did) that the external phenomenon which we call 'heat' is, in fact, molecular agitation. Another example of such a discovery is that water is H_2O, and yet other examples are that gold is the element with such and such an atomic number, that light is a stream of photons, and so on. These are all in some sense of 'identity statement' identity statements. Second, it is thought, they are plainly contingent identity statements, just because they were scientific discoveries. After all, heat might have turned out not to have been the motion of molecules. There were other alternative theories of heat proposed, for example, the caloric theory of heat. If these theories of heat had been correct, then heat would not have been the motion of molecules, but instead, some substance suffusing the hot object, called 'caloric'. And it was a matter of course of science and not of any logical necessity that the one theory turned out to be correct and the other theory turned out to be incorrect.

So, here again, we have, apparently, another plain example of a contingent identity statement. This has been supposed to be a very important example because of its connection with the mind–body problem. There have been many philosophers who have wanted to be materialists, and to be materialists in a particular form, which is known today as 'the identity theory'. According to this theory, a certain mental state, such as a person's being in pain, is identical with a certain state of his brain (or, perhaps, of his entire body, according to some theorists), at any rate, a certain material or neural state of his brain or body. And so, according to this theory, my being in pain at this instant, if I were, would be identical with my body's being or my brain's being in a certain state. Others have objected that this cannot be, because, after all, we can imagine my pain existing even if the state of the body did not. We can perhaps imagine my not being embodied at all and still being in pain, or, conversely, we could imagine my body existing and being in the very same state even if there were no pain. In fact, conceivably, it could be in this state even though there were no mind 'back of it', so to speak, at all. The usual reply has been to concede that all of these things might have been the case, but to argue that these are irrelevant to the question of the identity of the mental state and the physical state. This identity, it is said, is just another contingent scientific identification, similar to the identification of heat with molecular motion, or water with H_2O. Just as we can imagine heat without any molecular motion, so we can imagine a mental state without any corresponding brain state. But, just as the first fact is not damaging to the identification of heat and the motion of molecules, so the second fact is not at all damaging to the identification of a mental state with the corresponding brain state. And so, many recent philosophers have held it to be very important for our theoretical understanding of the mind–body problem that there can be contingent identity statements of this form.

To state finally what *I* think, as opposed to what seems to be the case, or what others think, I think that in both cases, the case of names and the case of the theoretical identifications, the identity statements are necessary and not contingent. That is to say, they are necessary if *true*; of course, false identity statements are not necessary. How can one possibly defend such a view? Perhaps I lack a complete answer to this question, even though I am convinced that the view is true. But to begin an answer, let me make some distinctions that I want to use. The first is between a *rigid* and a *nonrigid designator*. What do these terms mean? As an example of a nonrigid designator, I can give an expression such as 'the inventor of bifocals'. Let us suppose it was Benjamin Franklin who invented bifocals, and so the expression, 'the inventor of bifocals', designates or refers to a certain man, namely, Benjamin Franklin. However, we can easily imagine that the world could have been different, that under different circumstances someone else would have come upon this invention before Benjamin Franklin did, and in that case, *he* would have been the inventor of bifocals. So, in this sense, the expression 'the inventor of bifocals' is nonrigid: Under certain circumstances one man would have been the inventor of bifocals; under other circumstances, another man would have. In contrast, consider the expression 'the square root of 25'. Independently of the empirical facts, we can give an arithmetical proof that the square root of 25 is in fact the number 5, and because we have proved this mathematically, what we have proved is necessary. If we think of numbers as entities at all, and let us suppose, at least for the purpose of this lecture, that we do, then the expression 'the square root of 25' necessarily designates a certain number, namely 5. Such an expression I call 'a *rigid* designator'. Some philosophers think that anyone who even uses the notions of rigid or nonrigid designator has already shown that he has fallen into a certain confusion or has not paid attention to certain facts. What do I mean by 'rigid designator'? I mean a term that designates the same object in all possible worlds. To get rid of one confusion which certainly is not mine, I do not use 'might have designated a different object' to refer to the fact that language might have been used differently. For example, the expression 'the inventor of bifocals' might have been used by inhabitants of this planet always to refer to the man who corrupted Hadleyburg. This would have been the case, if, first, the people on this planet had not spoken English, but some other language, which phonetically overlapped with English; and if, second, in that language the expression 'the inventor of bifocals' meant the 'man who corrupted Hadleyburg'. Then it would refer, of course, in their language, to whoever in fact corrupted Hadleyburg in this counterfactual situation. That is not what I mean. What I mean by saying that a description might have referred to something different, I mean that in *our* language as *we* use it in describing a counterfactual situation, there might have been a different object satisfying the descriptive conditions *we* give for reference. So, for example, we use the phrase 'the inventor of bifocals', when we are talking about another possible world or a counterfactual situation, to refer to whoever in that counterfactual situation would have invented bifocals, not to the person whom people *in* that counterfactual situation would have called 'the inventor of bifocals'. *They* might have spoken a different language which phonetically overlapped with English in which 'the inventor of bifocals' is used in some other way. I am *not* concerned with that question here. For that matter, they might have been deaf and dumb, or there might have been no people at all. (There still could have been an inventor of bifocals even if there were no people – God, or Satan, will do.)

Second, in talking about the notion of a rigid designator, I do not mean to imply that the object referred to has to exist in all possible worlds, that is, that it has to necessarily exist. Some things, perhaps mathematical entities such as the positive integers, if they exist at all, necessarily exist. Some people have held that God both exists and necessarily exists; others, that he contingently exists; others, that he contingently fails to exist; and others, that he necessarily fails to exist:[8] all four options have been tried. But at any rate, when I use the notion of rigid designator, I do not imply that the object referred to necessarily exists. All I mean is that in any possible world where the object in question *does* exist, in any situation where the object *would* exist, we use the designator in question to designate that object. In a situation where the object does not exist, then we should say that the designator has no referent and that the object in question so designated does not exist.

As I said, many philosophers would find the very notion of rigid designator objectionable *per se*. And the objection that people make may be stated as follows: Look, you're talking about situations which are counterfactual, that is to say, you're talking about other possible worlds. Now these worlds are completely disjoint, after all, from the actual world which is not just another possible world; it is the actual world. So, before you talk about, let us say, such an object as Richard

Nixon in another possible world at all, you have to say which object in this other possible world would *be* Richard Nixon. Let us talk about a situation in which, as *you* would say, Richard Nixon would have been a member of SDS. Certainly the member of SDS you are talking about is someone very different in many of his properties from Nixon. Before we even can say whether this man would have been Richard Nixon or not, we have to set up criteria of identity across possible worlds. Here are these other possible worlds. There are all kinds of objects in them with different properties from those of any actual object. Some of them resemble Nixon in some ways, some of them resemble Nixon in other ways. Well, which of these objects is Nixon? One has to give a criterion of identity. And this shows how the very notion of rigid designator runs in a circle. Suppose we designate a certain number as the number of planets. Then, if that is our favourite way, so to speak, of designating this number, then in any other possible worlds we will have to identify whatever number is the number of planets with the number 9, which in the actual world is the number of planets. So, it is argued by various philosophers, for example, implicitly by Quine, and explicitly by many others in his wake, we cannot really ask whether a designator is rigid or nonrigid because we first need a criterion of identity across possible worlds. An extreme view has even been held that, since possible worlds are so disjoint from our own, we cannot really say that any object in them is the *same* as an object existing now but only that there are some objects which resemble things in the actual world, more or less. We, therefore, should not really speak of what would have been true of Nixon in another possible world but, only of what 'counterparts' (the term which David Lewis uses[9]) of Nixon there would have been. Some people in other possible worlds have dogs whom they call 'Checkers'. Others favour the ABM but do not have any dog called Checkers. There are various people who resemble Nixon more or less, but none of them can really be said to be Nixon; they are only *counterparts* of Nixon, and you choose which one is the best counterpart by noting which resembles Nixon the most closely, according to your favourite criteria. Such views are widespread, both among the defenders of quantified modal logic and among its detractors.

All of this talk seems to me to have taken the metaphor of possible worlds much too seriously in some way. It is as if a 'possible world' were like a foreign country, or distant planet way out there. It is as if we see dimly through a telescope various actors on this distant planet. Actually David Lewis's view seems the most reasonable if one takes this picture literally. No one far away on another planet can be strictly identical with someone here. But, even if we have some marvellous methods of transportation to take one and the same person from planet to planet, we really need some epistemological criteria of identity to be able to say whether someone on this distant planet is the same person as someone here.

All of this seems to me to be a totally misguided way of looking at things. What it amounts to is the view that counterfactual situations have to be described purely qualitatively. So, we cannot say, for example, 'If Nixon had only given a sufficient bribe to Senator X, he would have got Carswell through' because that refers to certain people, Nixon and Carswell, and talks about what things would be true of them in a counterfactual situation. We must say instead 'If a man who has a hairline like such and such, and holds such and such political opinions had given a bribe to a man who was a senator and had such and such other qualities, then a man who was a judge in the South and had many other qualities resembling Carswell would have been confirmed.' In other words, we must describe counterfactual situations purely qualitatively and then ask the question, 'Given that the situation contains people or things with such and such qualities, which of these people is (or is a counterpart of) Nixon, which is Carswell, and so on?' This seems to me to be wrong. Who is to prevent us from saying 'Nixon might have got Carswell through had he done certain things'? We are speaking of *Nixon* and asking what, in certain counterfactual situations, would have been true of *him*. We can say that if Nixon had done such and such, he would have lost the election to Humphrey. Those I am opposing would argue, 'Yes, but how do you find out if the man you are talking about is in fact Nixon?' It would indeed be very hard to find out, if you were looking at the whole situation through a telescope, but that is not what we are doing here. Possible worlds are not something to which an epistemological question like this applies. And if the phrase 'possible worlds' is what makes anyone think some such question applies, he should just *drop* this phrase and use some other expression, say 'counterfactual situation', which might be less misleading. If we say 'If Nixon had bribed such and such a Senator, Nixon would have got Carswell through', what is *given* in the very description of that situation is that it is a situation in which we are speaking of Nixon, and of Carswell, and of such and such a Senator. And there seems to be no less objection to *stipulating* that we are speaking of certain *people* than there can be objection to stipulating that we are speaking of certain *qualities*. Advocates of the other view take speaking of certain qualities as unobjectionable. They do not say, 'How do we know that this quality (in another possible world) is that of redness?' But they do find speaking of certain *people* objectionable. But I see no more reason to object in the one case than in the other. I think it really comes from the idea of possible worlds as existing out there, but very far off, viewable only through a special telescope. Even more objectionable is the view of David Lewis. According to Lewis, when we say 'Under certain circumstances Nixon would have gotten Carswell through', we really mean 'Some man, other than Nixon but closely resembling him, would have got some judge, other than Carswell but closely resembling him, through'. Maybe that is so, that some man closely resembling Nixon could have got some man closely resembling Carswell through. But *that* would not comfort either Nixon or Carswell, nor would it make Nixon kick himself and say '*I* should have done such and such to get Carswell through'. The question is whether under certain circumstances Nixon *himself* could have got *Carswell* through. And I think the objection is simply based on a misguided picture.

Instead, we can perfectly well talk about rigid and nonrigid designators. Moreover, we have a simple, intuitive test for them. We can say, for example, that the number of planets might have been a different number from the number it in fact is. For example, there might have been only seven planets. We can say that the inventor of bifocals might have been someone other than the man who *in fact* invented bifocals.[10] We cannot say, though, that the square root of 81 might have been a different number from the number it in fact is, for that number just has to be 9. If we apply this intuitive test to proper names, such as for example 'Richard Nixon', they would seem intuitively to come out to be rigid designators. First, when we talk even about the counterfactual situation in which we suppose Nixon to have done different things, we assume we are still talking about Nixon himself. We say, 'If Nixon had bribed a certain Senator, he would have got Carswell through' and we assume that by 'Nixon' and 'Carswell' we are still referring to the very same people as in the actual world. And it seems that we cannot say 'Nixon might have been a different man from the man he in fact was', unless, of course, we mean it metaphorically: He might have been a different *sort* of person (if you believe in free will and that people are not inherently corrupt). You might think the statement true in that sense, but Nixon could not have been in the other literal sense a different person from the person he, in fact, is, even though the thirty-seventh President of the United States might have been Humphrey. So the phrase 'the thirty-seventh President' is nonrigid, but 'Nixon', it would seem, is rigid.

Let me make another distinction before I go back to the question of identity statements. This distinction is very fundamental and also hard to see through. In recent discussion, many philosophers who have debated the meaningfulness of various categories of truths, have regarded them as identical. Some of those who identify them are vociferous defenders of them, and others, such as Quine, say they are all identically meaningless. But usually they're not distinguished. These are categories such as 'analytic', 'necessary', '*a priori*', and sometimes even 'certain'. I will not talk about all of these but only about the notions of *a priority* and necessity. Very often these are held to be synonyms. (Many philosophers probably should not be described as holding them to be synonyms; they simply *use* them interchangeably.) I wish to distinguish them. What do we mean by calling a statement *necessary*? We simply mean that the statement in question, first, is true, and, second, that it could not have been otherwise. When we say that something is *contingently* true, we mean that, though it is in fact the case, it could have been the case that things would have been otherwise. If we wish to assign this distinction to a branch of philosophy, we should assign it to metaphysics. To the contrary, there is the notion of an *a priori truth*. An *a priori* truth is supposed to be one which can be *known* to be true independently of all experience. Notice that this does not in and of itself say anything about all possible worlds, unless this is put into the definition. All that it says is that it can be known to be true of the actual world, independently of all experience. It may, by some philosophical argument, follow from our knowing, independently of experience, that something is true of the actual world, that it has to be known to be true also of all possible worlds. But if this is to be established, it requires some philosophical argument to establish it. Now, *this* notion, if we were to assign it to a branch of philosophy, belongs, not to metaphysics, but to epistemology. It has to do with the way we can know certain things to be in fact true. Now, it may be the case, of course, that anything which is necessary is something which *can* be known *a priori*. (Notice, by the way, the notion *a priori* truth as thus defined has in it *another* modality: it *can* be known independently of all experience. It is a little complicated because there is a double modality here.) I will not have time to explore these notions in full detail here, but one thing we can see from the outset is that these two notions are by no means trivially the same. If they are coextensive, it takes some philosophical argument to establish it. As stated, they belong to different domains of philosophy. One of them has something to do with *knowledge*, with what can be known in certain ways about the *actual* world. The other one has to do with *metaphysics*, how the world *could* have been; given that it is the way it is, could it have been otherwise, in certain ways? Now I hold, as a matter of fact, that neither class of statements is contained in the other. But, all we need to talk about here is this: Is everything that is necessarily knowable *a priori* or known *a priori*? Consider the following example: the Goldbach conjecture. This says that every even number is the sum of two primes. It is a mathematical statement and if it is true at all, it has to be necessary. Certainly, one could not say that though in fact every even number is the sum of two primes, there could have been some extra number which was even and not the sum of two primes. What would that mean? On the other hand, the answer to the question whether every even number *is* in fact the sum of two primes is unknown, and we have no method at present for deciding. So we certainly do not know, *a priori* or even *a posteriori*, that every even number is the sum of two primes. (Well, perhaps we have some evidence in that no counterexample has been found.) But we certainly do not know *a priori* anyway, that every even number is, in fact, the sum of two primes. But, of course, the definition just says '*can* be known independently of experience' and someone might say that if it is true, we *could* know it independently of experience. It is hard to see exactly what this claim means. It might be so. One thing it might mean is that if it were true we could *prove* it. This claim is certainly wrong if it is generally applied to mathematical statements and we have to work within some fixed system. This is what Gödel proved. And even if we mean an 'intuitive proof in general' it might just be the case (at least, this view is as clear and as probable as the contrary) that though the statement is true, there is just no way the human mind could ever prove it. Of course, one way an *infinite* mind might be able to prove it is by looking through each natural number one by one and checking. In this sense, of course, it can, perhaps, be known *a priori*, but only by an infinite mind, and then this gets into other complicated questions. I do not want to discuss questions about the conceivability of performing an infinite number of acts like looking through each number one by one. A vast philosophical literature has been written on this: Some have declared it is logically impossible; others that it is logically possible; and some do not know. The main point is that it is not trivial that just because such a statement is necessary it can be known *a priori*. Some considerable clarification is required before we decide that it can be so known. And so this shows that even if everything necessary is *a priori* in some sense, it should not be taken as a trivial matter of definition. It is a substantive philosophical thesis which requires some work.

Another example that one might give relates to the problem of essentialism. Here is a lectern. A question which has often been raised in philosophy is: What are its essential properties? What properties, aside from trivial ones like self-identity, are such that this object has to have them if it exists at all,[11] are such that if an object did not have it, it would not be this object?[12] For example, being made of wood, and not of ice, might be an essential property of this lectern. Let us just take the weaker statement that it is not made of ice. That will establish it as strongly as we need it, perhaps as dramatically. Supposing this lectern is in fact made of wood, could this very lectern have been made from the very beginning of its existence from ice, say frozen from water in the Thames? One has a considerable feeling that it could *not*, though in fact one certainly could have made a lectern of water from the Thames, frozen it into ice by some process, and put it right there in place of this thing. If one had done so, one would have made, of course, a *different* object. It would not have been *this very lectern*, and so one would not have a case in which this very lectern here was made of ice, or was made from water from the Thames. The question of whether it could afterward, say in a minute from now, turn into ice is something else. So, it would seem, if an example like this is correct – and this is what advocates of essentialism have held – that this lectern could not have been made of ice, that is in any counterfactual situation of which we would say that this lectern existed at all, we would have to say also that it was not made from water from the Thames frozen into ice. Some have rejected, of course, any such notion of essential property as meaningless. Usually, it is because (and I think this is what Quine, for example, would say) they have held that it depends on the notion of identity across possible worlds, and that this is itself meaningless. Since I have rejected this view already, I will not deal with it again. We can talk about *this very object*, and whether it could have had certain properties which it does not in fact have. For example, it could have been in another room from the room it in fact is in, even at this very time, but it could not have been made from the very beginning from water frozen into ice.

If the essentialist view is correct, it can only be correct if we sharply distinguish between the notions of *a posteriori* and *a priori* truth on the one hand, and contingent and necessary truth on the other hand, for although the statement that this table, if it exists at all, was not made of ice, is necessary, it certainly is not something that we know *a priori*. What we know is that first, lecterns usually are not made of ice, they are usually made of wood. This looks like wood. It does not feel cold and it probably would if it were made of ice. Therefore, I conclude, probably this is not made of ice. Here my entire judgement is *a posteriori*. I could find out that an ingenious trick has been played upon me and that, in fact, this lectern is made of ice; but what I am saying is, given that it is in fact not made of ice, in fact is made of wood, one cannot imagine that under certain circumstances it could have been made of ice. So we have to say that though we cannot know *a priori* whether this table was made of ice or not, given that it is not made of ice, it is *necessarily* not made of ice. In other words, if *P* is the statement that the lectern is not made of ice, one knows by *a priori* philosophical analysis, some conditional of the form 'if *P*, then necessarily *P*'. If the table is not made of ice, it is necessarily not made of ice. On the other hand, then, we know by empirical investigation that *P*, the antecedent of the conditional, is true – that this table is not made of ice. We can conclude by *modus ponens*:

$$P \supset \Box P$$
$$P$$
$$\overline{\Box P\star}$$

The conclusion – '$\Box P$' – is that it is necessary that the table not be made of ice, and this conclusion is known *a posteriori*, since one of the premises on which it is based is *a posteriori*. So, the notion of essential properties can be maintained only by distinguishing between the notions of *a priori* and necessary truth, and I do maintain it.

Let us return to the question of identities. Concerning the statement 'Hesperus is Phosphorus' or the statement 'Cicero is Tully', one can find all of these out by empirical investigation, and we might turn out to be wrong in our empirical beliefs. So, it is usually argued, such statements must therefore be contingent. Some have embraced the other side of the coin and have held 'Because of this argument about necessity, identity statements between names have to be knowable *a priori*, so, only a very special category of names, possibly, really works as names; the other things are bogus names, disguised descriptions, or something of the sort. However, a certain very narrow class of statements of identity are known *a priori*, and these are the ones which contain the genuine names.' If one accepts the distinctions that I have made, one need not jump to either conclusion. One can hold that certain statements of identity between names, though often known *a posteriori*, and maybe not knowable *a priori*, are in fact necessary, if true. So, we have some room to hold this. But, of course, to

---

★ The formalized argument can be read thus:
If *P*, then necessarily *P*
But *P*
Therefore, necessarily *P* (Edd.).

have some room to hold it does not mean that we should hold it. So let us see what the evidence is. First, recall the remark that I made that proper names seem to be rigid designators, as when we use the name 'Nixon' to talk about a certain man, even in counterfactual situations. If we say, 'If Nixon had not written the letter to Saxbe, maybe he would have got Carswell through', we are in this statement talking about Nixon, Saxbe, and Carswell, the very same men as in the actual world, and what would have happened to them under certain counterfactual circumstances. If names are rigid designators, then there can be no question about identities being necessary, because 'a' and 'b' will be rigid designators of a certain man or thing x. Then even in every possible world, a and b will both refer to this same object x, and to no other, and so there will be no situation in which a might not have been b. That would have to be a situation in which the object which we are also now calling 'x' would not have been identical with itself. Then one could not possibly have a situation in which Cicero would not have been Tully or Hesperus would not have been Phosphorus.[13]

Aside from the identification of necessity with *a priori*, what has made people feel the other way? There are two things which have made people feel the other way.[14] Some people tend to regard identity statements as metalinguistic statements, to identify the statement 'Hesperus is Phosphorus' with the metalinguistic statement, ' "Hesperus" and "Phosphorus" are names of the same heavenly body'. And that, of course, might have been false. We might have used the terms 'Hesperus' and 'Phosphorus' as names of *two* different heavenly bodies. But, of course, this has nothing to do with the necessity of identity. In the same sense '2 + 2 = 4' might have been false. The phrases '2 + 2' and '4' might have been used to refer to two different numbers. One can imagine a language, for example, in which '+', '2', and '=' were used in the standard way, but '4' was used as the name of, say, the square root of minus 1, as we should call it, '*i*'. Then '2 + 2 = 4' would be false, for 2 plus 2 is not equal to the square root of minus 1. But this is not what we want. We do not want just to say that a certain statement which we in fact use to express something true could have expressed something false. We want to use the statement in *our* way and see if it could have been false.

Let us do this. What is the idea people have? They say, 'Look, Hesperus might not have been Phosphorus. Here a certain planet was seen in the morning, and it was seen in the evening; and it just turned out later on as a matter of empirical fact that they were one and the same planet. If things had turned out otherwise, they would have been two different planets, or two different heavenly bodies, so how can you say that such a statement is necessary?'

Now there are two things that such people can mean. First, they can mean that we do not know *a priori* whether Hesperus is Phosphorus. This I have already conceded. Second, they may mean that they can actually imagine circumstances that they would call circumstances in which Hesperus would not have been Phosphorus. Let us think what would be such a circumstance, using these terms here as *names* of a planet. For example, it could have been the case that Venus did indeed rise in the morning in exactly the position in which we saw it, but that on the other hand, in the position which is in fact occupied by Venus in the evening, Venus was not there, and Mars took its place. This is all counterfactual because in fact Venus is there. Now one can also imagine that in this counterfactual other possible world, the earth would have been inhabited by people and that they should have used the names 'Phosphorus' for Venus in the morning and 'Hesperus' for Mars in the evening. Now, this is all very good, but would it be a situation in which Hesperus was not Phosphorus? Of course, it is a situation in which people would have been able to *say*, truly, 'Hesperus is not Phosphorus'; but we are supposed to describe things in our language, not in theirs. So let us describe it in our language. Well, how could it actually happen that Venus would not be in that position in the evening? For example, let us say that there is some comet that comes around every evening and yanks things over a little bit. (That would be a very simple scientific way of imagining it: not really too simple – that is very hard to imagine actually.) It just happens to come around every evening, and things get yanked over a little bit. Mars gets yanked over to the very position where Venus is, then the comet yanks things back to their normal position in the morning. Thinking of this planet which we now call 'Phosphorus', what should we say? Well, we can say that the comet passes it and yanks Phosphorus over so that it is not in the position normally occupied by Phosphorus in the evening. If we do say this, and really use 'Phosphorus' as the name of a planet, then we have to say that, under such circumstances, Phosphorus in the evening would not be in the position where we, in fact, saw it; or alternatively, Hesperus in the evening would not be in the position in which we, in fact, saw it. We might say that under such circumstances, we would not have called Hesperus 'Hesperus' because Hesperus would have been in a different position. But that still would not make Phosphorus different from Hesperus; but what would then be the case instead is that Hesperus would have been in a different position from the position it in fact is and, perhaps, not in such a position that people would have called it 'Hesperus'. But that would not be a situation in which Phosphorus would not have been Hesperus.

Let us take another example which may be clearer. Suppose someone uses 'Tully' to refer to the Roman orator who denounced Cataline and uses the name 'Cicero' to refer to the man whose works he had to study in third-year Latin in high school. Of course, he may not know in advance that the very same man who denounced Cataline wrote these works, and that is a contingent statement. But the fact that this statement is contingent should not make us think that the statement that Cicero is Tully, if it is true, and it is in fact true, is contingent. Suppose, for example, that Cicero actually did denounce Cataline, but thought that this political achievement was so great that he should not bother writing any literary works. Would we say that these would be circumstances under which he would not have been Cicero? It seems to me that the answer is no, that instead we would say that, under such circumstances, Cicero would not have written any literary works. It is not a necessary property of Cicero – the way the shadow follows the man – that he should have written certain works; we can easily imagine a situation in which Shakespeare would not have written the works of Shakespeare, or one in which Cicero would not have written the works of Cicero. What may be the case is that we *fix the reference* of the term 'Cicero' by use of some descriptive phrase, such as 'the author of these works'. But once we have this reference fixed, we then use the name 'Cicero' *rigidly* to designate the man who in fact we have identified by his authorship of these works. We do not use it to designate whoever would have written these works in place of Cicero, if someone else wrote them. It might have been the case that the man who wrote these works was not the man who denounced Cataline. Cassius might have written these works. But we would not then say that Cicero would have been Cassius, unless we were speaking in a very loose and metaphorical way. We would say that Cicero, whom we may have identified and come to know by his works, would not have written them, and that someone else, say Cassius, would have written them in his place.

Such examples are not grounds for thinking that identity statements are contingent. To take them as such grounds is to misconstrue the relation between a *name* and a *description used to fix its reference*, to take them to be *synonyms*. Even if we fix the reference of such a name as 'Cicero' as the man who wrote such and such works, in speaking of counterfactual situations, when we speak of Cicero, we do not then speak of whoever in such counterfactual situations *would* have written such and such works, but rather of Cicero, whom we have identified by the contingent property that he is the man who in fact, that is, in the actual world, wrote certain works.[15]

I hope this is reasonably clear in a brief compass. Now, actually I have been presupposing something I do not really believe to be, in general, true. Let us suppose that we do fix the reference of a name by a description. Even if we do so, we do not then make the name *synonymous* with the description, but instead we use the name *rigidly* to refer to the object so named, even in talking about counterfactual situations where the thing named would not satisfy the description in question. Now, this is what I think in fact is true for those cases of naming where the reference is fixed by description. But, in fact, I also think, contrary to most recent theorists, that the reference of names is rarely or almost never fixed by means of description. And by this I do not just mean what Searle says: 'It's not a single description, but rather a cluster, a family of properties which fixes the reference'. I mean that properties in this sense are not used *at all*. But I do not have the time to go into this here. So, let us suppose that at least one half of prevailing views about naming is true, that the reference is fixed by descriptions. Even were that true, the name would not be synonymous with the description, but would be used to *name* an object which we pick out by the contingent fact that it satisfies a certain description.

And so, even though we can imagine a case where the man who wrote these works would not have been the man who denounced Cataline, we should not say that that would be a case in which Cicero would not have been Tully. We should say that it is a case in which Cicero did not write these works, but rather that Cassius did. And the identity of Cicero and Tully still holds.

Let me turn to the case of heat and the motion of molecules. Here surely is a case that is contingent identity! Recent philosophy has emphasized this again and again. So, if it is a case of contingent identity, then let us imagine under what circumstances it would be false. Now, concerning this statement I hold that the circumstances philosophers apparently have in mind as circumstances under which it would have been false are not in fact such circumstances. First, of course, it is argued that 'Heat is the motion of molecules' is an *a posteriori* judgement; scientific investigation might have turned out otherwise. As I said before, this shows nothing against the view that it is necessary – at least if I am right. But here, surely, people had very specific circumstances in mind under which, so they thought, the judgement that heat is the motion of molecules would have been false. What were these circumstances? One can distill them out of the fact that we found out empirically that heat is the motion of molecules. How was this? What did we find out first when we found out that heat is the motion of molecules? There is a certain external phenomenon which we can sense by the sense of touch, and it produces a sensation which we call 'the sensation of heat'. We then discover that the external phenomenon which produces this sensation, which we sense, by means of our sense of touch, is in fact that of molecular agitation in the thing that we touch, a very high degree of molecular agitation. So, it might be thought, to imagine a situation in which heat would not have been the motion of molecules, we need only imagine a situation in which we would have had the very same sensation and it would have been produced by something other than the motion of molecules. Similarly, if we wanted to imagine a situation in which light was not a stream of photons, we could imagine a situation in which we were sensitive to something else in exactly the same way, producing what we call visual experiences, though not through a stream of photons. To make the case stronger, or to look at another side of the coin, we could also consider a situation in which we *are* concerned with the motion of molecules but in which such motion does not give us the sensation of heat. And it might also have happened that we, or, at least, the creatures inhabiting this planet, might have been so constituted that, let us say, an increase in the motion of molecules did not give us this sensation but that, on the contrary, a slowing down of the molecules did give us the very same sensation. This would be a situation, so it might be thought, in which heat would not be the motion of molecules, or, more precisely, in which temperature would not be mean molecular kinetic energy.

But I think it would not be so. Let us think about the situation again. First, let us think about it in the actual world. Imagine right now the world invaded by a number of Martians, who do indeed get the very sensation that we call 'the sensation of heat' when they feel some ice which has slow molecular motion, and who do not get a sensation of heat – in fact, maybe just the reverse – when they put their hand near a fire which causes a lot of molecular agitation. Would we say, 'Ah, this casts some doubt on heat being the motion of molecules, because there are these other people who don't get the same sensation'? Obviously not, and no one would think so. We would say instead that the Martians somehow feel the very sensation we get when we feel heat when they feel cold and that they do not get a sensation of heat when they feel heat. But now let us think of a counterfactual situation.[16] Suppose the earth had from the very beginning been inhabited by such creatures. First, imagine it inhabited by no creatures at all: then there is no one to feel any sensations of heat. But we would not say that under such circumstances it would necessarily be the case that heat did not exist; we would say that heat might have existed, for example, if there were fires that heated up the air.

Let us suppose the laws of physics were not very different: Fires do heat up the air. Then there would have been heat even though there were no creatures around to feel it. Now let us suppose evolution takes place, and life is created, and there are some creatures around. But they are not like us, they are more like the Martians. Now would we say that heat has suddenly turned to cold, because of the way the creatures of this planet sense it? No, I think we should describe this situation as a situation in which, though the creatures on this planet got our sensation of heat, they did not get it when they were exposed to heat. They got it when they were exposed to cold. And that is something we can surely well imagine. We can imagine it just as we can imagine our planet being invaded by creatures of this sort. Think of it in two steps. First there is a stage where there are no creatures at all, and one can certainly imagine the planet still having both heat and cold, though no one is around to sense it. Then the planet comes through an evolutionary process to be peopled with beings of different neural structure from ourselves. Then these creatures could be such that they were insensitive to heat; they did not feel it in the way we do; but on the other hand, they felt cold in much the same way that we feel heat. But still, heat would be heat, and cold would be cold. And particularly, then, this goes in no way against saying that in this counterfactual situation heat would still *be* the molecular motion, *be* that which is produced by fires, and so on, just as it would have been if there had been no creatures on the planet at all. Similarly, we could imagine that the planet was inhabited by creatures who got visual sensations when there were sound waves in the air. We should not therefore say, 'Under such circumstances, sound would have been light.' Instead we should say, 'The planet was inhabited by creatures who were in some sense visually sensitive to sound, and maybe even visually sensitive to light.' If this is correct, it can still be and will still be a necessary truth that heat is the motion of molecules and that light is a stream of photons.

To state the view succinctly: we use both the terms 'heat' and 'the motion of molecules' as rigid designators for a certain external phenomenon. Since heat is in fact the motion of molecules, and the designators are rigid, by the argument I have given here, it is going to be *necessary* that heat is the motion of molecules. What gives us the illusion of contingency is the fact we have identified the heat by the contingent fact that there happen to be creatures on this planet – (namely, ourselves) who are sensitive to it in a certain way, that is, who are sensitive to the motion of molecules or to heat – these are one and the same thing. And this is contingent. So we use the description, 'that which causes such and such sensations, or that which we sense in such and such a way', to identify heat. But in using this fact we use a contingent property of heat, just as we use the contingent property of

Cicero as having written such and such works to identify him. We then use the terms 'heat' in the one case and 'Cicero' in the other *rigidly* to designate the objects for which they stand. And of course the term 'the motion of molecules' is rigid; it always stands for the motion of molecules, never for any other phenomenon. So, as Bishop Butler said, 'everything is what it is and not another thing'. Therefore, 'Heat is the motion of molecules' will be necessary, not contingent, and one only has the *illusion* of contingency in the way one could have the illusion of contingency in thinking that this table might have been made of ice. We might think one could imagine it, but if we try, we can see on reflection that what we are really imagining is just there being another lectern in this very position here which was in fact made of ice. The fact that we may identify this lectern by being the object we see and touch in such and such a position is something else.

Now how does this relate to the problem of mind and body? It is usually held that this is a contingent identity statement just like 'Heat is the motion of molecules'. That cannot be. It cannot be a contingent identity statement just like 'Heat is the motion of molecules' because, if I am right, 'Heat is the motion of molecules' is not a contingent identity statement. Let us look at this statement. For example, 'My being in pain at such and such a time is my being in such and such a brain state at such and such a time' or, 'Pain in general is such and such a neural (brain) state'.

This is held to be contingent on the following grounds. First, we can imagine the brain state existing though there is no pain at all. It is only a scientific fact that whenever we are in a certain brain state we have a pain. Second, one might imagine a creature being in pain, but not being in any specified brain state at all, maybe not having a brain at all. People even think, at least prima facie, though they may be wrong, that they can imagine totally disembodied creatures, at any rate certainly not creatures with bodies anything like our own. So it seems that we can imagine definite circumstances under which this relationship would have been false. Now, if these circumstances are circumstances, notice that we cannot deal with them simply by saying that this is just an illusion, something we can apparently imagine, but in fact cannot in the way we thought erroneously that we could imagine a situation in which heat was not the motion of molecules. Because although we can say that we pick out heat contingently by the contingent property that it affects us in such and such a way, we cannot similarly say that we pick out pain contingently by the fact that it affects us in such and such a way. On such a picture there would be the brain state, and we pick it out by the contingent fact that it affects us as pain. Now that might be true of the brain state, but it cannot be true of the pain. The experience itself has to be *this experience*, and I cannot say that it is contingent property of the pain I now have that it is a pain.[17] In fact, it would seem that both the terms, 'my pain' and 'my being in such and such a brain state' are, first of all, both rigid designators. That is, whenever anything is such-and-such a pain, it is essentially that very object, namely, such-and-such a pain, and wherever anything is such-and-such a brain state, it is essentially that very object, namely, such-and-such a brain state. So both of these are rigid designators. One cannot say this pain might have been something else, some other state. These are both rigid designators.

Second, the way we would think of picking them out – namely, the pain by its being an experience of a certain sort, and the brain state by its being the state of a certain material object, being of such and such molecular configuration – both of these pick out their objects essentially and not accidentally, that is, they pick them out by essential properties. Whenever the molecules *are* in this configuration, we *do* have such and such a brain state. Whenever you feel *this*, you do have a pain. So it seems that the identity theorist is in some trouble, for, since we have two rigid designators, the identity statement in question is necessary. Because they pick out their objects essentially, we cannot say the case where you seem to imagine the identity statement false is really an illusion like the illusion one gets in the case of heat and molecular motion, because that illusion depended on the fact that we pick out heat by a certain contingent property. So there is very little room to manoeuvre; perhaps none.[18] The identity theorist, who holds that pain is the brain state, also has to hold that it necessarily is the brain state. He therefore cannot concede, but has to deny, that there would have been situations under which one would have had pain but not the corresponding brain state. Now usually in arguments on the identity theory, this is very far from being denied. In fact, it is conceded from the outset by the materialist as well as by his opponent. He says, 'Of course, it *could* have been the case that we had pains without the brain states. It is a contingent identity.' But that cannot be. He has to hold that we are under some illusion in thinking that we can imagine that there could have been pains without brain states. And the only model I can think of for what the illusion might be, or at least the model given by the analogy the materialists themselves suggest, namely, heat and molecular motion, simply does not work in this case. So the materialist is up against a very stiff challenge. He has to show that these things we think we can see to be possible are in fact not possible. He has to show that these things which we can imagine are not in fact things we can imagine. And that requires some very different philosophical argument from the sort which has been given in the case of heat and molecular motion. And it would have to be a deeper and subtler argument than I can fathom and subtler than has ever appeared in any materialist literature that I have read. So the conclusion of this investigation would be that the analytical tools we are using go against the identity thesis and so go against the general thesis that mental states are just physical states.[19]

The next topic would be my own solution to the mind–body problem, but that I do not have.

Notes

1. This paper was presented orally, without a written text, to the New York University lecture series on identity which makes up the volume in which it was first published. The lecture was taped, and the present paper represents a transcription of these tapes, edited only slightly with no attempt to change the style of the original. If the reader imagines the sentences of this paper as being delivered, extemporaneously, with proper pauses and emphases, this may facilitate his comprehension. Nevertheless, there may still be passages which are hard to follow, and the time allotted necessitated a condensed presentation of the argument. Occasionally, reservations, amplifications, and gratifications of my remarks had to be repressed, especially in the discussion of theoretical identification and the mind–body problem. The footnotes, which were added to the original, would have become even more unwieldy if this had not been done.

2. R. J. Butler (ed.), *Analytical Philosophy, Second Series* (Oxford: Blackwell, 1965), p. 41.

3. The second occurrence of the description has small scope.

4. In Russell's theory, $F(\imath xGx)$ follows from $(x)Fx$ and $(\exists!x)Gx$, provided that the description in $F(\imath xGx)$ has the entire context for its scope (in Russell's 1905 terminology, has a 'primary occurrence'). Only then is $F(\imath xGx)$ 'about' the denotation of '$\imath xGx$'. Applying this rule to (14), we get the results indicated in the text. Notice that, in the ambiguous form $\square(\imath xGx = \imath xHx)$, if one or both of the descriptions have 'primary occurrences' the formula does not assert the necessity of $\imath xGx = \imath xHx$; if both have secondary occurrences, it does. Thus in a language without explicit scope indicators, descriptions must be construed with the smallest possible scope – only then will $\sim A$ be the negation of A, $\square A$ the necessitation of A, and the like.

5. An earlier distinction with the same purpose was, of course, the medieval one of *de dicto–de re*. That Russell's distinction of scope eliminates modal paradoxes has been pointed out by many logicians, especially Smullyan.

So as to avoid misunderstanding, let me emphasize that I am of course not asserting that Russell's notion of scope solves Quine's problem of 'essentialism'; what it does show, especially in conjunction with modern model–theoretic approaches to modal logic, is that quantified modal logic need not deny the truth of all instances of $(x)(y)(x = y \cdot \supset \cdot Fx \supset Fy)$, nor of all instances of '$(x)(Gx \supset Ga)$' (where 'a' is to be replaced by a nonvacuous definite description whose scope is all of 'Ga'), in order to avoid making it a necessary truth that one and the same man invented bifocals and headed the original Postal Department. Russell's contextual definition of descriptions need not be adopted in order to ensure these results; but other logical theories, Fregean or other, which take descriptions as primitive must somehow express the same logical facts. Frege showed that a simple, non-iterated context containing a definite description with small scope, which cannot be interpreted as being 'about' the denotation of the description, can be interpreted as about its 'sense'. Some logicians have been interested in the question of the conditions under which, in an intensified context, a description with small scope is equivalent to the same one with large scope. One of the virtues of a Russellian treatment of descriptions in modal logic is that the answer (roughly that the description be a 'rigid designator' in the sense of this lecture) then often follows from the other postulates for quantified modal logic; no special postulates are needed, as in Hintikka's treatment. Even if descriptions are taken as primitive, special postulation of when scope is irrelevant can often be deduced from more basic axioms.

6. 'Modalities and Intensional Languages', *Boston Studies in the Philosophy of Science*, Vol. 1 (New York: Humanities Press, 1963), pp. 71 ff. See also the 'Comments' by Quine and the ensuing discussion.

7. It should. See her remark on p. 115, op. cit., in the discussion following the papers.

8. If there is no deity, and especially if the nonexistence of a deity is *necessary*, it is dubious that we can use 'he' to refer to a deity. The use in the text must be taken to be non-literal.

9. David K. Lewis, 'Counterpart Theory and Quantified Modal Logic', *Journal of Philosophy* LXV (1968), pp. 113 ff.

10. Some philosophers think that definite descriptions, in English, are ambiguous, that sometimes 'the inventor of bifocals' rigidly designates the man who in fact invented bifocals. I am tentatively inclined to reject this view, construed as a thesis about English (as opposed to a possible hypothetical language), but I will not argue the question here.

What I do wish to note is that, contrary to some opinions, this alleged ambiguity cannot replace the Russellian notion of the scope of a description. Consider the sentence, 'The number of planets might have been necessarily even.' This sentence plainly can be read so as to express a truth; had there been eight planets, the number of planets would have been necessarily even. Yet without scope distinctions, both a 'referential' (rigid) and a non-rigid reading of the description will make the statement false. (Since the number of planets is nine, the rigid reading amounts to the falsity that nine might have been necessarily even.)

The 'rigid' reading is equivalent to the Russellian primary occurrence; the non-rigid, to innermost scope – some, following Donnellan, perhaps loosely, have called this reading the 'attributive' use. The possibility of intermediate scopes is then ignored. In the present instance, the intended reading of $\diamondsuit\square$ (the number of planets is even) makes the scope of the description $\square$ (the number of planets is even), neither the largest nor the smallest possible.

11. This definition is the usual formulation of the notion of essential property, but an exception must be made for existence itself; on the definition given, existence would be trivially essential. We should regard existence as essential to an object only if the object necessarily exists. Perhaps there are other recherché properties, involving existence, for which the definition is similarly objectionable. (I thank Michael Slote for this observation.)

12. The two clauses of the sentence noted give equivalent definitions of the notion of essential property, since $\square((\exists x)\ (x = a) \supset Fa)$ is equivalent to $\square(x)\ (\sim Fx \supset x \neq a)$. The second formulation, however, has served as a powerful seducer in favour of theories of 'identification across possible worlds'. For it suggests that we consider 'an object b in another possible world' and test whether it is identifiable with a by asking whether it lacks any of the essential properties of a. Let me therefore emphasize that, although an essential property is (trivially) a property without which an object cannot be a, it by no means follows that the essential, purely qualitative properties of a jointly form a sufficient condition for being a, nor that *any* purely qualitative conditions are sufficient for an object to be a. Further, even if necessary and sufficient qualitative conditions for an object to be Nixon may exist, there would still be little justification for the demand for a purely qualitative description of all counterfactual situations. We can ask whether Nixon might have been a Democrat without engaging in these subtleties.

13. I thus agree with Quine, that 'Hesperus is Phosphorus' is (or can be) an

empirical discovery; with Marcus, that it is necessary. Both Quine and Marcus, according to the present standpoint, err in identifying the epistemological and the metaphysical issues.

14. The two confusions alleged, especially the second, are both related to the confusion of the metaphysical question of the necessity of 'Hesperus is Phosphorus' with the epistemological question of its *a priority*. For if Hesperus is identified by its position in the sky in the evening, and Phosphorus by its position in the morning, an investigator may well know, in advance of empirical research, that Hesperus is Phosphorus if and only if one and the same body occupies position *x* in the evening and position *y* in the morning. The *a priori* material equivalence of the two statements, however, does not imply their strict (necessary) equivalence. (The same remarks apply to the case of heat and molecular motion below.) Similar remarks apply to some extent to the relationship between 'Hesperus is Phosphorus' and '"Hesperus" and "Phosphorus" name the same thing'. A confusion that also operates is, of course, the confusion between what *we* would say of a counterfactual situation and how people *in* that situation would have described it; this confusion, too, is probably related to the confusion between *a priority* and necessity.

15. If someone protests, regarding the lectern, that it *could* after all have *turned out* to have been made of ice, and therefore could have been made of ice, I would reply that what he really means is that *a lectern* could have looked just like this one, and have been placed in the same position as this one, and yet have been made of ice. In short, I could have been in the *same epistemological situation* in relation to *a lectern made of ice* as I actually am in relation to *this* lectern. In the main text, I have argued that the same reply should be given to protests that Hesperus could have turned out to be other than Phosphorus, or Cicero other than Tully. Here, then, the notion of 'counterpart' comes into its own. For it is not this table, but an epistemic 'counterpart', which was hewn from ice; not Hesperus–Phosphorus–Venus, but two distinct counterparts thereof, in two of the roles Venus actually plays (that of Evening Star and Morning Star), which are different. Precisely because of this fact, it is not *this table* which could have been made of ice. Statements about the modal properties of *this table* never refer to counterparts. However, if someone confuses the epistemological and the metaphysical problems, he will be well on the way to the counterpart theory Lewis and others have advocated.

16. Isn't the situation I just described also counterfactual? At least it may well be, if such Martians never in fact invade. Strictly speaking, the distinction I wish to draw compares how we *would* speak *in* a (possibly counterfactual) situation, *if* it obtained, and how we *do* speak *of* a counterfactual situation, knowing that it does not obtain – i.e., the distinction between the language we would have used in a situation and the language we *do* use to describe it. (Consider the description: 'Suppose we all spoke German.' This description is in English.) The former case can be made vivid by imagining the counterfactual situation to be actual.

17. The most popular identity theories advocated today explicitly fail to satisfy this simple requirement. For these theories usually hold that a mental state is a brain state, and that what makes the brain state into a mental state is its 'causal role', the fact that it tends to produce certain behaviour (as intentions produce actions, or pain, pain behaviour) and to be produced by certain stimuli (e.g. pain, by pinpricks). If the relations between the brain state and its causes and effects are regarded as contingent, then *being such-and-such-a-mental state* is a contingent property of the brain state. Let X be a pain. The causal-role identity theorist holds (1) that X is a brain state, (2) that the fact that X is a pain is to be analysed (roughly) as the fact that X is produced by certain stimuli and produces certain behaviour. The fact mentioned in (2) is, of course, regarded as contingent; the brain state X might well exist and not tend to produce the appropriate behaviour in the absence of other conditions. Thus (1) and (2) assert that a certain pain X might have existed, yet not have been a pain. This seems to me self-evidently absurd. Imagine any pain: is it possible that *it itself* could have existed, yet not have been a pain?

If $X = Y$, then X and Y share all properties, including modal properties. If X is a pain and Y the corresponding brain state, then *being a pain* is an essential property of X, and *being a brain state* is an essential property of Y. If the correspondence relation is, in fact, identity, then it must be *necessary* of Y that it corresponds to a pain, and *necessary* of X that it correspond to a brain state, indeed to this particular brain state, Y. Both assertions seem false; it *seems* clearly possible that X should have existed without the corresponding brain state; or that the brain state should have existed without being felt as pain. Identity theorists cannot, contrary to their almost universal present practice, accept these intuitions; they must deny them, and explain them away. This is none too easy a thing to do.

18. A brief restatement of the argument may be helpful here. If 'pain' and 'C-fibre stimulation' are rigid designators of phenomena, one who identifies them must regard the identity as necessary. How can this necessity be reconciled with the apparent fact that C-fibre stimulation might have turned out not to be correlated with pain at all? We might try to reply by analogy to the case of heat and molecular motion; the latter identity, too, is necessary, yet someone may believe that, before scientific investigation showed otherwise, molecular motion might have turned out not to be heat. The reply is, of course, that what really is possible is that people (or some rational sentient beings) could have been in the *same epistemic situation* as we actually are, and identify *a phenomenon* in the same way we identify heat, namely, by feeling it by the sensation we call 'the sensation of heat', without the phenomenon being molecular motion. Further, the beings might not have been sensitive to molecular motion (i.e., to heat) by any neural mechanism whatsoever. It is impossible to explain the apparent possibility of C-fibre stimulations not having been pain in the same way. Here, too, we would have to suppose that we could have been in the same epistemological situation, and identify something in the same way we

identify pain, without its corresponding to C-fibre stimulation. But the way we identify pain is by feeling it, and if a C-fibre stimulation could have occurred without our feeling any pain, then the C-fibre stimulation would have occurred without there *being* any pain, contrary to the necessity of the identity. The trouble is that although 'heat' is a rigid designator, heat is picked out by the contingent property of its being felt in a certain way; pain, on the other hand, is picked out by an essential (indeed necessary and sufficient) property. For a sensation to be *felt* as pain is for it to *be* pain.

19. All arguments against the identity theory which rely on the necessity of identity, or on the notion of essential property, are, of course, inspired by Descartes' argument for his dualism. The earlier arguments which superficially were rebutted by the analogies of heat and molecular motion, and the bifocals inventor who was also Postmaster General, had such an inspiration; and so does my argument here. R. Albritton and M. Slote have informed me that they independently have attempted to give essentialist arguments against the identity theory, and probably others have done so as well.

The simplest Cartesian argument can perhaps be restated as follows: Let '*A*' be a *name* (rigid designator) of Descartes' body. Then Descartes argues that since he could exist even if A did not, $\Diamond$ (Descartes $\neq A$), hence Descartes $\neq A$. Those who have accused him of a modal fallacy have forgotten that '*A*' is rigid. His argument is valid, and his conclusion is correct, provided its (perhaps dubitable) premise is accepted. On the other hand, provided that Descartes is regarded as having ceased to exist upon his death, 'Descartes $\neq A$' can be established without the use of a modal argument; for if so, no doubt A survived Descartes when A was a corpse. Thus A had a property (existing at a certain time) which Descartes did not. The same argument can establish that a statue is not the hunk of stone, or the congery of molecules, of which it is composed. Mere non-identity, then, may be a weak conclusion. (See D. Wiggins, *Philosophical Review*, Vol. 77 (1968), pp. 90 ff.) The Cartesian modal argument, however, surely can be deployed to maintain relevant stronger conclusions as well.

Biographical Note

Saul Kripke is James McCosh Professor of Philosophy at Princeton University, and was previously Professor of Philosophy at Rockefeller University. In 1973 he gave the John Locke lectures at Oxford. Besides the lecture printed here and 'Naming and Necessity', he has published papers on modal logic and on philosophical subjects.

Further Reading

Kripke's essay on 'Naming and Necessity', mentioned in the editorial introduction, is to be found in *Semantics of Natural Languages*, edited by Donald Davidson and Gilbert Harman (Dordrecht: D. Reidel, 1972).

The standard point of departure for contemporary discussion of names, descriptions and identity is the work of Frege and Russell: see Frege's 'Sense and Reference', in *Translations from the Philosophical Writings of Gottlob Frege*, edited by Max Black and Peter Geach (Oxford: Blackwell, 1952), pp. 56–78, and Russell's 'On Denoting', *Mind* XIV (1905), reprinted in Russell's *Logic and Knowledge: Essays 1901–1950*, edited by R. C. Marsh (London: George Allen & Unwin, 1956), pp .41–56. Both these fundamental works may be found reprinted in numerous anthologies.

Two more recent papers relevant to Kripke's discussion are: David Wiggins: 'Identity Statements', in R. J. Butler (ed.), *Analytical Philosophy, Second Series* (Oxford: Blackwell, 1965), pp. 40–71. John Searle: 'Proper Names', *Mind* 67 (1958), reprinted in P. F. Strawson (ed.), *Philosophical Logic* (Oxford Readings in Philosophy, Oxford: Oxford University Press, 1967), pp. 89–96.

On necessity, and also analyticity, one standard point of departure is Quine's 'Reference and Modality', in W. V. Quine, *From a Logical Point of View* (New York: Harper & Row, 1961), pp. 139–57. This paper and a number of major contributions to the debate arising out of Quine's work are collected in *Reference and Modality*, edited by Leonard Linsky (Oxford Readings in Philosophy, Oxford: Oxford University Press, 1971). A less technical collection, more clearly attached to traditional metaphysical and epistemological concerns, is *Necessary Truth*, edited by John Woods and L. W. Sumner (New York: Random House, 1969). There is a symposium on Kripke's argument against the mind–body identity theory in *The Journal of Philosophy* LXXI (1974), comprising Fred Feldman: 'Kripke on the Identity Theory' (pp. 665–76) and William C. Lycan: 'Kripke and the Materialists' (pp. 677–89).

P. F. Strawson

Meaning and Truth

It is often said that it is the business of philosophy to analyse our fundamental conceptions, or, what comes to the same thing, to analyse fundamental features of the reality we experience. Certainly this sounds like at least one main business of philosophy. Analysing, however, is of different kinds. There is the kind, often done with great acuteness, and to the enlightenment of all, which is the setting-out or tracing of established connections between a certain concept and others, the latter concepts typically being somehow simpler or more basic than the one under scrutiny. There is also something else, an analysing of fundamental conceptions which can be fairly described as the *establishing* of connections between one concept and others, the latter typically being simpler or more basic. This second enterprise is one of construction or invention, although construction or invention which somehow is subject to truth, governed by the way things are.

Anyone of a philosophical bent will see that there are questions to be asked about the two things that have been distinguished, the setting-out of established conceptual connections, and *the establishing of conceptual connections, subject to truth*. Certainly the latter notion is less than crystal-clear, and quite likely to annoy persons of tidy mind. To use it, however, without waiting for its analysis, it does surely characterize Professor Strawson's sequence of reflection in his inaugural lecture, and also some of the two families of philosophical views from which he takes his departure.

The subject is meaning, principally the meaning of words and sentences. How is it to be elucidated? How are we to explain *linguistic meaning*? Simple reflection, perhaps on what it takes to master a foreign language, tells us that the meaning of words and sentences is a matter of semantic and syntactic rules and conventions: semantic rules to connect words and sentences with things in the world, syntactic rules to govern relationships between words or groups of words; syntactic rules include rules of grammar in the ordinary sense. Given these facts, our question becomes, How are we to explain these rules and conventions?

One family of answers, quickly summed up, is that these rules and conventions are to be explained in terms of something in fact distinct from them, *an utterer's meaning something*. This is to be understood as an utterer's having a certain complex intention, an intention which involves other intentions within its scope. He intends his audience to think he has a certain belief or, in the case of commands, requests and the like, to think he desires them to perform some particular action. But he also intends that this intention of his should be recognized by the audience as the intention behind his utterance. (To intend the second thing is to intend that his first intention be made wholly overt to his audience. If it were not made overt in this way, but discovered by his audience in a different way, there would be no *communication*.) The utterance is understood if the speaker is seen as intending these things.

The thesis before us, then, is that utterer's meaning, so conceived, is in a way prior to linguistic meaning. Utterer's meaning gives the explanation of the nature of linguistic meaning. If we want to understand the nature of semantic and syntactic rules, and we follow *the theorists of communication-intention*, as they can be called, we turn to a conception of pre-linguistic communication.

It will be as well to make clearer that what we have here is not some oddly confident speculation about the pre-history of language. It is not a speculation of the kind that might turn up near the very beginning of a linguist's book on the actual development of human speech and writing, or, for that matter, a linguist's book on the development of a child among adults with a full-blown language. One learns something of the nature of a thing, in our case linguistic meaning, by seeing that it could have come about in one way, and could not have come about in another way. This knowledge does not depend on knowing what actually did happen. By way of an analogy, one may be led to see something of the personality of a boy by seeing that it is in part the kind of personality he would have if he had been brought up in a certain way, even if in fact he was not.

A second family of answers to the given question is that linguistic meaning in its essential nature is not to be understood by way of any idea of communication, but rather by way of an idea still closer to words and sentences, the idea of *truth-conditions*. The essence of semantic and syntactic rules has nothing to do with communication, however useful those rules turn out to be for conveying one's beliefs and so on.

The reality comes into view by way of the fact, which certainly is a fact, whatever else is to be said of it, that to give the meaning of a statement is to give just the conditions under which it is or would be true, and hence, implicitly, the conditions under which it is or would be false. If a man knows all and the only conditions which must obtain, perhaps in his sitting-room, if a certain sequence of sounds is to count as true, he knows what statement it is that the sounds make, what they mean. A closely related account can be given of what it is to know that a sequence of sounds is a particular order or wish or question, none of which, of course, has either of the two truth-values.

For those who may be called *the theorists of formal semantics*, then, meaning is to be understood by way of the notion of truth-conditions. One sees the nature of semantic and syntactic rules when one sees that they specify truth-conditions for statements. Our two kinds of linguistic rules are what can be called, if loosely, truth-rules. If a man makes some sounds or marks, then whether or not they constitute a truth depends on two things: rules or conventions pertaining to them, and, let us say, the way things are in the sitting-room. It is the nature of the mentioned rules, the relevant linguistic rules, to give just the conditions under which the sounds or marks make a truth. One can give an account of what semantic and syntactic rules are, fundamentally, without bringing in communication at all.

Strawson, having drawn up into clear array these two opposing sides, is mainly concerned to examine the answers of the second one. By way of a constructive analysis of the kind mentioned at the beginning of this introduction, he comes in the end to the conclusion that the second family of answers fails. The formal-semantics account of meaning, if it is enlarged in a way in which it must be enlarged, turns into something else, an account that depends on the very idea put aside, the idea that meaning is at bottom to be understood by way of communication. The formal-semantics account of meaning, if adequately developed, is in fact an account significantly like that of the theorists of communication-intention.

There is little need to anticipate the orderly course of Strawson's inquiry, except perhaps in connection with its beginning, the matter of truth-conditions. When I know the truth-conditions for the statement that Helen is winsome, I know something particular to that statement, and *nothing whatever* about the truth-conditions for the statement, say, that the Albert Memorial is on Hampstead Heath. To know many sets of truth-conditions, even the truth-conditions for all the statements that can be made, is to know something quite other than what it is, *in general*, for statements to be true. Some follow the semanticist-philosopher Alfred Tarski and say that one has, nonetheless, an adequate understanding of the concept of truth. Strawson supposes otherwise. In effect he maintains, and it is hard to disagree with him, that we must guard against the natural tendency to run together two things: (i) knowing a different fact about each of no matter how many statements, and (ii) knowing the general fact, which applies to any statement, that it is true if things really are as the statement states them to be. The latter, and not the former, is a kind of definition or general concept of truth.

The formal-semantics account of meaning is one which depends on the notion of truth-conditions. However, while this notion is not identical with a general concept of truth, as just remarked, it does depend on such a general concept. Only the including of one will begin to finish the account. When we see this, we are started on a path which takes us to the notion of *statement* or *assertion* and hence, despite attempts to call a halt, or to turn aside, to the notion of communication. As Strawson remarks in ending his lecture, what we depend on ultimately in understanding meaning is *speech*. The last conceptual connection is with speech.

T. H.

P. F. Strawson

Meaning and Truth

During the last quarter of a century Oxford has occupied, or re-occupied, a position it last held, perhaps, six hundred years ago: that of a great centre of philosophy in the Western world. During the same period my predecessor in this Chair, Professor Gilbert Ryle, has been the centre of this centre. We owe much to his vision, his enterprise, and his devotion as a kind of overseer – a wholly non-autocratic overseer – of the subject's development and organization; we owe much more to his fertility, his brilliance, and his originality as a philosopher.

It is characteristic of philosophers to reflect on their own activity in the same spirit as they reflect on the objects of that activity; to scrutinize philosophically the nature, the aims, and the methods of philosophical scrutiny. When he has written in this metaphilosophical vein, Professor Ryle has sometimes presented the model philosopher in a somewhat austere light: as one whose rôle is to correct a slack, habitual mental stance; or to disentangle the traffic-jams of ideas; or to prescribe the right exercises for our intellectual cramps and confusions. Professor Ryle has done his share of this work of necessary correction. But when we survey his philosophical output as a whole, the impression is not of austerity, but of abundance; of profusion of insight, vividness of illustration, and readiness of devisal. Each recalcitrant topic in turn is brilliantly illuminated by a method in which detail, imagery, contrast, and generalization are powerfully combined. The topics cover a wide range; many of them fall in the broad regions of the philosophy of meaning and the philosophy of mind; and if I may, tentatively, express a judgement of preference here, I would select his treatment of *thinking*, on which he has already written much and on which he is still engaged, as perhaps the most subtle and sensitive of all his philosophical explorations.

In Professor Ryle's work, as in that of few other philosophers, the thought and the style are one: the accumulation of image and epigram, the sharp antithesis, the taut and balanced sentences are not decorative additions to his argument, but the very form of his thought. If one has to name a single quality as supremely characteristic of that thought and of that style, it will be one I have, perforce, named twice already: *brilliance*. His writings form a brilliant and lasting contribution, not only to philosophy, but also – which is as great a thing – to English letters.

What is it for anything to have a *meaning* at all, in the way, or in the sense, in which words or sentences or signals have meaning? What is it for a particular sentence to have the meaning or meanings it does have? What is it for a particular phrase, or a particular word, to have the meaning or meanings it does have? These are obviously connected questions. Any account we give of meaning in general (in the relevant sense) must square with the account we give of what it is for particular expressions to have particular meanings; and we must acknowledge, as two complementary truths, first, that the meaning of a sentence in general depends, in some systematic way, on the meanings of the words that make it up and, second, that for a word to have a particular meaning is a matter of its making a particular systematic contribution to the meanings of the sentences in which it occurs.

I am not going to undertake to try to answer these so obviously connected questions. That is not a task for one lecture; or for one man. I want rather to discuss a certain conflict, or apparent conflict, more or less dimly discernible in current approaches to these questions. For the sake of a label, we might call it the conflict between the theorists of communication-intention and the theorists of formal semantics. According to the former, it is impossible to give an adequate account of the concept of meaning without reference to the possession by speakers of audience-directed intentions of a certain complex kind. The particular meanings of words and sentences are, no doubt, largely a matter of rule and convention; but the general nature of such rules and conventions can be ultimately understood only by reference to the concept of communication-intention. The opposed view, at least in its negative aspect, is that this doctrine simply gets things the wrong way round or the wrong way up, or mistakes the contingent for the essential. Of course we may expect a certain regularity of relationship between what people intend to communicate by uttering certain sentences and what those sentences conventionally mean. But the system of semantic and syntactical rules, in the mastery of which knowledge of a language consists – the rules which determine the meanings of sentences – is not a system of rules *for* communicating at all. The rules can be exploited for this purpose; but this is incidental to their essential character. It would be perfectly possible for someone to understand a language completely – to have a perfect linguistic competence – without having even the implicit thought of the function of communication; provided, of course, that the language in question did not contain words explicitly referring to this function.

A struggle on what seems to be such a central issue in philosophy should have something of a Homeric quality; and a Homeric struggle calls for gods and heroes. I can at least, though tentatively, name some living captains and benevolent shades: on the one side, say, Grice, Austin, and the later Wittgenstein; on the other, Chomsky, Frege, and the earlier Wittgenstein.

First, then, as to the theorists of communication-intention. The simplest, and most readily intelligible, though not the only way of joining their ranks is to present your general theory of meaning in two stages: first, present and elucidate a primitive concept of *communication* (or communication-intention) in terms which do not presuppose the concept of *linguistic meaning*; then show that the latter concept can be, and is to be, explained in terms of the former.[1] For any theorist who follows this path, the fundamental concept in the theory of meaning is that of a speaker's, or, generally, an utterer's, *meaning something by* an audience-directed utterance on a particular occasion. An utterance is something produced or executed by an utterer; it need not be vocal; it could be a gesture or a drawing or the moving or disposing of objects in a certain way. What an utterer means by his utterance is incidentally specified in specifying the complex intention with which he produces the utterance. The analysis of the kind of intention in question is too complex to be given in detail here, so I shall confine myself to incomplete description. An utterer might have, as one of his intentions in executing his utterance, that of bringing his audience to think that he, the utterer, believes some proposition, say the proposition that *p*; and he might intend this intention to be wholly overt, to be clearly recognized by the audience. Or again he might have the intention of bringing his audience to think that he, the utterer, wants his audience to perform some action, say *a*; and he might intend this intention of his to be wholly overt, to be clearly recognized by the audience. Then, provided certain other conditions on utterer's intention are fulfilled, the utterer may be said, in the relevant sense, to mean something by his utterance: specifically, to mean that *p*, in the declarative mode, in the first case and to mean, in the imperative mode, that the audience is to perform action *a* in the second case. Grice, for one, has given us reason to think that, with sufficient care, and far greater refinement than I have indicated, it is possible to expound such a concept of communication-intention or, as he calls it, utterer's meaning, which is proof against objection and which does not presuppose the notion of linguistic meaning.

Now a word about how the analysis of linguistic meaning in terms of utterer's meaning is supposed to proceed. Here again I shall not go into details. The details would be very complex. But the fundamental idea is comparatively simple. We are accustomed, and reasonably, to think of linguistic meaning in terms of rules and conventions, semantic and syntactic. And when we consider the enormous elaboration of these rules and conventions – their capacity, as the modern linguists stress, to generate an infinite number of sentences in a given language – we may feel infinitely removed from the sort of primitive communication situation which we naturally think of when trying to understand the notion of utterer's meaning in terms which clearly do not presuppose linguistic meaning. But rules or conventions govern human practices and purposive human activities. So we should ask what purposive activities are governed by *these* conventions. What are *these* rules rules for doing? And the very simple thought I spoke of which underlies the suggested type of analysis is that these rules are, precisely, rules for communicating, rules by the observance of which the utterer may achieve his purpose, fulfil his communication-intention; and that this is their *essential* character. That is, it is not just a fortunate fact that the rules allow of use for this purpose; rather, the very nature of the rules concerned can be understood only if they are seen as rules whereby this purpose can be achieved.

This simple thought may seem too simple; and in several ways. For it is clear that we can, and do, communicate very complicated things by the use of language; and if we are to think of language as, fundamentally, a system of rules for facilitating the achievement of our communication-intentions, and if the analysis is not to be circular, must we not credit ourselves with extremely complicated communication-intentions (or at least desires) independently of having at our disposal the linguistic means of fulfilling those desires? And is not this absurd? I think this is absurd. But the programme of analysis does not require it. All that the analysis requires is that we can explain the notion of conventions of communication in terms of the notion of pre-conventional communication at a rather basic level. Given that we can do this, then there is more than one way in which we can start pulling ourselves up by our own linguistic boot-straps. And it looks as if we can explain the notion of conventions of communication in terms of the notion of pre-conventional communication at a rather basic level.

We can, for example, tell ourselves a story of the analytic-genetic variety. Suppose an utterer achieves a pre-conventional communication success with a given audience by means of an utterance, say *x*. He has a complex intention *vis-à-vis* the audience of the sort which counts as a communication-intention and succeeds in fulfilling that intention by uttering *x*. Let us suppose that the primary intention was such that the utterer *meant* that *p* by uttering *x*; and, since, by hypothesis, he achieved a communication-success, he was so *understood* by his audience. Now if the same communication-problem presents itself later to the same utterer in relation to the same audience, the fact, known to both of them, that the utterer meant that *p* by uttering *x* before, gives the utterer a reason for uttering *x* again and the audience a reason for interpreting the utterance in the same way as before. (The reason which each has is the knowledge that the other has the knowledge which he has.) So it is easy to see how the utterance of *x* could become established as between this utterer and this audience as a means of meaning that *p*. Because it has worked, it becomes established; and then it works *because* it is established. And it is easy to see how this story could be told so as to involve not just a group of two, but a wider group. So we can have a movement from an utterer pre-conventionally meaning that *p* by an utterance of *x* to the utterance-type *x* conventionally meaning that *p* within a group and thence back to utterer-members of the group meaning that *p* by a token of the type, but now *in accordance with the conventions*.

Now of course this explanation of conventional meaning in terms of utterer's meaning is not enough by itself. For it only covers the case, or only obviously covers the case, of utterance-types without structure – i.e. of utterance-types of which the meaning is not systematically derived from the meanings of their parts. But it is characteristic of linguistic utterance-types to have structure. The meaning of a sentence is a syntactic function of the meanings of its parts and their arrangement. But there is no reason in principle why a pre-conventional utterance should not have a certain complexity – a kind of complexity which allowed an utterer, having achieved one communication-success, to achieve another by repeating one part of the utterance while varying the other part, what he means on the second occasion having something in common with, and something which differentiates it from, what he meant on the first occasion. And if he does thus achieve a second success, the way is open for a rudimentary *system* of utterance-types to become established, i.e. to become conventional within a group.

A system of conventions can be modified to meet needs which we can scarcely imagine existing before the system existed. And its modification and enrichment may in turn create the possibility of thoughts such as we cannot understand what it would be for one to have, without supposing such modification and enrichment to have taken place. In this way we can picture a kind of alternating development. Primitive communication-intentions and successes give rise to the emergence of a limited conventional meaning-system, which makes possible its own enrichment and development which in turn makes possible the enlargement of thought and of communication-needs to a point at which there is once more pressure on the existing resources of language which is in turn responsive to such pressure . . .

And of course there is an element of mystery in this; but so there is in human intellectual and social creativity anyway.

All the foregoing is by way of the roughest possible sketch of some salient features of a communication-intention theory of meaning and of a hint as to how it might meet the obvious objection that certain communication-intentions presuppose the existence of language. It has all been said before, and with far greater refinement. But it will serve, I hope, as a sufficient basis for the confrontation of views that I wish to arrange.

Now, then, for the at least apparently opposed view, which I have so far characterized only in its negative aspect. Of course the holders of this view share some ground with their opponents. Both agree that the meanings of the sentences of a language are largely determined by the semantic and syntactic rules or conventions of that language. Both agree that the members of any group or community of people who share knowledge of a language – who have a common linguistic competence – have at their disposal a more or less powerful instrument or means of communicating, and thereby of modifying each other's beliefs or attitudes or influencing each other's actions. Both agree that these means are regularly used in a quite conventional way, that what people intend to communicate by what they say is regularly related to the conventional meanings of the sentences they utter. Where they differ is as to the relations between the meaning-determining rules of the language, on the one hand, and the function of communication, on the other: one party insists, and the other (apparently) refuses to allow, that the general nature of those rules can be understood only by reference to this function.

The refusal naturally prompts a question – namely: What *is* the general character of those rules which must in some sense have been mastered by anyone who speaks and understands a given language? The rejected answer grounds their general character in the social function of communicating, e.g., beliefs or wishes or instructions. If this answer is rejected, another must be offered. So we ask again: What is the general character of these meaning-determining rules?

It seems to me that there is only one type of answer that has ever been seriously advanced or developed, or needs to be seriously considered, as providing a possible alternative to the thesis of the communication-theorist. This is an answer which rests on the notion of truth-conditions. The thought that the sense of a sentence is determined by its truth-conditions is to be found in Frege and in the early Wittgenstein, and we find it again in many subsequent writers. I take, as an example, a recent article by Professor Davidson. Davidson is rightly concerned with the point that an adequate account of the meaning-rules for a language L will show how the meanings of sentences depend on the meanings of words in L; and a theory of meaning for L will do this, he says, if it contains a recursive definition of truth-in-L. The 'obvious connexion', he says, between such a definition of truth and the concept of meaning is this: 'the definition works by giving the necessary and sufficient conditions for the truth of every sentence, and *to give truth-conditions is a way of giving the meaning of a sentence.* To know the semantic concept of truth for a language is to know what it is for a sentence – any sentence – to be true, and *this amounts, in one good sense we can give to the phrase, to understanding the language.*'[2]

Davidson, in the article I quote from, has a limited concern. But the concern finds its place inside a more general idea; and the general idea, plainly enough, is that the syntactic and semantic rules together determine the meanings of all the sentences of a language and do this by means, precisely, of determining their truth-conditions.

Now if we are to get at the root of the matter, to isolate the crucial issue, it seems to me important to set aside, at least initially, one class of objections to the adequacy of such a conception of meaning. I say one class of objections; but it is a class which admits of subdivisions. Thus it may be pointed out that there are some kinds of sentences – e.g. imperatives, optatives, and interrogatives – to which the notion of truth-conditions seems inappropriate, in that the conventional utterance of such sentences does not result in the saying of anything true or false. Or again it may be pointed out that even sentences to which the notion of truth-conditions does seem appropriate may contain expressions which certainly make a difference to their conventional meaning, but not the sort of difference which can be explained in terms of their truth-conditions. Compare the sentence 'Fortunately, Socrates is dead' with the sentence 'Unfortunately, Socrates is dead'. Compare a sentence of the form '*p* and *q*' with the corresponding sentence of the form '*p* but *q*'. It is clear that the meanings of the members of each pair of sentences differ; it is far from clear that their truth-conditions differ. And there are not just one or two expressions which give rise to this problem, but many such expressions.

Obviously both a comprehensive general theory of meaning and a comprehensive semantic theory for a particular language must be equipped to deal with these points. Yet they may reasonably be regarded as peripheral points. For it is a truth implicitly acknowledged by communication-theorists themselves[3] that in almost all the things we should count as sentences there is a substantial central core of meaning which is explicable either in terms of truth-conditions or in terms of some related notion quite simply derivable from that of a truth-condition; e.g. the notion, as we might call it, of a compliance-condition in the case of an imperative sentence or a fulfilment-condition in the case of an optative. If we suppose, therefore, that an account can be given of the notion of a truth-condition itself, an account which is indeed independent of reference to communication-intention, then we may reasonably think that the greater part of the task of a general theory of meaning has been accomplished without such reference. And by the same token, on the same supposition, we may think that the greater part of the particular theory of meaning of a particular language *L* can also be given, free of any such, even implicit, reference; for it can be given by systematically setting out the syntactic and semantical rules which determine truth-conditions for sentences of *L*.

Of course, as already admitted, something will have to be added to complete our general theory and to complete our particular theories. Thus for a particular theory an account will have to be added of the transformations that yield sentences with compliance-conditions or fulfilment-conditions out of sentences with truth-conditions; and the general theory will have to say what sort of thing, semantically speaking, such a derived sentence in general is. But this, though yielding a large harvest in sentences, is in itself a relatively small addition to either particular or general theory. Again, other additions will be necessary in connection with the other objections I mentioned. But, heartened by his hypothesized success into confidence, the theorist may reckon on dealing with some of these additions without essential reference to communication-intention; and, heartened by his hypothesized success into generosity, he may be happy to concede rights in some small outlying portion of the *de facto* territory of theoretical semantics to the theorist of communication-intention, instead of confining the latter entirely to some less appetizing territory called theoretical pragmatics.

I hope it is now clear what the central issue is. It consists in nothing other than the simple-seeming question whether the notion of truth-conditions can itself be explained or understood without reference to the function of communication. One minor clarification is called for before I turn to examine the question directly. I have freely used the phrase 'the truth-conditions of sentences' and I have spoken of these truth-conditions as determined by the semantical and syntactical rules of the language to which the sentences belong. In such a context we naturally understand the word 'sentence' in the sense of a 'type-sentence'. (By a sentence in the sense of a type I mean the sense in which there is just one English sentence, say, 'I am feeling shivery', or just one English sentence, say, 'She had her sixteenth birthday yesterday', which one and the same sentence may be uttered on countless different occasions by different people and with different references or applications.) But for many type-sentences, such as those just mentioned, the question whether they, the *sentences*, are true or false is one that has no natural application: it is not the invariant type-sentences themselves that are naturally said to be true or false, but rather the systematically varying things that people say, the propositions they express, when they utter those sentences on different particular occasions. But if the notion of truth-*values* is in general inappropriate to type-sentences, how can the notion of truth-*conditions* be appropriate? For presumably the truth-conditions of something are the conditions under which it is true.

The difficulty, however, is quite easily resolved. All that needs to be said is that the statement of truth-conditions for many type-sentences – perhaps most that are actually uttered in ordinary conversation – has to be, and can be, relativized in a systematic way to contextual conditions of utterance. A general statement of truth-conditions for such a sentence will then be, not a statement of conditions under which that sentence is a truth, but a general statement of a type of conditions under which different particular utterances of it will issue in different particular truths. And there are other more or less equivalent, though rather less natural, ways of resolving the difficulty.

So now, at last, to the central issue. For the theorists of formal semantics, as I have called them, the whole weight, or most of the weight, both of a general theory of meaning and of particular semantic theories, falls on the notion of truth-conditions and hence on the notion of truth. We agree to let it rest there. But we still cannot be satisfied that we have an adequate general understanding of the notion of meaning unless we are satisfied that we have an adequate general understanding of the notion of truth.

There is one manoeuvre here that would completely block all hope of achieving adequate understanding; and, if I am not mistaken, it is a manoeuvre which has a certain appeal for some theorists of formal semantics. This is to react to a demand for a general explication of the notion of truth by referring us back to a Tarski-like conception of truth-in-a-given-language, L, a conception which is elucidated precisely by a recursive statement of the rules which determine the truth-conditions for sentences of L. This amounts to a refusal to face the general philosophical question altogether. Having agreed to the general point that the meanings of the sentences of a language are determined, or largely determined, by rules which determine truth-conditions, we then raise the general question what sort of thing truth-conditions are, or what truth-conditions are conditions *of*; and we are told that the concept of truth for a given language is defined by the rules which determine the truth-conditions for sentences of that language.

Evidently we cannot be satisfied with this. So we return to our general question about truth. And immediately we feel some embarrassment. For we have come to think there is very little to say about truth *in general*. But let us see what we can do with this very little. Here is one way of saying something uncontroversial and fairly general about truth. One who makes a statement or assertion makes a true statement if and only if things are as, in making that statement, he states them to be. Or again: one who expresses a supposition expresses a true supposition if and only if things are as, in expressing that supposition, he expressly supposes them to be. Now let us interweave with such innocuous remarks as these the agreed thoughts about meaning and truth-conditions. Then we have, first: the meaning of a sentence is determined by those rules which determine how things are stated to be by one who, in uttering the sentence, makes a statement; or, how things are expressly supposed to be by one who, in uttering the sentence, expresses a supposition. And then, remembering that the rules are relativized to contextual conditions, we can paraphrase as follows: the meaning of a sentence is determined by the rules which determine *what* statement is made by one who, in uttering the sentence in given conditions, makes a statement; or, which determine *what* supposition is expressed by one who, in uttering the sentence in given conditions, expresses a supposition; and so on.

Thus we are led, by way of the notion of truth, back to the notion of the *content* of such speech acts as stating, expressly supposing and so on. And here the theorist of communication-intention sees his chance. There is no hope, he says, of elucidating the notion of the content of such speech acts without paying some attention to the notions of those speech acts themselves. Now of all the speech acts in which something true or false may, in one mode or another, be put forward, it is reasonable to regard that of statement or assertion as having an especially central position. (Hot for certainties, we value speculation primarily because we value information.) And we cannot, the theorist maintains, elucidate the notion of stating or asserting except in terms of audience-directed intention. For the fundamental case of stating or asserting, in terms of which all variants must be understood, is that of uttering a sentence with a certain intention – an intention wholly overt in the sense required by the analysis of utterer's meaning – which can be incompletely described as that of letting an audience know, or getting it to think, that the speaker has a certain belief; as a result of which there may, or may not, be activated or produced in the audience that same belief. The rules determining the conventional meaning of the sentence join with the contextual conditions of its utterance to determine what the belief in question *is* in such a primary and fundamental case. And in determining what the belief in question is in such a case, the rules determine what statement is made in such a case. To determine the former *is* to determine the latter. But this is precisely what we wanted. For when we set out from the agreed point that the rules which determine truth-conditions thereby determine meaning, the conclusion to which we were led was precisely that those rules determined what statement was made by one who, in uttering the sentence, made a statement. So the agreed point, so far from being an alternative to a communication theory of meaning, leads us straight in to such a theory of meaning.

The conclusion may seem a little too swift. So let us see if there is any way of avoiding it. The general condition of avoiding it is clear. It is that we should be able to give an account of the notion of truth-conditions which involves no essential reference to communicative speech acts. The alternative of refusing to give any account at all – of just resting on the notion of truth-conditions – is, as I have already indicated, simply not open to us if we are concerned with the philo-sophical elucidation of the notion of meaning: it would simply leave us with the concepts of meaning and truth each pointing blankly and unhelpfully at the other. Neither would it be helpful, though it might at this point be tempting, to retreat from the notion of truth-conditions to the less specific notion of correlation in general; to say, simply, that the rules which determine the meanings of sentences do so by correlating the sentences, envisaged as uttered in certain con-textual conditions, with certain possible states of affairs. One reason why this will not do is that the notion of correlation in general is simply too unspecific. There are many kinds of behaviour (including verbal behaviour) – and many more kinds could be imagined – which are correlated by rule with possible states of affairs without its being the case that such correlation confers upon them the kind of relation to those possible states of affairs that we are concerned with.

Another reason why it will not do is the following. Consider the sentence 'I am tired'. The rules which determine its meaning are indeed such as to correlate the sentence, envisaged as uttered by a particular speaker at a particular time, with the possible state of affairs of the speaker's being tired at that time. But this feature is not peculiar to that sentence or to the members of the class of sentences which have the same meaning as it. For consider the sentence 'I am not tired'. The rules which determine its meaning are also such as to correlate the sentence, envisaged as uttered by a certain speaker at a certain time, with the possible state of affairs of that speaker's being tired at that time. Of course the kinds of correlation are different. They are respectively such that one who uttered the first sentence would normally be understood as affirming, and one who uttered the second sentence would normally be understood as denying, that the state of affairs in question obtained; or again they are such that one who utters the first sentence when the state of affairs in question obtains has made a true statement and one who utters the second sentence in these circumstances has made a false statement. But to invoke these differences would be precisely to give up the idea of employing only the unspecific notion of correlation in general. It is not worth labouring the point further. But it will readily be seen not only that sentences different, and even opposed, in meaning are correlated, in one way or another, with the same possible state of affairs, but also that one and the same unambiguous sentence is correlated, in one way or another, with very many different and in some cases mutually incompatible states of affairs. The sentence 'I am tired' is correlated with the possible state of affairs of the speaker's being at the point of total exhaustion and also with the state of affairs of his being as fresh as a daisy. The sentence 'I am over forty' is correlated with any possible state of affairs whatever regarding the speaker's age; the sentence 'Swans are white' with any state of affairs whatever regarding the colour of swans.

The quite unspecific notion of correlation, then, is useless for the purpose in hand. It is necessary to find some way of specifying a particular correlation in each case, viz. the correlation of the sentence with the possible state of affairs the obtaining of which would be necessary and sufficient for something *true* to have been said in the uttering of the sentence under whatever contextual conditions are envisaged. So we are back once more with the notion of truth-conditions and with the question, whether we can give an account of this notion which involves no essential reference to communicative speech acts, i.e. to communication-intention.

I can at this point see only one resource open, or apparently open, to the theorist of meaning who still holds that the notion of communication-intention has no essential place in the analysis of the concept of meaning. If he is not to swallow his opponent's hook, he must take some leaves out of his book. He sees now that he cannot stop with the idea of truth. That idea leads straight to the idea of *what is said*, the content of what is said, when utterances are made; and that in turn to the question of what is being *done* when utterances are made. But may not the theorist go some way along this path without going as far along it as his opponent? Might it not be possible to *delete* the reference to communication-intention while *preserving* a reference to, say, belief-expression? And will not this, incidentally, be more realistic in so far as we often voice our thoughts to ourselves, with no communicative intention?

The manoeuvre proposed merits a fuller description. It goes as follows. First: follow the communication-theorist in responding to the challenge for an elucidation of the notion of truth-conditions by invoking the notion of, e.g. and centrally, statement or assertion; (accepting the uncontroversial point that one makes a true statement or assertion when things are as, in making that assertion, one asserts them to be). Second: follow the communication-theorist again in responding to the challenge for an elucidation of the notion of asserting by making a connection with the notion of belief; (conceding that to make an assertion is, in the primary case, to give expression to a belief; to make a true assertion is to give expression to a correct belief; and a belief is correct when things are as one who holds that belief, in so far as he holds that belief, believes them to be). But third: part company with the communication-theorist over the nature of this connection between assertion and belief; deny, that is, that the analysis of the notion of asserting involves essential reference to an intention, e.g. to get an audience to think that the maker of the assertion holds the belief; deny that the analysis of the notion of asserting involves *any* kind of reference to audience-directed intention; maintain, on the contrary, that it is perfectly satisfactory to accept as fundamental here the notion of simply voicing or expressing a belief. Then conclude that the meaning-determining rules for a sentence of the language are the rules which determine *what* belief is conventionally articulated by one who, in given contextual conditions, utters the sentence. As before, determining what this belief is, is the same thing as determining what assertion is made. So all the merits of the opponent's theory are preserved while the reference to communication is extruded.

Of course, more must be said by this theorist, as by his opponent. For sentences which can be used to express beliefs need not always be so used. But the point is one to be made on both sides. So we may neglect it for the present.

Now will this do? I do not think it will. But in order to see that it will not, we may have to struggle hard against a certain illusion. For the notion of expressing a belief may seem to us perfectly straightforward; and hence the notion of expressing a belief in accordance with certain conventions may seem equally straightforward. Yet, in so far as the notion of expressing a belief is the notion we need, it may borrow all its force and apparent straightforwardness from precisely the communication-situation which it was supposed to free the analysis of meaning from depending on. We may be tempted to argue as follows. Often we express beliefs with an audience-directed intention; we intend that our audience should take us to have the belief we express and perhaps that that belief should be activated or produced in the audience as well. But then what could be plainer than this: that what we can do with an audience-directed intention we can also do without any such intention? That is to say, the audience-directed intention, when it is present, is something added on to the activity of expressing a belief and in no way essential to it – or to the concept of it.

Now what a mixture of truth and falsity, of platitude and illusion, we have here! Suppose we reconsider for a moment that analysis of utterer's meaning which was roughly sketched at the beginning. The utterer produces something – his utterance x – with a complex audience-directed intention, involving, say, getting the audience to think that he has a certain belief. We cannot detach or extract from the analysis an element which corresponds to his expressing a belief with no such intention – though we could indeed produce the following description and imagine a case for it: he acts *as if* he had such an intention though as a matter of fact he has not. But here the description depends on the description of the case in which he has such an intention.

What I am suggesting is that we may be tempted, here as elsewhere, by a kind of bogus arithmetic of concepts. Given the concept of Audience Directed Belief Expression (ADBE), we can indeed think of Belief Expression (BE) without Audience Direction (AD), and find cases of this. But it does not follow that the concept of ADBE is a kind of logical compound of the two simpler concepts of AD and BE and hence that BE is conceptually independent of ADBE.

Of course these remarks do not show that there is no such thing as an independent concept of belief-expression which will meet the needs of the anti-communication-theorist. They are only remarks directed against a too-simple argument to the effect that there is such a concept.

This much is clear. If there is such an essentially independent concept of belief-expression which is to meet the needs of the analysis of the notion of meaning, we cannot just stop with the phrase 'expressing a belief'. We must be able to give some *account* of this concept, to tell ourselves some intelligible story about it. We can sometimes reasonably talk of a man's actions or his behaviour as expressing a belief when, for example, we see those actions as directed towards an end or goal which it is plausible to ascribe to him in so far as it is also plausible to ascribe to him that belief. But this reflection by itself does not get us very far. For one thing, on the present programme, we are debarred from making reference to the end or goal of communication an essential part of our story. For another, the sort of behaviour we are to be concerned with must be, or be capable of being, formalized or conventionalized in such a way that it can be regarded as subjected to, or performed in observance of, rules; and of rules, moreover, which regulate the behaviour precisely in its aspect as expression of belief. It will not do to say simply: we might suppose a man to find *some* satisfaction (unspecified) or *some* point (unspecified) in performing certain formalized (perhaps vocal) actions on some occasions, these actions being systematically related to his having certain beliefs. For suppose a man had a practice of vocalizing in a certain way whenever he saw the sun rise and in another, partly similar, partly different, way whenever he saw it set. Then this practice would be regularly related to certain beliefs, i.e. that the sun was rising or that it was setting. But this description gives us no reason at all for saying that when the man indulged in this practice he was *expressing the belief* that the sun was rising or setting, in accordance with a rule for doing so. We really have not enough of a description to know *what* to say. As far as we could tell, we might say, he just seems to have this ritual of *saluting* the rising or the setting sun in this way. What need of his it satisfies we don't know.

Let us suppose, however – for the sake of the argument – that we can elaborate some relevant conception of expressing a belief which presupposes nothing which, on the present programme, we are debarred from presupposing; and that we draw on this concept of expressing a belief in order to give an account, or analysis, on the lines indicated, of the notion of linguistic meaning. Then an interesting consequence ensues. That is, it will appear as a quite contingent truth about language that the rules or conventions which determine the meanings of the sentences of a language are public or social rules or conventions. This will be, as it were, a natural fact, a fact of nature, in no way essential to the concept of a language, and calling for a natural explanation which must not be allowed to touch or modify that concept. There must be nothing in the *concept* to rule out the idea that every individual might have his own language which only he understands. But then one might ask: Why should each individual observe his own rules? or any rules? Why shouldn't he express any belief he likes in any way he happens to fancy when he happens to have the urge to express it? There is one answer at least which the theorist is debarred from giving to this question, if only in the interests of his own programme. He cannot say: Well, a man might wish to *record* his beliefs so that he could refer to the records later, and then he would find it convenient to have rules to interpret his own records. The theorist is debarred from giving this answer because it introduces, though in an attenuated form, the concept of communication-intention: the earlier man communicates with his later self.

There might be one way of stilling the doubts which arise so rapidly along this path. That would be to offer possible natural explanations of the supposed natural fact that language is public, that linguistic rules are more or less socially common rules; explanations which successfully avoided any suggestion that the connection of public rules with communication was anything but incidental and contingent. How might such an explanation go? We might say that it was an agreed point that the possession of a language enlarges the mind, that there are beliefs one could not express without a language to express them in, thoughts one could not entertain without a rule-governed system of expressions for articulating them. And it is a fact about human beings that they simply would not acquire mastery of such a system unless they were exposed, as children, to conditioning or training by adult members of a community. Without concerning ourselves about the remote origins of language, then, we may suppose the adult members of a community to wish their successors to have this mind-enlarging instrument at their disposal – and evidently the whole procedure of training will be simplified if they all teach the same, the common language. We may reasonably suppose that the learners, to begin with, do not quite appreciate what they will ultimately be doing with language; that it is for them, to begin with, a matter of learning to do the right thing rather than learning to say the true thing; i.e. a matter of responding vocally to situations in a way which will earn them reward or avoid punishment rather than a matter of *expressing their beliefs*. But later they come to realize that they have mastered a system which enables them to perform this (still unexplained) activity whenever they wish to; and *then* they are speaking a language.

Of course it must be admitted that in the process they are liable also to acquire the *secondary* skill of communicating their beliefs. But this is simply something added on, an extra and conceptually uncovenanted benefit, quite incidental to the description of what it is to have mastered the meaning-rules of the language. If, indeed, you pointedly direct utterances, of which the essential function is belief-expression, to another member of the community, he will be apt to take it that you hold whatever beliefs are in question and indeed that you intend him to take this to be so; and this fact may give rise, indeed, it must be admitted, does give rise, to a whole cluster of social consequences; and opens up all sorts of possibilities of kinds of linguistic communication other than that which is based on belief-expression. This is why, as already acknowledged, we may have ultimately to allow some essential reference to communication-intention into outlying portions of our semantic theory. But this risk is incurred only when we go beyond the central core of meaning, determined by the rules which determine truth-conditions. As far as the central core is concerned, the function of communication remains secondary, derivative, conceptually inessential.

I hope it is clear that any such story is going to be too perverse and arbitrary to satisfy the requirements of an acceptable theory. If this is the way the game has to be played, then the communication-theorist must be allowed to have won it.

But must the game, finally, be played in this way? I think, finally, it must. It is indeed a generally harmless and salutary thing to say that to know the meaning of a sentence is to know under what conditions one who utters it says something true. But if we wish for a philosophical elucidation of the concept of meaning, then the dictum represents, not the end, but the beginning, of our task. It simply narrows, and relocates, our problem, forcing us to inquire what is contained in the little phrase '. . . says something true'. Of course there are many ways in which one can say something which is in fact true, give expression, if you like, to a true proposition, without thereby expressing belief in it, without asserting that proposition: e.g. when the words in question form certain sorts of subordinate or co-ordinate clauses, and when one is quoting or play-acting and so on. But when we come to try to explain in general what it is to say something true, to express a true proposition, reference to belief or to assertion (and thereby to belief) is inescapable. Thus we may harmlessly venture: Someone says something true if things are as he says they are. But this 'says' already has the force of 'asserts'. Or, to eschew the 'says' which equals 'asserts', we may harmlessly venture: Someone propounds, in some mode or other, a true proposition if things are as anyone who believed what he propounds would thereby believe them to be. And here the reference to belief is explicit.

Reference, direct or indirect, to belief-expression is inseparable from the analysis of saying something true (or false). And, as I have tried to show, it is unrealistic to the point of unintelligibility – or, at least, of extreme perversity – to try to free the notion of the linguistic expression of belief from all essential connection with the concept of communication-intention.

Earlier I hinted that the habit of some philosophers of speaking as if 'true' were a predicate of type-sentences was only a minor aberration, which could readily enough be accommodated to the facts. And so it can. But it is not a simple matter of pedantry to insist on correcting the aberration. For if we are not careful, it is liable to lead us totally wrong. It is liable, when we inquire into the nature of meaning, to make us forget what sentences are *for*. We connect meaning with truth and truth, too simply, with sentences; and sentences belong to language. But, as theorists, we know nothing of human *language* unless we understand human *speech*

Notes

1. Not the *only* way; for to say that a concept ϕ cannot be adequately elucidated without reference to a concept ψ is not the same thing as to say that it is possible to give a classical analysis of ϕ in terms of ψ. But the *simplest* way; for the classical method of analysis is that in terms of which, in our tradition, we most naturally think.

2. 'Truth and Meaning' (*Synthese*, 1967, p. 310).

3. This acknowledgement is probably implicit, though not very clearly so, in Austin's concept of *locutionary meaning* (see *How to do things with Words*, Oxford, 1962); it is certainly implicit in Grice's distinction between what speakers *actually say*, in a favoured sense of 'say', and what they imply (see 'Utterer's Meaning, Sentence-Meaning and Word-Meaning' in *Foundations of Language*, 1968); and again in Searle's distinction between the *proposition* put forward and the illocutionary mode in which it is put forward (see *Speech Acts*, Cambridge, 1969).

Biographical Note

Sir Peter Strawson has been Waynflete Professor of Metaphysical Philosophy at Oxford since 1968, before which he was a Fellow of University College, Oxford. His books include *Introduction to Logical Theory* (1952), *Individuals* (1959), *The Bounds of Sense* (1966), *Logico-Linguistic Papers* (1971), *Subject and Predicate in Logic and Grammar* (1974) and *Freedom and Resentment and Other Essays* (1974). He is a Fellow of the British Academy.

Further Reading

Donald Davidson, 'Truth and Meaning', *Synthese* XVII (1967), pp. 304–13; H. H. P. Grice, 'Meaning', *Philosophical Review* LXVI (1957), pp. 377–88; 'Utterer's Meaning and Intentions', *Philosophical Review* LXXVIII (1969), pp. 147–77. John Searle, *Speech Acts* (Cambridge: Cambridge University Press, 1969). Jonathan Bennett, *Linguistic Behaviour* (Cambridge: Cambridge University Press, 1976). Samuel Guttenplan (ed.), *Mind and Language* (Oxford: Clarendon Press, 1975). Gareth Evans and John McDowell (edd.), *Truth and Meaning: Essays in Semantics* (Oxford: Clarendon Press, 1976).

A selection of books published by Penguin is listed on the following pages.

For a complete list of books available from Penguin in the United States, write to Dept. DG, Penguin Books, 299 Murray Hill Parkway, East Rutherford, New Jersey 07073.

For a complete list of books available from Penguin in Canada, write to Penguin Books Canada Limited, 2801 John Street, Markham, Ontario L3R 1B4.

If you live in the British Isles, write to Dept. EP, Penguin Books Ltd, Harmondsworth, Middlesex.

THE NATURE OF TIME

G. J. Whitrow

A foreigner, without a watch, asked a passer-by in the street, 'Please, what is time?' 'Why ask me?' came the answer. 'That's a philosophical question.' It is appropriate, however, to ask Professor G. J. Whitrow, a mathematician who for years has made a study of the thing that clocks keep (more or less). In this good-humored essay on an abstruse and elusive subject he discusses how man's ideas of time originated, how far they are inborn in animals and plants, how time has been measured from sundial and sandglass to the caesium clock, and whether time possesses a beginning, a direction, and an end. Professor Whitrow coaxes the diffident layman to contemplate with plea-sure the differences between cyclic, linear, biological, cosmic, and space time and relates time to gravity and the universe. In short, this is a delightful book and a source of endless arguments.

THE PROBLEM OF KNOWLEDGE

A. J. Ayer

What is knowledge, and how do we *know* things? Moreover, how do we know that we know them, in view of the doubts that the philosophic sceptic casts on our grasp of facts? The presentation of the sceptic's arguments leads here to a general discussion of the topic of scepticism and certainty. This is followed by a detailed examination of the philosophical problems of perception, memory, and our knowledge of other minds, which occupies the greater part of the book. In the course of the discussion Professor A. J. Ayer has also attempted to throw light upon the nature of the philosophical method and upon some of the problems connected with time, causality, and personal identity.

ETHICS: INVENTING RIGHT AND WRONG

J. L. Mackie

J. L. Mackie's new book is a complete and clear treatise on moral theory. His work on normative ethics – the moral principles he recommends – offers a fresh approach on a much neglected subject. The author deals first with the status of ethics, arguing that there are no objective values, that morality cannot be discovered but must be made. He examines next the content of ethics, seeing morality as a functional device, basically the same at all times but changing significantly in response to changes in the human condition. The book sketches a practical moral system, criticizing but also borrowing from both utilitarian and absolutist views. Thirdly, he examines the frontiers of ethics, areas of contact with psychology, metaphysics, theology, law, and politics. Throughout, his aim is to argue carefully, but forthrightly, on a wide range of questions that are both philosophical and practical.

CAUSING DEATH AND SAVING LIVES

Jonathan Glover

Questions about killing are among the most acute of moral problems, and yet very often our thinking about them is confused and clouded with emotion, so that someone who approves of contraception and abortion may very well deplore capital punishment, using diametrically opposed arguments in each case. With clarity and rigorous logic, Jonathan Glover examines the arguments we use in prohibiting or justifying the killing of others. He looks at the practical problems and the moral difficulties brought about by the advance of modern medicine, at theories of capital punishment, and at the justifications advanced for assassination, revolution, and war. Throughout, humanity and logic combine to make this a clear, concise, and necessary book.

A HUNDRED YEARS OF PHILOSOPHY

John Passmore

The critical acclaim that greeted the first edition of *A Hundred Years of Philosophy* showed that John Passmore had achieved what was long thought impossible: a history of modern ideas in knowledge, logic, and metaphysics which was both stimulating to the specialist and intelligible to the general reader. This edition contains much new material, including expanded discussions of A. J. Ayer, Karl Popper, Ludwig Wittgenstein, and Jean-Paul Sartre, enlarged sections on J. L. Austin, Karl Jaspers, and Martin Heidegger, an examination of Maurice Merleau-Ponty's phenomenology, and a final chapter on recent developments.

EXISTENTIALISM

John Macquarrie

This lucid discussion of existentialism reveals the vital contribution that existentialist thought has made to mankind. John Macquarrie's approach is original. After surveying the historical background, he evaluates existentialism by themes. Each chapter deals with a major theme of existentialist philosophy as exemplified by thinkers from Sören Kierkegaard to Albert Camus, and the chapters are arranged in the order of the existentialist dialectic. In the course of his evaluation Macquarrie shows what existentialism has brought to other branches of learning – ethics, art, psychology, theology, education – and he then examines the principal objections against it. Thus the book gives the reader not only a complete review of a philosophy that has formed modern man but also a sound analysis of the strengths and weaknesses of that formation.

THE VIKING PORTABLE LIBRARY

In single volumes, The Viking Portable Library has gathered the very best work of individual authors or works of a period of literary history, writings that otherwise are scattered in a number of separate books. These are not condensed versions, but rather selected masterworks assembled and introduced with critical essays by distinguished authorities. Over fifty volumes of The Viking Portable Library are now in print in paperback, making the cream of ancient and modern Western writing available to bring pleasure and instruction to the student and the general reader. An assortment of subjects follows:

WILLIAM BLAKE   CERVANTES
GEOFFREY CHAUCER   SAMUEL COLERIDGE
STEPHEN CRANE   DANTE
RALPH WALDO EMERSON   WILLIAM FAULKNER
EDWARD GIBBON   GREEK HISTORIANS
NATHANIEL HAWTHORNE   HENRY JAMES
THOMAS JEFFERSON   MACHIAVELLI
MEDIEVAL READER   JOHN MILTON
PLATO   EDGAR ALLAN POE
POETS OF THE ENGLISH LANGUAGE
MEDIEVAL AND RENAISSANCE POETS: LANGLAND TO SPENSER
ELIZABETHAN AND JACOBEAN POETS: MARLOWE TO MARVELL
RESTORATION AND AUGUSTAN POETS: MILTON TO GOLDSMITH
ROMANTIC POETS: BLAKE TO POE
VICTORIAN AND EDWARDIAN POETS: TENNYSON TO YEATS
ROMAN READER   BERNARD SHAW
JONATHAN SWIFT   VOLTAIRE
WALT WHITMAN   OSCAR WILDE

PENGUIN CLASSICS

The Penguin Classics, the earliest and most varied series of world masterpieces to be published in paperback, began in 1946 with E. V. Rieu's now famous translation of *The Odyssey*. Since then the series has commanded the unqualified respect of scholars and teachers throughout the English-speaking world. It now includes more than three hundred volumes, and the number increases yearly. In them, the great writings of all ages and civilizations are rendered into vivid, living English that captures both the spirit and the content of the original. Each volume begins with an introductory essay, and most contain notes, maps, glossaries, or other material to assist the reader in appreciating the work fully. Some volumes available include:

Aeschylus, THE ORESTEIAN TRILOGY
Honoré de Balzac, COUSIN BETTE
Geoffrey Chaucer, THE CANTERBURY TALES
Fyodor Dostoyevksy, THE BROTHERS KARAMAZOV
(2 volumes)
THE EPIC OF GILGAMESH
Gustave Flaubert, MADAME BOVARY
Nikolai Gogol, DEAD SOULS
Henrik Ibsen, HEDDA GABLER AND OTHER PLAYS
Friedrich Nietzsche, THUS SPOKE ZARATHUSTRA
Plato, THE LAST DAYS OF SOCRATES
Sophocles, THE THEBAN PLAYS
Stendhal, SCARLET AND BLACK
Leo Tolstoy, ANNA KARENIN
Ivan Turgenev, FATHERS AND SONS
Émile Zola, GERMINAL